UNITED STATES ARMY IN WORLD WAR II

The War in the Pacific

SEIZURE OF THE GILBERTS AND MARSHALLS

by

Philip A. Crowl

and

Edmund G. Love

MILITARY INSTRVCTION

CENTER OF MILITARY HISTORY
UNITED STATES ARMY
WASHINGTON, D.C., 1995

Library of Congress Catalog Card Number: 55-60002

First Printed 1955—CMH Pub 5-6-1

For sale by the Superintendent of Documents, U.S. Government Printing Office
Washington, D.C. 20402

UNITED STATES ARMY IN WORLD WAR II
Kent Roberts Greenfield, General Editor

Advisory Committee

(As of 17 March 1954)

James P. Baxter
President, Williams College

John D. Hicks
University of California

William T. Hutchinson
University of Chicago

S. L. A. Marshall
Detroit News

Charles S. Sydnor*
Duke University

Brig. Gen. Verdi B. Barnes
Army War College

Brig. Gen. Leonard J. Greeley
Industrial College of the Armed Forces

Brig. Gen. Elwyn D. Post
Army Field Forces

Col. Thomas D. Stamps
United States Military Academy

Col. C. E. Beauchamp
Command and General Staff College

Charles H. Taylor
Harvard University

Office of the Chief of Military History

Maj. Gen. Albert C. Smith, Chief**

Chief Historian	Kent Roberts Greenfield
Chief, War Histories Division	Col. George G. O'Connor
Chief, Editorial and Publication Division	Lt. Col. Thomas E. Bennett
Chief, Editorial Branch	Joseph R. Friedman
Chief, Cartographic Branch	Wsevolod Aglaimoff
Chief, Photographic Branch	Maj. Arthur T. Lawry

---

*Deceased.
**Maj. Gen. Orlando Ward was succeeded by General Smith on 1 February 1953.

. . . to Those Who Served

Foreword

Seizure of the Gilberts and Marshalls deals with amphibious warfare as waged by American forces against the Japanese-held atolls of the Central Pacific during World War II. The word *amphibious,* as here used, includes the landing and supply of troops in combat as well as the air and naval support of the operations.

The atoll operations described in this volume were amphibious from beginning to end. They were not simple seaborne hit-and-run raids of the Dieppe type. The objective was to secure the atolls as steppingstones to the next advance. The islands were relatively small, permitting continual naval and air support of the ground operations.

Some outstanding examples of the co-ordination of fire support by artillery, naval gunfire, and air are found in this book. The advantages of simple plans and the disadvantages of the more complicated will stand out for the careful reader.

The story of the capture of these atolls of Micronesia offers some of the best examples of combined operations that are available in the annals of modern war. Ground, sea, and air components were always present, and the effectiveness with which they were combined and co-ordinated accounts in large measure for the rapid success enjoyed in these instances by American arms. Units of the U.S. Navy and the U.S. Marine Corps were active participants in the operations and the role they played is treated in this volume as fully as is considered appropriate in a series devoted to the history of the U.S. Army in World War II.

From the point of view of strategy, the significance of this volume lies in the fact that it tells the story of the beginnings of the drive across the Central Pacific toward the Japanese homeland. This concept of defeating Japan by pushing directly westward from Hawaii through the island bases of the mid-Pacific was traditional in American strategic thinking, but had never been put to test and was seriously challenged in some quarters. As is shown here, the test was first made in the campaigns against the Gilberts and Marshalls, the outcome was successful, and the experience gained was of inestimable value in planning for the subsequent conduct of the war in the Pacific.

ORLANDO WARD
Washington, D. C.   Maj. Gen., U. S. A.
9 January 1953   Chief of Military History

The Authors

Philip A. Crowl, who has an M.A. from the State University of Iowa and a Ph.D. from the Johns Hopkins University, taught History at the Johns Hopkins University and at Princeton. Commissioned in the Navy in World War II, he became a lieutenant (senior grade) and commanding officer of an LCI gunboat that was in action at Leyte Gulf, Lingayen Gulf, and Okinawa. He is author of *Maryland During and After the Revolution* (1943) and co-author of *The U. S. Marines and Amphibious War* (1951). He was awarded the James V. Forrestal Fellowship for 1953–54 to prepare a study of command relationships in amphibious warfare in World War II.

Before World War II Edmund G. Love, with an M.A. from the University of Michigan, taught History in a Michigan high school. A captain of Infantry in World War II, he became historical officer of the 27th Infantry Division and observed the operations of that division on Makin, Eniwetok, Saipan, and Okinawa.

From 1946 to 1 August 1949 Mr. Love was a member of the Pacific Section of the Army's historical staff in Washington. Dr. Crowl has been a member of that staff since 1949.

Preface

This volume tells the story of the launching of the Central Pacific drive against Japan in late 1943 and early 1944. Specifically, it deals with the amphibious operations against five Central Pacific atolls—Makin, Tarawa, Kwajalein, Majuro, and Eniwetok. It was in these battles that American amphibious doctrine received its first critical test in the Pacific war, and the victories achieved made possible a continuation of the highly important drive against Japan's perimeter of island defenses in the Carolines, Marianas, Volcano Islands, and Ryukyus.

Numerically speaking, the Army's contribution to the forces responsible for the capture of these atolls was not as great as that of the Marine Corps. Yet the Army's role was a major one and is here set forth in minute detail. If the activities of other participating U.S. services receive less attention in these pages, it is only because this volume is by definition a part of the history of the U.S. Army in World War II.

For a variety of reasons this book has been a long time in preparation. A draft was prepared by Mr. Edmund G. Love, then set aside, to be taken up later by the undersigned for extensive revision, correction, and elaboration. The authors' debts for aid and assistance are too numerous to acknowledge in detail. Dr. Louis Morton and Dr. John Miller, jr., during their respective tenures as Chief of the Pacific Section, Office of the Chief of Military History, read every page with care and discrimination and offered invaluable guidance. In addition, Dr. Miller prepared a separate study of the strategic background of the operations which was used as the basis for the first and part of the second chapter. Dr. Kent Roberts Greenfield, Chief Historian, Department of the Army, gave liberally of his time and advice. To Maj. Gen. Orlando Ward, formerly Chief of Military History, Col. George G. O'Connor, Chief of War Histories Division, and the military members of their staff a great debt is owed for their sympathetic interest, technical assistance, and supervision of the publication of the volume.

Mr. Wsevolod Aglaimoff and Mr. Charles von Luettichau not only prepared the maps but offered many important suggestions regarding tactical details. Mr. Thomas Wilds did a distinguished job of piecing together the complicated and often obscure story of Japanese defensive preparations and battle operations. Miss Margaret Plumb checked all the footnotes of the original draft for accuracy. Miss Mary Ann Bacon edited the manuscript and prepared the index with imagination as well as meticulous care, and Mr. Allen R. Clark was copy editor. Maj. Arthur T. Lawry and Miss Margaret Tackley are responsible for the selection of photographs. Mr. Israel Wice and his staff, Miss Lois Aldrich of the Departmental Records Branch, Office of the Adjutant General, U.S. Army, and Mrs. Vivian McCoy and Mr. Paul Rugen of the Records and Research Section, Historical Branch, G-3, Headquarters, U.S. Marine Corps, are to be thanked for their aid in the gathering of the documents and other source materials that made up the frame work of the volume. Mrs. Martha Willoughby and Mrs. Marguerite Bartz typed the manuscript.

To the historical sections of the other U.S. services special thanks are due for unfailing co-operation. Lt. Col. Frank Hough, USMC, Lt. Col. Harry Edwards, USMC, and the staff of the Historical Branch, G-3, Headquarters, U.S. Marine Corps were especially generous in their assistance. The large number of officers of the Army, Navy, Marine Corps, and Air Force who read and criticized various portions of the manuscript, corresponded with the authors, or permitted themselves to be interviewed, is acknowledged in the bibliographical note appended to the volume.

Washington, D. C.   PHILIP A. CROWL
28 January 1954

Contents

Tables

Charts

Maps

Illustrations

Photographs are from the Department of Defense files.

SEIZURE OF THE
GILBERTS AND MARSHALLS

CHAPTER I

The Decision To Strike
Through the Central Pacific

In November 1943 American forces successfully invaded the Gilbert Islands, which the Japanese had wrested from British control shortly after the attack on Pearl Harbor almost two years earlier. Thus the United States initiated the great westward drive across the Central Pacific that would eventually bring Allied forces to the very doorstep of the Japanese homeland. This drive would constitute the northern or upper part of a two-pronged movement against the heart of Japanese military and economic power in the Pacific. The lower prong would be represented by General Douglas MacArthur's steady progress up the Solomon Islands, up the northern coast of New Guinea, and into the Philippine Islands. But it was to the Central Pacific route, westward from Hawaii through the myriad islands and atolls of Micronesia, that the American strategic planners had assigned the "main effort" in the war against Japan. Along this path U.S. naval, ground, and air forces under command of Admiral Chester W. Nimitz were to begin a series of amphibious assaults of size and scope unparalleled in the history of oceanic warfare.

Prewar Plans

There was nothing new in the idea that the United States would have to seize strategic island bases in the Central Pacific in the event of a war against Japan. Throughout the 1920's and 1930's strategic planners in Washington had prepared a series of plans, designated the ORANGE plans, to provide for that contingency. All of these chose the Central Pacific as the main avenue of approach for a decisive move against the prospective enemy. The first ORANGE plan, approved by the Joint Army and Navy Board in 1924, conceived of an offensive war against Japan that would be essentially naval in character. By cutting the Japanese Empire's sea routes, and by air and naval operations, Japan, it was believed, could be isolated. The plan further provided that troops from the continental United States would be assigned to seize and hold islands in the Central Pacific, including the Marshall group, and that large bodies of troops would be dispatched to reinforce the Philippines.

Between 1925 and 1938 this original ORANGE plan was revised many times. In the final revision it was decided that the Philippines could be defended by their peacetime garrison plus whatever other local forces were available, without reinforcements from the United States. But none of the changes affected one basic aspect of the plan—U.S. naval forces would move westward through the islands of the Central Pacific to establish naval dominance in the western waters of that ocean.

The ORANGE plans had been prepared on the assumption that only the United States and Japan would be at war. By 1941 this assumption was no longer valid. The emergence of the Rome–Berlin–Tokyo Axis, the American decision to support Great Britain in her struggle against Germany and Italy, and the growing realization that the United States was likely to become involved in war against the Axis caused American and British officials to prepare tentative plans for combined action. The last American plan made before 7 December 1941 was prepared on the assumption that the United States and Britain would be allied and at war with a combination of enemy powers and was designated RAINBOW 5. Although never formally approved by President Franklin D. Roosevelt, it was the plan put into effect at the outbreak of war between the United States and the Axis Powers. In the belief that Germany was the major enemy and would have to be defeated first, RAINBOW 5 declared the Atlantic-European theater to be the main area of operations. In the Pacific and the Far East the Allies would assume a role primarily defensive, although limited naval offensive measures were to be undertaken at the earliest possible moment.

Specifically, the U.S. Army was to help defend the Hawaiian and the Philippine Islands, and to help hold the entrance to Manila Bay. The U.S. Navy's role in the Pacific was naturally more extensive. The Navy was to conduct raids, defend such American bases as Wake, Guam, Midway, and Samoa, "prepare to capture" the Japanese Mandated Islands and establish a fleet base at Truk, maintain the line of communications between the United States and the Philippines, and establish naval superiority in the western Pacific.[1] Thus, with the assignment to the U.S. Navy of the task of seizing the Japanese Mandated Islands, including Truk, the role of the Central Pacific in the forthcoming war was reaffirmed.

Pacific Organization and Early Strategy

The success of Japan's offensive moves in late 1941 and the first months of 1942 did not completely invalidate all Pacific provisions of RAINBOW 5, but it did postpone any attempt to carry out the offensive provisions in the early part of 1942.[2] By May 1942 the Japanese had seriously weakened the U.S. Pacific Fleet, had seized the Philippines, Wake, Guam, and the Gilberts, had captured Malaya, Burma, and the Netherlands Indies, and had installed themselves in the Bismarck Archipelago-New Guinea-Solomons area. They held an enormous perimeter of bases that included the Kurils, the Marianas, Wake, the Marshalls, Rabaul in New Britain, the Netherlands Indies, and Malaya, with outposts in the Gilberts, the

---

[1] Information on ORANGE and RAINBOW plans is derived from Louis Morton, *The Fall of the Philippines,* UNITED STATES ARMY IN WORLD WAR II (Washington, 1953), Ch. IV.

[2] Morton, *Fall of Philippines,* p. 79. An exception must be made for U.S. submarine warfare. As Admiral Richmond Kelly Turner, USN (Ret), points out, ". . . the first major naval offensive—that of the Pacific Fleet submarines—began the day war broke out." (Ltr, Adm Turner to Maj Gen Orlando Ward, 12 Feb 52, Incl 1, p. 3, OCMH.)

Solomons, and New Guinea. They apparently expected the United States to grow war-weary launching attacks against these strong positions, and to give up the fight and agree to a negotiated peace.[3]

But by mid-1942 the Japanese had overreached themselves. Confident after their first successes, they decided to capture positions in the Aleutians, the Fijis, Samoa, New Caledonia, and Midway, enlarge their holdings in New Guinea, and then to expand the main perimeter to include the newly won bases as well as the Gilberts. Seizure of Port Moresby in New Guinea and of the Fijis, Samoa, and New Caledonia would have cut the line of communications between the United States and Australia. Thus isolated, Australia could not be used as a base for Allied counteroffensives.

Frustrated in their attempt to take Port Moresby by the Allied Coral Sea victory in early May 1942, the Japanese turned to Midway and the Aleutians and met with disaster. Although they did obtain footholds in the Aleutians, their effort against Midway was a costly failure. In the Battle of Midway, 3–4 June 1942, the U.S. Pacific Fleet destroyed four large aircraft carriers plus hundreds of planes and many of their best-trained pilots. Thus crippled, the Japanese *Combined Fleet* was no longer capable of offensive action. The time had come for the Allies to seize the initiative. The groundwork had already been laid since the U.S. Joint Chiefs of Staff (JCS), who had been assigned responsibility for the strategic direction of the war in the Pacific, had already organized the Pacific theater and undertaken measures to initiate at least limited offensives.

The Joint Chiefs on 30 March 1942, with the approval of President Roosevelt and the Allied governments concerned, had organized the Pacific theater into two

great commands—the Southwest Pacific Area and the Pacific Ocean Areas. *(Map 1)* The Southwest Pacific Area, under General MacArthur, consisted principally of Australia, New Guinea, the Bismarck Archipelago, the Netherlands Indies, the Philippines, and adjacent waters.

The Pacific Ocean Areas[4] included nearly all the rest of the Pacific Ocean. It encompassed virtually everything south of the Bering Strait, west of continental United States, north of the South Pole, and east of the Southwest Pacific Area and China. The Pacific Ocean Areas was divided into three commands: the North Pacific, which stretched north of latitude 42° north; the South Pacific, which lay south of the equator and east of the Southwest Pacific; and the Central Pacific, lying between the equator and latitude 42° north. Major islands and groups in the Central Pacific were the Hawaiian Islands, Wake, part of the Gilberts, the Marshalls, the Carolines, the Marianas, the Bonins, the Ryukyus, Formosa, and the Japanese home islands.[5]

Commander in Chief, Pacific Ocean

---

[3] For a detailed discussion of Japanese strategy, strength, and dispositions see below, Ch. IV.

[4] The directive establishing the command used "Area." Memo, JCS for President, 30 Mar 42, incl Directive to CINCPOA and Directive to Supreme Commander, SWPA, ABC 323.31 POA (1–29–42), 1-B. Usage has authorized the plural, however.

[5] By the 30 March directive a third command, the Southeastern Pacific Area, was set up but never became a theater of operations and so lapsed into insignificance. Directly under Admiral Ernest J. King rather than Admiral Nimitz, its western limit ran from Antarctica northward along the meridian of 100° west to latitude 11° north and thence east to the coast of Central America.

On 2 July 1942 the boundary between the South and Southwest Pacific Areas was moved from 160° to 159° east longitude in order to place Guadalcanal and adjacent islands in the South Pacific Area. (Joint Directive for Offensive Opns in SWPA Agreed on by U.S. Chiefs of Staff, 2 Jul 42, OPD 381, Sec. II, Case 83).

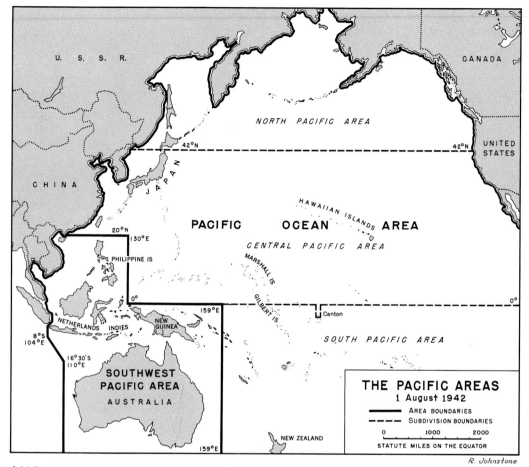

MAP 1

Areas, with headquarters at Pearl Harbor, was Admiral Nimitz, who concurrently served as Commander in Chief, U.S. Pacific Fleet. By the terms of his orders from the Joint Chiefs of Staff, Nimitz commanded virtually all Allied forces in his areas. He directly commanded the Central and North Pacific Areas, but according to his instructions he appointed a subordinate as Commander, South Pacific Area. After October 1942 this post was held by Admiral William F. Halsey, Jr.

Missions assigned Nimitz and Mac-Arthur were practically the same. They were to hold bases essential to the security of the U.S.–Australia line of communications, support operations that would contain the Japanese, support the defense of North America, protect necessary sea and air communications, and prepare for major amphibious offensives.

The first offensive moves of the Allies in the Pacific were undertaken in accordance with the basic Allied strategy for the conduct of the war—Germany would be defeated first and, pending the defeat of the

German forces, the Allies would defend in the Pacific. But it had long been agreed that the Commonwealth of Australia and the Dominion of New Zealand, valuable as integral economic and political units of the British Commonwealth of Nations and as bases for future operations, would not be allowed to fall to the enemy. It was therefore necessary that the Allies hold the British Pacific possessions and retain control of the vital lines of communications to them. In early 1942 a substantial number of forces were sent from the United States to Australia and the bases along the line of communications. Defense of that line was also a primary mission of the U.S. Pacific Fleet.

Thus, when that fleet thrashed the Japanese at Midway, the Joint Chiefs' next move was clear. With the Japanese infiltrating southward from Rabaul through the Solomons and New Guinea toward the line of communications and Port Moresby, General George C. Marshall, Chief of Staff, U.S. Army, and Admiral Ernest J. King, Commander in Chief, U.S. Fleet, and Chief of Naval Operations, on 2 July 1942 ordered the South and Southwest Pacific forces to advance through the Solomons and New Guinea to seize Rabaul and remove the enemy threats. Forces of the two areas moved promptly to the attack, and in the lengthy Guadalcanal and Papua Campaigns, which dragged on until early 1943, succeeded in halting the enemy's southward advance.[6]

By February 1943 the armed forces of the two areas were still far from capturing Rabaul, but they had insured the safety of the line of communications between the United States and the British Pacific dominions. With the Japanese on the defensive, the supply lines fairly safe, and Allied

air and surface strength on the increase, the Joint Chiefs of Staff could consider the possibility of further offensive operations in the Pacific, especially in the areas under Nimitz' immediate command.

The Casablanca Conference

While the Guadalcanal and Papua Campaigns were slowly drawing to a close, American and British planners met once more to decide, among other things, a future course of operations for the Pacific theater. The meeting was convened in Casablanca, French Morocco, in January of 1943. In attendance were President Roosevelt with the U.S. Joint Chiefs of Staff and Prime Minister Winston S. Churchill accompanied by the British Chiefs of Staff.[7]

At Casablanca, although the British and Americans were agreed on such larger issues as the necessity for beating Germany first, there were some points of disagreement that had to be settled before the Allied program for 1943 could be determined. The British were generally reluc-

[6] See John Miller, jr., *Guadalcanal: The First Offensive*, UNITED STATES ARMY IN WORLD WAR II (Washington, 1949); Samuel Milner, *Victory in Papua*, UNITED STATES ARMY IN WORLD WAR II (Washington, 1955); Samuel Eliot Morison, HISTORY OF UNITED STATES NAVAL OPERATIONS IN WORLD WAR II, Vol. IV, *Coral Sea, Midway, and Submarine Actions* (Boston: Little, Brown and Company, 1949), and Vol. V, *The Struggle for Guadalcanal* (Boston: Little, Brown and Company, 1949); Maj. John L. Zimmerman, USMCR, *The Guadalcanal Campaign* (Washington, 1949); Wesley Frank Craven and James Lea Cate, eds., THE ARMY AIR FORCES IN WORLD WAR II, Vol. IV, *The Pacific: Guadalcanal to Saipan, August 1942 to July 1944* (hereafter cited as *AAF IV*) (Chicago: University of Chicago Press, 1950).
[7] The Joint Chiefs of Staff together with the British Chiefs of Staff, or their representatives in Washington, constituted the Combined Chiefs of Staff (CCS).

AMERICAN REPRESENTATIVES AT CASABLANCA CONFERENCE. *Back row, standing, left to right: Mr. Harry L. Hopkins; Lt. Gen. Henry H. Arnold, Commanding General, Army Air Forces; Lt. Gen. Brehon B. Somervell, Commanding General, Services of Supply; Mr. W. Averell Harriman, Lend-Lease Coordinator in Great Britain. Front row, seated, left to right: General George C. Marshall, Chief of Staff, U.S. Army; President Franklin D. Roosevelt; Admiral Ernest J. King, Commander in Chief, U.S. Fleet, and Chief of Naval Operations.*

tant to go immediately as far in the Pacific as the Americans desired.[8]

The position taken by the American representatives was that, having seized the the initiative from Japan the previous August at Guadalcanal, it would be unwise to relinquish it and allow the Japanese to dig in too strongly or to mount a counteroffensive. Throughout the conference they continually stressed the importance of keeping constant pressure on Japan. The British, on the other hand, expressed their opposition to greater efforts in the Pacific at that time. They reminded

their American colleagues of the extreme importance of beating Germany first, and in that connection of giving substantial aid to the Soviet Union. The Japanese, they suggested, should be contained by limited offensives until Germany fell.[9]

The most articulate spokesman for the American position was Admiral King, who introduced the question of a Central

---

[8] For a more complete discussion see John Miller, jr., "The Casablanca Conference and Pacific Strategy," *Military Affairs,* XIII (1949), 209–15.

[9] CCS 135, 26 Dec 42, title: Basic Strategic Concept for 1943; CCS 135/1, 2 Jan 43, title: Basic Strategic Concept for 1943—The European Theater.

Pacific offensive to the Combined Chiefs in the afternoon of 14 January. He began his discussion with an analysis of the strategic situation in the Pacific, where, he declared, the Allies were engaging the enemy on four fronts: the Alaska-Aleutians area, the Hawaii–Midway line, the South and Southwest Pacific Areas, and the China-Burma-India theater. After pointing out that the object of the Guadalcanal and Papuan operations was to secure the approaches to northeast Australia, and that Rabaul was the key to the situation there, he brought forward the problem of where to go after Rabaul was captured by the Allies.

The Philippine Islands, King advocated should certainly be a major objective, although he was not prepared at that time to rule out completely the possibility of driving through the Aleutians against the Japanese home islands. As between the East Indies and the Philippines, the latter was preferable since an attack on the Indies would be a frontal assault against a strong position, whereas the Philippines could be taken on the flank. Although King did not make the point explicitly, implicit in his analysis was the fact that seizure of the Philippines would cut off Japan from the vast riches of the Indies, especially oil, since the Philippines squarely blocked the sea routes between Japan and the Indies.

With the Philippines as a major objective, King argued, the next problem was the selection of a route of approach. He did not definitely commit himself on that point, though from his analysis it appears that he favored the Central Pacific. For years, he observed, the Naval War College had been studying the question of how to recapture the Philippines in the event they were taken by the enemy. Three routes of

approach had been considered: an approach from the north to Luzon via the Aleutians; a southern route that was outflanked by enemy bases; and a direct route through the Central Pacific. The direct thrust, King declared, would necessitate "establishing a base in the northwestern Marshalls and then proceeding to Truk and the Marianas." Later in the meeting he spoke strongly in favor of taking Truk and the Marianas. Both Admiral King and General Marshall re-emphasized the importance of keeping the Japanese under pressure by retaining the initiative, for, as King warned, there was always the danger that the Japanese might mass their remaining aircraft carriers for another great strike at either Midway or Samoa.[10]

Three days later the American representatives at Casablanca submitted a more detailed proposal for immediate operations in the Pacific. Again arguing that it was essential that the Japanese be kept under "continual pressure sufficient in power and extent to absorb the disposable Japanese military effort," they proposed that the following steps be taken:

1. Seizure and consolidation of positions in the Solomons and in eastern New Guinea up to the Huon Peninsula, and of the New Britain-New Ireland area;

[10] Min, 56th mtg CCS, 14 Jan 43. Proceedings and papers of the Casablanca Conference are filed in sequence with the CCS and JCS minutes and papers. They were also printed and bound, along with the proceedings of the meetings between the President and Prime Minister, in a volume entitled Casablanca Conference: Papers and Minutes of Meetings (edited and printed by the CCS, 1943) and filed in the office of the G-3. See also Robert E. Sherwood, *Roosevelt and Hopkins: An Intimate History* (New York: Harper & Brothers, 1948), Ch. XXVII, for an analysis of the conference from Harry Hopkins' point of view. The discussion of strategy at the Casablanca Conference will be more fully treated in Maurice Matloff, The Strategy of Coalition Warfare, 1943–1944, a volume now in preparation for this series.

2. Seizure of Kiska and Agattu in the Aleutians;

3. Seizure of the Gilberts, Marshalls, and Carolines (including Truk) after the capture of Rabaul;

4. Occupation of New Guinea as far as the Dutch border as an extension of the Truk operation; and

5. Operations in Burma to keep China in the war and to intensify attacks by China-based planes against shipping.

Increases in Allied forces for the Pacific and Burma in 1943 would partly depend on what the Japanese did, but the reinforcements were planned: 250,000 air and ground troops, 500 planes, the larger portion of new U.S. warships, 1,250,000 tons of shipping, and reinforcements to the British Eastern Fleet for Burma.[11]

Once more the British objected on the ground that Pacific operations might divert enough Allied strength to jeopardize the fight against Germany. Again both King and Marshall rose to defend the American position. To the British suggestion that the Allies confine their Pacific operations in 1943 to Rabaul and Burma alone, King replied that there were resources available to include the Marshalls as well. The month of May might find Rabaul in Allied hands, he argued, and since the Burma campaign would not begin until November, combat forces would remain idle in the interim unless they could be re-employed in the Marshalls. General Marshall was able to allay the British worries that Pacific offensives would cut into operations against Germany by proposing that the Gilberts-Marshalls-Carolines invasions be undertaken "with the resources available in the theater." The British finally assented, and there were no more disagreements at Casablanca over Pacific strategy.[12]

Thus, for their Pacific program for 1943, the Allies decided to "make the Aleutians as secure as may be," to advance northwest from Samoa to protect the line of communications to Australia, and to mount diversionary operations against the Malay Barrier. They decided to advance directly west "as practicable" through the Central Pacific toward the line Truk–Guam, particularly against the Marshall Islands, in conjunction with operations against Rabaul, whose capture in 1943 was practically taken for granted. The advance through the Central Pacific would not be allowed to prejudice the recapture of Burma, nor would there by any northward advance from Rabaul toward Truk and Guam unless sufficient forces were available to complete the task and follow up.[13]

As far as Pacific strategy was concerned, the U.S. Joint Chiefs of Staff had accomplished much at Casablanca. They had expounded in some detail the significance of Pacific operations to their British colleagues, and had secured approval of at least a start on the drive across the Central Pacific in 1943. The possibility of beginning the advance was of course closely connected with MacArthur's and Halsey's operations against Rabaul.

MacArthur's Strategic Plans

At his headquarters in Brisbane, General MacArthur had been preparing for the recapture of Rabaul for some time, and

[11] CCS 153 (Revised), 17 Jan 43, title: Situation to be Created in the Eastern Theater (Pacific and Burma) in 1943.

[12] Min, 60th mtg CCS, 18 Jan 43.

[13] Proceedings of the last meeting, Casablanca Conf, pp. 154–69; CCS 155/1, 19 Jan 43, title: Conduct of the War in 1943; CCS 168, 22 Jan 43, title: Conduct of the War in the Pacific Theater in 1943; CCS 170/2, 23 Jan 43, title: Final Report to the President and Prime Minister Summarizing Decisions by the CCS.

by February 1943 had completed a detailed, comprehensive plan known as ELKTON.[14] In addition, he and his staff were considering ways and means to accomplish the ultimate defeat of Japan. Looking far into the future, they concluded that the recapture of Rabaul would gain "important, but not decisive advantages" that would help future operations but would not adversely affect Japan's war economy. In order to strike a great blow at the enemy's capacity to wage war, MacArthur and his planners reasoned, Japan should be cut off from the Netherlands Indies with its great quantities of oil, tin, and rubber. If the Allies seized the Philippines and developed air and naval bases there, Japan could be denied access to the Indies. Thus far MacArthur's conclusions agreed with those expressed by the U.S. Chiefs of Staff at Casablanca. But there was one major difference—the route of approach.

Whereas the Joint Chiefs had clearly intimated that the Philippines were to be approached through the Central Pacific, MacArthur concluded that a drive through the Marshalls and Carolines would have to be made without land-based air support, would be slow, would cost heavily in naval power and shipping, and would "require a re-orientation of front." Since according to his reasoning the Central Pacific route was unwise, MacArthur desired that after he and Halsey had captured Rabaul, Southwest Pacific forces should advance west along the north coast of New Guinea and thence into Mindanao in the southern Philippines. Neutralization of the Palaus and seizure or neutralization of various islands in the Banda and Arafura Seas would protect the flanks of the advance.[15] This long-range plan prepared by General MacArthur's headquarters was designated RENO.

In March 1943 representatives of the Central, South, and Southwest Pacific Areas convened in Washington to meet with the Joint Chiefs and Joint Staff Planners in a series of sessions known as the Pacific Military Conference. This conference paid only slight attention to the Central Pacific; its primary purpose was to decide what should be the next immediate steps in the South and Southwest Pacific theaters. The Joint Chiefs of Staff were not at this time apprised of MacArthur's RENO plan, but they were given the full details of ELKTON.

ELKTON contemplated a drive against Rabaul along two axes—through New Guinea and New Britain on the west and through the Solomons to New Ireland on the east—to culminate in a converging assault on Rabaul. But to execute ELKTON would have required 22⅔ divisions and 45 groups of aircraft. The South and Southwest Pacific Areas together had a total of only 15⅔ trained divisions and less than half enough aircraft. Some reinforcements could be provided, but the everlasting scarcity of troop transports and cargo ships prevented reinforcement on anything like the scale required by ELKTON. As a result, the Joint Chiefs decided not to try to take Rabaul in 1943. Cutting the objectives for 1943 in half, they ordered MacArthur and Halsey to take Woodlark Island and Kiriwina (Trobriand Islands) in the Solomon Sea, to seize the Lae-Salamaua-Finschhafen-Madang area of

---

[14] GHQ SWPA, ELKTON Plan for the Seizure and Occupation of the New Britain-New Ireland-New Guinea Area, 12 and 28 Feb 43 versions. A copy of the 12 February ELKTON is in OCMH files; a copy of the 28 February version is in G-3 files. For a more detailed treatment, see John Miller, jr., CARTWHEEL: The Reduction of Rabaul, a forthcoming volume in this series; for MacArthur's earlier plans see Milner, *Victory in Papua.*

[15] GHQ SWPA, Estimate of Situation and Rough Draft, RENO Plan, 25 Feb 43, OCMH.

New Guinea, to capture western New Britain, and to drive through the Solomons to southern Bougainville.[16]

Thus, the Pacific Military Conference of March settled for the time being the immediate future in MacArthur's and Halsey's theaters of operation. By curtailing the list of objectives to be captured in 1943, the conference also indirectly gave impetus to the Central Pacific drive since any addition to the total shipping, manpower, and equipment that might be made available to the Pacific in the future would not have to be sent to bolster the capture of Rabaul. Instead, it could be assigned to Nimitz' Central Pacific theater. It remained for the Combined Chiefs of Staff to come to a final decision at their next meeting in respect to forthcoming operations in the Central Pacific and to determine which of the two theaters, MacArthur's or Nimitz', should be allocated priority in the drive against Japan.

The Washington Conference and the Strategic Plan for the Defeat of Japan

In May 1943 President Roosevelt and the Joint Chiefs of Staff met once more with Prime Minister Churchill and the British Chiefs of Staff, this time in Washington. The purpose of the Washington conference, which is generally known by its code name TRIDENT, was to re-examine Allied strategy for 1943 in the light of changes in the situation since the meeting at Casablanca. Little had developed in the Pacific since early February, and the conference concerned itself primarily with the European bomber offensive, the cross-Channel attack, possible operations after the seizure of Sicily, and the Burma-China-India theater.[17] But the conference was called upon to consider a tentative plan for

the war in the Pacific drawn up after Casablanca by the highest American strategists.

This plan, prepared by the U.S. Joint Chiefs of Staff and their subordinate committees [18] and submitted to the Washington conference on 20 May 1943, was entitled "The Strategic Plan for the Defeat of Japan." [19] "Strategic Plan" was actually a misnomer. It was not a plan according to strict military definition, for it gave no estimates of enemy strength and dispositions, did not mention the types and numbers of Allied forces that would be required to accomplish the missions it described, said nothing about command or commanders, and did not establish time schedules. Nevertheless, although more of a set of ideas than a plan, the "Strategic Plan" became the cornerstone of Pacific strategy for the remainder of 1943 and for 1944. Furthermore, it diverged widely from MacArthur's strategic concepts as expressed in RENO.

The plan as it stood in May 1943 involved operations by China, Great Britain, and the United States. It also apparently encompassed action by the Pacific domin-

---

[16] GHQ SWPA, ELKTON Plan for the Seizure and Occupation of the New Britain-New Ireland-New Guinea Area, 28 Feb 43; Notes on Pacific Conf Held in March 1943, DRB AGO; JCS 238/5/D, 28 Mar 43, Directive: Plan for Opns for Seizure of the Solomon Islands-New Guinea-New Britain-New Ireland Area. In the end, Rabaul was never assaulted, but was neutralized by air action. For a fuller discussion of these and related points see Miller, CARTWHEEL.

[17] Records of the conference are in the volume, TRIDENT Conference, May 1943, Papers and Minutes of Meetings (edited and printed by CCS, 1943), copy in G-3 files.

[18] The subordinate committees included the Joint War Plans Committee (JWPC), the Joint Strategic Survey Committee (JSSC), and the Joint Staff Planners (JPS).

[19] JSSC 40/2, 3 Apr 43; JPS 67/4, 28 Apr 43; JCS 287, 7 May 43; JCS 287/1, 8 May 43; CCS 220, 14 May 43. All bear the title "Strategic Plan for the Defeat of Japan" or something very similar.

ions of the British Commonwealth of Nations, although these were not mentioned by name.

The ultimate objective of all operations was naturally the unconditional surrender of Japan. It was then thought that securing unconditional surrender might require an Allied invasion of the Japanese home islands, although the U.S. Chiefs of Staff and their subordinates agreed that control of the sea, especially of the western Pacific, might bring about unconditional surrender without invasion, and even without an air offensive. If invasion proved necessary, it could not be successful unless the Japanese will to resist had been seriously weakened. Undermining the enemy's powers of resistance and his desire to keep fighting by a large, sustained air offensive against the home islands was regarded as the best method. The possibility of employing air bases in the Kuril Islands, Formosa, and Siberia to mount the offensive was discussed, but it was agreed that China offered the best sites.[20] China would thus have to be maintained, and United States and British forces would need to fight their way to China in order to secure a good port, preferably Hong Kong.

The two Allies would, according to the plan, get to China by three general routes: through Burma; through the Strait of Malacca and the South China Sea to Hong Kong from the west; and from the east across the Pacific and through the Celebes Sea to Hong Kong. The British, assisted by the Americans and Chinese, would recapture Burma, and would make the drive through the Strait of Malacca to Hong Kong by a series of amphibious operations. The Chinese would help capture Hong Kong and with American aid would seize and defend the necessary air base sites. Meanwhile, United States forces would be driving through the Celebes Sea to Hong Kong. Then China, Great Britain, the United States, and apparently the Pacific dominions would join forces in a grand air bombardment of Japan. Nothing was said about the invasion of Japan beyond the statement that it might be necessary. Although exact timing was not discussed, it was then generally thought that the final advances would not be undertaken before the fall of Germany, and might last until 1948.

The next problem dealt with by the plan was that of the selection of the route and methods by which U.S. forces would approach Hong Kong from the east. Here was one of the basic strategic decisions of the Pacific war. United States forces, it was decided, were to advance westward from Pearl Harbor through the Central Pacific, and through the South and Southwest Pacific Areas to open a line of communications to the Celebes Sea, recapture the Philippine Islands, secure control of the northern part of the South China Sea, and join in the descent upon Hong Kong.

The main effort in the westward advance would be made in the Central Pacific,[21] a subsidiary effort through the South and Southwest Pacific. This choice of the Central Pacific as the most advantageous route of advance was dictated by several considerations. It was much shorter and less roundabout than the southern route and would not require as many ships, troops, and supplies. It was far more healthful than the pest-ridden jungles of the Solomons and New Guinea. Through the Central Pacific, the Allies could strike the enemy's most

---

[20] The Marianas were not mentioned as a possible base for B-29's, whose capabilities had been briefly discussed at Casablanca.

[21] Italics are the authors'.

vulnerable flank and isolate Japan from her overseas empire. Furthermore, if Allied fleets destroyed or contained the enemy fleet, they could then strike directly from the Pacific against the Japanese home islands, without relying exclusively on aerial bombardment from fields in China. The Japanese could deploy only limited air and ground forces in the islands and atolls of the Central Pacific, whereas on the southern route only the availability of troops, planes, and ships would limit the size of the Japanese forces. The Allies, on the other hand, were under no such handicap because of their superiority in carrier-based air power. In the absence of land-based aircraft, carrier-based planes could support amphibious operations against island fortresses.

A successful drive through the Central Pacific would outflank the Japanese in New Guinea, whereas operations along the northern New Guinea coast would neither eject them from nor outflank them in the Central Pacific, and the Japanese would retain relative freedom of naval maneuver. And, as Admiral King had pointed out at Casablanca, an Allied drive exclusively along the southern route would expose flanks and rear to enemy attacks. Whereas an attack through New Guinea into the Philippines or the Indies would be a head-on push against large islands containing positions closely arranged in depth, one directed through the Central Pacific would strike at vulnerable positions separated from one another by vast ocean reaches, and thus not quite so well placed to support one another. Seizure of the Marshalls and Carolines would give the Allies control of much of the Pacific and place them in position to isolate Japan from the Philippines–Indies salient, perhaps by the seizure of Formosa. Further,

the great American naval shipbuilding program would be largely wasted if the southern route were used, and certainly the U.S. Pacific Fleet could best be used in long-range offensives.

But if all these factors favored the Central Pacific as the area where the "main effort" against Japan should be launched, other considerations argued for continuing the South-Southwest drive at least as a secondary effort in support of the principal offensive. In the first place, it was believed that Australia would doubtless object to a redirection of all offensive effort to the Central Pacific. Besides, the oil fields of the Vogelkop Peninsula of New Guinea, then in Japanese hands, might be of some use to the Allies. Furthermore, Allied forces in the South and Southwest Pacific Areas were already in close contact with the Japanese, and shifting them all to the Central Pacific would waste time and shipping. Finally, and most important, was the fact that twin drives along the central and southern axes would provide more opportunities for mutual support, and by preventing the Japanese from being able to guess the time and place of forthcoming advances would keep them strategically off balance. For these reasons, then, American strategic planners decided to make the twin drives, with the main effort through the Central Pacific.

On 20 May the "Strategic Plan for the Defeat of Japan" was submitted to the Combined Chiefs of Staff. It was accepted as a "basis for combined study and elaboration of future plans." [22] Next day Admiral King spoke to the Combined Chiefs at some length to explain the American proposals. He reverted to many of the statements he and Marshall had made at

---

[22] Min, 90th mtg CCS, 20 May 43.

Casablanca regarding routes across the Pacific, the importance of the various Allied lines of communications, and the necessity for maintaining constant pressure on the Japanese communication lines and recapturing the Philippines. In pursuit of these goals, Rabaul, Truk, and the Marianas were important intermediate objectives. The Marianas, which King stated were an important base on the Japanese lines of communications, he regarded as a key to success.[23]

Two days later the Combined Chiefs of Staff approved a lengthy paper containing the U.S. Joint Chiefs' proposals for Allied objectives in the Pacific and Far East in 1943 and 1944. This paper, based on the "Strategic Plan," repeated previous arguments and provided estimates of forces required and forces actually available for particular operations.

Offensives in 1943 and 1944 should aim at the following:

1. Conduct of air operations in and from China;
2. Conduct of operations in Burma designed to increase the movement of supplies to China;
3. Ejection of the Japanese from the Aleutians;
4. Seizure of the Marshalls and Carolines;
5. Seizure of the Solomons, the Bismarck Archipelago, and enemy-held New Guinea; and
6. Intensification of operations against the Japanese lines of communications.

It was estimated that capture of the Bismarck Archipelago, which would secure the line of communications to Australia and help provide access to the Celebes Sea, would require perhaps seven divisions of which five would be amphibious units. If Rabaul were effectively neutralized by air bombardment, perhaps only five—three amphibious—would be needed. Assuming that Allied forces could capture western New Britain and southern Bougainville by December 1943, the Joint Chiefs concluded that the Bismarck Archipelago operations would not be completed before April 1944.

Seizure of the Marshalls, it was agreed, was essential to an extension of the line of communications to the Celebes Sea, and would also shorten and secure the routes to Australia. From the Marshalls, land-based aircraft could help support naval surface operations against the enemy's communication lines, and there was always the possibility that an Allied push into the Marshalls would force the Japanese fleet to come out fighting. The Marshalls operation would require two reinforced amphibious divisions, four heavy bombardment and two fighter groups of land-based planes, and aircraft from four standard and four auxiliary aircraft carriers, in addition to four battleships, three more auxiliary carriers, twelve cruisers, sixty-three destroyers, twenty-four attack transports, forty-four tank landing ships (LST's), plus landing craft. Garrison forces would include one reinforced division, 10 defense battalions, 545 planes, and 18 motor torpedo boats. The entire operation, from the initial invasion to the time the assault troops were withdrawn and readied for the invasion of the Carolines, would last six and three-fourths months.

Capture of the Carolines would be a much larger affair. Possession of this enormous string of atolls would help give the Allies control of the Central Pacific, provide them with a major fleet base at Truk,

---

[23] Min, 92d mtg CCS, 21 May 43.

and put them in position to push on to the southwest or to threaten the Japanese archipelago directly. Truk and Ponape, as well as various other atolls, would have to be captured; air raids against Guam and Saipan in the Marianas would be necessary. It was agreed that the Carolines should be approached through the Marshalls even if Rabaul were in Allied hands.

No specific time limit was set, but the Combined Chiefs of Staff agreed that the proposed Carolines campaign would be lengthy. And it would require, they estimated, 3 reinforced amphibious divisions, 2 heavy bomber groups, 10 carriers of the *Enterprise* and *Essex* classes, 7 auxiliary carriers, 4 modern battleships, 9 old battleships, 31 cruisers, 108 destroyers, 20 submarines, 45 attack transports, 15 attack cargo ships, 6 LSD's (landing ships, dock), 3 headquarters ships (AGC's), and miscellaneous auxiliaries. To garrison the islands would take two reinforced divisions and three defense battalions, plus aircraft.

Controlling factors would include amphibious equipment and availability of divisions with amphibious training. There were then two Marine divisions (the 1st and 2d, in the Southwest and South Pacific Areas, respectively) that were ready to go, with the 3d Marine Division in the South Pacific supposed to be ready for combat by 15 July. The 4th Marine Division in California was expected to complete its training before the end of the year. Since transferring divisions from the South and Southwest Pacific to the Central Pacific would take many ships that were urgently needed elsewhere, it was agreed that two more Marine divisions and two more Army amphibious divisions were required in the Pacific.

As far as naval forces were concerned, the picture was bright. The huge fleet

could be provided, the Combined Chiefs asserted, and they concluded that the forces listed would be sufficient to carry on simultaneous operations in the Central and South Pacific Areas in 1943 and 1944.[24]

The final resolutions of the conference, as approved by President Roosevelt and Prime Minister Churchill, established the Allied objectives for the remainder of 1943 and part of 1944, and allotted certain forces for reaching those objectives. All decisions reached at Casablanca that did not square with the Washington resolutions were canceled. The Americans and British restated their determination to force the unconditional surrender of the Axis at the earliest possible date. They decided to "maintain and extend unremitting pressure" on Japan to reduce her war-making power and to gain new bases with the expectation that Britain, the United States, and all Allied Pacific powers (including the Soviet Union if possible) would direct all their resources to force the surrender of Japan soon after Germany's defeat.

The program for the Pacific and Far East was ambitious and complicated. Using as a basis the U.S. "Strategic Plan for the Defeat of Japan," the Combined Staff Planners were to prepare an "appreciation leading to a plan for the defeat of Japan," including an estimate of the necessary forces. Recapture of Burma in 1943 was considered impossible, but preliminary operations were to be started, air operations intensified, and the flow of supplies to China augmented.

In the Pacific, the objectives recommended by the Joint Chiefs—ejection of

---

[24] CCS 239/1, 23 May 43, title: Opns in the Pacific and Far East in 1943–44.

the Japanese from the Aleutians,[25] seizure of the Marshalls and Carolines, seizure of the Solomons, Bismarck Archipelago, and Japanese-held New Guinea, and intensification of operations against the Japanese lines of communication—were all accepted.

Unlike Casablanca, the Washington decisions included estimates of forces required, concluding on the cheering note that the Allies had enough of everything, granted that the rate of losses, especially in shipping, did not markedly increase.[26] By 1 January 1944, according to existing plans, one Marine and three Army divisions would be in the Central Pacific; the South Pacific would have two Marine, five U.S. Army, and one New Zealand divisions; the Southwest Pacific, four U.S. Army infantry, one U.S. Army airborne, one Marine, and eleven Australian Army divisions, of which three would be available for offensive operations. According to the Joint Chiefs' estimates of 12 May two more divisions were thus needed for the Marshalls, two more for the Carolines, and three additional for New Guinea.[27]

Thus the Washington conference of May 1943, although not primarily concerned with Pacific strategy, made important decisions regarding the conduct of the Pacific war. By approving in a general way the "Strategic Plan for the Defeat of Japan," it set the pattern of strategy for the duration of the war against Japan. By authorizing the drive through the Marshalls and Carolines and approving allocation of the required forces, it determined the course of Admiral Nimitz' operations for about a year.

With the selection of the classic Central Pacific route, the Joint Chiefs now faced the tasks of deciding on exact objectives and of picking the precise units for the forthcoming drive across the Pacific.

---

[25] In May 1943, while the Washington conference was under way, naval forces from Nimitz' command and the 7th Infantry Division from the Western Defense Command recaptured Attu. The Japanese evacuated Kiska shortly before the landing of a joint U.S.-Canadian force there in August. The Aleutians were thus free of Japanese.

[26] CCS 242/6, 25 May 43, title: Draft of Agreed Resolutions. See also CCS 232/1, 18 May 43, title: Agreed Essentials on the Conduct of the War.

[27] CCS 244/1, 25 May 1943, title: Implementation of Assumed Basic Undertakings and Specific Operations for the Conduct of the War in 1943-1944.

CHAPTER II

Selection of Targets and Tactical Planning

Selection of the Targets

The Washington conference of May 1943 (TRIDENT) set forth the general outline of proposed operations in the Pacific for the second half of 1943 and for 1944, but much work, thought, and discussion remained before detailed plans could be devised to carry out these broad concepts. Two main problems were still to be decided. The first of these was the choice of exact targets within the Marshalls group. The group consists of a double chain of coral atolls lying between latitude 5° and 15° north and longitude 162° and 173° east. There are altogether thirty-two islands and atolls and some selection had to be made between them.[1] Also, the possibility early presented itself that the Marshalls might best be approached by way of the Gilberts, a group of sixteen islands and atolls formerly belonging to the British and lying athwart the equator in the general area of longitude 173° east.[2] (*Map 2*)

More difficult of solution was the second problem, which involved the balance and co-ordination of the Allied offensive as between the Central Pacific theater and General MacArthur's Southwest Pacific Area. Although the "Strategic Plan for the Defeat of Japan" had clearly indicated that the "main effort" in the westward advance would be through the Central Pacific, there were still those among the various planning staffs in Washington—in addition of course to General MacArthur himself—who doubted the wisdom of giving the Central Pacific offensive priority over MacArthur's proposed drive against Rabaul. These doubts had to be resolved or the objections overruled before final plans for a Marshalls operation could be developed. Any troops, aircraft, and shipping that were to be made available to the Central Pacific drive would have to be diverted from the pool either already under MacArthur's control or potentially assignable to his theater. It was to these delicate and difficult problems that planners in Washington addressed themselves in June and July of 1943.

Work began immediately after the Washington conference. On 27 May the Joint Staff Planners directed the Joint War Plans Committee to estimate the forces required for an invasion of the Marshalls and to recommend target dates.[3] The War Plans Committee promptly delivered a preliminary report suggesting that the in-

---

[1] R. W. Robson, *The Pacific Islands Handbook, 1944* (New York: The Macmillan Company, 1946), p. 146.
[2] *Ibid.*, p. 161.
[3] Memo, JPS for JWPC, 27 May 43, sub: Examination into Pacific Theater, with JWPC 39/D in ABC 384 Marshall Islands (10 Jun 43), 1.

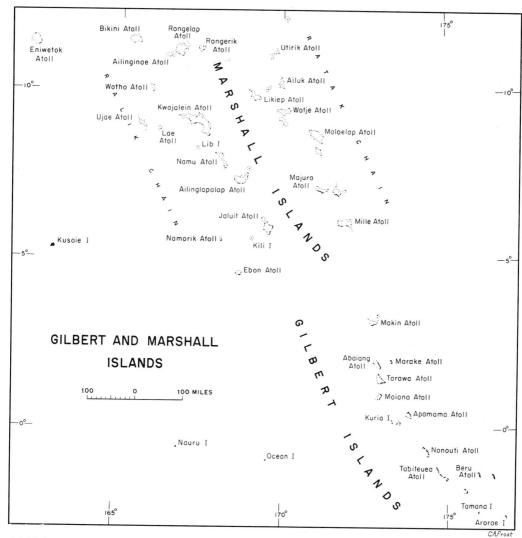

Bikini Atoll   Rongelap Atoll
Eniwetok Atoll   Rongerik Atoll   Utirik Atoll
Ailinginae Atoll
—10°—   Wotho Atoll   Ailuk Atoll
MARSHALL   Likiep Atoll
Kwajalein Atoll   Wotje Atoll
Ujae Atoll
Lae Atoll   Maloelap Atoll
Lib I
Namu Atoll
Ailinglapalap Atoll
Majuro Atoll
Jaluit Atoll
Mille Atoll
—5°—   Kusaie I   Namorik Atoll
Kili I
Ebon Atoll   —5°—

GILBERT
Makin Atoll

GILBERT AND MARSHALL

ISLANDS
Abaiang Atoll   Marake Atoll
Tarawa Atoll
Maiana Atoll
100   0   100 MILES
Kuria I.   Apamama Atoll
—0°—   —0°—
Nauru I
Ocean I   ISLANDS   Nonouti Atoll
Tabiteuea Atoll   Beru Atoll
Tamana I
165°   170°   175°   Aroroe I

C.A.Frost

MAP 2

vasion of the Marshalls be carried out in three phases: (1) seizure of Kwajalein, Wotje, and Maloelap Atolls in the center; (2) occupation of Eniwetok and Kusaie as outposts to the north and west; and (3) mopping up to seize or neutralize the entire Wake–Gilberts–Marshalls system. The operation, it was recommended, should be launched toward the end of October to coincide with planned Burma operations. Since the initial attacks against the Marshalls would be the first attempt in U.S. military history to assault defended atolls, it was believed that "battle-tested shock troops with amphibious training" totaling one corps of two divisions would be needed for the first phase. The committee recognized that the best assault craft for the invasions would be amphibian tractors (landing vehicles, tracked) which, when launched from tank landing ships outside the range of shore batteries, could deploy and proceed shoreward without much danger of being stopped by the fringing reefs so abundant in that part of the world.

The only available battle-tested amphibious troops were the 1st Marine Division in the Southwest Pacific and the 2d Marine Division in the South Pacific, although it was thought possible to substitute the 7th Infantry Division for one of the Marine divisions once the Aleutian operations were concluded. Invasion of the Marshalls in October would necessarily deprive MacArthur and Halsey of their only amphibious divisions with combat experience and thus require that South–Southwest Pacific operations be halted by early August. The Joint War Plans Committee therefore recommended that Mac-Arthur and Halsey be ordered to conduct a holding action along the line Russell Islands–Woodlark–Kiriwina–Buna until the Marshalls operation was concluded.[4]

The proposition that MacArthur and Halsey merely conduct a holding action until the conclusion of the Marshalls operation was met with little favor in the Operations Division of the War Department General Staff or by General Mac-Arthur. Members of the Operations Division argued that for both political and military reasons MacArthur's campaign against Rabaul (CARTWHEEL) should not be impeded. Halting this campaign, it was held, would cause difficult political repercussions "both in Australia–New Zealand, and in this country." On the military side, any such cessation of the offensive would decrease pressure on the Japanese, warn them that they would be attacked

elsewhere, create a lull in an area where Allied air operations were most effective, and eliminate operations tending to relieve pressure on Burma. A defeat in the Marshalls, continued the Operations Division's thesis, would leave the United States for a time without forces to bring pressure on Japan, and might expose the line of communications to the Southwest Pacific. If forces were transferred from Mac-Arthur's area to Nimitz', any stalemate that might develop in the Marshalls could only result in an interval of complete inactivity. The commitment of all available amphibious equipment would postpone for a long time the renewal of amphibious operations in the South-Southwest Pacific. There were other logistical difficulties as well. There probably would not be enough cargo ships and transports. Besides, delivery of amphibian tractors (LVT's) in quantity had just begun, and it was doubtful that enough would be ready by October. Success in these operations would be dependent on this "new and untried type of equipment," and the troops would need to be trained in its use.[5]

Both the Joint Planners and the Joint Chiefs of Staff agreed that MacArthur's campaign against Rabaul should not be interrupted but concluded that the Central Pacific drive could be launched concurrently anyway. The Joint War Plans Committee was ordered to prepare a plan for an offensive against the Marshalls to be executed in November or December of

---

[4] JPS 205, 10 Jun 43, title: Opns Against Marshall Islands.

[5] OPD brief, title: Notes on Preliminary Rpt by JWPC, Opns Against Marshall Islands, atchd to JPS 205, ABC 384 Marshall Islands (10 Jun 43), 1.

OPD was wrong about the amphibian tractor, which was neither new nor untried. It had given excellent service during the landings in the Solomons in August 1942.

1943, but with the understanding that MacArthur's campaign should proceed according to schedule.[6] The Joint Chiefs directed Nimitz to prepare a tactical plan for seizing the Marshalls and submit it to Washington. They also radioed MacArthur explaining to him that more extensive operations in the Pacific were warranted by the increasing Allied naval strength, and that they were contemplating invading the Marshalls about mid-November, employing the 1st and 2d Marine Divisions plus all assault transports and cargo ships and the major portion of naval forces from Halsey's area.[7]

General MacArthur's response was immediate and unfavorable. On 20 June he radioed the Chief of Staff that he was disturbed over the effect the proposed invasion of the Marshalls would have on future operations in the South and Southwest Pacific. Withdrawal of the two Marine divisions would prevent the ultimate assault against Rabaul toward which his current operations were leading. He refused to accept the proposition already agreed to by the joint planners in Washington that the main effort against Japan should be made through the Central Pacific. On the contrary, he argued that "a diversionary attack [in the Marshalls] would of course assist the main effort in this theater [Southwest Pacific]," but that troops should come from the continental United States, "rather than be subtracted from the main attack to the extent that may result in its collapse. . . . I am entirely in ignorance regarding the discussions and decisions of the recent Washington conference and request that I be advised in this respect insofar as it affects the broad concept of operations in this theater. . . ." MacArthur went on to urge the principles of the RENO plan, long cherished by his head-

quarters. "From a broad strategic viewpoint," the best method of defeating Japan would be to move from Australia through New Guinea to Mindanao with "utterly essential" land-based air support all the way. In this fashion could Japan best be cut off from her conquered territory. An attack through the Marshalls, he argued, would involve a series of carrier-supported amphibious attacks against objectives defended by naval units, ground troops, and land-based aircraft. He made reference to Midway as an example of what he considered such folly.[8] "Moreover," he maintained, "no vital strategic objective is reached until the series of amphibious frontal attacks succeed in reaching Mindanao."[9]

In the end, none of these arguments was deemed compelling enough to dissuade the Joint Chiefs of Staff from their intention to launch the Central Pacific drive in 1943. But the fear of diverting too large a force from MacArthur's theater was primarily responsible for the eventual decision to initiate that drive against the Gilberts rather than directly against the Marshalls.

Even before the receipt of General MacArthur's radiogram, the Joint War Plans Committee had proposed as a possible alternative to a direct strike against the Marshalls the preliminary capture of islands in the Gilberts as well as Nauru, some 390 miles to the westward. The committee's general concept embraced simul-

---

[6] Min, 80th mtg JPS, 13 Jun 43; JWPC 54/1/D, 14 Jun 43, title: Sequence of Certain Pacific Opns.

[7] Min, 92d mtg JCS, 15 Jun 43; Rad, COMINCH to CINCPAC, CM-IN 9983, 16 Jun 43; Rad, JCS to MacArthur, CM-OUT 6093, 15 Jun 43.

[8] MacArthur was referring here to the attempted Japanese invasion of Midway, which was supported exclusively by carrier aircraft.

[9] Rads, MacArthur to Marshall, CM-IN 13149, 20 Jun 43, and CM-IN 13605, 22 Jun 43.

taneous landings on Nauru, and on Makin and Tarawa in the Gilberts, to be covered by carrier attacks against other Japanese bases in the Gilberts and Marshalls. These islands, once secured, could then be employed as air bases from which to attack the Marshalls and reconnoiter the Carolines. Invasion of the Gilberts and Nauru would require, in addition to naval forces, one Marine division and and one regimental combat team, several amphibian tractor battalions and other reinforcing units, five heavy bomber squadrons, and one fighter group. The committee still considered this approach to be inferior to a direct invasion of the Marshalls, but recommended that it be undertaken if enough forces could not be mustered for the Marshalls.[10]

This proposal to attack the Gilberts rather than the Marshalls found immediate favor with the Operations Division. It would obviously require fewer forces and thus be less likely to interfere with MacArthur's plans. Although recognizing that heavy and medium bombers for the Gilberts could only be provided by taking them from somewhere else, the division nevertheless expressed itself to Col. Frank N. Roberts, then acting as Army member of the Joint Staff Planners, as favoring this alternative plan.[11]

While various staff planners were thus approaching what might be considered a compromise between the Central and Southwest Pacific concepts of strategy, the idea of giving priority to the Central Pacific once again received strong support on 28 June when the Joint Strategic Survey Committee presented its views of Pacific strategy to the Joint Chiefs of Staff. This committee, consisting of Lt. Gen. Stanley D. Embick of the Army, Vice Adm. Russell Willson of the Navy, and

Maj. Gen. Muir S. Fairchild of the Army Air Forces, pointed out that the Allies in the South and Southwest Pacific, by driving northward against Rabaul, had been attempting to reverse the polarity of the Japanese campaign of early 1942. This reversal held "small promise of reasonable success in the near future." The committee therefore recommended that a campaign in Nimitz's area be given priority over MacArthur's campaign against Rabaul. Only in operations against the Marshall and Caroline Islands, argued Embick, Willson, and Fairchild, was there a chance to use the fleet to best advantage. Central Pacific advances would also support the defense of Australia and shorten the line of communications to the Southwest Pacific. The Strategic Survey Committee therefore recommended that seizure of the Marshalls and Carolines, which it regarded as the best action that could be inaugurated in 1943, be the first step in the drive toward the Celebes Sea.[12]

Next day this committee sat with the Joint Chiefs and discussed the suggestions. Admiral William D. Leahy, always a strong supporter of MacArthur and his strategic ideas, pointed out that granting priority to the Central Pacific would be a "complete reversal" of existing policy and projected plans.[13] On the other hand Admiral King, expressing dissatisfaction with the slow "inch-by-inch" progress to date, asserted that although Rabaul was important, Luzon was even more so, and that

[10] JPS 205/2, 18 Jun 43, title: Opns Against Marshall Islands.

[11] OPD brief, title: Summation of Memo on Opns in CENPAC, with JPS 205/2 in ABC 384 Marshall Islands (10 Jun 43), 1; OPD brief, Notes on 94th Mtg JCS, 29 Jun 43, with JCS 386 in OPD 384 Pacific (28 Jun 43).

[12] JCS 386, 28 Jun 43, title: Strategy in the Pacific.

[13] Fleet Admiral William D. Leahy, *I Was There* (New York: Whittlesey House, 1950).

the latter could best be approached by way of the Japanese Mandated Islands and the Marianas. The Joint Chiefs then turned over the committee's recommendations to the Joint Staff Planners for further study.[14] What emerged was in general a vindication of the Central Pacific concept, with the qualification that the first steps in that direction be made by way of the Gilberts.

On 19 July the Joint Staff Planners submitted to the Joint Chiefs a long analysis summing up the relative importance of Central and Southwest Pacific operations as well as a draft of a directive to Admiral Nimitz. The Staff Planners recommended that continued pressure be applied against Rabaul and then in detail spelled out the reasons for the desirability of a concurrent push through the Central Pacific. Such a move, they argued, would have advantages: (1) it would force the Japanese to disperse their air strength; (2) it would allow the United States to use its superior naval forces in an area where enemy ground and air forces were weak; and (3) it would enlarge the Allied front facing the Japanese and at the same time take place near enough to the Solomons to allow naval forces to support operations in either or both areas.

The first step in the Central Pacific drive, they recommended, should be an invasion of the Gilberts and Nauru. Good air photographs of the Marshalls would be required before an invasion there, and the islands to the south would provide convenient bases for air reconnaissance. Capture of the Gilberts and Nauru, however, was considered only a preliminary to the main offensive against the Marshalls and Carolines—a drive already agreed on by President Roosevelt, Prime Minister Churchill, and the Combined Chiefs of Staff. The Staff Planners therefore recommended that the Gilberts and Nauru be invaded by Admiral Nimitz' forces about 1 December 1943.[15]

Next day (20 July) the Joint Chiefs of Staff met to discuss this analysis. Once again Admiral Leahy expressed his sympathy with MacArthur's point of view by insisting that the proposed Central Pacific drive not be allowed to "interfere with . . . operations being conducted by General MacArthur. . . ." To this Admiral King replied that the invasion of the Gilberts would augment rather than curtail MacArthur's campaigns. General Marshall added that the United States could ill afford to let her great carrier forces in the Pacific stand idle and agreed that a campaign in the Central Pacific would be helpful to MacArthur's planned offensive against Rabaul. General Henry H. Arnold, the commanding general of the Army Air Forces, agreed with the concept behind the new offensive and stated that four additional bomber squadrons could be provided. The Joint Chiefs thereupon approved the Joint Planners' directive but, on Admiral King's motion, set 15 November rather than 1 December as the date for the invasion of the Gilberts.[16]

The Joint Chiefs sent Nimitz his orders the same day. He was instructed to organize and train necessary forces, to "capture, occupy, defend, and develop bases in the GILBERT GROUP and NAURU" on 15 November, and to occupy other islands and develop "airfields and facilities thereon" as necessary to support the invasion of the principal objectives.

All surface forces of the Pacific Fleet

[14] Min, 94th mtg JCS, 29 Jun 43.
[15] JCS 386/1, 19 Jul 43, title: Strategy in the Pacific.
[16] Min, 97th mtg JCS, 20 Jul 43.

were available to Nimitz. The Joint Chiefs estimated he would require five modern battleships, seven old battleships, seventeen carriers (including four light and seven escort carriers), and twelve cruisers, plus thirty-seven troop transports and cargo ships as well as other amphibious craft assigned the Central Pacific. Air units would include all Pacific Fleet naval aircraft except those in the South and Southwest Pacific, in addition to elements of the Seventh Air Force and the additional bomber groups. Ground troops would include the 2d Marine Division and one Army division not yet designated, three Army aviation engineer or construction battalions, one port battalion, and three Marine defense battalions. Task force commanders would be appointed by Nimitz. The general concept, the Joint Chiefs announced, involved mounting out the task forces from Pearl Harbor and the Fijis, or from both, and seizing the target areas in simultaneous attacks. CARTWHEEL would meanwhile be continued.

Purpose of the invasion of the Gilberts and Nauru, the Joint Chiefs told Nimitz, was "to improve the security of lines of communication," "to inflict losses on the enemy," and "to prepare to gain control of the Marshalls." They therefore ordered him to prepare plans for seizing the Marshalls about 1 February 1944, under the assumption that MacArthur would be operating against positions in New Guinea, the Admiralties, and New Ireland about the same time.[17]

With the transmission of these orders to Nimitz, there remained but one problem—selection of the other division for the Gilberts. Admiral King for some time had been advocating withdrawing the 1st Marine Division from the Southwest Pacific, and General Marshall for some time

had been opposing its withdrawal.[18] On 22 July King wrote Marshall to urge withdrawal of the 1st Marine Division and of the 3d Marine Division from the South Pacific to "avoid the inevitable consequences of 'mixed forces.' The Marines are by tradition, experience, and training eminently suited for amphibious operations," especially on the small islands of the Central Pacific as contrasted with the large land areas in the South and Southwest Pacific.[19] Marshall replied seven days later. He pointed out that removal of the two Marine divisions would cause profound dislocations in shipping as well as seriously affect CARTWHEEL. In his view, the 27th Division in Hawaii was the only unit, Army or Marine, that could be made available without creating great shipping problems. It had not yet received its first amphibious training but Marshall, stating that amphibious training could start at once and that by November the division should be able to render good service, offered the 27th Division.[20]

This offer must have satisfied King, for on the last day of July Marshall was informed that King acceded to the employ-

[17] JCS 386/2, 20 Jul 43, title: Strategy in the Pacific; Rad, JCS to CINCPAC, CM-IN 14465, 20 Jul 43.
[18] Memo, CNO for CofS, 14 Jun 43, sub: Withdrawal of 1st Marine Div, and Memo, CofS for CNO, 23 Jun 43, sub: Withdrawal of 1st Marine Div and Change of Allocation of 2 Army Divs. Both in OPD 320.2 Australia 184.
[19] Ltr, CNO to CofS, 22 Jul 43, OPD 381 Security 196.
[20] Capt. Edmund G. Love, The 27th Infantry Division in World War II (Washington: Infantry Journal Press, 1949), p. 21; Memo, CofS for CNO, 29 Jul 43, sub: Release of 1st or 3d Marine Divs for Opns in CENPAC, OPD 381 Security 196. General Marshall does not seem to have been quite satisfied with the status of the 27th Division. See his informal memo for Maj. Gen. Thomas T. Handy in OPD 381 Security 196.

ment of the 27th Division in the Gilberts–Nauru operation.[21]

With the preparation of the directive of 20 July and the designation of ground combat forces, then, the Joint Chiefs of Staff had laid the strategic groundwork for launching the Central Pacific drive that would eventually bring American and Allied forces almost to the doorstep of Japan. Tactical planning for the operation was left to the theater commanders involved. The code name established for the operation was GALVANIC.

Planning for Galvanic

Planning and training responsibilities for the forthcoming landings fell eventually to six separate headquarters. As in all Pacific operations outside of General MacArthur's theater, Admiral Nimitz, as Commander in Chief, Pacific Fleet and Pacific Ocean Areas (CINCPAC-CINCPOA), exercised supreme command and held ultimate responsibility for the success of the endeavor. Next in the chain of command was Vice Adm. Raymond A. Spruance, then designated Commander, Central Pacific Forces, the highest operational fleet command in the theater. Under him was the Fifth Amphibious Force, an organization that was established on 24 August 1943 and commanded by Rear Adm. Richmond Kelly Turner.

For purposes of training and controlling the troop elements of future amphibious landings in the Central Pacific, a separate command was created on 4 September 1943. This was the V Amphibious Corps, commanded by Maj. Gen. Holland M. Smith, USMC.[22] For this particular operation General Smith had at his disposal the 2d Marine Division, commanded by Maj. Gen. Julian C. Smith, USMC, and the

27th Infantry Division, commanded by Maj. Gen. Ralph C. Smith, USA, both of whom prepared their own tactical plans for assaulting their separate targets.

Responsibility for preliminary training and logistical supply of the Army troops committed to the operation fell to the headquarters of the Commanding General, Central Pacific Area, Lt. Gen. Robert C. Richardson, Jr., USA. This organization was activated on 14 August 1943 and was charged among other things with the duty of administering and training all Army ground forces and Army air forces in the Central Pacific, subject to the direction of Admiral Nimitz.[23]

In view of the fact that both the Fifth Amphibious Force and V Amphibious Corps were undergoing organization during the planning phase of the Gilberts operation, much of the burden of devising tactical plans for the troops fell originally to the staffs of the two divisions involved, the 27th Infantry Division and the 2d Marine Division. Both were under some handicaps. The 2d Marine Division was stationed in New Zealand. Its commanding general, General Julian Smith, had been alerted by Admiral Spruance early in August to the fact that the capture of Tarawa and Apamama (Abemama) Atolls would be assigned to his forces, but not until 15 September was the division formally attached to V Amphibious Corps

---

[21] Memo, Vice Adm Richard S. Edwards [CofS to King] for Gen Marshall, 31 Jul 43, sub: Designation 27th Div to Gilbert Opn, OPD 381 Security 196.

[22] Cmdr Fifth Amph Force, U.S. Pacific Fleet, Rpt of Amph Opns for the Capture of the Gilbert Islands, 4 Dec 43 (hereafter cited as Fifth Amph Force Rpt, Capture of Gilbert Islands), p. 1.

[23] History of United States Army Forces Middle Pacific and Predecessor Commands During World War II, 7 December 1941–2 September 1945 (hereafter cited as USAFMIDPAC Hist) p. 100, MS in OCMH.

and not until 2 October did General Smith and his staff personally report to General Holland Smith, the corps commander, in Pearl Harbor.[24] Meanwhile, the division staff prepared its own plans, which were eventually approved with modifications by the corps commander.

For the 27th Infantry Division, tactical planning for its particular task was complicated by a midstream change of objectives. The original directive from the Joint Chiefs of Staff had assigned the entire division to the capture of Nauru. Acting on this directive, the division's staff proceeded to gather intelligence data about that island from various sources and by early October had devised a tentative plan of attack employing two regiments in the assault with the third regiment (less one battalion) in floating reserve. Landing beaches were laid out on the northwest coast of the island.[25]

Meanwhile, higher headquarters were beginning to doubt the feasibility of attacking Nauru at all. On 19 September V Amphibious Corps submitted a revised estimate of the situation that "envisaged considerable difficulty in the capture of Nauru" with the forces made available. After further study in conjunction with the various Navy echelons involved, it became evident that the original concept of GALVANIC should be revised. Nauru offered too many hitherto-unsuspected hazards for an amphibious attack at this particular time. It was about 390 miles west of the westernmost of the Gilberts and hence would place an additional strain on available shipping. Simultaneous landings in the two places would furthermore necessitate a wide dispersal of supporting fleet elements—a dangerous division of forces in view of the presumed possibility of a Japanese naval counterattack. Finally, the pre-

cipitous terrain on Nauru would make an amphibious assault and the land fighting thereafter too costly to be warranted by the strategic advantages to be gained. Makin Atoll was considered no less suitable than Nauru as an air base for operations against the Marshalls and was thought to be considerably less well defended. Furthermore, the fact that it was only about 105 miles north of Tarawa made it possible to concentrate the supporting fleet in one area and thus avoid the danger of excessive dispersion.[26]

Hence, on 24 September Admiral Spruance recommended to Admiral Nimitz that the projected invasion of Nauru be dropped and that an amphibious landing on Makin be substituted. After obtaining the consent of the Joint Chiefs of Staff, Nimitz accepted this recommendation, and early in October a revised plan was issued to his command.[27] Spruance was ordered to seize Makin, Tarawa, and Apamama, to cover the amphibious landings on each of these targets with air and naval surface forces, and to deny to the enemy use of land bases in the Marshalls and on

---

[24] Capt. James R. Stockman, USMC, *The Battle for Tarawa* (Washington, 1947).

The present approved (Board of Geographic Names) spelling is "Abemama." As of 1943–44, however, "Apamama" was in accepted usage and it was this spelling that was uniformly employed in American military plans and reports. Therefore, the spelling "Apamama" will be used in this volume.

[25] Participation of the United States Army Forces in the Central Pacific Area in GALVANIC Operation (hereafter cited as USAFICPA Participation Rpt GALVANIC), pp. 131–37; 27th Inf Div Rpt of G–2 Activities, GALVANIC Opn.

[26] Ltr, Cmdr Fifth Amph Force to COMCENPAC, 24 Sep 43, sub: GALVANIC Opn, Discussion of Substitution of Makin as Assault Objective Instead of Nauru, Ser 0037, File 1975 Operation and Training (GALVANIC), Folder I, VAC files, Naval Records Management Center, Mechanicsburg, Penna.

[27] V Phib Corps GALVANIC Rpt, 11 Jan 44, p. 2.

Nauru during the operation.[28] D Day for the landings was originally set as 19 November 1943. A month later this was postponed one day, to 20 November.[29]

Intelligence on the Gilberts

From the very outset of the planning phase of the Gilberts operation, the chief hurdle to be overcome was the initial absence of much reliable information about the physical nature of the target islands and of the disposition of the enemy defenses thereon. The most critical gap in American intelligence, and one never satisfactorily filled, was the lack of any very precise hydrographic data. Charts published by the Navy's Hydrographic Office were so out of date and so inaccurate as to be worse than useless. Also, published tide tables were sketchy in the information they contained. They listed only a few of the Central Pacific islands and for these the figures given for high and low tides were in reference to points as distant as Valparaiso in Chile and Apia in Samoa, thus rendering them highly unreliable.[30]

It is axiomatic that in amphibious operations reasonably accurate data on tides and on hydrographic conditions offshore of the proposed landing beaches are essential. On such information hinges the solution to such important problems as what is the best time of day, month, and year to launch the operation, what beaches are most accessible, and what type of landing craft can be employed to get troops ashore in proper order with a minimum danger of capsizing, grounding, broaching, or being swept off course by tidal currents.

In obtaining this essential information, as well as intelligence of the probable number and disposition of enemy troops and defense installations on the islands, intelli-

gence officers of the appropriate staffs had to rely on three main sources—aerial reconnaissance, submarine reconnaissance, and reports from British citizens who had lived or traveled in the Gilberts.

Photographic coverage of Tarawa was made on 18–19 September and on 20 October, and of Makin on 23 July and 13 October. Excellent vertical and oblique shots of Tarawa were obtained, both of great value in studying beaches and locating weapons and installations. For Makin, the vertical photographs were good, but no large-scale obliques were turned in and this hampered considerably the study of hydrographic conditions as well as the interpretation of installations.[31]

Additional and highly detailed information was received from a reconnaissance mission of the submarine USS *Nautilus* conducted in late September and early October. From this vessel's report much of the missing data on hydrographic and beach conditions on both of the main islands could be filled in. Information as to condition of surf, reefs, and beaches, characteristics of lagoon entrances, current data, tidal data, and so forth, was supplied. Periscopic photographs of the beach lines showed many more details than had appeared on the aerial photographs.[32]

---

[28] CINCPAC-CINCPOA Opns Plan 13-43, 5 Oct 43.

[29] Fifth Amph Force Rpt, Capture of Gilbert Islands, Annex A, p. 5. Both of these target dates were arbitrarily fixed as west longitude dates, although the Gilberts lie in east longitude about seven degrees west of the international date line. During this operation then, the target islands were presumed to be in plus-twelve time zone, although actually lying west of it. In effect this meant that all local date-time groups during the operation were computed as Greenwich civil time minus twelve hours.

[30] Fifth Amph Force Rpt, Capture of Gilbert Islands, Incl C, p. 2.

[31] V Phib Corps GALVANIC Rpt, Incl C, p. 2.

[32] Fifth Amph Force Rpt, Capture of Gilbert Islands, Incl C, p. 2.

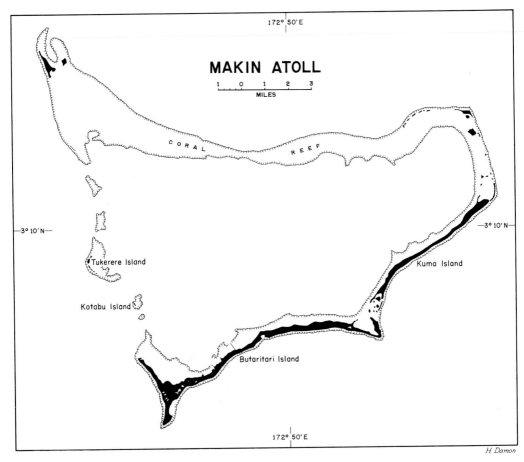

172° 50' E

MAKIN ATOLL

1   0   1   2   3
MILES

CORAL   REEF

—3° 10' N—

Tukerere Island

Kuma Island

Kotabu Island

Butaritari Island

172° 50' E

—3° 10' N—

H. Damon

MAP 3

Finally, during September and October, a total of sixteen former residents or travelers in the islands were attached to Admiral Turner's staff to supply additional information from memory. These included Australian, New Zealand, and Fiji naval reserve officers, officials of the Western Pacific High Commission, Australian Army reserve officers and enlisted men, and civilians. Part of this group was sent to Wellington to assist the 2d Marine Division.[33] Others, more familiar with Makin, worked directly with the staff on Oahu. Among the latter were Lt. Comdr. Ger-

hard H. Heyen, R.A.N., and Pvt. Fred C. Narruhn, 1st Fiji Infantry Regiment, a native of Makin. Private Narruhn was assigned directly to the 27th Division's intelligence section and was particularly helpful in providing necessary information for planning that operation. Another source of information made available to the division shortly before it sailed was Lt. Col. James Roosevelt, USMCR, who had been a member of the 2d Marine Raider Battalion under Lt. Col. Evans F. Carlson,

---

[33] Stockman, *Tarawa,* p. 4.

BUTARITARI FROM THE AIR. *Navy Wildcat fighters over the island on 20 November 1943.*

USMC, which had staged a raid on Makin on 16 August 1942.[34]

Final Intelligence Estimates: Makin

On the basis of these various sources of information, V Amphibious Corps and the two division headquarters committed to the Gilberts were able to draw up reasonably complete and on the whole not too inaccurate estimates of the geographical nature and defensive strength of the target islands.

Makin is an atoll located approximately 2,000 nautical miles southwest of Oahu. It is north of Tarawa by about 105 miles, southeast of Kwajalein in the Marshalls by 450 miles, and east of Truk by 1,265 miles. The atoll is triangular in shape enclosing a large lagoon. (*Map 3*) The southeastern leg of the triangle holds the main land formation, consisting of two long islands, Butaritari and Kuma, which with their connecting reef are about thirteen miles long and average five hundred yards in width with the highest land point rising no more than twelve feet above sea level. Butaritari was rightly believed to contain the largest number of natives, the entire population of the atoll being estimated as about 1,700 at

---

[34] 27th Inf Div Rpt of G–2 Activities, GALVANIC Opn, p. 6; Ltr, Maj Gen Ralph Smith, USA (Ret), to Chief, HD SSUSA, 31 Jan 49, Incl, p. 2, OCMH.

the time of the Japanese occupation in December 1941.

Butaritari, according to the 27th Division's G-2 terrain study, was "shaped like a crutch with the armrest facing generally West and the leg of the crutch pointing East and slightly North."[35] For purposes of tactical study the island was divided into three parts. The extreme western area, that is the armrest of the crutch, was thought to be generally of good substantial footing with scattered coconut trees and sand brush on the northern part and thick coconut groves interspersed with *bobai* (taro) pits in the southern. East of this area was a stretch of land designated the inland lagoon area. Except near the shore this was believed swampy, covered with saltbrush, and impassable in many parts for vehicles. Near the geographical center of the island was the main village of Butaritari situated on fairly dry ground. The easternmost segment of the island was believed to contain good land, with some *bobai* pits and gradually thickening coconut growth as the extreme eastern tip was approached. A road had been observed running from Ukiangong Village, near the southwest point, in a northerly direction about half way out Flink Point, a promontory on the northwest side. The road connected with another that ran in a northeasterly direction along the north shore of the island to its eastern tip. A short cross-island road ran through Butaritari Village from the northern (lagoon) to the southern (ocean) shore.

On the all-important question of suitable spots for landing, it was believed that the best beaches were those on the lagoon (north) shore and on the southern half of the west coast of the island. On the west coast the reef was thought to be very close to the beach, therefore offering no particular hazard to ordinary landing craft. On the lagoon side, the reef was estimated to extend 500 to 1,500 yards out from the shore, but was considered to be flat and even enough to permit troop landings at the reef's edge. Four prominent landmarks presented themselves on the lagoon side. These were, from west to east, On Chong's Wharf, King's Wharf, Stone Pier, and Government Wharf. All projected far enough into the lagoon to be useful as guide marks for landing craft.

No particular difficulties were contemplated by the division planners from tidal or hydrographic conditions. It was believed that single boats could land at almost any point on the island during high water and two hours before and after high water. This was an error as events were soon to prove. Had the division planners carefully consulted Admiral Turner's operation plan, they would have discovered that during periods of neap tide (and 20 November fell in such a period) standard Navy landing craft would be grounded on the reef off the lagoon shore some 100–150 yards out.[36]

The Japanese garrison on Butaritari was estimated to be from 500 to 800 troops consisting of one rifle company, one field battery of four heavy antiaircraft guns, and two antiaircraft machine gun batteries totaling four medium antiaircraft guns and twenty machine guns.[37] It was apparent

---

[35] 27th Inf Div FO 21, 23 Oct 43, App 1 to Annex 2, p. 1. The account given here of intelligence estimates of Makin is derived from this appendix and the situation map of Butaritari Island, Makin Atoll, prepared by G-2, V Phib Corps.

[36] TF 54 Opn Plan A2-43, 23 Oct 43, Annex B, p. 21.

[37] 27th Inf Div FO 21, Annex 2, p. 1; V Phib Corps GALVANIC Rpt, Incl C, p. 3. The estimate given in the situation map prepared by G-2, V Phib Corps, differed as follows: heavy AA guns, 3 definite; medium AA guns, 1 definite, 10 possible; machine guns, 24 definite, 89 possible.

from aerial photographs that the enemy had concentrated the major part of his defenses in the central area of the island around Butaritari Village. This fortified area was bounded on east and west by tank traps running generally in a zigzag path from lagoon to ocean shore.[38]

Final Intelligence Estimates: Tarawa

Tarawa, like Makin, is a triangular coral atoll and is roughly 18 miles long on the east side, 12 miles long on the south side, and 12.5 miles long on the west side. None of the small islands comprising the atoll rises to more than ten feet above sea level. (*Map 4*)

The entire west leg of the triangle consists of a barrier reef through which there is only one entrance into the lagoon passable by deep-draft vessels. Just 3.5 miles south of this entrance lies the island of Betio, resting on the southwest corner of the triangle. It was here that the Japanese had constructed an airfield and had concentrated their major defenses. It was here that the first major amphibious assault by American forces in the Central Pacific would take place.

Betio itself is surrounded on all sides by reefs. Along the south shore the reef extends to a uniform distance of about 600 yards from the high-water line. On the narrow west shore it varies from 800 to 1,200 yards at the extreme southwest point of the island where strong rip currents occur. Off the north shore, facing the lagoon, also lies a fringing reef, but this is wider and shelves more gradually than the reefs elsewhere. This, plus the fact that the lagoon was on the lee side of the island and somewhat sheltered from heavy swells, made this coast line the most desirable for landing operations.[39]

Most of these facts were known to planners of the operation as a result of aerial and submarine photographs and consultation with former residents and visitors familiar with the atoll. What was not known with any certainty, however, was the condition of prevailing tides in the area. The central problem that plagued all planners of the Tarawa operation was the question of the probable height of water over the fringing reef off the north coast of Betio. The 2d Marine Division, which was assigned to the operation, had available only a limited number (eventually 125) of amphibian tractors. These vehicles, which could carry about twenty troops each, were equipped to operate both through water and overland, and to them reefs offered no particular obstacle. However, there were not enough on hand to transport all of the necessary assault troops from ship to shore. The remainder would have to be carried in standard "Higgins boats" (LCVP's) which, when fully loaded, drew at least 3.5 feet. Thus about four feet of water above the reef was essential if the landing craft were to carry the assault troops from ship to shore without interruption.

To complicate matters further the date chosen for the invasion was in a period of neap tide at Tarawa. Neap tides occur during the first and third quarters of the moon. During these times the range of tide, that is the difference between high and low water, is at its lowest point and high tides are lower than usual. Thus, the probability of there being sufficient water over the reef even at high tide on the par-

---

[38] V Phib Corps G-2 Situation Map, Butaritari Island.

[39] 2d Marine Div, Special Action Rpt, 6 Jan 44, Incl A, Narrative Account of the Gilbert Islands Opn, p. 3.

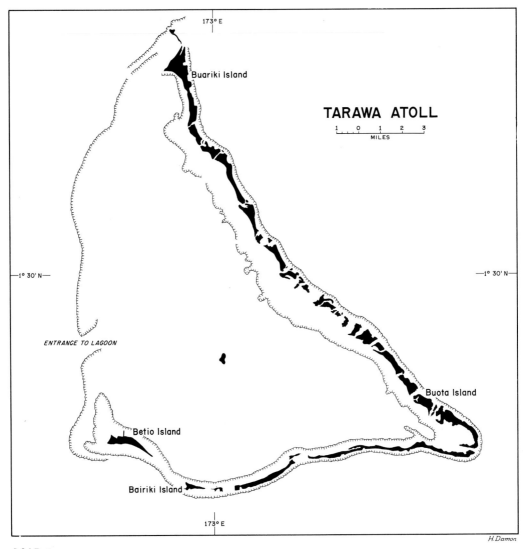

MAP 4

ticular date chosen for the invasion was decreased.[40]

These problems were all appreciated by planners on both corps and divisional levels, but their sources of information were contradictory. Admiral Turner's intelligence staff, as for Makin, made a correct estimate of tidal conditions at Tarawa on the proposed day of landing. His operation plan reads in part: "During high water neap tides the reef [that is, the lagoon reef]

---

[40] For a more complete discussion of the question of tides at Tarawa, see Jeter A. Isely and Philip A. Crowl, *The U. S. Marines and Amphibious War* (Princeton, New Jersey: Princeton University Press, 1951), Ch. VI.

off the north coast of Betio is covered by from one to two feet of water. . . ."[41] If this analysis were to be believed, then it was obvious that nothing but amphibian tractors could negotiate the reef on 20 November, which was known to fall in the period of neap tide. Standard landing craft drawing from three to four feet would be grounded on the reef. Admiral Turner's staff also knew that during neap tides a "dodging" tide frequently occurred at Tarawa, that is, the tide instead of following the usual semidiurnal pattern, ebbed and flowed several times in twenty-four hours.[42] This might further complicate the problem of getting standard landing craft ashore, even through channels blown in the reef.

Either this information was improperly understood or it was disbelieved, because up to the very date of the landing there was still hope that at Betio there would be enough water over the reef to float standard landing craft. This hope was nurtured by several former residents of the Gilberts and shipmasters who had navigated the adjacent waters. All but one of these consulted by the staff of the 2d Marine Division affirmed that five feet of water could be expected over the reef at Betio at high tide. The single exception was Maj. F. L. G. Holland, a British officer who had lived on Bairiki, the island adjacent to Betio, for fifteen years. During the Marine division's final rehearsals on Efate in the New Hebrides before sailing for the target island, Major Holland announced that during neap tide periods less than three feet of water could be expected at high tide.[43]

Major Holland was right and in general his pessimism was shared by General Julian Smith, the 2d Marine Division's commander. At least his troops were briefed to expect no more than a fifty-fifty chance of

getting into the shore on Betio in boats.[44] As events turned out even this was far too optimistic an estimate.

Although hydrographic information for Tarawa was faulty, the prelanding intelligence of Japanese troop strength and defense dispositions was excellent. This was largely derived from aerial and submarine photographs assembled by the Joint Intelligence Center, Pacific Ocean Areas, and interpreted by that headquarters and by the intelligence section of the 2d Marine Division. As of 11 November, the division estimated enemy troop strength on Betio alone to be not less than 2,500 and not more than 3,100,[45] a prediction that postbattle studies proved to be remarkably accurate. Betio was known to be far more heavily fortified than Makin. From aerial photographs it appeared that the north shore was defended by an elaborate system of fire trenches, rifle pits, coastal and antiaircraft weapons, antiboat emplacements, and machine gun positions. Defenses on the west and south shores were thought to be similar in all respects, including density.

On this tiny, narrow island only three miles long and less than six hundred yards across at its widest point, the Japanese were believed to have 8 or 9 coastal defense guns, 12 heavy antiaircraft guns ranging from 75-mm. to 12-cm., 12 medium antiaircraft guns from 40-mm. to less than 75-mm., 81 antiboat positions for weapons

---

[41] TF 54 Opn Plan A2-43, 23 Oct 43, Annex B, p. 11.
[42] Ibid., p. 29.
[43] Stockman, Tarawa, p. 4; Interv, Jeter A. Isely with Lt Gen Julian C. Smith, USMC (Ret), 28 Oct 48, on file, Princeton University Library, Princeton, N. J.
[44] Interv cited n. 43; Memo, Lt Col William C. Chamberlin, USMC, for Jeter A. Isley, 29 May 50, on file, Princeton University Library, Princeton, N. J.
[45] 2d Marine Div Opn Order 14, 25 Oct 43, Addendum 1 to App 1 to Annex D, 11 Nov 43.

CHART 1—TASK ORGANIZATION OF VARIOUS COMMANDS FOR THE ATTACK ON THE GILBERT ISLANDS

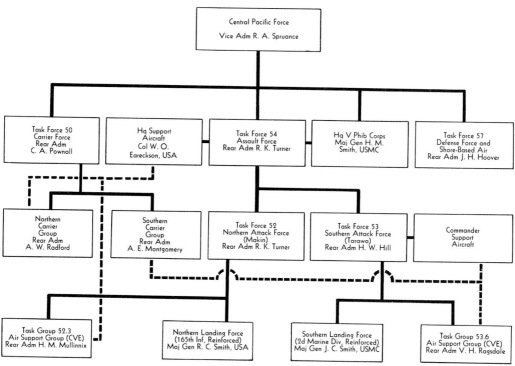

- - - - - Operational control of aircraft overhead in combat area

of sizes ranging from heavy machine guns to 40-mm. guns, and 52 light weapons.[46] There was good reason to believe that this would be the fiercest amphibious battle yet fought in the Pacific.

Organization and Command of the American Forces

Admiral Spruance's Operation Plan Number Cen 1-43 was issued on 25 October and, subject to some subsequent modifications, set forth the command organization of the GALVANIC operation and outlined the tasks assigned to each subordinate command. The immediate task of capturing and occupying Makin, Tarawa,

and Apamama, of destroying inferior enemy surface forces attempting to interfere with the landing operations, and of initiating the establishment of advance bases and the construction of airfields on the three islands was assigned to Admiral Turner's assault force (Task Force 54). This was in turn subdivided into a Northern Attack Force (Task Force 52), also commanded by Admiral Turner, and a Southern Attack Force (Task Force 53) under Rear Adm. Harry W. Hill, USN, plus sundry other lesser task groups including a reconnaissance group for Apamama, and

---

[46] 2d Marine Div Opn Order 14, 25 Oct 43, App 1 to Annex D; *Ibid.*, Addendum 1, 11 Nov 43.

garrison groups for the three islands. The duty of the Northern Attack Force was to capture Makin; that of the Southern Attack Force to take Tarawa and Apamama. (*Chart 1*)

The main troop components of the Northern Attack Force were to consist of the 165th Regimental Combat Team (reinforced) of the 27th Infantry Division. This combat team plus units of the 7th Army Defense Battalion and various service units were to constitute the Northern Landing Force, under command of General Ralph Smith. The parallel command for the seizure of Tarawa was the Southern Landing Force, consisting mainly of the 2d Marine Division plus assigned units of the 2d and 8th Marine Defense Battalions, all under command of General Julian Smith. A separate task group was set up for occupying Apamama. The commanding officer of the submarine *Nautilus,* Comdr. Donald G. Irvine, USN, was directed to land a reconnaissance platoon of V Amphibious Corps on that presumably undefended island some time after the main landings on Tarawa and Makin.

To transport the 165th Regimental Combat Team and its supplies and equipment to Makin, Admiral Turner was able to allocate four attack transports (APA's), one attack cargo ship (AKA), one LSD, and nine LST's. To screen the transports and LST's, and to provide naval gunfire and aerial support for the landing on Makin, a total of four old battleships, four heavy cruisers, thirteen destroyers, and three escort carriers (CVE's) was provided.[47] To the 2d Marine Division for the assault on Tarawa was assigned one transport (AP),[48] twelve attack transports, three attack cargo ships, one LSD, and twelve LST's. To screen these vessels and to bombard the shore at Tarawa, Southern Attack Force had a total of three battleships, three heavy cruisers, three light cruisers, twenty-one destroyers, and five escort carriers.[49]

Thus, about equal shares of naval gunfire support were apportioned to the Makin and Tarawa landings, although it was known that the latter would be by far the more formidable target. If the only problem involved in the operation had been that of landing troops on the two islands, then logic would have dictated allocating a far heavier portion of naval gunfire support to the Southern Landing Force. As it was, purely naval considerations prompted a more equal division of fire power. Makin was more than a hundred miles closer than Tarawa to the Marshalls and if any major sortie by the elements of the Japanese fleet should develop, it would probably be from that direction. Hence, it was considered prudent to dispose a good part of the American combat vessels in a position where it could more quickly intercept a Japanese naval counterattack.[50]

Within Admiral Turner's assault force (Task Force 54), but not enjoying any clear-cut authority, was the Commander, V Amphibious Corps, General Holland Smith. During the planning and training phase, both the 2d Marine Division and the 27th Infantry Division were clearly attached to Holland Smith's headquarters

---

[47] TF 52 Amph Attack Order A3-43, 23 Oct 43; Fifth Amph Force Rpt, Capture of Gilbert Islands, p. 5.

[48] The main differences between the AP and APA were that the latter carried more landing craft and was better constructed and rigged to unload assault troops and their supplies rapidly.

[49] Fifth Amph Force Rpt, Capture of Gilbert Islands, p. 5; TF 53 Opn Order A104-43 (Revised), 4 Nov 43, pp. 1–2.

[50] COMCENPACFOR, Gen Instr to all Flag Officers, CENPACFOR, for Gilberts Opn, 29 Oct 43, Naval History Division.

and were under his command.[51] But for the operational phase, his position in the chain of command was ambiguous. Admiral Spruance's operation plan provided that the "Commanding General Fifth Amphibious Corps will be embarked in the flagship of the *Assault Force* [Task Force 54] and will command all landing force troops." [52] However, by the same order, all directives by Commander, V Amphibious Corps, had to be approved by Admiral Turner as Commander, Assault Force, before they could be issued. Furthermore, the only authority specifically delegated to Holland Smith under Admiral Turner's own operation plan was that "Commanding General, Fifth Amphibious Corps, embarked in the Force Flagship of the Commander *Assault Force*, will advise the Commander *Assault Force* in regard to the employment of the Landing Forces at each objective and the employment of reserve troops . . . ." [53]

On the question of the immediate command of troops to be committed ashore at Makin and Tarawa, both Spruance's and Turner's orders bypassed Holland Smith. At both objectives the related attack force commanders—Turner, Commander, Task Force 52, at Makin, and Hill, Commander, Task Force 53, at Tarawa—were to command the troops through the appropriate landing force commanders (that is, General Ralph Smith, USA, at Makin and General Julian Smith, USMC, at Tarawa). These last two officers would assume command ashore only when Admiral Turner, as commander of the assault force, should so direct.[54]

In other words, General Holland Smith was given no tactical command over troops.[55] His capacity during the operation was merely that of an adviser to Admiral Turner. However, there is evidence that in his own mind General Smith believed that he held a more exalted position. Later, he wrote, "As soon as the assault waves hit the beach the status of my command was parallel, not inferior to, Kelly Turner's." [56] This misconception could easily have arisen from the paragraph of Admiral Spruance's operation plan cited above, which seemed to give the V Amphibious Corps commander command over "all landing force troops." The confusion was further compounded when at the last minute Admiral Nimitz issued a directive removing General Holland Smith's name from the command. Smith protested and at last, in his own words, "Admiral Spruance insisted that I go along." [57] Go he did, but as an adviser, not a troop commander.

Comparable to, but not exactly analogous with, the position of General Smith in the chain of command was that of the Commander, Support Aircraft, Col. William O. Eareckson, AAF. At this juncture in the Pacific war, the Navy's development of a centralized system of ground control of support aircraft in amphibious operations was still in a formative stage. At Guadalcanal Admiral Turner had set up a rather hasty, temporary control organization for aircraft assigned to troop support. Under his plan, during the amphibious phase of the operation, all troop support aircraft were controlled by an air support director group attached to his staff

---

[51] Stockman, *Tarawa*, p. 3; USAFMIDPAC Hist, Vol I, pp. 108–09.

[52] COMCENPACFOR Opn Plan Cen 1-43, p. 11.

[53] TF 54 Opn Plan A2-43, 23 Oct 43, p. 9.

[54] COMCENPACFOR Opn Plan Cen 1-43, p. 12; TF 54 Opn Plan A2-43, 23 Oct 43, p. 10.

[55] Ltr, Adm Turner to Maj Gen Harry J. Malony, USA, Chief, HD SSUSA, 17 Jan 49, OCMH.

[56] Holland M. Smith, *Coral and Brass* (New York: Charles Scribner's Sons, 1949), p. 113.

[57] *Ibid.*, p. 117.

and aboard his flagship, the USS *McCaw-ley*, with a similar stand-by group aboard the USS *Neville*, which was assigned to waters off Tulagi. In addition, a fighter squadron, flown from carriers located far out at sea and assigned the duties of combat air patrol in the immediate area of the landing, was controlled by Rear Adm. Victor A. C. Crutchley, R.N., Turner's second in command, through a fighter director group located aboard the USS *Chicago*.[58]

Although this plan did not permit completely centralized control, it did embody two important principles. First, all aircraft in the objective area were under command of units on board ships actually present. Secondly, after the initially scheduled strikes, all missions for troop support aircraft were established by the air support director group aboard the force flagship as a result of requests from the commanders of the landing forces, that is, of the troops ashore.

After his appointment to the post of Commander, Fifth Amphibious Force, Central Pacific, Admiral Turner sought to capitalize on his experience at Guadalcanal by setting up an air support control organization on a permanent basis. But he found little enthusiasm for the project among naval air circles at Pearl Harbor and no naval aviator who, in his opinion, had sufficient rank or experience to do the job. However, in the person of Colonel Eareckson, then temporarily attached to Admiral Nimitz's headquarters, he discovered an aviator who met his requirements. Colonel Eareckson had acted as an air co-ordinator and air-ground liaison officer for close support missions flown by planes of the Eleventh Air Force during the invasion of Attu in May 1943.[59] Although he had not previously worked with

naval aircraft, he was borrowed from Admiral Nimitz's staff for the Gilberts operation and designated Commander, Support Aircraft.

The scope of his duties and authority for the forthcoming invasion was not made entirely clear in the covering operation plans, the ambiguity being a reflection of a yet unmatured conception of the role of close air support control in naval amphibious doctrine. According to Operation Plan A2-43, issued by Admiral Turner as commander of the assault force for the entire Gilberts operation (Task Force 54), "The Commander Support Aircraft, GALVANIC [Eareckson], embarked in the Force Flagship of the Commander Assault Force [Turner], will advise the Commander Assault Force in regard to the employment of support aircraft at all objectives."[60] In another paragraph of the same plan it is stated, "At each objective, during the assault, the related Attack Force Commanders [that is, Turner at Makin, and Hill at Tarawa] will command the support aircraft through the Air Commander of the base to be established at the objective. . . ."[61]

This would seem to indicate that Colonel Eareckson's position in the chain of command was, like General Holland Smith's, merely that of adviser to the assault force commander, Admiral Turner. Also, according to the above cited plan, the attack force commander at each objective would presumably exercise direct command over support aircraft through the air base commander ashore, once such bases were established. However, in prac-

[58] Ltr, Adm Turner to Gen Ward, 30 Oct 50, pp. 1–2, OCMH; Miller, *Guadalcanal*, pp. 37–39.
[59] Craven and Cate, *AAF IV*, pp. 382–86.
[60] TF 54 Opn Plan A2-43, 23 Oct 43, par. 5(d).
[61] *Ibid.*, par. 5(f).

tice, this was not to be the case. Since this command setup had been ordained by directives from higher authority, it could not be changed. But Admiral Turner did succeed in radically modifying the arrangement by directing that at both Tarawa and Makin flight leaders of combat air patrols, upon being relieved from this type of duty, should report to the Commander, Support Aircraft, and be prepared to strafe ground installations as directed by him before returning to their carriers. To insure safety to the ground troops, pilots were warned that it was "imperative that strafing attacks be delivered *only* as directed by the Support Aircraft Commander." [62] Also, supporting aircraft at both Makin and Tarawa were ordered to maintain twelve scout bomber planes and six torpedo bomber planes on each station during daylight at an "initial point" designated by the support aircraft commander to give direct support to ground troops and to replace the Support Aircraft Group as requested by the support aircraft commander. In addition, antisubmarine patrol aircraft were ordered to report to the support aircraft commander upon arrival on and departure from station. [63]

As it finally went into effect, then, the duties of the support aircraft commander both at Makin and at Tarawa were made more positive than had originally been contemplated. Colonel Eareckson, who would sail aboard Turner's flagship, was given general direction over close air support and antisubmarine patrol for the whole assault force (Task Force 54). In addition, he had direct command duties with respect to support aircraft of the attack force at Makin (Task Force 52). For the Tarawa phase, a second commander of support aircraft was assigned to Task Force 53 and accompanied Admiral Hill on his flagship *Maryland,* from which he

too would directly command close air support and antisubmarine patrol at that objective. [64] In later amphibious landings in the Central Pacific this allocation of air responsibilities was formalized and clarified, but it was in the Gilberts operation, in spite of some confusion in the covering plans, that this subsequent development was clearly forecast.

Aerial support, both tactical and strategic, was to be provided in the main by two separate task forces. The carrier force (Task Force 50) was under command of Rear Adm. Charles A. Pownall, USN, and consisted of six large and five small carriers with their accompanying battleships, cruisers, and destroyers. The bulk of this force was assigned the task of destroying enemy aircraft and defenses on Tarawa on D minus 2 and D minus 1 and on Mille, Jaluit, and Makin on D minus 1. At the same time, planes from this force were to photograph both Makin and Tarawa and deliver copies, together with information of sea conditions at landing beaches, to Admirals Turner and Hill on their respective flagships. On D Day and daily thereafter they were to conduct early morning searches to the north and west of the Gilberts and to provide air support for the land operations. One relief group of this task force was ordered to destroy aircraft and air harbor facilities on Nauru by both air and surface bombardment. [65]

All shore-based aircraft for the operation were organized into Task Force 57 under the command of Rear Adm. John H. Hoover. The Seventh Air Force provided Admiral Hoover with both fighters and bombers. Ninety heavy bombers were

---

[62] TF 54 Opn Plan A2-43, 23 Oct 43, Annex C, pp. 4, 10.
[63] *Ibid.*, pp. 4, 10, 11.
[64] Ltr, Turner to Ward, 30 Oct 50, pp. 4–6.
[65] CENPACFOR Opn Plan Cen 1-43, pp. 4–5, 8–9.

organized into Task Group 57.2, commanded by Maj. Gen. Willis H. Hale, AAF. Fifty-six Navy patrol bombers were placed in Task Group 57.3 under direct command of Admiral Hoover. A third task group (57.4) consisted of ninety Marine fighter planes, seventy-two Marine scout bombers, twenty-four scout and utility planes, and sundry Army and Navy transport planes—all to be based on the Ellice Islands and all under command of Brig. Gen. Lewie G. Merritt, USMC.

Task Force 57 was to attack enemy air bases at Tarawa, Nauru, Mille, Jaluit, and such other enemy positions in the Marshalls as were within range. The force was to conduct photographic reconnaissances of Kwajalein, Wotje, Maloelap, Mille, and Jaluit, all in the Marshalls. Starting on D minus 3, it was to conduct long-range searches in areas not covered by carrier planes. Other general duties were to attack enemy ships and shipping, defend American bases in the Ellice and Gilbert Islands, and provide air transportation.[66]

All of this air power was in addition to the planes attached to the two attack forces. At Makin, three escort carriers would accompany Admiral Turner's Northern Attack Force. Admiral Hill's Southern Attack Force at Tarawa would enjoy the support of five such vessels.[67]

Admiral Turner's Plan for the Attack

The general plan for the operation, as worked out by Admiral Turner in conjunction with the staff of V Amphibious Corps, contemplated the simultaneous capture of Makin by the 165th Regimental Combat Team of the 27th Infantry Division and of Tarawa by the 2d Marine Division, reinforced. One regimental combat team of the Marine division (later designated the 6th RCT) was to be held as

corps reserve for the support of one or both of these operations or for the subsequent occupation of Apamama. This corps reserve was to be employed only as authorized by Admiral Turner as Commander, Task Force 54, on the advice of General Holland Smith.[68]

The assault was to be made initially by troops carried in amphibian tractors, some fitted with grapnels for destroying wire and thus opening boat routes to the beaches. The tractors would be carried to the target areas in LST's, each of which had space in its tank deck for seventeen vehicles. The amphibian tractors would be followed by troops in LCVP's (landing craft, vehicle and personnel) and by medium tanks transported in LCM's (landing craft, mechanized), which would be carried forward by Navy transports and by LSD's.

On D Day at both Makin and Tarawa Navy planes were to strike from 0545 to 0615, attacking coast defense guns, heavy antiaircraft guns, observation towers, radio installations, aircraft, and personnel, as well as any barracks and buildings undamaged by previous attacks. From about H Hour minus 5 minutes to H Hour plus 15 minutes (that is from 5 minutes before to 15 minutes after the first troops hit the beach), planes would attack installations on the landing beaches. They were to strafe along the water's edge until the first wave of landing craft approached to within 100 yards of the beach, then shift fire inland to a depth of 100 yards. Immediately thereafter, they were to bomb all secondary defense installations behind the beaches clear across each island as well as all beach installations between 500 and 1,000 yards to both sides of the landing

[66] *Ibid.*, pp. 5–6, 12–13.
[67] See above, pp. 00–00.
[68] TF 54 Opn Plan A2-43, 23 Oct 43, Annex A.

areas. Following these scheduled missions, aircraft were to fly combat air patrol and antisubmarine patrol and carry out bombing and strafing attacks in close support of the ground troops.[69]

For Makin, naval gunfire support would be provided by four old battleships, four cruisers, and six destroyers.[70] For Tarawa, three battleships, two heavy cruisers, three light cruisers, and nine destroyers would be assigned to this duty.[71] The general plan for the employment of these vessels at both objectives was as follows: During the early morning of D Day, commencing about 0615, the heavy ships would deliver prearranged neutralization and counterbattery fires at moderately long range. As mine sweepers gradually closed the beaches off Makin and swept the lagoon off Betio, support vessels would move to closer range. Battleships and heavy cruisers were permitted to move in as close as 2,000 or 3,000 yards (that is, one to one and a half nautical miles) in order to knock out heavy turret guns ashore. Shortly before the landing, light cruisers and destroyers were instructed to move to still closer range for a last-minute saturation fire. This was to terminate at H minus 5 minutes so as to permit a final air strike on the beaches immediately before the first wave of troops hit. Under no circumstances were ships and planes to bombard the same areas simultaneously. After the landings had been made ships were to stand by to fire on targets of opportunity on request of shore fire control parties attached to troop units and to deliver slow neutralization fire on areas 400 to 800 yards or more from the nearest troops.[72]

It was believed by some naval planners of the operation that this tremendous volume of preliminary naval gunfire coupled with the proposed aerial bombardment would surely be ample to knock out most of the heavier Japanese installations and at the very least neutralize the beaches during the assault phase of the operation. Just before the 2d Marine Division sailed from Efate, one of the ranking naval officers is reported to have stated of Betio: "We do not intend to neutralize it, we do not intend to destroy it. Gentlemen, we will obliterate it."[73] Such optimism was extravagant, as the course of the battle would show, but it was based on the knowledge that in no previous amphibious operation had such a tremendous weight of naval and air power been available to landing troops. That a mere two and a half hours of preliminary naval bombardment, no matter how concentrated, was still not enough to "obliterate" even tiny islands the size of Betio and Butaritari was still to be proved.

The 27th Division's Plan: Butaritari

For the landing on Butaritari, total troop strength of the 165th Regimental Combat Team with its attached units came to 6,470 men. This included, besides the infantry troops of the 165th, detachments from the 105th Infantry Regiment of the 27th Division, part of the 193d Tank Battalion, the 152d Engineer Battalion, coastal artillery and antiaircraft batteries of the 98th and 93d Coastal Artillery Battalions, a platoon from the V Amphibious Corps Reconnaissance Company, plus sundry

---

[69] *Ibid.*, Annex C, pp. 2–4, 8–9.
[70] TF 52 Amph Attack Order A3-43, 23 Oct 43, p. 1.
[71] TF 53 Opn Order A104-43 (Revised), 4 Nov 43, pp. 1–2.
[72] TF 54 Opn Plan A2-43, 23 Oct 43, p. 5; *Ibid.*, Annex C, pp. 2–3, 8–9.
[73] Earl J. Wilson, Jim F. Lucas, Samuel Shaffer, and C. Peter Zurlinden, *Betio Beachhead* (New York: The Putnam Company, 1945), p. 32.; Interv, Isely with Julian Smith, 28 Oct 48, p. 4.

medical, signal, ordnance, quartermaster, and bomb disposal detachments.

The plan for getting these troops ashore on Butaritari was elaborate in the extreme and unlike any adopted before or since in the Pacific war. It was devised by General Ralph Smith, Commanding General, 27th Division, and approved somewhat reluctantly by General Holland Smith, commander of the V Amphibious Corps.[74] The basic principle of the plan was to land two battalions on the west coast of Butaritari, followed quickly by tanks and artillery pieces. Two hours after the main landing, a third battalion was to be put ashore on the north (lagoon) side of the island roughly 4,000 yards east of the main landing beaches. This battalion would then split into two groups, one heading eastward, the other westward in the general direction of the main landing force. The object was to envelop in an amphibious pincers movement the Western Tank Barrier that lay athwart the island between the main landing beaches on the west coast and the most heavily fortified area in the center— the so-called Citadel area. (Map I)

The first wave to land on the west coast (at Red Beaches) was to consist of thirty-two LVT's embarked on two LST's, manned by separate detachments of the 105th Infantry (called Detachments X and Y). These were to land at Red Beaches at H Hour and to clear a passage through any barbed wire or other underwater obstacles that might impede the succeeding landing craft. On hitting the shore, the troops were to move south and north respectively and cover the right and left flanks of the main landing beaches.[75]

This scheme of manning the first wave of LVT's with troops drawn from a regiment outside of the one that made up the main landing force was a product of necessity rather than choice. Because of the pre-

vailing shortage of LVT's at the time of the operation, General Ralph Smith could not be certain that any of these vehicles would be available for the Makin landing. Not until about two weeks before sailing from Pearl Harbor did the tractors assigned to the 27th Division actually arrive. Hence, in working out a landing plan, General Smith had to take into account the possibility that no amphibian tractors might be ready for the operation, and therefore assigned all of the assault troops of the 165th Regimental Combat Team to LCVP's. Against the contingency that the desired tractors would show up at the last minute, he detached special units from the 105th Regimental Combat Team of his division to make up the first wave and to perform whatever duties thereafter that might be considered desirable.[76]

Following this first wave of LVT's would come the assault troops of the 1st and 3d Battalion Landing Teams, 165th Regiment, boated in LCVP's. On the right, the 3d Battalion Landing Team would land on Red Beach 2 and seize the right half of the division beachhead to about 1,600 yards inland. It would then move right to clear the area around Ukiangong Village and Ukiangong Point. On the left, the 1st Battalion Landing Team would land on Red Beach, seize the division beachhead in its zone of action and move left to capture the area from the north end of Red Beach to Flink Point. Upon capture of the division beachhead, it was to relieve the right battalion on the entire front line and

[74] General Ralph Smith's personal diary, which he kindly loaned to the authors, gives evidence of an original disagreement between himself and General Holland Smith on the landing plan. Holland Smith at first favored a head-on assault from the lagoon, instead of landing two battalions on the west coast and a third, later, on the lagoon shore. (Entry, 9 Oct 43).
[75] 27th Inf Div FO 21, 23 Oct 43.
[76] Interv, Philip A. Crowl with Maj Gen Ralph C. Smith, USA (Ret), 30 Oct 50, OCMH.

push reconnaissance as far east as "Jill" Lake. Upon being relieved, the 3d Battalion would assemble in dispersed formation as division reserve in the area north of Ukiangong Village.

Two hours later, at W Hour (1030), the second landings were to be made on Yellow Beach 2 on the north shore between On Chong's Wharf and King's Wharf, both of which projected out into the lagoon. Here, too, the first wave would consist of sixteen LVT's mounted aboard an LST and would be manned by Detachment Z of the 105th Infantry Regiment. On arrival at the beach the troops were to dismount, half of them moving directly east to clear the enemy from King's Wharf and establish a beach block and defensive position on the left flank of the beach. The other half was to move directly west, clearing any Japanese found on On Chong's Wharf and protecting the right flank of the beach. Following this wave would come the assault troops of the 2d Battalion Landing Team, 165th, with Company A of the 193d Tank Battalion attached and boated in LCVP's and LCM's. Upon seizing the beachhead, this battalion was to make its main effort to the westward to effect contact with the 1st Battalion Landing Team, which at that juncture was supposed to be moving eastward from the main division beachhead.

Meanwhile, at H Hour the platoon of the V Amphibious Corps Reconnaissance Company with one reinforced infantry platoon from the 2d Battalion, 165th Infantry, was to have landed on tiny Kotabu Island just north of Flink Point so as to secure the seaward approaches into the lagoon from possible enemy fire from that quarter. As soon after H Hour as was permissible, the three artillery batteries of the 165th Regiment were to be landed over Red Beach 2 and take position on Ukian-

gong Point. Two of these batteries consisted of the standard 105-mm. howitzers organic to regiment. Because of limitations in shipping space, 75-mm. pack howitzers had to be substituted for the third battery.[77]

The basic premise upon which this plan was made was that the first main obstacle to a quick capture of the island would be the West Tank Barrier. This consisted of a trench about six feet deep and over fourteen feet wide and extended by log fences. The whole system was laid out in a north-south direction across the island about 3,400 yards east from Red Beaches.[78] It was believed that this barrier would seriously impede the progress of tank-infantry teams approaching from the west coast, and that the best method of eliminating the hazard was to envelop it. Since this would necessitate two battalions moving toward each other, each was instructed to use special colored-smoke grenades and to maintain close radio contact. By these safeguards it was hoped that the danger of a fire fight between the American units would be minimized.[79]

What this plan failed to take into account was the potentiality of naval gunfire. The tank barrier offered an ideal target for enfilade fire by destroyers lying off either the lagoon or the ocean side of the island. However, as of the autumn of 1943, the efficacy of naval gunfire against shore targets had not been proved to the satisfaction of 27th Division planners. General Ralph Smith and his staff were still skeptical of this particular type of fire,[80] hence they felt compelled to rely almost entirely on their tank-infantry teams to overcome

[77] Ltr, cited n. 34.
[78] V Phib Corps G-2 Situation Map, Butaritari Island.
[79] Ltr cited n. 34.
[80] Interv cited n. 76.

the western tank barrier and establish a foothold on Butaritari.

Another defect in the plan was that it relied too heavily on the assumption that communications between separate units would be adequate. To avoid the danger of a fire fight between the two infantry forces as they approached each other, it was essential that they be in perfect communication with each other. Also, if artillery was to be used at all in the gap between the two forces, it would be imperative that close radio or telephone contact be maintained between the artillery battalion and the various infantry commanders. As it turned out, no such contact was established during the first day's fighting on Makin.

2d Marine Division's Plan: Betio

By contrast, the plan for landing the 2d Marine Division on Betio was a model of simplicity. General Julian Smith had under his control only two reinforced regiments of his division, the 2d and 8th Regimental Combat Teams. The 6th Regimental Combat Team was to be held in corps reserve to be landed at Tarawa, Makin, or Apamama as the situation dictated. General Smith's plan called for the landing of three battalion landing teams abreast on Red Beaches 1, 2, and 3 on the north (lagoon) shore of Betio. (*Map II*) The first three assault waves were to be made up of amphibian tractors, the fourth wave would be tanks boated in LCM's, the fifth would be LCVP's, each carrying about thirty-six troops.[81]

The first troops to land would be, from east to west (left to right) the 2d Battalion, 8th Marines; 2d Battalion, 2d Marines; and 3d Battalion, 2d Marines. The 1st Battalion, 2d Marines, was to be held in regimental reserve. In division reserve, to be committed when and where the situation warranted, would be the 1st and 3d Battalions of the 8th Marines.

As soon as the beachhead was secured, the assault troops were to move directly across the island to the south, seizing the airfield and mopping up enemy positions along the ocean beaches. When this task had been completed, the two battalions on the east were to pivot and move to the left along the axis of the island to clean it off to its eastern tip. The artillery regiment (10th Marines) was to land on order on the main beaches and prepare to mass the bulk of its fires from Central Pier (which jutted out into the lagoon almost on the boundary between Red Beaches 2 and 3) to the eastern end of Betio.

With the withdrawal of the 6th Marines from division control, General Julian Smith could count on having only about a two-to-one superiority over the Japanese, who were reckoned to number somewhere between 2,500 and 3,100.[82] This was considerably under the classic three-to-one superiority which, according to standard amphibious doctrine, is the minimum ratio desirable. If the assault was to proceed with the speed and ease hoped for, this deficiency in troop strength would have to be made up for by the preliminary naval and aerial bombardment and by the sustained momentum of the first five waves of assault troops and tanks. If any of these failed to materialize—that is, if aerial and naval bombardment proved less destructive than expected or if the ship-to-shore movement broke down—then the burden imposed on the invading troops would be unduly heavy. Events at Tarawa were soon to prove this to be the case.

---

[81] 2d Marine Div Opn Order 14, 25 Oct 43, with annexes.

[82] Stockman, *Tarawa*, p. 4.

CHAPTER III

Preparing for the Attack

Training

The Marine V Amphibious Corps, under General Holland Smith, was responsible for supervision of the ship-to-shore amphibious training of all units scheduled to take part in the invasion of the Gilbert Islands. General Richardson, commanding general of United States Army Forces in the Central Pacific Area (USAFICPA), was in charge of the rest of the training of Army units for this operation in addition to discharging the logistical and administrative duties of his command.

Before its specific assignment to the Gilberts operation, the 27th Infantry Division had been conducting preliminary amphibious training for a period of about eight months.[1] The division had been a National Guard unit from New York State and was called into Federal service in October 1940. Beginning in March 1942 it was transferred to Hawaii and for the next year and a half served as base defense force, first in the outer islands and later on Oahu after the 25th Infantry Division was sent to Guadalcanal in November 1942. While in Hawaii the division was triangularized, losing its fourth regiment, the 108th Infantry, to the 40th Division. This left it with the 165th, the 105th, and the 106th Infantry Regiments.[2]

Since November of 1942 the division's commanding general had been General Ralph Smith. His previous wartime duty had been with Military Intelligence Division of the War Department General Staff (G-2) and with the 76th Infantry Division at Fort George G. Meade.[3]

In spite of the fact that its original duties in the Hawaiian area were largely defensive in character, the division early commenced to make preparations against the day when it might be called upon to participate in amphibious operations. In December 1942 two of its officers were detailed to attend an amphibious school conducted by the U.S. Marine Corps in San Diego. On their return an amphibious school was opened in Hawaii. This school, conducted from 7 April to 12 May 1943, was attended by regimental and battalion commanders and their executive officers, and staff intelligence, operations, and logistics officers, and others.

Between May and August each battalion landing team was assembled at Schofield Barracks on Oahu and given instructions in the use of ropes, cargo net climbing and descending, boat team drill, debarking and deployment from mock-up boats, passage through wire entanglements and other obstacles, and various other tech-

---

[1] USAFICPA Participation Rpt GALVANIC, p. 29.
[2] Love, *27th Infantry Division*, pp. 1–2.
[3] General Officers Service Biographies, Public Information Division, Department of the Army.

niques peculiar to amphibious warfare. Battalion staffs prepared boat assignment tables, boat diagrams, shore party organization, landing diagrams, and debarkation and approach schedules. Next, each battalion landing team received one week's instruction at the Waianae Amphibious Training Center where a pier was used to simulate a Navy transport, and where a specially constructed barge was anchored offshore to give the troops experience in embarking and debarking from a listing vessel.[4]

In August, when General Richardson assumed command of United States Army Forces in the Central Pacific Area, steps were taken forthwith to expand the amphibious training program in the Hawaiian area with special attention given to the units of the 27th Division scheduled to participate in the forthcoming Gilberts operation. Construction of three new training centers had already commenced and before the end of August these were completed and ready for use. They were located at Waimanalo on the southeastern shore of Oahu, at Kahuku Point on the northernmost tip of Oahu, and in the Pali region in the central part of the island. All were equipped with mock-up ships' platforms and other facilities for specialized amphibious training. It was planned that each combat team of the 27th Division would be rotated through each of these camps as well as through the Schofield training area. Each team was to spend three weeks at each center.[5]

In addition to this general "preamphibious" training, various specialist courses were set up. Shore fire control parties were trained by division artillery for the purpose of directing naval gunfire after hitting the beach. The division's G-4 (supply) officer, Lt. Col. Charles B. Ferris, set up a

school for transport quartermasters, commencing on 17 September. Officers and noncommissioned officers were made familiar with the characteristics of Navy transports by visiting Pearl Harbor, measuring the ships, and observing the loading of ships. Stowage plans used in the Attu operation were studied and tentative stowage plans for the forthcoming operation were devised.[6]

One of the main sources of amphibious training doctrine available at this time was the War Department Field Manual 31-5, entitled Landing Operations on Hostile Shores (1941). This was based in large part on a previous Navy Department publication, Fleet Training Publication 167 (1938), which in turn originated in earlier studies in amphibious warfare produced by the Marine Corps in 1934 and 1935.[7] In addition, at the suggestion of General Ralph Smith, General Richardson's headquarters obtained copies of a detailed set of notes prepared by the 9th Infantry Division covering its training at Navy amphibious training centers on the east coast of the United States. These items and other literature obtained from the Marine training base at Camp Elliott, San Diego, made up the bulk of the theoretical doctrine upon which the training in Hawaii was based.[8]

Only one serious shortcoming in the training program was subsequently noted. No systematic training of Army tanks in conjunction with small infantry units was attempted. In view of the importance of a smoothly functioning tank-infantry team

---

[4] USAFICPA Participation Rpt GALVANIC, pp. 129–30.
[5] USAFMIDPAC Hist, Vol. 9, pp. 1847–48.
[6] USAFICPA Participation Rpt GALVANIC, p. 131.
[7] USAFMIDPAC Hist, Vol. 9, pp. 1943–44; Isely and Crowl, U.S. Marines and Amphibious War, Ch. II.
[8] USAFMIDPAC Hist, Vol. 9, pp. 1944–45.

TRAINING OPERATIONS ON OAHU, HAWAII. *Soldier hurdles barbed-wire obstacles (above); troops practice a landing operation (below).*

in the forthcoming Makin operation, the omission was serious.[9]

Following this period of shore-based training, the 165th Regimental Combat Team conducted joint amphibious training on beaches in the Hawaiian area with ships of Transport Division 20. Adverse weather conditions and poor beaches detracted somewhat from the success of this program. Also, no fire support or control vessels were available, thus adding undesirable artificialities to the maneuvers.[10]

Finally, after all transports were loaded, last-minute rehearsals were held between 31 October and 3 November 1943. Admiral Turner's Task Force 52, with the troops and the equipment of the Northern Attack Force aboard, proceeded from Pearl Harbor to the vicinity of Maalaea Bay, Maui, on the night of the 31st. Next morning rehearsals were held off the coast of Maui, with simulated naval gunfire and air support. All troops were landed but no supplies and equipment were sent ashore for fear of damage to landing craft and equipment, which could not be repaired before final embarkation for Makin. This exercise was repeated at daylight on 2 November. Finally, at dawn of 3 November a full-scale dress rehearsal was held off the coast of Kahoolawe Island employing actual gunfire and air support. Assault troops were embarked and proceeded to the line of departure, but did not land because Kahoolawe's beaches were rocky and therefore dangerous to the safety of landing craft. After the completion of this final exercise, the task force returned to Pearl Harbor for final loading, repairs, and briefing before sailing for Makin.[11]

Meanwhile at Wellington, New Zealand, the 2d Marine Division was carrying on its own training program. One of its regiments, the 2d Marines, had already made one amphibious landing at Guadalcanal and the other two, the 6th and 8th Marines, had participated in the subsequent land fighting on that island. In the words of General Holland Smith, "They were veterans of a campaign and needed little training other than amphibious training." [12] This the division got during the month of October as Navy transports were made available.

Final rehearsals of the entire Southern Attack Force, less its escort carriers, were held at Efate in the New Hebrides between 7 and 12 November. Two separate landing exercises were conducted at Mele Bay and fire support ships held bombardment practice on Erradaka Island. Communications equipment was tested and communications exercises were held at the same time.[13] Although this training was valuable, especially for the personnel who had recently joined the division to replace losses at Guadalcanal, the rehearsals were still not as satisfactory as desired, principally because the forces involved had too short a time to prepare and co-ordinate their plans.[14]

Logistics

The chief logistical problem in preparing for the Gilberts operation was the shortage of amphibian tractors in the Pacific Ocean Areas. This vehicle was one of the few truly amphibian pieces of equipment to be put to extensive use throughout

[9] Ltr, Hq 27th Inf Div to TAG, 14 Dec 43, sub: Participation of TF 52.6, 27th Div, in GALVANIC (Makin) Opn, p. 10, AG 327-0.3(429) 16–25 Nov 43, DRB AGO.

[10] Fifth Amph Force Rpt, Capture of Gilbert Islands, Incl A, pp. 2–3.

[11] Ibid., pp. 3–4.

[12] V Phib Corps GALVANIC Rpt, p. 5.

[13] Stockman, Tarawa, p. 9.

[14] V Phib Corps GALVANIC Rpt, p. 5.

the war in the Pacific. It was capable of about 4.5 knots in the water, and its tracks enabled it to traverse coral reefs and other obstacles not negotiable by standard landing craft. About twenty-six feet in length, it could carry (at this date) upward of twenty troops.

The LVT (sometimes called the "Alligator") had been first designed by one Donald Roebling, a retired manufacturer, for rescue work in the Everglades of Florida. Shortly thereafter the vehicle was brought to the attention of Marine officers stationed at Quantico, Virginia, who set about adapting it to military purposes. By 1940, under Marine Corps pressure, the Navy Department set aside funds for further development and by the outbreak of the war the amphibian tractor's utility both as a troop carrier and as a cargo carrier for amphibious landings had been satisfactorily demonstrated.[15] At Guadalcanal a few were used logistically to carry supplies and ammunition directly from shipboard to inland dumps, to move guns, and to evacuate the wounded.[16]

Early during the planning stage for the Gilberts, it was realized that certainly at Tarawa and possibly at Makin standard landing craft could not pass through the protective wire and log barricades that were known to have been erected to seaward on the reefs and beaches. Also, there was some doubt as to whether there would be enough water over the reef at Tarawa to permit Higgins boats to get through. Experiments in breaking up such barricades as were expected in the Gilberts were made with these amphibian tractors and turned out favorably.[17]

Steps were then taken to procure enough amphibian tractors to carry the assault troops ashore at both Tarawa and Makin. At Efate the 2d Marine Division had on hand about one hundred tractors, of which seventy-five were considered to be operational. These were old models (LVT(1)'s), unarmored and susceptible to mechanical failure. The division requested the assignment of a hundred new models (LVT(2)'s) from San Diego. The request was granted but sufficient transport to carry the vehicles into the combat area could not be provided. In the end, naval authorities released three LST's to do the job and fifty additional amphibian tractors reached the 2d Marine Amphibian Tractor Battalion at Samoa just before it set sail for Tarawa. Thus, for the attack on Betio, the marines had a total of 125 amphibian tractors which, excluding those earmarked for purely logistical duties, was sufficient to make up the first three waves of the assault.[18]

The 27th Division received forty-eight LVT's for use at Makin. These were not delivered at Oahu until 29 October, only thirteen days before sailing for the island. Before the 29th only one tractor had been available for training. Nevertheless, a provisional company from Headquarters, 193d Tank Battalion, had been organized on 21 October to operate these vehicles and was felt to be trained sufficiently to warrant use in the operation.[19]

Another amphibious development introduced into the Central Pacific Area during the Gilberts operation was the extensive employment of pallets for unloading supplies. Pallets had been employed

[15] Secretary of the Navy, Continuing Board for the Development of Landing Vehicle, Tracked, History of Landing Vehicle, Tracked (Washington, 1 Dec 45).

[16] Miller, *Guadalcanal*, p. 75.

[17] Fifth Amph Force Rpt, Capture of Gilbert Islands, p. 10.

[18] Stockman, *Tarawa*, pp. 4–5.

[19] USAFICPA Participation Rpt GALVANIC, pp. 65–66, 97–98; 193d Tk Bn Rpt of Makin Opn, Sec. XIII, Rpt of Provisional Amph LVT Co, p. 34.

by the 7th Infantry Division in the Aleutians and had been reported upon favorably by that division after its arrival in the Hawaiian Islands. Pallets are sledlike structures to which supplies are strapped. Those used in the Aleutians had measured about four by six feet and were smooth-bottomed, like toboggans. Experiments were conducted on Oahu both with this type and with one that had runners attached. The toboggan type was found to be more satisfactory on rough coral, while the sled type was discovered to be better on sand and finger coral. Fifteen hundred pallets of the toboggan type and 350 of the sled type were built for the Makin operation.[20] In the end, the assault force palletized virtually all of its supplies with the exception of 55-gallon drums.[21] These pallets, heavily loaded with supplies, could be unloaded from landing craft by tractor and moved to inland dumps so rapidly that under ideal conditions a lighter could be unloaded in an estimated one twelfth of the time taken by the standard manhandling method.[22]

In the Gilberts operation, this technique of palletization was used to an appreciable degree only at Makin. The 2d Marine Division constructed few pallets. However, the one battalion commander at Tarawa who reported on the subject considered that the employment of pallets there would have been feasible, and the transport quartermaster of Holland Smith's V Amphibious Corps later commented favorably on the experiment conducted by Army troops at Makin.[23]

Troops, supplies, and equipment of the Northern Attack Force were loaded in the Hawaiian area aboard four APA's and one AKA.[24] Three LST's carried between them the forty-eight amphibian tractors assigned to the assault force and a company of medium tanks was carried aboard the LSD Belle Grove. These four amphibious vessels also carried between them 791 troops. All of the transports were combat loaded—this is to say, each tactical unit was embarked aboard a single ship with its supplies and equipment stowed in inverse order to their probable tactical employment during the landing. High-priority material was normally stowed near the top and center of ships' holds; low-priority near the bottom and on the outside. Thus, the 1st Battalion Landing Team of the 165th Regimental Combat Team, consisting of 1,044 officers and men with their essential supplies and equipment, was loaded aboard the Neville; 2d Battalion Landing Team, numbering 1,219, aboard Leonard Wood. In addition, each of these vessels carried shore parties from the 3d Battalion, 105th Infantry, and sundry other personnel including air liaison parties, shore fire control parties, observers, and newspaper correspondents. The attack cargo ship Alcyone carried, in addition to its load of supplies and equipment, miscellaneous units of the 165th Regimental Combat Team such as the Service Company, the Cannon Company, 27th Division Quartermaster Company Detachment, 27th Division Signal Company Detachment—in all 288.[25]

---

[20] USAFICPA Participation Rpt GALVANIC, p. 46.
[21] Ibid., p. 27.
[22] Interv, Edmund G. Love with Col Charles B. Ferris, Sep 47.
[23] V Phib Corps GALVANIC Rpt, Incl F, Rpt by Special Staff Officers, Sec. VIII, Rpt by Transport Quartermaster, p. 4.
[24] The troopships were Leonard Wood, Calvert, Neville and Pierce; the cargo ship (which also carried some troops) was Alcyone.
[25] Ltr, Hq 27th Inf Div to CG Port of Embarkation, Fort Mason, California, 7 Dec 43, Incl 2, sub: Capacities of Listed Ships Cargo and Actual Combat Load Details, AG 327–Inf (165)–4.8(25054), DRB AGO.

SUPPLIES PALLETIZED *for the Gilberts operation. Method of loading and strapping (above); an LVT towing a loaded pallet during the actual operation (below).*

Besides their troops, each of the three attack transports was loaded with the following supplies and equipment: all Table of Basic Allowance equipment and individual and organizational property for the units aboard except for certain items, such as chemical warfare equipment, that were ordered left behind; 10 days' rations plus 2 days' K rations carried by each individual on board; one 5-gallon container of water per man on board; 7 days' motor fuel for bulldozers and other vehicles aboard, 5 units of fire for all weapons, 10 days' medical supply for all units, and 7 days' supply of ordnance cleaning and preserving materials, and spare gun parts. Average poundage per soldier on these three ships came to 1,322.

The *Alcyone*, the only attack cargo ship assigned to the Northern Attack Force, carried in addition to the troops mentioned, the following supplies and equipment: 24 days' B rations for the entire force; approximately 3,000 5-gallon cans of water; sufficient gasoline for 8 days' operation for all motor vehicles; approximately 18,750 gallons of white gasoline; over 70,000 gallons of diesel oil; 28,200 gallons of high-octane gasoline for the amphibian tractors; 7,684 gallons of motor oil; 3,655 pounds of grease; 5 units of fire for all weapons on board; 5 units of fire for one battery of 105-mm. howitzers; 4 units of fire for the weapons of the medium tanks carried aboard the *Belle Grove*; 4 units of fire for the two .30-caliber and one .50-caliber machine guns on each of the amphibian tractors carried aboard the 3 LST's; slightly more than 30 days of medical supplies; 30 days of maintenance for all items in ordnance; about 1.5 tons of chemical warfare supplies; approximately 30 days' quartermaster supplies for the entire force; 30 days' signal supplies; and 30

days' engineer maintenance for an engineer combat battalion and 20 days' maintenance requirements for an infantry division less the combat battalion.[26]

The 2d Marine Division, loading in New Zealand, experienced somewhat more difficulty than did the 165th Regimental Combat Team. This was because in many cases ships assigned to the division failed to arrive in Wellington until just before the scheduled time for loading. Before their actual arrival, division headquarters had little information about ships' characteristics. Not knowing in many cases the names of the ships or even the type of ships to be assigned, Marine planners had no reliable information on such vital matters as the size of ships' holds and hatches, troop spaces, and so forth. Hence, loading plans could be only tentative and had to be revised at the last minute as individual vessels put in their appearance at Wellington.[27]

Nevertheless, the ships were combat loaded in a manner at least satisfactory enough to elicit no adverse comment from the division commander. Thirteen APA's, three AKA's and one LSD completed loading and left Wellington on 1 November 1943.[28] In addition, three LST's carrying amphibian tractors met the division at Samoa.

---

[26] *Ibid.*, Incl 1, Logistics of Makin Island Opn, 27th Div Task Force; S. L. A. Marshall, Makin Notes (2d draft), p. 182, OCMH.

[27] V Phib Corps GALVANIC Rpt, Incl F, Rpt of Special Staff Officers, Sec. VIII, Rpt of Transport QM, p. 1; *Ibid.*, Incl G, Rpt by Special Observers, Sec. II, Rpt by Capt Richard F. Whitehead, USN, p. 1.

[28] The following ships were used to lift the 2d Marine Division: *Zeilin, Heywood, Middleton, Biddle, Lee, Monrovia, Sheridan, La Salle, Doyen* (all APA's); *Thuban, Bellatrix* (AKA's); and *Ashland* (LSD). 2d Marine Div Special Action Rpt, 6 Jan 44, Incl A, Narrative Account of Gilbert Islands Opn, p. 1.

Preliminary Air and Naval Action

Well before the crystallization of plans for the invasion of the Gilberts, bombers of the Seventh Air Force had commenced to harass those islands as well as nearby Nauru. In January and February reconnaissance missions were sent over the Gilberts and on 20 April a flight of twenty-two B-24's took off from Funafuti for a thousand-mile run to Nauru. There, in spite of heavy interception, they hit the runway recently constructed by the Japanese as well as the local phosphate plant. Two days later twelve B-24's struck Tarawa with moderate success.[29]

At this time Funafuti and Canton were the only two Allied bases within range of the Gilberts, and these were so far away as to make regular bombing runs difficult and hazardous. Hence, in order to strengthen American control of air approaches to these islands, the Joint Chiefs in July authorized the seizure of other islands for the construction of new airfields from which to conduct neutralization and reconnaissance.[30] Accordingly, early in August, Admiral Nimitz ordered three Marine defense battalions to "occupy, organize, and defend the atolls of Nukufetau and Nanomea at the earliest practicable date . . . and to construct airfields thereon."[31] These two islands, both in the Ellice group, were respectively about 600 miles south and 350 miles east of Tarawa. An advance survey party landed at Nanomea Atoll on 18 August to determine whether it was occupied by the enemy and, after reconnoitering, to select a site for an airfield. No Japanese were discovered on the atoll, and ten days later the advance party was followed ashore by the forward echelon of the 7th Marine Defense Battalion and detachments from two naval construction battalions. Meanwhile, on 22 August, an advance party of the 2d Marine Airdrome Battalion landed at Nukufetau, and was followed five days later by the remainder of the battalion and elements of a naval construction battalion. The Marine contingent at Funafuti was strengthened and naval construction troops sent there. All units began at once the construction of new airfields and the improvement and enlargement of existing facilities.

The transformation of these atolls into air bases progressed rapidly. By 7 September a 5,000-foot airstrip was ready for use at Nanomea, and by the end of the month a full squadron of planes was operating from there. Work at Nukufetau was somewhat slower, but the strip was ready for use by 9 October.[32]

On 11 August a small task force was sent by General Richardson to develop Baker Island, a U.S. possession about 480 miles due east of the Gilberts. This expedition was composed of the 804th Aviation Engineer Battalion, a provisional antiaircraft artillery battalion, a provisional air service support squadron, a fighter squadron, and miscellaneous service elements. The force carried equipment and supplies sufficient to construct, operate, and maintain a base for ninety days. It arrived at Baker on 1 September. A week later a strip capable of supporting fighter planes was already in use.[33]

Thus, on the eve of the invasion of the Gilberts, the Seventh Air Force had five

[29] Craven and Cate, *AAF IV*, pp. 286–88.
[30] Rad, JCS to CINCPAC, CM-IN 14465, 20 Jul 43.
[31] CINCPAC-CINCPOA Opns in POA, Aug 43, par. 56.
[32] CINCPAC-CINCPOA Opns in POA, Sep 43, pp. 3–4.
[33] USAFICPA Participation Rpt GALVANIC, p. 145.

bases within bombing range of those islands. Funafuti, Nukufetau, and Nanomea each had two bomber squadrons; on Canton were stationed one bomber squadron, one fighter-bomber squadron, and one fighter squadron; Baker had one fighter squadron.[34] Advance headquarters of the Seventh Air Force was opened at Funafuti on 6 November, and at approximately the same time Admiral Hoover's flagship *Curtis* anchored in the lagoon.[35]

The first air attack in the Gilberts operation occurred on 13 November when eighteen B-24's took off from Funafuti to bomb Tarawa. They dropped about fifteen tons of bombs on the target, starting a large fire but causing no other observable damage. Although no enemy interception was met, antiaircraft fire was unusually heavy. On the next day nine B-24's bombed Tarawa again, causing some damage to the airstrip. The same day, the first strike was launched against Mille Atoll, the nearest of the Marshalls. Of the twenty planes that started for Mille, only nine reached the target. They dropped four tons of bombs on the airfield. Although antiaircraft fire from both Tarawa and Mille was heavy, there was still no interception by enemy planes. On 15 November the strikes were extended to include Jaluit in the Marshalls. Seventeen bombers hit that atoll, causing damage to the seaplane base and sinking ships in the lagoon. Another strike by eight B-24's was conducted against Mille and Makin the same day. The airfield at Mille was again damaged and again there was no air opposition.

On 16 November the air offensive moved farther west, to Kwajalein Atoll. Of twenty planes assigned the mission that day, only one reached the primary target. The others turned back and dropped their bombs on Jaluit, in the Marshalls, and

Tarawa and Little Makin, in the Gilberts. The same day six B-24's set out for Maloelap, but were unable to drop their bombs because of poor weather. For the first time, enemy fighters arose to intercept the attack. On 17 November, the day immediately preceding the scheduled arrival of the American carrier force in the target area, twenty bombers hit Tarawa, Mille, and Maloelap. Considerable damage was reported to have been done to the airfields at Tarawa and Mille. At Maloelap the bombers were intercepted by Japanese fighters and in the ensuing action one B-24 was badly damaged and crashed at Baker Island on its return flight.

In all, the heavy bombers of the Seventh Air Force had flown 141 bombing sorties against the Gilberts and Marshalls between 13 and 17 November. They dropped about 173 tons of bombs and destroyed at least five enemy aircraft. Of course, it is impossible to calculate the extent of the damage done to the airfields and defense installations in the Gilberts, since the same area was later covered by carrier aircraft and then by naval guns just before the invasion.[36]

While the bases for the air offensive against the Gilberts were being built and reinforced, other preliminary moves against the targets were taking place. A fast carrier task force (Task Force 50) under command of Admiral Pownall was organized early in September to strike the Gilberts in order to "decrease enemy pressure on our holdings in the Ellice Islands," which the Japanese had bombed from Tarawa and Makin. This force was to de-

---

[34] Craven and Cate, *AAF IV*, p. 298.

[35] Operational Hist of Seventh Air Force, 7 Dec 41–6 Nov 43, p. 66, MS filed in Air University Historical Liaison Office, Washington, D. C.

[36] *Ibid.*, pp. 88–90; Craven and Cate, *AAF IV*, pp. 299–302.

stroy aircraft and installations at Tarawa, Makin, and Apamama and to conduct such reconnaissance as was possible.[37]

The naval force that approached the Gilberts during the night of 17–18 September consisted of three carriers, three cruisers, and eleven destroyers. It was to be supported by twenty-four B-24's flying from Canton and Funafuti and fourteen flying from Guadalcanal. The planes of the first group were to attack Tarawa just before dawn on 18 September; those from Guadalcanal were to hit Nauru at the same time. Twenty-eight photoreconnaissance planes from Canton and Funafuti were to join the task force in the area of Tarawa and combine bombing runs on that island with their photographic mission.

Arriving near Tarawa during the early morning hours of 18 September, the carriers launched their first flight at approximately 0330, hoping to take advantage of moonlight for their initial runs. There was not enough light, however, and the planes had to hover over the island until daybreak. Between then and 1822 of the same day six separate attacks were made against Tarawa, during which eighty tons of bombs were dropped and all visible installations strafed. One attack was launched against Makin at daylight and another against Apamama later in the morning.

The airfield at Nauru was reported to be neutralized. At Tarawa considerable quantities of fuel and ammunition were destroyed, several buildings were wrecked, and a small freighter was sunk. At Makin three large flying boats were set on fire, and some damage was done to shore installations. The most important single achievement of the strike was the photographic coverage of Tarawa and Makin by both carrier- and land-based aircraft. At Tarawa opposition from antiaircraft artillery was intense, but at Makin it was extremely weak. No fighter interception was encountered at either target, but two Japanese medium bombers were shot down northwest of Makin.

The carrier force retired to the south during the night. Next day the attack was continued by twenty B-24's from Canton and Funafuti. The bombers were intercepted by enemy fighters over Tarawa, where the airfield had been repaired during the night. Of the eighteen Japanese fighters that rose to meet the attackers, six were definitely destroyed and four more listed as probably destroyed. During these two days of operations American losses were five planes, one of them a bomber that crash-landed at Nanomea on its return from the second flight.

The raid on the Gilberts was followed eighteen days later by a naval carrier strike against Wake. Led by Rear Adm. Alfred E. Montgomery, USN, Task Force 14, the largest carrier striking force yet assembled in the Pacific, hit Wake on 5 and 6 October. Sixty-seven Japanese planes were reported destroyed in the air and on the ground, and shore installations were heavily damaged.[38]

Then, commencing on 13 November, the land-based bombers of Admiral Hoover's Task Force 57 made nightly attacks on Tarawa and Makin as well as on Nauru and islands in the central Marshalls. A total of sixty-six planes participated in these raids before November 20.[39]

Finally, during the two days before the landings, both Navy and Army planes delivered last-minute softening-up blows. The

[37] CINCPAC-CINCPOA Opns in POA, Sep 43, pp. 7–10.
[38] CINCPAC-CINCPOA Opns in POA, Oct 43, pp. 5–8.
[39] CINCPAC-CINCPOA Opns in POA, Nov 43, Annex E, p. 20.

NAURU ISLAND *under attack by Liberator bombers of the Seventh Air Force.*

first strike was against Nauru. At 0300 on 18 November one group of Admiral Pownall's task force launched eighteen fighter planes for a dawn strike against that island. They were followed, three hours later, by twenty more fighters and then, at intervals of two to three hours, by dive bombers, torpedo bombers, and more fighters. All day long these planes bombed and strafed Nauru. By the day's end about ninety tons of bombs had been dropped. Installations on the island were reported to have been severely damaged. One Japanese ship was left burning, and three or four medium bombers were destroyed on the ground. Four or five enemy fighters sought to intercept the attack, but all were shot down.[40]

The carrier attack on Nauru was fol-

lowed next day with strikes by land-based planes. Seventh Air Force bombers, accompanied by Navy photoreconnaissance aircraft, bombed both airfields and shipping, causing considerable damage and removing Nauru as a threat to operations in the Gilberts.[41]

At the same time the Gilberts themselves were brought under heavy aerial attack. On 19 November, nineteen B-24's from Nukufetau and Funafuti dropped about ten tons of bombs on Tarawa, causing fires throughout the area and damaging the airfields. Twelve more planes, from Nanomea, dropped twenty-three tons on

[40] *Ibid.*, p. 26.
[41] Operational Hist of Seventh Air Force, 6 Nov 43–31 Jul 44, pp. 91–93, MS filed in Air University Historical Liaison Office, Washington, D. C.

TABLE 1—AMMUNITION EXPENDED BY JAPANESE ON TARAWA AND MAKIN 13–19 NOVEMBER 1943

	Type of Ammunition	Rounds Expended	Rounds Remaining
Tarawa	127-mm. AA	a 1, 437	3, 290
	75-mm. AA	a 1, 312	1, 345
	13-mm. MG	a 51, 160	14, 903
	8-inch	46	b
	14-cm.	104	b
Makin.	13-mm. MG	a 9, 100	2, 400

a Minimum rounds expended.
b Not available.
Source: CINPAC-CINCPOA Translation 10018, Summary of the American Army Counterattack in the Gilbert Area of November 1943, Imperial Headquarters, Army Department, dated January 1944; PACMIRS Captured Japanese Document MR-50 (D-65), Military Action in the Gilbert Islands (Girubato shoto ni okeru sento), translated by Joseph Guilfoyle, filed in OCMH.

Makin.[42] Planes from the Northern and Southern Carrier Groups released ninety-five tons of bombs on Makin and sixty-nine on Betio Island. One enemy plane was shot down by the Northern Carrier Group off Makin while three were disposed of near Tarawa. Cruisers and destroyers of the Southern Carrier Group moved close to Tarawa shortly before noon on 19 November and, between air strikes, bombarded ground defenses.

The same day the Interceptor Carrier Group of Admiral Pownall's task force moved into position northwest of Makin and, from a point about midway between the Gilberts and the Marshalls, launched a series of attacks against Jaluit and Mille. One hundred and thirty tons of bombs were dropped on these two atolls. Power stations at both places were destroyed, hangars burned, and other buildings hit. Runways were rendered unserviceable at Mille and three vessels in the lagoon were damaged. Seven aircraft were destroyed on the ground.

Although it is impossible to determine the exact amount of damage wrought by this pre-D-Day bombardment, one certain fact emerges—the Japanese wasted a considerable amount of their precious ammunition against these aerial attacks. Whatever else the preliminary bombardment may or may not have accomplished, it wreaked havoc on the enemy's ammunition supply. (Table 1, above.)

The heavy expenditure of 13-mm. machine gun ammunition was particularly important since these weapons were to form the main basis of ground fire defense. It is clear that the Japanese recognized the seriousness of the problem. One of their dispatches sent back to Tokyo warned, "We must quickly replenish ammo for the 13 mm. MGs on both Tarawa and Makin."[43]

Movement Overseas

Following the final rehearsal at Maui on 4 November the Northern Attack Force had returned to Pearl Harbor, where most of the troops debarked for a week's rest

[42] *Ibid.*, pp. 90–91.
[43] CINCPAC-CINCPOA Translation 10018.

SOUTHERN ATTACK FORCE *steaming toward the Gilberts; in the foreground a TBF-1 Avenger performs an antisubmarine patrol.*

and rehabilitation. Part of the task force had already left for the Gilberts. On 31 October six LST's, escorted by a destroyer, had left Oahu carrying part of the garrison troops that would occupy Makin after its capture. Five days later, as soon as refueling could be completed after the return from the rehearsal, the three LST's carrying amphibian tractors and the special landing groups that would man them departed for Makin with a destroyer escort. They traveled by a shorter route than the first convoy and were scheduled to arrive at their destination at precisely the same time as the main body of the assault force, which was to leave Pearl Harbor on the afternoon of 10 November.[44] Although the Northern Attack Force, the Northern Carrier Group, and the Interceptor Car-

rier Group all departed from the Hawaiian Islands at the same time, they did not travel together; the two carrier groups moved along a course parallel to that followed by the Northern Attack Force but about 300 miles to the northwest. The two routes of approach changed approximately 800 miles east of the Gilberts, with the Northern Attack Force turning to meet the Southern Attack Force, the two carrier groups diverging and moving directly to their assigned stations.

Meanwhile, following rehearsals in Efate, the Southern Attack Force, composed of transports, fire support ships, and auxiliaries, sortied from that island on 13

[44] TF 54 Movement Order A1-43, 20 Oct 43; CINCPAC-CINCPOA Opns in POA, Nov 43, Annex E, Plate II.

BRIEFING TROOPS *on scale models of Butaritari. This training during the voyage to Butaritari facilitated the landings.*

November. It was followed by the fast battleships, cruisers, and carriers of the Southern Carrier Group. Two days later, on 15 November, the Relief Carrier Force, composed of two carriers, three cruisers and four destroyers, left Espíritu Santo, also in the New Hebrides. The last-named force moved almost directly north, toward Nauru. The Southern Carrier Group and the Southern Attack Force moved along courses roughly parallel to each other, which brought them to points just south of Funafuti, where all ships refueled. From there the courses diverged, the Southern Carrier Group going directly to its appointed area west of Apamama and Tarawa, and the Southern Attack Force

moving in a northerly direction to a rendezvous on 18 November with the Northern Attack Force coming from Pearl Harbor.[45] Thereafter, ships of the two convoys moved along parallel courses toward the Gilberts to the northwest, the Northern Attack Force pulling slightly to the north as the islands were approached.

Late on the afternoon of 18 November the northern LST group, still ahead of the rest of the assault force, had been discovered by Japanese planes. One enemy bomber attacked the little convoy but was driven off by antiaircraft gunfire. On 19 November at 1435 another Japanese plane

[45] CINCPAC-CINCPOA Opns in POA, Nov 43, Annex E, p. 3 and Plate II.

appeared overhead, but just as it was about to launch an attack, four U.S. fighter planes arrived on the scene and shot it down in flames. A more determined attack on the LST's was made after dark when two other Japanese bombers swooped low over the slow-moving vessels. The first, hit by ships' antiaircraft fire, burst into flames and fell into the sea, just missing the bow of one of the vessels. Burning gas lighted up the entire convoy for several minutes. Soon afterwards the second enemy plane left without inflicting any damage.[46]

Aboard the transports, troops were undergoing their final briefing. At the last minute (on 19 November) General Ralph Smith decided to make one minor revision in the landing plan for the 165th Infantry on Makin. He requested permission to land one infantry company and one shore fire control party on the northeast tip of Butaritari on the afternoon of D Day and to land the balance of the battalion and one shore fire control party on the south end of Kuma Island on the morning of D plus 1.[47] The object of this scheme was to set up a second envelopment of the Japanese—to catch the enemy as he was pushed eastward by the main attack or as he attempted to move across the reef to Kuma Island.[48] Whatever merit the plan may have had, it went untested. On General Holland Smith's advice, Admiral Turner turned down the request and reaffirmed his intention to go through with the original landing plan.

In the early hours of 20 November the two attack forces reached their separate destinations. The transports moved toward their debarkation areas and the fire support ships moved into shore for the initial bombardment. In the dim light of the early morning, the invasion of Butaritari and Betio began.

[46] USS *LST 31* War Diary, pp. 50–52.

[47] Fifth Amph Force Rpt, Capture of Gilbert Islands, Incl A, p. 14.

[48] Interv, Philip A. Crowl with Maj Gen Ralph C. Smith, 30 Oct 50.

CHAPTER IV

The Enemy

Japanese Invasion of the Gilberts

Japanese interest in the Gilberts dated from the earliest days of the war. The primary strategic purpose of the empire at the beginning of the war was the occupation and development of what was called the Southern Resources Area—the Netherlands Indies and adjacent regions. It was this part of the Pacific that contained most of the raw materials considered essential to Japan's economic welfare and military potential. As a corollary to the seizure of these islands, it was also believed necessary to maintain free lines of communication between the Japanese homeland and the Southern Resources Area. Finally, to guarantee the permanent success of its ventures, Japan hoped to cripple Allied naval strength in the Pacific and establish a strong defensive perimeter to protect the homeland and its new economic adjunct to the south. To accomplish these objectives, Japanese strategists contemplated three successive steps: the establishment of a perimeter along a line from the Kurils through the Marshalls, the Bismarcks, Timor, Java, Sumatra, and Malaya to Burma; the consolidation and strengthening of this perimeter; and the defense of the perimeter.[1]

The responsibility for carrying out this plan in the Central Pacific and in the Bismarcks area fell to the *4th Fleet,* which before Pearl Harbor commanded naval ground force garrisons in the mandated islands from its headquarters at Truk. According to Imperial Navy plans formulated in November 1941, the mission of the *4th Fleet* at the beginning of the war was:

1. Defend the South Sea Islands, patrol, maintain surface communications, capture Wake. At opportune time attack and destroy enemy advanced bases in South Pacific Area. In co-operation with Army capture Guam and then Bismarck Area.

. . . .

4. Defend and patrol points in South Sea Islands and Bismarcks. Maintain surface communications. Search for and attack enemy shipping. Make surprise attacks and destroy enemy bases on our perimeter.[2]

The main offensive thrust was to reach southward to the Bismarcks area, while in the east the perimeter was to be held and strengthened by the capture of Wake. A minor part of this plan was the seizure of Makin Atoll in the Gilberts in order better to protect the more important Marshall Islands to the north. Makin, lying 0°40′ east of the boundary of the Japanese Mandate, offered the advantage of being located about 240 nautical miles southeast of Jaluit, the most important seaplane base in the lower Marshalls. The seizure of Makin and its subsequent development

---

[1] United States Strategic Bombing Survey (USSBS) (Pacific), Naval Analysis Division, *The Campaigns of the Pacific War* (Washington, 1946), pp. 2–3.

[2] *Ibid.*, pp. 47–48.

into a seaplane base would make it possible to extend air patrols closer to Howland, Baker, and the Ellice Islands and to protect the eastern flank of the Japanese perimeter from possible Allied advance through the Ellice-Gilberts chain. Also, since Makin was the northernmost of the Gilberts, it could be the most easily supplied by transport from the Marshall Islands.[3]

On 3 December 1941 one company was detached from the *51st Guard Force* based on Jaluit and constituted the *Gilberts Invasion Special Landing Force* under Air Force command. This force, consisting of from 200 to 300 troops plus laborers, left Jaluit by ship on 8 December and on the 10th reached Makin Atoll, which was forthwith occupied. One of the troopships also visited Tarawa on 24 December. The entire operation yielded nine prisoners.[4]

After the invasion the Makin garrison set about constructing a seaplane base and coastal defenses. By August of 1942 the garrison had dwindled to only 43 men under a warrant officer, and it was this tiny group that was called upon to defend the atoll against the first American landing in the Central Pacific.[5]

Carlson's Raid and Its Aftermath

On 17 August 1942 the 2d Marine Raider Battalion, consisting of 221 marines under the command of Colonel Carlson, landed on Makin from two submarines. The primary purpose of this raid was to confuse the Japanese and cause them to divert forces that might otherwise be assigned to the Guadalcanal area.[6] Carlson himself stated the secondary purposes of the raid:

This task group will execute landings on Makin from the USS NAUTILUS and USS ARGONAUT on 17 August for the purpose of destroying enemy troops and vital installations and to capture important documents and prisoners.[7]

In the early hours of 17 August the raiders disembarked from the two submarines into rubber boats powered by outboard motors and landed on the southern coast of Butaritari. Heavy swells and mechanical failures in some of the engines prevented the party from making two separate landings as originally planned, but eventually fifteen out of the eighteen boats managed to get ashore at one landing beach, while two others landed a mile north and another a mile south.[8]

Just after the landing one of the marines accidentally discharged his rifle. Believing that all chance of surprise was lost, Colonel Carlson ordered Company A of his battalion to proceed across the island

[3] USSBS (Pacific), Naval Analysis Division, *The American Campaign Against Wotje, Maloelap, Mille* and *Jaluit* (Washington, 1947), pp. 18–19.

[4] The *51st Guard Force* was part of the *6th Base Force,* which was under command of *4th Fleet.*

Base Forces, Guard Forces and Defense Forces (*Konkyochitai, Keibitai, Bobitai*), Vol. 1, Dec 41–May 42, in U.S. National Archives, World War II Seized Enemy Records, Record Group 242, NA 12029, WDC 161090; *6th Base Force* War Diary (*Dairoku konkyochitai senji nisshi*), NA 12654, WDC 160599. Hereafter documents contained in the National Archives collection will be cited by title, National Archives (NA) number, and Washington Document Center (WDC) number.

[5] Land Forces (*Rikujo butai*), Vol. 2, NA 11665, WDC 161013.

[6] Ltr, CinC US Pacific Fleet to CinC US Fleet, 20 Oct 42, sub: Solomon Islands Campaign—Makin Island Diversion, 6-13.0002/42(20756), Hq USMC Historical Division.

[7] TUG 7.15.3 (2d Marine Raider Bn) Opn Order 1-42, 7 Aug 42.

[8] This account of Carlson's raid is taken from the following sources: CO 2d Marine Raider Bn, Rpt of the Raid Against Makin, 17–18 Aug 42, dated 3 Sep 42; Ltr cited n. 6; Ltr, CTG 7.15 (USS *Nautilus*) to CTF 7, sub: Rpt of Marine-Submarine Raider Expedition. All of these reports are on file at Headquarters, USMC Historical Division.

to the lagoon shore. By 0545 the company commander, Capt. Merwin C. Plumley, USMC, reported that he had captured Government House without opposition, and he was then ordered west along the lagoon road. By this time it had become apparent that the Japanese defenses were concentrated at the base of On Chong's Wharf on the lagoon shore and at Ukiangong Point, the southwesternmost promontory of Butaritari. Carlson asked for naval gunfire in this area, and *Nautilus* complied by firing some twenty-four rounds. Throughout the day isolated groups of Japanese were encountered, spirited fire fights ensued, and a number of enemy were killed. The chief Japanese response to the landing was from the air. At 1130, two Japanese naval reconnaissance planes scouted the island, dropped two bombs and then flew back north to a base in the Marshalls. About two hours later, twelve enemy planes arrived and bombed and strafed for an hour and a quarter. Two of the planes landed in the lagoon and were destroyed by Marine machine gun and antitank rifle fire. The third and last air raid occurred at 1630.

Shortly thereafter, at 1700, the marines began an orderly withdrawal to the southern coast, and within two hours the bulk of the battalion was boated, but only a few were able to get through the heavy surf and back to the submarines. A hundred and twenty men were left on the beach that night. By the following morning still more marines made their way through the surf, but at 0920 further evacuation was halted by an air raid, leaving seventy men, including Colonel Carlson, stranded on the beach.

At this point, the battalion commander discovered that Japanese resistance was practically nonexistent, consisting of only a few troops scattered about the island. He sent out patrols to search for food and destroy the Japanese radio station at the base of On Chong's Wharf. A cache of aviation gasoline of 700 to 1,000 barrels was fired, and the marines ranged freely about the island, meeting only the most feeble resistance. The office of the Japanese commandant was searched and all available papers secured. Finally, on the evening of the second day, evacuation was completed and all of the rubber boats reached the *Nautilus*.

This expedition cost the lives of thirty marines. Left ashore were twenty-one dead and nine others who were later captured and beheaded.[9] In retrospect, the entire expedition appears to have been ill advised. Though little of any importance was learned and no subsequent attempt was ever made in the Pacific war to emulate the Makin raid, the observations of Major Roosevelt, who was Carlson's executive officer, were later of some value to the intelligence staff of the 27th Infantry Division in preparing plans for the ultimate invasion of Makin. Otherwise, there is no evidence that the raid of August 1942 made any significant contribution to Allied victory in the Pacific.

On the other hand, there is every reason to believe that this raid induced the Japanese to commit to the Gilberts far heavier forces than they had originally contemplated. To that extent the progress of American arms across the Central Pacific was made more difficult. The Japanese response to Carlson's expedition was immediate. Troops were drawn from the Marshalls, the Carolines, and Japan and sent to garrison hitherto-unoccupied islands in the British Mandates. The Gilberts now

---

[9] Morison, *Coral Sea, Midway and Submarine Actions,* pp. 240–41.

were occupied in force, and garrisons were established as well on Nauru and Ocean Islands. Before August, in all the islands south of the Marshalls the enemy had only the small force on Makin. After August they began a build-up in this area that was to result in several island strongholds under an entirely new base force command. Even if it cannot be proved conclusively that Carlson's expedition was the sole cause of this change in policy, the raid can with certainty be credited with a rapid acceleration in the Japanese program of building up defenses in the Gilberts.

No time was lost in replacing the Makin garrison. On 19 August, four reconnaissance seaplanes from Kwajalein made a close search of the Makin area and found no trace of the Americans. This indicated that the coast was clear for a counterlanding, in full company strength, which the Japanese had started to organize at Jaluit as soon as news of the raid was received. On the 20th a small advance detachment was flown to Makin from Jaluit and was shortly followed by the bulk of the force transported by ship. The nine marines left on Butaritari were taken prisoner and the equipment that Carlson was forced to abandon was captured.[10]

Now began a series of small troop movements from all directions into the fringe of British island possessions bordering the Marshalls. Nauru was invaded on 25 August and Ocean Island on the 26th. On the 29th a landing force composed of one company of the *43d Guard Force* (western Carolines) took over Nauru. Two days earlier a company detached from the *62d Guard Force* (Jaluit) commenced to garrison Ocean. This unit was joined a few days later by a company from the *41st Guard Force* from Truk. Another company, from

the *5th Special Base Force,* left Saipan on 28 August and on the 30th arrived at Makin, where it was to remain pending the arrival of a special naval landing force from the Japanese homeland.[11]

These moves were followed by the invasion of Apamama, which lasted from 31 August to 4 September.[12] More important still, the entire *Yokosuka 6th Special Naval Landing Force (SNLF)* was dispatched from Japan to the Gilberts in September. This force consisted of 1,509 officers and men and was the first unit of any considerable size to arrive in the area. It was these troops that were to remain in the Gilberts, chiefly on Tarawa, until the American invasion in November 1943.[13] On 15 September the main portion of the *6th SNLF* arrived at Tarawa, and detachments were subsequently transferred to Apamama and Makin.

In September and October small parties were sent from Tarawa to snuff out the few remaining communications centers maintained by the Allies in the area. Since the beginning of the war a number of Australian and New Zealand coastwatchers had stayed in various islands of the central and southern Gilberts, observing Japanese air and surface movements and radioing important information to the Allies. These the Japanese now proceeded to eliminate quickly. On 26 September a small party landed on Beru Atoll and destroyed a British wireless station there. Next day Tamana Atoll was invaded. Here the Jap-

[10] *6th Base Force* War Diary, NA 12654, WDC 160599; Base Forces, Guard Forces, and Defense Forces, Vol. 2, Jun 42–Nov 42, NA 12053, WDC 161110.

[11] *Ibid.; 41st Guard Force* War Diary, NA 12134, WDC 161744.

[12] Land Forces, Vol. 2, NA 11665, WDC 161013.

[13] JICPOA Translation 3998, *6th Base Force* Secret Directive 104-43.

anese destroyed communications equipment and captured two Allied soldiers and one wireless operator. Also on the 27th, a second landing party captured communications equipment on Maiana, Nonouti, and Kuria Atolls. Later, in October, Maiana and Nonouti were revisited and Abaiang and Beru raided, netting more wireless sets and a few prisoners. By 6 October the Japanese declared that the Gilberts were completely cleared of enemy personnel, and that all communications installations had been destroyed.[14]

Thus the Makin raid of August 1942 constitutes a clear line of demarcation in Japanese policy in the Gilberts. Before that time there were only forty-three men, under command of a warrant officer, stationed in the whole area. Within a month after Carlson's battalion landed on Makin, the total garrison for the Gilberts came to more than 1,500 troops plus four companies on Nauru and Ocean. Just as significant was the change in the command structure for the area. Before August 1942 the only command located in the Gilberts was the *Special Landing Force* at Makin. This force was subordinate to the *62d Guard Force* based on Jaluit, which was subordinate to the *6th Base Force* on Kwajalein, in turn subordinate to the *4th Fleet* at Truk.[15] The *Yokosuka 6th SNLF,* assigned to the Gilberts with headquarters at Tarawa after the Carlson raid, was immediately under the *6th Base Force* at Kwajalein. Under this headquarters two subordinate commands were set up at Makin and Apamama. In addition, two new commands were set up under the *6th Base Force*—the *43d Guard Force Dispatched Landing Force* on Nauru and the *62d Guard Force Dispatched Landing Force* on Ocean Island.[16] The Gilberts and the nearby islands of Ocean and Nauru were obviously achiev-

ing greater status in Japan's defensive strategy.

Throughout the winter and early spring of 1943 other steps were taken to improve defenses in the Gilberts. Another recognition of the increased importance of this area came on 15 February 1943 when the *Yokosuka 6th Special Naval Landing Force* was deactivated and the command in the Gilberts was renamed the *3d Special Base Force.* The new command was made responsible not only for the defense of Tarawa, Makin, and Apamama Atolls, but also of Nauru and Ocean Islands.[17] This was a significant command reorganization reflecting clearly the change in Japanese attitude toward the importance of the Gilberts after Carlson's raid. In the beginning of 1942 Japan had nothing more than a lookout station in the Gilberts subordinated to a guard force command, which was in turn responsible to a base force at Kwajalein. Now, in February 1943, Japanese forces in the Gilberts were constituted as a base force command on an echelon equal to that of the Kwajalein base force command.

Parallel to these developments in command organization was the steady progress being made in fortifying the various islands and improving their military potentialities. Beginning about 1 January 1943, the Japanese steadily shipped *4th Fleet* laborers, mostly Koreans, to the islands south of the Marshalls for construction work. Some in-

dication of the cost involved in the fortifications under construction is afforded by
the fact that, on 4 March 1943, 7,409,000
yen ($1,736,669.60) was earmarked for air
base construction in the Gilberts and land
fortifications on Nauru.[18]

An even stronger indication of the increasing importance of the Gilberts to
Japanese defensive strategy was the detachment of the *Sasebo 7th Special Naval
Landing Force* from the *Southeastern Area
Fleet* (Rabaul) and its commitment to
Tarawa under the *4th Fleet.* Arriving in
May, the force remained on Tarawa until
the American invasion in November.[19]
This move as much as any other single
event was evidence of the declining significance attached by the Japanese high
command to the Solomons-New Guinea
area, and by the same token of the increasing importance of the Central Pacific, including the Gilberts. Also in May, the
Japanese established a new plan of overall defense called the *Z Operation.* According to this plan the defensive perimeter
was drawn through the Aleutians, Wake,
the Marshalls, the Gilberts, Nauru, Ocean,
and the Bismarcks. The principal positions
along the perimeter were to be strengthened and local commanders were to be responsible for defense in case of invasion.
Garrison forces at the point of attack were
instructed to destroy the enemy at the
shore line. If the enemy should succeed in
forcing a landing, local forces were to
counterattack persistently in an effort to
delay the invaders as long as possible and
to prevent the establishment of bases.[20]

Meanwhile, construction of fortifications and airfields was proceeding apace.
The main concentration of effort was on
Tarawa. Concrete and log emplacements
for guns of all sizes up through 14 centi-
meters were constructed, transmitting and

receiving stations set up, coconut trees
logged and transported from outlying
islands, tank barricades and tank pits constructed, underwater obstacles emplaced,
and dugouts made for individual riflemen
and machine gunners.[21] Similar though
not nearly so extensive preparations were
being made concurrently on Makin.

The air base on Makin was completed
and ready to accommodate reconnaissance
and fighter seaplanes by July 1943. At
Tarawa construction on an airstrip was
begun in October 1942, and a trial landing of a land-based bomber was made on
28 January 1943. By 31 May the major
runway on Betio, Tarawa Atoll, was 80
percent completed, positions for planes
100 percent, and a secondary runway 40
percent.[22]

Thus, while high-level staff planners of
the Allied forces were gradually coming to
the decision to institute a drive across the
Central Pacific, the Japanese in that area
were preparing against the expected attack as rapidly as conditions permitted.
Necessity had compelled the Japanese to
admit the probability of defeat in the
Solomons-New Guinea area though Rabaul, it is true, had not yet been given up
as lost, and valiant efforts were to be made
in the autumn of 1943 to save that bastion
from disaster. As the year wore on, however, it became more and more apparent
that the most immediate threat to Japan's
perimeter defense was in the Central Pacific, and it was here that the Japanese

[18] Special Forces (*Tokusetsu butai*), Vol. 3, Part 1,
NA 12032, WDC 161106.
[19] Tabular Records of Special Landing Forces, NA
11651, WDC 161406.
[20] USSBS, *Campaigns of the Pacific War*, pp. 6–7.
[21] JICPOA Translation 5085, Construction of Fortifications at Tarawa, Nauru, and Ocean Islands; Special Forces, Vol. 3, Part 2, NA 12028, WDC 161705.
[22] Japanese Bases in the Mandated Islands and
Gilberts, MS, Office of Naval History.

JAPANESE COASTAL DEFENSES. *8-cm. naval guns installed in log emplacements on Makin (above) and Tarawa (below).*

high command hoped to force a show-down with the invading forces from the east.

American Attacks and Japanese Responses

September witnessed the opening of the first large-scale American aerial attacks against the Gilberts and nearby islands. Planes of Admiral Pownall's fast carrier force, assisted by Army Air Forces B-24's from Canton and Funafuti, struck Makin, Tarawa, and Nauru on 18–19 September. According to one Japanese diary, twenty-eight laborers were killed during the strike on Makin, probably from a direct hit on a shelter.[23] The damage done by the raid on Betio was more serious. The runway was hit, although not seriously enough to prevent repair by labor troops.[24] The antenna mast of a receiving station was knocked half down, and a transmitting station completely destroyed. A storehouse and a hospital were completely destroyed, as were the entire air force kitchen and half of the *Sasebo 7th Special Naval Landing Force* kitchen. The damage to air communications installations was particularly serious. The transmitting station destroyed by the air raid was evidently the chief means of communication with other islands and on Betio itself, judging by the measures taken to restore it—two transmitters were borrowed from the *Sasebo 7th Special Naval Landing Force* (one set from the receiving room and one from the medium attack plane command post) and another from the *3d Special Base Force*.[25]

Following the raid, one of the island defenders wrote in his diary: "The island is a sea of flames. . . . Seven of our medium attack bombers were destroyed and a great number of our guns were damaged. Moreover, shell dumps, ammunition

dumps, various storehouses and barracks on Bairiki [the island just east of Betio] were destroyed. A great number of men were killed and wounded."[26]

Whether or not this individual report was exaggerated, the response of the Japanese at Tarawa was immediate. On 24 September, Rear Adm. Keiji Shibasaki, IJN, commanding officer of the *3d Special Base Force*, ordered the commanding officers of the *111th Construction Unit* and the *4th Fleet Construction Department Detachment* to build immediately a bombproof shelter for communications equipment.[27] Later, it was reported: "Work was started immediately and is scheduled to be completed during October. After the work is completed, one transmitter and three receivers will be installed in the station. No matter what happens, we hope to be able to maintain radio communications."[28] At the same time work was begun on a transmitting station, which according to plans was to be of concrete and to contain three short-wave transmitters and one long-wave transmitter with attachments. Completion date was scheduled for December.[29]

Another important result of the September raids was the evacuation of aircraft from Tarawa. Before the raids there had been three air installations in the *3d Special Base Force* area, airfields at Nauru and Tarawa, and a seaplane base at Makin.

[23] JICPOA Translation 4991, Extracts from a Diary at Makin.
[24] Base Forces and Guard Forces, Vol. 4, Jun 43–Nov 43, NA 12030, WDC 161091.
[25] JICPOA Translation 4051, Report of Present Conditions at Tarawa Air Base on 29 September 1943, *755th Naval Air Group, Tarawa Detachment*.
[26] JICPOA Translation 3872, Diary of an Artilleryman in *Yokosuka 6th SNLF*.
[27] JICPOA Translation 5071, *Gilbert Area Defense Force* Special Order No. 18.
[28] JICPOA Translation 4051.
[29] *Ibid.*

One of the most important duties of these installations was to maintain patrols in the southeast corner of the Japanese-held Central Pacific. Patrols from Nauru covered the area south of that island; patrols from Makin covered the area to the east; and patrols from Tarawa extended to the southeast between the other two.[30] The Japanese had originally intended to build up the Tarawa airfield and plane complement to considerable strength, and by early September there were 330 air personnel on the island and 18 planes. However, the Allied carrier strike of 18–19 September seriously disrupted operations and installations and destroyed nine of the planes.[31] After this it was decided to evacuate the air units, and Tarawa was never again used as a Japanese air base. After the removal of the planes from Tarawa, Makin assumed full responsibility for patrolling the Gilberts. By November there were only four amphibious reconnaissance planes at Makin charged with the dual mission of reconnaissance and antisubmarine patrol.[32] For all practical purposes, Japanese local air defenses were eliminated by the strikes of 18–19 September.

Meanwhile, the Japanese Navy was preparing its own plans for a defense of the Gilberts-Marshalls area and for a decisive engagement with the U.S. Pacific Fleet. Plans for the defense of the Gilberts by the Japanese Fleet were drawn up about 8 September 1943 and included the following moves: (1) Large and, if possible, small submarines in the Rabaul area were to move up and operate in the vicinity of the Gilberts. (2) The *2d Fleet* was to advance and operate in an area west and north of Nauru so as to decoy the U.S. Pacific Fleet. Then, after thirty-six land-based attack planes from Rabaul had carried out attacks against the invading fleet,

the *2d Fleet* was to move up to the Mille area and continue operations. (3) If necessary, a destroyer squadron was to come up from the Rabaul area and participate in the operations. (4) Planes of the *3d Fleet* that were undergoing training were to join in these operations if necessary, regardless of the amount of training they had completed.[33]

In September 1943 the main striking force of the Japanese Navy was based at Truk and was under the command of Admiral Mineichi Koga, Commander in Chief, *Combined Fleet*. It consisted chiefly of the superbattleships *Yamato* and *Musashi,* and two battleships and a destroyer squadron from the *1st Fleet.* Also included in Koga's force were the *2d* and *3d Fleets,* which had the combined strength of 3 carriers, 2 battleships, 11 heavy cruisers, 3 light cruisers, and a large number of destroyers.[34] It was this force that Koga tried to hold together for a decisive blow against the U.S. Fleet. His was ". . . not a plan of any positive action to draw the American Fleet into a decisive action, but rather to wait until the American Fleet came up; and he felt sure that they were bound to come up if he only waited." [35]

On two occasions before the American landings on Makin and Tarawa, Koga sortied from Truk with part of this formidable task force in the hope of meeting American warships. Each time he had to

---

[30] JICPOA Translation 3590, Incl 1, Location of Patrols.

[31] JICPOA Translation 4051.

[32] JICPOA Bull 8-44, Japanese Forces in the Gilbert Islands, p. 1.

[33] USSBS, *Campaigns of the Pacific War,* p. 200.

[34] Tabular Records of Daily Movements of Japanese Battleships, Carriers and Cruisers, NA 11792, WDC 160677.

[35] USSBS (Pacific), Naval Analysis Division, *Interrogations of Japanese Officials,* 2 vols. (Washington, 1946), Vol. II, p. 512.

return to his home base without having given battle. The first expedition occurred in September when the admiral learned that Pownall's fast carrier force was approaching the Marshalls-Gilberts area. Immediately he dispatched a large force, composed of elements of the *2d* and *3d Fleets*, which proceeded to Eniwetok, the location from which he considered it best to base an attack. The force consisted of 3 carriers, 2 battleships, 7 heavy cruisers, and 3 light cruisers.[36] It left Truk on 18 September and arrived at Eniwetok on the 20th. Not finding the expected American task force (then operating well to the south and east) the Japanese fleet returned to Truk.

The second large fleet sortie from Truk occurred in October when Koga's radio intelligence indicated the strong possibility of an Allied raid against Wake or the Marshalls. Koga, hoping that this was the opportunity for the decisive engagement he had missed the previous month, once again dispatched a large fleet from Truk to Eniwetok on 17 October. The October force was even more powerful than the September one. Included were the same 3 carriers, plus 6 battleships, 8 heavy cruisers, and 3 light cruisers. These ships remained in Eniwetok for a few days then sailed north some 300 miles toward Wake and returned once again to Truk.[37] No elements of the American fleet were encountered. Pownall's carriers, which had conducted a highly successful strike against Wake on 5–6 October, were by that time safely back in the Pearl Harbor area.

While Admiral Koga was playing cat and mouse with the elusive American task forces in the Marshalls, American pressure was threatening the Japanese Southeast Area. At the end of September Imperial General Headquarters adopted an opera-

tional policy for the Rabaul area "consisting merely of a whittling-down campaign against the enemy which relied upon the momentary use of crucial battle forces when conditions were favorable."[38] This policy was embodied in the *RO Operation*, which was to utilize the planes of Koga's *Carrier Division 1* from land bases in the Rabaul area, and was to have been activated around the middle of October. Since the carriers of *Division 1* were the only vessels of this type in the entire Japanese Navy with anywhere near full plane complements at the time, the *RO Operation* would partially incapacitate the Japanese Fleet. It was undoubtedly this consideration that led Koga to postpone the *RO Operation* in order to make one last attempt at a decisive naval engagement while he still had his fleet intact. After failing in this attempt and after his arrival at Truk on 26 October, he ordered the *RO Operation* activated and took steps to dispatch the planes of *Carrier Division 1* to the Rabaul area.[39] This decision had a profound, and from the American point of view, wholly beneficial effect on the forthcoming invasion of the Gilberts and Marshalls.

Leaving their carriers behind at Truk, a total of 173 planes of *Carrier Division 1* flew down to Rabaul on 1 November and remained in the area until the 13th.[40]

---

[36] Tabular Records of Battleships . . . , NA 11792, WDC 160677.

[37] *Ibid.*

[38] Historical Section, G-2, General Headquarters, Far East Command, Japanese Studies in World War II, No. 50, Southeast Area Naval Operations, Vol. III, p. 5, OCMH.

[39] Aircraft Carriers *(Kubo)*, Vols. 3 and 4 in Merit Board of the Imperial Japanese Navy, Greater East Asia War Campaigns: Materials for Investigation of Meritorious Service *(Daitōa sen'eki kōseki chōsa shiryō tsuzuri)*, NA 12552 WDC 161734, and NA 12060, WDC 161102.

[40] Tabular Records of Battleships . . . , NA 11792, WDC 160677.

While there, they engaged in three air battles and lost 121 planes or roughly two thirds of the entire force.[41] At the same time, on receiving word of the Allied landing at Bougainville (1 November), Admiral Koga dispatched the *2d Fleet* along with elements of the *3d Fleet* to Rabaul. The force arrived at Rabaul on 5 November and was immediately subjected to a fierce attack by planes from Rear Adm. Frederick C. Sherman's fast carrier force (Task Force 38) and again on the 11th not only by Sherman's force but also by Admiral Montgomery's Task Group 50.3.[42] Altogether, four of Koga's heavy cruisers (*Takao, Maya, Atago,* and *Mogami*) were so damaged during these strikes as to be non-operational during the Gilberts invasion. Another two (*Myoko* and *Haguro*) had been put out of operation by gunfire and by collision during the initial landings on Bougainville at Empress Augusta Bay. Still another (*Tone*) was in dry dock undergoing periodic check-up. Thus, of the eleven heavy cruisers that Koga had had under his command in September of 1943, only four remained operational in mid-November. All but one of the remainder had been temporarily put out of operation at Rabaul or Bougainville.[43]

The loss of these cruisers, coupled with the tremendous attrition of carrier planes at Rabaul, meant that the Japanese battleships based at Truk were virtually immobilized, since they would not dare enter combat without proper protection. The sorry plight in which the Japanese Navy now found itself, facing as it did an impending American invasion of the Central Pacific, can best be summarized in the words of Vice Adm. Shigeru Fukudome, IJN:

But in November, as Bougainville landing operations commenced, he [Koga] was forced to send his air strength to Rabaul. As it turned out, practically all of them were lost at Rabaul and Bougainville. Consequently, the Fleet air strength was almost completely lost, and although the Gilberts fight appeared to be the last chance for a decisive fight, the fact that the fleet's air strength had been so badly depleted enabled us to send only very small air support to Tarawa and Makin. The almost complete loss of carrier planes was a mortal blow to the fleet since it would require six months for replacement. . . . In the interim, any fighting with carrier force was rendered impossible.[44]

No better testimony could be adduced to the mutual interdependence of the various Allied forces operating in different areas of the Pacific. Without the tremendous losses inflicted on the Japanese by forces under General MacArthur and Admiral Halsey, the Central Pacific forces under Admiral Nimitz would certainly have faced far greater odds in their invasion of the Gilberts.

Japanese Defenses on the Eve of the Attack

By the morning of 20 November when the ships of Admiral Turner's Northern Attack Force hove into view of Makin

---

[41] Japanese Studies in World War II, No. 50, Vol. III, p. 26.
[42] Samuel Eliot Morison, HISTORY OF UNITED STATES NAVAL OPERATIONS IN WORLD WAR II, Vol. VI, *Breaking the Bismarcks Barrier, 22 July 1942–1 May 1944* (Boston: Little, Brown and Company, 1950), pp. 323–36.
[43] Tabular Records of Battleships . . . , NA 11792, WDC 160677; USSBS, *Campaigns of the Pacific War,* pp. 152–53.
[44] USSBS, *Interrogations of Japanese Officials,* Vol. II, p. 516. Perhaps even more important than the plane losses was the attrition of carrier pilots. Of 192 flight crews from *Carrier Division 1* dispatched to the Rabaul area in November 1943, 86 were lost. Japanese Studies in World War II, No. 50, Vol. III, p. 26.

Atoll, the Japanese had on the main island of Butaritari an estimated 798 men under command of Lt. (j.g.) Seizō Ishikawa, commander of the *3d Special Base Force Makin Detachment*. This figure by no means represents the enemy's combat strength since the majority were labor troops (mostly Korean) whose combat effectiveness was only slightly more than nil. The organization of Japanese forces on D Day was roughly as follows:

Unit	Number
Total	798
3d Special Base Force Makin Detachment	284
Air personnel	100
111th Construction Unit	138
4th Fleet Construction Department Detachment	276

The air personnel were ground crews left marooned on the island after the planes had escaped. How well they were armed or how effective they were as combat troops it is impossible to know. Of the labor troops, about 220 were Korean, the remainder Japanese who were not in the service either because of age or physical infirmities.[45] None of the labor troops was assigned a battle station and none had any training, although it appears that the Japanese workers and perhaps a few Koreans were issued rifles on D Day. Thus, the maximum total of trained combat troops on Makin came to no more than 384, and the actual number was probably no more than 300.

As to defense installations, the Japanese had been able or willing to fortify Butaritari with only a bare minimum. A perimeter defense had been established around the seaplane base on the lagoon shore. (*See Map II*.) Defenses on the lagoon shore were comparatively light, consisting mainly of three dual-purpose 8-cm. guns at the base of King's Wharf and a few machine guns. Running from the lagoon to the ocean were two tank barrier systems, each partially guarded by strands of trip wire and covered by antitank guns, machine guns, and rifle pits. The West Tank Barrier was made up of a wide ditch and a coconut log barrier. The ditch extended from the lagoon approximately two thirds of the way across the island, was 12 to 13 feet wide, and about 5 feet deep. The log barrier, starting at the south end of the ditch and extending to the ocean shore, was about 4.5 feet high and braced from the east by diagonal logs. Altogether a total of one antitank gun, one concrete pillbox, 6 machine gun positions, and 50 rifle pits covered this barrier.

The East Tank Barrier, more heavily fortified than that to the west, consisted of a trench 14.5 feet wide by 6 feet deep stretching from the lagoon about two thirds of the way across the island and bent in the middle toward the westward. From the southern terminus of this trench to the ocean shore a log antitank barricade had been erected and a similar barricade lay to the east of the northern section of the trench. Double-apron wire and trip wire had been laid in continuous lines across the entire island in the same area. West of the trap itself was an intricate system of gun emplacements and rifle pits. Three pillboxes of either log or cement barred the approach to the trap. Lying between these emplacements and connecting them was a series of forty-three rifle pits, interspersed with machine guns. Immediately to the west of this line in the center of the island was another group of twenty-three rifle pits. On the south shore between the terminus of the road running from the end of Stone Pier and the southern end of the tank barrier were located nineteen more rifle pits, two machine guns, and a 70-mm.

---

[45] JICPOA Bull 8-44, pp. 8–9.

JAPANESE TANK DEFENSES ON MAKIN. *The West Tank Barrier (above); one of the antitank gun emplacements at the East Tank Barrier (below).*

howitzer, all placed to protect the ocean shore.[46]

Along the ocean shore a series of strong points had been established, incorporating 3 8-cm. coast defense guns, 3 antitank positions, 10 machine gun emplacements, and 85 rifle pits. Obviously, the Japanese expected that any invasion of the island would be made on the ocean shore, following the example of Carlson's raid. On either side of the heavily defended area was an outpost consisting of a squad of men, a lookout tower approximately 70 feet high, and telephone communication to command posts within the fortified area.

The defended area was divided into three parts. Aviation personnel were quartered in the eastern portion, the majority of the garrison force lived in the center, and the Korean laborers were billeted in the western part.

The island of Betio in Tarawa Atoll was much more heavily manned and fortified. There the garrison, commanded by Admiral Shibasaki, consisted of an estimated 4,836 men organized as follows: [47]

Unit	Number
Total	4,836
3d Special Base Force	1,122
7th SNLF	1,497
111th Construction Unit	1,247
4th Fleet Construction Department Detachment	970

Of this number, the members of the *3d Special Base Force* and the *Sasebo 7th Special Naval Landing Force* were trained combat troops. The extent of combat effectiveness of the labor troops on the island is more difficult to determine. The combat importance of these construction units usually varied with the number of Japanese personnel since the Koreans were almost never given weapons. The *4th Fleet Construction Department* was about 85 percent Korean and the *111th Construction Unit* about 30

percent Korean.[48] Thus, if all of the Japanese laborers at Tarawa were trained and equipped for combat, the total effective strength on that atoll would have been over 3,600. However, it appears that the military organization of the labor troops may have existed mostly on paper, and the training program set up for them by the Japanese, even if carried out, would at best have provided a reserve force of limited value.[49] Thus, a safe guess as to the number of combat effectives on Tarawa would probably be about 3,000.

Betio itself had been built into an island fortress of the most formidable aspect. The island had been organized for an all-round decisive defense at the beach. (*See Map II.*) The basic beach defense weapon along the entire north coast and on both sides of the eastern tip was the 13-mm. machine gun. Along the western and southwestern coasts the 7.7-mm. machine gun was used for the same purpose. The guns were located in open emplacements to allow the additional mission of antiaircraft fires. Those on the northern coast were so positioned as to permit flanking fire to the front of artificial barriers (tetrahedrons) that had been emplaced along the reef, or frontal fire on the direct approaches to the beach.

Inshore, organization for defense was more haphazard. Bombproof ammunition and personnel shelters were put to use as defensive positions in depth, although they had not originally been constructed for that purpose. In some cases, the fire from the doorways of these shelters was mutu-

---

[46] JICPOA Bull 4-44, Study of Japanese Installations on Butaritari Island, Makin Atoll, map facing p. 1.
[47] JICPOA Bull 8-44, p. 4.
[48] JICPOA Translation 4096, Projected Installations at Jaluit and Truk.
[49] JICPOA Bull 8-44, p. 4.

ally supporting, but this was only by accident. For the most part they were blind to attack from several directions, and since they had not been designed as blockhouses, had only a few firing ports. The basic weapons were complemented by a network of obstacles including antitank ditches, beach barricades, log fences and concrete tetrahedrons on the fringing reef, double-apron high-wire fences in the water near the beach, and double-apron low-wire fences on the beach itself. The larger obstacles on the reef were designed to canalize the approach of boats into areas that could be swept effectively by antiboat fires from 127-mm., 80-mm., 7-cm., 37-mm., and 13-mm. guns. The lighter double-apron fences were laid along diagonal lines from the beaches, and machine guns were emplaced in every case so that flanking fires could be laid parallel to the wire and just forward of it. Altogether, on Betio there was a total of four 8-inch guns, four 14-cm., four 12.7 cm., six 8-cm., ten 75-mm. mountain guns, six 70-mm. howitzers, eight 7-cm. dual-purpose single mounts, nine 37-mm. field guns, twenty-seven 13-mm. single mounts, four 13-mm. double mounts, and seven tanks mounting 37-mm. guns.

Fire control equipment was installed for the coast defense, and antiaircraft batteries, including range finders, directors, and searchlights, had been set up. For the most part weapons were mounted in carefully and strongly constructed emplacements of coconut logs, reinforced concrete, and revetted sand. Ammunition and personnel were protected from shelling and bombing by log and concrete bombproof shelters covered with sand to increase safety and improve camouflage. These shelters were ordinarily placed opposite the interval between, and inshore of, pairs of guns. Heavy gun ammunition was handled from bombproof shelters to ready boxes in concrete emplacements by narrow-gauge railway and overhead chain hoist gear.[50]

This bare recital of enemy defense installations on Betio does only scant justice to the really horrible obstacles that the attacking forces would have to overcome. Tarawa was the most heavily defended atoll that would ever be invaded by Allied forces in the Pacific. With the possible exception of Iwo Jima, its beaches were better protected against a landing force than any encountered in any theater of war throughout World War II. Makin, by comparison, was lightly held. But any beach guns that are manned and ready to fire are formidable enough to the men of the first waves of an amphibious landing force. Boated in slow-moving craft, as they make their way from ship to shore they offer ideal targets to the waiting defenders—unless the latter have been destroyed, or at least dispersed, by the attackers' naval and aerial bombardment. It was the hope of the landing forces at both Makin and Tarawa that this would be accomplished before the first troops touched shore.

[50] JICPOA and Intelligence Section, 2d Marine Division, Study of Betio Island, Tarawa Atoll, 2 parts, Part I, pp. 4–7.

CHAPTER V

The Landings on Makin

Red Beaches

On 20 November sunrise at Makin came at 0612. Weather was fair. Wind was east-southeast at thirteen knots, which meant there was relatively little surf either at the main landing beaches on the west coast or inside on the protected lagoon.[1] At 0603 the first of the troop-carrying transports, *Leonard Wood,* arrived on station in the transport area off Red Beaches on the western coast of Butaritari and commenced to lower her boats. Within four minutes the three other transports and the cargo ship carrying the 165th Regimental Combat Team had followed suit. Admiral Turner sent the signal that H Hour would be at 0830 as planned and that William Hour for the landing on Yellow Beach on the north shore of the island would tentatively be 1030, a time subsequently confirmed. *(Map III)*

From 0610 to 0640 carrier-based planes, as scheduled, bombed, dive-bombed, and strafed the western beaches and inland. As they drew away, naval guns of the accompanying battleships, cruisers, and destroyers opened fire and kept up a steady rain of shells until 0825, just five minutes before the first troops hit the shore. While this was taking place a half-hour rain squall almost hid the island from the anxious watchers aboard ship. Happily, by 0800 the rain lifted and landmarks, though still obscured slightly by smoke

and dust raised by naval fire, came into fairly clear relief. As the ships ceased fire, aircraft again flew in low to strafe the beaches in a five-minute attack. Twenty minutes later naval guns again took up the chorus, keeping their bombardment well to the front of the advancing troops.[2]

The damage wrought during this first day by naval and aerial bombardment was considerable. In the immediate region of the main beaches and eastward little real damage was done—the destruction was generally confined to coconut trees, native huts, and a few dummy gun positions. In the area of the West Tank Barrier, neither the ditch nor the log barricade of the trap was seriously damaged except for one direct hit from a heavy bomb near the northern terminus of the trench system. Just to the east of the main tank trap lay a well-defined trench system running at right angles to the beach. These trenches were comparatively shallow and were revetted at ends and intervals with coconut logs. The area was reported to be badly shot up. One trench received a direct hit from a 2,000-pound bomb which,

---

[1] TF 54 Opn Plan A2-43, 23 Oct 43, Annex B, p. 43; Commander Central Pacific Force U.S. Pacific Fleet, War Diary, 1–30 November 1943, Annex A, p. 1.

[2] Fifth Amph Force Rpt, Capture of Gilbert Islands, Annex A, pp. 14–15; V Phib Corps GALVANIC Rpt, Annex B, Rpt by G-3, pp. 1–2; 165th Infantry Regiment Combined Journal Events and Message File, 20 Nov 43, located in AGO Records Administration Center, Kansas City, Missouri.

in the words of Admiral Turner, "considerably scrambled the trench, Japs and trees for some distance." Sixty-two enemy dead were later counted in this one area, most of whom were the victims of a combination of concussion and air bursts. In the area south of Yellow Beach and east to the East Tank Barrier all buildings were reported destroyed. Three 80-mm. antiaircraft positions at the base of King's Wharf and two light tanks revetted to act as pillboxes were severely damaged. Forty-one enemy dead were counted, of whom twenty-five were apparently killed by concussion from heavy bombs.[3]

Although the covered shelters in this area were not destroyed, a careful examination made by the 27th Division's artillery commander after the landing showed that there was little in the area around Yellow Beach that was not covered either by a direct hit or by fragmentation. In his opinion, "a high degree of neutralization was obtained."[4] Admiral Turner's final conclusion was that "the effect of naval and air bombardment was highly satisfactory; and contributed materially in the reduction of hostile resistance." "However," he added, "there was not enough of it."[5]

While the ships of the naval gunfire support group pounded away at Butaritari, troops of the 165th Infantry continued to debark. In the early morning light they clambered down rope cargo nets into the waiting LCVP's. As soon as each craft had received its allotted quota of men (about thirty-six each), it moved off for a short distance and joined other small boats circling in the assembly area.[6]

At 0643 two LCVP's left the side of *Neville.* Carrying a special detachment of the reinforced 2d Platoon of Company G, 165th Infantry, and nineteen marines of the 4th Platoon of the V Amphibious

Corps Reconnaissance Company, they were headed for Kotabu Island about a mile and a half north of Flink Point. Naval bombardment preceded them as they plunged into the ground swell for a ride of almost an hour's duration.[7]

Shortly thereafter the three tractor-laden LST's that had moved in separate convoy to Butaritari hove into view through the morning mist and took station in the transport area at about 0700. Within an hour all the amphibian tractors bound for Red Beaches were in the water, circling and waiting the signal to approach the beaches.[8]

At 0750 the order was given to move to the line of departure.[9] The amphibian tractors formed two inverted V's, each pointed toward a beach, and one by one the other landing craft pulled off from their circles and formed a series of triangular formations constituting the subsequent landing waves. Two destroyers, *Phelps* and *MacDonough,* had taken station approximately 2,800 yards west of Red Beaches. When the first landing wave was between them, the two ships began to move slowly toward the island firing their 5-inch guns. At 0815 the first wave of amphibian tractors passed through the escorting destroyers and headed for the beach.

---

[3] Fifth Amph Force Rpt, Capture of Gilbert Islands, Incl H, pp. 6–10; V Phib Corps GALVANIC Rpt, Incl F, Rpt by Special Staff Officers, Sec. II, Naval Gunfire Rpt, pp. 1, 3.

[4] Ltr, 27th Inf Div Artillery Officer (Col Harold G. Browne) to CTF 52.6, 7 Dec 43, sub: Rpt on Naval Gunfire in Makin Opn, p. 2, AG 327 Art 0.3.0 (22866), DRB AGO.

[5] Fifth Amph Force Rpt, Capture of Gilbert Islands, Incl H, p. 10.

[6] USS *Leonard Wood* Action Rpt, 20 Dec 43, p. 2; USS *Calvert* Action Rpt, 28 Nov 43, p. 2.

[7] V Phib Corps GALVANIC Rpt, Incl C, p. 342.

[8] Fifth Amph Force Rpt, Capture of Gilbert Islands, Incl A, p. 15.

[9] USS *Leonard Wood* Action Rpt, 20 Dec 43, p. 3.

They were followed by two waves of LCVP's carrying the main body of the 1st and 3d Battalion Landing Teams at approximately five-minute intervals. The first wave of the 1st Battalion headed for Red Beach on the left and contained 233 men in seven boats; the following waves consisted of only six boats each. In the first wave, at the rear center, was Lt. Col. Gerard W. Kelley, the battalion commander, together with the commander of Company D, the air-ground and Navy liaison parties, and some battalion communications personnel. To the right was the first wave of the 3d Battalion, heading for Red Beach 2. It had a similar boat schedule, with Lt. Col. Joseph T. Hart, the battalion commander, and the commanding officer of Company M riding in the same boat. Each battalion was accompanied by two LCM's carrying light tanks with their crews, one light machine gun squad, two rifle squads, and other personnel.[10]

As the leading wave of LVT's approached the beaches they commenced to fire their rockets, but with less than even moderate success. Many fell short into the water; others would not fire at all because of defects in their firing mechanisms caused by salt water. At 1,000 yards the amphtracks' (amphibian tractors') .50-caliber machine guns opened fire, joined 200 yards farther in by their .30-caliber machine guns. No sustained fire from the beaches was encountered. Off Red Beach 2 enemy rifle fire wounded one seaman and killed another, but these were the only casualties recorded during the ship-to-shore movement. About forty yards offshore the amphibians came over the coral reef. No barbed wire, mines, or other obstacles impeded them. At approximately 0831 the tractors touched the rocks and

lumbered up the beaches. The men of the special landing groups scrambled over the sides.[11] Some sought cover, but many stood still, waiting first for enemy fire before taking precautions. Maj. Edward T. Bradt, commanding the 3d Battalion, 105th Infantry, and in charge of the special landing groups, later described his action. "I jumped down from my boat [sic] and stood straight up for two or three minutes, waiting for somebody to shoot me. Nobody shot! I saw many other soldiers doing the same thing."[12]

Following the LVT's came the first three waves of landing craft at about five-minute intervals. The first wave was scheduled to put a total of 460 men and eight tanks ashore in an area removed by approximately 3,000 yards from the main defenses on the island. Although intelligence had revealed the presence of rocks and coral pinnacles along the approaches to the shore, Admiral Turner's staff was satisfied that landing boats could get ashore there at any time.[13]

They were wrong. The reef was studded with coral boulders about forty yards off shore. Coming in on a rising tide, some of the landing craft were able to slip past the boulders and were held less than a boat's length (thirty-six feet) from the water's edge, but many were broached, stranded, or forced to put to sea again. The tanks,

---

[10] USS *Phelps* Action Rpt, 20–26 Nov 43, p. 2; USS *MacDonough* Action Rpt, Bombardment of Makin Island, 20 Nov 43, pp. 2, 3; BLT 165-1 FO 4, 11 Nov 43, Annexes B and C.
[11] 193d Tk Bn Rpt of Makin Opn, Sec. XIII, Rpt of Provisional Amph LVT Co, p. 34; Marshall, Makin Notes, p. D1; Maj Millard C. Inskeep, Tanks in the Makin Action, and Sgt Frederick A. Baxter, Armored Force Action on Makin, MSS, OCMH. Major Inskeep was Executive Officer, 193d Tank Battalion.
[12] Marshall, Makin Notes, p. D1.
[13] TF 52 Amph Attack Order A3-43, 23 Oct 43, Annex I.

LANDINGS ON RED BEACH *were hazardous because of coral rock formations.*

waterproofed for the landing, rolled off the ramps into water which did not quite drown them out. Ahead of them, the men struggled in swells sometimes over their heads, stumbled over rocks and slipped on boulders, or sought cover at the edge of the beach.

Red Beach, on the left, was a rubble of coral boulders and proved usable for only fifteen yards of its width. The seven landing craft of the first wave encountered great difficulties getting ashore. Some did not make it. The amphibian tractors that preceded the first wave had to abandon their original objectives to assist the boats stranded on the reef. Those few landing craft that did reach shore, moreover, found it difficult to withdraw and allow later assault waves to land. As the tide receded, landing operations were further compli-

cated. Only the absence of enemy opposition in this area made possible a landing without heavy casualties. Under any kind of enemy fire the natural obstacles to a landing here would have probably proved catastrophic to the attacking troops.[14]

The carefully prepared sequence for the arrival of various elements of the assault and shore parties on Red Beach was thrown into confusion by these conditions. At best, only three boats could be landed at one time, and the fifth wave was not able to get ashore until shortly after 1000, over an hour behind schedule.[15]

The landing on Red Beach 2, despite better conditions, was also delayed. The

---

[14] Marshall, Makin Notes, p. D1; 193d Tk Bn Rpt of Makin Opn, Sec. XIII, Rpt of Provisional Amph LVT Co.

[15] 27th Inf Div G-2 Jnl, 20 Nov 43.

3d Battalion Landing Team, composed of 1,250 men, was scheduled to land there in seven waves at five-minute intervals. Beginning at 0840 the first three waves landed, but the remaining boats landed singly, and it was 1022 before the seventh wave arrived off the beach. During D Day, in addition to these troops, *Leonard Wood* sent ashore 4 tanks, 1 bulldozer, 5 jeeps, 4 antitank guns, and other portable equipment.[16] For the same period the transport *Calvert* disembarked 913 troops (of the 1st Battalion Landing Team) and eighty-two tons of equipment, but at nightfall much of the cargo was still afloat in landing craft.[17]

Establishing the Beachhead

General Ralph Smith's plan called for the rapid capture of Flink Point and Ukiangong Point and the occupation of all of the area east of Red Beaches to the first beachhead line about 1,300 yards inland. The 1st Battalion Landing Team on the left was to take Flink Point and the left half of the beachhead line. The 3d Battalion Team on the right was to capture Ukiangong Village and Point and was responsible for the right half of the beachhead line. On the completion of this phase of the action, the 1st Battalion Landing Team would relieve the 3d and the latter was to go into division reserve in the area north of Ukiangong Village.[18]

The main force of the 1st Battalion moved directly forward toward the beachhead line, meeting only insignificant rifle fire but retarded somewhat by the thick vegetation and by debris and water-filled craters resulting from the air and naval bombardment. Their supporting light tanks were of no assistance to the infantry until late in the day. Bad communications

between tanks and infantry and terrain difficulties slowed up the former's advance. Except by staying on the road, they could make no headway against the combined obstacles of debris, shell holes, and marsh, and on the main road inland they were held up by large craters left by naval shells.[19]

The 1st Battalion advanced with two companies abreast. On the right, Company B and part of the 1st Platoon of Company D, a heavy machine gun platoon, covered the widest zone; their first action was the seizure of an undefended observation tower that was protected by barbed wire and log barricades. On the left, Company C moved straight ahead without waiting for its heavy weapons platoon to land. Company A remained in dispersed formation in battalion reserve.[20]

At the end of the first phase, at approximately 1030, Companies B and C held the left half of the beachhead line just east of Rita Lake, the largest of several shallow ponds. The eastern edge of this pond stretched almost the entire length of the beachhead line south of the point at which it was crossed by the island highway. There, Company B had established contact with Company K of the 3d Battalion just across the highway on its right flank. Meanwhile, Company A had been dispatched northward to occupy Flink Point and had progressed about halfway out that peninsula.[21]

While the 1st Battalion was pushing

[16] USS *Leonard Wood* Action Rpt, 20 Dec 43, p. 3.
[17] USS *Calvert* Action Rpt, 28 Nov 43, pp. 2–3.
[18] 27th Inf Div FO 21, 23 Oct 43.
[19] 193d Tk Bn Rpt of Makin Opn, pp. 71–77; V Phib Corps GALVANIC Rpt, Incl F, Rpt by Special Staff Officers, Incl 3, Rpt of Engineer Officer, p. 3.
[20] Marshall, Makin Notes, pp. B2–B4.
[21] 27th Inf Div G-3 Msg File, 20 Nov 43, Msgs 26, 29, 35, 39, 40, 42.

DENSE VEGETATION ON BUTARITARI *retards the advance of the troops.*

DUMMY COAST DEFENSE GUN *made from a coconut log.*

forward against practically no opposition in its sector, the 3d Battalion on the right was making almost equally rapid progress against an area that it had been believed would be more vigorously defended. The special landing group of Detachment X had swung to the right after landing in amphtracks and established a defensive position on the southern flank. Company K moved almost straight eastward; Company I fanned out in a triangular area between the main highway and the ocean south of Company K's sector; and Company L, assisted by a part of the special landing group, turned south to take Ukiangong Village and to clear the whole point beyond it.[22]

Contrary to expectation, no enemy fire came out of the huts of Ukiangong Village, and the native residents had all deserted.

By 1040 Company L could report practically all of Ukiangong Point secured without opposition.[23] What had been thought to be defense installations proved instead to be a stone-crushing plant, two large dummy guns, some square piles of coral rock, and a few bomb shelters.[24] Sixty natives were discovered on Ukiangong Point, but thus far no enemy had shown himself.[25]

Meanwhile, Company K was pressing its advance on toward and beyond Rita Lake. Finally, almost two hours after the landing, one unit of this company met the first Japanese to be encountered. Five of

[22] Marshall, Makin Notes, 3d BLT map, after p. F3.
[23] 27th Inf Div G-3 Msg File, 20 Nov 43, Msg 30, and G-2 Msg File, Msg 55.
[24] JICPOA Bull 4-44, Part III, pp. 65, 73–77.
[25] 27th Inf Div G-3 Msg File, 20 Nov 43, Msgs 42, 43.

the enemy were killed. At 1055 Company K reached the first beachhead line on the east shore of Rita Lake and shortly thereafter was relieved by elements of the 1st Battalion and went into reserve.[26]

Thus within less than two and a half hours after the initial landing, the beachhead had been secured to a line 1,300 yards inland. Ukiangong Point had been occupied and preparations were already under way for making that area suitable for the establishment of artillery positions from which the main attack eastward to the tank barrier could be supported. Part of Flink Point had been secured and nothing stood in the way of securing the whole of that peninsula, which was completed, in fact, by 1240. No opposition of any consequence had yet developed. Except for the initial difficulties in getting the troops ashore against natural rather than man-made obstacles, the landing had been a pushover.

Yellow Beach

Early in the morning of D Day, Admiral Turner had confirmed that William Hour for the landing on Yellow Beach would be 1030. According to the plan this beach, which lay between On Chong's Wharf and King's Wharf on the northern (lagoon) shore of Butaritari, would be assaulted by the 2d Battalion Landing Team of the 165th Infantry reinforced by tanks of the 193d Tank Battalion. This force was to move the short distance across the island to the ocean shore, then branch to right and left (west and east). The group on the right would move toward the West Tank Barrier in conjunction with a simultaneous push from the other side of that barrier by the 1st Battalion Landing Team. The group on the left would establish

positions west of the East Tank Barrier and hold there pending the reduction of the West Tank Barrier and the capture of the entire "Citadel" area including the village of Butaritari.

The troops charged with assaulting Yellow Beach were carried aboard the transport *Neville,* the LSD *Belle Grove,* and the LST *179.* Aboard *Neville* were the 2d Battalion of the 165th Regiment, commanded by Lt. Col. John F. McDonough, and the reconnaissance platoon that was scheduled for tiny Kotabu Island just north of Flink Point. *Belle Grove* carried the tanks of Company A, 193d Tank Battalion, boated in LCM's. Embarked on LST *179* was Detachment Z of the 105th Infantry loaded in the sixteen LVT's that would make up the initial assault wave.

After receiving the word at 0800 that the Kotabu detail had taken that island without opposition, this naval task unit moved into its assigned transport area just west of the lagoon and commenced debarking its landing craft. The LST proceeded through the channel and into the lagoon before launching its amphtracks with the special landing groups aboard. As the tractors circled, the landing craft behind them slowly formed assault waves. By 0915 they were ready to move toward the beach. In the first wave were the sixteen amphibian tractors. Following it at an interval of about one minute came the second wave, eight LCM's carrying medium tanks, followed about two minutes later by the third wave, seven LCM's carrying medium tanks. In the fourth wave, which came two minutes later, were two troop-carrying LCVP's accompanied by four LCM's with light tanks aboard. The next four waves were made up of LCVP's

---

[26] *Ibid.,* Msg 43.

carrying the bulk of the assault troops with
one bulldozer embarked in the seventh
wave.[27]

As the landing forces moved toward
Yellow Beach the destroyers *MacDonough*
and *Phelps* opened fire with their 5-inch
guns, commencing at 1005.[28] The sun by
now was bright, and the lagoon calm. The
beach, in flames, was covered by billowing
smoke.[29] About 1,100 yards from the
beach the LVT's discharged their rockets—six from each boat—laying down an
area barrage along the beach's edge. In
contrast to what had happened earlier in
the morning during the approach to Red
Beaches, the rockets worked.[30] At 1025,
with the first wave still about 600 yards off
the beach, the two destroyers ceased firing
to allow a last-minute strafing run by the
carrier planes.[31] As the planes neared the
beach, the first waves of amphtracks
slowed down for fear of coming under their
fire. The later waves slowed down too, and
kept their proper intervals, except for
those carrying medium tanks, which
bunched up slightly. These delays caused
the landing schedule to be set back about
ten minutes, but at least there was no piling up of waves as there had been during
the approach to Red Beach.[32]

As the troops renewed their progress toward shore, they came under enemy fire
for the first time about 500 yards from the
beach. This may have come from two steel
hulks that lay sunk in the shallow water
of the lagoon, or from On Chong's Wharf,
or from a small green and white patrol
boat moored to the wharf, or from the
shore itself. Also, from King's Wharf on
their left, the amphtracks were hit by bullets. Under this cross fire the men crouched
low in their tractors as they made the last
three hundred yard run into the beach.
The first touchdown was at 1041.[33]

One of the amphtracks ran up the seaplane ramp on King's Wharf. The men
disembarked and worked their way inland
by crawling along the western slope of the
causeway, which masked them from enemy fire. Unable to bring their weapons to
bear, the Japanese quickly fled and the
pier was taken by the attackers without
further contest.[34] On the far right of the
first landing wave one of the tractors developed a defective steering device and
landed too far to the west in the On
Chong's Wharf area. All of the others
landed properly on Yellow Beach and began to move inland, swerving to the right
or left before disembarking the men of the
special landing group. Enemy shellfire
struck two of these vehicles, and among
the dismounting men five were reported
killed and twelve wounded.[35] One lone
tractor went completely out of control and
drove straight across the island toward the
ocean shore through the main Japanese
defenses. It finally hung up in a shell crater
and two of its crew were killed by enemy
machine gun fire while the others escaped
to take cover in the brush.[36]

The first mission of the two halves of the
special landing group was to clear the enemy from the two wharves and construct

[27] USS *Neville* Action Rpt, 5 Dec 43, pp. 1–3.
[28] USS *Phelps* Action Rpt, Seizure and Occupation
of Makin Island, 5 Dec 43, p. 3.
[29] Marshall, Makin Notes, p. G1.
[30] *Ibid.*, p. F36.
[31] Fifth Amph Force Rpt, Capture of Gilbert
Islands, Incl A, p. 16.
[32] V Phib Corps GALVANIC Rpt, Incl B, G-3 Rpt,
p. 3.
[33] *Ibid.*, pp. 3–4; USS *Neville* Action Rpt, 5 Dec 43;
Interv, Capt Bernard E. Ryan, CO Co E, 165th Inf,
in S. L. A. Marshall, file of intervs (hereafter cited as
Marshall Intervs), p. 38, OCMH.
[34] Marshall, Makin Notes, p. F37.
[35] Interv, Capt William Ferns, CO Co M, 105th
Inf, Marshall Intervs, p. 55.
[36] Marshall, Makin Notes, pp. F36–F41.

YELLOW BEACH LANDING AREA. *Landing craft head for the beach under the smoke of the preinvasion bombardment (above); King's Wharf (below).*

defensive beach blocks from the base of each wharf to points about 150 yards inland. King's Wharf fell without a contest, once the first troops had landed. On Chong's Wharf, although beaten to kindling wood, still offered some cover to the enemy and a force moved in to seize it at once.

Deploying by squads, the right half of the special landing group swung forward against light opposition, pivoting on the base of the wharf. It continued to move westward in a line stretching about 150 yards from the base of the wharf. Little except light rifle fire was encountered. Two machine gun positions were found at the base of the wharf, but they were manned by dead Japanese, evidently killed by naval fire. While a squad worked out along the pier, the inland end of the group's line came up against a series of dugouts or bombproof shelters. Grenades were thrown inside, killing some of the enemy immediately. Others were taken prisoner as they emerged and still others stayed within and temporarily avoided capture. Now and then the Americans received a random shot, but no one was injured. All the shelters inland from On Chong's Wharf were cleaned out before noon. About thirty-five prisoners, mostly Koreans, were taken and an estimated twenty of the occupants were killed.[37]

Only 100 yards behind the first wave of amphibian tractors came the LCM's with their medium tanks. They hit the reef lying from 150 to 200 yards offshore and could proceed no farther since there was only about 2.5 to 3 feet of water over the reef. Ramps were lowered and the medium tanks lumbered forward through the shallow water. All but two of the fifteen tanks reached the shore safely. These two foundered in shell holes in the reef. In one

of them was Capt. Robert S. Brown, who commanded the medium tanks and who was thus left out of the action during the critical phase when his presence ashore was most needed.[38] The difficulties of the other foundered tank were later described by the sergeant in command:

We . . . went forward about 25 yards and hit a shell hole. We got out of that and went about 15 yards more and hit another. The water was about 7 feet deep and our tank drowned out. The tank immediately filled with smoke after hitting the second shell hole. My driver said the tank was on fire. The crew dismounted right there with great speed through the right sponson door. I remained inside the tank. As soon as the crew got out of the tank they were machine gunned from the shore and with more speed they came back inside the tank. Something like an hour and a half later we were picked up by an alligator.[39]

Two of the mediums to land were hung up in taro pits, although one eventually freed itself and succeeded in getting into the action before being hung up again. The remaining eleven made their way to the ocean shore of the island, then split up and moved east and west against the two tank barriers. There was no effective coordination between tanks and infantry, the tanks operating independently. One ran over a shelter while the infantry stood by and killed about a dozen Japanese who came out. Another wiped out a machine gun nest at the base of the sandpit before proceeding across the island to join the other tanks going east. One tank moved directly into Butaritari Village but encountered no opposition. Machine gun nests and pillboxes were found in fair

———
[37] Marshall, Makin Notes, p. F37.
[38] Marshall, Makin Notes, p. EE2; 193d Tk Bn Rpt of Makin Opn, p. 44.
[39] 193d Tk Bn Rpt of Makin Opn, p. 56.

YELLOW BEACH LANDING *of the 2d Battalion, 165th Infantry.*

abundance, but no difficulty was reported in wiping them out. No personnel casualties were reported by any of the tank crews.[40]

Behind the tanks in the fourth and fifth waves came the troops of the 2d Battalion, 165th Infantry, boated in LCVP's. Like the tank-carrying craft ahead of them, these too grounded on the reef.[41] After a short hesitation the men debarked into knee-deep water and began their slow passage into shore. The intensity of fire from the enemy increased. Radios, flame throwers, bazookas, and other equipment were soaked or lost. Yet, in spite of the fact that the troops were fairly closely bunched in the water, they escaped with few casualties. Most of the fire was low in the water and generally inaccurate. Only two were killed; none wounded.[42]

At the beach the men of Companies E and F, constituting the fourth and fifth waves, divided. Up to this time the landing troops had had little or no opportunity to locate definitely the almost incessant fire that was being poured upon them from the right flank as they approached the beaches. At the outset it was believed that at least a portion of this fire originated from the two battered and scuttled hulks that rested on the bottom just off the end of On Chong's Wharf. The first effort to eliminate this source of fire was made by an LCVP from *Neville.* Under command of Bosn. Joseph V. Kasper, this boat

---

[40] *Ibid.,* pp. 41–59.

[41] Marshall, Makin Notes, p. G2.

[42] Intervs, Capt Bernard E. Ryan and Capt Francis P. Leonard, CO Co F, 2d Bn 165th Inf, Marshall Intervs, pp. 38, 48.

HULKS OFF ON CHONG'S WHARF *being bombed (above), while soldiers on the reef cease activities to watch (below).*

mounted three of its guns on the starboard side and ran for the hulks at an angle permitting all guns to fire at once. Until one gun jammed and the cross fire from the beach compelled it to withdraw, the boat poured a rain of lead against the supposed enemy position. The fact that Boatswain Kasper was fatally wounded during the run added weight to the belief that these derelicts constituted a serious menace to the attacking troops.[43]

For the next two hours naval attention centered around the two wrecked ships, somewhat to the detriment of the troops already ashore. All landing operations were held up for over an hour, from 1125 to 1250, while carrier planes bombed and strafed the hulks. Five bombers missed by wide margins and when an attempt was made to skip-bomb the targets, the bombs merely bounced over the hulks.[44] Then at 1219 the destroyer *Dewey* opened fire on the same targets and kept it up until 1257.[45] In such close quarters, firing on the hulks endangered American forces approaching the beach. Some of the destroyer's shells hit the old ships and inflicted observable damage, but others passed over the heads of the special landing groups and hit inland. As a result Capt. William Ferns, who commanded the special landing group, pulled his men back

100 yards east onto On Chong's Wharf and immediately requested the cessation of all naval and aerial bombardment. Soon the bombardment ceased.[46]

Meanwhile, landings of later waves on Yellow Beach had been interrupted. Medical aid men, who were needed ashore, and Maj. Dennis D. Claire, who was supposed to command the forces moving to the left from Yellow Beach against the East Tank Barrier, were still afloat in landing craft waiting to go in.[47] In spite of the distraction caused by the hulks, the assaulting troops had penetrated the Citadel area, the most strongly fortified on the island, lying between the two tank barriers. In spite of adverse hydrographic conditions and in spite of moderate fire from the shore, the first phase of the assault on Yellow Beach had been successfully completed with only minor casualties.

---

[43] USS *Neville* Action Rpt, 5 Dec 43, pp. 7, 8; V Phib Corps GALVANIC Rpt, Incl B, G-3 Rpt, p. 4.

[44] Marshall, Makin Notes, p. F30a; V Phib Corps GALVANIC Rpt, Incl F, Rpt by Special Staff Officers, Sec. 1, Rpt by Air Officer, p. 4.

[45] Fifth Amph Force Rpt, Capture of Gilbert Islands, Incl A, p. 17.

[46] Interv, Capt Ferns, Marshall Intervs, p. 56.

Captain Ferns states that there were two destroyers participating in this shelling. Admiral Turner's narrative of the action, however, indicates that only one, *Dewey*, was firing at this time. Fifth Amph Force Rpt, Capture of Gilbert Islands, Incl A, p. 17.

[47] Marshall, Makin Notes, p. F30a.

CHAPTER VI

Reduction of the West Tank Barrier

*Advance of the 2d Battalion
to the Barrier*

Following the leading waves of amphibian tractors and medium tanks in to Yellow Beach of Butaritari came the assault companies of the 2d Battalion Landing Team, Company E on the left and Company F on the right. To Company E, commanded by Capt. Bernard E. Ryan, was assigned the task of establishing a line across the island west of the East Tank Barrier and holding there against possible attack from the east until the West Tank Barrier had been eliminated. This was intended to be primarily a defensive mission and the details of the company's actions on D Day will be treated later.[1] Company F, under command of Capt. Francis P. Leonard, with elements of Company G later attached, had the main offensive mission of moving against the West Tank Barrier in co-ordination with the 1st Battalion Landing Team, which was supposed to be approaching the same objective simultaneously from the opposite direction. (*See Map III.*)

The preliminary mission of Company F was for its two assault platoons, the 2d on the left and the 1st on the right, to move directly across the atoll. This mission completed, the 1st and 3d Platoons were to swing right, with the 1st on the left flank, and head westward for the West Tank Barrier. The 2d Platoon was to revert to company reserve and follow the center of the line some fifty yards behind. Two light machine guns were stationed between the assault platoons, and the 60-mm. mortars remained in the vicinity of Yellow Beach to support the attack from that area.[2] To the rear of Company F, Company G (minus 2d Platoon), commanded by Capt. Paul J. Chasmar, was to land and to act as reserve force for Captain Leonard's company as it moved to the south and west.[3]

The main enemy installations of the West Tank Barrier were first encountered by Company F rather than by the right half of the special landing group of the 105th Infantry, which had been landed in amphibian tractors. That group had become involved almost immediately in cleaning up the lower end of On Chong's Wharf and in demolishing various shelters between the wharf and the highway in the area through which they were to deploy for the move westward.

---

[1] See below, pp. 17–22.
[2] Interv, Capt Leonard, Marshall Intervs, p. 48. *Note:* Because of poor visibility the mortars were not used at any time to support Company F's attack against the West Tank Barrier.
[3] Interv, Capt Chasmar, Marshall Intervs, p. 62.

As soon as the two assault platoons of Company F waded ashore and finished their reorganization at the beach, they plunged inland. Only scattered rifle fire greeted them during this movement. The only established enemy positions found by the assault troops during the first two hours in this area were two machine gun emplacements and seven wholly or partly demolished buildings located at the base of On Chong's Wharf and abandoned by the enemy.

Company F's initial move from the beach was, as planned, almost due south. The 1st and 2d Platoons, with the two light machine guns of Company H, the heavy weapons company, carried along between them, started out for the ocean shore. It took them until shortly after noon to reach the opposite side of the island. They struggled through the debris and over the marshy ground beyond the east-west highway without coming to grips with the unseen and scattered Japanese riflemen. Some of the defenders withdrew deeper into the woods, but some remained behind in concealment to keep up a nerve-wracking fire on the American infantrymen as they advanced across the island. Company F lost one man killed and one wounded from this harassment and managed to eliminate four Japanese and four Korean laborers.[4] Although a number of shelters were encountered, no fire was received from them.

The only serious handicap to the troops as they moved southward was the terrain and vegetation and a breakdown of communications between the 1st and 2d Platoons of Company F. Their radios had become waterlogged and messenger service between the platoons was inadequate. The result was a gap between the two assault platoons. To fill this growing hole in the line, Company F's 3d Platoon was brought forward from reserve and committed. This meant moving Company G (less 2d Platoon) closer to the advance where it could be used if further strength was needed. However, Company G's 3d Platoon had already been ordered to take a light machine gun squad and relieve the special landing group at the base of On Chong's Wharf. This relief started at 1145, and the diversion of 3d Platoon, Company G, from the main line of advance necessitated calling on some elements of Company H as reinforcement for Company G in its role as reserve.[5] These reserve troops now moved into the center of the island and combed the area behind the advancing line.

The mopping-up operations were described in detail by 1st Sgt. Pasquale J. Fusco:

Smoking out the snipers that were in the trees was the worst part of it. We could not spot them even with glasses and it made our advance very slow. When we moved forward, it was a skirmish line, with each man being covered as he rushed from cover to cover. That meant that every man spent a large part of his time on the ground. While at prone, we carefully studied the trees and the ground. If one of our men began to fire rapidly into a tree or ground location, we knew that he had spotted a sniper, and those who could see the tree took up the fire. When we saw no enemy, we fired occasional shots into trees that looked likely.[6]

As the advance elements of Company F reached the ocean shore they found no live installations. The center platoon did come upon two unoccupied machine gun emplacements with a barbed-wire barricade

---

[4] Marshall, Makin Notes, p. F26.
[5] Intervs, Capt Leonard and Capt Chasmar, Marshall Intervs, pp. 48–50, 62–63.
[6] Quoted in Marshall, Makin Notes, p. F30.

and a rifle trench—all abandoned by the enemy. Though these positions had been primarily designed to resist a landing from the south and to control the road along the ocean shore, they could have been used upon troops advancing from the lagoon. Luckily they were not. Company F's first mission was accomplished with amazing ease.[7]

On arrival at the ocean Company F immediately began to reorganize its lines, a movement completed by about 1230. The platoon of Company G that had relieved the special landing group near On Chong's Wharf had been forced to withdraw during the time the destroyer *Dewey* shelled the hulks, but it now recovered the ground it had given up and took position straddling the island highway on the right flank of Company F.

Meanwhile, Colonel McDonough, 2d Battalion commander, had accompanied Company F in its advance toward the southern shore. Shortly before its reorganization, he left the line and returned to Yellow Beach in an effort to bring up the medium tanks to support the coming advance toward the West Tank Barrier. He ordered Capt. Wayne C. Sikes, a tank officer, to take charge of the tanks in the center of the line while Lt. Col. Harmon L. Edmondson, commander of the 193d Tank Battalion, proceeded at once to the south shore with two of the mediums. By 1230, five more had crossed the island and were ready to assist on the left flank of Company F's line.[8]

With these five tanks in support, Company F immediately jumped off for the main attack to the westward. The tank-trap clearing still lay some 300 to 400 yards away. As the troops approached it they found a number of underground shelters that yielded both Japanese soldiers and

labor troops. Some of the labor troops were armed with knives and at least one carried a rifle. After the tanks had moved up and put heavy fire against the shelters, infantrymen followed with TNT pole charges, which were shoved into the openings of shelters. Flame throwers, which would have been the ideal weapon against such emplacements, had been doused during the landing and were of no use. During this first engagement Company F lost eight killed and six wounded. By that time it had come within range of fire from entrenchments running along the West Tank Barrier. Later, five machine gun nests buttressing the trench defenses in this area were discovered. For two hours no advance was made on the right. Meanwhile, on the left, the 1st Platoon, which was supported by Colonel Edmondson's five tanks, reached the barrier by 1330.[9]

On the right half of the line advancing westward, the 3d Platoon of Company F found the going tougher, partly because it had only three tanks to support it. Directly south of On Chong's Wharf and about half way across the island was a large enemy air raid shelter in the path of the advance. It was about thirty feet long with blast-proof entrances on either end. Hand grenades tossed into the shelter had been tossed out again. One medium tank had come up and shelled it with 75-mm. with no apparent success. Finally the same tank, accompanied by two infantrymen and four engineers, succeeded in reducing it. The tank, covering the dismounted personnel,

[7] Lt Col William R. Durand to G-3 USAFICPA, 8 Dec 43, Rpt on Makin Island Expedition, p. 4; Interv, Capt Chasmar, Marshall Intervs, pp. 62–63.
[8] Baxter, Armored Force Action on Makin, pp. 13–14; Marshall, Makin Notes, pp. EE2–EE6; Interv, Capt Leonard, Marshall Intervs, pp. 48–50.
[9] Interv, Capt Leonard, Marshall Intervs, pp. 48–50; Baxter, Armored Force Action on Makin, p. 14.

DEFENSIVE POSITIONS ON MAKIN. *West Tank Barrier (above); a typical dugout (below).*

moved slowly in from the left flank. Two BAR[10] men, one on the flank of the tank and one in the rear of it, moved with it until they got to ground where they could cover the baffle entrance. The four engineers, one of whom was 1st Lt. Thomas B. Palliser, a platoon commander of Company C, 102d Engineers, advanced to the rear of the tank and then between the two BAR men. Palliser himself took the lead. Behind him came the platoon sergeant. Both were covered by two engineer riflemen. At first they tried to use a flame thrower, but as in all other efforts to use this weapon on Makin, the attempt failed because of the soaking the equipment had received during the landing. This failing, a TNT pole charge was employed. The platoon leader placed the charge between the outside of the baffle entrance and the interior wall of the shelter. A fifteen-second fuze gave the detail ample time to clear back to cover. The resulting explosion did not collapse the shelter, but it killed all the personnel inside—twelve Japanese.[11]

In spite of this successful engagement in the center of the line, the men on the right remained pinned down by fire from rifle pits fringing on the eastern edge of the barrier. At this juncture Colonel McDonough sent in the 3d Platoon of Company G with orders to take three medium tanks and move around the Japanese left (north) flank.[12] On each side of the highway, along which the center of this platoon advanced, were three machine gun positions. Two that faced the lagoon between road and beach were connected by a trench with a small shelter.[13] To knock out these two emplacements, two eight-man squads crawled forward to within about fifteen yards of them and then took stations according to available cover. The BAR men and their assistants covered the main entrances. Two

men from each squad armed with grenades made ready on either side of the entrances. They rushed the pits and heaved grenades in them; then, without stopping, dashed to the other side and blasted the entrances with several more grenades. Once the grenades exploded, the BAR men and assistants followed up with bayonets. Two other men then inspected the pits covered by the rest of the squad. Not a man was lost in this action, and the enemy positions were silenced.[14]

This left one remaining machine gun position in the area assigned to the 3d Platoon of Company G. Efforts on the part of infantrymen to direct their supporting tanks to attack it failed. No radio communications existed between tanks and infantry and an attempt on the part of one lieutenant to direct one tank against this target by pounding his rifle butt on the top of the tank failed to elicit any response from the crew inside. As the three tanks moved on past the emplacement without attacking it, S. Sgt. Michael Thompson, commanding Company G's 3d Platoon, undertook to rush the position singlehanded. His action can best be described in his own words:

I worked my way slowly forward, hugging the ground. I could see the muzzle of the gun, projecting beyond the pit, but it did not seem to be manned. . . . I rushed the pit, jumped in and seized the machine gun to swing it around and face it down the connecting trench. . . . I dropped the machine gun . . . and grabbed my rifle. Three Japs in the trench, a short distance from me, were beginning to stir. They looked as if they had been stunned by an explosion. So I shot them. Then

[10] Browning automatic rifle.

[11] Marshall, Makin Notes, p. EE14a.

[12] Interv, Capt Leonard, Marshall Intervs, pp. 48–50.

[13] JICPOA Bull 4-44, map facing p. 1.

[14] Marshall, Makin Notes, p. F30.

I walked down the trench and came to an object, well covered with palm leaves. I pulled the leaves back and discovered a much-alive Jap soldier. So I shot him also. Then the rest of the platoon came up and took over.[15]

The three tanks that had left this emplacement undisturbed continued on across the tank barrier without serious opposition. About 1600 they met some light tanks attached to the 1st Battalion that had come along the main highway from the western beaches. Thus, a preliminary junction of the two attacking forces on the northern end of the line was achieved.[16] Meanwhile, at the south end of the line an advance patrol from Company B had succeeded in contacting Company F at about 1500.[17] In the center resistance continued until about 1650, by which time most of the enemy fire had been eliminated by the guns of the four medium tanks leading the assault in that area. By 1655 firm contact was established on the southern end of the line between Companies B and F and an hour later the troops of the 1st and 2d Battalions had established contact all along the West Tank Barrier.[18]

Advance of the 1st Battalion

While the 2d Battalion was moving across the island from Yellow Beach and gradually wiping out resistance east of the West Tank Barrier, Colonel Kelley's 1st Battalion was moving toward the same objective from the opposite direction. On the right (south) was Company B, commanded by Capt. Henry Berger; on the left Company C with Capt. Charles E. Coates, Jr., commanding. Company A, commanded by Capt. Lawrence J. O'Brien, after securing Flink Point went into reserve. From the heavy weapons company a machine gun platoon was assigned to each of the two

companies in attack. The mortar platoon was assigned to operate as a separate entity in support of the whole battalion, although actually mortars were not used by the battalion during the first day's operation because of the thin deployment of the enemy and because of the narrow gap between troops of the 1st and 2d Battalions that were approaching each other from opposite directions.[19]

About 1130 Colonel Kelley set up his command post on the beachhead line on the west edge of Rita Lake and began personally to direct the advance westward.[20] The first objective was the Second Phase Line, which ran through the east end of Joan Lake about 1,200 yards ahead. Between these two lines the enemy was afforded excellent opportunities to set up positions easily covering the firm ground. The defenders had taken advantage of the first of these opportunities. In the area around Jill Lake the Japanese had established two machine gun positions and an antitank gun emplacement commanding the main east-west highway, while fire trenches and another machine gun nest covered the ocean shore and the area immediately to the north of it. However, these were unmanned and no fortifications were to be found at the Second Phase Line.[21]

[15] *Ibid.*, pp. F33–F34.
[16] Baxter, Armored Force Action on Makin, p. 13.
[17] Interv, Capt Henry Berger, Marshall Intervs, pp. 25–26; 1st Bn 165th Inf Regt Combined Jnl, 20 Nov 43, Msg 56; 165th Inf Regt Combined Jnl, 20 Nov 43, Msg 65.
[18] Intervs, Col McDonough and Capt Leonard, Marshall Intervs, pp. 48–50, 59–60; Msgs cited n. 17; 27th Inf Div G-3 Msg File, 20 Nov 43, Msg 100.
[19] Intervs, Capt Berger, Capt Coates, Capt O'Brien, and Capt Paul E. Ryan, CO Co D, Marshall Intervs, pp. 25–26, 24, 22–23, 19.
[20] 1st Bn 165th Inf Regt Combined Jnl, 20 Nov 43, Msg 24.
[21] JICPOA Bull 4-44, I, p. 28; Interv, Capt Berger, Marshall Intervs, pp. 25–26.

M3 LIGHT TANK, *bogged down in a shell crater, holds up the advance on the narrow causeway north of Jill lake.*

Only occasional rifle fire met the advancing American troops. Most of this came from lone riflemen, or snipers, stationed in trees or in the underbrush. Undoubtedly the prevalence of tree snipers on Makin was sometimes exaggerated by the American troops that fought there, with the result that there was much promiscuous and sometimes dangerous strafing of tree tops. Nevertheless, in this particular area the Japanese had prepared among the fronds at the tops of certain trees places where they cached rifles and left gourds of water and sake. To mark such trees they tied to them girdles of fronds about four feet above the ground so that a rifleman could run to a tree, snatch off the marker, climb up by notches cut in the trunk and wait for likely targets.[22]

The light tanks had not come forward beyond Jill Lake because on the highway, between that pond and another just north of it, a large crater made by a naval shell had engulfed the leading tank of the column causing a roadblock. The highway at that point was a causeway off of which other tanks could not move to bypass the first. Hence, the lead tank had to be towed off and the shell hole filled before the column could proceed.[23]

By about 1400 the troops had reached the Second Phase Line just east of Joan Lake. In the advance from Jill Lake only

[22] Interv, Capt Berger, Marshall Intervs, pp. 25–26; Marshall, Makin Notes, p. G4.
[23] V Phib Corps GALVANIC Rpt, Incl F, Rpt by Special Staff Officers, Sec. 3, Rpt of Engineer Officer, p. 3; 193d Tk Bn Rpt of Makin Opn, p. 68.

two Japanese were reported killed. About the same time, the light tank mired on the causeway was extricated, and the entire tank platoon commenced moving to the front to support the infantry. Meanwhile, no direct radio communication had been established with the 2d Battalion. Frantic radio messages from Colonel Kelley to the supporting planes and to regimental and division command posts failed to elicit any very clear information as to the position of the 2d Battalion, which was advancing toward his own troops. At the same time fire from friendly troops had pinned down his own front lines.[24] In spite of these difficulties, division headquarters dispatched the message, "Continue your attack vigorously to effect a junction with McDonough without delay." The advance was resumed.[25]

Company B on the right made the most rapid progress. Fire from the east side of the West Tank Barrier, then under attack by the 2d Battalion, held them up for a while, but an advance patrol under 1st Lt. Patrick J. Raleigh was sent forward and about 1500 succeeded at last in establishing contact with Company F.[26] On the left, Company C ran into more difficulty when it encountered the only determined resistance between Red Beach and the West Tank Barrier. About 150 yards west of the barrier and to the south of the east-west road, the enemy had emplaced a Lewis machine gun concealed by a natural dip in the terrain and protected by riflemen concealed in and among surrounding trees. The gun's fire cut obliquely across the main highway, between two sharp bends, and stopped the 1st Platoon, Company C, in a small clearing south of the highway.[27] North of this emplacement, on the lagoon side of the highway, was a large palm tree that had around its base a square of heavy coconut logs and raised earth. The platoon

leader, 2d Lt. Daniel T. Nunnery, took cover at the base of this tree and proceeded to study the surrounding area. He was shortly joined by Captain Coates, Company C's commander.

In a moment, Colonel Kelley, the 1st Battalion commander, moved to reconnoiter the position indicated by Lieutenant Nunnery. In an effort to keep Company C moving to the tank trap and join with the 2d Battalion, he sought out Captain Coates. On the way, he met Col. Gardiner J. Conroy who was ordering a tank up to fire into the enemy position. Colonel Kelley advised that his troops would be endangered by such fire and informed the regimental commander that he would have Captain Coates continue the advance, bypassing the pocket, and leave his support platoon to reduce it.

Colonel Kelley moved out to the trees to instruct Captain Coates, who promptly shouted "get down." Just in time Colonel Kelley threw himself to the ground, avoiding an enemy machine gun burst. When Captain Coates signaled to his left platoon, that unit moved over to the lagoon, and under the cover of a three-to-four-foot bank proceeded east and around the clearing toward the tank barrier.

In the meantime Lieutenant Nunnery, still under the palm tree, was shot through the head and killed. Between his body and the machine gun lay an American rifleman, shot through the arm. Chaplain Joseph A. Meany, who had come up with Colonel Conroy a few minutes before, rushed out to the wounded man and dropped down beside him. He too was

---

[24] 1st Bn 165th Inf Regt Combined Jnl, 20 Nov 43, Msgs 28, 31, 34, 39, 40, 41.

[25] *Ibid.*, Msg 43; 27th Inf Div G-3 Msg File, 20 Nov 43, Msgs 56, 62.

[26] Interv, Capt Berger, Marshall Intervs, pp. 25-26.

[27] Interv, Capt Coates, Marshall Intervs, p. 28.

shot, although his life was saved by a small medal and identification disk that deflected one of the bullets. Another soldier dashed out to aid the chaplain and dropped dead at his feet. The whole area was now alive with the cracking of rifles and the rattle of the machine gun.

From the lagoon side now appeared a lone figure walking into the center of the scene. It was Colonel Conroy, erect, evidently believing that only a few Japanese riflemen were holding up the company. Colonel Kelley shouted to him to get down. He hesitated, and as he did a rifle cracked and the regimental commander went down with a bullet between his eyes. The time was then 1455.[28]

Command of the regiment now passed to Colonel Kelley, while that of the 1st Battalion was assumed by its executive officer, Maj. James H. Mahoney.[29] The light tanks that had been brought forward by Colonel Conroy retired on Colonel Kelley's order without firing a shot because of the danger of their hitting friendly troops. For the same reason mortar and machine gun fire had to be withheld.

1st Lt. Warren T. Lindquist, leader of the Intelligence and Reconnaissance Platoon was ordered to await the reduction of the position by the support platoon of Company C, or under cover of darkness (whichever occurred first) to crawl out and bring Chaplain Meany in. The latter proved to be the solution, and as darkness fell Lieutenant Lindquist and several of his men crawled out, found the chaplain, who had administered first aid to himself, and carried him back to the 1st Battalion aid station.[30]

Meanwhile, Company C had advanced to the edge of the West Tank Barrier clearing. Company A, which had been in reserve throughout the first phase of attack,

was ordered to advance from its position near Rita Lake and mop up in the rear of Company B. By the time it had come up to Company B, the latter unit had established contact with Company F on the opposite side of the barrier. By 1755, after Company F had finally destroyed the last of the enemy in the center of its line, contact between the two battalions extended the length of the barrier.[31]

The first portion of the plan for occupying Butaritari Island was accomplished, therefore, late on D Day. In the entire zone from the western beaches to the center of the Citadel area, enemy resistance had been overcome except for one small wedge-shaped pocket northwest of the West Tank Barrier clearing. On orders from division headquarters the attack was halted, and positions for the night were selected and secured.[32]

Holding Action on the East

While Company F, with elements of Company G attached, was moving across the island and toward the West Tank Bar-

---

[28] This account of the incidents leading up to the death of Colonel Conroy was derived from the following sources: Interv, Capt Coates, Marshall Intervs, p. 24; Marshall, Makin Notes, pp. F18–F19; Ltr, Col Gerard W. Kelley to Maj Gen Harry J. Malony, 31 Jan 49, OCMH; 27th Inf Div G-3 Msg File, 20 Nov 43, Msg 89.
Colonel Conroy's body was buried in Gate of Heaven Cemetery on Makin Island on 21 November 1943, L. W. Yarwood conducting burial services. (Sworn affidavit of L. W. Yarwood, 14 Sep 50, filed in OCMH.) General Holland Smith's report that Colonel Conroy's body was still lying where it had fallen two days after his death is erroneous. Smith, *Coral and Brass,* p. 126.)
[29] 27th Inf Div G-3 Msg File, 20 Nov 43, Msgs 89–91.
[30] Ltr, Col Kelley to Gen Malony, 31 Jan 49.
[31] 27th Inf Div G-3 Msg File, 20 Nov 43, Msgs 98, 100.
[32] *Ibid.,* Msgs 87, 88.

rier, a second force of the 2d Battalion moved to the left to take up a holding position. This left-wing force consisted of Company E, half of Detachment Z of the 105th Infantry aboard LVT's, and before the end of the day a platoon of light tanks. Company H, the heavy weapons company, was in reserve on the beach.

The prescribed plan was for the 1st Platoon of Company E to push due south across the island to the ocean shore on the left flank of Company F. It was then to turn left and act as company reserve behind the 2d Platoon. The mission of this latter unit was to advance inland from the beach to a point roughly fifty yards behind the main east-west highway and then to swing left and extend its line to the ocean shore. The 2d Platoon would then form the right flank of a line, running from the lagoon to the ocean, which was intended to seal off the eastern portion of the island. One reinforced squad of the 3d Platoon was to mop up the sandspit near King's Wharf, while the main body of this platoon pivoted to the left and tied in with the 2d Platoon. The extreme left flank of the new line would be manned by the left half of the special landing group, Detachment Z. It was expected that by nightfall this composite force would reach a line along a dirt road that crossed the island from the foot of King's Wharf, an advance of about 500 yards from the point of pivot on Yellow Beach. During most of D Day these maneuvers would be commanded by the Company E commander, Captain Ryan, since the battalion commander, Colonel McDonough, was personally supervising the drive on the West Tank Barrier. Colonel McDonough's executive officer, Major Claire, had been detained in his small boat off the reef while the hulks were being brought under fire.[33]

As Captain Ryan's 1st Platoon moved south across the island it met only desultory resistance—chiefly random fire from lone riflemen in trees and bushes. On its left flank, near the main island highway, the platoon encountered two fortified positions, one a machine gun and the other an antitank emplacement containing a 37-mm. gun commanding the highway. The first had been abandoned and the second, with its cover still on, had been disabled by preliminary bombardment.

Near the ocean shore road the troops discovered storage buildings for bombs and food, but these too were undefended. Just beyond the road was a machine gun emplacement that had been designed principally to cover the ocean approach and was flanked by rifle pits and double-apron barbed wire. The gun was turned against the Americans approaching from the north but was shortly put out of action by the 75-mm. gun of a medium tank. Ten Japanese were killed. Altogether the 1st Platoon suffered only three killed and one wounded during its trek across the island.[34]

The 2d Platoon of Company E met even lighter opposition in an area having fewer enemy installations. It moved up quickly to take its position on the right flank of the eastern line across the island. The platoon met sniper resistance but continued to move forward slowly to the line, only being held up for a short while until the 3d Platoon on its left was able to move forward. Three men were wounded during this movement.

Mopping up the sandspit proved to be an easy job for the reinforced squad of the

[33] Interv, Capt Bernard E. Ryan, Marshall Intervs, pp. 38–41; Marshall, Makin Notes, pp. F22–F24.
[34] Interv, Capt Ryan, Marshall Intervs, pp. 38–41; 193d Tk Bn Rpt of Makin Opn, p. 53; JICPOA Bull 4-44, map facing p. 3.

3d Platoon. All resistance in that area had previously been eliminated either by preliminary aerial and naval bombardment or by the amphibian tractors that had landed part of Detachment Z on the left flank of the first wave. The squad, its mission completed, waited for the left wing of the Company E line to move along the beach as far as the base of the sandspit.[35]

Just southwest of King's Wharf, the main body of the 3d Platoon, Company E, was stopped before a group of positions, strongly constructed and cleverly disguised, lying directly opposite the sandspit south of the island's main highway. Essentially, this emplacement consisted of a well-reinforced pit, three feet deep, immediately off the road and a tunnel that ran some thirty-five yards south connecting the pit to a concrete pillbox. The American troops approached the tunnel's west side, which was "blind," that is, had no apertures. It was merely a part of a dirt bank that rose about eight feet from the taro patch before it. The top of the tunnel was no different in appearance from the surrounding terrain, except that it contained small concealed burrow holes large enough to permit a man to squirm out. Running across the top was a shallow trench about fifteen yards long. The east wall contained a number of oblong apertures wide enough to permit ingress and egress. The entire structure was heavily constructed and may have served as an air raid shelter as well as an entrenchment.[36]

In front of this position the 3d Platoon was stopped for about four hours. As the troops came up to the position, the Japanese held their fire and the nature of the emplacement was not at first discerned. Three men climbed the west wall and took positions in the kneeling trench, apparently not realizing that there were Japa-

nese beneath them and not noticing the burrow holes. Meanwhile, the machine gun on the right flank of the tunnel had pinned down the body of the platoon, thus leaving the men on top unsupported. Suddenly from the apertures on the east, or far side of the tunnel, a group of Japanese emerged and charged the men on top with bayonets. One of the Americans was killed and another wounded before the platoon's fire cut the Japanese down. More came out. The wounded man was bayoneted to death and the third man was bayoneted but later escaped. Other skirmishers who had not approached the tunnel embankment withdrew immediately.

Next, bazookas and rifle grenades were brought to bear against the tunnel position but with small success. Enemy fire was now holding back the entire line. Finally the battery of 105-mm.'s, which had by now come ashore and set up positions on Ukiangong Point, was requested to fire into the area. A total of five missions was fired, chiefly to interdict reinforcements that might be brought to the tunnel from the woods beyond King's Wharf. Company E's 60-mm. mortars also laid down a barrage for the same purpose.[37]

Upon completion of the artillery fire, Captain Ryan sent a detail of seven men under S. Sgt. Hoyl Mersereau to work around to the rear, east of the position. Their mission was to take the apertures under fire and keep any more enemy raiding parties from emerging. Mersereau and his men crawled and crept in a wide circle, eventually reaching a point about forty yards away from the reverse slope of the

---

[35] Interv, Capt Ryan, Marshall Intervs, pp. 38–41.
[36] *Ibid.*, pp. 44–45; Marshall, Makin Notes, p. F31.
[37] Marshall, Makin Notes, pp. F31–F32, EE10; Interv, Capt Ryan, Marshall Intervs, pp. 38–41; 105th FA Bn Makin Rpt, 8 Dec 43, p. 6.

mound. Here, taking shelter behind a low bank, they began firing into the openings. With this protection, Company E now worked men forward on the west side of the tunnel. An attempt to use flame throwers at this juncture failed since these weapons were still out of commission. The company commander then turned to the engineers, who brought up charges of TNT and dropped them into the machine gun positions at either end of the tunnel. After these were detonated, light tanks were brought up to fire their 37-mm. shells into the entrances. At last the enemy, driven to desperation, began to emerge from the apertures with bayonets fixed, only to be cut down by rifle fire from Mersereau's detail. About 1600, some four hours after the mound was first encountered, it was possible to leave it and move forward. Eight Americans had been killed or wounded in the action. A small detail was left to mop up as Ryan's company moved on.[38]

Another fifty yards eastward the advance was again halted, this time by enemy fire coming from a log emplacement and a trench about five feet deep and thirty-five yards in length. The terrain in the area was too thickly wooded to set up all-night positions, so, under orders received at 1720, Company E withdrew to an area south of the sandspit's western edge near the center of the island. As it was digging in for the night, a platoon of Company G appeared to reinforce it.[39]

First Day: The Summing Up

Thus by the end of the first day of fighting a firm foothold had been established on Butaritari. The 2d Battalion occupied an area between the West Tank Barrier and a line extending from the base of King's Wharf across the island to the ocean shore. The 1st Battalion was in contact with the 2d all along the West Tank Barrier, although a small wedgelike pocket northwest of the barrier, which was contained by Company C, remained to be cleaned out.[40]

Artillery was in position on Ukiangong Point and had already fired missions in support of the 2d Battalion on the eastern front. About 1100, the 105th Field Artillery had commenced landing immediately behind the combat elements of the infantry. All three batteries (less B Battery's 105-mm. howitzers) were in position by 1430.[41]

However, no artillery support was called for or delivered in the main battle zone. The scheme of maneuver did not permit firing in support of the 1st and 3d Battalions after the landing of the 2d Battalion on Yellow Beach. With the two forces moving toward each other, the gap between them was too narrow to permit safe delivery of supporting fire.[42]

American casualties on the first day were low. The total reported for 20 November was twenty-five killed and sixty-two wounded seriously enough to require evacuation.[43] Estimates as to Japanese casualties are impossible to arrive at with any degree of accuracy. As of 2100 on D Day, division intelligence estimated that fifty Japanese had been killed. But next morning, the 2d Battalion reported a total of 200 Japanese dead to have been discovered in the Citadel area alone as of

---

[38] Marshall, Makin Notes, p. F32; Interv, Capt Ryan, Marshall Intervs, pp. 38–41.
[39] 27th Inf Div G-3 Msg File, 20 Nov 43, Msg 88.
[40] V Phib Corps GALVANIC Rpt, Incl B, G-3 Rpt, p. 5, and overlay attached.
[41] B Battery carried in addition to its organic 105's four 75-mm. pack howitzers.
[42] 105th FA Bn Makin Rpt, 8 Dec 43.
[43] USAFICPA Participation Rpt GALVANIC, Annex 10, Table IV.

0700. In addition, the battalion reported the capture of forty-one prisoners, mostly labor troops.[44]

One thing was clear. A far smaller number of enemy had been engaged by the attacking infantry and tanks than had been anticipated. From Yellow Beach south to the ocean and west to Red Beaches, only a few fortifications and entrenchments had been located and many of these were abandoned. The supposition upon which the landing plan had been based—that the western end of the island would be the main area of resistance—had proved false. By the end of the day it was clear that the bulk of enemy troops (estimated next morning to be about 200)[45] had abandoned whatever defenses they had built up in the area and had withdrawn to the eastern end of the island to await the advance of the attacking troops.

[44] 27th Inf Div G-2 Msg File, 21 Nov 43, Msgs 73, 75, 133, 145.
[45] Ibid., Msg 17.

CHAPTER VII

Consolidating the Beachhead

Build-up of the Assault

In the initial landings on Butaritari a platoon of Company C, 102d Engineers, was attached to each of the infantry battalion landing teams. One squad of each platoon was distributed over the first-wave boats of the assault companies and came ashore prepared to clear beach and underwater obstacles with Bangalore torpedoes. The remainder of the platoon of engineers landed with the reserve of the infantry battalion landing team.

Shore parties were furnished by the 152d Engineers. Company A was attached to the 3d Battalion Landing Team at Red Beach 2, Company B to the 1st Battalion Landing Team at Red Beach, and Company C to the 2d Battalion Landing Team at Yellow Beach.

All three shore parties encountered unexpected difficulties. As the 27th Division's engineer reported, "Red Beach was a beach in name only and afforded landing with difficulty for about six boats at flood tide." At Red Beach 2, landings could be made only for about three hours before and after flood tide, and even then only with considerable difficulty. Since the tide was high at H Hour, troops and supplies could be landed there with relative ease for the first few hours, but as the tide approached the ebb, progress in unloading was slowed down. The lagoon off Yellow Beach was of course too shallow to float LCVP's or LCM's closer than 200 yards

offshore, and up to noon of the second day of the operation the only supplies to reach this beach had to be transferred from landing craft to amphibian tractors at the reef's edge. By that time, sectional pontoons, brought along by naval vessels and set up on all beaches, projected far enough to seaward to permit all types of landing craft to debark their supplies directly without transferring them first to amphibian tractors. Also by then, King's Wharf, including the seaplane runway, was sufficiently repaired to accommodate all the shore parties of the 152d Engineers, which moved to the pier and organized two shifts to assist in unloading.[1]

The difficulties at Red Beaches clouded an otherwise successful landing. By the close of the first day's action, only a small part of the supplies and equipment had been unloaded, and even some of the troops were still far from shore aboard small craft as night closed in. By evening of D Day, *Leonard Wood* had unloaded approximately 38 percent of her supplies and equipment and *Calvert* about 23 percent. Not all of this had reached shore, however. Some was still embarked in landing craft at nightfall. By 1800 all the transports had completed their unloading for the day and got under way for night cruising dispositions.[2]

---

[1] Makin Task Force Engineer (Col Brendan A. Burns), Rpt and Recommendations, 20 Dec 43, pp. 1–2.

[2] USS *Calvert* Action Rpt, 28 Nov 43, pp. 3–4; USS *Leonard Wood* Action Rpt, 20 Dec 43, p. 4.

UNLOADING SUPPLIES AT KING'S WHARF

Also among the first waves to land at all beaches were communications personnel carrying both radio and telephone equipment. These were provided by the Detachment, 27th Signal Company, the communications platoon of the 165th Regimental Combat Team, and three teams of the 75th Signal Company, each attached to a battalion landing team. Shortly after landing they were able to establish radio contact between the troops ashore and the division and regimental commanders still afloat. Uninterrupted radio contact between ship and shore, however, was at first difficult to maintain. Radio sets were wet from the brief rain squall that had occurred early in the morning and were further damaged by waves and spray breaking over the landing craft during the long wait between loading from the transports and landing at the beaches. Landing craft grounded on the reefs, and since all personnel had to wade ashore in water from waist to shoulder depth, radio and telephone equipment was further damaged. Some difficulty was also encountered in maintaining contact by wire run laterally along Red Beaches—amphibian tractors churning across the beach, for example, often tore up the wire. Wires strung from trees later in the day made communications more reliable.[3]

---

[3] 27th Inf Div Rpt of Participation of TF 52.6 in GALVANIC (hereafter cited as TF 52.6 GALVANIC Rpt), p. 3; Signal Officer 27th Inf Div Task Force (Lt Col Thomas J. Murray), Summary of Signal Communications During the GALVANIC Operations of 27th Inf Div Task Force, p. 3; Ltr, Maj Rex R. Stillwell, USMC, to G-3 V Phib Corps, 4 Dec 43, in V Phib Corps GALVANIC Rpt, Incl F, Rpt by Special Staff Officers, Sec. V, p. 2.

More serious was the fact that during the first day of landing no direct radio communication was established between the 1st and 3d Battalion Landing Teams on Red Beaches and the 2d Battalion Landing Team on Yellow Beach, although previous arrangements had been made for this by the allocation of an appropriate frequency and the assignment of necessary radio sets. Late in the day, it is true, occasional messenger service connected the 2d Battalion Landing Team with the rest of the force on the west end of the island, but not until the morning of the second day of operations was full radio, wire, and messenger service established between Red and Yellow Beaches.[4] In view of the fact that these two forces were approaching each other in a delicate maneuver that required precise timing and complete coordination, the absence of direct radio contact between them was a serious handicap.

Another defect in communications noted during the first days of the Makin operation was faulty communications procedures. Greenwich civil time and local time were used interchangeably in the date-time groups of messages and in the time specified in the contents of the messages. Authenticators were seldom used, although standard procedure required it. Many message centers were apparently under the impression that local time was zone plus-9½ (that is, Greenwich civil time plus 9½ hours) whereas it was actually zone plus-12, thus causing a 2½-hour error in their dispatches. None of this was fatal, but it did cause some avoidable confusion at headquarters.[5]

Most serious was the failure, or rather absence, of communications between tanks and the infantry units that they were supposed to support. The tanks attached to the 27th Division for this operation were equipped with radio sets that could not operate on either the infantry or artillery nets. From the outset this caused considerable confusion and was largely responsible for the poor infantry-tank co-ordination that characterized the fighting on Makin. The only sets in the division that could operate with the tanks were those of the 27th Cavalry Reconnaissance Troop. Therefore, it was necessary to attach a radio team from that unit to each battalion landing team headquarters. In the lower echelons (rifle companies, platoons, and squads, and tank platoons and individual tanks) there was no communication agency capable of linking the components of the infantry-tank teams.[6]

In spite of these difficulties and defects in establishing and maintaining direct contact between lower echelons, communications between the task force commander (Admiral Turner) and the various units ashore and between the regimental and division commanders and the elements under them were reported generally satisfactory. This was provided in part by the air liaison parties, and the shore fire control parties, which were landed fairly early in the operation and were attached to each battalion landing team.[7]

Two shore fire control parties were assigned to each battalion. These landed

[4] Signal Officer 27th Inf Div Task Force, Summary of Signal Communications, GALVANIC, p. 3.

[5] 27th Inf Div G-3 Msg File, G-2 Msg File, *passim;* Ltr, Maj Stillwell to G-3 V Phib Corps, 4 Dec 43, in V Phib Corps GALVANIC Rpt, Incl F, Rpt by Special Staff Officers, Sec. V, p. 2.

[6] TF 52.6 GALVANIC Rpt, pp. 2–3.

[7] ALP U-13, attached to 3d BLT, was in position ashore by 0910; ALP U-11, attached to 1st BLT, by 1110; ALP U-12, attached to 2d BLT, was held up off Yellow Beach by the air attack against the hulks but was landed by 1258. V Phib Corps GALVANIC Rpt, Incl F, Special Staff Officers Rpt, Sec. I, Air Officer Rpt, pp. 3–4.

with their respective infantry battalions and were immediately able to furnish close supporting fires on call. On D Day one cruiser *(Minneapolis)* and two destroyers *(Dewey* and *Phelps)* were designated to deliver fires on request from these parties. However, no requests were received, either on that day or later in the operation. This failure to call upon naval guns can be explained in part by the relatively limited area lying between Yellow Beach and Red Beaches, an area apparently considered by troop commanders to be too restricted to risk calling on naval fire for support. In spite of the fact that the shore fire control parties were not called upon to perform the functions for which they were primarily intended, they did provide a valuable and sometimes the only communications liaison between ship and shore.[8]

To each battalion landing team was also attached an air liaison party whose function was to call for air strikes in support of ground troops at the request of the respective troop commanders. Air Liaison Party U-13, attached to the 3d Battalion Landing Team, was in position ashore about 100 yards from the beach by 0910. The party attached to the 1st Battalion Landing Team (ALP U-11) reported in position at 1110. That attached to the 2d Battalion Landing Team (ALP U-12) was held up off Yellow Beach by the air attack against the hulks, but was able to get ashore by 1258.[9] As in the case of naval fire, no close air strikes were called for against land targets on D Day, but again the air liaison parties had reliable and consistent communications with the various headquarters afloat and in many instances, especially during the early hours after the landing, these groups and the shore fire control parties were the only sources of information available to higher echelons.[10]

One other important communications net was that established between the field artillery batteries and the division commander, once the latter got ashore. Although communications by wire between artillery units and infantry units was impossible to maintain because of the damage wrought by tanks and tractors, radio communications were deemed satisfactory. Also, the radios manned by artillery personnel often filled the gap created by the failure of communications between infantry units and command posts. It was rare that the division commander could not secure information from the front lines of any battalion landing team through the artillery communications setup.[11]

One result of these initial failures in communications ashore (contrasted with the comparatively superior ship-to-shore communications setup) was to delay moving the entire division headquarters from *Leonard Wood* until the second day of the

[8] Ltr, 27th Inf Div Artillery Officer (Col Harold G. Browne) to CTF 52.6, 7 Dec 43, sub: Rpt on Naval Gunfire in Makin Opn, p. 2, AG 327 Art 0.3.0 (22866), DRB AGO; Fifth Amph Force Rpt, Capture of Gilbert Islands, Incl H, p. 4.

[9] V Phib Corps GALVANIC Rpt, Incl F, Special Staff Officers Rpt, Sec. I, Air Officer Rpt, pp. 3–4.

[10] *Ibid.;* Ltr, Maj Stillwell to G-3 V Phib Corps, 4 Dec 43, p. 2.

[11] Signal Officer 27th Inf Div Task Force, Summary of Signal Communications, GALVANIC, p. 4; TF 52.6 GALVANIC Rpt, p. 8; Ltr, 1st Lt James B. Sullivan to Lt Col Arthur W. Tyson, 7 Dec 43, sub: Observations on Makin Island Opn, p. 4.

The report of Admiral Turner's communications officer is far less sanguine in its estimates of the efficiency of communications ashore than are the official Army reports. It reads, in part, "Landing Force Communications ashore were largely non-existent. There were no beach laterals and no command channels. Some breakage of equipment, delays in loading, usual losses and confusion and a lack of command organization appear to be the major causes of an outstanding lack of communications. Equipments which were finally gotten ashore and in working condition were not utilized on channels as planned." Fifth Amph Force Rpt, Capture of Gilbert Islands, Incl D, pp. 7–8.

operation.[12] In spite of these difficulties all other command posts were set up on the island before nightfall of the first day's action. Colonel Conroy had left his ship as early as 0900, and by 1100 the regimental command post was set up ashore.[13] Meanwhile, Colonel Hart, commanding the 3d Battalion Landing Team, had opened his command post, as had Colonel Kelley of the 1st Battalion Landing Team.[14] By 1800 General Smith was ashore, although his command post still remained afloat.[15]

First Night on Butaritari

By the time action against the enemy had been closed in the late afternoon of 20 November, the first objectives of the invasion of Makin had in the main been accomplished. Except for the small pocket contained by Company C, the West Tank Barrier system had been reduced. Other secondary aims had also been realized. A solid holding line facing east had been established, and the likelihood of any substantial Japanese reinforcement of the West Tank Barrier reduced to a minimum. Beachheads had been secured on two shores and were in process of development. Artillery was ashore and had already fired a few missions in support of Company E's advance eastward. All command posts were ashore except the division's. *(Map 5)*

With the virtual reduction of the West Tank Barrier, the troops facing the main body of Japanese on the eastern part of the island automatically became the front-line units. The principal element in the east on the night of D Day was Company E, reinforced by one platoon of Company G and a part of Detachment Z of the 105th Infantry, one of the special landing groups.

The nearest American position behind the front-line elements was the medium tank park established by the 193d Tank

Battalion near the center of Yellow Beach. This was some 500 yards to the rear of Company E's line. Tank crews either stayed in their vehicles or joined Company H and the Yellow Beach shore party in digging a perimeter defense. The command post of the 2d Battalion was also located on Yellow Beach, adjacent to the perimeter established by the tank battalion.[16]

About five hundred yards farther to the west, dug in near the lagoon along the eastern edge of the West Tank Barrier system, was Company G, less the platoon that had joined Company E. Company F dug in directly south of Company G, in the same area. Beyond the tank trap, Company C set up its night position just east of the "pocket" that had caused so much trouble during the afternoon. The other three companies of the 1st Battalion were in position along the southern half of the west barrier system, bending back to the west along the ocean shore. The remainder of the 165th Regimental Combat Team was spread out over the island from the West Tank Barrier to Red Beaches. The 3d Battalion had assembled just southwest of Rita Lake shortly after its relief and dug in there for the night. General Ralph Smith, after coming ashore at 1800, had ordered Colonel Hart to prepare his men for a movement to Kuma Island, northeast of Butaritari, at 0900 the next morning. Disturbing news from Tarawa prompted Admiral Turner to disapprove this projected move, however. The 3d Battalion was to be maintained in readiness at Rita

---

[12] 27th Inf Div G-3 Jnl, 20 Nov 43, Msg 95.
[13] 165th Inf Regt Combined Jnl, 20 Nov 43, Msg File, Msg 22.
[14] 1st Bn 165th Inf Regt Combined Jnl, 20 Nov 43, Msg 16.
[15] 27th Inf Div G-3 Jnl, 20 Nov 43, Msg 95.
[16] Baxter, Armored Force Action on Makin, pp. 10–14.

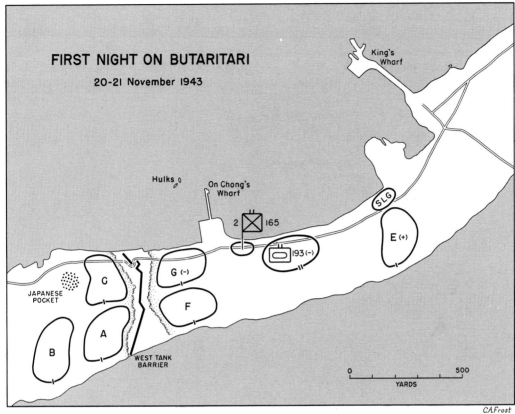

FIRST NIGHT ON BUTARITARI

20-21 November 1943

MAP 5

Lake for transshipment to Tarawa if it should be needed there.[17]

The 105th Field Artillery Battalion dug in for the night near its guns south of Ukiangong Village and was prepared, if called upon, to furnish night fires for the units farther to the east. Nearby was the second bivouac area of the 193d Tank Battalion, occupied mainly by the amphibian tractors of the Red Beach special landing groups and by light tanks. Another platoon of light tanks was situated at Red Beach 2, where practically all the remaining troops ashore had assembled.[18]

As night closed in on the island, it appeared probable that the enemy would adopt one or more of three courses. He could defend his current positions in depth, withdraw to the eastern part of Butaritari and then cross over to Kuma Island, or counterattack in force.[19]

Actually, no major counterattacks were undertaken by the Japanese during the first night, nor was there any organized withdrawal eastward. Some successful attempts were made to bolster defenses along the eastern line and a few positions at the base of King's Wharf were reoccupied and new machine gun emplacements

---

[17] 27th Inf Div G-3 Msg File, 20 Nov 43, Msgs 86–91.

[18] Baxter, Armored Force Action on Makin, pp. 10–14.

[19] 27th Inf Div G-2 Periodic Rpt, Rpt 1, 20 Nov 43.

constructed facing the American lines. One machine gun was placed in the wrecked seaplane lying in the lagoon off of King's Wharf, another at the base of King's Wharf, and three more were set up in buildings in the area immediately southward.[20]

Also, a few efforts were made to work small patrols into the area of the West Tank Barrier system. Some of these were intercepted. One, of from twelve to sixteen men, tried to move around the left flank of Company E near the sandspit, but was stopped by rifle fire.[21] In the sector assigned to Detachment Z, 105th Infantry, several enemy infiltrated American positions. Three were killed and two wounded by rifle fire and grenades.[22] One twelve-man patrol did manage to slip along the ocean shore and reach a point between Companies A and B. Only twenty feet from Company A its members stopped to fire at Company B, which had been discovered to the front. When dawn came the enemy was revealed only a few yards away and the whole patrol was killed without trouble.[23]

The communications breakdown among units of the Japanese militated against any successful reinforcement of the West Tank Barrier system, for while patrols were attempting to infiltrate the system, survivors behind the American lines were trying to get out. For example, one ten-man group was killed by grenades and BAR fire as it tried to escape toward the ocean early in the morning.[24]

These instances constituted the only recorded cases of organized Japanese counteractivity during the first night after the landing on Butaritari, and there is no evidence that these various movements of small patrols were in any way co-ordinated. Other than that, the enemy's countermeasures were limited to sniper fire from lone riflemen located within or close to the U.S. lines. This was kept up all night and was reportedly accompanied by a variety of ruses such as dropping lighted firecrackers to attract American fire and calling out messages in garbled English.[25]

One effect of these tactics was to precipitate a breakdown of fire discipline among the green and nervous American troops. "Trigger-happy" soldiers peppered away indiscriminately at unseen targets throughout the night, not only wasting ammunition but, more important, drawing frequent counterfire. The worst example occurred just after daybreak when a man from the 152d Engineers ran along the lagoon shore from the direction of On Chong's Wharf toward the command post of the 2d Battalion, shouting, "There's a hundred and fifty Japs in the trees!" A wave of shooting hysteria swept the area. When the engineer admitted that he had seen no enemy but had merely heard firing, shouted orders to cease fire proved ineffectual. Direct commands to individuals were necessary. The harassing tactics of the enemy were to this extent effective.[26]

Final Mop-up at the West Tank Barrier and Yellow Beach

The first problem to be solved on the morning of the second day was the elimination of the enemy still left alive in or near the West Tank Barrier system. The

[20] Interv, Capt Ferns, Marshall Intervs, pp. 55–58.
[21] Interv, Capt Ryan, Marshall Intervs, pp. 39–41.
[22] Interv, Capt Ferns, Marshall Intervs, pp. 55–58.
[23] Marshall, Makin Notes, p. F14.
[24] Interv, 1st Sgt Bartholomew Mooney, Marshall Intervs, pp. 20–21.
[25] Intervs, Capt Ben Krugman and Sgt Mooney, Marshall Intervs, pp. 9–10, 14, 20–21.
[26] Marshall, Makin Notes, p. F45; Durand, Rpt on Makin Island Expedition, p. 4.

M3 MEDIUM TANKS *shell the hulks off On Chong's Wharf.*

Japanese still held a small wedgelike pocket just northwest of the barrier and from that position could bring guns to bear on the east-west highway, which was now the main supply route from Red Beaches. Also, the approaches to Yellow Beach were not yet secure, and any attempts to bypass the pocket by bringing supplies through the lagoon would be handicapped by fire from the west. The two hulks on the reef near On Chong's Wharf, which had been so heavily attacked from the air and sea on D Day, were once more believed to be occupied by the enemy.

As landing craft came into Yellow Beach early on the second morning, some of them "returned" fire against the hulks, aiming at the top decks of the ships. On shore, among the American troops in or near the

West Tank Barrier clearing, intermittent bursts of machine gun fire were received for as long as two hours after dawn. These were probably "overs" directed at the hulks from the landing craft. At 0818, while landing craft stayed clear, the first of a long series of air strikes, which continued until 1630, began against the hulks.[27] At 0920 several of the medium tanks went to the water's edge and shelled the derelicts with their 75-mm. guns. They were reported to be overshooting by some 2,000 yards, their shells falling into the lagoon in the middle of the boat lanes. Whether from enemy or from friendly fire, the approach to Yellow Beach was so dangerous

---

[27] V Phib Corps GALVANIC Rpt, Incl F, Rpt by Special Staff Officers, Sec. I, Air Officer's Rpt, Incl A, pp. 6–8.

for the landing craft that, as late as 1230 when the tide was beginning to ebb, about forty of them were still circling well out in the lagoon, afraid to come in.[28]

Finally, late in the afternoon, Captain Coates, commanding officer of Company C, was ordered to dispatch a detail to investigate the hulks. He ordered 2d Lt. Everett W. McGinley to take sixteen men in two LVT's to board the two vessels and eliminate whatever he found there in the way of enemy positions. They found nothing. The top deck of each ship was so wrecked, twisted, and torn that in McGinley's opinion no enemy could have fired from there without being in plain view. From the top deck there was a sheer drop to the bottom of the hulks without any intervening deck. Water, waist-high, covered the bottom. The only possible location for hidden Japanese was a two-foot ledge that ran around the interior walls of both hulks. Although he found no empty shells or weapons McGinley admitted that some might have been on the lagoon bottom hidden from view by the water.[29]

Whether or not the hulks had ever contained enemy positions remains doubtful. Lt. Col. William R. Durand, the official observer sent to Makin by General Richardson's headquarters, had no doubts. On the question as to whether the hulk contained machine guns he reported, "I am certain that it did; not only because it interrupted landing operations and actually caused a few casualties but also because a captured overlay showed the positions."[30] The testimony was corroborated by all the officers and men of Company F who were interviewed on the subject. This was the company that dug in along the West Tank Barrier about 300 to 500 yards from the hulks. All claimed that on the second morning, for about an hour or more at intervals of every few minutes, direct fire from the hulks hit into the dirt right along their line of positions.[31]

On the other hand, in Colonel Kelley's opinion, the belief that fire was being directed from the sunken vessels both against the lagoon and inland was a hallucination from beginning to end. It was his belief that the fire that observers thought to be coming from the hulks against landing craft as they came through the lagoon was actually coming from the shore. He also believed that fire later received by troops on shore from the direction of the lagoon came not from the hulks but from landing craft that were firing at the hulks and sending "overs" into the areas occupied by friendly troops. This conclusion was confirmed by Lt. Col. S. L. A. Marshall, the official historian assigned to the operation by the Historical Branch, G-2, War Department General Staff.[32]

With all this conflicting testimony, it is impossible for the historian to reach any final conclusion except to say that the weight of the evidence would seem to indicate that the hulks had been unoccupied by the enemy from the very beginning of the operation. In any case, it is certain that after the investigation conducted by Lieutenant McGinley, no more fire was heard from the hulks or the area near them.

Meanwhile, operations against the pocket west of the tank barrier had begun at 0800 under the direction of Major Mahoney, the 1st Battalion commander. He ordered S. Sgt. Emmanuel F. DeFabees to skirt the pocket with a patrol and enter it

[28] 27th Inf Div G-4 Jnl, 21 Nov 43, p. 5.
[29] Marshall Intervs, p. 37.
[30] Durand, Rpt on Makin Island Expedition, p. 2.
[31] Marshall, Makin Notes, p. F42.
[32] Ibid.; Interv, Edmund G. Love with Col Gerard W. Kelley, Sep 47; Ltr, S. L. A. Marshall to Dr. Kent Roberts Greenfield, 2 Apr 52, OCMH.

from the right flank. The sergeant cut sharp right for fifty yards and then sought to force an entrance, his men crawling on their bellies. The patrol "found the fire too heavy." It then went obliquely for seventy-five yards and was again turned back. By this time DeFabees was convinced that much of the fire was coming from friendly forces and the patrol was withdrawn. It was about this time that Company A was firing toward a supposed Japanese machine gun nest on the lagoon side of the island and Company F along the tank trap was receiving fire from the direction of the lagoon itself, which may or may not have been from American landing craft. In any case, there was considerable confusion on the part of all hands as to just what were the sources of fire against U.S. positions in the west of the West Tank Barrier.[33]

Thirty minutes after DeFabees had withdrawn his patrol, at 0840, Major Mahoney announced that Company C had cleared out the pocket and was reorganizing and extending to Company B.[34] This announcement was slightly premature since the flank was not considered entirely secure until about noon.[35]

The liveliest action in the West Tank Barrier zone occurred in a coconut grove along the eastern edge of the barrier clearing, just north of the middle of the island. About 1030 a group of Japanese began firing rifles and light machine guns into the platoon of Company F that was mop-

ping up along the former stronghold. Captain Leonard asked for three light tanks to come up and give him help. The tanks, after reporting, moved over to the highway, which skirted the northern edge of the clearing, so that their line of fire was toward the ocean. While the tanks were spraying the tree tops with machine gun fire and canister they were approached by a fourth towing fuel along the highway. After the latter's tow cable snapped it also joined the other tanks in the attack.

The four tanks had been firing for about five minutes when a Navy bomber suddenly swung over them at a very low altitude and dropped a 2,000-pound fragmentation bomb about twenty-five feet from one of the tanks. 1st Lt. Edward J. Gallagher, the tank officer in charge, was killed, as were two enlisted men nearby. Several others were injured. By the time the tank crews had recovered from surprise and concussion, the Japanese were giving no further trouble.[36]

This episode at the tank trap closed the action at the West Tank Barrier. No further important difficulty was encountered with enemy stragglers in that zone. Attention could now be fully centered on the drive eastward to secure the remainder of the island.

---

[33] Marshall, Makin Notes, p. F17.
[34] 1st Bn 165th Inf Regt Combined Jnl, 21 Nov 43, Msg 8.
[35] Marshall, Makin Notes, p. F17.
[36] Interv, Lt Robert Welch, Marshall Intervs, pp. 32–33; Marshall, Makin Notes, pp. F43, EE6–EE7.

CHAPTER VIII

Makin Taken

The plan for the capture of Makin, though divided into three phases, was a continuing process that involved no major regroupings of forces. After the establishment of the beachheads on Butaritari the first objective had been the reduction of the West Tank Barrier, and this was followed by a drive to the east and pursuit of the enemy to outlying islands. The West Tank Barrier had been reduced during the first day's action. The second day would see—in addition to the mopping up of the area around the West Tank Barrier and of the western end of Butaritari—the beginning of the drive to the east. The situation at Tarawa had prevented General Ralph Smith from moving the 3d Battalion, 165th Infantry, to Kuma Island early on the morning of the second day, a move that would have eliminated much of the need for the third phase of the operation. He dispatched that morning, however, a small party under Maj. Jacob H. Herzog, assistant intelligence officer of the division, with orders to investigate Kuma for the presence of Japanese forces.[1] Also, air observers were instructed to keep a close watch for any signs of a large enemy movement to the outlying islands.[2] With these precautions, the main attention of the 165th Regimental Combat Team was centered during the second day on the drive to the eastern end of Butaritari.

The Main Action of the Second Day

The plan of attack for the second day provided that Company E and attached elements should immediately push eastward from positions of the night before while Company F should remain in reserve near Yellow Beach. General Smith's order, sent out the previous evening, had set the jump-off hour at 0700, following an intense artillery preparation.[3] Colonel McDonough, however, elected to defer the advance of the infantry until the medium tanks were ready, and these were delayed until enough fuel could be brought forward.[4]

During the interim aircraft pounded the area in front of the 2d Battalion. At 0843 the air liaison party attached to McDonough's battalion requested bombing and strafing of the zone ahead of Company E as far as the East Tank Barrier. This was complied with. As soon as McDonough had ascertained that the tanks would be fueled by 1045 he ordered the attack to

---

[1] TF 52.6 GALVANIC Rpt, p. 8.
[2] It was possible for troops to move to Kuma from Butaritari along the reef at low tide without recourse to boats.
[3] 27th Inf Div G-3 Msg File, 20 Nov 43, Msg 92.
Note: In spite of this order clearly specifying 0700 as jump-off hour, Captain Ryan, Company E's commander, was under the impression that the renewed attack "was slated for 0800." Interv, Capt Ryan, Marshall Intervs, pp. 38–41.
[4] Durand, Rpt on Makin Island Expedition, p. 4.

jump off at 1100. Meanwhile, at 1026 he radioed to his supporting aircraft that "tanks and troops are moving forward" and that all bombing and strafing should cease. Although this cancellation was acknowledged and confirmed, the air columns formed for the bombing runs kept coming in as originally ordered. Fortunately, Captain Ryan, Company E's commander, exercised firm control over his troops and was able to hold back their advance until the air attacks had ceased. Thus the faulty air-ground co-ordination caused no damage beyond delaying the attack even longer.[5]

By 1110 the attack was at last in progress.[6] Ten medium tanks had been refueled and had moved into position to support the troops,[7] and Colonel McDonough chose to rely exclusively on these vehicles to support his infantry. Although both the forward observer and the liaison officer from the artillery battalion repeatedly suggested that fire be placed well in advance of the front line to soften up the enemy, the infantry commander declined it. He even refused to allow the forward observer to register the artillery battalion until after the day's action had ceased.[8] Although the 105-mm. pieces on Ukiangong Point fired a total of twenty-one missions early in the morning, not a single howitzer was fired after 0630.[9]

On the extreme left was Detachment Z of the 105th Infantry. Next to it came the 1st Platoon, Company G, which had reinforced the 3d Platoon, Company E, throughout the night. In the center was the 1st Platoon and on the right the 2d Platoon of Company E. All units moved forward in a skirmish line. Fifty yards to the rear, mopping up Japanese stragglers, was a second formation consisting of the 3d Platoon, Company E, the 2d and 3d Platoons,

Company G, and a detail of marines consisting of the 4th Platoon of the V Amphibious Reconnaissance Company.[10] (*Map 6*)

The line advanced steadily, though slowly, averaging about three yards a minute. 1st Sgt. Thomas E. Valentine of the front echelon of Company E described the opposition encountered:

> On the second day we did not allow sniper fire to deter us. We had already found that the snipers were used more as a nuisance than an obstacle. They would fire, but we noted little effect by way of casualties. We learned that by taking careful cover and moving rapidly from one concealment to another we could minimize the sniper threat. Moreover, we knew that our reserves would get them if we did not. So we contented ourselves with firing at a tree when we thought a shot had come from it and we continued to move on.[11]

West of the tunnel that had been taken during the previous afternoon but subsequently relinquished, the enemy fell back again. In the next 200 yards, from the tunnel to the road crossing the island from the base of King's Wharf, the stiffest resistance of the day was encountered.

---

[5] V Phib Corps GALVANIC Rpt, Incl F, Rpt by Special Staff Officers, Sec. I, Air Officer's Rpt, Incl A, pp. 6–7; Durand, Rpt on Makin Island Expedition, pp. 4–5.

[6] 27th Inf Div G-3 Msg File, 21 Nov 43, Msg 24.

[7] 193d Tk Bn Rpt, pp. 41–57.

[8] 105th FA Bn Informal Rpt of A Battery, Rpt of Liaison Officer No. 2, 105th FA Bn, Kansas City Records Center, AGO (KCRC).

[9] Marshall, Makin Notes, p. EE11; 105th FA Bn S-3 Rpt on Action, Butaritari Island, Makin Atoll, p. 4, KCRC.

[10] V Phib Corps GALVANIC Rpt, Incl C, G-2 Rpt, Incl D, Rpt of 1st Lt Harvey C. Weeks, USMCR, p. 2; Interv, Capt Ryan, Marshall Intervs, pp. 38–41. These marines had been part of the reinforced 2d Platoon of Company G, which had been landed from *Neville* at Kotabu and Tukerere Islands on D Day. Having reconnoitered the tiny islets and discovered no opposition, they had returned to their ship the same day and were subsequently landed on Butaritari.

[11] Interv, 1st Sgt Thomas E. Valentine, Marshall Intervs, pp. 42–43.

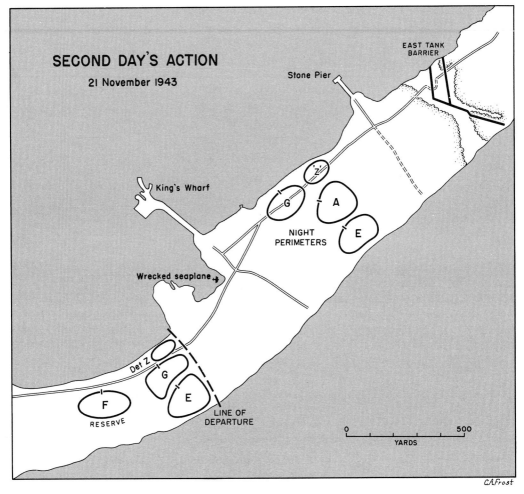

SECOND DAY'S ACTION

21 November 1943

MAP 6

From an enemy seaplane beached on the reef, machine gun and rifle fire struck at the left flank and in toward the center of the line. To allay this nuisance, four of the medium tanks finally pumped enough shells from their primary weapons at close range to annihilate the eighteen occupants concealed in the plane's body and wings.[12] On the right an emplacement, intended mainly for defense against landings from the ocean, contained three dual-purpose 3-inch guns. Farther on, at the ocean end of the cross-island road, a twin-barreled, 13-mm. dual-purpose machine gun also covered part of the zone of advance.[13]

In the center, about thirty yards beyond the tunnel, there was a large underground

---

[12] Interv, Capt Ryan, Marshall Intervs, pp. 38–41. From the air an explosion in the seaplane was observed at 1146. V Phib Corps GALVANIC Rpt, Incl F, Rpt by Special Staff Officers, Sec. I, Air Officer's Rpt, Incl A, p. 7.

[13] JICPOA Bull 4-44, map facing p. 1.

BEACHED SEAPLANE AND RIFLE PITS *(above and below, respectively)* were *Japanese points of resistance.*

shelter, and about thirty yards farther on, six rifle pits connected by a trench. Squarely across the King's Wharf road, a little south of the middle of the island, was a longer trench with eleven rifle pits.[14]

Between noon and 1400 the advance passed through one of the most heavily defended areas on the island. On the lagoon shore at the base of King's Wharf, along the east-west highway, and along King's Wharf road were buildings and tons of fuel and ammunition used by Japanese aviation personnel. A group of hospital buildings was situated near the lagoon at the base of the wharf. Under coconut trees along the ocean shore at the right were four machine gun emplacements supported by ten rifle pits, the whole group being protected on the east and west flanks by double-apron wire running inland from the water across the ocean-shore road.[15]

One after another, all of these positions were overrun. On the left Detachment Z of the 105th Infantry moved steadily along the lagoon shore, wiping out trenches and emplacements with the help of one medium tank. Combat engineers using TNT blocks were also employed. By the close of the day the detachment unit had advanced from six to seven hundred yards east of King's Wharf, suffering only six casualties.[16] In the center and on the right of the line, Company E met with equal success. Moving slowly but steadily forward, by 1700 it had pushed some 1,000 yards east of Yellow Beach. Tank-infantry co-ordination was much improved over that of the previous day. Infantry troops pointed out enemy strong points to their supporting tanks, covered them as the tanks moved in for close-range fire, and mopped up the positions once the tanks had withdrawn or moved forward.[17] Meanwhile, in the rear

areas, Company A joined Company F at 1300 in the vicinity of the West Tank Barrier and proceeded to mop up stranded enemy riflemen in that area.[18]

The day's advance had wrested from the Japanese their long-range radio receiving station, a heavily revetted, seventy-eight by thirty-three foot underground building at the south edge of a cleared rectangular area east of King's Wharf. Other installations captured or destroyed left the main area of enemy military positions entirely in American hands.[19] When action ceased about 1700, all Japanese resistance from Red Beaches to Stone Pier had been eliminated with the exception of a few isolated snipers.[20] Total U.S. casualties for the day were even fewer than on the previous day—eighteen killed and fifteen seriously wounded.[21] Still ahead lay the East Tank Barrier system, resembling that on the west and designed primarily to stop an assault from the east.

The job of continuing the next morning's attack would not fall to McDonough's battalion, which had carried the main burden of advance from Yellow Beach to Stone Pier. Shortly after the day's fighting had ceased, the 2d Battalion was ordered into reserve by General Ralph Smith. At the same time, Colonel Hart's 3d Battalion was ordered to relieve the 2d, commencing at daylight on 22 November, and to attack eastward vigorously, commencing at 0800.

---

[14] *Ibid.*

[15] *Ibid.*

[16] Interv, Capt Ferns, Marshall Intervs, pp. 55–58.

[17] Interv, Capt Ryan, Marshall Intervs, pp. 38–41.

[18] Interv, Capt O'Brien, Marshall Intervs, pp. 22–23.

[19] JICPOA Bull 4-44, II, p. 24.

[20] 27th Inf Div G-3 Msg File, 21 Nov 43, Msg 37; 27th Inf Div G-2 Msg File, 22 Nov 43, Msg 167.

[21] USAFICPA Participation Rpt GALVANIC, Annex 10, Table IV.

Hart was directed to employ, as the situation dictated, Companies A and C of the 193d Tank Battalion, the 105th Field Artillery Battalion, and whatever naval gunfire and aerial support he required. This relief was approved by General Holland Smith, who had by that time come ashore and was with the division commander.[22]

The Second Night

As night closed down on the second day's fighting on Butaritari, the supply situation was still unsatisfactory. Earlier in the afternoon Colonel Ferris, the 27th Division's supply officer, had reconnoitered Yellow Beach and discovered that only amphibian tractors could negotiate the reef, that vehicles were being drowned out when they struck potholes created in the reef shelf by naval shells, and that pallets were being dunked as they were pulled off landing craft at the edge of the beach. Also, the beachhead itself was so cluttered with foxholes, tree trunks, and other obstacles that it was highly unsatisfactory as a point of supply. Meanwhile, Admiral Turner had ordered all ships excepting *Pierce* to unload on Yellow Beach, with the result that many landing craft that might otherwise have been unloaded on Red Beaches were tied up in the lagoon unable to dump their loads because of adverse hydrographic and beach conditions. Ferris consulted with Admiral Turner late in the afternoon on board the flagship *Pennsylvania,* and the admiral approved using Red Beaches as much as possible until conditions on Yellow Beach had improved. A request to permit night unloading was denied since Turner had already ordered his ships to put to sea during the hours of darkness.[23]

Ashore, Company A was ordered to relieve at 1630 the advanced elements of Company E and Company G on the front line. The latter withdrew to the lagoon shore west of Company A and dug in. A little later Company E retired to a line about 300 yards west of the Stone Pier road. In the center of the forward line Company A established its perimeter and to the north, along the lagoon shore, was Detachment Z, 105th Infantry.[24]

To the rear, Company B spread out to cover the West Tank Barrier. In an effort to prevent the indiscriminate firing that had characterized the previous night, orders were passed out to the troops to use hand grenades instead of rifles. About a hundred grenades in all were thrown from Company B's perimeter during the night. Next morning five dead Japanese were found lying beyond the perimeter, all apparently killed by grenade fire. Then, just before the men withdrew from their foxholes, they killed two more Japanese by machine gun fire directed at surrounding tree tops.[25]

Early in the morning hours a sentry on the lagoon shore threw the troops in that area into a brief fright by reporting the approach of landing craft carrying Japanese reinforcements. "There are 200 Japs out there," he claimed as he aroused Colonel Durand and Colonel McDonough in their foxholes. The two officers got up and reconnoitered the beach, talking in loud voices to avoid being shot by their own men. The boats proved to be American, and the "200 Japs" an illusion.[26]

---

[22] 27th Inf Div G-3 Msg File, 21 Nov 43, Msgs 24, 34, 37.
[23] 27th Inf Div G-4 Jnl, pp. 5–6.
[24] Intervs, Capts O'Brien, Ryan, and Ferns, Marshall Intervs, pp. 22–23, 38–41, 55–58, respectively.
[25] Interv, Capt Berger, Marshall Intervs, pp. 25–26.
[26] Marshall, Makin Notes, pp. F30a–F30b.

The Third Day: Capture of the East Tank Barrier

Well before nightfall on the second day of fighting General Ralph Smith had requested permission to use the 3d Battalion, 165th Regiment, which was still held in reserve against the possibility of being employed at Tarawa. Since the situation on that island had improved considerably during the day, his request was granted at 1705.[27] The 27th Division commander immediately ordered Colonel Hart to leave his reserve area at daylight on the 22d and move to the relief of the 2d Battalion facing the East Tank Barrier system. At 0800 the 3d Battalion, aided by light and medium tanks as well as artillery, naval gunfire, and carrier-based air support, was to attack vigorously to the east. All command posts were to be moved forward to a point near Yellow Beach where closer control could be exercised.[28]

In conjunction with the continuation of the drive eastward, an expedition under Major Herzog would set out in LVT's early in the morning for Kuma Island to intercept any Japanese who might seek refuge there. Another party was to attempt an amphibious encirclement, going through the lagoon to a point east of the front line and establishing there a strong barrier line across the narrowest part of the island to stop any Japanese fleeing eastward from the pressure of the 3d Battalion.[29] Meanwhile, harassing artillery fire was to be directed into the eastern end of the island from time to time.

Commencing at 0600, 22 November, the 3d Battalion moved along the island highway in column of companies toward Yellow Beach. Elements of Company K led the column, followed by a platoon of tanks. Company I, the battalion's antitank platoon, the headquarters and headquarters company, two platoons of Company M, medical units, and Company L followed in that order.[30] As the column passed along Yellow Beach, approximately thirteen medium and light tanks and some engineer units fell in. Beyond King's Wharf, Company K swung to the right as far as the ocean, while Company I filled the area at the left to the lagoon. Together they moved ahead in a skirmish line, all other elements being in reserve.[31] (*Map 7*)

At 0700 artillery on Ukiangong Point commenced shelling the East Tank Barrier, while Company A and Detachment Z, 105th Infantry, withdrew. From then until 0820 artillery fired a total of almost 900 rounds. The 3d Battalion's line moved swiftly ahead across the area taken on the previous afternoon but abandoned during the night. At 0820, as the artillery preparation was lifted, the tanks and infantry moved against the enemy. By 0915 the first 250 yards had been traversed with only light opposition, but resistance became more stubborn as the forces reached the road running south from Stone Pier.[32]

The first mission of the tanks was to shell the buildings ahead of them while the infantry grenaded surface installations and small shelters. The infantry-tank tactics that had been developed in the two preceding days for the reduction of large shelters were employed. As the infantry approached air raid shelters, tanks opened

[27] 27th Inf Div G-3 Msg File, 21 Nov 43, Msg 34.
[28] 27th Inf Div G-2 Jnl, 22 Nov 43, Serial 10.
[29] 27th Inf Div G-3 Msg File, 22 Nov 43, Msgs 8, 9, 10, 17, 19, 27.
[30] Marshall, Makin Notes, p. DD1.
[31] Baxter, Armored Force Action on Makin, p. 16; Interv, 1st Lt Vernal E. Edlund, Marshall Intervs, pp. 66–68.
[32] 27th Inf Div G-3 Msg File, 22 Nov 43, Msgs 11, 14, 16; Marshall, Makin Notes, p. EE11; 105th FA Bn Makin Rpt, pp. 6–7, KCRC.

up with their 75-mm. guns, knocking the shelters out as the infantry line continued on. Surface structures and smaller shelters were disposed of with hand grenades.[33]

At the ocean end of the Stone Pier road, and along the shore east of it, Company K came upon a series of rifle pits and machine gun nests with one 70-mm. howitzer position, all abandoned by the enemy.[34] At 0945, as the barrier defenses came within range of the tanks, field artillery resumed its fire, first on the clearing and then to the east of it. After twenty-five minutes the shelling from Ukiangong Point ceased.[35] The 105th Field Artillery Battalion then began moving forward to a new position closer to the front while tanks and troops entered the zone just shelled.[36]

With the 3d Battalion's attack moving steadily eastward, Colonel Hart, as previously planned, sent a special detachment to cut off the enemy from retreat to the eastern end of Butaritari. For this mission two reinforced platoons of Company A, which had only that morning been relieved from its position in the line, were sent with additional reinforcement of one section of light machine guns and one platoon of heavy machine guns from Company D. This detail, under command of Captain O'Brien, embarked at 1100 in six LVT's on a three-mile run across the lagoon to a point on the north shore well to the east of the East Tank Barrier. Around noon Captain O'Brien's men landed without opposition and set up a line across the island. Ten natives encountered near the beach informed the captain that the remaining Japanese were fleeing eastward across the reef to Kuma.[37]

The longer U.S. amphibious move to Kuma Island was made by a detail under Major Bradt. This group, in ten LVT's,

was guided to Kuma by Major Herzog, who had reconnoitered that island the day before. At 1400 nine of the amphtracks landed without opposition in the vicinity of Keuea, about a mile from the southwestern tip of the island. The enemy on Butaritari was now entirely cut off from retreat.[38]

Meanwhile, tanks and infantry were moving upon and through the East Tank Barrier. Although more heavily fortified than the West Tank Barrier, this strong defensive system offered no opposition whatever. The enemy had apparently abandoned the barrier during the night. Only a few dead Japanese were found, evidently killed by earlier bombardment, in the barrier system.[39]

The Advance Beyond the East Tank Barrier

After passing through the tank barrier system, troops of the 3d Battalion did not pause, but pushed eastward. Tanks were operating 200 to 300 yards east of the barrier in the barracks area between the highway and the lagoon as early as 1042. Two hours later, while men from Company A were forming a line across the island neck, tanks had reached a clearing about 800 yards short of that line, and the two forces were in communication.[40]

[33] Marshall, Makin Notes, p. DD1.
[34] Interv, Lt Edlund, Marshall Intervs, pp. 66–68.
[35] Marshall, Makin Notes, p. EE11.
[36] 27th Inf Div G-3 Periodic Rpt 3, p. 1.
[37] 27th Inf Div G-3 Msg File, 22 Nov 43, Msgs 8, 9, 10, 17, 19; Interv, Capt O'Brien, Marshall Intervs, pp. 22–23.
[38] 27th Inf Div G-3 Msg File, 22 Nov 43, Msgs 2, 20, 27.
[39] Marshall, Makin Notes, p. DD1.
[40] V Phib Corps GALVANIC Rpt, Incl F, Rpt by Special Staff Officers, Sec. I, Air Officer's Rpt, Incl A, p. 10; 27th Inf Div G-2 Msg File, 22 Nov 43, Msg 185; 27th Inf Div G-3 Msg File, 22 Nov 43, Msg 28; Interv, Capt O'Brien, Marshall Intervs, pp. 22–23.

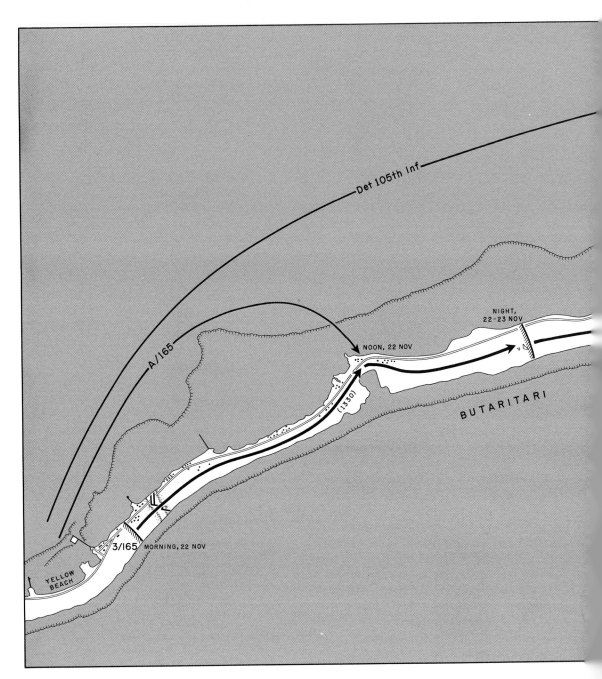

Det 105th Inf

A/165

NIGHT,
22-23 NOV

NOON, 22 NOV

(1330)

BUTARITARI

3/165 MORNING, 22 NOV

YELLOW
BEACH

MAP 7

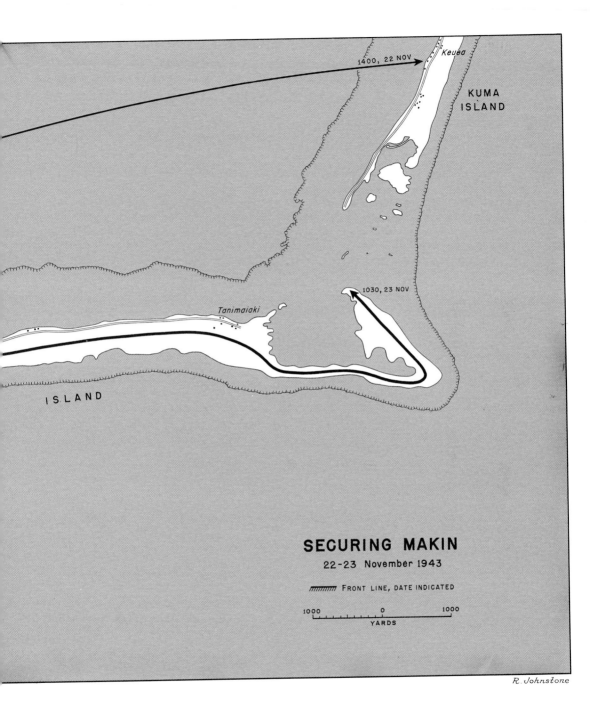

1400, 22 NOV   *Keuea*

KUMA
ISLAND

1030, 23 NOV

Tanimaiaki

ISLAND

SECURING MAKIN
22-23 November 1943

////////// FRONT LINE, DATE INDICATED

1000   0   1000
YARDS

R. Johnstone

It was believed that the Japanese remaining between these two forces would be trapped. In fact, no such event took place. By the time the 3d Battalion had reached Company A's barricade line at 1330, they had encountered no opposition. Either the enemy remnants had evaded discovery or had slipped east of the island's neck before noon when Company A had landed from its LVT's. The only sign of life in that area occurred shortly after the junction of forces when about three hundred natives emerged to be taken under custody by the American soldiers and escorted outside of the line of advance. After a short rest the 3d Battalion pressed forward again, while the Company A platoons and their attached units went to the rear.[41]

At this point General Ralph Smith, in pursuance of the original plans, assumed full command of the island forces at 1510.[42] Shortly thereafter he was ordered to reembark the 1st and 2d Battalions, all medium tanks, all except five light tanks, and all naval gunfire and air liaison parties the next morning (23 November).[43]

Beyond the narrow neck of the island where they had joined forces with the Company A detachment, the 3d Battalion advanced some 2,100 yards, stopping about 1645. With Company I on the right, Company K on the left, and Company L in the rear, the battalion dug in for the night in perimeter defense.[44]

Ahead lay about 5,000 yards of Butaritari Island still unsecured by the attacking forces. The escape of any enemy that might remain in that area across the reef to Kuma was barred by Major Bradt's detachment on that island. From his positions at the southwestern end of Kuma he could effectively cover any crossing and in fact did repulse two enemy attempts to land on Kuma during the night.[45]

The day's activity had been easy, except for the heat and the tangled tropical growth through which the 3d Battalion had had to advance. Enemy resistance in the area of the East Tank Barrier and eastward had been nominal. At the day's end Admiral Turner announced the capture of Makin "though with minor resistance remaining" and congratulated General Ralph Smith and his troops. All that seemed to remain was to mop up a now thoroughly disorganized enemy trapped in the extreme northeastern tip of Butaritari.[46]

The Last Night

After a wearisome but generally unopposed day's advance, the 3d Battalion dug in in a series of separate company perimeters, stretching across the width of the island in a line of about 300 yards in length.[47] At the north Company I covered the lagoon shore, the main highway, and about one half of the island's width. In an oval clearing in the center of the island two small ponds intervened between Company I and Company K, which set up a perimeter covering the distance from there to the ocean shore. West of these two companies in a long, narrow oval running all the way across the island was Company L, facing west. Spaced along this entire position were the light machine guns of the various company weapons platoons, and

[41] Marshall, Makin Notes, p. DD1; Interv, Capt O'Brien, Marshall Intervs, pp. 22–23.

[42] 27th Inf Div G-3 Msg File, 22 Nov 43, Msg 29.

[43] *Ibid.*, Msg 32.

[44] 3d Bn 165th RCT Combined Jnl, 22 Nov 43, Serial 33.

[45] 27th Inf Div G-3 Msg File, 23 Nov 43, Msg 3.

[46] *Ibid.*, 22 Nov 43, Msg 36.

[47] This account is derived, except when noted, from Marshall, Makin Notes, pp. DD1–DD13.

the heavy machine guns of Company M. The battalion antitank guns were placed at the point where the lines of defensive positions crossed the highway. One pair faced to the west along the road while the second pair faced to the east. The two antitank gun batteries were covered by heavy machine guns of the antitank platoon and a few riflemen. The men from Company M covered their own guns, while riflemen from the three rifle companies protected the remainder.

No very serious effort was made to establish a strong perimeter. No thorough reconnaissance of the ground just ahead was made, although about an hour and a half elapsed between the time the battalion began to dig in (1645) and sunset (1818) and another hour and a quarter remained before total darkness set in (1931).[48] During the heat of the day's activity most of the men had dropped their packs to the rear, including their entrenching tools. Foxholes were therefore shallower than usual. In some cases men did not even bother with them. Instead, they dragged coconut logs into place and built themselves barricades above ground. The truth is that very few, if any, of either officers or men entertained serious notions that there was much danger from the remnant of Japanese facing them. This opinion was most succinctly expressed by 1st Lt. Robert Wilson who later said, "Many of us had the idea there were no Japs left; when the firing began, I didn't believe it was the real thing."[49]

The first effort of the enemy to penetrate the perimeter occurred shortly after dark. Following close on the heels of a party of natives who had safely made their way into the American lines, a group of Japanese advanced close to the line, imitating baby cries as they came. The ruse was

recognized by a member of the engineer detachment, who opened fire with his machine gun killing about ten Japanese. Thereafter until dawn, the night was broken by intermittent fire fights, infiltrations, and individual attacks on the American positions.

This was no organized counterattack or banzai charge such as occurred later on Saipan. Rather, it was a series of un-coordinated small unit, sometimes individual, fights. In an effort to unnerve the Americans, the Japanese periodically set up a tom-tom-like beating all over the front of the perimeter. Periodically, also, they would yell or sing, apparently under the influence of sake.[50] They came on sometimes in groups and sometimes singly. A number of them filtered into the American lines, and their fire engaged the perimeter from both sides. The brunt of the attack fell on a few machine gun and heavy weapons positions that were covering the front from the right and left of the line. To the crews of these weapons the attack naturally appeared formidable indeed. Actually, although from three to four hundred men of the battalion were under Japanese mortar, machine gun, rifle, and grenade fire from time to time, the enemy onslaught broke and disintegrated around these relatively few positions held down by the heavy weapons and machine guns on the front. Those who were only slightly to the rear of the guns were in the position of uneasy onlookers, bound by the character of the defense to take relatively little hand in the repulse given the enemy.

---

[48] TF 54 Opn Plan A2-43, 23 Oct 43, Annex B, p. 43 (sunrise-sunset tables, Makin).

[49] Marshall, Makin Notes, p. DD9.

[50] Recently emptied bottles and canteens, which had apparently contained this liquor, were reported discovered the following morning.

When daylight finally came it was apparent that the night's attack had been both less massive and less deadly than it had seemed while it was going on. Fifty-one enemy dead were counted in front of American guns, although more were later found east of these positions. Some or all of these may have been wounded during the night's activity and dragged themselves away from the perimeter to die. American casualties for the night came to three killed and twenty-five wounded.[51]

A few of the enemy also had tried to escape from Butaritari over the reef to Kuma. At midnight about ten came upon the defense line set up by Major Bradt's detail from the 105th Infantry and were either killed or wounded while making an effort to cross it. Unless some had previously escaped beyond Kuma to the other northern islets of the atoll, the last remnants of the original Japanese forces were destined to be pinched off on 23 November, D plus 3.[52]

Mop-Up

The sixty-odd Japanese killed during the night represented the bulk of the remaining enemy soldiers on Butaritari. All that was left to be secured was the eastern extremity of the island, including Tanimaiaki Village, and the few scattered enemy left here were mostly labor troops and airmen.

The American attack was launched at 0715 with Company I in the advance. As many men as possible rode on the five light and sixteen medium tanks that had been sent up earlier to spearhead the drive. Behind them, Company K on the left and Company L on the right formed a skirmish line across the island. Still farther to the rear came the men of Company B from the 1st Battalion, as reserve support. With the left flank rode a special detail equipped with loudspeakers through which nisei interpreters were to broadcast appeals for surrender to whatever enemy troops might be left in Tanimaiaki Village. About 1015 it was discovered that some Japanese had moved across the rear of the advance unit and cut its wire. Colonel Marshall, who was in temporary command of the nisei detail, was ordered to return to the rear with a message requesting Colonel McDonough to get his support element forward. As his jeep started back from the front line it ran into an ambush that the Japanese had set up for about 300 yards along the road, somewhat more than a half a mile to the rear. At that point a support element making its way forward arrived on the scene and cleared out the ambush in a short, sharp fight. This was the last tactical encounter on Makin.[53]

By 1030 advanced elements of the 3d Battalion had reached the tip of Butaritari, and organized resistance was declared to be over.[54] Only a few Japanese had been encountered on the way and these had been quickly silenced. An hour later General Smith radioed to Admiral Turner, "Makin Taken! Recommend command pass to Commander Garrison Force."[55] Except for minor mopping-up activities, the operation was over.

At 1400 the 2d Battalion under Colonel McDonough started to board *Pierce* from Red Beach 2.[56] At 1630 Admiral Turner ordered General Smith to turn over com-

[51] 27th Inf Div G-3 Msg File, 23 Nov 43, Msg 9.
[52] Marshall, Makin Notes, pp. F11–F12.
[53] 27th Inf Div G-3 Msg File, 23 Nov 43, Msg 9; Marshall, Makin Notes, pp. DD14–DD15; Ltr, S. L. A. Marshall to Dr. Kent Roberts Greenfield, 2 Apr 52, p. 8, OCMH.
[54] 27th Inf Div G-3 Msg File, 23 Nov 43, Msg 18.
[55] *Ibid.*, Msg 19.
[56] 27th Inf Div G-4 Jnl, p. 10.

mand of the island to the garrison force commander, Col. Clesen H. Tenney, the following day at 0800.[57] From 1900 to 2120 that evening and again during the next morning, the 27th Division staff and the improvised staff of Colonel Tenney conferred. It was decided to leave on the island a considerable quantity of communications equipment already in operation, with the personnel to operate it. All the LVT's were left, and with them a Navy boat pool of nine officers and 1,943 enlisted men. Many of the trucks, bulldozers, and jeeps were also to remain.[58]

During the morning Major Mahoney's 1st Battalion went aboard *Calvert,* while other detachments embarked on other transports. At noon the special detail returned from Kuma and began to board *Leonard Wood,* following the headquarters staff.[59] The 3d Battalion under Colonel Hart was left behind to assist and protect the construction forces. Also remaining for the time being on the island were Battery C, 105th Field Artillery; one platoon of Company C, 193d Tank Battalion; the LVT detachment from Headquarters Company, 193d Tank Battalion; the Collecting Platoon and the Clearing Company and surgical team, 102d Medical Battalion; Company C, 102d Engineers; the 152d Engineers; Batteries K and L, 93d Coast Artillery (AA); Batteries A, B, C, and D, 98th Coast Artillery (AA); and the Intelligence and Reconnaissance Platoon, 165th Infantry.[60]

The remainder of the troops that had fought on Butaritari were boated and ready to sail by noon of 24 November. A short delay caused by the report of nearby enemy planes held up the convoy until 1400, but at that time the ships finally shoved off for the more inviting shores of Oahu.[61] The capture of Makin was history.

Profit and Loss

Reckoned in terms of the casualties sustained by the 27th Division, the seizure of Makin at first glance appears to have been cheap. Total battle casualties came to 218, of which 58 were killed in action and 8 died of wounds. Of the 152 wounded in action and the 35 who suffered nonbattle casualties, 57 were returned to duty while action was going on.[62] At the end of the fighting, enemy casualties were estimated to come to 550 including 105 prisoners of war, all but one of whom were labor troops.[63] Later mopping-up activities accounted for still more, and in the end the total enemy garrison, none of whom escaped, was either captured or killed. Thus, a total of about 300 combat troops and 500 laborers was accounted for at Makin.[64]

In view of the tremendous superiority of American ground forces to those of the enemy and the comparatively weak state of Japanese defenses, the ratio of American combat casualties to those of Japanese combat troops was remarkably high— about two to three. In other words, for every three Japanese fighters killed, two Americans were either killed or wounded. Thus the cost of taking Makin was not quite so low as it had first seemed.

Naval casualties incident to the capture of Butaritari were much higher than those of the ground forces. During the prelimi-

[57] 27th Inf Div G-3 Msg File, 23 Nov 43, Msg 38.
[58] 27th Inf Div G-4 Jnl, Min of Conf, 23 Nov 43.
[59] USS *Calvert* Action Rpt, 28 Nov 43; USS *Leonard Wood* Action Rpt, 20 Dec 43.
[60] 27th Inf Div G-3 Msg File, 24 Nov 43, Msg 26; USAFICPA Participation Rpt GALVANIC, pp. 17–18.
[61] 27th Inf Div G-4 Jnl, p. 11; 27th Inf Div G-2 Jnl, 24 Nov 43, Serial 9, 11.
[62] USAFICPA Participation Rpt GALVANIC, Annex X, Tables I and IV.
[63] 27th Inf Div G-2 Periodic Rpt 5.
[64] See above, p. 71.

nary naval bombardment on 20 November, the battleship *Mississippi* had a turret explosion resulting in the death of forty-three men and the wounding of nineteen others. More important was the sinking of the escort carrier *Liscome Bay*. On the morning of 24 November she was operating about twenty miles southwest of Butaritari in company with two other escort carriers, all under command of Rear Adm. Henry M. Mullinix, USN. At 0513 *Liscome Bay* was hit admidship by one or more torpedoes fired from an undetected enemy submarine. Her bombs and ammunition exploded and within twenty-three minutes she sank. Fifty-three officers, including Admiral Mullinix, and 591 enlisted men were lost and many others seriously wounded and burned.[65]

This sinking, occurring on D plus 4, gave point to an argument repeatedly put forth in naval circles that in amphibious operations time was of the essence, that ground operations prolonged beyond the time compelled by absolute necessity constituted an unacceptable risk to naval shipping and to the lives of naval personnel. *Liscome Bay* when torpedoed was standing by to furnish air cover for Admiral Turner's attack force on its voyage back to Oahu. Had the capture of Makin been conducted more expeditiously, she would have departed the danger area before 24 November, the morning of the disaster.

General Holland Smith was later of the opinion that the capture of Makin was "infuriatingly slow."[66] Considering the size of the atoll, the nature of the enemy's defenses, and the great superiority of force enjoyed by the attacking troops, his criticism seems justified. It is all the more so when to the cost of tardiness is added the loss of a valuable escort aircraft carrier with more than half the hands aboard.

[65] Samuel Eliot Morison, HISTORY OF UNITED STATES NAVAL OPERATIONS IN WORLD WAR II, Vol. VII, *Aleutians, Gilberts, and Marshalls, June 1942-April 1944* (Boston: Little, Brown and Company, 1951), pp. 140–41.

[66] Smith, *Coral and Brass*, p. 125.

CHAPTER IX

The Capture of Tarawa

The seizure of Makin by the Northern Attack Force had proceeded with relative ease. The Southern Attack Force, commanded by Admiral Hill, which had the mission of capturing Tarawa, was faced with a numerically stronger and far better prepared enemy.[1] The landing force consisted of the 2d Marine Division less the 6th Marine Regiment, the latter originally being held in corps reserve for employment at either Makin or Tarawa. The division was commanded by General Julian Smith. His plan of attack called for the original assault landings to be made on the three westernmost beaches of the northern (lagoon) shore of Betio Island at the southwestern corner of the atoll. These landing beaches were designated, from west to east, Red Beaches 1, 2, and 3. The attack was to be made by three battalion landing teams under command of Col. David M. Shoup, commander of the 2d Marine Regimental Combat Team. The first three assault waves were to be carried from ship to shore in amphibian tractors, of which 125 had been made available to the division. Tanks would be boated in the fourth wave in LCM's, and the successive waves of infantry would be carried by standard personnel landing craft (LCVP's). One battalion of the 2d Marines was to be held in regimental reserve, and two battalions of the 8th Marines would be in division reserve.[2] *(Map IV)*

The Americans were opposed at Tarawa by an enemy garrison whose combat strength ran upward of 3,000 well-trained men. Most of these troops were concentrated on Betio Island. For about nine months fortifications along the island's perimeter and obstacles in the water approaches had been in process of construction. By 20 November 1943, the date of the invasion, Betio bristled with guns of all calibers, well protected in emplacements of steel, concrete, and thick coconut logs.[3]

Preliminaries to the Invasion

On 7 November most of the ships of Admiral Hill's Southern Attack Force (Task Force 53) had assembled at Efate for last-minute rehearsals. The 2d Marine Division had arrived in transports from Wellington, New Zealand, and Rear Adm. Howard F. Kingman had brought the supporting combat ships from Pearl Harbor. Following rehearsals and critiques, the force sailed for Betio on 13 November.[4]

Shortly after 2330 on 19 November the

---

[1] It is impossible in this volume, which is primarily a history of Army operations, to give to the capture of Tarawa the detailed attention that the comparative size and nature of the operation would otherwise warrant. For a fully detailed and accurate account of the capture of Tarawa see Stockman, *Tarawa*. This is the official Marine Corps account of the operation, published by the Historical Section, Division of Public Information, Headquarters, U.S. Marine Corps.
[2] See above, p. 43.
[3] See above, pp. 70–74.
[4] Stockman, *Tarawa*, p. 9.

JAPANESE NAVAL GUNS EMPLACED ON BETIO. *These 8-inch (200-mm.) guns were part of the fortifications installed on the island.*

convoy entered the seventeen-mile-wide channel between Maiana and Tarawa Atolls and, on reaching the open sea west of the atolls, swung north. The ships now moved directly to assume their station west of Betio. At 0356 the first transport began to lower its boats; the others followed within a few minutes. With the approach of daylight at 0550, it became apparent that the transports were too far to the south. The error, made because of a heavy southward current and the inaccuracy of the charts, brought the transports within range of the enemy's coastal guns on Betio.[5]

Japanese patrol planes had spotted the convoy on the 19th if not earlier, and therefore by D Day the enemy had had time to man his defensive positions.[6] Shortly after 0200 on 20 November the approaching convoy had been detected, evidently by radar, and the Japanese had made their final preparations for defense. They held fire until the vessels halted and preparations for landing were begun.[7] At 0441 the island commander, Admiral Shibasaki, ordered a red star cluster fired over Betio Island, the signal for the garrison to prepare to fire. Twenty-six minutes later a coastal battery on the western end of Betio opened up.[8]

---

[5] TF 53 Rpt of Tarawa Opns, 13 Dec 43, Incl A, p. 9.

[6] CINCPAC-CINCPOA Translation 10018.

[7] Army Section, Imperial GHQ, Special Report on Lessons from the War, Vol. 25, Military Action in the Gilbert Islands Area, Nov 43, p. 3. (Translation in OCMH.)

[8] TF 53 Rpt of Tarawa Opns, 13 Dec 43, Incl A, p. 30.

The first Japanese shells landing in the midst of the American transports caused little damage. American warships returned fire immediately. The first salvo from the battleship *Colorado* was away at 0507, followed almost at once by shells of other support vessels including Admiral Hill's flagship *Maryland*. Within a short time one enemy gun was reported destroyed and its magazine exploded in a great cloud of fire. Other direct hits were believed scored soon afterwards. As U.S. naval gunfire grew in intensity, the Japanese were forced to take cover with resultant lack of accuracy.[9]

By 0542 the action of the naval gunfire support ships had neutralized, to some extent, Japanese attempts to halt the debarkation. The warships then ceased in order to allow the planes to begin their dawn air strike as planned. The planes, however, failed to arrive on schedule and with no naval gunfire to harass them, the enemy batteries resumed full fire and for thirty minutes peppered the transport area with shells. One transport after another reported near misses. Finally, at 0605, Admiral Hill ordered the fire support ships to reopen fire. Eight minutes later the planes arrived over the target for the scheduled air strike on the beaches. This lasted until 0622.[10]

Meanwhile, it had become apparent that the transports would have to move north out of range of the coastal batteries and the move was undertaken at 0619, being carried out during the period of the resumed naval gunfire and the air strikes. At approximately the same time Admiral Hill announced that W Hour, the scheduled time for the prelanding naval bombardment, would be at 0620.[11]

While the transports were making their way to safer berths, two mine sweepers, *Pursuit* and *Requisite,* moved toward the

entrance of the Tarawa lagoon. Close astern came two escorting destroyers, *Ringgold* and *Dashiell,* which were to take up fire support positions inside the lagoon once the entrance had been swept for mines. Following closely behind the destroyers were several small landing craft equipped with smoke pots designed to conceal the movements of the first waves as they crossed the line of departure. As *Pursuit,* which was in the lead, neared the lagoon entrance, shore batteries turned

[9] *Ibid.*

[10] *Ibid.;* 2d Marine Div Special Action Rpt Tarawa, 13 Jan 44, pp. 4–5.

Admiral Turner has offered as a possible explanation for the delay in the air strike the following: According to the original Air plan issued on 23 October, the dawn air strikes at both Makin and Tarawa were to begin at 0545 and end at 0615. Later, the Air representatives on the various naval staffs objected to such an early strike because their experience had demonstrated that shortly before sunrise airplane pilots, themselves high up in sunshine and thus good targets, could not distinguish their own individual targets hidden in the darkness below. Hence, on 5 November it was agreed by all the principal commanders present at the rehearsals of Task Force 52 in the Hawaiian area that the air strike should be postponed from 0545 until 0610. Admiral Pownall, in command of the carrier task force, was informed of this change of plan and in fact his pilots came in at Tarawa only three minutes late according to the revised schedule. Admiral Hill was at Efate when the revised plan was decided upon, and it is apparent that he was not aware of the change. Admiral Turner suggests one of three possibilities to explain the failure of co-ordination of the dawn strike at Tarawa: (a) either Turner's staff did not send the change in plan to Hill; or (b) due to a failure in fast mail or radio communications, Hill did not receive the change; or (c) having received the change, Hill's staff failed to act on it. (Ltr, Adm Turner to Gen Ward, 12 Feb 52, Incl 1, p. 12.) When interviewed, Admiral Hill was unable to throw further light on this subject (Interv, Philip A. Crowl with Vice Adm Harry W. Hill, 9 Apr 52), nor do the records consulted help to solve the mystery. At any rate, if Admiral Turner's conjecture is sound, the aviators of Task Force 50 must be absolved from blame in delivering their dawn strike later than was expected.

[11] TF 53 Rpt of Tarawa Opns, 13 Dec 43, Incl A, p. 31.

their attention to this little vessel. Water-spouts rose in the air as shells landed near-by. Aboard the mine sweeper, machine guns and heavier weapons returned fire, and *Ringgold* and *Dashiell* joined with their 5-inch guns. At 0646 *Pursuit* pushed through the entrance channel. No mines were found, and at 0715 the mine sweeper took position as control vessel at the line of departure inside the lagoon. Still returning fire, the vessel swung to face the lagoon entrance. Behind it dense clouds of dust and smoke obscured the island and hung low over the water. To make certain that the line of departure would be clearly marked, *Pursuit* turned on her searchlight. The vessel still had suffered no serious damage.[12]

The two destroyers pushed into the lagoon a few minutes behind the mine sweepers and immediately came under heavy fire.[13] *Ringgold* started firing with all batteries as soon as she was inside the reef line. At 0711 she suffered a direct hit from a 5-inch gun, the shell entering the after engine room, completely disrupting the water, steam, and electricity supply to the after part of the ship. Moments later another shell glanced off the barrel of a forward torpedo tube, passing through sick bay and into the emergency radio room. The ship continued to maneuver in spite of the damage, trying to locate the larger weapons that were firing on the ships inside the lagoon.[14]

While the fire support vessels were moving to the lagoon, the first waves of amphibian tractors and landing craft began their move from the rendezvous areas toward the line of departure inside the lagoon. It soon became apparent that they would be late in arriving. The LVT's had to contend with choppy seas, a strong head wind, and a receding tide. Furthermore,

many of the vehicles were in poor mechanical condition.[15]

Pursuit, which had begun to track the landing waves by radar, reported that they were approximately forty minutes behind schedule.[16] Fifteen minutes later, further reports showed that only a little over 500 yards had been traversed. In the air above, observation planes gave various estimates of the distance to be traveled to the beaches and the probable times of landing. There were many discrepancies in the reports, but all agreed that the landings would be late. As a result, Admiral Hill notified all vessels and troop commanders at 0803 that H Hour would be delayed until 0845. Twenty minutes later it was changed once more—to 0900. These messages, however, failed to reach the fighter planes that were scheduled to strafe the beaches immediately before the first troops landed. Operating on the assumption that H Hour was still 0830 the planes started their strafing mission at 0825, and naval fire had to lift until the planes had cleared from the area.[17]

Even this much of a delay proved overly optimistic. In fact, the first amphibian tractor to touch the beach did not arrive until 0910. Although the mine sweeper *Pursuit* and one observation plane had already reported that 0900 was too early by at least fifteen minutes to expect the first touchdown, Admiral Hill nevertheless ordered all naval gunfire, except for that of two destroyers, to cease by 0855.

[12] *Ibid.;* CINCPAC-CINCPOA Opns in POA, Nov 43, Annex E, p. 10.
[13] USS *Ringgold* Action Rpt, 21 Oct 43–2 Dec 43, pp. 9–10.
[14] *Ibid.*
[15] CINCPAC-CINCPOA Opns in POA, Nov 43, Annex E, p. 11.
[16] USS *Pursuit* Action Rpt, 6 Dec 43, p. 4.
[17] TF 53 Rpt of Tarawa Opns, 13 Dec 43, Incl A, p. 32.

WESTERN END OF BETIO AFTER BOMBARDMENT. *Open area in right center is the end of the airstrip runway. Red Beach 1 is shown in upper right. Note coastal fortifications in foreground.*

He reasoned that to continue naval fire through the heavy smoke that lay over the lagoon was too risky to the assault troops as they moved toward shore. Planes came in again for a five-minute strike at 0855, but from 0900 until 0910, except on Red Beach 3 at which two destroyers were still firing, the Japanese were left unhampered to reinforce their beach positions and direct accurate fire of all types on the approaching vehicles.[18]

What had been the effect of all this terrible pounding of Betio from air and ship on the morning of the landing? A total of about 3,000 tons of naval projectiles alone had been thrown against the enemy in the four hours before the first troops touched down.[19] From the point of view of one observer, Admiral Kingman, who commanded the fire support group responsible for the island's bombardment, "it seemed almost impossible for any human being to be alive on Betio." [20]

This of course proved to be an illusion, as the marines ashore were soon to discover to their sorrow. Yet certain concrete results can be attributed to the preliminary bombardment. At least one 8-inch coast defense battery and two 120-mm. antiaircraft batteries were silenced by naval gunfire after receiving direct hits. Everything above ground or in open pits, such as personnel,

---

[18] *Ibid.*
[19] V Phib Corps GALVANIC Rpt, Incl F, Sec. II, p. 2.
[20] TG 53.4 (Fire Support Group) Action Rpt, 17–22 Nov 43, p. 2.

bombs, and trucks, was probably destroyed. Camouflage screens over dugouts and bombproof shelters were wiped away. Most important was the fact that Shibasaki's network of telephone wire, most of which was laid above ground, was to all intents and purposes obliterated, and his system of signal communications was completely paralyzed.[21]

However, even this destruction was not enough. Along the beaches there were many pillboxes of concrete, coconut logs, and steel, most of which were not destroyed.[22] On Red Beaches 2 and 3 there were at least five machine guns manned and firing at the troops as they advanced over the reef toward the shore. As Admiral Hill put it, "that was five too many." [23] To the marines who led the assault on Betio without any armor heavier than their helmets and the shirts on their backs, this was a gross understatement.

The Landings on Red Beach 1

The 3d Battalion, 2d Marines, which was to land on Red Beach 1, had placed two companies in the first three waves of LVT's. Company K was to land on the left of the battalion zone, while Company I, on the right, was to touch down on the extreme northwest corner of the island. Each was to be supported by elements of the heavy weapons unit, Company M. The third rifle company of the battalion, Company L, was boated in the fourth and fifth waves along with the mortar platoon of Company M. Maj. John F. Schoettel, battalion commander, was with the fourth wave.[24]

Red Beach 1 presented the only irregular shore line on Betio Island, a deep cove indenting the island just east of its western tip. The boundary between the zone of action of the 3d Battalion and the 2d Battalion, 2d Marines, just east of it, lay almost at the point where the shore line straightened out to sweep in a fairly regular line toward the island tail. All along the reaches of Red Beach 1 lay a coconut log barricade, erected as an obstacle over which invading troops must crawl. The barricade was separated from the water on the western half of the beach by approximately twenty yards of coral sand. On the east the beach was much narrower, and in most places the water lapped at the base of the logs. High tide would cover all of the beach strip within the cove.

The amphibian tractors of the 3d Battalion were the first by two or three minutes to land on Betio Island. As they reached the reef and clambered over it they met heavy fire from machine guns and antiboat weapons. The LVT's had been under scattered fire since leaving the line of departure, but the volume that fell upon the tractors as they waddled over the reef toward the beach was so heavy that it caused considerable disorganization in the three waves. The principal source of enemy fire seemed to be one large emplacement at the left extremity of Red Beach 1, between it and Red Beach 2. The Japanese here were in a position to rake the entire approach formation. By the time the initial wave climbed out of the water at 0910, casualties in Company K were already so great as to make it extremely doubtful whether that unit could establish a foothold on the shore.

---

[21] TF 53 Rpt of Tarawa Opns, 13 Dec 43, Incl A, p. 48.

[22] V Phib Corps GALVANIC Rpt, Incl F, Sec. II, p. 2.

[23] TF 53 Rpt of Tarawa Opns, 13 Dec 43, Incl A, p. 48.

[24] 2d Marine Regt Rpt of Opns on Betio Island, 20–24 Nov 43, Incl G, Account of Tarawa Opns by 3d Bn 2d Marines (hereafter cited as 3d Bn 2d Marine Action Rpt), p. 1.

RED BEACH 1. *Damaged LVT's and floating bodies testify to the ferocity of Japanese resist-ance at the junction of Red Beaches 1 and 2.*

In Company I, which was farther away from the troublesome strong point, casualties were less heavy at the outset, though by 1100 both companies had sustained 50 percent casualties.[25] The movement toward the island had been steady. Here and there, a tractor, hit and burning, was stopped dead in the water. If its occupants were alive and able to do so, they climbed over the sides and tried to wade ashore. From those vehicles that pulled up before the log barricade, the marines jumped to seek whatever cover the barricade afforded. Company K found itself under heavy machine gun fire from the strong position on its left and the bullets sweeping up the narrow sand shelf kept the men's heads to the ground and forbade movement. Company I found the barricade offered some

protection from the fire. Within a few minutes, the riflemen of this company began to infiltrate inland. As already indicated, during movement of the 3d Battalion toward the beaches LVT's had been hit and were either destroyed or burning. As the fourth wave, including some tanks, approached the beach, the men could see, ahead of them through the smoke and dust from the island, the disabled vehicles.

Everywhere the lagoon was marked with the telltale splashes of bullets and larger caliber shells. The first LCM's and LCVP's discovered there was not enough water to float their landing craft beyond the reef line. Coxswains of some of the tank lighters turned their craft away, seemingly

[25] *Ibid.*, pp. 1–2.

in search of another more favorable landing site. The command boat came up just as the LCM's were turning, and Major Schoettel immediately ordered them to the beach.[26] Company L, under the command of Maj. Michael P. Ryan, arrived at the reef at this critical moment and the company commander ordered his men into the water to wade ashore.

On the beach most of Company K and part of Company I were drawn up before the log barricade. To the left of Red Beach 1 the formidable emplacement at the battalion boundary had a clear field of fire all along the narrow strip of sand between the water and the sea wall. Company K, which had already suffered heavily during the landing, now had to lie in the exposed area under constant fire, incurring further casualties. Company I, which had had fewer losses during the ship-to-shore movement and on the beach, had pushed inland for fifty yards. Until 1100 there was little if any communication between the two assault companies. Company K, after being pinned down to the narrow sand beach, had finally managed to push a few men over the coconut barrier and to a point fifty yards inland from the shore, about the same distance as that reached by the unit on the right.

More than half of Red Beach 1 was still in the hands of the enemy. Along the eastern half, particularly at the main emplacement on the Red Beach 2 boundary, the Japanese were still active and causing considerable damage to troops trying to get ashore. Company L was severely hit while wading in, losing about 35 percent of its strength before reaching the beach on the west end of the island.[27]

The platoon of medium tanks attached to the 3d Battalion had been ordered by Major Schoettel to debark and the tanks were put into the water at the reef line, about 1,200 yards from dry land, while Company L was still struggling through the water toward shore. In front of them went the tank reconnaissance men to place guide flags in the potholes offshore.

As soon as the guides entered the water, they were subjected to fierce fire from the enemy. Although the tanks came in safely in spite of this fire, most of the guides were killed or wounded. The vehicles came ashore on the left half of Red Beach 1, in the area swept most severely by Japanese fire. The sand was covered with the bodies of dead or wounded marines who could not yet be moved because of the intense fire. Rather than run the heavy tanks over these inert forms, the platoon commander decided to go back into the water, around to the extreme right flank of the beach, and then move inland from there. As the tanks executed this maneuver, four of them fell into potholes in the coral reef and were drowned out. Only two were able to make shore and these were shortly knocked out by 40-mm. gun fire.[28]

Major Schoettel had returned to the reef after rounding up the tank lighters and dispatching them to the reef's edge. The scene confronting him was extremely confused. The men of Company L were in the water and Schoettel could see most of them wading ashore. The heavy fire from the beaches was readily apparent. It was obviously coming from the position on the boundary between the two beaches, and when the battalion commander and his group began to debark from their landing craft they were brought under the same fire. Faced with the choice of wading ashore and probably losing all of his com-

[26] *Ibid.*, p. 2.
[27] *Ibid.*, p. 2.
[28] *Ibid.*, p. 3.

DISABLED LVT *in the water at the junction of Red Beaches 1 and 2. Note shattered M1 rifle on the deck and tank turret showing above the water off the stern of the LVT.*

mand group or remaining on the reef where he could direct fire against the enemy position, Schoettel chose the latter. Having established his command post on the reef and made contact with Company K by radio, Major Schoettel reported to Colonel Shoup, commander of the 2d Marine Regimental Combat Team, who was located on Red Beach 2, and explained the situation to him. Colonel Shoup ordered the major to land with the fourth wave on Red Beach 2 and work from there onto Red Beach 1. Major Schoettel, however, was unable to get ashore until late afternoon.[29]

During the morning several requests were made for air strikes against the main beach position.[30] One air strike was eventually delivered at approximately 1120, but immediately brought complaints from Company K that friendly troops were being strafed and was accordingly discontinued.[31]

Operations at Red Beach 2

The 2d Battalion, 2d Marines, was scheduled to land at Red Beach 2 with Company F on the left and Company E on the right and Company G in support.[32] Red Beach 2 extended from the eastern curve of the cove to Central Pier. As on Red Beach 1, a four-foot-high log barri-

[29] 2d Marine Div D-3 Jnl, 19–20 Nov 43, p. 9.
[30] *Ibid.*, pp. 9–13.
[31] 2d Marine Regt Unit Jnl Tarawa Opn, 20 Nov 43, p. 2.
[32] 2d Marine Regt Rpt of Opns on Betio Island, 20–24 Nov 43, Incl F, Summary of Tarawa Opn by 2d Bn 2d Marines (hereafter cited as 2d Bn 2d Marines Action Rpt), p. 2.

LANDINGS AT RED BEACH 2. *Troops wade ashore (above). The beach after the attack (below); note half-submerged tanks in center background.*

cade had been constructed to form a sea wall. For the most part the barricade lay about twenty yards from the water's edge, thus leaving a narrow open strip of deep coral sand over which the marines would have to move after leaving the water. The enemy had constructed pillboxes and shelters along the barricade at intervals, and the defenders in these positions could keep the narrow sand strip and its approaches under heavy fire.

As the three original landing waves headed for Red Beach 2 they were subjected to heavy concentrated fire from all along the beach, the heaviest coming from the same positions on the boundary that were causing the 3d Battalion so much trouble on the right.

There was no possibility of sideslipping out of range of the enemy's guns, although troops that were not mounted on LVT's could find some protection by wading ashore under Central Pier. As soon as the first LVT's climbed over the reef on their way to shore, the scene in the 2d Battalion zone became one of almost indescribable confusion. LVT's were hit by all types of gunfire. Some of them were disabled and lay helpless in the water. Crews and assault troops climbed over the side and waded toward shore. When their vehicles were hit, the drivers of some LVT's lost control and veered off course. Others, seeking vainly to escape the direct frontal fire, eventually landed on Red Beach 1. Even before the first waves had landed on Red Beach 2, reserve elements coming to the reef in LCVP's found that there was not enough water to float the small craft over the shelf. The men in the boats without hesitation leaped into the water for the long trek to shore.

Company F landed on the left half of the beach, near the base of the pier. This unit,

decimated on the way to shore, could do little more than take possession of the sand strip in its immediate area. Some of the men pushed over to the coconut log barrier and took cover behind it. A few others were able to crawl over the barrier and move inland, but at no point did the hold on the beach extend more than fifty yards inland. For the time being everyone was forced to dig in and hold the small area gained in landing. From hidden dugouts on either flank, from pillboxes just behind the barrier, and from trees just inland, the Japanese poured a merciless fire into the men lying in the coral sand.[33]

Once ashore, the units on Red Beach 2 found it impossible to establish firm physical contact. One platoon of Company E had landed on Red Beach 1 in an isolated position. The other two platoons had established a toe hold comparable to that seized by Company F, but so far toward the western end of Red Beach 2 as to prevent coordination of the efforts of the two companies. When Company G, the reserve, landed in the center of Red Beach 2, it was also immediately pinned down on the narrow coral strip and was unable to move forward over the sea wall. There was no opportunity for the men to organize when they reached the beach. In little groups of two and three, sometimes even as individuals, they dug foxholes in the sand or sought shelter beneath the log barricade. The few men who were able to crawl over the retaining wall were isolated and cut off.[34]

Companies G and E made physical contact soon after reaching the beach, but it was not until late in the day that a firm line was formed by all three companies of the battalion. The complete disorganiza-

[33] *Ibid.*, pp. 1–3.
[34] *Ibid.*

tion of the troops on Red Beach 2 may be seen from the composition of Company F in the late afternoon. At that time the company commander had under his control six men from Company F, sixteen from Company E, ten from Company C, and fifteen from Company H.

The 2d Battalion lost its commander, Lt. Col. Herbert R. Amey, during the landing. Approaching the reef in an LCM in the fourth wave, which included half of the battalion headquarters group and a few observers, and discovering that there was not enough water to float the lighter beyond that point, Colonel Amey hailed two passing LVT's on their return from the beach. The headquarters group scrambled into the tracked vehicles and started toward shore. While still 200 yards from land, the tractor containing Colonel Amey was stopped by barbed wire. Rather than spend time circling to look for a passage the battalion commander ordered his men over the side to wade ashore. As the group waded toward the barbed wire, a burst of machine gun fire killed Colonel Amey and wounded three others. The remainder of the headquarters immediately splashed to cover behind an abandoned boat. Since Maj. Howard J. Rice, the battalion executive, had landed on Red Beach 1, Lt. Col. Walter I. Jordan, an observer from the 4th Marine Division, assumed command of the 2d Battalion until Major Rice could rejoin his men. The command post was eventually set up in a shell hole in the middle of Red Beach 2. Salt water or enemy machine gun fire had rendered the battalion's radios useless, and communication with the widely scattered elements, except by runner, was impossible. It was not until well after 1000 that a runner system began functioning on Red Beach 2. Even then, no attempt could be made to expand the area

seized by the first landing waves. Each of the companies and the command post group had to give full attention to survival. Huddled along the coconut log barrier, moving only when necessary, the battalion turned its efforts to eliminating the enemy positions that jutted out onto the beach itself. Groups from the 18th Marines (Engineers) that had landed with the first waves moved up and down the narrow beach area blowing up dugouts and emplacements with demolitions. Behind the battalion the water was filled with amphibian tractors and debris. Troops still struggled to get ashore, some wading, others approaching gingerly in commandeered landing tractors. Practically all the marines who came ashore in this area had chosen the relative shelter of Long Pier and were trying to push toward the beaches by threading their way along the piling.

Unlike the situation at Red Beach 1, where ship-to-shore movement all but ceased during the period immediately following the original assault, attempts to get troops ashore on Red Beach 2 were continuous. Command groups and reserve elements landed through the lagoon in amphibian tractors or waded in beside Central Pier throughout the day. During the whole period, the approaches to Red Beach 2 were under constant heavy machine gun and antiboat fire.[35]

The Landings at Red Beach 3

The original landings on the extreme left were scheduled to be made by the 2d Battalion, 8th Marines, under Maj. Henry P. Crowe. The battalion had been attached to the 2d Marines for the operation. The two assault companies were E and F, sup-

---

[35] 18th Marines Combat Rpt, Incl A, Rpt of Co A, 1st Bn 18th Marines, pp. 3–7; Stockman, *Tarawa*, p. 17.

ported by one platoon of Company G. One reason that this landing was considerably more successful than the others was the longer period of naval bombardment before the landing. The fire from the two destroyers in the Red Beach 3 area lasted until seven minutes before the first LVT reached shore. Although heavy fire of all types greeted the first waves, it was not as effective as that on the other beaches. One LVT received a direct hit and was stopped in the water, and a few casualties were inflicted on other landing craft. The number of men lost in the battalion totaled under twenty-five. Five of these casualties, officers of Company E, were hit as they debarked from their respective landing craft on the beach next to Central Pier.

Two of Company E's LVT's found a hole in the coconut log barricade and drove through, continuing as far inland as the triangle formed by the main airstrip and taxiways. The rest of Company E lost no time in following on foot, and within a few minutes after the first wave was ashore a substantial beachhead extending to the airfield had been established. Company F, on the extreme left flank of Red Beach 3, had less success but did establish a hold with its left flank anchored on the short pier known as Burns-Philp Wharf. Before this company could expand its hold to reach the inland line of Company E, it was met by serious counterfire from a strong Japanese position a few yards to its left front. The supporting platoon of Company G landed without incident, moved along in the wake of Company E, mopping up several enemy positions, and eventually extending the left flank of the assault back toward Company F. No firm physical contact between the left and right companies was established, however, until late in the day.[36]

Reinforcing the Beachhead

Colonel Shoup and the command group of the 2d Marines had followed close behind the assault waves in an LCVP and arrived at the reef a few minutes after the first wave reached the beach. When it became apparent that the landing craft in which he was boated could not get over the reef, the regimental commander hailed an LVT that was ferrying casualties back from the beach. The wounded men were transferred to the LCVP and Colonel Shoup and his party started for Red Beach 2. After three separate attempts to reach shore, all of which were halted by heavy gunfire, the party was forced to debark when the tractor's engine stopped. By 1030 the whole group was wading ashore along Central Pier. Shortly afterwards the command post was established ashore on Red Beach 2.[37]

Colonel Shoup had maintained constant radio communication with all three of his landing team commanders until Colonel Amey was killed. Shoup later regained contact with Colonel Jordan through the radio of the 2d Battalion, 8th Marines. Information from Red Beach 1 was scanty, owing to the failure of Major Schoettel to get ashore.

In addition to the three companies of the 3d Battalion, 2d Marines, other scattered units of the assault force had come ashore on Red Beach 1, principally from the 2d Battalion, 2d Marines, originally scheduled for Red Beach 2. The landing craft carrying these battalion units had been driven to the right, either by the heavy fire

---

[36] 2d Marine Regt Rpt of Opns on Betio Island, 20–24 Nov 43, Incl H, Rpt of Tarawa Opns by 2d Bn 8th Marines (hereafter cited as 2d Bn 8th Marines Action Rpt), pp. 1–2.

[37] *Ibid.*, pp. 1–2; Stockman, *Tarawa*, pp. 16–17.

RED BEACH 3. *Marines take cover behind the sea wall on the beach (above). A medium tank supports the attack, Burns-Philp Wharf in the background (below).*

from the strong point between the two beaches or by mechanical failures of the LVT's. One platoon of Company E, one platoon of Company G, two platoons of Company H, the 2d Battalion executive officer, Major Rice, and a portion of the battalion headquarters company landed at the northwestern corner of the island on Red Beach 1. Immediately upon landing, Major Rice attempted to rejoin his own battalion on Red Beach 2, but because of the strong point between the two beaches his attempts were to prove unsuccessful.[38]

While still afloat, Colonel Shoup decided to commit his reserve. The reports from the 2d Battalion, at this time principally from Major Rice who described his unit as isolated and pinned on the beach, and the absence of information from Red Beach 1, seemed to indicate to the regimental commander that the situation was more precarious on the two right-hand beaches. At 0958 he therefore ordered Maj. Wood B. Kyle, commander of the 1st Battalion, 2d Marines, to land on Red Beach 2 and work to the west toward Red Beach 1 in an attempt to assist the 3d Battalion in that area.[39]

Major Kyle moved at once to the reef but found, as others had before him, that the landing craft in which he was boated could not negotiate the shallow water between there and shore. By this time, approximately 1030, more LVT's from the original landing waves were returning to the reef line. Major Kyle set about at once to secure as many of these as possible. At 1100 he had commandeered enough of them to boat Companies A and B. Company C remained at the reef until additional vehicles could be procured and did not land until after 1300.[40] Meanwhile, during the transfer of the two assault companies of the battalion, enemy fire had

continued heavy throughout the lagoon. Three of the 1st Battalion's boats were sunk by direct hits during the debarkation. When the LVT's turned and started again for the beach they were met by the same intense fire that had greeted the units landing earlier. In the ensuing twenty minutes many of the tractors received hits from large-caliber shells or were riddled with bullets. As in the case of the early assault waves, many marines were forced to take to the water and wade ashore with resultant heavy casualties. The tractors on the right were forced off course. A total of one officer and 110 men thus landed on Red Beach 1 and eventually joined the 2d and 3d Battalions.

The orders committing the reserve battalion had been intercepted aboard the flagship *Maryland* and at 1018 General Julian Smith ordered Col. Elmer E. Hall, commander of the 8th Marine Regimental Combat Team, to release one battalion landing team of his regiment, which was in division reserve, to Colonel Shoup at the line of departure.[41] The 3d Battalion, 8th Marines, at this time debarking from its transport, was designated for the job. The landing craft bearing this battalion left the line of departure at 1200 for Red Beach 3. The battalion, boated in LCVP's, found it impossible to proceed farther than the reef line and, like others before them, debarked to wade ashore. At the particular point of debarkation the water was deep, and a few of the heavily laden marines drowned. The others were taken under heavy fire from the beaches as they waded their way

---

[38] 2d Bn 2d Marines Action Rpt, pp. 2–4.
[39] 2d Marine Regt Rpt of Opns on Betio Island, 20–24 Nov 43, Incl E, Rpt of Tarawa Opns by 1st Bn 2d Marines (hereafter cited as 1st Bn 2d Marines Action Rpt), p. 1.
[40] *Ibid.*, pp. 1, 2.
[41] 2d Mar Div D-3 Jnl, 19–20 Nov 43, p. 9.

to shore. Within the space of a few minutes severe casualties had been suffered by the battalion, and the survivors gravitated to Central Pier to make their way inland. It was late afternoon before elements of the battalion were able to take an effective part in the action.[42]

*Development of the Situation
on 20 November*

By early afternoon of D Day five battalions of marines had been committed at Tarawa. All but one had sustained heavy casualties and were in a badly disorganized state. On Red Beach 1 elements of three battalions supported by two medium tanks were fighting virtually separate actions. On Red Beach 2 elements of two battalions struggled to hold the ground they had seized in the landings and fought to clear out the positions from which fire was being placed on the narrow beach area. Some attempt was made to expand the beachhead, but with little success. On Red Beach 3 the early successes of Company E, 8th Marines, were consolidated, and the major effort was directed toward the reduction of the troublesome enemy positions near Burns-Philp Wharf.

*The Action Along the Western End
of the Island*

As already related, Major Ryan, the commander of Company L, had assumed command of all elements of the 3d Battalion, 2d Marines, ashore on Red Beach 1 shortly after his arrival there. For two hours after the two assault companies had established firm physical contact, Major Ryan sought to organize the battalion's remnants for a drive across the island. With the arrival of the two medium tanks

early in the afternoon, this aggressive officer was finally able to drive forward toward the south shore of Betio. Working from shelter to shelter, small detachments made steady progress. The support of the two tanks was extremely valuable, but midway in the engagement one was disabled by a direct hit from an enemy gun and the other was damaged in a duel with an enemy tank. By that time Major Ryan's force had moved to within 300 yards of the south shore of the island, and the commander was anxiously trying to reach higher headquarters with the information that part of Green Beach, on the west coast of Betio, was available for landing reserves.[43]

Major Ryan's reports of the conditions on Red Beach 1 failed to reach their destination, and the suitability of Green Beach for landings was not yet realized. Neither General Julian Smith nor Colonel Shoup was optimistic about the situation on Red Beach 1. Both officers, who had received their information during the morning from reports of Major Schoettel, were under the impression that the position of the 3d Battalion, 2d Marines, was extremely tenuous.[44] It was only at 1800, when Colonel Shoup finally succeeded in establishing radio contact with Major Ryan, that the real situation became known. Major Ryan, in the meantime, had withdrawn his lines into a more compact defensive position and reported that the 3d Battalion held a beachhead approximately 300 yards deep and 150 yards wide.

Elsewhere in the Red Beach 1 area little progress had been made. Throughout the afternoon the units under Major Rice's

---

[42] 3d Bn 8th Marines Special Action Rpt, 1 Dec 43, pp. 1–2.

[43] 3d Bn 2d Marines Action Rpt; Stockman, *Tarawa*, p. 22.

[44] 2d Marine Div D-3 Jnl, 19–20 Nov 43, p. 10.

DAMAGED MEDIUM TANK M4

command had fought to destroy the positions separating the western beach from Red Beach 2. Many of the marines who had landed near the northwestern tip of the island continued to be pinned down on the narrow coral sand strip between the water's edge and the coconut barricade that had been erected twenty yards inland. The stubborn system of Japanese defensive positions at the boundary between beaches continued to pour fire into this confined space. As darkness fell, several hundred yards still separated the landing forces on the two beaches.[45]

Completion of the Action on D Day

Elsewhere on Betio Island the situation of the troops improved only slightly during the day. On Red Beach 3, Major Crowe's battalion bent its efforts toward eliminating the strong steel-reinforced position on its left flank. In vicious fighting throughout the afternoon, the Japanese resisted efforts to destroy the position. Buildings near it were set on fire by marines, tanks and flame throwers were brought into play, and one section of 37-mm. guns was lifted above the sea wall to take the position under direct fire. The 1st Platoon of Company F, nearest the beach, was pinned down most of the afternoon by a constant shower of grenades and machine gun fire. Late in the afternoon the 2d Platoon of Company F was virtually wiped out while trying to circle the emplacement on its inland side. The action of the tanks and guns did succeed in breaking up one tank-supported Japanese counterattack.[46]

[45] Stockman, *Tarawa*, p. 22.
[46] 2d Bn 8th Marines Action Rpt, pp. 2, 3.

DAMAGED JAPANESE TYPE 95 LIGHT TANK ON BETIO

On the right of Major Crowe's line, Companies E and G, supported and reinforced by elements of the 3d Battalion, 8th Marines, consolidated their hold on the area between the beach and the airstrip triangle. The advanced positions, however, were under constant rifle and machine gun fire from bypassed Japanese defenders who had utilized every conceivable hiding place from which to harass the invaders.

The most confused situation on the island at nightfall was on Red Beach 2 where the 2d Battalion, 2d Marines, had been unable to organize a sustained attack from the narrow toe hold originally established on the beach. Some small detachments had penetrated 125 yards inland from the sea wall, while others still remained pinned down on the narrow sand strip at the water's edge. Units were disor-

ganized and scrambled, and large gaps existed in the lines throughout the zone of action. The 1st Battalion, 2d Marines, had bolstered the 2d Battalion at various places, but there was no organized line. One company commander later described the situation as "impossible to control." No officer knew where all the component elements of his command were, nor did he have the necessary communications to control those he could not see.[47]

Supply, Communications, and Command

Original supply plans of the 2d Division had called for a routine discharge of cargo from the transports into available lighterage following debarkation of assault troops.

---

[47] 2d Bn 2d Marines Action Rpt, pp. 2ff.

These barges were to follow the landing waves ashore, at first in waves and later, as dumps were established ashore, moving as directed by the control boat as fast as the beach could handle them. Attempts to follow this plan soon failed. Discharge of cargo from transports was effected rapidly, but the supply barges, when they arrived at the reef line, found it impossible to reach the beaches. During the earlier part of the day LVT's were kept busy ferrying reserve troops ashore and had little time for transporting supplies. In this situation many of the small craft loaded with supplies returned to the line of departure and waited there for further orders. By early afternoon a confused jam of boats had concentrated near the entrance to the lagoon. Some supply craft did move to the end of Central Pier and there discharged their loads, but the movement of supplies along the pier to the beaches was as difficult from that point as it was from the reef itself. This was partly because a section of the log structure had been burnt out by earlier American action and partly because of the intense fire that the enemy placed along the pier. In many cases the reserve troops that worked their way shoreward along the pier throughout the day carried some of the more vitally needed supplies, such as water, ammunition, and plasma, ashore with them. By nightfall several carrying parties had been organized under the direction of Brig. Gen. Leo D. Hermle, assistant division commander, and Maj. Stanley E. Larsen, executive officer of the 3d Battalion, 8th Marines. The carrying parties worked throughout the night to get supplies ashore. Some supplies were also ferried ashore in LVT's on D Day, but the amount was negligible.[48]

The supply situation brought into sharp focus another pressing problem of the Tarawa invasion force—that of communications. Colonel Shoup had radioed to the transports intermittently throughout the day asking for more ammunition, water, and medical supplies. As these calls reached the ships they heightened the confusion there. The transport commanders had been dispatching boatloads of cargo since early morning, under the impression that they were arriving safely at the beaches. Because no accurate picture of the situation between the transports and the beach was available, the transport group commander, Capt. Henry B. Knowles, USN, sent Maj. Ben K. Weatherwax, assistant supply officer of the division, ashore to determine the exact status of supplies there. This mission, begun at 2100, took until dawn to complete. Major Weatherwax found that Colonel Shoup had received virtually none of the supplies dispatched to him and that the majority of boats containing the badly needed materials was still at the line of departure. One of the ironical features of Major Weatherwax's mission came when he tried to transmit this information back to Captain Knowles by radio. Two different attempts to reach the naval commander failed, and eventually the supply officer had to make the long, tortuous trip back along the pier to a landing boat and report to the transport in person.[49]

The failure of communications had other serious consequences. Aboard *Maryland,* the only information that the division commander, General Julian Smith, had,

[48] TG 53.1 Rpt on Tarawa Opns, 1 Dec 43, p. 2; Stockman, *Tarawa,* pp. 25–26; Ltr, CG 2d Marine Div to CG V Phib Corps, 2 Jan 44, sub; Recommendations Based on Tarawa Opn, No. 3, Ship-to-Shore Supplies, Beach and Shore Parties, p. 2, A 7–17, 2d Mar Div/Recommendation Tarawa, Gilbert Area files, Hist Branch, G-3, Hq USMC.
[49] Stockman, *Tarawa,* pp. 26–27.

came from the reports of observers in planes, intercepted radio messages, and a few direct reports from Colonel Shoup. At 1343 General Smith ordered General Hermle to proceed at once to the end of the pier, form an estimate of the situation ashore, and relay the estimate to *Maryland*.[50] The assistant division commander reported at 1710 that he was at the pier, but subsequent efforts to forward information to General Smith from that point proved unsuccessful. The messages had to be sent by hand to the nearest ship for relay to *Maryland*, with the result that they did not arrive at the command post for some time. For two hours General Hermle was able to talk to Colonel Shoup and Major Crowe and to assist in organizing supply and evacuation procedure at the pier. At 1930 all radio communications with the shore ceased, and General Hermle sent two officers along the pier to Colonel Shoup's command post on the beach. They returned at 0345 with an estimate of the situation ashore.[51] To transmit this to General Smith, General Hermle had to go to the destroyer *Ringgold*. Even then General Smith never received the message which included, among other things, a recommendation that the 1st Battalion, 8th Marines, be committed on Red Beach 2. Meanwhile, General Smith had ordered General Hermle to take command of troops ashore. This order, issued at 1750 on D Day, was never received by the assistant division commander.[52] Colonel Carlson, veteran of the Makin raid and now an observer who had landed with the assault troops, had left the beach at 1230 at the request of Colonel Shoup. He eventually reached *Maryland* with the first complete picture of Colonel Shoup's situation.[53]

The absence of a detailed estimate had not prevented General Smith from acting vigorously to relieve what he understood to be a precarious situation ashore. After releasing one battalion (the 3d) of the 8th Marines to Colonel Shoup, he ordered, at 1130, all the remaining elements of the 8th Marines to be boated. Next, he sent an inquiry to Shoup asking whether these elements were needed ashore.[54] The answer, received an hour and a half later, was a succinct "Yes."[55]

At 1625 General Smith ordered Colonel Hall, commander of the 8th Marines, to land on the eastern beaches. Colonel Hall was already afloat, waiting at the line of departure with the 1st Battalion for orders to land. General Smith's message was never received by him, and the remainder of the 8th Marines stayed afloat throughout the night waiting for the orders that never came. At division headquarters a message was received at 2019 that Colonel Hall had landed at Red Beach 2, and so no further orders were issued.[56] This erroneous report came from an air observer who had mistakenly identified the landing craft of the 1st Battalion, 10th Marines (Artillery), then heading for the shore as those belonging to the 1st Battalion, 8th Marines.[57]

The waves of the three assault battalions and the elements of the two reserve battalions had spent the day on or near the beaches with little or no resupply and very little in the way of support. Only two medium tanks had joined the force on Red Beach 1. Another platoon of mediums

---

[50] 2d Marine Div D-3 Jnl, 19–20 Nov 43, p. 17.

[51] Stockman, *Tarawa*, pp. 25, 26.

[52] 2d Marine Div D-3 Jnl, 19–20 Nov 43, p. 24; Stockman, *Tarawa*, p. 26.

[53] Stockman, *Tarawa*, p. 25.

[54] 2d Marine Div D-3 Jnl, 19–20 Nov 43, p. 9.

[55] *Ibid.*, p. 15.

[56] 2d Marine Div D-3 Jnl, 20–21 Nov 43, p. 2.

[57] Stockman, *Tarawa*, p. 24.

managed to get three vehicles ashore on Red Beach 2. These were eventually ordered by Colonel Shoup to move across the front to support the 3d Battalion, 2d Marines, on Red Beach 1. As they approached the formidable Japanese position between Red Beach 1 and Red Beach 2, however, they were halted by marines who told them they could not get through. The tanks were eventually put to work by the 2d Battalion, 2d Marines, and aided materially in eliminating several of the pillboxes and reinforced emplacements behind Red Beach 2. Two of the three vehicles were put out of action during the first day.

Four medium tanks of the 3d Platoon, Company C, 2d Tank Battalion, landed on Red Beach 3 shortly after the first waves had landed. Three were put out of action during the first two hours. The other, although set afire early on D Day, continued to operate in support of the 2d Battalion, 8th Marines, throughout the engagement.[58]

Most of the support afforded the men ashore on D Day was furnished by warships and carrier-based aircraft. It had been planned to land artillery on Red Beach 1 as soon as a sufficient beachhead had been established. The battalion selected for this mission was the 1st Battalion, 10th Marines (75-mm. pack howitzers), under Lt. Col Presley M. Rixey, USMC. Colonel Rixey landed on Tarawa as a member of Colonel Shoup's command group and took an active part in the direction of the landing operations. The artillery was held at the line of departure, however, until conditions ashore improved. Later in the afternoon it was decided to bring the howitzers ashore on Red Beach 2, rather than Red Beach 1 where the situation was still obscure. By the end of the day five gun sections of the battalion

had been brought ashore either in LVT's or by boat and hand-carry. This completed the build-up of assault forces on D Day.[59]

Consolidating the Beachhead: D plus 1

As night fell on Betio, the 2d Division faced its most critical period—everyone expected the Japanese to counterattack. At every point on the beachhead the hold was precarious. At 1911 General Smith had radioed Colonel Shoup, "Hold what you have."[60] Efforts to expand the beachhead were to be discontinued until morning. Under cover of darkness, however, the task of resupply and reinforcement was to proceed.

Activities during the night proved anticlimactic. Instead of making vicious attempts to drive the marines back into the sea, the Japanese allowed the hours of darkness to pass in relative quiet. Here and there small infiltrating groups of the enemy wandered into American lines. Some detachments even managed to swim out into the lagoon and man machine guns on old hulks west of Central Pier or to occupy burnt-out LVT's from which they could place fire on the approaches to the beaches. One Japanese unit attempted to recapture Burns-Philp Wharf, but was driven off by a patrol of the 2d Battalion, 8th Marines.[61]

As the second day on Betio dawned, the furious battle was renewed. The first American effort of the morning was aimed at landing the 1st Battalion, 8th Marines, which had remained afloat at the line of departure throughout the night. Division

[58] Ibid.
[59] Ibid., p. 28.
[60] 2d Marine Div D-3 Jnl, 20–21 Nov 43, p. 2.
[61] 2d Bn 8th Marines Action Rpt, p. 3.

headquarters had not learned the whereabouts of this battalion until after midnight when Colonel Hall was finally reached through the radios on *Pursuit*. First plans envisioned the landing of the remainder of the 8th Marines at the eastern end of the island. At 0513, however, division headquarters was notified that Colonel Shoup would prefer to have the battalion on Red Beach 2.[62] Accordingly, at 0615 the commander of the 1st Battalion, 8th Marines, Maj. Lawrence C. Hays, Jr., and his men clambered out of their landing craft at the reef line, just to the west of Central Pier. An hour later the first four waves were ashore, having suffered heavy casualties while wading to the beach.[63] Colonel Shoup immediately ordered Major Hays to reorganize and take up a position on the right flank of the 2d Battalion, 2d Marines. When ready, he was to launch an attack against the stubbornly defended position at the juncture of the two right-hand beaches in an effort to re-establish contact with the 3d Battalion, 2d Marines.[64]

Earlier, a serious attempt to eliminate the blockhouses on the battalion boundary had been made. During the landing of the 1st Battalion, 8th Marines, Colonel Rixey had put the pack howitzers of his 10th Marines in position to fire directly upon these emplacements. Using delay fuzes in order to penetrate the coral and log shelters, the howitzers succeeded in silencing the enemy's guns in this area, though only temporarily.[65]

Coincident with the attempt to bolster the men ashore with reinforcements, was the effort to straighten out the supply situation. The key to this seemed to lie in the assembly of landing craft and amphibian tractors that had been near the line of departure throughout most of the first night.

Early on the morning of 21 November, Capt. John B. McGovern, USN, commander of Transport Group 4, was sent to *Pursuit* to take control of the ship-to-shore movement of supplies. By 1000 Captain McGovern had commandeered eighteen LVT's with which, in conjunction with Marine Corps supply officers, he instituted a ferrying system in which the amphibian tractors shuttled supplies to shore and evacuated wounded from the beaches to the control vessel.[66]

Colonel Shoup from dawn until 1000 on D plus 1 sought to launch a drive to expand the narrow beachhead held during the night. On Red Beach 3 the primary objective of Major Crowe's battalion was the reduction of the strong system of emplacements near Burns-Philp Wharf. Although virtually all of the attention of the U.S. troops in this zone was centered on the position, little progress was made in reducing it or in eliminating the heavy fire that poured along the beach from it.[67]

In the center of Betio, with support from Colonel Rixey's artillery, the 2d Battalion, 2d Marines, soon consolidated a line just short of the taxiway on the airfield and began to move men into the triangle formed by the taxiway and airstrip where a few isolated individuals had spent the night. Between the airfield and the northern beach, demolition groups moved against Japanese stragglers. One by one the stubborn positions that had harassed landing operations for twenty-four hours

---

[62] 2d Marine Div D-3 Jnl, 20–21 Nov 43, pp. 1, 8–9.
[63] 8th Marines Special Action Rpt, 1 Dec 43, p. 1; 1st Bn 8th Marines Combat Rpt, 28 Nov 43, p. 1.
[64] 1st Bn 8th Marines Combat Rpt, 28 Nov 43, p. 1.
[65] Stockman, *Tarawa*, pp. 37–38.
[66] CINCPAC-CINCPOA Opns in POA, Nov 43, Annex E, p. 12; Stockman, *Tarawa*, pp. 36–37.
[67] 2d Bn 8th Marines Action Rpt, pp. 3–4.

BEACH DEFENSIVE POSITIONS, *which had to be eliminated by small unit action.*
Note wire beach obstacles in left background.

were reduced and some freedom of movement was at last achieved by the marines on and near the water's edge. Also on Red Beach 2, the 1st Battalion, 2d Marines, concentrated first on removing enemy machine guns that interdicted the approaches to the airstrip and then began a drive toward the south shore of Betio.[68] On Red Beach 1 Major Ryan by 1100 had organized a drive that was to carry all the way across the island and to secure Green Beach—the western coast of Betio—so that it could be freely used for subsequent landings. Close gunfire support by two destroyers paved the way for this advance.[69]

The attacks launched on the fronts during the afternoon were successful on all but the left zone of action, where no advance was made. On Red Beach 2 and Red Beach 1 elements of three battalions drove all the way across the island to the opposite shore.[70] Shortly after 1700 Colonel Shoup, in the first encouraging message to division headquarters, ended by adding the hopeful words "We are winning."[71]

About mid-afternoon on D Day, when the situation ashore was most confused and precarious and while reports of extremely heavy casualties were reaching *Maryland,* Admiral Hill had radioed Admiral Turner, at Makin, asking for the release of the Expeditionary Troop Reserve for use at Tarawa.[72] As a result Col. Maurice G. Holmes, commanding officer of the 6th Marine Regimental Combat Team, was notified some two hours later that his regiment had been released from corps reserve to 2d Marine Division control. The next morning (21 November), at a conference aboard *Maryland,* General Smith and Colonel Holmes discussed several possibilities for the employment of the reserve regiment. No decision was made at the conference but shortly after noon it was decided to land one battalion over Green Beach on the western coast of Betio. Colonel Holmes directed his 1st Battalion, commanded by Maj. William K. Jones, to prepare to go ashore.[73] This was accomplished at 1640. The battalion landing team was followed about two hours later by a platoon of light tanks—the 3d Platoon, Company B, 2d Tank Battalion.[74]

Shortly after noon, Lt. Col. Raymond L. Murray, commanding officer of the 2d Battalion, 6th Marines, received orders to land on Bairiki Island, less than three and a half miles to the southeast of Betio.[75] The movement, designed to intercept enemy troops that might be escaping across the reef between the two islands and thence into the far reaches of the atoll, was accomplished later in the afternoon following an intensive naval and aerial bombardment. No live Japanese was discovered.[76]

Tarawa Is Secured

The afternoon of D plus 1, 21 November, was the turning point in the battle for Tarawa. At the close of the day there were seven battalions of Marine infantry ashore on Betio, the 1st Battalion, 6th Marines, having landed at 1840 over Green Beach, supported by a company of light tanks. Early the next morning, a battalion of Marine artillery (2d Battalion, 10th Marines) went ashore on Bairiki. Troops on Red Beaches 1 and 2 had driven to the south coast of Betio, although the stubborn

---

[68] 1st Bn 2d Marines Action Rpt, p. 4.
[69] 3d Bn 2d Marines Action Rpt, p. 2.
[70] 2d Marine Div Special Action Rpt, p. 3.
[71] 2d Marine Div D-3 Jnl, 20–21 Nov 43, p. 25.
[72] *Ibid.,* 19–20 Nov 43, p. 16.
[73] 6th Marines Special Action Rpt, 20 Dec 43, p. 6.
[74] Stockman, *Tarawa,* p. 40.
[75] 6th Marines Special Action Rpt, 20 Dec 43, p. 6.
[76] Stockman, *Tarawa,* p. 40.

pocket on the boundary between the two beaches still defied all attempts to destroy it and continued to harass, to some extent, landing activities at both Red Beaches and on Central Pier. At 2030 Col. Merritt A. Edson, Chief of Staff, 2d Division, established an advance command post on Red Beach 2, for the first time providing a centralized headquarters ashore that would not be subject to the vagaries of communication failures. Colonel Edson immediately assumed the burden of command until General Smith could come ashore.[77]

Plans for the Third Day

Colonel Edson spent virtually the entire night of 21–22 November in consultation with Colonels Shoup and Hall before issuing the orders for the co-ordinated attack of the next morning. Two of the great deficiencies of the 21 November operations were provided for during the conference. The first, air and naval gunfire support, which had been present but in large measure ineffective because of the inaccurate knowledge of American positions, was now co-ordinated to provide thorough and complete coverage of all target areas in front of the proposed attack.[78] In addition, at 0330, Colonel Edson ordered that the 2d Battalion, 10th Marines (Artillery), less one battery, be landed on Bairiki Island to provide supporting fire for the advance.[79] To overcome many of the communications difficulties, the radios of the separate landing teams of the 6th Marines were brought into the command net of the 2d Division.[80] Added precaution was taken by sending information of the attack by officer courier to the units on Red Beach 1 and Green Beach.[81]

The attack of 22 November was to have two objectives. The first was to advance to the east along the south shore of the island. This movement was to be made by the 1st Battalion, 6th Marines, attacking from Green Beach through the lines then held by the 3d Battalion, 2d Marines. The advance was to continue through the area of the 1st and 2d Battalions, 2d Marines, tying in eventually with the right flank of the 8th Marines, which was to change its direction of attack from south to east. This latter change was actually only a formality inasmuch as Major Crowe's full attention since shortly after landing had been centered on the position just inland from the base of Burns-Philp Wharf, which was to the east. This main attack was to be reinforced in the zone of the 6th Marines by the 3d Battalion of that regiment, which was held in reserve just off Green Beach. Two battalions of the 8th Marines, the 2d and 3d, were to make the main effort on the left (north).

The second objective of the day was to be the reduction of the pocket between Red Beaches 1 and 2. This attack was to be made by the 1st Battalion, 8th Marines. The battalion was to pivot on the beach, swing to the west, and move toward Red Beach 1 through the pocket, which would be contained on the opposite side by the 3d Battalion, 2d Marines.

Gains on 22 November

The 1st Battalion, 6th Marines, jumped off at 0800. Moving with two companies abreast down the narrow hundred-yard strip of heavily fortified ground between

---

[77] Stockman, *Tarawa*, pp. 40–41.
[78] 2d Marine Div D-3 Jnl, 21–22 Nov 43, p. 4.
[79] 6th Marines Special Action Rpt, 20 Dec 43, p. 5.
[80] Stockman, *Tarawa*, p. 43.
[81] 2d Marine Div D-3 Jnl, 21–22 Nov 43, p. 6.

JAPANESE BOMBPROOF SHELTERS, *stubborn points of resistance, were reduced only after hard and prolonged fighting.*

the airfield and the south shore, Major Jones and his men progressed rapidly and by 1100 had reached the area held by the 1st Battalion, 2d Marines. An estimated 250 Japanese were killed and only light casualties were incurred by the marines.[82] During the forenoon the rest of the 3d Battalion, 6th Marines, landed over Green Beach and began moving up in the rear of the assault.[83]

Upon completion of the first phase of the attack new orders were issued for a continuation of the advance up the island as far as the eastern end of the airfield. This advance began about 1300 and continued in the face of stronger resistance until the objective was reached late in the afternoon.[84]

Elsewhere on Betio gains had also been made during the day against heavier resistance and with less evident results. Company F, 8th Marines, aided by Company K of the same regiment and detachments of the 18th Marines (Engineers), finally succeeded in reducing the steel pillbox just inland from Burns-Philp Wharf, together with two strong supporting positions. One of the positions, a large blockhouse, was counterattacked by the Japanese shortly after it had been captured, but the attempt to retake it was broken up.[85] It was the successful completion of this action during the morning that brought about the issuance of the new orders for the afternoon of the third day.[86] Once the evidently strong enemy positions there had been reduced, the 8th Marines would be relieved while the relatively fresh battalions of the 6th Marines continued to the eastern tip of the island.

The attack on the strong point between the westernmost beaches proceeded slowly. The two companies farthest inland made some gains, but Company B, 8th Marines, nearest the shore, met firm resistance and was little nearer to the reduction of the position at nightfall than it had been in the morning. During the afternoon the 1st Battalion, 2d Marines, was relieved by the advance of the 1st Battalion, 6th Marines.[87]

At nightfall on the third day Americans were in possession of all the western end of Betio Island as far east as the eastern end of the airfield, except for the pocket between Red Beaches 1 and 2. General Julian Smith came ashore on Green Beach shortly before noon and then moved to Red Beach 2 by LVT and assumed command ashore.[88] Despite the relatively substantial gains, it was estimated that at least five days of heavy fighting remained before the atoll would be completely subdued.[89]

Events of the Third Night

General Julian Smith had already begun the preparation of the attack order for the fourth day when this pessimistic prediction was made. On the next morning Colonel Holmes was to assume command of the final drive to the eastern tip of Betio Island. The two battalions of the 6th Marines already on Betio were to be joined by the 2d Battalion, which would be moved from Bairiki.[90] This plan for further reinforcement was to be rendered unnecessary before it could be executed, for, as the order was being prepared, events

[82] 6th Marines Special Action Rpt, 20 Dec 43, p. 6.
[83] 2d Marine Div D-3 Jnl, 21–22 Nov 43, p. 15.
[84] 1st Bn 6th Marines Special Action Rpt, 3 Dec 43, pp. 4, 5.
[85] 2d Bn 8th Marines Action Rpt, p. 4.
[86] 2d Marine Div D-3 Jnl, 21–22 Nov 43, p. 17.
[87] 1st Bn 8th Marines Combat Rpt, 28 Nov 43, p. 2.
[88] 2d Marine Div D-3 Jnl, 21–22 Nov 43, pp. 18, 22.
[89] *Ibid.*, p. 27.
[90] 6th Marines Special Action Rpt, 20 Dec 43, p. 6.

were already transpiring that were to end Japanese resistance. Throughout the battle the enemy had shown little inclination to counterattack and seemed un-co-ordinated and lacking in offensive leadership, apparently because of the breakdown in communications caused by the preliminary aerial and naval bombardment. By the evening of 22 November most of the remaining enemy, approximately 1,000 in number, were squeezed east into the narrow tail of the island. There, although unable to maneuver, they could effect a closer-knit organization than had heretofore been possible. The Japanese leaders seemed to have determined, therefore, on an offensive action against the invaders, and this move they planned carefully. At approximately 1930 a group of about fifty Japanese attacked American positions established only a short time before.[91] The 1st Battalion, 6th Marines, had already assumed responsibility for the whole cross-island line, and Major Jones had placed all three of his rifle companies in position with his weapons company, just in the rear, in reserve. The Japanese succeeded in finding a small gap between two of the front-line units, but the battalion moved in to close the hole and helped destroy the attacking force without sustaining serious damage. One significant feature of this action was the employment of grenades, bayonets, and literally hand-to-hand action by the marines.[92] The reliance on close-in methods of defense defeated the whole purpose of the enemy's infiltration attempt, which seems to have been to secure accurate information as to American positions. The Japanese were forced to risk a second probing attack later in the evening with the consequent attrition of their already dwindling strength. Artillery was brought within seventy-five yards of the

Marine front lines and acted as an effective screen before the infantry. The second Japanese attack was a two-pronged movement, one group striking at Company B on the right of the line and another group of about the same size against the left center of the line in the Company A sector. Both enemy groups were destroyed—that attacking Company A was annihilated by artillery fire and the one in front of Company B by a combination of close-in artillery fire and hand-to-hand infantry fighting.[93]

The final and heaviest counterattack was launched by the enemy at 0300 after an hour of intense enemy machine gun fire all along the line. Several of the Japanese guns were destroyed by American grenades and counterfire from heavy machine guns. The final attack, when it came, was launched by about 300 enemy troops and hit both Company A and Company B. It was repulsed within an hour. Within an area fifty yards deep in front of the Marine positions, over 200 Japanese were found dead next morning, while in the impact area of the artillery, somewhat farther removed, another 125 badly mangled bodies were found.[94]

Betio Island Secured

While the 1st Battalion, 6th Marines, was repulsing the counterattack, preparations were made for the fourth day's action. The 3d Battalion, 6th Marines, had been moved before 2300 into position directly behind the front line. At the time of the second counterattack one company was

---

[91] 1st Bn 6th Marines Special Action Rpt, 3 Dec 43, p. 5.

[92] Stockman, *Tarawa*, pp. 52, 53.

[93] 1st Bn 6th Marines Special Action Rpt, 3 Dec 43, p. 6.

[94] Stockman, *Tarawa*, p. 54.

already in position there and before morning the whole battalion had formed a secondary line.[95] At 0800 the 3d Battalion passed Companies I and L through the 1st Battalion and attacked to the east down the narrow tail of Betio. Only at one time during the morning did the demoralized remnants of the Japanese garrison offer any resistance. At a point 350 yards beyond the eastern end of the airfield a concentration of pillboxes and fire trenches held up the advance of Company I. On the left Lt. Col. Kenneth F. McLeod, the battalion commander, immediately moved Company L around the right of the strong point, leaving the position to be mopped up by Company I, and proceeded with only one company in the advance. At 1310 the battalion reached the island's tip. Four hundred and seventy-five Japanese were reported killed during the advance.[96]

The last organized Japanese resistance on Betio was to cease a few minutes later. By 1000 on the fourth day, the 1st Battalion, 8th Marines, and the 3d Battalion, 2d Marines, had joined to form a semicircular attack upon the position on the boundary between Red Beaches 1 and 2. To accomplish the juncture, a platoon of marines, under the command of Maj. Hewitt D. Adams and supported by two 75-mm. guns, waded out onto the reef in front of the emplacement and made a direct frontal assault on the strong point, eliminating completely the positions that faced the lagoon.[97] The 3d Battalion, 2d Marines, then advanced toward the beach. One last pillbox had to be destroyed, and the weary marines moved to mop up the stragglers still holding out in holes and shelters. Major Schoettel then notified division headquarters that the task was complete.[98]

At 1330 the same afternoon, General Smith announced the end of organized resistance on Betio.[99] Three jobs still remained, however, before the Gilberts operation could be considered completed: the rest of the islands of Tarawa Atoll had to be taken; Apamama Atoll must be captured; and Abaiang, Marakei, and Maiana Atolls occupied.

Conclusion of the Operation

During the afternoon of 23 November, the 2d Battalion, 6th Marines, which had moved from Bairiki to Betio during the morning, learned that it was to mop up the remaining islands of Tarawa Atoll. At 0500 on 24 November it embarked for Buota Island to begin the northward march up the atoll. It was expected that approximately a hundred Japanese would be found somewhere along the eastern leg of the atoll. A thorough search on 24 November failed to reveal the enemy, however, and a continued march on 25 November brought the battalion to Buariki, the northernmost island of the atoll, where enemy troops were at last encountered. Here, on the evening of 26 November and throughout the following day, a sharp engagement was fought in which approximately 150 Japanese were killed at a cost of 32 American dead and 60 wounded in action.[100]

Abaiang, Maiana, and Marakei Atolls lie respectively north, south, and northeast of Tarawa. On 29 November Company D,

---

[95] 1st Bn 6th Marines Special Action Rpt, 3 Dec 43, p. 6.
[96] 6th Marines Special Action Rpt, 20 Dec 43, Narrative Rpt of Opns of Landing Team 3d Bn 6th Marines, pp. 3, 4.
[97] Stockman, *Tarawa*, p. 58.
[98] 3d Bn 2d Marines Action Rpt, p. 3.
[99] Stockman, *Tarawa*, p. 59.
[100] 6th Marines Special Action Rpt, 20 Dec 43, Narrative Account of Opns of 2d Bn 6th Marines, 21–29 Nov 43, pp. 1–2.

2d Tank Battalion, was dispatched aboard the mine sweeper *Pursuit* to reconnoiter these atolls on the assumption that they might be sheltering Japanese coastwatchers. On Abaiang, five Japanese were flushed out but managed to escape by boat. On the other two atolls only natives were discovered.[101]

Apamama, an atoll lying seventy-six miles south of Tarawa, was captured by the V Amphibious Corps Reconnaissance Company, less one platoon. Carried to their destination aboard the submarine *Nautilus,* the company landed on the atoll in rubber boats in the early morning of 21 November. Aided by naval gunfire from their submarine as well as from an escorting destroyer, the marines were able to complete the occupation of the atoll by 24 November. The operation yielded twenty-three Japanese dead, mostly by their own hands. Next day General Hermle, in command of a landing force built around the 3d Battalion, 6th Marines, relieved the reconnaissance company and completed the organization of the atoll's defenses. Thus from Makin southward 180 miles to Apamama the whole island chain constituting the northern Gilberts was captured or occupied by the American forces. The capture of Tarawa yielded an estimated 4,690 Japanese killed, and 17 Japanese and 129 Korean prisoners of war. Marine Corps casualties, including killed, wounded, and missing in action, came to 3,301.[102] This was a high price to pay for a few hundred acres of coral. Yet in the minds of most American military planners and strategists the cost of the capture of the Gilberts was justified both in the terms of the strategic gains realized and the tactical lessons learned.

---

[101] Stockman, *Tarawa*, p. 65.
[102] *Ibid.,* p. 72.

CHAPTER X

Strategic and Tactical Significance of the Gilberts Operation

Strategic Consequences

Writing some six years after the event, General Holland Smith posed the question, "Was Tarawa worth it?" "My answer," he said, "is unqualified: No." General Smith continued:

From the very beginning the decision of the Joint Chiefs to seize Tarawa was a mistake and from their initial mistake grew the terrible drama of errors, errors of omission rather than commission, resulting in these needless casualties. . . . Tarawa had no particular strategic importance. . . . Tarawa should have been by-passed. Its capture . . . was a terrible waste of life and effort. . . . [We] should have let Tarawa "wither on the vine." We could have kept it neutralized from our bases on Baker Island, to the east, and the Ellice and Phoenix Islands, a short distance to the southeast.[1]

General Smith was alone among high-ranking officers to voice this opinion. Admirals King, Nimitz, and Spruance, as well as General Julian Smith, were all in agreement that the capture of Tarawa and Makin was a necessary prelude to the invasion of the Marshalls.[2]

The strategic value of the Gilberts lay in their geographic proximity to the Mar-

shalls and therefore in their utility as air bases for the forthcoming operations in the Central Pacific. Before launching the Gilberts campaign, the United States had no airfields within range of the Marshalls, the closest being at Funafuti in the Ellice Islands and at Canton—1,300 and 1,600 nautical miles from Kwajalein, respectively. The occupation of Baker Island and Nanomea, which was incident to the capture of the Gilberts, closed this range somewhat and allowed American planes to operate from bases about 1,020 and 1,050 nautical miles from Kwajalein. But even if these islands could have been held without the elimination of the Japanese air potential in the Gilberts, which is in itself doubtful, Baker and Nanomea were still too distant from the Marshalls to allow steady

---

[1] Smith, *Coral and Brass*, pp. 111–12.

[2] Admiral King, Official Rpt Covering Combat Opns Up to March 1, 1944, p. 42; Admiral Nimitz, quoted in New York *Sun*, November 16, 1948, Sec. II, p. 1; Admiral Spruance, Address to the Royal United Service Institution, London, October 1946, quoted in Capt. Walter Karig, USNR, Lt. Comdr. Russell L. Harris, USNR, and Lt. Comdr. Frank A. Manson, USN, *Battle Report*, Vol. IV, *The End of an Empire* (New York: Rinehart & Company, 1948), p. 77; Lt. Gen. Julian C. Smith, USMC (Ret), "Tarawa," *United States Naval Institute Proceedings*, LXXIX (1953), 1163–76.

bombing and photographic reconnaissance. The capture of key islands in the Gilberts halved the distance between American airfields and Kwajalein and made possible the effective employment of land-based aircraft against that target. Almost immediately upon completion of infantry fighting in the Gilberts, naval Seabees and Seventh Air Force engineers commenced work on airfield construction at Tarawa and Makin. By 18 December the field at Makin was well enough along to base its first planes. Less than a week later two fields at Tarawa (one on Betio and one on Buota) were ready to fly and service bombers. By mid-January a field at Apamama was in operation.[3]

The completion of these airfields in the Gilberts changed the entire character of operations against the Marshall Islands. The long-distance raids with light bomb loads now gave way to shorter flights with heavier loads, and allowed flights of planes with shorter ranges. Medium bombers, attack bombers, and fighters were brought into the attack. Army Air Forces B-25's (medium bombers) were based at Tarawa and Apamama; A-24's (fighter-bombers) and P-39's (fighters) were based at Tarawa and Apamama; A-24's and P-39's were brought to Makin; and P-40's (fighters) were based on Makin and Apamama. Most of the B-24 (heavy bomber) squadrons that had been bombing the Gilberts and southern Marshalls were moved to Tarawa by the first week in January. Advance headquarters of the VII Bomber Command and of the VII Air Service Command were set up at Tarawa by 7 January.

During November the B-24's, which were then carrying the entire load alone, had totaled 237 sorties against the Gilberts and Marshalls. In December these planes, able to stage through Tarawa late in the month, flew 365 bombing and photographic sorties against the Marshalls alone. They were augmented by the B-25's that were brought to Tarawa on 28 December and the A-24's based at Makin.

The Gilbert bases allowed the use of land-based fighters for the first time in the Central Pacific. The two P-39 squadrons and the one P-40 squadron based at Makin and Apamama accompanied bombing sorties over the Marshalls from the day they arrived in the Gilberts. In addition to protecting the heavier planes, the fighters also bombed and strafed Japanese installations and shipping. No longer did B-24's have to assume sole responsibility for land-based photographic and bombing missions against the Marshalls. Those of shorter range could be turned over in part to medium bombers and fighters based in the Gilberts. Also, the shortened distances between the new forward bases and the B-24 targets in the Marshalls allowed the heavy bombers to fly with still heavier loads and more frequently.[4] Finally, as Admiral Spruance pointed out, the superior photographic techniques of land-based aviation made possible a more accurate picture of terrain, hydrographic conditions, and enemy defenses in the Marshalls than could otherwise have been obtained.

Tactical Lessons Learned

The Gilberts operation, especially the invasion of Tarawa, was the first instance in the Pacific war of a large-scale amphibious assault against a well-fortified shore line. Before the outbreak of the war the

[3] Operational History of the Seventh Air Force, 6 Nov 43–31 Jul 44, p. 14; Craven and Cate, *AAF IV*, pp. 303–04.
[4] Operational History of the Seventh Air Force, 6 Nov 43–31 Jul 44, pp. 14–19; Craven and Cate, *AAF IV*, pp. 304–06.

United States armed forces, chiefly the Navy and the Marine Corps, developed a systematic doctrine for landing waterborne troops on hostile shores, supporting them both before and after the landing by naval guns and carrier-based air, and providing the necessary logistical support by overseas shipping. This doctrine had been set forth in abundant detail in a series of military manuals published by the two services.[5] Yet, until Tarawa, it had never been put to a severe test in the Pacific. The landings in the Solomons, New Guinea, and the Aleutians had all been conducted against light opposition or no opposition at all. Tarawa was the first occasion in the Pacific war when the enemy had heavily fortified the beachhead that had to be seized if the attacking force was to achieve its objective.

The fact that the atoll was captured with acceptable casualties (about 20 percent) provided incontestable proof that American amphibious doctrine was sound and that the most formidable island fortress could be taken even with the relatively slender means then available to Allied forces in the Pacific. Just as significant, however, as the ultimate success of the invasion were the various deficiencies in equipment and techniques and the errors in execution that the operation revealed. It was the experience gained in the Gilberts, coupled with a tremendous expansion of all U.S. arms in the Pacific, that made the more nearly perfect execution of subsequent amphibious operations possible.

Naval Support

According to the later testimony of Admiral Hill, the "first and foremost" among lessons learned during the Gilberts operation was "that naval task forces accompanying the assault forces had the power to move into an area, obtain complete naval and air control of that area, and remain there with acceptable losses throughout the entire assault and preliminary consolidation phases." "This," he continued, "is a lesson which had never been demonstrated before the Gilberts operation and which formed the basis for all subsequent operations in the Central Pacific Area."[6]

Just as the invasion of Tarawa demonstrated that naval task forces could seize control of the air and sea long enough to support a successful landing, so did it indicate that a period of preliminary naval fire, much longer than a few hours, was necessary if all beach defenses were to be eliminated or effectively neutralized. The consensus among observers at Tarawa was that the three hours allotted for preliminary naval bombardment was insufficient.[7] Any hopes that had been pinned on the ability of naval gunfire and aerial bombardment to "obliterate" the target proved false. In spite of the more than 3,000 tons of explosives thrown at or dropped on the island of Betio immediately before the landing, the majority of Japanese weapons there were still in operation when the troops reached shore.

---

[5] The most important of these manuals were The Tentative Manual for Landing Operations (Marine Corps School, Quantico, 1934); Fleet Training Publication 167, Landing Operations Doctrine, United States Navy (Office of Naval Operations, Division of Fleet Training, 1938); and Basic Field Manual 31-5, Landing Operations on Hostile Shores (War Department, 1941). For the prewar evolution of amphibious doctrine, see Isely and Crowl, *U.S. Marines and Amphibious War*, pp. 14–71.

[6] Ltr, Adm Hill to Gen Malony, 14 Feb 49, p. 4, OCMH.

[7] *Ibid.*, pp. 4–5; V Phib Corps GALVANIC Rpt, pp. 16–17; Ltr, CG 2d Marine Div to CG V Phib Corps, 4 Jan 44, sub: Recommendations Based on Tarawa Opn, Recommendation 5, Naval Gunfire, p. 1, A 7-17, 2d Mar Div/Recommendation Tarawa, Gilbert Area files, Hist Branch, G-3, Hq USMC.

The difficulty was that there were too many targets to be destroyed for the time allowed. Naval ships had time to deliver pinpoint destructive fire only against such well-defined targets as coastal defense weapons and heavy antiaircraft batteries. If the beach preparation had been spread over a longer period of time, with slower fire to allow ships to observe their targets and determine the effectiveness of that fire, it would have been far more effective. As it was, with the limited time available, ships' guns had to resort to mere area bombardment, or neutralization fire, long before it could be accurately determined how many of the enemy's guns had been actually knocked out of action. Neutralization is not destruction, as the marines who went ashore soon discovered. One solution for the deficiencies of naval gunfire at Tarawa was clear. For naval ships effectively to support landing operations they would have to deliver slow, deliberate, pinpoint fire against selected targets and maintain constant observation of the damage actually done by their salvos. This would require time—more time than was allotted to the support ships at either Tarawa or Makin.

Another conclusion in respect to naval gunfire support that emerged from the Tarawa operation was that an insufficient proportion of major-caliber armor-piercing shells was employed by the firing ships. Against the steel-reinforced concrete pillboxes found on Betio, 5-inch antiaircraft and 6-inch bombardment shells had little effect. For future operations against well-fortified positions of this sort, it was recommended that greater reliance be put on the heavy guns of battleships and that a larger proportion of armor-piercing shells be employed.[8]

Still another deficiency in both the plan and the execution of preliminary naval gunfire at Tarawa was the rapid shifting of fire from one target to another. This was based on the principle of keeping the enemy guessing as to where to jump next by placing fire into areas in an unpredictable sequence. Experience at Tarawa showed that although this type of bombardment was useful for neutralization, it failed to achieve the degree of destructiveness desired. Destructive fire called for accurate control, which was rendered impossible by sudden, large, and frequent shifts of fire. For future operations, it was recommended that less radical shifting be employed, and that naval fire be laid directly toward or away from, and right or left of an established reference point. Thus, it was believed, more accurate fire control could be maintained and greater damage be done to well-covered enemy emplacements.[9]

Also at Tarawa, naval gunfire on the beaches was lifted too soon. One reason for this was to permit a last-minute aerial strafing and bombing run along the shore line, but the precaution was unnecessary. Actually, the planes did not fly low enough to be endangered by ships' gunfire. The desirability of a last-minute naval barrage, more effective than aerial bombardment, was clearly demonstrated. At Makin this had been partially provided for by equipping some of the leading amphibian tractors with 4.5-inch rockets, which were fired to good effect on Yellow Beach.[10] At Tarawa only two small support craft (LCS's)

[8] CINCPAC-CINCPOA GALVANIC Opns, Preliminary Study of Action Rpts, 31 Dec 43, p. 2; TF 53 Rpt of Tarawa Opns, 13 Dec 43, Incl A, p. 49; Ltr cited n. 7, Recommendation 5, Naval Gunfire, p. 1.
[9] TF 53 Rpt of Tarawa Opns, 13 Dec 43, Incl A, p. 45.
[10] Ltr, Hq 27th Inf Div to CG V Phib Corps, Rpt of Opns GALVANIC, 18 Dec 43, p. 7.

were furnished with rockets. These were fired from the flanks of the leading wave with indeterminate effects. An alternative to a last-minute rocket barrage would have been the employment of armored amphibians (amphibian tanks) in the first wave. These could be equipped with 37-mm. or 75-mm. guns and would have provided excellent close support fire for the assault waves. Another device that was clearly suggested by the landing on Betio was the continued employment of destroyer fire in support of the leading waves until just before the landing. In the one instance where this was done, on Red Beach 3 at Tarawa, casualties to the troops in the ship-to-shore movement were reduced to a minimum. In the opinion of General Julian Smith, close support fires by destroyers should have been maintained all along the beach until the troops were within a hundred yards of the shore line.[11]

These various deficiencies in both the quantity and quality of naval preparatory fire at Tarawa pointed up a corollary lesson—the desirability of an early landing of artillery on islands adjacent to the main target to assist the attendant naval ships and aircraft in laying down a heavy bombardment preliminary to the principal landings. The configuration of Central Pacific atolls was such as to make this tactic feasible, other conditions permitting. In every case the larger islands, which were invariably the most heavily fortified, were separated by only short distances from smaller neighboring islets within easy artillery range. During the invasion of Tarawa it was not thought practicable to emplace artillery on the islets adjacent to Betio well in advance of the main landing for the same reason that it was not believed wise to provide for a more prolonged preliminary naval bombardment—the fleet

should not be exposed to enemy action any longer than could possibly be helped. By the time that the Marshall Islands were invaded this danger was no longer so acute, and it was possible for the planners of those operations in each case to make provision for placing artillery on the smaller islets of the atolls some hours before the initial landings on the main islands.[12]

Close Air Support

Clearly, the most disappointing aspect of the entire Tarawa operation was the execution of air support for the landing. The inadequacy of air support was attributed in about equal measure to poor communications, poor co-ordination, and the poor training of the carrier pilots.

The plans called for a dawn strike on the beaches from 0545 to 0615. This strike was twenty-five minutes later than was expected by the ground troops and naval surface forces present. Admiral Hill's support aircraft commander aboard the flagship *Maryland* was unable to establish communication with the striking groups to determine their status. *Maryland's* main batteries were firing and the concussion apparently disrupted her radio communications. The majority of planes attacked between 0610 and 0620.

The H-Hour air strike was scheduled for the period from H minus 5 to H plus 15 minutes, with H Hour set at 0830. At 0820 the air groups were informed that H Hour would be delayed until 0900. This change of plans was either not received or was disregarded by the planes, and fighters commenced strafing the beaches at 0825 as originally scheduled. At 0842 they were

---

[11] Ltr cited n. 7, Recommendation 2, Ship-to-Shore Movement, pp. 12–13.

[12] See below, Ch. XI, pp. 19, 27.

finally reached and directed to cease firing. At 0855, on the anticipation that H Hour would be 0900, surface ships were directed to stop firing and fighters were ordered to strafe the beaches. In fact, the fighters did not arrive to strafe until just before 0910, and by that time the first troops were coming ashore and the mission had to be canceled.[13]

In addition to the poor co-ordination of air support with the other arms, it was evident that the carrier squadrons were not fully enough trained to provide efficient air support of amphibious operations. One carrier commander reported that carrier flights operated over the target area on D Day with little semblance of orderly procedure. Serious confusion resulted when dive and glide bombing and strafing was carried out to the taste of the individual leaders.[14] Pilots experienced considerable difficulty in locating and striking targets as requested, both before and after the troops landed. It became apparent that the pilots had not been thoroughly briefed and that they lacked sufficient knowledge of the general techniques employed by landing forces in an amphibious operation. One solution to the problems thus raised was suggested by General Holland Smith—to assign at least one Marine aircraft wing specifically to give direct air support to landing operations. The wing, he recommended, should make direct air support a specialty, should train specifically for that purpose, and should be given a complete background of amphibious operations and a period of thorough training in the problems peculiar to air support of landings.[15]

Communications

The failure of communications aboard the battleship *Maryland* on several critical occasions during the landing on Betio served to point clearly to the need for specially constructed and equipped headquarters ships in future amphibious operations. The simple fact was that no battleship was suited to perform the duties imposed on *Maryland*. Her transmitters, receivers, and antennae were too close together and caused mutual interference. Several of her radio communications installations were so damaged by the shock of her own naval guns as to be completely inoperative. Furthermore, if a situation had arisen where the vessel would have had to leave the immediate area of Tarawa to engage in a surface fleet action, the ability of both Admiral Hill and General Julian Smith to exercise command would have been seriously impaired.[16]

All of these shortcomings were well recognized before the operation. Specially equipped headquarters ships were already under construction, but none was ready in the Pacific in November 1943. The ships would make their appearance in the Marshalls operations, but until they were completed the only alternative was to make the best of the means available. The experience with *Maryland* at Tarawa merely confirmed what had already been realized—that the battleship was inadequate as an amphibious command ship.[17]

The other outstanding communications deficiency revealed in the Gilberts operation was in tank-infantry liaison. On Tarawa as at Makin the communications equipment carried by the tanks broke

[13] TF 53 Rpt of Tarawa Opns, 13 Dec 43, Incl A, p. 55; V Phib Corps GALVANIC Rpt, p. 15.
[14] CINCPAC-CINCPOA GALVANIC Opns, Preliminary Study of Action Rpts, p. 5.
[15] V Phib Corps GALVANIC Rpt, p. 16.
[16] TF 53 Rpt of Tarawa Opns, 13 Dec 43, Incl A, pp. 22, 54–55, 62.
[17] Ltr cited n. 6, Adm Hill to Gen Malony, p. 5, OCMH.

down completely. Tanks could communicate neither with each other nor with the infantry units they were supposed to be supporting. On Betio not a single member of a tank crew was killed inside a tank, but several became casualties getting out of their tanks in an effort to communicate with infantrymen. This deficiency could only be remedied by the installation of improved radio sets.[18]

Weapons

At Tarawa the 37-mm. gun, which was mounted on the light tank, proved virtually useless in knocking out pillboxes and various other enemy emplacements. However, fire delivered from the light tank was effective for holding the enemy down while infantry advanced. Whatever its merits in this connection, the light tank was generally incapable of the duties imposed on it. The consensus among most commentators was that in future operations against the Japanese the light tank be replaced by the medium tank mounting a 75-mm. gun.[19]

Perhaps the most valuable weapon at Tarawa proved to be the flame thrower. The greatest obstacle facing the troops in their advance was the extensive layout of Japanese pillboxes and heavy emplacements. Against these, flame throwers firing through ports and pillbox entrances proved invaluable. However, not enough had been assigned to the 2d Marine Division, and it was recommended that for future operations at least one per rifle platoon be issued. Another suggestion made as a result of this experience was that tanks be equipped with large-capacity flame throwers.[20]

Logistics

The plans for unloading supplies and equipment on Betio followed the standard doctrine as set forth in current naval manuals on the subject.[21] Control over small boats was vested in the commander of the naval transport group and priority in unloading was given to the assault transport division on which were embarked the assault troops. Each assault landing team had a shore party that was to function on its own beach, the 2d Marine Division shore party commander co-ordinating the activities of the separate shore parties. Parallel to the division shore party commander was a naval senior beachmaster whose job was to co-ordinate the activities of three platoons of naval personnel assigned to unloading duties on the beach and to advise the transport group commander on the best methods of getting supplies and equipment from ship to shore.

As events worked out, none of these plans could be put into effect until late on the second day of the operation. During most of the first two days of fighting, the beachhead was neither deep enough nor safe enough to allow shore parties to function normally. Boats, on returning to parent ships, were loaded and dispatched to various beaches without awaiting the call of shore party commanders. Direct requests placed by the troops to the ships did not give adequate information and therefore many boats were loaded with nonessential matériel. Finally and most important, there was an insufficient number of control stations established off the beaches

[18] Ltr cited n. 6, Recommendation 4, Tanks, pp. 5, 7.
[19] *Ibid.*, p. 8; V Phib Corps GALVANIC Rpt, p. 17; *Ibid.*, Incl G, Rpt by Special Observers, Part A, Rpt by Brig Gen James L. Underhill, USMC, p. 9, and Part F, Rpt by Maj Clifton A. Woodrum, Jr., USMCR, p. 2.
[20] V Phib Corps GALVANIC Rpt, p. 17; Ltr cited n. 6, Recommendation 4, Tanks, p. 8.
[21] Fleet Training Publications 167 and 211.

to regulate the traffic of boats returning to the beach after their initial trips.

Much of this confusion was of course unavoidable, given the extreme difficulties of establishing the beachhead. The whole concept of the shore party in amphibious doctrine presumes the establishment of a protected area along the shore line sufficient in depth to permit the physical unloading of boats and the dumping of supplies and equipment on land in a relatively orderly fashion at places where troops can get what they need when they need it. None of these conditions obtained during the first two days of fighting on Betio. Yet this was not all that was amiss. Even had a comparatively safe beachhead been established, the offshore control system was inadequate to meet the requirements imposed on it.

Hence, it was recognized that in future operations control boats should be stationed at or near the line of departure for the purpose of directing traffic to and from the beach. After the initial assault, only such equipment and supplies as would probably be immediately required ashore should be boated and the boats should then be dispatched to a central control vessel offshore for assignment to separate beaches. The control vessels, it was recommended, should be under control of a senior naval officer assisted by an officer representing the landing force. In this manner, it was hoped, much of the confusion evident at Tarawa could be avoided.[22]

One final logistical lesson that was pointed up by the Gilberts operation was the desirability of pallet loading in amphibious landings. Pallets had been used extensively at Makin and with excellent results.[23] None had been made available to the 2d Marine Division for Tarawa and the lack had been noted. Holland Smith's headquarters concluded, "pallets are unquestionably necessary in landing operations," and set forth immediately to provide Marine divisions with the requisite number for future landings.[24]

The Amphibian Tractor

Of all types of amphibious equipment used in the Gilberts operation, the amphibian tractor was the most indispensable. "Without the amphibian tractor," reported Holland Smith, "it is believed that the landing at Tarawa would have failed."[25] Speaking from his experience at Makin, General Ralph Smith concurred. "The use of amphibian tractors in this type of operation," he said, "is considered mandatory to insure success and reduce casualties. . . . Their necessity cannot be over-emphasized."[26]

Yet if the presence of these vehicles spelled the difference between success and failure in the Gilberts, it remained true that there were not enough on hand, at least at Tarawa. The 125 amphibian tractors assigned to the 2d Marine Division were not enough. Only the first three assault waves could be initially carried ashore by amphtracks. Subsequent waves boated in standard Navy landing craft were stopped at the reef, and the troops had to wade into the beach or await transfer to LVT's. Thus, the momentum so necessary to amphibious assault against a well-defended shore line was halted. The

---

[22] TF 53 Rpt of Tarawa Opns, 13 Dec 43, Incl A, pp. 21–22; Ltr cited n. 7, Recommendation 2, Ship-to-Shore Movement, pp. 5–6.

[23] Ltr, Hq 27th Inf Div to CG V Phib Corps, Rpt of Opns GALVANIC, 16 Dec 43.

[24] V Phib Corps GALVANIC Rpt, p. 13; *Ibid.*, Incl D, p. 3.

[25] V Phib Corps GALVANIC Rpt, p. 12.

[26] Ltr cited n. 10.

result was only short of disaster for the attacking troops.

General Julian Smith recommended that in the future no less than three hundred troop-carrying LVT's be furnished each Marine division, plus an additional twenty-five for cargo-carrying purposes.[27] Admiral Nimitz concurred.[28] Never again in the Pacific war would the assault troops be so handicapped as they had been at Tarawa for lack of these essential vehicles.

Conclusion

Strategically speaking, the Gilberts operation was not a turning point in the Pacific war. It was only a prelude to the invasion of the Marshalls, which in turn was a prelude to more decisive naval and land victories in the Carolines and the Marianas. The chief strategic significance of this operation is that it was the beginning of the Central Pacific drive against Japan. It had been decreed by the Joint Chiefs of Staff that the Central Pacific drive would constitute the "main effort" in the Pacific war.

Largely because of the limited means available to Admiral Nimitz' forces, the drive was initiated not against the geographic center of Japanese power in the mid-Pacific, but against the perimeter. Yet victory in the Gilberts certainly paved the way for the relatively easy conquests in the Marshalls that were to follow. Air bases were obtained without which adequate bombardment and photographic reconnaissance of these more important targets would have been difficult if not impossible to obtain.

Tactically speaking, the Gilberts landings, especially that on Tarawa, were chiefly important as a testing ground of established amphibious doctrine. Never before in the Pacific war had such an experimental opportunity presented itself. After Tarawa there was no doubt that the techniques, tactics, and procedures set forth in the basic U.S. manuals for landing operations were workable even under the most difficult conditions. Some shortcomings and deficiencies in the execution of the landings were revealed. The most serious deficiencies stemmed from shortages of amphibious equipment and from lack of sufficient naval power or previously emplaced artillery to permit as prolonged a period of preliminary bombardment as was desirable. These could only be corrected as production of the necessary arms caught up with the needs of the Central Pacific drive. Meanwhile, avoidable errors and omissions in execution were carefully noted and studied by all echelons concerned in the Gilberts operation. And, what is more important, steps were immediately taken to avoid their repetition in the future.

---

[27] Ltr, CG 2d Marine Div to CG V Phib Corps, 27 Dec 43, sub: Recommendations Based on Tarawa Opn, Recommendation 1, Amphibian Tractors, p. 2.
[28] CINCPAC-CINCPOA GALVANIC Opns, Preliminary Study of Action Rpts, 31 Dec 43, p. 11.

CHAPTER XI

Tactical Planning for the Marshalls

In projecting the initial drive into the Central Pacific, it had always been understood that the first big prize would be the capture of strategic positions in the Marshall Islands. (*See Map 2.*) These consist of 32 island groups and 867 reefs scattered over more than 400,000 square miles of ocean. The islands lie in two roughly parallel chains about a hundred miles apart. The northeastern chain, called Ratak—meaning "sunrise"—contains the large atolls of Mille, Maloelap, and Wotje. The southwestern or "sunset" chain is called Ralik and contains Jaluit, Kwajalein, Rongelap, Bikini, and Eniwetok, as well as numerous smaller atolls. Kwajalein is located approximately in the geographic center of the group at longitude 167° 30' east and latitude 9° north. From Pearl Harbor it is about 2,100 nautical miles in a southwesterly direction. Tarawa lies 565 miles to the southeast. Slightly south of west and about 980 miles away is Truk, which was believed to be the key bastion of the Japanese in the Carolines.

All of the islands are coral and most of them are atolls, each consisting normally of a low-lying chain of islands connected partially by reefs and surrounding a lagoon. Most of the lagoons are circular in formation and have good passages through the reefs. The largest coral atolls in the world are found in this part of the Pacific. The coral chain of some of the larger atolls extends upward of a hundred miles, encircling vast areas of water. The individual islands contained in the atolls are small, rarely more than two or three miles in length, quite narrow, and flat, never rising to more than a few feet above sea level. The larger islands are covered with coconut palms, breadfruit trees, and pandanus. The smaller ones are barren or covered only with brush.[1]

The first European contact with the Marshalls dates back to the period of Spanish and Portuguese explorations in the sixteenth century. The Marianas were discovered by the Spaniards in 1521, the Carolines by the Portuguese in 1527, and the Marshalls by the Spanish navigator Miguel de Saavedra in 1529. In 1686 the Marshalls were formally annexed by Spain and remained nominally attached to that nation until late in the nineteenth century. Then the German Empire began to expand its influence into the South Seas and in the 1890's commenced negotiations with Spain for transfer of her holdings in

---

[1] Intelligence Center Pacific Ocean Areas (ICPOA), Bull 30-43, Enemy Positions Marshall–Gilbert Area, Vol. I, Marshall Islands, Ralik Chain, pp. 7–11; R. W. Robson, *The Pacific Islands Year Book* (Sydney, Australia: Pacific Publications, Ltd., 1943), p. 99.

the area. The latter's defeat in the Span-
ish-American War sounded the death
knell to Spain's long-moribund empire in
the Pacific. She agreed to dispose of all her
possessions in the Marshalls, Carolines,
and Marianas to Germany except for
Guam, which was ceded to the United
States. The Germans commenced a vigorous colonization policy interrupted only
by the outbreak of World War I.[2]

In October of 1914 the Japanese Navy
commenced the seizure and occupation of
the main islands in this area. In December
of the following year, a military headquarters was established at Truk, and the
islands were divided into six administrative districts, each governed by a resident
garrison commander. At the conclusion of
the war all of the islands of the North
Pacific formerly under German possession
were turned over to Japan as a Class C
mandate as provided in Article 22 of the
Covenant of the League of Nations. Under
the terms of the mandate, Japan was
bound to prevent "the establishment of
fortifications or military and naval bases,"
and the neutralization of other islands in
the Pacific was further guaranteed by a
treaty between Japan and the United
States in 1922.[3] The manner in which the
Japanese Empire honored these commitments will be treated later.[4]

Early Planning

Initial planning for the Marshalls invasion necessarily had to be conducted concurrently with that for the Gilberts operation, which would precede it, yet everyone
concerned realized that final plans could
not be matured until after the Gilberts
had been occupied. One of the chief reasons for taking those islands was, after all,
to provide bases from which the Marshalls

could be more easily bombed and photo-
graphed.

Nevertheless, as early as August 1943,
Admiral Nimitz requested of the Joint
Chiefs of Staff a specific directive authorizing him to seize the Marshalls. His reasons
were that the necessary strength appeared
to be available, that the islands would provide bases for further advance toward
communications lines vital to the enemy,
that Allied lines of communication to the
South and Southwest Pacific would thereby be strengthened, that the operation
might precipitate a fleet action with the
enemy on favorable terms, and that it
should cause the Japanese to divide their
available forces among various theaters.
"Thus," he concluded, "we get on with
the war."[5]

On 1 September the Joint Chiefs, as was
expected, dispatched an affirmative answer to Admiral Nimitz. He was ordered
to seize and control the Marshalls and, on
completion, seize or control Wake, Eniwetok, and Kusaie (the easternmost island
of the Carolines). The purposes of the
operation, as stated in the Joint Chiefs directive, were to be fourfold: (1) to prepare
to gain control of the Carolines; (2) to inflict losses on the enemy; (3) to improve
the security of the lines of communication;

---

[2] Robson, *Year Book*, p. 91.
[3] *The Japan Year Book, 1940–41* (Tokyo: The Japan
Times Press), pp. 917–18; Denys P. Myers, *Handbook
of the League of Nations* (Boston: The World Peace
Foundation, 1935), p. 378; International Military
Tribunal for the Far East (IMTFE), International
Prosecution Section (IPS) Document 6257, Prepared
Statement and Report on Japanese Naval Prepara-
tions 1931–1941, p. 13. The proceedings of the
IMTFE and attached documents are filed in the Law
Library, Office of the Judge Advocate General, De-
partment of the Navy.
[4] Ch. XIII, below.
[5] Ltr, CINCPAC–CINCPOA to COMCENPAC,
22 Sep 43, Serial 00190, Incl A, CINCPAC to
COMINCH, 20 Aug 43, Serial 00151.

and (4) to support other operations in the Pacific and Indian Ocean theaters by extending pressure on the Japanese. The target date was to be 1 January 1944, although this was made contingent upon the successful completion of operations in the Gilberts. Ground troops assigned to the landing and capture of the principal islands were to be the 4th Marine Division, the 22d Marine Regiment (reinforced), and the 7th Infantry Division.[6]

Nimitz then proceeded to prepare a study of the forthcoming operation and recommended that the advance into the Marshalls be accomplished by the simultaneous seizure of Kwajalein, Maloelap, and Wotje Atolls. Maloelap and Wotje were on the eastern fringe of the group, closest to Pearl Harbor, while Kwajalein was roughly in the geographic center. These three atolls, according to Nimitz' estimate, contained 65 percent of the aircraft facilities in the Marshalls. The remaining 35 percent, located chiefly on Jaluit and Mille, could, it was estimated, be easily neutralized by operations from the center.[7]

The code name settled upon for the Marshalls operation was FLINTLOCK, and immediately upon receipt of the Joint Chiefs directive, appropriate staffs set to work devising tentative plans for the landings. As planning progressed it soon became apparent in Pearl Harbor that the Central Pacific forces would be unable to meet the original target date of 1 January 1944. On 25 October Admiral Nimitz wrote Admiral King in Washington, "With considerable regret I now recommend that the Flintlock target date be 31 January, although every effort will be made to anticipate the date given."[8] The reasons set forth for the desired delay were that troop training would be incomplete;

that time would have to be allowed to repair damage done to ships returning from the Gilberts operation; that the Gilberts bases would not be ready in time to be useful against the Marshalls; and, finally and most important, that more time was needed for photographic reconnaissance.

As further intelligence of the proposed target in the Marshalls became available and as news of the difficulties of the Gilberts operations reached Pearl Harbor, Admiral Nimitz proposed another radical revision of the original FLINTLOCK plan. Instead of attacking Wotje, Maloelap, and Kwajalein simultaneously, he proposed bypassing the former two atolls and concentrating all his forces against Kwajalein Atoll. In this he was opposed by all the other Central Pacific commanders consulted on the matter, except for Rear Adms. Charles H. McMorris and Forrest P. Sherman of his own staff.[9] Admiral Spruance later recollected:

I argued as strongly as I could with Admiral Nimitz against Kwajalein, proposing instead Wotje and Maloelap. My argument was based . . . on the insecurity of our line of communications in to Kwajalein after the withdrawal of the Pacific Fleet. . . . With the air pipe line through Eniwetok open back to Japan and with the activity which had been shown by Japanese air in the Marshalls in their attacks on our fleet forces during the Gilberts operation, I felt that our support shipping moving into Kwajalein would have

[6] Ltr, CINCPAC–CINCPOA to COMCENPAC, 22 Sep 43, Serial 00190, Incl B, Dispatch, JCS to CINCPAC, 1 Sep 43.
[7] Ltr, CINCPAC to CINCPOA, 22 Sep 43, Serial 00190, Incl C, CINCPAC Study of Marshalls Opn.
[8] Ltr, CINCPAC–CINCPOA to COMINCH, 25 Oct 43, Serial 00247.
[9] Ltr, Adm Nimitz to Jeter A. Isely, 18 Jan 49; Interv, Isely with Adm Hill, 29 Oct 48; Ltr, Adm Spruance to Isely, 3 Jul 49; all filed in Princeton University Library; Ltr, Gen Richardson to Gen Malony, 31 Jan 49, OCMH.

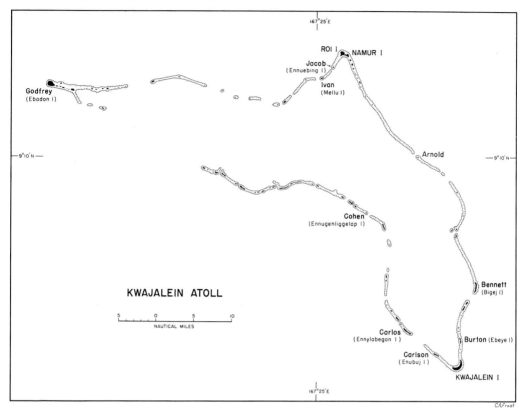

MAP 8

a tough time of it. In my arguments I was supported by Admiral Turner and General Holland Smith, but I was overruled by Admiral Nimitz.[10]

Thus, Nimitz alone was responsible for initiating the decision to hit straight into the center of the Marshall Islands. Events were to prove his boldness justified; the dangers feared by his more cautious advisers never materialized.

The Joint Chiefs approved these changes recommended by the theater commander and, on 14 December, Admiral Nimitz issued his revised Operation Plan 16-43, which definitely assigned Kwajalein Atoll as the target in the forthcoming operation. The 7th Infantry Division was to take the

southern group of islands in the atoll, including Kwajalein Island. The 4th Marine Division was to capture Roi-Namur and the other northern islands of the atoll.[11] (Map 8) Roi-Namur, lying at the northeastern corner of Kwajalein Atoll, is about forty-four nautical miles from Kwajalein Island, which is at the southeastern corner.

One final change in the plan was made on 26 December. Admiral Spruance, after being overruled on the question of bypassing Wotje and Maloelap, asked that Majuro, one of the easternmost of the

---

[10] Ltr, Spruance to Isely, 3 Jul 49.
[11] CINCPAC–CINCPOA Opn Plan 16–43 (Revised), 14 Dec 43.

Marshalls, be included as an additional objective. He wanted the atoll at the earliest possible moment as a fleet base, and he believed that airfields constructed there would help cover the line of communications to Kwajalein. A Navy reconnaissance plane flying over that area in early December had drawn no antiaircraft fire and had seen no activity, thus leading Nimitz to believe that if a Japanese garrison was there, it was small. Hence, it was agreed to send a small expeditionary force consisting of 2d Battalion Landing Team of the 106th Infantry with the 1st Marine Defense Battalion attached, and the Reconnaissance Company of V Amphibious Corps to occupy the atoll.[12] D Day for all landings was to be 31 January 1944.

Spruance's Plan

As always in the Central Pacific, the highest operational command for the Marshalls invasion went to Admiral Spruance, now designated Commander, Fifth Fleet (Task Force 50).[13] Once again Admiral Turner commanded the Joint Expeditionary Force (Task Force 51). Command of the expeditionary troops fell to General Holland Smith (Task Force 56). General Smith's position in the chain of command in relation to Admiral Turner was made clearer than it had been in the Gilberts operation, and his authority was more precisely defined.[14] He was put in direct command of all landing forces and garrison forces once they were ashore. The troop commanders of each of the landing forces, that is of the 7th Infantry Division and the 4th Marine Division, were expressly placed under General Smith until such time as Admiral Spruance should determine that the capture and occupation phase of the operation had been com-

pleted. However, General Smith's authority as commander of expeditionary troops had one limitation. Since it was recognized that "the employment of troops, including the reserve troops engaged in the seizure of objectives, is subject to the capabilities of the surface units to land and support them," any directives issued by General Smith as to major landings or as to major changes in tactical plans had to have the approval of Admiral Turner before they could be issued. To this extent, the expeditionary troops commander was still subordinate to Admiral Turner.[15]

Immediately subordinate to Admiral Turner as Commander, Expeditionary Force, were the three attack forces. The Southern Attack Force (Task Force 52), commanded also by Admiral Turner, was assigned the task of capturing Kwajalein Island and the surrounding islands in the southern half of the atoll. The Northern Attack Force (Task Force 53), commanded by Rear Adm. Richard L. Conolly, was charged with the capture of Roi-Namur and all other islands in the northern half of the atoll. The Majuro Attack Group (Task Group 51.2) was to be commanded by Admiral Hill.

Under Holland Smith's immediate command were the three landing forces, one assigned to each of the major objectives. The Southern Landing Force (Task Group 56.1), composed primarily of the 7th Infantry Division, was commanded by Maj.

---

[12] Ltr, Spruance to Isely, 3 Jul 49; V Phib Corps FLINTLOCK Rpt, Incl B, G-5 Rpt, p. 4; Rad, CINCPAC-CINCPOA to JCS, 17 Dec 43.

[13] COMCENPAC Opn Plan Cen 1-44, 6 Jan 44. Spruance's old designation, Commander, Central Pacific Force, and his new title, Commander, Fifth Fleet, were used interchangeably in the planning stage of the Marshalls operation.

[14] See above, Ch. II, pp. 43–46.

[15] COMCENPAC Opn Plan Cen 1-44, 6 Jan 44, p. 18.

CHART 2—TASK ORGANIZATION OF MAJOR COMMANDS FOR THE ATTACK ON KWAJALEIN AND MAJURO ATOLLS

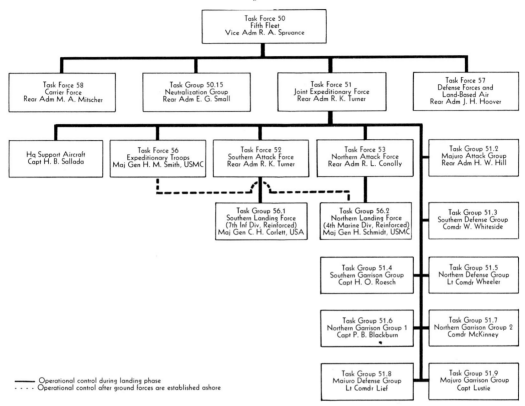

— Operational control during landing phase
- - - - Operational control after ground forces are established ashore

Gen. Charles H. Corlett, USA. The Northern Landing Force (Task Group 56.2), consisting of the 4th Marine Division with attached units, was commanded by Maj. Gen. Harry Schmidt, USMC. The Majuro Landing Force, commanded by Lt. Col. Frederick B. Sheldon, USA, was made up of the 2d Battalion, 106th Infantry, and the V Amphibious Corps Reconnaissance Company. At each objective the attack force commander (naval) was to command the landing force through the landing force commander (ground troops) until the situation permitted the latter to assume command ashore.

Under Admiral Spruance and parallel to Admiral Turner were three other commands. The first was the newly organized Carrier Force (Task Force 58), under Rear Adm. Marc A. Mitscher, which comprised four groups of fast carriers each with a varying number of the newest and fastest battleships, cruisers, and destroyers. The second was the Neutralization Group (Task Group 50.15), under Rear Adm. Ernest G. Small, consisting of three heavy cruisers, four destroyers, and two mine sweepers. The third was named Defense Forces and Land Based Air (Task Force 57) and was commanded by Admiral Hoover. Its chief components were the Strike Command (Task Group 57.2) under

General Hale, consisting of eleven land-based Army bomber squadrons; three Army fighter squadrons; and a Marine Search and Patrol Group (Task Group 57.3) under the command of General Merritt.

As outlined in Admiral Spruance's plan, the jobs assigned to Mitscher's fast carrier force were manifold. The force was to move into the Marshalls area on 29 January (D minus 2) and destroy enemy aircraft and air facilities at Wotje, Maloelap, Roi-Namur, and Kwajalein. The following day it was to co-ordinate air operations against Wotje and Maloelap with bombardment of those islands by cruisers from Turner's task force and Small's Neutralization Group. At the same time, other ships of Mitscher's force would deliver both air and surface bombardment against Roi-Namur and Kwajalein Islands. Concurrently, Eniwetok was to be denied to the enemy as an airfield. On D Day (31 January) the force was to furnish air support over Kwajalein Atoll as requested by Admiral Turner.

The job of softening up the target islands as well as other islands in the Marshalls group was assigned to Admiral Hoover's task force. Before the fast carriers moved into the area the land-based planes of Task Force 57 were to keep Mille and Jaluit neutralized; destroy enemy aircraft and air facilities at Roi-Namur, Kwajalein, and Maloelap; mine the waters around Jaluit, Mille, Maloelap, and Wotje; furnish air support at Kwajalein on D Day as requested by Admiral Turner; and be responsible for the photographic reconnaissance of the Marshalls as directed by Admiral Nimitz. From 25 December through D Day they were to search the entire Marshalls area for enemy plane and ship movements, attack enemy ships and shipping, protect

the Ellice and Gilbert Islands, and provide air transportation. Finally, to this headquarters was assigned the duty of developing the advance bases in Kwajalein and Majuro once these had been captured by ground and naval forces.

Finally, Admiral Small's little force of cruisers and destroyers was ordered to operate off the atolls of Wotje and Maloelap and bombard those islands intermittently commencing on 29 January. The purpose of this maneuver was to deny the enemy the use of his airfields there.[16]

Admiral Turner's Attack Plan

The plan for the invasion of the Marshalls differed in many important details from that for any previous amphibious operation in the Pacific. The differences resulted partly from the experiences gained in the Gilberts and partly from the fact that by this time a far greater quantity and variety of amphibious equipment had been made available to the Central Pacific forces.

No longer did the attack force commanders have to rely on the faulty communications systems of battleships to maintain proper radio liaison between ship and shore and ship and air. Two newly constructed headquarters ships, each equipped with the latest developments in radio and radar gear and unburdened by gunfire support duties, were provided for this operation. Admiral Turner at Kwajalein carried his flag aboard the USS *Rocky Mount* and Admiral Conolly at Roi-Namur rode the USS *Appalachian*. In addition, Admiral Hill was given a new flagship, the APA *Cambria*, which had been partially converted into a headquarters ship.

---

[16] *Ibid.*, pp. 14–16.

In the interim between the Gilberts and Marshalls invasions, several improvements were made in the techniques of softening up the enemy defenses before the first troops touched shore. These all added up to one factor: a great increase in both the quantity and accuracy of fire power to be delivered before the invasion. Provision was made for a longer period of preliminary aerial bombardment both from the newly acquired island bases in the Gilberts and from the newly organized fast carrier force. Naval ships and planes were ordered to move into the target area and shell and bombard enemy installations one day before the initial landings in the Marshalls and a full two days before the main landings were executed. Also, provision was made to land field artillery on islands adjacent to Kwajalein Island and Roi-Namur a day before these two main objectives were assaulted by ground troops. The field pieces were to be registered on the larger islands in time to support the assault troops as they moved from ship to shore.

To provide a last-minute saturation of the beaches, two new, or rather modified, forms of older types of amphibious equipment were introduced. The first of these was the armored amphibian or amphibian tank (LVT(A)).[17] This vehicle was merely the standard amphibian tractor equipped with extra armor plating and mounting a 37-mm. gun housed in a turret. It was to precede or accompany the first wave of troops from the line of departure to the shore and provide extra fire support for them. The second was the LCI gunboat (LCI(G)). This little vessel (153 feet in length), originally designed to land infantry troops at the shore line, had been converted into a gunboat by the addition of three 40-mm. guns and banks of 4.5-inch rocket launchers. The LCI(G)'s were to precede the first wave of amphibian vehicles close into shore, firing their rockets and guns in an effort to knock out any enemy personnel and machine guns that might still be functioning on the beaches after the heavier naval and aerial fire had lifted.

Finally, a sufficient number of amphibian tractors was provided to the battalion landing teams to permit them to land their assault waves *in toto*. This, it was hoped, would provide the necessary momentum to the assault, so noticeably lacking at Tarawa, and would eliminate the necessity of transferring assault troops from landing craft to amphibian tractors at the reef line.

To transport the troops and equipment of the 7th Infantry Division to Kwajalein Island, Admiral Turner was able to plan on a total of 11 attack transports, one troop transport ship, 3 attack cargo ships, 2 landing ships dock to carry the tanks, and 16 LST's to carry amphibian tractors and trucks. To escort these ships to the target area and provide naval and aerial support, mine sweeping, and other functions, he had 4 old battleships, 3 heavy cruisers, 21 destroyers, 2 high-speed transports (APD's), 3 escort carriers, 12 LCI's (landing craft, infantry), and 4 mine sweepers (AM's and DMS's). About the same number of troop and cargo ships were assigned to Admiral Conolly's Northern Attack Force to transport the 4th Marine Division to Roi-Namur. Conolly's support shipping was less than Turner's by one old battleship, one heavy cruiser, and eleven destroyers, but in partial recompense he was awarded two light cruisers. The Majuro Attack Group under Admiral Hill consisted of one heavy cruiser, two escort car-

---

[17] In Marine Corps terminology, this vehicle was called the armored amphibian tractor; in the Army it was called the amphibian tank.

riers, four destroyers, one mine sweeper, one attack transport, one troop transport, and two high-speed transports. The attack force reserve group, which carried the 22d Marine Regiment and the two battalions of the 106th Infantry Regiment not assigned to Majuro, consisted of five attack transports, one troop transport, two attack cargo ships, and seven destroyers.[18]

Admiral Turner's plan called for extensive prelanding bombardment both from surface ships and from the air. On D minus 1 (30 January) eight battleships from Mitscher's fast carrier force, accompanied by about a dozen destroyers, were to deliver a dawn bombardment against Kwajalein Island and Roi-Namur. The object was to destroy aircraft, coast defense guns, and personnel, and to render the airfields temporarily useless. At the same time, two advance units of cruisers and destroyers from Turner's task force were to bombard the airfields at Wotje and Maloelap. These dawn bombardments were to be followed by air strikes against each of the objectives. After the strikes were completed the surface ships would again take up the bombardment and maintain a steady fire until about noon.[19]

On D Day (31 January) the schedule called for initial landings on islands adjacent to Kwajalein and Roi-Namur upon which artillery could be emplaced for the main assaults. Cruisers, old battleships, and destroyers of Turner's task force were to conduct an all-day bombardment against both the smaller islands and the main targets in order to support landings on the smaller islands, to destroy coastal batteries, antiaircraft defenses, and beach defenses on the main islands, and to continue the destruction of aircraft and airfield installations. Fifteen minutes before the first wave of boats was scheduled to hit

the shore at Carlson (Enubuj),[20] which lies just northwest of Kwajalein Island, flights of torpedo bombers, dive bombers, and fighter planes were to deliver a last-minute attack against the beaches. A similar strike was to be delivered against Ivan (Mellu) and Jacob (Ennuebing) Islands, which lie southwest of Roi-Namur.

On D plus 1 (1 February) cruisers and battleships and as many destroyers as could be spared from screening duties were to conduct bombardments in support of the main landings on Kwajalein and Roi-Namur. Other islands that could be used by the Japanese to interfere with these landings were to be kept neutralized by surface bombardment. At daylight the heavy ships were to open up with counter-battery fire to protect the transports as they unloaded the troops, and with area bombardment to destroy secondary defenses behind the beaches. As H Hour approached, destroyers and LCI gunboats were to move into very close range of the beaches. Close supporting fire for advancing boat waves as they moved in to the shore line was to be delivered by cruisers firing 8-inch and 5-inch shells from medium ranges and by destroyers and LCI(G)'s at close ranges. Cruisers were ordered to cease fire when the first wave was about 1,000 yards from the beach. Destroyers and LCI(G)'s were to continue fire until the first landing wave was 500 yards or less from the beach. Thereafter they would shift to the flanks to protect succeeding waves.

Commencing forty-five minutes before

<hr>

[18] TF 51 Opn Plan A6-43, 3 Jan 44, Serial 0013.
[19] *Ibid.*, Annex C.
[20] Carlson is the code name used by the American forces. In this volume the code names and, sometimes, the native names (in parenthesis) will be used to identify the lesser islands of Kwajalein Atoll. See list, p. 375.

the first waves touched shore, air strikes by the maximum available number of planes were to be carried out against the main landing beaches both at Kwajalein Island and at Roi-Namur. These were to cease twenty-five minutes before the first wave touched shore in order to allow a resumption of ships' fire and of artillery fire from Carlson, Ivan, and Jacob. In addition to this air support provided by planes from the escort carriers in Turner's task force, Admiral Hoover's Task Force 57 was ordered to provide one squadron of land-based heavy bombers to attack various strong points and blockhouses, commencing sixty minutes before the first landings on the main islands.[21] With this tremendous bombardment by aircraft, surface ships, and artillery, all to be executed before the first troops hit the shore line, it was hoped that the bitter experience of Tarawa would not be repeated.

The Landing Force Plans

Southern Kwajalein

Kwajalein Island is shaped like a crescent, its concave side being the lagoon or north shore. It is approximately two and a half miles in length and averages 800 yards in width for two thirds of its length from west to east, then tapers, after bending to the north, to less than 300 yards in width at its northeastern tip. It is the largest island of the atoll.[22] The island nearest to the western end of Kwajalein is Carlson (Enubuj), approximately two miles to the northwest. (*Map 9*) Next to the northeastern end are two tiny pieces of land, Byron and Buster Islands (no known native names), then the larger Burton (Ebeye), which is nearly two and a half miles from Kwajalein. Photographs and intelligence

surveys showed that Carlson was weakly defended if at all, while the Burton garrison was estimated to be at least 1,000 troops. Closer scrutiny of Burton also revealed extensive prepared positions. It was estimated that there were eight antiaircraft guns near the ramps and service apron, and the island seemed to be ringed by a series of pillboxes. In the opinion of General Corlett, 7th Division commander, and of his division artillery officer, Brig. Gen. Archibald V. Arnold, the artillery could be placed on either Carlson or Burton and deliver fire on the landing beaches in support of the main assault on Kwajalein Island. The absence of defenses on Carlson made this island seem to be the more desirable, but in order to utilize the fire power of the division artillery to the fullest, it was necessary to decide at exactly what spot on Kwajalein Island the assault troops were to go ashore. Should the landing beaches be toward the northeastern end of the island, Burton would serve better for artillery emplacements, even though it was defended.

The reef along the ocean side of Kwajalein Island is from 100 to 130 yards wide and precipitous. At low tide it is completely bared and fairly smooth except near the ends of the island. Heavy surf strikes the eastern shore and rolls along the southern shore, but at the southwestern corner the swell becomes moderate, a circumstance that favored landings in that area. On the lagoon side, although the water is smooth, the reef is from 500 to 800 yards wide. Boulders and smooth coral outcroppings

---

[21] TF 51 Opn Plan A6-43, 3 Jan 44, Serial 0013, Annexes C, E.

[22] Terrain data are from 7th Infantry Division Report on Operation FLINTLOCK 31 January–4 February 1944 (hereafter cited as 7th Inf Div FLINTLOCK Rpt), Vol. II, Field Orders and Report of Operation, FO 1, 6 Jan 44, Intelligence Annex.

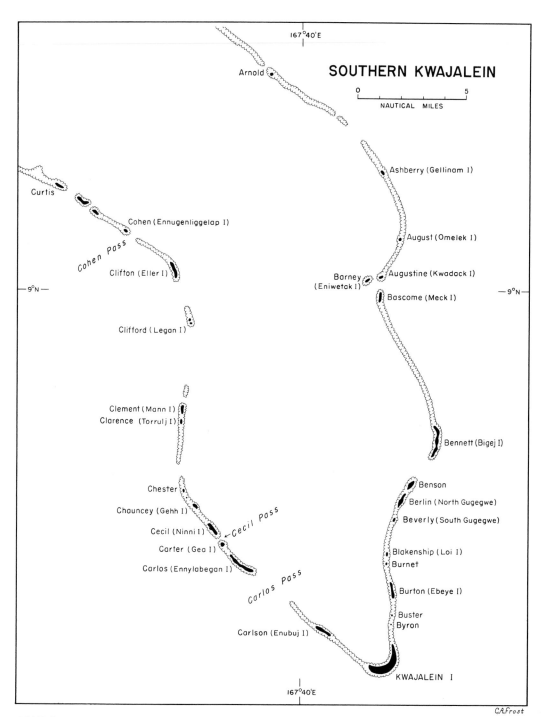

Arnold

SOUTHERN KWAJALEIN

167°40'E

0   5
NAUTICAL MILES

Ashberry (Gellinam I)

Curtis

Cohen (Ennugenliggelap I)

August (Omelek I)

Cohen Pass

Clifton (Eller I)

Barney
(Eniwetak I)

Augustine (Kwadack I)

— 9°N —

Bascome (Meck I)

— 9°N —

Clifford (Legan I)

Clement (Mann I)
Clarence (Torrulj I)

Bennett (Bigej I)

Chester

Benson
Berlin (North Gugegwe)
Beverly (South Gugegwe)

Chauncey (Gehh I)

Cecil (Ninni I)

Cecil Pass

Blakenship (Loi I)
Burnet

Carter (Gea I)

Carlos (Ennylabegan I)

Burton (Ebeye I)

Carlos Pass

Buster
Byron

Carlson (Enubuj I)

KWAJALEIN I

167°40'E

C.A.Frost

MAP 9

promised to make the approach to the lagoon beaches even more difficult than those at Tarawa or at Red Beaches, Makin. The beaches along both the ocean and the lagoon shore vary normally from ten to twenty yards in width after rising from the reef. At the two tips of the island, however, the beaches rise more gradually and are considerably more extensive, a smooth beach of coral sand extending for approximately 250 yards inland at the northeastern tip and 450 yards at the western end.

It was generally believed that the Marshalls, having been prewar Japanese territory and being nearer to the heart of Japan, would be more strongly fortified than the Gilberts. Should the prepared positions that had furnished such a costly obstacle at Tarawa be excelled by those on Kwajalein Island, the forthcoming attack would have to be carefully planned to strike the weaker portions of the Japanese defensive system. The preliminary reconnaissance had shown that the enemy had apparently long expected attack from the seaward side. But photographs taken on 4 December showed that the garrison had begun the erection of positions along the lagoon, apparently on the ground that Tarawa had been attacked from the lagoon shore and an invasion of Kwajalein might possibly come from the same direction.

After weighing these various considerations, the planners decided that the 7th Infantry Division should land at either end of the island rather than in a frontal attack against either the ocean or lagoon shore line. Because reef and surf conditions were more favorable at the western end, and because Carlson Island would probably be much easier to take quickly than would Burton, plans were laid for the division to land on the beaches at the western extremity. This would take place after the D-Day

invasion of Carlson Island, where the division artillery would be placed to support the main landing on Kwajalein.[23] Such a course of action would give the assault troops on Kwajalein Island the benefit of high-angle artillery fire to supplement the fire of the flat-trajectory naval guns.

Three other small islands in addition to Carlson were to be captured during the preparatory phase of the operation. These were Carlos (Ennylabegan), Carter (Gea), and Cecil (Ninni) Islands, all lying north of Carlson. They guarded Cecil Pass, the best deep-water channel into the lagoon at southern Kwajalein, and were thought to be lightly defended, if at all. It was Admiral Turner's desire to move many of the transports and fire support vessels into the lagoon, where they would be protected from submarine attack and where naval gunfire could be brought to bear directly on the lagoon beach defenses. The 7th Division's operation order, therefore, called for the capture of four islands during Phase I, which was to begin on D Day, 31 January.[24] Artillery was to be landed on Carlson and moved into firing position at the earliest possible moment after troops had landed.

The assault on Kwajalein Island, the main objective, was to take place on the morning of D plus 1 (1 February) if, by then, Carlson had been captured and the artillery placed in position. By close planning between division artillery representatives, Army and Navy air services, and naval gunnery officers, all bombardment and naval gunfire and Army artillery support were carefully co-ordinated for the support of the main attack. Following a preliminary (prelanding) bombardment of one hour, each type of fire would lift in-

[23] Ibid., FO 2, 6 Jan 44.
[24] Ibid., FO 1, 6 Jan 44, p. 1.

land. Army artillery would be nearest in advance of the troops; naval gunfire next; and the aerial coverage still farther inland.[25]

The 7th Division had no organic 155-mm. howitzer battalions, but during the planning stage the 145th Field Artillery Battalion was attached for the operation. During the night of D Day (31 January–1 February) the 145th and two other field artillery battalions were to deliver interdictory fire from Carlson on all the principal fortified areas of Kwajalein Island and place counterbattery fire on any enemy artillery that might be emplaced on Burton. They were also to fire general support missions for the infantry.[26]

The reduction of Kwajalein Island itself was to constitute Phase II of the 7th Division operations. In the allocation of targets, the 7th Division had been assigned all islands south of the line running between Arnold Island in the eastern side of the atoll and Cohen (Ennugenliggelap) Island in the western side. Of these, Burton was believed to be the only one besides Kwajalein defended by a sizable garrison.

Plans for Phases III and IV to complete the conquest of southern Kwajalein were laid, but the time of execution was to depend upon progress made in Phase II. The forces that were to seize Cecil, Carter, Carlos, and Carlson on D Day would then constitute a reserve for landing teams operating on Kwajalein Island.[27] Once the need for this reserve had passed, the forces could be committed in Phase III, the reduction and occupation of Burton Island and the investigation of Buster, Byron, Burnet, and Blankenship (Loi) Islands. The final phase was to include the seizure of Beverly (South Gugegwe), Berlin (North Gugegwe), Benson, and Bennett (Bigej) Islands in the eastern chain.[28]

To accomplish its mission at southern Kwajalein, the 7th Division was organized into nine battalion landing teams, each consisting of three rifle companies, a heavy weapons company, a platoon of engineers from the 13th Engineer Battalion, a platoon of medium tanks from the 767th Tank Battalion, a platoon from one of the regimental cannon companies, and small detachments of service troops.[29] A tenth landing team, for use against small objectives, was formed by the 7th Cavalry Reconnaissance Troop and Company B, 111th Infantry, a regiment that was part of the prospective Kwajalein Garrison Force but had been attached to the division for the assault phase of the operation. In the event that a battalion landing team was called upon to act separately, it could be made self-sufficient by the addition of a shore party team.

With the prospect of different elements of the division operating at widely scattered points in the atoll and depending on many varied arms for support, communications promised to be a major difficulty. This problem was anticipated. A provisional communications unit, known as the 75th Joint Assault Signal Company (JASCO), was organized for the 7th Division, and elements of the 295th JASCO were furnished to the 106th Regimental Combat Team.[30] The 75th Provisional JASCO, made up of the 75th Signal Company reinforced by naval and air force

[25] Ibid., FO 2, Annex 6, p. 1.
[26] 7th Inf Div FLINTLOCK Rpt, Vol. XII, Arty Jnl, Msg 35, 31 Jan 44.
[27] 7th Inf Div FLINTLOCK Rpt, Vol. II, FO 1, 6 Jan 44, p. 2.
[28] Ibid., FO 4, 1 Feb 44.
[29] Ibid., FO 1, 6 Jan 44, Annex 1, p. 5.
[30] USAFICPA Report of Participation in the Kwajalein and Eniwetok Operations, 30 Nov 44 (hereafter cited as USAFICPA Participation Rpt Kwajalein and Eniwetok), pp. 143, 144.

personnel, totaled 592 officers and men. It was to co-ordinate naval gunfire support missions and direct air strikes, whether performed by land-based bombers of the Army Air Forces or carrier-based planes of the Navy. It was also the channel through which troops ashore communicated with command posts afloat.

For operational purposes the 75th Provisional JASCO was divided into a headquarters, ten shore and beach party teams, and nine shore fire control teams. Each of the shore and beach party teams would serve with a battalion landing team and would be made up of thirty-two men, drawn from both Army and Navy. The nine shore fire control teams, composed of Navy officers and Army signal men, were to be distributed among the nine assault landing teams. Also operating with, but not a part of, the 75th JASCO were thirteen air-ground liaison teams of five men each. Each battalion received one of these teams, the other four being apportioned among the various regimental headquarters and division artillery. Seventy-nine men of the 75th Provisional JASCO were retained by division headquarters to perform administrative functions and co-ordinate work of the various teams.

For the Kwajalein Island operation, enough LVT's were provided to carry the first four waves of assault troops into the beach. A total of 174 amphibian vehicles was assigned to the 7th Infantry Division. Of these, 79 were amphibian tanks (or armored amphibians) mounting 37-mm. guns and designed primarily for close support of the first waves both during and after the ship-to-shore movement. The remainder were standard amphibian tractors. For this operation, the tanks and tractors were divided into four combat tractor groups, each with 14 amphibian

tanks and 20 amphibian tractors, plus one additional detachment of 17 amphibian tanks to be distributed among the four groups as the situation required. Twenty-one vehicles were placed in a reserve LVT pool that was to provide immediate replacement to the combat tractor groups. One of the tractor groups was assigned to the D-Day landings on Carlson Island and one to Carlos Island. Two were assigned to Kwajalein Island for the D-plus-1 landings. After carrying the troops of the first four assault waves to the beaches, the tractors of these groups were either to support the infantry advance inland, or, in the case of Kwajalein Island, were to return to the reef line and pick up reserve troops boated in standard landing craft.[31] By these measures, it was hoped to guarantee an uninterrupted movement of the assault troops from ship to shore and an avoidance of the breakdown of momentum such as had occurred at Tarawa.

The first phase of the operations of the Southern Attack Force was to open with a predawn landing of one platoon of the 7th Cavalry Reconnaissance Troop on each of the two channel islands, Carter and Cecil. These landings were to be accomplished with the greatest secrecy, and the conquest of the outposts was to be completed as quickly as possible before the defenders could reinforce the garrisons that might be there. The reconnaissance troop was embarked on two high-speed transports (APD's), along with two platoons of Company B, 111th Infantry. The landings were

---

[31] 7th Inf Div FLINTLOCK Rpt, Vol. II, FO 1, 6 Jan 44, Annex 8, pp. 1–2, and FO 2, 6 Jan 44, Annex 8, pp. 1–2; *Ibid.*, Vol. VII, G-4 Rpt, Annex E, Ordnance Rpt, p. 5; 7th Infantry Division Report of Participation in Operation FLINTLOCK, 8 Feb 44 (hereafter cited as 7th Inf Div Participation Rpt FLINTLOCK), p. 34; 708th Amph Tk Bn Special Action Rpt, Kwajalein Opns, 12 Mar 44, pp. 1–2.

to be made in rubber boats that would be paddled ashore from 800 yards off the beaches. The men would go over the side of the APD's into their landing craft and land at 0330. It was hoped the capture would be completed shortly after daylight. The next moves of the first phase were to be the simultaneous landings on Carlos and Carlson Islands. The 1st Battalion, 17th Infantry, was to land on the former while the 2d Battalion, 17th Infantry, invaded the latter. The 3d Battalion, 17th Infantry was to be held in reserve, ready to go to the aid of either landing team. While the capture of Carlson Island was in progress, the division artillery, loaded for the most part on amphibious trucks, was to debark and proceed to a rendezvous area offshore. Upon a signal from the commander of the Carlson landing force, the guns were to be moved ashore and into position.

The major part of the Southern Attack Force plan was that dealing with Kwajalein Island, the main objective. After the landing on the western tip of the island with the two regimental combat teams abreast—the 184th on the left and the 32d on the right—the attack was to proceed directly up the axis of the island with the boundary between regiments drawn roughly along a line that divided the island into halves. In the left zone of action the assault force would consist of the 2d and 3d Battalions, 184th Infantry; in the right zone the 1st Battalion, 32d Infantry, was to make the initial landings. The 1st Battalion, 184th Infantry, and the 2d and 3d Battalions, 32d Infantry, were to be held either at the line of departure or in the lagoon ready for use in later aspects of the attack.

Phases III and IV were dependent upon the progress of the attack on Kwajalein Island. The 17th Regimental Combat Team, upon conclusion of the Carlson and Carlos invasions, was to be held as division reserve for the landings on the main island. If it became evident that operations there were going well and the 17th would not be needed, the capture of the remaining islands could proceed, using battalion landing teams of this reserve regiment and the 7th Reconnaissance Troop.[32] Operations in the last two phases were not clearly defined as to tactics; the exact procedure to be used was left until the target was reached and a closer survey made.

Northern Kwajalein Atoll

The plans drawn up by the 4th Marine Division for the capture of Roi-Namur and the adjacent islands in the northern half of Kwajalein Atoll were similar in most respects to those of the 7th Division. The only important difference in the landing plan stemmed from the choice of beaches. Whereas the 7th Division proposed to land on a narrow front on the west end of Kwajalein Island and fight its way up the long axis of the island, the 4th Marine Division was able to undertake a more orthodox amphibious maneuver and land two regiments abreast on a broad front on the lagoon shore of Roi-Namur. (*Map 10*)

Roi Island measures 1,250 yards north and south by 1,200 yards east and west. At the time of the landing it was almost entirely cleared and was the site of the largest enemy airfield in Kwajalein Atoll. The field had three runways and was shaped in the form of a figure 4. It also had four turning circles, two service aprons, two hangars, numerous service buildings, a

---

[32] 7th Inf Div FLINTLOCK Rpt, Vol. II, FO 1, 6 Jan 44, p. 2, and FO 2, 6 Jan 44, pp. 2, 3.

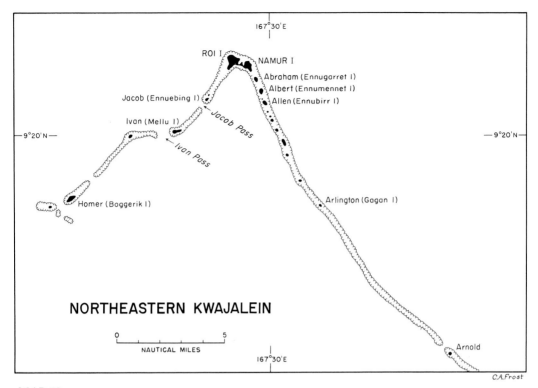

MAP 10

control tower, and some thirty revetments. The dispersal area covered practically the whole island. Namur Island, located 500 yards southeast of Roi, is connected with the latter by a sand beach on the lagoon (southern) side and a causeway between the islands halfway between the lagoon and ocean beaches. The island measures approximately 900 yards east-west and 800 yards north-south. Unlike Roi, it was heavily wooded at the time of the landings, in spite of the fact that it contained a large number of buildings.

The beaches along the seaward side of Roi and Namur, as elsewhere in the atoll, are approached over a reef from 125 to 400 yards wide that falls away sharply to seaward and has a ragged outer edge. This reef, plus the fact that surf on Roi-Namur's ocean coast was extremely heavy, made landings from that side unfeasible. The only possible location for a landing, therefore, was from the lagoon where the reef fell gradually and was under water at high tide, and where there was no considerable surf.[33]

The 4th Marine Division's plan of attack closely paralleled that of the 7th Infantry Division in the south. On D Day, while the Southern Attack Force would be busy with the capture of islands adjacent to Kwajalein, the 25th Marine Regimental Combat Team, commanded by Brig. Gen. James L. Underhill, USMC, would

[33] 4th Marine Div Opn Plan 3-43 (Revised), App 2 to Annex Fox, 30 Dec 43.

capture five islets near Roi-Namur. Two of these guarded passes into the lagoon. The most important of the northern channels was Ivan Pass guarded by Ivan (Mellu) Island, about five miles to the west of the main base at Roi. A nearer pass was also guarded by Ivan as well as Jacob (Ennuebing) Island, from which it took its name. Just to the southeast of Namur lay five other islets, three of them large enough to be usable, the other two being simply reef outcroppings. The three larger were named Abraham (Ennugarret), Albert (Ennumennet) and Allen (Ennubirr). These three, as well as Ivan and Jacob, were thought to be suitable for the emplacement of artillery.[34]

On D Day, General Underhill's landing group was to seize Jacob and Ivan Islands and establish thereon the 3d and 4th Battalions of the 14th Marine Regiment (Artillery). Thereupon, the group was to move to Albert and Allen Islands where the other two battalions of the Marine artillery regiment were to be emplaced. The occupation of these islands, none of which was expected to be heavily defended, was to be completed before darkness on D Day.

On the next day the main landings were to take place on Roi and Namur. The 23d Regimental Combat Team was ordered to land two regiments abreast on Red Beaches 2 and 3 on the lagoon shore of Roi. The 24th Regimental Combat Team was to conduct simultaneous landings on Green Beaches 1 and 2 on the lagoon shore of Namur. The third and final phase of the operation would include capture of the remaining islands in northern Kwajalein and would be conducted on order depending upon the speed with which the main objectives were attained.

These landings would of course follow the same intense aerial, naval, and artillery preparatory fire outlined for southern Kwajalein. The assault troops would all be boated in amphibian tractors, which would be preceded by a wave of LCI gunboats and a wave of armored LVT's. The LCI(G)'s were instructed to proceed to within 1,000 yards of the beach, fire their rockets, and continue to support the landing of troops by gunfire. The armored amphibians were to pass through the LCI(G)'s and open fire with their 37-mm. guns and machine guns. Finally, the amphibian tractors mounting the infantry were to follow the armored amphibians and pass through them if the latter had to be stopped short of the beaches. Tanks, boated in LCM's, would follow the first waves of troops.[35]

Coincident with the seizure of Kwajalein, the separate task group (Task Group 51.2) under Admiral Hill was to invade Majuro Atoll. This force was made up principally of the 2d Battalion, 106th Infantry, from the 27th Infantry Division, and the V Amphibious Corps Reconnaissance Company. Majuro was thought to be lightly defended, perhaps not at all. For this reason, plans for the occupation of the atoll were dependent upon the results of a preliminary reconnaissance to be carried out by the reconnaissance company on D Day after its seizure of Calalin Island, which guarded the principal entrance pass into the lagoon.[36]

---

[34] 4th Marine Div Final Rpt on FLINTLOCK Opn, 17 Mar 44, Incl C.

[35] 4th Marine Div Opn Plan 3-43 (Revised), 31 Dec 43, pp. 1-2; *Ibid.*, Annex M.

[36] TG 51.2 Action Rpt Majuro Atoll, Marshall Islands, 15 Feb 44, p. 4.

CHAPTER XII

Training, Logistics, and Preliminary Operations

Training the Army Ground Troops

Of the troops who were to make the invasion of Kwajalein Atoll, only the 17th and 32d Regimental Combat Teams of the 7th Infantry Division had seen previous combat. The two Army regiments had conducted successful amphibious landings on Attu and captured it in May 1943.[1] The 184th Infantry had made an unopposed landing at Kiska. Neither the 106th Regimental Combat Team of the 27th Infantry Division, nor the 4th Marine Division, nor the 22d Marines, an independent Marine regiment, had engaged in any previous operations. Even those units that had been in combat were now faced with entirely new problems. The two combat teams of the 7th Division that had landed on Attu had fought under conditions very different from those to be found on a coral atoll. Each unit therefore underwent a period of intensive training with emphasis on the amphibious techniques that would be used at Kwajalein Island and Roi-Namur.

Initial training of the 7th Division for the Marshalls operation fell under the control of General Richardson's headquarters (USAFICPA). The entire division spent a week at a jungle training center on Oahu, where it was put through battle-conditioning courses and received instruction in jungle fighting, jungle living, booby traps and demolitions, sniping and infiltration, and defense against various types of tactics that might be employed against it in the forthcoming campaign. Each company conducted exercises in the attack of fortified positions involving the use of chemical mortars, flame throwers, grenades, engineer-infantry teams, tanks, and machine guns and rifles.[2]

One of the chief tactical defects that had been revealed in the ground fighting at Makin and Tarawa was the poor communications and co-ordination between tanks and infantry. Steps were taken before the invasion of the Marshalls to rectify this deficiency. On 5 November the 767th Tank Battalion was attached to the 7th Infantry Division and, as soon as reports began to flow in from the Gilberts, tank and infantry officers worked in close conjunction to prevent repetition of errors committed in that operation. To improve co-ordination, tank companies and platoons, as nearly as possible, were trained with the infantry battalion with which

[1] Edmund G. Love, *The Hourglass: A History of the 7th Infantry Division in World War II* (Washington: Infantry Journal Press, 1950), Part II.
[2] USAFICPA Participation Rpt Kwajalein and Eniwetok, p. 33.

they were to work. Frequent conferences were held and a standard tank-infantry doctrine was worked out. It was agreed that tanks should precede infantry in the assault against organized positions, but not beyond the range of infantry covering fire. Tanks were not to be used to eliminate sniper fire, but should be employed against automatic weapons holding up the infantry line. Tanks should be used as forward scouts whenever the infantry was advancing into enemy country via a road. The tank commander was always to be subordinate to the infantry commander.[3]

The difficulty of maintaining communications between infantry front-line companies and the supporting tanks, especially when under machine gun and rifle fire, had been made too painfully evident in the Gilberts. As a solution a phone was devised that could be used from the outside of the tank. The phone was located in a metal box attached to the rear of each tank. On the outside of the phone box was placed a switch that operated a light on the inside of the tank. An infantryman wanting to communicate with his supporting tank had merely to flick the switch to stop the tank, remove the phone, and then talk to the tank commander inside.[4]

In addition to its responsibility for ground combat training, General Richardson's headquarters also supervised the preliminary amphibious training of the 7th Division and its attached units. Battalion landing teams were rotated through a three-day period of advanced training with floating equipment. Each team practiced embarkation, debarkation, and the formation of boat waves. Following this came battalion landing exercises, ending in a tactical firing exercise ashore. One combat company from each battalion and the 7th Cavalry Reconnaissance Troop

were given intensive training in rubber boats.[5]

Special schools were set up on Oahu at Waianae and Makua to train 7th Division troops to handle amphibian tractors and amphibian trucks.[6] These schools were conducted under the direct supervision of the 7th Division Ordnance Company. The trainees for the DUKW's came from the infantry regiment service companies and the field artillery battalions. Those for the LVT's were taken from the infantry regiment antitank companies.[7]

One of the most pressing problems facing the 7th Division after its arrival in the Hawaiian Islands was the procurement and training of shore party personnel. General Corlett had requested of General Richardson's headquarters that his division be assigned three extra engineer battalions in addition to the organic combat engineer battalion. These were to be employed exclusively for shore party work. General Richardson was unable to meet the request and informed the 7th Division commander that he would have to draw his shore parties from garrison troops assigned to the occupation of Kwajalein after the assault phase was completed, that is the 3d and 4th Army Defense Battalions. Consequently, seven engineer companies and two infantry companies of the garrison force were used as a nucleus for

---

[3] 767th Tank Battalion Report of Tank Operation FLINTLOCK, 28 Feb 44 (hereafter cited as 767th Tk Bn FLINTLOCK Rpt), pp. 2–3; S. L. A. Marshall, Notes on Kwajalein Opn, MS, 3 vols, OCMH (hereafter cited as Marshall, Kwajalein Notes), Vol. III, pp. 64–65.

[4] 767th Tk Bn FLINTLOCK Rpt, p. 35.

[5] USAFICPA Participation Rpt Kwajalein and Eniwetok, pp. 33–34; 7th Inf Div Participation Rpt FLINTLOCK, p. 2.

[6] On the tactical employment of the DUKW, see below, pp. 17–18.

[7] 7th Inf Div FLINTLOCK Rpt, Vol. VII, G-4 Rpt, Annex E, Ordnance Rpt, p. 3.

the shore parties assigned to the nine battalion landing teams of the division. There was not enough heavy equipment for both the shore party operation and the garrison resident engineer work so it was decided to use the same equipment for both tasks. Each shore party received five bulldozer crawler tractors of various sizes, one 20-ton 20-foot boom crane, one five-kilowatt floodlight system, one sled-mounted four-ton power winch, nine 2½-ton trucks, 200 feet of steel roller conveyor, 1,000 feet of beach mat, and a five-horn portable loudspeaker system.

After being issued this equipment each shore party received its training along with the battalion landing team to which it was to be attached. To indoctrinate the shore party personnel with the idea that they "were as important members of the *fighting* troops as any other component" of the battalion, the shore parties were designated "beach combat teams." Training included "dry boat" exercises in which beaching conditions were simulated and "wet boat" exercises in which each battalion and its shore party made actual landings in the beaches at Waianae Amphibious Training Center on Oahu.[8]

The amphibious training centers at Waianae and Waimanalo were also used to train joint assault signal company (JASCO) personnel in the special signal and communications problems involved in joint operations. The 75th JASCO, assigned to the 7th Division, totaled 592 officers and men, drawn both from the Army and the Navy. Elements of a similar organization, the 295th JASCO, were assigned to the 106th Regimental Combat Team of the 27th Division. Included in this signal company were three shore fire control teams and three beach and shore party teams. Operating with the 295th

JASCO were four air liaison teams.[9]

On 11 December, after the completion of its preliminary training, the 7th Division and its attached units were turned over to General Holland Smith's V Amphibious Corps for operational control and advanced amphibious training. Shipboard exercises were conducted for the 184th Regimental Combat Team, which had had the least amphibious experience of the three regiments of the division. Then, just before sailing, final rehearsals were held at Maui and Kahoolawe, Hawaii. On the former island actual landings were made, although naval gunfire was only simulated. The next day, naval ships fired live ammunition against the beaches of uninhabitated Kahoolawe. This completed the training for the amphibious units scheduled for the landings on the southern half of Kwajalein Atoll.[10]

Meanwhile, the 106th Regimental Combat Team had been undergoing a similar training program. By 3 October, when it was alerted for the Marshalls operation, it had already completed approximately eight weeks of intensive training as part of the 27th Division's Nauru task force. Thereafter, until it was turned over to V Amphibious Corps on 11 December, the regiment continued to be trained under the supervision of 27th Division headquarters. All officers and noncommissioned officers were thoroughly briefed upon the division's experiences at Makin during the week after the return of the Makin force to Oahu. Attempts were made to correct many of the deficiencies that had been found in the Makin plan.

[8] 7th Inf Div FLINTLOCK Rpt, Vol. VII, G-4 Rpt, Annex D, Engineer Rpt, pp. 2–3.
[9] USAFICPA Participation Rpt Kwajalein and Eniwetok, pp. 143–44; see above, pp. 178–79.
[10] USAFICPA Participation Rpt Kwajalein and Eniwetok, p. 34; V Phib Corps FLINTLOCK Rpt, p. 5.

Particular attention was given, as it had been in the 7th Division, to the problem of tank-infantry co-operation. The 106th Infantry was also trained in co-ordination with the 295th JASCO. Upon being assigned to V Amphibious Corps, it reviewed all amphibious training, and on 21 December the regiment embarked on a nine-day practice cruise and rehearsal off Maui.[11]

Training the 4th Marine Division

The 4th Marine Division was activated on 15 August 1943 at Camp Pendleton, California, General Schmidt commanding. On 20 September it was assigned to the V Amphibious Corps with the understanding that it would participate in some undesignated Central Pacific landing and that it must be fully trained and equipped by 1 December. The division held frequent boat exercises throughout September and October, using boats furnished by the Amphibious Training Command.[12]

Late in October, Group Three of the V Amphibious Force was organized under command of Admiral Conolly. Conolly's task force (later designated Task Force 53) was assigned the duty of carrying and supporting the 4th Marine Division in the invasion of Kwajalein Atoll. Admiral Conolly established his headquarters at Camp Pendleton and worked in close conjunction with division headquarters in preparing a training schedule. The proximity of the two headquarters made for excellent co-ordination of their activities. Each regimental combat team of the Marine division was given a two-week period of actual ship-to-shore training from transports. One division rehearsal landing was conducted on the Aliso Canyon beaches of Camp Pendleton during December. After

word arrived late in that month that the target would be the northern part of Kwajalein Atoll, plans for a final rehearsal were drawn up to simulate as far as possible the actual conditions that could be expected in the Marshalls.[13]

The 1st Joint Assault Signal Company, with functions similar to the Army JASCO's, was attached on 2 December and commenced training with its assigned infantry and naval units. On 20 November the 1st Armored Amphibian Battalion was attached. As soon as the reports of the 2d Marine Division's experiences at Tarawa were received by 4th Marine Division headquarters, training in the employment of amphibian tractors was stepped up. Early in December a new amphibian tractor battalion—in addition to the one already organic to the division—was organized. Later still, an amphibian tractor company was added. This led to an undesirable dilution of trained personnel. Also, the fact that the tractors had to be equipped with additional armor kept many of them out of operation at the time when intensive training of tractor crews was most necessary. The result was that the marines assigned to man the amphibian tractors were inadequately trained, a defect that was to have serious effects on the ship-to-shore movement at Roi-Namur.[14] It was the opinion of General Schmidt that "the greatest deficiency in amphibious training [in the 4th Marine Division] appeared to be in methods of boat control, especially during the critical stage of forming boat waves and groups for the assault." He also noted that his LVT

---

[11] USAFICPA Participation Rpt Kwajalein and Eniwetok, pp. 197–99.

[12] 4th Marine Div Final Rpt FLINTLOCK, p. 2.

[13] TF 53 Rpt of Amph Opns for the capture of Roi and Namur Islands, 23 Feb 44, pp. 1–2.

[14] 4th Marine Div Final Rpt FLINTLOCK, p. 2.

crews lacked adequate training in troop-carrying operations, elementary seamanship, and in the use of the compass.[15]

Logistics

Supplying and Loading Army Ground Troops

The burden of initial supply support for the 7th Infantry Division and the 106th Regimental Combat Team fell jointly on Headquarters, United States Army Forces, Central Pacific Area; the V Amphibious Corps; and Commander, Service Force, Pacific Fleet—all in Oahu. This division of responsibility caused some confusion and delay. The main source of difficulty was that the place and responsibility of V Amphibious Corps was never clearly defined in regard to supply, at least to the satisfaction of the logistics officers of the 7th Division.[16] General Holland Smith was in tactical command of the operation and General Richardson was charged with training and supplying the Army troops that would participate. This dichotomy tended to handicap the easy flow of supplies into the hands of the troops. As the 7th Division's logistics officer, Lt. Col. David X. Angluin, reported: "On the one hand there was the supply headquarters without tactical authority or especial tactical consideration [USAFICPA], and on the other hand there was the [ultimate] tactical headquarters without supply responsibility [V Amphibious Corps]. Considerable valuable time was lost in processing requests because of the lack of early definition of responsibility."[17] Logistical planning on the division level was always complicated by the necessity for working through several responsible parties instead of one. For example, during the four months of planning and equipping, Class III supply (fuels and lubricants) was passed back and forth between Army and Navy authorities until finally it was decided that the Navy would be responsible for supplying bulk fuels and the Army for filling and marking five-gallon containers, while certain other types of oils and greases would be bought on the open market.[18] Luckily, the division was allowed ample time to prepare for the Marshalls invasions and most of the difficulties arising from divided responsibility were overcome.

The basic logistics plan was originally prescribed by Admiral Nimitz on 11 November.[19] Only one major change was later made; this was in the amount of ammunition to be carried by the combat troops. The original directive had provided that the combat troops embarking on the Marshalls expedition would carry five units of fire for each weapon except for antiaircraft guns, which were allowed ten.[20] As a result of the experience in the

---

[15] *Ibid.,* Annex J, p. 18.

[16] V Phib Corps FLINTLOCK Rpt, Annex F, G-4 Rpt, p. 2; 7th Inf Div FLINTLOCK Rpt, Vol. VII, G-4 Rpt, Annex F, QM Rpt, p. 2.

[17] 7th Inf Div FLINTLOCK Rpt, Vol. VII, Part III, p. 6.

[18] *Ibid.,* Annex F, QM Rpt, p. 2.

[19] CINCPAC-CINCPOA Opn Plan 16-43, 12 Oct 43, Annex A, Logistic Plan for Land-Based Forces, 11 Nov 43.

[20] A unit of fire is by definition the number of rounds of ammunition that will normally be used by one weapon in one day. In the Central Pacific, the Army unit of fire for each of the main weapons was as follows:

Weapon	Rounds
.30-caliber carbine M1	30
.30-caliber rifle M1903 (Springfield)	70
.30-caliber rifle M1 (Garand)	70
.30-caliber automatic rifle M1918A2 (BAR)	750
.30-caliber machine gun	1,800
60-mm. mortar	100
81-mm. mortar	90
75-mm. howitzer (field)	300
75-mm. gun (field and tank)	300
90-mm. gun (AA)	125
105-mm. howitzer	200
155-mm. howitzer	150

Source: 7th Inf Div FLINTLOCK Rpt, Vol. VII, G-4 Rpt, Annex E, Ordnance Rpt, Incl 3.

Gilberts, officers of the 7th Division became dissatisfied with this allotment, particularly the allowance to artillery weapons. Late in the preparatory phase, the division initiated a request for an increase in the total number of units of fire to be taken to the Marshalls.[21] This was finally approved by Admiral Nimitz on 5 January, and the total units of fire for 105-mm. howitzers were increased from five to ten and for other ground weapons from five to eight.[22]

As finally drawn up, the logistics plan for the Marshalls operation provided that assault forces would carry 30 days of B rations, 5 days of C rations, 5 days of K rations, 2 days of D rations, and 5 days of water in cans. Thirty days of Class II (maintenance), Class III (fuels and lubricants), and Class IV (medical, aviation, and construction) supplies were also to be carried by the assault troops. The garrison forces were supplied with like amounts except that the number of units of fire provided for them was reduced.[23]

The 7th Division had been the first in the Pacific to experiment with pallets, and once again, as at Attu, these amphibious sleds were used extensively. The division engineer was charged with the responsibility of palletizing supplies and certain items of equipment. By the end of the preparatory phase a total of 4,174 sled loads were palletized. This included 3 days of K and C rations, 3 days of Class III supplies carried in five-gallon cans, 3 units of fire for all weapons except the artillery howitzers and chemical mortars, 2 units of fire for four 105-mm. howitzer battalions, 8 units of fire for one 155-mm. howitzer battalion, 4 units of fire for the 4.2-inch chemical mortars, and sundry items of engineer, medical, signal, ordnance, and hospital equipment. None of the supplies carried in LST's or LSD's were palletized since these ships were not considered suitable for easy handling of pallets.[24]

No single item of equipment was more eagerly sought by planners at all echelons than the amphibian tractor, whose utility as a carrier of assault troops had been so fully demonstrated at Tarawa and Makin. Late in November Admiral Nimitz informed General Richardson that a minimum of four tractor battalions per division was desirable for atoll operations. One of these battalions, he added, should consist of amphibian tanks—amphibian tractors carrying extra armor plate and mounting 37-mm. guns. Richardson promptly requested the War Department to make the allocation.[25] This could not be honored in its entirety, but the newly formed 708th Amphibian Tank Battalion, then training in California, was dispatched to Oahu. Although the personnel of the battalion had scarcely become acquainted with their vehicles, the unit was attached to the 7th Division on 15 December for the Marshalls operation.[26]

An antitank company from each of the three regiments of the 7th Division was converted into an LVT group and added to the amphibian tank battalion. When finally organized the battalion's total came to one company of amphibian tanks of seventeen LVT(A)'s and four amphibian tractor groups of thirty-four each. Each of these groups was then organized into waves to carry the assault troops. The first wave

---

[21] Hist AFMIDPAC, I, 130.
[22] CINCPAC Opn Plan 16-43 (Revised), Annex A, Logistic Plan for Land-Based Forces, CINCPAC-CINCPOA Secret Serial 000204, 5 Jan 44. This plan replaced the original plan of 11 November 1943. V Phib Corps Adm Order 1-44, 5 Jan 44.
[23] V Phib Corps Adm Order 1-44, 5 Jan 44.
[24] 7th Inf Div FLINTLOCK Rpt, Vol. VII, G-4 Rpt, Part V, pp. 5–6, and Annex I, pp. 1–2.
[25] Rad, USAFICPA to WD, 28 Nov 43, CPA 7528.
[26] 7th Inf Div G-4 Jnl, 15 Dec 44.

was to consist of eight amphibian tanks, the second of six amphibian tanks and two amphibian tractors, the third and fourth of eight amphibian tractors each. In addition, two tractors in each group were designated as free vehicles. All were loaded on LST's, seventeen vehicles per ship. Finally, twenty-one tractors were formed into a reserve LVT pool that was to provide immediate replacements to the combat teams when necessary. These spare vehicles were loaded on an LSD. In all, a total of 174 amphibian tanks and tractors was provided for the 7th Division's invasion of Kwajalein. In order to maintain and repair them it was necessary to make provision for shops to be assigned exclusively to this work. Four LST's were designated as repair ships and to each were assigned mechanics who were specialists in this field.[27]

One of the novel features of the Marshalls operation was the tactical employment for the first time on any extensive scale in the Pacific of a newly developed amphibian vehicle, the 2½-ton amphibian truck or DUKW. It was a six-wheeled truck with a boat hull, a tunnel propeller, and a small rudder, and could carry twenty-five troops or 5,000 pounds of cargo.[28] Just as the U.S. Navy and Marine Corps had been primarily responsible for the development of the LVT, so the Army can be credited with the pioneer work that produced the DUKW. Since 1940 various organizations within the Army had been experimenting with amphibian trucks of the smaller variety, and several models had been perfected, chiefly for employment as personnel carriers. In April 1942 the War Department authorized the Quartermaster Corps to develop an amphibian truck based on the standard Army 2½-ton six-by-six truck. Research was turned over to

the National Defense Research Committee, which in turn designated the New York yacht designing firm of Sparkman and Stephens to work out the details. A contract was signed with General Motors Corporation, and by June 1942 the first model was ready for demonstration. After a series of tests conducted under the auspices of the Quartermaster Corps and the Transportation Corps, the original model, with modifications, was accepted, and production on a large scale commenced. The vehicle was designated "DUKW" according to the code system employed by General Motors and this was inevitably translated into "duck" by the troops in the field.[29]

The 7th Division was allowed a total of a hundred DUKW's for the invasion of southern Kwajalein. Forty DUKW's were organized into two groups of twenty each and assigned to the infantry, chiefly for logistical purposes. Sixty were allocated to division artillery.

The DUKW's for the artillery were divided into four groups of fifteen vehicles, each group serving one firing battalion, five DUKW's to each 105-mm. howitzer battery. They were to be carried aboard LST's, one ship being assigned to each 105-mm. howitzer battalion. Certain changes had to be made before the DUKW could be used to carry artillery pieces.

[27] 7th Inf Div FLINTLOCK Rpt, Vol. VII, G-4 Rpt, Annex E, Ordnance Rpt, pp. 5–6; 708th Amph Tk Bn Special Action Rpt, Kwajalein Opn, 12 Mar 44, pp. 1–2.
[28] Office of Naval Intelligence, Confidential Publication 226 (Washington, 1944). Two DUKW's had been used at Makin with altogether favorable results, but the number was insufficient to demonstrate conclusively how efficiently these vehicles could be used in amphibious operations.
[29] Col. Edwin S. Van Deusen, "Trucks That Go Down to the Sea," Army Ordnance, XXV (1943), 555–58.

First, the center of gravity had to be lowered so that the truck would not capsize in rough water with a top-heavy load. This was accomplished by lowering the floor boards in the cargo box. The second change would have involved widening the cargo space by from six to eight inches but no way was found to do this. It was discovered, however, that the oversize combat wheels on the pieces could easily be replaced by ordinary truck-type wheels and tires, allowing the howitzers to fit perfectly into the DUKW's. In addition, out of each group of fifteen artillery DUKW's, three were fitted with A-frames by which the pieces could be easily lifted from the cargo box into position.

As in the case of the LVT's it was realized that floating shops for repair of DUKW's would be needed. Certain LST's were assigned this duty and were issued special parts and a sizable stock of patching and welding material for the purpose.[30] The precaution was to prove its worth in the fighting to come.

One final logistical lesson that had emerged from the Tarawa operation was that pointing to the necessity for establishing some system of floating supply until the beachhead had been expanded sufficiently to permit the uninterrupted operation of inland supply dumps. Shortly after the termination of the Tarawa fight, logistics officers of the 7th Division held a series of conversations with Captain Knowles, naval transport group commander, and Lt. Col. Jesse S. Cook, USMC, the D-4 officer of the 2d Marine Division. On the basis of the information gained from these interviews it was decided that at Kwajalein a better system of combat supply would have to be set up. It was essential that plans be made for the immediate delivery of priority supplies to the fighting troops ashore

before the shore parties were organized. On the suggestion of Warrant Officer (j.g.) John T. Dalton, it was finally decided to stow initial combat supplies on LST's and use DUKW's to carry them to the shore as needed. Thus the LST's would act as floating supply dumps until such time as it was possible to set up inland dumps.

A plan of supply was compiled that required stowage space aboard seven LST's for two units of fire for all weapons except artillery, four days' emergency rations, one and a half days of water, two days of Class III supplies, quartermaster and ordnance cleaning and preserving kits, and approximately fifty-five tons of explosives. A portion of these supplies was "preloaded" in the forty infantry DUKW's that were embarked in two of the seven LST's. The remaining five LST's embarked seventeen amphibian tractors each in addition to the priority supplies.

This proposal was presented to Captain Knowles for recommendations and comments. He approved the solution as presented. It was then presented to Admiral Turner, who gave his approval and made the necessary arrangements for the shipping required to carry out the plan.[31]

In addition to the 7th Division, other Army units scheduled for the Marshalls had to be supplied in the Hawaiian area. These were the 106th Infantry Regiment of the 27th Division and the 3d and 4th Army Defense Battalions, the latter two being designated as the chief components of the garrison force for the Marshalls.

The 106th Infantry Regiment, as a reserve, expected to land, if at all, over

---

[30] 7th Inf Div FLINTLOCK Rpt, Vol. VII, G-4 Rpt, Annex E, Ordnance Rpt, p. 10; 7th Inf Div Rpt, Use of DUKW's by the Artillery of the 7th Infantry Division in the FLINTLOCK Operation, 4 Apr 44.

[31] 7th Inf Div FLINTLOCK Rpt, Vol. VII, G-4 Rpt, Annex A, Initial Combat Supply, p. 1.

beaches already secured and was therefore equipped to operate as a combat team only in land operations. The regiment had originally begun training with the 27th Division for operations against Nauru. When that target was dropped in favor of Makin, the Gilberts force was reduced to a single regimental combat team, the 165th. Only a five-day interval elapsed, however, before Admiral Nimitz included the 106th in his plans for the Marshalls invasion. Although under the operational control of the V Amphibious Corps, the regiment remained attached to the 27th Division until 11 December and during this period was brought up to strength and fully equipped by the 27th Division and General Richardson's headquarters.

The 106th Infantry was reinforced during this period by the addition of one provisional clearing company, a provisional hospital, a tank maintenance ordnance detachment, and a bomb disposal squad. Two tank companies were also added. Company B of the 102d Engineer Battalion and elements of that battalion's headquarters were attached to the 27th Division, and from it to the 106th Infantry, as were various special troop detachments from the division's headquarters. When the 295th JASCO was attached to the division after Makin, detachments were in turn assigned to the 106th Infantry.[32]

The 106th was to carry a thirty-day level of supplies with it to Kwajalein in all classes except ammunition. Five units of fire of all types were allotted. As a result of the Makin experience, 27th Division supply officers sought and received approval of a modification in the USAFICPA unit of fire tables to provide increased supplies of 60-mm. illuminating shells and 37-mm. canister as well as more 81-mm. heavy mortar shells for use against concrete emplacements. In contrast to the regiments of the 7th Division, which altogether used only 4,174 pallets, the 106th Infantry alone used 3,000 for the Kwajalein reserve mission.[33]

Soon after the regiment's formal attachment to the Marshalls force, further changes in the supply plan had to be made. Late in December the 2d Battalion was assigned to the Majuro mission and all logistic and loading plans had to be revised. Enough supplies were turned over to the Majuro battalion to make it self-sufficient. The regiment's shipping, which was reduced by two vessels after the subtraction of those assigned to the 2d Battalion, proved insufficient, thereby causing shifts on loading plans.[34]

The plans for loading the various ships that would carry the assault troops and their supplies and equipment were worked out by consultation between representatives of the staffs of Admiral Turner, General Holland Smith, and the 7th Infantry Division. Since it was decided to increase the number of units of fire to be carried by the 7th Division, it was impossible to combat-load all the ships assigned to carry the troops. Accordingly, the attack transports and their accompanying attack cargo ships were loaded between decks with initial combat equipment and supplies; the bulk of the remaining supplies was stowed in the holds of the cargo ships without any attempt at genuine combat loading. Loose emergency supplies of all classes were carried aboard the LST's. This resulted in a combat load of about 600 short tons in each APA and AKA, with an additional 1,000 tons of maintenance supplies in each

---

[32] USAFICPA Participation Rpt Kwajalein and Eniwetok, pp. 197–99.

[33] Ibid., p. 199.

[34] Ibid., p. 201.

AKA and emergency supplies on the LST's. The LST's that carried the amphibian tractors also were stowed with an average load of 350 tons of miscellaneous supplies.[35]

The procedure established for working out the details of loading was as follows: each regimental commander upon receiving approval of his equipment list conferred with the naval transport division commander to which his regiment was assigned. Together they allocated personnel and cargo to ships in such manner as to support the tactical plans of the ground troops and provide for a balanced unloading of the ships. The next step was for the battalion landing team commander or the senior troop officer embarking on each ship to confer with the ship's commanding officer, who was responsible for proper loading plans for his ship. Actual loading was performed by troop working details with ships' crews manning the winches and supervising the stowing of cargo in the holds. The port authorities at Honolulu and Pearl Harbor furnished the necessary dock equipment and the personnel to man it. Each troop unit had a transport quartermaster who dealt with the ships' transport quartermaster in supervising the actual details of loading.[36]

When the loading was finally completed, the 21,768 officers and men of the 7th Infantry Division, reinforced, with all their initial supplies and equipment were embarked aboard one headquarters ship, eleven attack transports, three attack cargo ships, nineteen LST's, three LSD's, and two high-speed transports. The corps reserve, consisting of the 22d Marine Regimental Combat Team and the 106th Infantry (totaling 9,325 officers and men), was carried aboard six attack transports, one troop transport, one attack cargo ship

and one cargo ship (AK). The 2d Battalion Landing Team of the 106th Infantry Regiment, scheduled to land on Majuro, was for the most part embarked on an attack transport, USS *Cambria*, which was also Admiral Hill's flagship. Two accompanying LST's carried the remainder of the troops. The V Amphibious Corps Reconnaissance Company, also assigned to this mission, was aboard a high-speed transport.[37]

4th Marine Division Logistics

Navy and Marine Corps authorities in the San Diego area assumed responsibility for supplying and loading the 4th Marine Division. In the matter of special amphibious equipment the Marine division was both more and less fortunate than the 7th Division. Altogether the Marines took with them to Roi-Namur 280 amphibian tractors and 75 armored amphibians, a far larger number than was allowed to the 7th Division. These were organized into the 4th Amphibian Tractor Battalion, the 10th Amphibian Tractor Battalion with Company A of the 11th Amphibian Tractor Battalion attached, and the 1st Armored Amphibian Battalion.[38] On the other hand no DUKW's were made available to the Marine division and it had to rely exclusively on landing craft and amphibian

[35] Commander in Chief U.S. Fleet, Publication P-002, Amphibious Operations in the Marshall Islands January–February 1944, 20 May 44 (hereafter cited as COMINCH P-002), Ch. V, p. 1.

[36] *Ibid.*, Ch. V, pp. 4–5.

[37] 7th Inf Div FLINTLOCK Rpt, Vol. VII, G-4 Rpt, Annex H. Transport QM Rpt, p. 2; V Phib Corps, Summary of Units and Ships Upon Which Embarked, FLINTLOCK; TF 51 Rpt FLINTLOCK, p. 3.

[38] TF 51 Rpt FLINTLOCK, Annex J to Incl J; V Phib Corps, Summary of Units and Ships Upon Which Embarked, FLINTLOCK.

tractors to carry its artillery and supplies ashore.[39]

The division was also handicapped by the fact that shipping was available for only 30 percent of its transportation. Only eight one-ton cargo trucks and twenty-five 2½-ton dump trucks could be taken along and all the 2½-ton cargo trucks had to be left behind. According to the division commander, at least twice the amount of transportation taken should have accompanied his troops on the invasion.[40]

To carry the marines to their destination Admiral Conolly's Task Force 53 included one headquarters ship, eleven attack transports, one troop transport, three attack cargo ships, one high-speed transport, fifteen LST's, and two LSD's. Four attack transports and one attack cargo ship constituted a transport division, lifting the personnel, equipment, and supplies of a regimental combat team. Each battalion landing team embarked in one attack transport, and the fourth attack transport of each transport division carried the regimental support group and headquarters. The attack cargo ship of each transport division lifted a few personnel and a great part of the regimental supplies.[41]

The division headquarters was embarked aboard the AGC USS *Appalachian,* which was Admiral Conolly's flagship. All the 105-mm. artillery was embarked in one LSD *(Epping Forest),* each weapon with its supply of ammunition preloaded on an LCM. All the Marine 75-mm. pack howitzers were preloaded in LVT's, which were carried aboard three LST's. Medium tanks were preloaded in LCM's and embarked in the other LSD *(Gunston Hall),* light tanks in the attack transports, amphtracks and armored amphibians in LST's and LSD's.[42]

The only serious problem to arise while

these vessels were being loaded came about as a result of Admiral Nimitz' order to increase the number of units of fire from five to ten for 105-mm. howitzers and from five to eight for all other weapons. This had been done in the instance of the 7th Division, but the staff of the 4th Marine Division was opposed to it. Five units, said General Schmidt, would have been sufficient.[43] Certainly this midstream change in the amount of required ammunition complicated the division's loading in San Diego. Prepared loading plans had to be scrapped and various desired items of supply and equipment left ashore to make room for ammunition. "Of utmost importance," complained the division commander, "is the cessation of logistical planning once the loading has begun."[44]

Preliminary Army Air Operations

The first strikes against the Marshalls by land-based aircraft took place as part of the plan to neutralize them in preparation for the landings in the Gilberts on 20 November. Following the seizure of Makin and Tarawa, operations against the various important Marshalls atolls continued without interruption. The previous mission of temporary neutralization now gave way to one of permanent neutralization or destruction of defenses. Until the middle of December all operations were conducted by B-24's based south and east of the Gilberts and were restricted by the dis-

[39] 4th Marine Div Final Rpt FLINTLOCK, Incl J, p. 27.
[40] *Ibid.,* p. 29.
[41] TF 53 Rpt FLINTLOCK, Incl H, p. 1.
[42] *Ibid.,* p. 2; V Phib Corps, Summary of Units and Ships Upon Which Embarked, FLINTLOCK.
[43] 4th Marine Div Final Rpt FLINTLOCK, Incl J, p. 28.
[44] *Ibid.,* p. 46.

tances that had to be flown; after 23 December flights could be made by planes based in the Gilberts, and in January the B-24's began operating from the Gilberts to strike more deeply and more powerfully into the Marshalls.

During November and December two atolls received more attacks than the others. Mille, nearest to the Gilberts and therefore more easily reached and immediately dangerous, was the center of attention, but Maloelap with its large air facilities had to be kept under constant surveillance and attack. Jaluit was a less important target. Kwajalein and Wotje received most attention during January as the softening-up before the invasion went into high gear.

Mille

Mille Atoll was subjected to a carrier strike on 18–19 November, by which time most of its air facilities had been damaged extensively. Because it was their only base within fighter range of the Gilberts, the Japanese concentrated every effort to get the runways back into condition at the earliest possible moment and to keep the base well reinforced with planes. Their success was attested to by the appearance of several Japanese fighters west of Makin as early as 20 November.[45] That same night enemy bombers were over Tarawa.

On 24 November eleven B-24's staged through Baker Island for a raid on Mille Atoll. At the target they were intercepted by approximately eight fighters that caused minor damage to the bombers but did not prevent the dropping of bombs on Mili, the main island of the atoll. Between that date and 19 December 106 heavy bombers dropped a total of 122 tons of bombs on the runways and installations.

All of these missions were flown from Canton, staging through Baker, or from Nanomea, Nukufetau, or Funafuti. The largest single mission was flown on 4 December when thirty-four B-24's bombed Mili Island. Throughout the period Japanese fighters operated from the Mille base and rose to intercept the American formations.

Beginning on 18 December the pattern of attacks against Mille changed. That day saw the first strike by American attack bombers and land-based fighters. Twelve A-24's, escorted by thirteen P-39's, appeared over the atoll and damaged three enemy fighters on the ground. On the same day six more P-39's destroyed six out of eight interceptors in the air and four more planes on the ground. The following day, the 19th, the last B-24 strike on Mille was executed. Approximately twenty-five interceptors arose to meet the flight of nineteen B-24's, and seven of the Japanese planes were shot down. From then until 25 December, fighters and attack bombers kept up daily attacks on Mille. Confirmed damage to the enemy during the period 18 through 25 December included virtually all the fuel dumps on the atoll bombed and most of the buildings leveled. A total of eleven enemy planes were destroyed on the ground. There was no further Japanese interception from Mille after 25 December. On only two occasions after that date were enemy aircraft found on this eastern atoll. Three planes were observed on the ground on 3 January and destroyed. Five days later a routine reconnaissance flight discovered approximately four more parked along the runways. By the time an attack group hit the island on 10 January, even these few planes had disappeared.

---

[45] CINCPAC-CINCPOA Opns in POA, Nov 43, Annex E, p. 21.

MILLE UNDER AIR ATTACK

After 25 December, with both attack bombers and fighters regularly available from the new bases at Makin, Tarawa, and Apamama, the neutralization of Mille entered its final phase. Fighters conducted daily reconnaissance over the atoll. Their findings were usually transmitted to their home bases, and a task group of either fighters or attack bombers made a flight on the same day to knock out whatever had been uncovered by the reconnaissance flight. On four occasions between 1 January and 31 January American planes were on station over Mille for the whole day. The airfield was rendered useless. Ships disappeared from the lagoon, and even antiaircraft fire became scarce and ineffective. Strafing and bombing had left the installations virtually in ruins and had

so completely isolated the atoll that after 22 December only submarines and small fishing craft ventured into the area. All of the latter were destroyed.[46]

Maloelap

Although Mille was extremely dangerous to American bases and offensive efforts because of its nearness to the Gilberts, Maloelap was considered the greatest potential threat to operations in the Marshalls. Taroa, the principal island of this atoll was, except for Kwajalein, the most

[46] Operational History of the Seventh Air Force, 6 Nov 43–31 Jul 44. This account of operations against all the Marshall atolls has been reconstructed from the chronological log attached to the operations report. See also Craven and Cate, *AAF IV*, pp. 302–10.

TAROA AFTER BEING BOMBED

important air base between Tarawa and Truk. It bristled with antiaircraft installations and heavy guns; its airfields supported by far the largest number of planes in the eastern Marshalls; its garrison was well armed.

The first post-Gilberts air strike on this formidable base was carried out by ten B-24's flying from Nanomea on 26 November. Primarily directed against Taroa's runways, the planes dropped twenty-two tons of bombs from an altitude of approximately 10,000 feet. Of the two interceptors that arose to meet the attack one was shot down.

Between 26 November and 10 January all flights against Maloelap were made by B-24's, flying from Nanomea, Nukufetau, and Canton. The round-trip distance from the two former bases was 2,000 to 2,200 miles, and the Canton squadrons staged through Baker Island on round-trip flights of approximately 3,100 miles. All flights were met by interceptors. For thirty to fifty minutes on each flight bomber crews were forced to fight their way into the target and out again. During the period nine B-24's were shot down by enemy action and fifty-nine Japanese fighters were destroyed. Damage to the Maloelap base was extensive, but not crippling. Large fires were started, buildings destroyed, and two ships bombed with inconclusive results. Runways were never put entirely out of operation, always being repaired the same day they were damaged.

The second period of the offensive against Maloelap can be said to have begun on 11 January, when the long flights from the south were superseded by shorter and more frequent strikes by B-25's. The character of the fighting did not greatly change, however. As late as 26 January about twenty-five interceptors rose to meet the attack. The pounding of Taroa and adjacent islands in the atoll continued. Between 11 and 25 January inclusive, approximately seventy tons of bombs were dropped from the light bombers flying at treetop level, and the island was systematically strafed by machine gun fire and 75-mm. shells from the B-25's. Fifteen enemy fighters were destroyed as against an American loss of six B-25's. Shipping was thoroughly cleared from the lagoon, and the ground installations seemed to be totally destroyed; but the airfield remained in operation.

The last phase of the attack on this stubborn base was begun on 26 January with the introduction of fighter escorts for the B-25's. On the first day nine B-25's, followed at a considerable distance by twelve P-40's, flew into Taroa for a low-level attack. The B-25's destroyed nine interceptors on the ground and five more after they were airborne. The control tower and two other buildings on the airfield were set afire and four tons of bombs were dropped in fuel dump and dispersal areas, starting large fires. As the B-25's left the target to return to Makin they were followed by about fifteen Japanese fighters. Thirty miles south of Maloelap the twelve P-40's met the bomber formation and immediately engaged the enemy fighters, destroying eleven of them and severely damaging two more.

The strike of 26 January was decisive. Practically all of the remaining enemy air strength at Maloelap had been destroyed, and the once formidable base was rendered almost powerless to defend itself against air strikes. On 27 January a formation of seven B-24's struck Taroa from Makin, dropping seventeen tons of bombs on the airfield area, setting fire to more dumps and damaging the runway. No interception was attempted although a few planes were sighted on the ground. On 28 January, the tactics of the first bomber-fighter attack were repeated, the airfield on Taroa again being the target. Five enemy planes managed to become airborne, but their pilots were neither aggressive nor experienced. One was shot down by the B-25's, but when the formation attempted to lead the other enemy planes back toward the fighter escort, the engagement was broken off. The last low-level attack was made on 29 January, the B-25's attacking ammunition dumps and buildings on the outer islands. There were no signs of enemy planes. Maloelap had been almost completely neutralized at last, and only on the day the carrier task force moved into the Marshalls.

Jaluit

Because of its reduced importance as a naval base and its lack of air installations, Jaluit received much less attention than Mille and Maloelap. Two strikes against this former administrative center of the Marshalls had been conducted during the action preliminary to the Gilberts invasion. On 23 November, as the action at Makin and Tarawa was drawing to a close, eight B-24's struck Jaluit from Nukufetau, dropping eight tons of bombs on the target and meeting little opposition. Three float-type fighters were seen, but instead of attacking the bombers they flew off in the opposite

WOTJE UNDER AIR ATTACK. *Note columns of smoke rising from hits on the runway.*

direction. Only two more strikes were directed at Jaluit before the opening of bases in the Gilberts. In both cases large fires were started. There was no interception on either raid and only moderate antiaircraft opposition.

From 12 December through 29 January Jaluit was subjected to a total of thirteen separate strikes, mostly by attack bombers and fighters from Makin and Tarawa. Concentrating on low-level bombing and strafing, the strikes reduced Jaluit to rubble. Oil and ammunition dumps, communications facilities, and buildings were destroyed. Three ships were sunk in the lagoon. At no time during this entire period were the attackers intercepted by enemy planes, although antiaircraft fire was usually intense and accurate. By the time the carrier task force approached, two days before the invasion of Kwajalein, Jaluit had been reduced to impotence. It could send neither reinforcements nor air support to the garrison that would need help.

Wotje

No American strike at Wotje was conducted until 13 December, when ten B-24's made the 3,100 mile round trip from Canton, staging through Baker. One subsequent raid by the same route was made before 23 December, on which day bombers based at Canton carried out the first of a series of three flights through Tarawa. After 8 January both B-24's and B-25's, using the new bases at Makin and Tarawa, made ten strikes on Wotje in the period through 29 January. On only one occasion did Japanese fighters intercept the flights. On 26 December six planes attacked a formation of seventeen B-24's.

During the period 13 December–29 January approximately 325 tons of bombs were dropped on Wotje. As in the other Marshalls atolls the primary targets were airfields, dumps, and shipping. A few cargo vessels were found in Wotje Lagoon as late as 29 January, but every other form of communication with the outside world, except possibly radio, had been destroyed.

Kwajalein

Because, with the exception of Eniwetok, it was the farthest west of all the principal atolls of the Marshalls, Kwajalein received relatively little attention from the Seventh Air Force bombers. During the preliminaries to the Gilberts invasion a group of eight B-24's had attempted the flight from Nanomea, but because of bad weather and the great distance only one plane managed to get through to drop fragmentation bombs on Roi-Namur. The next Seventh Air Force strike against Kwajalein (there was in the meantime a carrier strike on 4 December) came on 21 December, when four B-24's and four PB4Y photoreconnaissance planes from Nanomea succeeded in dropping six tons of bombs on various islands of the atoll and in taking valuable pictures of installations. Although they were intercepted by nine fighters, none of the planes was lost.

In nine subsequent missions during December and January, about 200 tons of bombs were distributed throughout the atoll, causing some damage to installations and shipping. No interception of American land-based bombers was made after 22 January. As late as 29 January, however, the airfield at Roi-Namur was still

operative, and the Japanese had continued to bring in planes.

Preliminary Naval Action

One naval strike was delivered against the Marshalls in the period between 24 November and 29 January. The force for this strike, Task Groups 58.1 and 58.3, was organized from Task Force 50,[47] which had supported the Gilberts invasion while the ships were still west of Makin and Tarawa late in November. Admiral Pownall combined most of the vessels of his Interceptor and Northern and Southern Carrier Groups into two new task groups for movement to the target area. Upon arrival there the two groups were brought together for operation against Kwajalein Atoll and Wotje.

Pownall's task groups consisted of six fast carriers, five heavy cruisers, two light cruisers, three of the new class of antiaircraft cruisers, and twelve destroyers. After a rendezvous for refueling 820 miles northeast of Kwajalein Atoll on 1 December, the force moved southwest and arrived unobserved near Kwajalein on the morning of 4 December. The first planes were launched at 0630. A total of 246 took part in the various attacks on this atoll.[48]

At Roi-Namur the early flights discovered Japanese planes parked on the airstrip and many fighters airborne. In addition, two light cruisers and one large freighter were at anchor off the islands. In the ensuing engagement, nineteen of the

---

[47] In January 1950, the designation Task Force 50 was taken over by Admiral Spruance's Fifth Fleet. The fast carrier force of the Central Pacific became Task Force 58, and was commanded by Admiral Mitscher.

[48] CINCPAC-CINCPOA Opns in POA, Dec 43, Annex A, pp. 6–8.

ACTION AT KWAJALEIN. *Cargo ships at anchor in the lagoon (left-hand page) are sitting ducks*

for U.S. carrier-based planes. Japanese torpedo planes strike back at the U.S. task force (right-hand page.)

interceptors were destroyed, and one Japanese medium bomber was shot down as it
tried to escape from the field. Three more
bombers were destroyed on the ground,
but most of the remainder of the Japanese
aircraft on the ground escaped damage
because the American pilots did not receive word of their camouflaged locations.
Several hits were scored on the cruisers
and the freighter.

No planes were found at Kwajalein
Island since the field there was still under
construction. Nearly thirty cargo vessels
of various types were anchored, however,
in the lagoon off this island. Seven of these
were sunk and several others damaged. At
a nearby island two large multiengined
flying boats were strafed and set on fire.

At noon, while the strikes on Roi-
Namur and Kwajalein Island were still in
progress, twenty-nine aircraft attacked
Wotje, where they destroyed five planes on
the ground and set fire to hangars, machine shops, and barracks. At both Kwajalein and Wotje complete photographic
coverage was secured.

The original plans for the carrier attack
on Kwajalein had contemplated a two-
day strike, but shortly before noon of the
first day enemy planes, evidently from
Roi-Namur, began a series of counterattacks on the carrier groups. Although no serious damage was inflicted in these daylight
attempts to sink the carriers, recovery of
planes was hampered by the maneuvers
the attacks made necessary. One of the
carriers received a torpedo hit but fortunately was not sunk. The task groups
withdrew the next day, and the rest of the
strike was abandoned.

Damage to the enemy's bases had been
extensive. It was considered necessary,
however, for the land-based planes of the
Seventh Air Force to continue attacks
upon Kwajalein and Wotje, and in actual-

ity a considerable portion of the task of
softening Japanese resistance upon Kwajalein was left to the larger carrier force
that would arrive in the area on 29 January just ahead of the landing forces.

Approach of the Invasion Force

By 20 January 1944 all preparations in
the Hawaiian Islands for the invasion of
the Marshalls were completed. Although
it was to be surpassed in size later, the
combined ground, air, and naval force
that was ready to sail for the Marshalls at
that time comprised the largest expedition
ever assembled in the Pacific under the
American flag. About half of the expedition had originated in the Hawaiian
Islands, but its other elements had moved
there from points as widely separated as
San Diego on the west coast, the Fiji
Islands, the Samoan Islands, and the Ellice
Islands.

Plans called for the neutralization phase
to be followed by simultaneous assaults on
Majuro, northern Kwajalein, and southern Kwajalein. After the month of intensive bombing and strafing raids by the
Seventh Air Force against airfields and
shipping, Mille and Jaluit were almost
useless to the enemy. Wotje and the great
base at Maloelap were largely neutralized,
but there were numerous Japanese aircraft
at Roi-Namur at the time of the carrier
strike on 29 January. Task Force 58—with
its four separate groups of carriers, battleships, cruisers, and destroyers and its 700
carrier-based planes—was to enter the
Marshalls area on 29 January, two days
before D Day, to complete the neutralization.[49]

All of the task groups sailed from the
Hawaiian Islands within a few hours of

[49] CINCPAC-CINCPOA Opns in POA, Feb 44,
Annex A, pp. 10, 11.

their scheduled times of departure. For the assault troops the day of departure was 22 January. The Southern Attack Force departed from Pearl Harbor and Honolulu, while the Northern Attack Force sailed on the same day from Lahaina Roadstead in the outer islands after a thirty-hour break in their journey from San Diego. The southern force moved about thirty-five miles ahead of the northern group. Embarkation had taken most of the preceding day, and the slower-moving LST groups carrying the amphtracks and a detachment of the 1st Marine Defense Battalion for the defense of Majuro had cast off and departed while the main convoy was being prepared. The Attack Force Reserve and the Majuro Attack Group left together on 23 January. The reserve force was to go to no specified destination other than the general vicinity of the three landings, any one of which might require reinforcement.[50]

The American submarines that had been operating throughout the Marshalls area for the past month now took stations to the west. Three patrolled near Truk, one near Ponape, one near Kusaie, and one near Eniwetok.[51]

The week's voyage to the area of the eastern Marshalls was made by all the groups without mishap. At dawn on 29 January the four task groups of Task Force 58 and the Neutralization Group (Task Group 50.15) moved into the first attack positions assigned to them. Despite squally weather and overcast skies, which severely handicapped action, Rear Adm. John W. Reeves of Task Group 58.1 launched aircraft from *Enterprise*, *Yorktown*, and *Belleau Wood*. A few moments later the planes were attacking Taroa, giving special attention to the airfields and shipping. Air strikes were continued all day, and by nightfall Taroa's airfield, which had still been con-

sidered able to put up interceptors, was completely neutralized. The second task group (Task Group 58.2) of Task Force 58, under Admiral Montgomery, had meanwhile attacked Roi-Namur. Planes from *Essex*, *Intrepid*, and *Cabot* bucked northeasterly winds to bomb and strafe once more the important airfield at that base. Ninety-two enemy planes were based on Roi airfield when the attack developed. Command of the air was seized by American planes at the outset and after 0800 no enemy planes was seen airborne over Roi-Namur. Numerous hits were made on runways, hangars, fuel dumps, and gun positions.

The third group (Task Group 58.3) of Task Force 58 had sortied from Funafuti under the command of Admiral Frederick Sherman. An hour before sunrise the group took position southwest of Kwajalein Island and planes of *Cowpens*, *Monterey*, and *Bunker Hill* took off for the target. The airfield and adjacent buildings on Kwajalein Island were bombed on the first strike. During the rest of the day the remainder of Kwajalein Island was subjected to strafing and bombing. During the evening Admiral Sherman's group moved northwestward toward Eniwetok to be in position to launch an attack at dawn of D minus 1. The fourth task group (Task Group 58.4), under Rear Adm. Samuel P. Ginder, included the carriers *Saratoga*, *Princeton*, and *Langley*. It sent a succession of flights against Wotje, beginning early in the day and met very little serious opposition.[52] In addition to the attack, Wotje was subjected to fire by units of Task Group 50.15.

While the carriers were still operating in the vicinity of the targets, land-based

---

[50] *Ibid.*, Annex A, p. 21.
[51] *Ibid.*, p. 17.
[52] *Ibid.*, pp. 10–15.

ROI AIRFIELD. *The causeway connecting Roi and Namur is shown in upper left. Note height of smoke columns as indicated by ground shadows.*

planes from the Gilberts joined in the general attack. At Kwajalein one flight of seven B-24's dropped fifteen tons of bombs on Roi-Namur and three more tons on Kwajalein Island during the morning and early afternoon. As the carrier planes retired at dusk another seven heavy bombers arrived for a night attack, dropping twenty tons of bombs on Kwajalein Island.[53]

At Wotje, flying through heavy overcast, one flight of three B-24's dropped seven tons of bombs, causing fires and damaging the runways. A few hours later a flight of nine B-25's dropped three tons of bombs on the island in a low-level attack and strafed and sank a small cargo vessel in the lagoon. During this late attack carrier planes from the task force mis-

takenly intercepted the B-25's and shot down two before it was realized they were American planes.

Maloelap, Jaluit, and Mille also received land-based attacks during the day. At Taroa, two and a half tons of bombs were dropped by B-25's, which then joined carrier planes in strafing the island. At Jaluit, attack bombers and fighters dropped seven tons of bombs and afterwards strafed the island. Mille was covered all day by twenty fighters, flying in flights of four. Planes that had been scheduled to strike these targets but that were unable to get through because of weather or mechanical difficulty flew over Mille on the

[53] Operational History of Seventh Air Force, 6 Nov 43–31 Jul 44, pp. 121, 122.

way back to American bases in the Gilberts and dropped their bomb loads on the islands of that atoll.

The air strikes from the various task groups were supplemented by naval bombardment from battleships, cruisers, and destroyers in the carrier groups. In the cases of Wotje and Maloelap the Neutralization Group moved in when the faster ships had finished their day's work late on the afternoon of 29 January.

While the initial strikes of this day were going forward, Task Forces 52 and 53, conveying the two landing forces, were about to enter the waters between the two chains of atolls. Approaching from the northeast, their gradually converging courses finally met north of Ailuk Atoll in the eastern chain, approximately 200 miles east of Kwajalein. The tractor groups were still ahead although their lead was being steadily reduced. In another twenty-four hours it disappeared.

On the morning of 30 January the destroyers and cruisers accompanying the landing forces turned aside to bombard Maloelap and Wotje, joining the other forces already there. During the afternoon the vessels resumed their journey to Kwajalein, joining the main convoys there in time for the bombardment preparatory to the landings of the two assault groups. On 30 January the strikes of carrier-based aircraft continued at Kwajalein, Wotje, Taroa, and Roi-Namur, but with some adjustment in forces to allow one task group to take Eniwetok under attack. This task group, which on the previous day had struck Kwajalein Island, had now moved northwestward toward the new target. Its place was taken by Task Group 58.1, which had previously been engaged at Taroa. Task Group 58.4, which had previously been concerned only with Wotje,

now assumed responsibility for continued neutralization of Taroa as well. Task Group 58.2 continued to be primarily concerned with Roi-Namur.

The group attacking Wotje and Taroa concentrated upon runways at Taroa and airfield installations and buildings at Wotje. At Kwajalein Island and Roi-Namur over 400 sorties were flown. During the afternoon surface ships of the force conducted a four-hour bombardment of both targets. Task Group 58.3 launched its planes for the attack on Eniwetok at 0450. Torpedo bombers, which made the first sweep over the atoll, and later fighters found and destroyed nineteen planes on the ground. In subsequent action virtually every building in the atoll was destroyed, the runways were filled with craters, and various defensive positions were taken under gunfire from the surface ships. Task Group 58.3 was to remain south of Eniwetok until 6 February and was to be joined there by Task Group 58.4, which would move from the Wotje–Maloelap area on 3 February.

While the second day's bombardment was being carried out, the Northern and Southern Attack Forces remained on course together for approximately half the distance between Ailuk and Kwajalein, then separated, each going directly to its own transport and fire support area off Kwajalein. All elements arrived in their assigned places during the night of 30–31 January. Lights could be seen on Kwajalein Island by troops aboard the ships of the Southern Task Force as the vessels neared the end of their journey. These lights were presumably from fires started by the air strikes of the day just passed. Before the sun rose on the new day, the first phase of the occupation of Kwajalein Island was to begin.

CHAPTER XIII

Japanese Defenses in the Marshalls

Before Pearl Harbor

Under the terms of Article 22 of the Covenant of the League of Nations, Japan was bound to prevent "the establishment of fortifications of military and naval bases" in the former German possessions in the Pacific mandated to her—the Marianas, Palaus, Carolines, and Marshalls. The neutralization of other Japanese-held islands was guaranteed by the Washington Naval Limitations Treaty of 1922, signed by the United States and Japan, as well as by the British Empire, France, and Italy.[1] On 27 March 1933, Japan gave the required two years' notice of her intention to withdraw from the League, and the official withdrawal was consummated on 27 March two years later. This action, being unilateral, did not relieve Japan of her obligation not to fortify the mandated islands under the terms of the Covenant.[2] However, the League was powerless to enforce the Covenant and after 1935 the islands were for the most part closed to foreign visitors. From 1935 until 1944 the nature and extent of Japanese activities in the mandated islands remained veiled in mystery. One inevitable result of this policy of exclusion, coupled with the known aggressive intentions of the Japanese Empire on the Asiatic mainland, was in the late 1930's to raise grave suspicions among the Western powers that Japan was fortifying the islands contrary to her commitments stipulated under the terms of the League Covenant. One Australian commentator put it, "It is believed that Japan has assembled, in these islands, equipment and supplies which would be of great value to her in any policy of aggression."[3] Evidence brought to light since the close of World War II amply justifies the suspicion.

From 1934 through 1941 the Japanese undertook considerable construction activity in their island possessions, allegedly for nonmilitary purposes. According to the testimony of Capt. Hidemi Yoshida, IJN, who was intimately connected with naval construction in the mandates, this program was aimed primarily at the building of "cultural and industrial facilities."[4] Under the category of "cultural and industrial facilities" were listed such items as ramps and runways for aircraft, wireless stations, direction finders, meteorological stations, and lighthouses. These improvements, Yoshida claimed, were necessary for safe navigation, promotion of commerce, and other peaceful pursuits.

---

[1] Myers, *Handbook of the League of Nations*, p. 378; IPS Document 6257, p. 13.
[2] IMTFE Proceedings, pp. 39, 43, 205–16, 408–15.
[3] Robson, *Year Book*, p. 94.
[4] IMTFE Defense Document 1518, pp. 4–5.

Unquestionably many of these installations could be employed for commercial purposes. It is equally true that their nature was such as to permit an easy conversion to military uses, if the situation so demanded. It also appears certain that the Japanese made a deliberate effort to disguise military construction projects in the cloak of harmless peaceful endeavors. For example, in 1940 the Naval Secretariat set aside the sum of 4,635,750 yen ($1,086,619.80) for lighthouse construction throughout the Palaus, Carolines, and Marshalls. Among the items authorized for these "lighthouses" were military barracks, generators, ammunition storage buildings, command posts, lookout stations, roads, and water storage facilities. No mention was made of towers, searchlights, bells, foghorns, or the other paraphernalia usually associated with such aids to navigation.[5]

Whatever the extent of Japanese military construction in the Pacific islands was before 1940, it is clear that from that year until the outbreak of war with the Allied Powers in December 1941 the mandated islands were being fortified as rapidly as conditions would permit.

Late in 1939 the *4th Fleet* of the Imperial Japanese Navy was organized and charged with the mission of protecting the mandated area. With headquarters at Truk, the *4th Fleet*'s area of command roughly coincided with the area mandated to Japan. After the commencement of hostilities Wake, Guam, the Gilberts, Nauru and Ocean Islands were added. This "fleet" had only a few combat vessels under its command, its primary duties being to build up and defend air and naval bases in Japan's island possessions. Throughout 1940 the *4th Fleet* existed mostly on paper, and did not really start to grow until the end of the year.

About the same time that the *4th Fleet* was being activated, the Imperial Navy sent a large team to survey the Marshalls with the object of laying plans for a fairly large-scale construction program. Up until late 1939 far more attention had been devoted to the Carolines and Marianas than to the more distant Marshalls. Now, improvements in warships and naval weapons, and especially the advent of heavy land-based bombers, forced the Japanese to re-evaluate the importance of the Marshalls and to concentrate more heavily on their defense.[6]

In January 1941, the *6th Base Force* was activated as a subordinate command and assigned to the Marshalls, where it remained to command the Marshalls sector until destroyed by the American invasion of Kwajalein. At the same time, a subordinate unit, the *6th Defense Force,* was also activated and arrived in the Marshalls in March.[7] Finally, in September 1941, three guard forces (the *51st, 52d* and *53d*) were activated and ordered to the Marshalls where they were made directly responsible to the *6th Base Force* for the defense of Jaluit, Maloelap, and Wotje.[8] Similar units were dispatched to the other mandates at the same time.

Concurrently with this movement of troops and workers into the Marshalls, airfield construction in the area was accelerated. Early in 1941 the *4th Fleet* assumed control of all unfinished aircraft installa-

---

[5] Special Forces, Early Series, Vol. 9, NA 12226, WDC 160867.

[6] USSBS (Pacific), Naval Analysis Division, *The Reduction of Truk* (Washington, 1947), p. 2; Japanese Studies in World War II, No. 173, Marshall Islands Operations, pp. 5–6, OCMH.

[7] Base Forces, Early Series, Vol. 9, NA 12245, WDC 160869.

[8] Base Forces, Early Series, Vol. 10, NA 12229, WDC 160867; Special Forces, Early Series, Vol. 10, NA 12255, WDC 161009.

tions and also commenced many new projects. Most of the money appropriated for
the defense of the mandated islands was
allocated to the building of airfields and
other aircraft facilities. During the period
16 November 1940 to 31 May 1941, a total
of 49,526,396 yen ($11,608,987.22) was
appropriated for airfield and seaplane base
construction and this figure represented
about 70 percent of the total sum appropriated for the erection of defenses in the
islands.

Work on other types of installations was
also commenced and in most cases completed before the attack on Pearl Harbor.
Communications installations were concentrated on the four islands or atolls
where four base force headquarters were
located—Truk, Saipan, Palau, and Kwajalein. Barracks were placed on the most
important islands and atolls, while office
construction was concentrated mostly at
Truk, with lesser concentrations at Saipan
and Palau. Saipan and Palau were supply
centers and staging points for the advance
into the Philippines and into the south
after the start of the war. Fuel oil and coal
storage facilities, including tanks and
pumps, were highly important since they
extended the effective range of the Japanese fleet beyond the main bases in the
homeland. Such facilities had been located
at Saipan, Truk, Palau, Ponape, and Jaluit
according to earlier appropriations. Later
construction projects activated near the
close of 1941 under *4th Fleet* administration
included fueling facilities at Wotje, Taroa,
Roi, Eniwetok, and Kwajalein, all in the
Marshalls. Submarine bases were established at Truk, Ponape, and Roi. Gun positions were placed on Palau, Saipan, Taroa,
Roi, Wotje, and Jaluit in the latter part of
1941. As was the case in fueling facilities,
the Marshalls were developed as military

bases later than the Marianas and Carolines. First, priority went to Truk, Saipan,
and Palau, with concurrent but less important developments of Ponape, Pagan, and
Tinian. Later, priority was given to four
atolls in the Marshalls—Jaluit, Wotje,
Maloelap, and Kwajalein—with minor
attention to Majuro and Eniwetok. Water
installations, command posts, ammunition
storage facilities, and minor fortifications
were ubiquitous.[9]

Prewar Japanese records of garrison
forces stationed in the Marshalls leave no
doubt that extensive military developments
were undertaken before Pearl Harbor. The
6th Base Force, which was assigned the mission of defending these islands, reached
Wotje early in 1941. It was transferred the
following August to Kwajalein, which then
became the administrative center of the
Marshalls sector of the *4th Fleet*'s area of
responsibility. The main troop concentrations under the *6th Base Force* coincided
with the concentration of construction
projects on the four atolls of Kwajalein,
Wotje, Jaluit, and Maloelap. Mille, which
was to be extensively developed during the
war, was at this time merely a lookout station. The mission of the *6th Base Force* was
to defend the Marshall Islands and adjacent sea areas, plan the rapid completion
of accelerated military preparations within
the area and strengthen preparations for
actual combat, plan and supervise all types
of measures relating to defense and attack
and for supply and transportation service,
engage in all types of combat training, and
conduct weather observation in the Marshalls area.[10]

[9] *4th Fleet* Construction File, Special Forces, Early
Series, Vols. 9 and 10, NA 12226 and 12255, WDC
160867 and 161009.
[10] Base Forces, Early Series, Vol. 10, NA 12229,
WDC 160867.

The *6th Defense Force,* which reached the Marshalls in March 1941, included four gun batteries distributed, one battery apiece, to Wotje, Kwajalein, Maloelap, and Jaluit. Its mission was to construct gun positions and other defense installations on each of these islands; supply ships, special lookout stations, and weather stations; send out antiair and antisubmarine patrols; and conduct accelerated training for all types of warfare.[11]

Still another group assigned to the Marshalls was the *6th Communications Unit,* whose prewar missions were to maintain communications and liaison in the Marshalls area, with fleet units, and with the homeland, and to intercept foreign communications.[12] Finally, the *51st, 52d,* and *53d Guard Forces* arrived at Jaluit, Maloelap, and Wotje in October and November 1941 with the general duties of defense of those atolls.[13]

Thus it can be seen that, in the year or more preceding the attack on Pearl Harbor, the Marshalls along with the other mandated islands were becoming rapidly integrated into the Japanese defensive system. Contrary to the Covenant of the League of Nations and to the treaty of Washington, Japan had fortified those islands, established air bases there for military purposes, and garrisoned them with armed troops. With the outbreak of actual hostilities this program was to be rapidly accelerated.

From Pearl Harbor to the Eve of Invasion of the Marshalls

The period from the beginning of the war to the middle of 1943 saw considerable expansion of the *6th Base Force.* Wake, after its seizure, was placed under *6th Base Force* command and extensively developed.

Early in 1942 Makin was made a seaplane base and, after Carlson's raid, the Gilberts with Nauru and Ocean were strongly garrisoned by forces under *6th Base Force* command. During this eighteen-month period, Mille was transformed from a lookout station to a major base, while installations and fortifications on Kwajalein, Jaluit, Maloelap, and Wotje were constantly improved. In June of 1943 the *66th Guard Force* was activated at Yokosuka and assigned to Mille.[14] Originally, the Japanese had intended to use this atoll as a staging point for aircraft in a proposed campaign against the Ellice, Fiji, and Samoan Islands, a plan abandoned after the American invasion of the Gilberts.[15] Some air facilities were completed by November 1942, but the atoll was not fully developed until a year later. By that time Mille was one of the best defended atolls and had the largest garrison in the Marshalls if Kwajalein and Roi-Namur are counted separately.

The latter half of 1943 was distinguished by a marked increase in the number of troops, especially Army personnel, dispatched to the Marshalls. Up to that time the Marshalls had been garrisoned exclusively by Navy units, but in early 1943 it had become apparent to the Japanese that they were faced with a series of probable defeats so long as their forces continued to be tied up in the Solomons–New Guinea area. The deterioration of the

[11] Base Forces, Early Series, Vol. 9, NA 12245, WDC 160869; Special Forces, Early Series, Vol. 10, NA 12255, WDC 161009.

[12] Special Forces, Early Series, Vols. 9 and 10, NA 12226 and 12255, WDC 160867 and 161009.

[13] Base Forces, Early Series, Vol. 10, NA 12229, WDC 160867.

[14] Tabular Records of Special Landing Forces, NA 11651, WDC 161406.

[15] USSBS, *The American Campaign Against Wotje, Maloelap, Mille and Jaluit,* p. 18.

Japanese position in the southeast posed a threat to the island garrisons of the Central Pacific, which were considered too weak to ward off American attack. The Japanese responded by drawing Army units from the Philippines, Manchuria, and the homeland and dispatching them to the Central Pacific.[16]

By the end of August 1943 the Japanese position in the Southeastern Pacific Area was such that all thought of offensive operations had to be abandoned. The surrender of Italy on 8 September was a further blow to the Japanese Empire, for it was felt that a powerful portion of the British fleet would be freed to bring pressure on the Indian Ocean front. Until this time, the Japanese defense perimeter had run through the Marshalls, Gilberts, the Southeastern Pacific Area, the Netherlands Indies, and Burma. Now the Solomons and New Guinea were cracking, exposing the Gilberts and Marshalls to the ever-increasing danger of American attack. Hence, the old defensive perimeter had to be abandoned and a new one erected in its place. On 15 September Imperial General Headquarters decided to contract the perimeter to a line running from the Banda Sea through the Carolines and Marianas. The new line was to be made impregnable to American assault during the time gained by delaying actions in the Marshalls and Gilberts, and in the Japanese Southeastern Pacific Area. Thus, these areas were written off as a loss as early as September, but the Japanese were determined to make the American advance toward their new perimeter as costly as possible in order to gain time and wear down the American will to fight. It was in accordance with this strategic concept of fighting a delaying action in the Marshalls that Imperial General Headquarters de-

cided to send large numbers of Army reinforcements there in September 1943.[17]

Army units in Japan, the Philippines, and Manchuria were reorganized as amphibious brigades and South Seas detachments, and dispatched to the Central Pacific as fast as possible.[18] Even though the Marshalls had been written off as indefensible from the long-range point of view, they received a considerable share of the Army reinforcements because of the Japanese intention to conduct strong delaying actions there. The troops were distributed mostly on the periphery—on the atolls and islands of Wake, Eniwetok, Kusaie, and Mille. Kwajalein, Jaluit, Maloelap, and Wotje already had sizable garrisons, while those on the peripheral islands, except Wake, had been previously quite small.

By January of 1944 Army troops in the Marshalls, Wake, and Kusaie totaled 13,721. The units involved were the *1st South Seas Detachment;* the *1st Amphibious Brigade, A Detachment;* the *2d South Seas Detachment;* and the *3d South Seas Garrison Detachment.* They were distributed among the islands and atolls as follows: Kwajalein, 933; Jaluit, 620; Maloelap, 404; Wotje, 667; Mille, 2,530; Eniwetok, 2,586; Wake, 2,050; and Kusaie, 3,931.[19]

---

[16] Japanese Studies in World War II, No. 72, History of the Army Section, Imperial General Headquarters, 1941–45, p. 77, OCMH.

[17] *Ibid.,* pp. 87–88; Japanese Studies in World War II, No. 55, Operations in the Central Pacific, pp. 8–9, and No. 50, Southeast Area Naval Operations, Vol. III, pp. 1–5, OCMH. The Japanese Southeastern Pacific Area conformed roughly to the American Southwest Pacific Area.

[18] CINCPAC-CINCPOA Translation 9499A, Order of Battle for Palau Sector, Marshalls, Marcus, Wake and Kusaie.

[19] JICPOA Translation 6234, Distribution of Forces and Dispositions of the *1st South Seas Detachment;* JICPOA Bull 88-44, *1st Amphibious Brigade,* Japanese Army, 13 Jun 44; JICPOA Bull 89-44, Japanese Defense of Eniwetok Atoll, 12 Jun 44; CINCPAC-CINCPOA Translation 9614, Summary of the Re-

The military background of these Army units was not especially impressive. The *1st South Seas Detachment* was the only one experienced in combat. As part of the *122d Infantry Regiment,* it had arrived in the Philippines late on New Year's Day 1942 and saw action shortly after landing. Although originally designed as a garrison unit, it was pressed into action on Bataan peninsula and fought there until the American surrender on 9 April.[20] Most of *A Detachment* was organized from the *107th Infantry Regiment,* which had been stationed in Japan since its activation in the autumn of 1940.[21] The *1st Amphibious Brigade* was organized from the *2d Independent Garrison Unit,* which had functioned as a railway guard in Manchuria since its activation.[22]

The arrival of these Army troops put considerable strain on the facilities existing on the islands, which had already been garrisoned by Navy personnel. Apparently no provision had been made to prepare minor fortifications for the Army reinforcements. Thus D Day on Kwajalein found the members of the *1st Amphibious Brigade* in the process of digging in with desperate haste. As one soldier put it: "Since landing on this island there have been no days off because of continuous duties and details. Most of my time has been spent digging trenches." [23]

Enemy air strength in the Marshalls in the few months before the American invasion fluctuated greatly as the Japanese fought a losing battle to replace their mounting losses from the homeland and other parts of the Empire. As of January 1944 their air installations in the area included, in the Kwajalein Atoll, an incompleted land base on Kwajalein Island, a land base on Roi, and a seaplane base on Burton; elsewhere in the Marshalls, land bases on Maloelap, Wotje, Mille, and Eniwetok, and seaplane bases on Jaluit, Wotje, Majuro, Taongi, and Utirik.[24]

During the month of November 1943 the Japanese lost about 71 planes in the Marshalls, chiefly as a result of carrier and land-based strikes incident to the American invasion of the Gilberts. Nevertheless, they were able to balance almost all of these losses with reinforcements flown from the homeland and from the *3d Fleet* at Truk.[25] The planes from Truk, 32 in number, represented virtually all the remaining carrier air, and most of these fell victim to American attack by the end of November. By 25 January 1944, Roi had about 35 planes; Kwajalein Island, about 10 reconnaissance planes; Maloelap, 50 planes; Wotje, 9; and Eniwetok, 15.[26] As American aerial attacks on the Marshalls were stepped up in December and January, Japanese air strength dwindled rapidly.

organization of the *Third, Fifth,* and *Thirteenth Divisions,* the Independent Mixed Brigades, the Amphibious Brigades, and the South Seas Detachments, and of the 250th Return Demobilization, War Ministry Order, 16 Nov 43; CINCPAC-CINCPOA Translation 9499A; CINCPAC-CINCPOA Translation 9536, Excerpts Taken from the *31st Army* Monthly Reports for March and April 1944, dated 30 Apr 44; JICPOA Translation 5545, *Inner South Seas Force* Secret Opn Order 26-43.

[20] See Louis Morton, *The Fall of the Philippines,* Ch. XV, and *passim.*

[21] Military Intelligence Division, War Department, Order of Battle of the Japanese Armed Forces (Washington, 1945), p. 116.

[22] JICPOA Bull 88-44, *1st Amphibious Brigade,* Japanese Army, 13 Jun 44, p. 1.

[23] JICPOA Translation 7224, Extracts from the Diary of Kinichi Ijiya, entry of 25 Jan 44.

[24] JICPOA Air Target Folders 50A (1 Dec 43), 53A (15 Dec 43), 58A (20 Dec 43), 3A (20 Jan 44); JICPOA Bull 46-44, Base Installations Roi, Namur and Ennubirr Islands, Kwajalein Atoll, 15 Apr 44; CINCPAC-CINCPOA Translation 9138, Naval Air Headquarters: Digest of Japanese Naval Air Bases, Sep 43.

[25] *4th Fleet* War Diary, NA 11398, WDC 160336.

[26] USSBS, *The Campaigns of the Pacific War,* pp. 201–02.

Mille, Jaluit, and Wotje ceased to be effective as air bases. Wotje had from 30 to 35 planes in November, but this force was almost completely destroyed by two American carrier strikes. By 29 January there were only twelve "Kates" on Wotje; that day six failed to return from a mission and the rest were evacuated to Roi. The Japanese managed to keep the air strength at Maloelap at 50 planes throughout November and into December, but by January only 13 fighters were operational; 40 had been damaged and grounded. On 29 January, the American carrier raid reported the destruction of 10 planes in the air, and all that were on the ground. By 1 February, the only remaining Japanese planes in the Marshalls proper were the few on Eniwetok.[27] Thus, by the time of the American invasion, the enemy's power to resist by aerial attack had wasted away to almost nothing. Complete mastery of the air, so essential to success in amphibious operations, had been assured to the attackers.

The Defenses of Kwajalein Atoll, January 1944

Kwajalein Atoll had been the hub of Japanese military activity in the Marshalls since August 1941. As headquarters of the *6th Base Force,* it was the nerve center of the surrounding bases. Reinforcements coming into the Marshalls almost invariably passed through Kwajalein, to be parceled out from there. Supplies were usually distributed from this atoll, which was the closest major base to Truk and to the supply lines from the homeland. Branches of various departments of the *4th Fleet* were located there to supervise supply, transportation, and the more technical aspects of construction. Kwajalein was the center of communications not only for all other bases in the Marshalls, but for the Gilberts, Nauru, and Ocean as well. The air base on Roi commanded all Japanese air forces in the Marshalls and Gilberts. All this gave Kwajalein some of the characteristics of a rear area, with more red tape than bullets, far from the front-line outposts on the periphery of the Marshalls. As a matter of fact, an American amphibious landing on Kwajalein was discounted by most Japanese as only a remote possibility, and it was fortified accordingly. As one Japanese naval commander put it, speaking of the Japanese estimate of American intentions after the Gilberts campaign: "There was divided opinion as to whether you would land at Jaluit or Mille. Some thought you would land on Wotje but there were few who thought you would go right to the heart of the Marshalls and take Kwajalein."[28]

Japanese island defense doctrine in the campaigns in the Gilberts and Marshalls stressed defense at the beaches. Every attempt was to be made to annihilate the enemy before he could get ashore, and if he did reach the beaches, the defenders were to counterattack before he could consolidate his positions. Since it was assumed that the enemy might be destroyed at the beaches, the island defenses were strung in a thin line along the shores, with little or no defense in depth. This doctrine was the product of the offensive character of Japanese military thought in general, and also was influenced by the geography of coral atolls, which were composed chiefly of thin flat islands surrounding a lagoon. Most of the islands had very little depth to defend, and the occasional wider islands

[27] USSBS, *The American Campaign Against Wotje, Maloelap, Mille and Jaluit,* pp. 35–36.
[28] USSBS, Naval Analysis Division, *Interrogations of Japanese Officials* (Washington, 1946), Vol. I, Interrogation of Comdr Chikataka Nakajima, IJN, pp. 143–44.

or wider sections of islands were usually occupied by airstrips. Later, on Iwo Jima, which was larger than most coral islands, the American attack encountered prepared defenses in depth. Later still, on Okinawa, the Japanese abandoned completely the concept of shore defense and retired to prepare defenses some distance away from the landing beaches. This change in Japanese island defense doctrine came about as a result both of experience and of the recognition of geographic realities.[29] But at the time of the Marshalls invasion, Japanese tactical doctrine still stressed beach-line defense to the neglect of defense in depth.[30]

Originally the plan for defending the atoll had been based on the assumption that the attack would come from the sea. After the experience at Tarawa, the Japanese appear to have changed their minds about American intentions and shifted their emphasis from defending the ocean shores to defending the lagoon beaches of the islands. Gun positions were set up along the lagoon, trenches dug, and antitank obstructions erected to prevent or delay a landing over these beaches.[31]

The three most heavily defended islands of the atoll were Roi-Namur, Kwajalein, and Ebeye (Burton), in that order of strength.[32] Roi-Namur was somewhat better fortified than Kwajalein Island, but neither approached Tarawa as to the size and number of weapons or the construction and concentration of positions. These northern islands contained four 12.7-cm. twin-mount dual-purpose guns that were divided into two batteries of two, one located near the northwest corner of Roi and the other on the northernmost tip of Namur. (See Map VII.) Four 37-mm. gun positions were established. One was located on the west shore of Roi near the

southwest tip of the island, another near the northeastern corner of Roi; the other two were on the southeastern tip and in the center of the east coast of Namur. Nineteen 13.2-mm. single-mount dual-purpose guns were located in strong points mostly along the ocean shores, from the east coast of Namur to the west coast of Roi. Ten 20-mm. antiaircraft guns were emplaced, most of them along the shore line and near the airfield taxi circles on Roi; three were part of the strong point on the northwest tip of Namur and one was located on the south shore of that island. Machine guns were emplaced in concrete pillboxes, although many of the light machine guns were not permanently emplaced, but shifted from position to position as the battle demanded. The many rifle pits and fire trenches were located in the beach areas of both islands. There were three concrete blockhouses on Roi. One was located on the southwest tip, one in the northwest corner, and one in the northeast corner. Another was in the center of the east shore of Namur. The blockhouses were all located in strong point areas, housed 13-mm. machine guns, and were probably used as command posts.

The reefs off Roi-Namur were not mined, and very few antipersonnel mines

[29] War Department Technical Manual E 30-480, Handbook on Japanese Military Forces, 1 Jun 45, Ch. VII, Part III, pp. 64–68; Roy E. Appleman, James M. Burns, Russell A. Gugeler, and John Stevens, Okinawa: The Last Battle, UNITED STATES ARMY IN WORLD WAR II (Washington, 1948), Ch. IV.
[30] JICPOA Bull 48-44, Japanese Defenses, Kwajalein Atoll, 10 Apr 44, p. 1.
[31] War Department Mission, Marshall Islands, Japanese Defenses and Battle Damage, 14 Mar 44, p. 10; Japanese Studies in World War II, No. 73, Marshall Islands Operations, pp. 34–36, OCMH.
[32] The following detailed description of enemy defenses on Kwajalein Atoll is derived, unless otherwise indicated, from JICPOA Bull 48-44, Japanese Defenses, Kwajalein Atoll, 10 Apr 44.

were encountered inland. Wire entanglements were found at two points—on the beach around the northeast taxi circle on Roi, and on the narrow bit of land connecting Roi with Namur. The beach around the northeast taxi circle also boasted a tank obstacle in the form of large rocks jutting out of a rock wall. Antitank ditches had been dug throughout the two islands.

The defenses of Roi-Namur were quite clearly organized around a series of seven strong points, four on Roi and three on Namur, all on the ocean side. Starting from the southwest tip of Roi, the first was located along the southern shore of the west coast. The second and third were to the south and north of the northwest taxi circle. The fourth was on both sides of the wire and stone barriers next to the northeast taxi circle. The fifth, sixth, and seventh were on the northwest, north, and east tips of Namur, respectively. From the lagoon side the approaches were covered mostly by nothing heavier than 7.7-mm. machine guns.[33]

Kwajalein Island was less well fortified. A study of enemy defenses, made there by the engineering officer of V Amphibious Corps after the operation was concluded, stated, "The prepared defenses of this island were surprisingly weak. . . ."[34]

On Kwajalein, four 12.7-cm. dual-purpose twin-mount guns were divided into batteries of two, one located at each end of the island. *(Map V)* Each battery was protected by 7.7-mm. and 13-mm. machine guns along the nearby beaches. Near each gun were two 150-cm. searchlights. In addition, the northern end of the island was guarded by a twin-mount dual-purpose 13-mm. machine gun on the lagoon shore. Several 7.7-mm. machine guns were in position on the western end and other heavy machine guns were scattered about

the center of the island, some mounted on wooden sleds for easy movement to critical points.

On the ocean shore were six 8-cm. dual-purpose guns, divided into two batteries of three guns each. One battery was east of the tank ditch and the other was opposite the center of the airfield. The first had a 360-degree traverse and could fire either to seaward or landward. The other formed the nucleus of a strong point composed of a semicircle of rifle pits facing the beach supported by one heavy and one 13-mm. machine gun, and also included an observation tower, a range finder, and a 110-cm. searchlight.

Two other 8-cm. guns were in position on the lagoon shore, and the blockhouse on the main pier (Nob Pier), which jutted out into the lagoon near the northern tip of the island, had a 13-mm. dual-purpose gun on its roof and firing ports on the ground floor allowing machine guns to fire in all directions.

Other sheltered positions included about forty reinforced concrete pillboxes on the beaches of the ocean shore and at the northern and western ends of the island, and about twelve U-shaped standing pits. Fire trenches encircled the island, just inland from the beach. At intervals along the ocean shore were squad positions with ten to fifteen rifle pits each. These were usually arranged in a semicircle facing the beach and were camouflaged with grass.

There was a concrete sea wall along most of the ocean shore and around the northern and western ends of the island. The section at the northern end had posts set into it, probably to act as a tank barricade. East of the area cleared for the air-

[33] See JICPOA Bull 48-44, Map 4.
[34] Ltr Rpt, Kwajalein Atoll, Study and Report of Japanese Defenses by Engineers, V Phib Corps, 15 Feb 44, p. 1.

TABLE 2—JAPANESE STRENGTH IN SOUTHERN KWAJALEIN ATOLL ON D DAY

Unit	Number
Total	about 5,000
Army troops	933
6th Base Force headquarters	250
61st Guard Force (main body)	557
SNLF attached to 6th Base Force headquarters	250
Casuals	250
4th Fleet Construction Department Detachment	1,400
Sankyu Transportation Company	260
952d Air Unit	160
6th Communications Unit	350
6th Submarine Base Force	105
Other 4th Fleet detached personnel and naval stragglers	a

ᵃ Unknown.

Source: JICPOA Bull 88-44, 1st Amphibious Brigade, Japanese Army, 13 Jun 44; JICPOA Bull 89-44, Japanese Defense of Eniwetok Atoll, 12 Jun 44; CINCPAC-CINCPOA Bull 11-45, Japanese Naval Ground Forces, 15 Jan 45; JICPOA Translation 3998, 6th Base Force Secret Directive 104-43; Marshall, Kwajalein Notes, Vol. III, pp. 54–55; JICPOA Translation 7354, Personnel Figures of the Fourth Construction Unit; JICPOA Preliminary POW Interrogation Reports 42, Interrogation of Shoan Gishifu, 43, Interrogation of Toshio Nabata, S1c, 952d Air Group, 48, Interrogation of Katsuhide Okueno, Superior Seaman, Kwajalein SS Base.

field was a tank ditch extending halfway across the island, and three smaller tank ditches ran between the ocean shore and the road in the vicinity of the airfield. The lagoon shore was protected by a two-strand barbed-wire fence at the water's edge. The large tank ditch was supported by trenches, rifle pits, and machine guns.

The fortifications on Burton were much lighter than those on Kwajalein, mostly machine gun positions and rifle pits. (See Map 14.) These were organized at the beaches with a concentration of dual-purpose machine guns grouped around the seaplane base in the lagoon. At the base of the south seaplane ramp was a 20-mm. antiaircraft machine gun. Near it, and between the two seaplane ramps, were two 13-mm. single-mount machine guns, three 7.7-mm. machine guns, and a concrete pillbox. Two 8-cm. dual-purpose guns were located on the ocean shore. The large number of empty machine gun emplace-

ments would seem to indicate that the defenses of the island had not been completed at the time of the invasion. The few pillboxes found in the vicinity of the seaplane base were small, reinforced concrete shelters, each with two firing ports facing seaward. Most of the fire trenches and rifle pits were on the ocean side at the center of the island and at the north and south ends of the island.

The total number of Japanese on Kwajalein, Burton, and other islands in the southern part of the atoll on D Day came to about 5,000 men. (Table 2)

The Army troops on Kwajalein consisted of the Kwajalein and part of the Wotje detachment of the 1st Amphibious Brigade. The Kwajalein detachment, under a Capt. Kenzo Tsuyuki, numbered 204 men and consisted of one rifle company and one mortar platoon. The 729 men of the Wotje detachment had arrived on Kwajalein about 10 January 1944 and

were awaiting transportation to their assigned location when the invasion began.
They were commanded by a Col. Tarok-
ichi Aso and comprised the *2d Battalion*
(less the *1st* and *3d Companies*), three signal
squads, and an engineer platoon.[35]

The *6th Base Force* headquarters in January of 1944 included about 80 military personnel and somewhere in the neighborhood
of 200 civilians.[36] This unit, the headquarters for all shore and surface forces in
the Marshalls, was commanded by Rear
Adm. Monzo Akiyama, IJN, who was the
highest-ranking officer in the Kwajalein
garrison at the time of the American assault. Under the *6th Base Force* was the *61st
Guard Force*, which since before Pearl Harbor had borne the chief responsibility for
defending the atoll. The main body of this
force was stationed in Kwajalein Island
and a detached force was on Roi. The main
body was divided into two small battalions,
four antiaircraft batteries, and six lookout
stations, of which three were on Kwajalein and one each on Bigej (Bennett), Gea
(Carter), and Ennylabegan (Carlos).[37] Also
attached to the *6th Base Force* was one company of about 250 men from the *Yokosuka
4th Special Naval Landing Force*, which arrived in Kwajalein in October 1942.[38]

The labor troops on Kwajalein and adjacent islands were engaged in the construction of the airfield on Kwajalein and
other projects. Fourteen hundred of these
were provided by the *4th Fleet Construction
Department Detachment* and were either Koreans or Japanese unfit for ordinary military duties. Their combat effectiveness was
probably close to nil. Another 260 laborers,
from Okinawa, were provided by the
Sankyu Transportation Company, which
was a purely civilian organization. These
were used as stevedores and are not considered combat effectives.

The three remaining military units in

the area were the *952d Air Unit*, the *6th
Communications Unit*, and the *6th Submarine
Base Force*. The air unit, consisting of about
160 men, was stationed on Burton, and
when the invasion began the duty of defending the island fell to that unit. Since
there were only enough rifles for about half
the men and not even one hand grenade
apiece, their combat effectiveness cannot be
regarded as very important. The *6th Communications Unit* handled communications
command, code and voice signal, code signal dispatch and reception, and the radio
direction finder equipment on Kwajalein
and Enubuj (Carlson). No information is
available as to the combat potential of this
group of 350 men, but it was probably
slight.[39] The *6th Submarine Base Force*, consisting of about a hundred electricians,
mechanics, seamen, doctors, corpsmen,
and maintenance men, had some weapons
including thirteen machine guns and sixty
rifles, but the force was established chiefly
for the purpose of providing a rest and
recreational depot for submarine crews
and is not to be regarded as a combat
unit.[40]

All together, of the enemy personnel in
southern Kwajalein, only about 1,820
could be considered combat effectives at
the time of the invasion. The remainder
can be classified as only partially effective
or not effective at all. (*Table 3*)

---

[35] JICPOA Bull 88-44, *1st Amphibious Brigade*, Japanese Army, 13 Jun 44, pp. 6–7.

[36] Answers Received by a Representative of Capt.
Samuel Eliot Morison, USNR, from Japanese Naval
Officers, Tokyo, 1946, MSS on file at Office of Naval
History.

[37] *61st Guard Force* War Diary, NA 12147.

[38] Special Landing Forces, Early Series, Vol. 8, NA
11647, WDC 160871 (2).

[39] *6th Base Force* War Diary, NA 12654, WDC
160599; CINCPAC-CINCPOA Special Translation
51, Japanese Land-Based Communications Units,
p. 18.

[40] JICPOA Preliminary Interrogation Rpt 48, Interrogation of Katsuhide Okueno.

TABLE 3—COMBAT EFFECTIVENESS OF JAPANESE IN SOUTHERN KWAJALEIN ATOLL
ON D DAY

Unit	Effective	Partially Effective	Not Effective
Total	1,820	865 plus	1,830
Army troops			
6th Base Force headquarters	933	0	0
61st Guard Force (main body)	80	0	170
SNLF attached to 6th Base Force headquarters	557	0	0
Casuals	250	0	0
4th Fleet Construction Department Detachment	0	250	0
Sankyu Transportation Company	0	0	1,400
952d Air Unit	0	0	260
6th Communications Unit	0	160	0
6th Submarine Base Force	0	350	0
4th Fleet detached personnel and naval stragglers	0	a	0

a Unknown.

Source: See sources for Table 2.

Roi-Namur and the other islands of northern Kwajalein, although somewhat more elaborately fortified than the southern islands, had fewer people on hand to resist the invasion. Actual figures for northern Kwajalein are harder to come by than those for the southern part of the atoll. A postbattle count of enemy killed and prisoners taken would indicate that on the northern islands there were 3,563 enemy, including Korean laborers.[41] No complete breakdown is available, but Table 4 represents the best possible estimate from known sources.

The *61st Guard Force Dispatched Force* had been on Roi since before Pearl Harbor and constituted the main body of combat troops. It was responsible for operating most of the weapons on Roi-Namur above the small arms category. It was probably under the tactical if not the administrative control of *Headquarters 24th Air Force,* and itself exercised tactical command over all or part of the *4th Fleet* laborers.[42]

The *24th Air Force* headquarters com-

manded all air units in the Marshalls except the *952d* at Burton, which was controlled by the *6th Base Force.*[43] This headquarters was commanded by Rear Adm. Michiyuki Yamada, who was responsible to *4th Fleet* headquarters at Truk and who was the highest-ranking officer at Roi.[44] On 25 January there were two medium bomber units, one with twelve land-based planes and one with three, and a fighter unit of twenty planes under this headquarters command.[45]

As to the combat effectiveness of these people, it is difficult to hazard anything more than a guess since the extent of mili-

[41] V Phib Corps FLINTLOCK Rpt, Incl D, G-2 Rpt, p. 12.

[42] *61st Guard Force* War Diary, NA 12147.

[43] *6th Base Force* War Diary, NA 12654, WDC 160599.

[44] CINCPAC-CINCPOA Bull 43-45, Register of Japanese Naval Officers, Parts I and II, 20 Feb 45; CINCPAC-CINCPOA Bull 90-45, Command and Staff List, Japanese Navy, 17 Apr 45.

[45] CINCPAC-CINCPOA Bull 16-45, Japanese Naval Air Organization, 22 Jan 45.

TABLE 4—JAPANESE STRENGTH IN NORTHERN KWAJALEIN ATOLL ON D DAY

Unit	Number
Total	2,852 plus
	345
61st Guard Force Dispatched Force	
Air Force personnel	150
24th Air Force headquarters	2,000
Other air units [a]	357
4th Fleet Construction Department Detachment	c
Other units [b]	

[a] *281st, 275th, and 753d Air Units.*
[b] *Attached Special Landing Force,* communications personnel, and naval stragglers.
c Unknown.
Source: JICPOA Bull 48–44, Japanese Defenses, Kwajalein Atoll, 10 Apr 44, Map 3; Answers Received by a Representative of Capt Samuel Eliot Morison, USNR, from Japanese Naval Officers, Tokyo, 1946; JICPOA Translation 7354, Personnel Figures of the *Fourth Construction Unit.*

tary preparedness of the air force personnel is not known. The best estimate would be that on Roi-Namur there were 345 combat effectives of the *61st Guard Force Dispatched Force;* 2,150 air force personnel partially effective as combat troops; 357 *4th Fleet* laborers, ineffective; and about 700 miscellaneous personnel including marooned sailors whose combat effectiveness was probably nonexistent.

It would appear, then, that neither Roi-Namur nor Kwajalein Island was a formidable island fortress in the category of Tarawa or, later, of Iwo Jima. The Japanese had skimped on fortifications of this central atoll in favor of the atolls in the eastern sector of the Marshalls, which they considered more likely to be the objects of attack. By D Day Japanese air power throughout the entire Marshalls area had been reduced to ineffectiveness. Manpower in the islands under attack was of limited military value. On Roi-Namur the bulk of the enemy consisted of air force personnel; on Kwajalein a large percentage was labor troops. Even before American naval guns and aircraft and artillery

placed on nearby islands had completed their bombardment of the main defenses, the capacity of the Japanese to ward off the attack was comparatively slight.

The invasion of Kwajalein Atoll was notable for the innovations in amphibious techniques and amphibious equipment used there. To these can be given much of the credit for the ease with which the operation was completed, in contrast to the earlier landings at Tarawa. But equally or more notable was the fact that the strategic planners for the operation, especially Admiral Nimitz, correctly estimated that this was a weak spot in the Japanese defense of the Central Pacific and exploited it accordingly. The decision to bypass the eastern Marshalls and strike directly at Kwajalein was fully justified by the comparatively weak state of enemy defenses there. Hitting the enemy where he was not was impossible in the Central Pacific, since all the islands and atolls of any strategic importance were fortified. The only alternative was to hit him where he was least able to defend himself, and this was done in the invasion of Kwajalein Atoll.

CHAPTER XIV

The Invasion of Southern Kwajalein

The Landings on D Day

Occupation of Carter and Cecil Islands

As the Southern Attack Force approached its transport and fire support areas located six to ten miles southwest of Kwajalein, the APD's *Overton* and *Manley* slipped ahead in the early morning of 31 January toward the two channel islets that were the first points to be seized by the invading troops.[1] *(See Map 9.)* Carter (Gea) Island lay about nine miles northwest of Kwajalein Island. A half mile farther, on the opposite side of the channel, was Cecil (Ninni). Each of the two APD's was carrying 155 men organized into a provisional unit, in part from the 7th Cavalry Reconnaissance Troop and in part from Company B, 111th Infantry. Troop A, on *Overton,* consisted of the headquarters platoon of the reconnaissance troop plus sixty-one officers and men of the infantry company, all under command of Capt. Paul B. Gritta. In Troop B, transported on *Manley* and commanded by 1st Lt. Emmett L. Tiner, the 1st and 3d Platoons of the reconnaissance troop were supplemented by ninety-three infantry officers and men. Both units were attached for the forthcoming operation to the 17th Regimental

Combat Team, under Col. Wayne C. Zimmerman.[2]

Troop A was to take Cecil Island and Troop B, Carter Island. The islets were tiny, without known defenses, and were assumed to have but small garrisons. Once the two islands were under control, the four platoons of the 7th Cavalry Reconnaissance Troop were to be reunited and taken aboard *Overton* to their next mission, which was tentatively set as the reconnoitering of Chauncey (Gehh) Island, about one mile northwest of Cecil. The infantry elements of the two provisional units would remain as garrison and defense forces on the channel islands.[3]

In the darkness of the moonless night, the islands could not be seen from the ships. The sea was running high as the high-speed transports, about 2,600 yards out, each dispatched one motor launch and a number of rubber boats filled with reconnaissance troops followed by the in-

[1]TF 51, Rpt of Opns for the Capture of the Marshalls (hereafter cited as TF 51 Marshalls Rpt), Incl C, p. 2.

[2] 7th Cavalry Reconnaissance Troop, Rpt of Kwajalein Opn, 20 Feb 44 (hereafter cited as 7th Cav Rcn Tr Rpt), p. 1; 111th Infantry Report After Action Against Enemy, 31 Jan–1 Feb 44, 15 Apr 44 (hereafter cited as 111th Inf AAR).

[3] 7th Inf Div FLINTLOCK Rpt, Vol. II, FO 1, 6 Jan 44, Phase I, pp. 1–2; 7th Cav Rcn Tr Rpt, pp. 1–2.

fantry carried in Higgins boats.[4] The plan for landing on each island required that the rubber boats be towed by a launch to within 800 yards of the shore and then be paddled to a rendezvous halfway in. There they were to wait until two men went forward on an electric-powered raft, made a beach reconnaissance, and set up directional lights marking the best landing spot. The rest of the men in the rubber boats were to follow them ashore and, while establishing a beach defense, guide the Higgins boats in with red lights. Leaving the infantry to defend the beach, the two reconnaissance platoons were first to occupy the side of the island nearest the channel and then to reconnoiter and make secure the remainder of the island.

At the outset some delay was encountered in dispatching Troop B from *Manley* because of the difficulty in finding Carter Island. Then the lead boat mistook Cecil for Carter and by the time this confusion righted itself it was almost daylight. Hence, plans for a preliminary beach reconnaissance were abandoned, and the rubber boats were paddled to shore at the southern end of Carter at 0620. No resistance was met on the beach. Defenses were set up and the infantry boats guided in while a reconnoitering patrol struck through the fringe of brush at the edge of the beach and entered the heavy tropical undergrowth beyond.

The patrol returned without discovering any enemy, and the reconnaissance platoons, with an infantry platoon providing flank and rear protection, pushed off toward an observation tower at the northwest corner of the island. The area around the tower was soon discovered to be unoccupied except for one Japanese soldier, who was killed. The first reconnaissance platoon then turned around to comb back down the island again, concentrating this time on the ocean side. As the skirmish line pushed back into the tangle of undergrowth again, it was suddenly taken under fire from Japanese concealed in a shell crater and surrounding trees. The platoon leader, 2d Lt. Claude V. Hornbacher, ordered a machine gun set up in the crotch of a tree, and with it in position a covering fire was laid down on the whole area. Under protection of this fire, Sgt. Leonard C. Brink took personal charge of the situation. In ten or fifteen minutes he hurled grenade after grenade into the crater while the machine gun fired over his head. The Japanese replied in kind. Finally, after enemy resistance seemed to have dwindled, Sergeant Brink and other members of the platoon crawled forward and jumped into the hole with knives and bayonets. Within seconds the skirmish was over and nineteen Japanese soldiers were dead at the cost of one American wounded. The island again fell silent. A few more Japanese were flushed from their hiding places near the ocean shore, and by 0930 the capture of Carter Island was completed.

Intelligence materials were gathered up and sent to Admiral Turner's flagship, *Rocky Mount,* and at 1000 responsibility for controlling the island was transferred to the infantry elements. The southeast side of the channel was secured.

At the same time that Troop B was seizing Carter, Troop A was engaged in a parallel mission. At 0430 Troop A started from *Overton* toward what was supposed to be Cecil Island. The craft moved against a strong current and an offshore wind.

---

[4] 7th Cav Rcn Tr Rpt, p. 2. Unless otherwise indicated, the account of the action on Chauncey, Carter, and Cecil Islands is drawn from this report or that of the 111th Infantry.

Although the rubber boats were cast loose too soon and had to be rounded up and again taken in tow until brought within paddling distance of the shore, they made an unopposed landing at 0545, thirty-five minutes earlier than Troop B's on Carter. Guide lights were placed and the infantry's landing craft came in just at daybreak, while the beachhead defense was being established.

After a brief reconnaissance during which four enemy were killed and two captured, Captain Gritta, commanding Troop A, came to the conclusion that he was on the wrong island. He suspected that his party had been landed at Chauncey, the small island next northwest of Cecil. This was confirmed by General Corlett, who at 0810 ordered Troop A to "forget about Chauncey; proceed on regular mission." [5]

Leaving a small party of infantrymen to stand guard over a Japanese tugboat stranded near the beach, Captain Gritta embarked the remainder of his troop in rubber boats and proceeded along the reef to Cecil. That island was found to be unoccupied and by 1235 was reported secured.[6] The pass into the lagoon could now be swept in preparation for the entry of ships to provide fire support for the landings planned the next day.

Back on Chauncey, Capt. Gilbert Drexel and his men of Company B, 111th Infantry, kept the stranded tugboat under surveillance and started to comb the woods and underbrush thoroughly. An enemy force estimated at 100, which had escaped the initial reconnaissance, engaged the infantry near the center of the island.[7] Others appeared on the tugboat, fired on strafing planes and on the American detail left to guard the tugboat, and were in turn taken under fire by *Overton*. Under orders to

move to Cecil, the company broke off the engagement in the woods, which had cost them two deaths in return for an estimated forty-five enemy killed. The infantrymen set up a defensive perimeter for the night and waited for boats to transfer them to Cecil the following day. Chauncey was left for a later date to be cleared of the remaining enemy on it. Only one squad of infantrymen reinforced by members of *Overton's* crew were left to guard the stranded tug. On 1 February they were reinforced by a platoon and ordered to set up a perimeter defense at the beach until more troops could be landed to clean out the remnant of Japanese still on the island.[8]

Carlson and Carlos

The seizure of Carlson and Carlos Islands on D Day was assigned to the 17th Regimental Combat Team. Carlson was to be used for the emplacement of divisional artillery and Carlos for supply dumps and repair stations. The capture of Carlson was considered the most important D-Day mission for the Southern Landing Force because of its proximity to Kwajalein Island and its importance as a site for the forty-eight 105-mm. and twelve 155-mm. howitzers that were to provide artillery support for the main landing the next day.

Carlos and Carlson Islands extended along the reef northwest of Kwajalein.[9] Both islands were long and narrow. Carlson was about two-thirds of a mile in length and under 300 yards in width; Carlos about a mile long and 300 yards

[5] 7th Inf Div FLINTLOCK Rpt, Vol. VI, G-3 Jnl, 31 Jan 44, Msgs 22a, 23; Marshall, Kwajalein Notes, Vol. II, pp. 20–21.
[6] 7th Inf Div G-3 Jnl, 31 Jan 44, Msg 90.
[7] 111th Inf AAR, p. 3.
[8] 7th Cav Rcn Tr Rpt, p. 6.
[9] 7th Inf Div FO 1, Annex 3, App 4, p. 9.

wide. Between the two lay a gap of approximately 4,300 yards, but the water over the connecting reef was never deep enough to float even small boats. Reconnaissance flights had revealed on Carlson the presence of radio towers and other installations including a 100-yard finger pier on the lagoon side. It was estimated that a force of from 250 to 300 was stationed on the island to defend it and maintain defense communications there. Carlos Island, it was believed, would contain a much smaller garrison, if any.[10]

The 17th Regimental Combat Team's plan called for simultaneous attacks of battalion strength on the northwestern tip of each island.[11] The 1st Battalion, Lt. Col. Albert V. Hartl commanding, was to attack Carlos; the 2d Battalion, commanded by Lt. Col. Edward P. Smith and supported by one platoon of Company A, 708th Amphibian Tank Battalion, was to land on Carlson. The 3d Battalion, Lt. Col. Lee Wallace commanding, was to remain afloat in landing craft at the line of departure and be available for either island as needed. Two light tanks were designated for the fourth wave of those landing on Carlos and four were allocated to the fourth landing wave for Carlson. The tanks were provided by Company D, 767th Tank Battalion. Company C of the tank battalion was to stand by to provide support missions if called on.

The transports carrying the three battalion landing teams arrived in the transport area six miles to seaward of Carlson at 0544 on 31 January.[12] Five LST's carrying four amphibian tractor groups had already arrived in an assigned area westward from Carlos Island, and on order they moved through the pitch darkness to the transport area to take aboard the assault troops of the first four waves. The men were to disembark from the transports into Higgins boats, move about 600 yards to their assigned LST's, and then distribute themselves among the amphibian tractors at the rate of fifteen men per vehicle. On order, the LST's were then to move close in to the line of departure and disgorge their amphibian tractors through their open bow doors.

This complicated maneuver, carried out as it was in total darkness, inevitably resulted in confusion. The LST's were unable to find the transports until the latter turned on identification lights. This caused delay and Admiral Turner found it necessary to postpone H Hour from 0830 to 0910.[13]

As the LST's left the transport area, one pair carried the LVT group taking the 1st Battalion to Carlos, and another pair carried the LVT group conveying the 2d to Carlson. Other craft followed, including six tank lighters, twelve LCI(G)'s equipped with 40-mm. guns and rockets, and an additional LST carrying the fifteen amphibian tanks of Company A, 708th Amphibious Tank Battalion.[14]

Preparatory naval bombardment opened at 0618 when *Pennsylvania* and *Mississippi* commenced firing on the western end of Kwajalein Island. As daylight revealed three enemy merchant ships in the lagoon, these also received fire from the destroyer *Ringgold* and the cruiser *San Francisco*. In spite of squally showers and a low ceiling, the first of the carrier planes

---

[10] 7th Inf Div FLINTLOCK Rpt, Vol. II, FO 2, 6 Jan 44, pp. 1–4.

[11] *Ibid.*, Vol. VIII, RCT 17 FO 1, 17 Jan 44, p. 2.

[12] TF 51 Marshalls Rpt, Incl A, p. 2: 7th Inf Div FLINTLOCK Rpt, Vol. VIII, RCT 17 Rpt of Opns, 15 Feb 44 (hereafter cited as RCT 17 Rpt), pp. 3, 63, 64; 767th Tk Bn FLINTLOCK Rpt, pp. 84–85.

[13] 7th Inf Div G-3 Jnl, 31 Jan 44, Msg 14.

[14] LST *224* Action Rpt Kwajalein, 8 Feb 44; 767th Tk Bn Jnl, 31 Jan 44, p. 3.

reported on station at 0840 to commence the first of many strafing and bombing runs on Kwajalein Island.[15] Observation planes later spotted fire for the battleships and cruisers. At 0810 the scheduled plotted bombardment began with shells from four battleships (*New Mexico, Mississippi, Idaho,* and *Pennsylvania*), three cruisers (*Minneapolis, San Francisco,* and *New Orleans*) and four destroyers (*Stevens, McKee, Ringgold,* and *Sigsbee*) systematically striking Carlos, Carlson, Kwajalein, Burton, and Beverly Islands.[16]

The line of departure for the landing on Carlos lay about 3,000 yards west of the island's northwestern tip, Harvey Point. The plan called for the first four waves of the 1st Battalion Landing Team to start for the shore in thirty-two LVT's manned by seven officers and 140 enlisted men. Each of the first two waves was to consist of eight amphtracks in staggered rows of four, the two waves to be spaced three minutes apart. The third wave was to contain five armored LVT's in the first row and four in the second. Wave four consisted of more LVT's in a similar formation; wave five, LCM's carrying tanks and self-propelled mounts (75-mm. howitzers); and wave six, standard landing craft carrying one heavy machine gun platoon, battalion headquarters elements, advance personnel of the battalion aid station, and a squad of engineers.[17]

The ship-to-shore movement proceeded in general according to plan, and the first troops, two infantry platoons and part of the 1st Platoon, Company A, 13th Engineers, reached shore at 0910. They came into a wide, shallow cove near the northwestern end of the island, which seemed wild and uninhabited. On the left, on Harvey Point, and to the right, tall palms could be seen in small groves, but waist-high underbrush interspersed with small patches of bare sand extended across the island directly back of the beachhead line. Vegetation had been only slightly disturbed by the preliminary bombardment. Behind the first two waves of infantrymen were landed a platoon of heavy machine guns, the communications section of the beach and shore parties, forward observers for the mortars, advance elements of the Signal Corps detachment, infantry reserves, light tanks, self-propelled mounts, battalion headquarters elements, and medical personnel. By 1040, the first five waves were ashore. The landings were unopposed.[18]

The occupation of Carlos was easily accomplished. Company A, which landed on the right, pushed southward along the ocean side of the island; Company C, on the left, made its way across to the lagoon side and then proceeded in a southerly direction. Near the pier on the lagoon shore, men of Company C encountered their first enemy—three unarmed Japanese, whom they promptly killed. Five others in this area were found to have committed suicide. Company A captured seven or eight prisoners in their southward march. When the front had advanced two thirds of the way down the island, Company C halted and Company A took over the entire line. About two hundred yards from the southern point of the island, Company A met a group of nine Japanese, who were cut down by rifle fire as they tried to rush the Americans. The southern point of the

[15] TF 51 Marshalls Rpt, pp. 32–33 and Incl E, App 2, p. 1.

[16] *Ibid.,* Incl E, App 2, p. 1.

[17] 7th Inf Div FO 1, Annex 8; Marshall, Kwajalein Notes, Vol. II, p. 12; RCT 17 Rpt, Jnl, 31 Jan 44, Msgs 31, 37.

[18] Marshall, Kwajalein Notes, Vol. II, p. 12; RCT 17 Jnl, 31 Jan 44, Msgs 31, 37.

LANDING ON CARLSON ISLAND. *Note DUKW (right center) equipped with A-frame device.*

island was reached by 1400. The force found an observation tower and sheds with a radio in working order. At 1615 the 1st Battalion reported the island secured. No casualties were reported. No prepared defenses had been found.[19]

Resistance on Carlson Island was expected to be considerably stronger than that on Carlos or any of the other islands occupied on D Day.[20] The first four assault waves of the 2d Battalion Landing Team were carried ashore in amphibian tractors. The later waves approached the reef in LCVP's from which they were obliged to wade in for the last seventy-five yards. The wave formations were similar to those at Carlos, and the support from destroyers and LCI(G)'s was the same.

The first wave hit the sandy beach at the northwestern corner of Carlson at 0912. The beach was about 300 yards wide with a treeless sandspit at the left and a thin growth of coconut palms behind a shoulder in the coast line at the right. The amphibians crawled up the beach, meeting no resistance. Company E came in on the left and Company F on the right, while Company G was kept in floating reserve, prepared to land at a point near the middle of the island if the tactical situation so required. In the first wave with the rifle squads were rocket grenadiers, demolition engineers, flame thrower operators, and wire-cutting specialists, all of the 13th

---

[19] Marshall, Kwajalein Notes, Vol. II, p. 14; RCT 17 Rpt, S-2 Worksheets, p. 133.
[20] Marshall, Kwajalein Notes, Vol. II, pp. 14–15; RCT 17 Rpt, pp. 4, 137–39.

Engineers. The second wave landed at 0920, and the third was ashore ten minutes later. LCI gunboats continued their fire until the third wave had landed. Carrier planes strafed and bombed the island, moving to the southeastern extremity by 0938.

Company F on the right pushed straight across the island to the lagoon, and at 0941 swung southeastward for the push along the length of the island. Company E on the left mopped up the northern end before starting down the ocean side, somewhat behind Company F. At 0958 enemy artillery fire from Kwajalein was reported, but by 1120 naval gunfire and an air attack had put a stop to all Japanese shelling from that quarter.[21]

Meanwhile, a section of the shore party in two amphibian tractors had reconnoitered the reef during the initial landings and selected a route ashore for the four light tanks and four self-propelled 75-mm. howitzers, which came in by 1010.[22] The tanks disembarked from their LCM's on the reef and made their way to the shore, minus one vehicle that broke its final drive and remained incapacitated for the rest of the operation. Once ashore, the tanks found passage through the thick underbrush and coral extremely difficult and a second tank was temporarily disabled.[23]

The infantrymen accompanied by combat engineers continued southeastward toward the communications center, which was almost in the middle of the island, arriving there at 1105.[24] The preliminary bombardment had knocked down one radio tower and weakened another as well as smashing the major buildings, even those constructed of reinforced concrete. The enemy fled, offering no resistance as Company F searched the area. Company E on the ocean side discovered three sets of dummy emplacements but only light enemy resistance. Small arms fire fell briefly among the infantrymen as the two companies moved in line abreast southeastward from the radio tower. Only one man was wounded, however. No further opposition was met. By noon the southeastern tip of the island was reached, and at 1210 the battalion reported the island secured. Twenty-one Korean prisoners were captured. No live Japanese were found on the island, although the battalion commander reported, somewhat ambiguously, that "it is believed that some of the Koreans were part Japanese."[25]

Development of Positions

The unexpected ease with which Carlson was occupied led to an early landing of the divisional artillery—even before the island was officially declared secured. At 1125 General Corlett sent orders to the 7th Division artillery group to begin getting its pieces ashore.[26] This group, commanded by General Arnold, consisted of four battalions of 105-mm. howitzers (31st, 48th, 49th, and 57th Field Artillery), and one battalion of 155-mm. howitzers (145th Field Artillery), plus headquarters, medical, communications, and special troops. The 105-mm. howitzer battalions were loaded mostly on LST's. The 145th Field Artillery with its 155-mm. pieces had to be loaded on two larger transports—the AKA *Virgo* and the APA *President Polk*. Liaison and forward observation parties were on

---

[21] RCT 17 Jnl, 31 Jan 44, Msgs 15, 23, 24, 26.
[22] 767th Tk Bn Jnl, 31 Jan 44, p. 3; RCT 17 Rpt, p. 4.
[23] Lt Paul R. Leach, Tanks on Kwajalein Atoll, MS, p. 7, OCMH.
[24] *Ibid.*
[25] *Ibid.*, p. 4.
[26] 7th Inf Div G-3 Jnl, 31 Jan 44, Msgs 67, 72.

DEMOLISHED COMMUNICATIONS CENTER AND STRONGPOINT
(above and below, respectively). Preliminary bombardment destroyed many defensive installations and demoralized the defenders.

the transports with the infantry to which they were attached; the five air observers were on three cruisers of the attack force; and the division artillery command party was on *Rocky Mount* with General Corlett.[27]

The 155-mm. howitzers with their tractors, equipment, and ammunition were loaded onto LCM's. These craft grounded in three feet of water offshore but the howitzers were hauled to the beach and dragged to their designated areas, where some were ready for registration fire by 1525. However, the last were not emplaced until long after dark.[28]

The 105-mm. howitzers were, on the other hand, more expeditiously unloaded. Their DUKW's moved with relative ease from their mother LST's about 1,000 yards offshore to the positions where the batteries were to be emplaced. Certain DUKW's, especially equipped with A-frame hoists mounted in the rear, took their places near the battery positions. The other vehicles with guns aboard were driven one at a time at right angles across the rear ends of the A-frame DUKW's and halted under the hoists. There, each piece was lifted clear of the DUKW that had transported it, lowered to the ground, hooked to the pintle of the same vehicle and pulled into position. Under the most favorable conditions, a whole battalion could be brought into position in seven minutes.[29]

The 31st Field Artillery Battalion was the first to commence unloading its howitzers. Its DUKW's proceeded from the beach across the island and along the lagoon shore to a spot opposite the battalion area. Then, with the aid of a bulldozer and much tree cutting, they hauled the pieces to a thick coconut grove, unloaded them, and returned to the beach to pick up ammunition. Shortly after 1500 the 105's commenced registration fire on a Kwaja-

lein Island check point, using smoke shells to distinguish their fire from that of the naval vessels, which were concurrently bombarding that island. Observation posts were later established in the radio tower, on the end of the pier, and in an LVT out in the lagoon, while registration was accomplished with the help of an observation plane launched from one of the cruisers.[30]

The 48th, 49th, and 57th Field Artillery Battalions followed a similar pattern, occupying areas in the center and on the southern half of Carlson Island. At nightfall the last registration fire was being delivered on a check point on Kwajalein Island by the 49th Battalion. Ammunition was being rapidly loaded into DUKW's from beached LST's, and before dawn a large supply of shells was on hand to support the main attack on Kwajalein.[31]

The divisional artillery was concentrated within an unusually limited area. The twelve batteries of 105's were crowded together in an area only 900 yards long by 150 yards wide. The guns of the 49th Battalion were at the southeastern end of the island; those of the 57th Battalion in the adjacent area to the northwest on the ocean side of the island; those of the 31st in a zone west of the pier line on the ocean side; and those of the 48th Battalion closely grouped south of the radio tower. The 155-mm. howitzers of the 145th Battalion

---

[27] 7th Inf Div Southern Landing Force Arty Rpt Kwajalein Opn, 12 Mar 44, pp. 3–11.

[28] 145th FA Bn Rpt of FLINTLOCK Opn, p. 4.

[29] 7th Inf Div Rpt, use of DUKW's by the Artillery of the 7th Infantry Division in the FLINTLOCK Operation, 4 Apr 44, p. 5.

[30] 7th Inf Div Southern Landing Force Arty Rpt Kwajalein Opn, pp. 7, 13.

[31] Of these, 45 percent were high explosive, 40 percent time-fuzed, and 15 percent smoke. 7th Inf Div FLINTLOCK Rpt, Vol. XII, Arty Rpt, S-4 Rpt on Kwajalein, p. 2.

105-MM. M2 HOWITZERS *in position on Carlson Island.*

were emplaced farthest from Kwajalein Island between two roads near the middle of Carlson. Following registration, the batteries prepared for an irregular schedule of harassing fire on both Kwajalein and Burton Islands so that the enemy would be prevented, if possible, from repairing and reorganizing his defenses.[32]

The night of D Day on southern Kwajalein found the Southern Attack Force, despite the unfinished business on Chauncey Island, with all its scheduled objectives attained. The channel islands were secured; the channel itself and an anchorage in the lagoon had been swept for mines; and a part of the invading force had entered the lagoon to take stations there. On Carlos and Carlson the Americans were in full possession.

During the early afternoon, the 3d Bat-

talion Landing Team of the 17th Infantry and one platoon of the 31st Field Hospital had been brought ashore on Carlos. By 1200 men of Company A of the 7th Medical Battalion were ashore and operating a collecting station at the beach.[33] The 1st Battalion had returned to the northwest section of Carlos and the 3d Battalion, the reserve force, occupied the southeastern half.

Supply sections of the 7th Division, which had been separated during the journey to the island, had assembled ashore, co-ordinated their work, arranged their communications, and were beginning to

[32] Cpl Millard Rogers, The Artillery Action of the Battle of Kwajalein Atoll, MS, p. 21, and App II, Map 1, OCMH.
[33] 7th Inf Div Med Bn Rpt of Activity During FLINTLOCK Opn, 22 Jan–8 Feb 44, pp. 12, 23.

build dumps. At 1800, on the northern tip of Carlos, a detachment of the 707th Ordnance Company had set up the LVT maintenance shop capable of handling heavy repairs.[34] At the southern end of the island a consolidated ammunition dump was prepared during the night and was ready for use by 0800 on 1 February.

Carlson Island was the scene of even greater night activity. As planned, the 7th Division's headquarters, rear section, had remained on board Admiral Turner's flagship, *Rocky Mount*, together with that of the V Amphibious Corps, but during the afternoon the command posts and headquarters had been set up on Carlson by the 2d Battalion, 17th Infantry, by the division artillery, and by the 7th Division forward echelon, the latter commanded by Brig. Gen. Joseph L. Ready. At 1645 General Corlett, having observed the early landing of the division artillery, ordered harassing fire placed on Kwajalein Island throughout the night. As a result, there was a much longer preliminary artillery bombardment than the one-hour preparation indicated in the plans as a minimum. During the night both Kwajalein and Burton Islands were treated to a continuing harassing fire by the artillery emplaced on Carlson.[35]

After dark, naval support vessels joined with the artillery to keep a constant harassing fire over Kwajalein and Burton. The larger island was shelled by *San Francisco, Idaho, New Mexico,* and their screening destroyers, while Burton was covered by the destroyer *Hall.* Troops of the 32d and 184th Regimental Combat Teams had moved during the afternoon from their transports to LST's, which were spending the night either west of Kwajalein Island or in the lagoon with orders to return to the transport area at 0530. The remaining vessels of the Southern Attack Force operated in waters southwest, south, and southeast of Kwajalein Island with orders to be in the transport area at 0600.[36]

One of the novel experiments of the Marshalls operation had also been carried out on D Day with successful, although in a sense inconclusive, results. This was the employment for the first time in the Pacific of an underwater demolition team, composed in this instance of both Army and Navy personnel, whose duties were to conduct close reconnaissance of the beaches at the western end of Kwajalein Island and, if necessary, detonate any underwater obstacles found there. At high tide on the morning of 31 January, shortly after 1000, and again at low tide at approximately 1600, this detachment worked its way to points within 300 yards of the beach. Fire from the battleships *Pennsylvania* and *Mississippi* covered these intrepid individuals as they ranged over the approaches to the main landing beaches in rubber boats. Having ascertained that surf and reef conditions were satisfactory and that no underwater obstacles or antiboat mines were located off the beaches, they returned without casualty. Since there were no underwater obstacles present, no opportunity was allowed the team to test its detonation equipment technique under combat conditions. Nevertheless, the team performed valuable service later in the operation in the demolition of wrecks, coral heads, and other underwater obstructions along the lagoon shore of the island.[37]

---

[34] 7th Inf Div FLINTLOCK Rpt, Vol. VII, G-4 Rpt, Annex F, QM Rpt, p. 1, and Annex E, Ordnance Rpt, 707th Ord Co Narrative Rpt, p. 1.

[35] 7th Inf Div Southern Landing Force Arty Rpt Kwajalein Opn, p. 11; 145th FA Bn Rpt of FLINTLOCK Opn, p. 171; 7th Inf Div G-3 Jnl, 31 Jan 44, Msgs 87, 125.

[36] TF 51 Marshalls Rpt, Incl A, p. 4.

[37] *Ibid.*, Incl E, pp. 7–8.

With all the conditions for a successful landing deemed favorable, Admiral Turner issued the order at 1622 on 31 January that the main assault on the western beaches of Kwajalein Island should proceed the following day. The scheduled time of landing, H Hour, was set at 0930. The attack would be carried out according to the original plan.[38]

The Landings on Kwajalein Island

Long before sunrise on the morning of 1 February 1944 the Southern Attack Force at Kwajalein Atoll moved from its night cruising dispositions to the positions assigned for the day's operations against Kwajalein Island. The eight LST's on which the leading wave of assault troops had spent the night were the first to approach their rendezvous, at 0530, and within half an hour the larger transports and the warships that were to provide fire support were taking stations. At 0618 *Mississippi* and *Pennsylvania* took up the harassing fire, which had been maintained during the night by other ships and by the artillery on Carlson.[39] Squalls, frequent rain showers, and scudding clouds lowered visibility. They threatened to hamper the attack but not to compel either its postponement or the adoption of the alternative plan for a complicated landing from the lagoon.[40] The assault was to be made from the ocean against the western end of Kwajalein Island.

As the sun rose at 0712, *Mississippi* moved to a range of about 1,500 yards to fire broadsides on visible targets. The other support vessels closed to about the same range when the systematic preparatory fire was begun at 0745. At that time *Mississippi* switched her salvos to Burton, northeast of Kwajalein, and *Pennsylvania, New Mexico,*

Minneapolis, New Orleans, and *San Francisco,* screened by eight destroyers, directed their main batteries at the western end of Kwajalein Island in direct preparation for the landings. The destroyers *Ringgold* and *Sigsbee* entered the lagoon and prepared to prevent interisland movement by the enemy.[41]

The preparatory bombardment of Kwajalein Island was unprecedented in the Pacific in both volume and effectiveness. During one period two shells per second were hitting specific targets or areas in the path of the assault troops. The 14-inch naval shells of the battleships were most effective in piercing and destroying reinforced concrete structures. From the cruisers and destroyers, 8-inch and 5-inch shells ploughed into bunkers and tore up the thick growth of pandanus and palm trees. All together on 1 February, almost 7,000 14-inch, 8-inch, and 5-inch shells were fired by supporting naval vessels at Kwajalein Island alone,[42] and the bulk of these were expended against the main beaches before the landing. The field artillery on Carlson also joined in the preparatory fire. Its total ammunition expenditure on 1 February against Kwajalein was about 29,000 rounds.[43] Finally, aerial bombardment added its bit to the pulverization of Kwajalein's defenses. At 0810 six Liberators (B-24's) of the 392d Bombardment Squadron based on Apamama reported on station. Between 0830 and 0910 they flew above the trajectory of the naval and artillery shells and dropped fifteen 1,000-pound and 2,000-pound bombs on the blockhouse

[38] 7th Inf Div G-3 Jnl, 31 Jan 44, Msg 122.
[39] TF 51 Marshalls Rpt, Incl E, App 2, p. 4.
[40] *Ibid.*, Incl F, p. 3.
[41] *Ibid.*, Incl E, App 2, p. 4.
[42] *Ibid.*, Incl E, App 1, Table 3.
[43] 7th Inf Div Southern Landing Force Arty Rpt Kwajalein Opn, p. 11.

EFFECT OF BOMBARDMENT OF KWAJALEIN. *Preinvasion attacks reduced defensive positions in the beach area to rubble.*

and dual-purpose twin-mount guns at the northwestern end of Kwajalein Island.[44] This was followed almost immediately by bombing and strafing attacks carried out by carrier-based aircraft. From the carriers *Enterprise, Yorktown, Belleau Wood, Manila Bay, Corregidor,* and *Coral Sea* eighteen dive bombers and fifteen torpedo bombers struck the western part of Kwajalein Island while as many fighters strafed the area with machine guns and rockets. All together ninety-six sorties were flown from the carriers in support of the troop landing on Kwajalein Island.[45]

The results of all this expenditure of explosives were devastating. The damage was so intensive that it is impossible to determine the relative effectiveness of the three types of bombardment—naval, artillery, and air. The area inland of Red Beaches was reduced almost completely to rubble. Concrete emplacements were shattered, coconut trees smashed and flattened, the ground pock-marked with large craters, coral ripped to splinters. As one observer reported, "The entire island looked as if it had been picked up to 20,000 feet and then dropped." [46]

The Assault Landings

The first touchdowns were to occur at 0930. As the time for departure approached, ships, amphibian vehicles, and landing craft began to take their assigned places. The line of departure was 5,000 yards northwest of Kwajalein Island, south of the center of Carlson Island, and the transport area was about 3,000 yards southwest of the line.[47] Control over the landing waves was vested in the commanding officers of the 184th and 32d Regimental Combat Teams, who were located on the control ship, a subchaser (SC 539).[48] The LST's carrying the amphibian tractors went into position about 1,000 yards west of the line of departure, lowered their ramps, and launched their amphtracks with the troops loaded. The tractors began to circle slowly in a column of waves, waiting the signal to move into line. The LSD's *Lindenwald, Belle Grove,* and *Ashland* in an area west of the LST's launched the LCM's containing the medium tanks of Companies A, B, C, and part of D of the 767th Tank Battalion.[49] Two small control boats, assigned to keep the landing craft moving toward the shore at proper intervals, took stations just seaward of the line of departure. Near the ends of the line the amphibian tanks of Company A, 708th Amphibian Tank Battalion, circled after being released from their mother LST, waiting to take their wing positions with the first waves to go ashore.[50] Farther back in the transport area, the landing craft on the transports were swung out from the decks and launched. They were to carry the supporting waves with extra ammunition and equipment. Two LST's with high priority supplies and the DUKW groups waited to move near enough to the beaches to send in supplies quickly.[51]

The northern (left) part of the 500-yard

---

[44] Operational History of the Seventh Air Force, 6 Nov 43–31 Jul 44, p. 125; Craven and Cate, *AAF IV*, p. 306.

[45] CINCPAC-CINCPOA Opns in POA, Feb 44, Annex A, p. 35; TF 51 Marshalls Rpt, Annex F, p. 3.

[46] CINCPAC-CINCPOA Opns in POA, Feb 44, Annex A, p. 35; TF 51 Marshalls Rpt, Incl E, p. 11.

[47] TF 52 Attack Order A1-44.

[48] 7th Inf Div FLINTLOCK Rpt, Vol. XI, RCT 184 Rpt of Opns and Jnl, 31 Jan–6 Feb 44 (hereafter cited as RCT 184 Rpt and RCT 184 Jnl), p. 2.

[49] 7th Inf Div G-3 Jnl, 1 Feb 44, Msg 13; 767th Tk Bn Jnl, 31 Jan 44, pp. 2, 32.

[50] LST *224* Action Rpt Kwajalein, 8 Feb 44.

[51] 7th Inf Div G-4 Rpt, Annex A, Initial Combat Supply, p. 3.

western shore line had been designated Red Beach 1, and the southern (right) part was Red Beach 2. *(Map VII)* Preliminary reconnaissance had indicated the existence of the stronger fortifications along the ocean side, and for that reason the combat-seasoned 32d Regimental Combat Team, under Col. Marc J. Logie, was assigned the landing on Red Beach 2. The 184th Regimental Combat Team, under Col. Curtis D. O'Sullivan, was to land on Red Beach 1 at the same time. The two combat teams were to make their assaults in columns of battalions, led by the 1st Battalion of the 32d, containing 84 officers and 1,628 enlisted men, and the 3d Battalion of the 184th, consisting of 73 officers and 1,489 enlisted men. Of the three companies of the 767th Tank Battalion, Company B would support the landing of the 184th on Red Beach 1 and Company A that of the 32d on Red Beach 2, while Company C would be held in reserve under division control.[52]

The enemy offered some resistance to the gathering attack in spite of the overwhelming preparatory fire that had already wrecked most of their guns on the western end of Kwajalein Island. A few antiaircraft shells fell among the assembling landing craft, one of them striking an LVT, injuring two men and knocking the vehicle out of action. The rest of the amphibian tractors, separated by about twenty yards between vehicles and about 100 yards between waves, continued to circle under excellent control. Nevertheless, one accidental collision between two amphibians occurred, damaging one of them and interfering slightly with the landing schedule.[53]

The first waves of the 3d Battalion, 184th, commanded by Lt. Col. William P. Walker, and of the 1st Battalion, 32d, under Lt. Col. Ernest H. Bearss, started for the shore precisely on time at 0900 after receiving the signal from the control boat.[54] The LVT's mounted at least two, sometimes three, machine guns each, and, in addition, twenty of them had specially mounted infantry-type flame throwers that could be operated from the assistant driver's seat.[55] At each outside wing and in the center between the first two waves, platoons of amphibian tanks were echeloned. From their turrets, 37-mm. guns protruded. Behind the first wave came three succeeding waves of infantry at two-minute intervals.

As the tractors set out for their thirty-minute run from the line of departure to the shore, Navy aircraft strafed the beaches in a last-minute blow. At 0905 artillery and naval ships resumed fire against the beaches and kept it up until 0928, two minutes before the touchdown, after which they moved their fire inland. LCI gunboats added the final touch. Firing from outside the lanes of approach at the northern and southern extremities of the landing area, they let go their 4.5-inch rockets at 1,100 yards from the shore line and again at 800 yards and fired their 20-mm. and 40-mm. guns at still closer ranges. The seventeen amphibian tanks on the wings and in the center, and the tractors in between them also rode in firing. Small arms and mortar fire from the Japanese inflicted few injuries among the incoming troops, and for the most part the waves preserved their formation.[56]

There was, however, some shifting to the right (south). The steering mechanism of

---

[52] 7th Inf Div FO 1, p. 7; 7th Inf Div FO 2, p. 2.

[53] Marshall, Kwajalein Notes, Vol. I, pp. 5–6.

[54] 7th Inf Div G-3 Jnl, 1 Feb 44, Msg 22.

[55] Flame throwers were also installed on eighteen light tanks. 767th Tk Bn FLINTLOCK Rpt. pp. 52, 53; Marshall, Kwajalein Notes, Vol. I, p. 2.

[56] Marshall, Kwajalein Notes, Vol. I, pp. 1–6.

INVASION OF KWAJALEIN. *Following the preinvasion bombardment (above), landing craft head for the beaches (below).*

the LVT that had been damaged in the collision caused it to veer from its position and move to the right among the tractors of the 1st Battalion, 32d Regiment. All the landing vehicles inclined slightly to the right toward the southern boundaries of the boat lanes, and after they crossed the reef the current took them still farther in that direction. The result was some crowding on the south, but not enough to interfere seriously with the landing.[57]

Artillery fire from Carlson was still falling on the beaches as the LVT's reached positions only thirty-five yards offshore. Thereupon it was shifted to a zone 200 yards inland. Although most of the defensive positions immediately inland of the shore line had been obliterated, shell craters and piles of debris everywhere remained to deter the invaders. The first wave landed on schedule at 0930. In the zone of the 32d Regimental Combat Team enough of the enemy survived in their underground shelters or filtered back through the curtain of artillery and naval gunfire to greet the attackers with small arms fire and grenades. From a few undestroyed pillboxes inland of the beaches, the Japanese opened up with light mortar and automatic fire—fire heavy enough to cause a few casualties among the first waves.[58]

As the first troops dropped down from the high sides of the amphtracks into the shallow water or onto the beach itself, most of them ran over the dune and sought shelter behind the wreckage of a sea wall until the artillery and naval fire lifted inland. On Red Beach 1, where the sea wall was almost at the water's edge, the LVT's were tilted up enough to obtain a fair field of fire inland. On Red Beach 2 the amphibians stopped at the water line, their fire sweeping barely above the men of the

1st Battalion. For about two minutes the men of the first wave on Red Beach 2 waited in the shelter of the sea wall while LVT's poured fire over their heads. Then, while a detail demolished one remaining pillbox on the beach itself, the rest of the men moved forward rapidly to seek out the enemy just beyond the beach.[59] On the left, the two assault companies (Companies I and K) of the 3d Battalion, 184th Infantry, were also making progress. By 1122 both assault battalions were reported to have advanced 150 yards inland against only slight resistance.[60]

Combat engineers carrying demolition charges and wire cutters were distributed among the first wave of infantrymen and were prepared to clear the way for the second and subsequent waves to move inland. The preparatory fire, however, had been so effective that further demolition work was unnecessary. Both engineers and covering infantry were therefore able to advance inland with the second wave.[61]

The amphibian tanks of the first line of attack were expected to proceed inland, striking targets found within a hundred yards of the shore. The LVT's in the second and third waves were to move to the flanks and circle back to the ships to bring in the men of the later waves who were embarked in landing craft too deep-drafted to get over the reef. All vehicles met serious difficulties on the beaches. Some found the undestroyed portions of the sea wall too high to cross; others fell into shell holes or

---

[57] *Ibid.*, pp. 6–7.

[58] *Ibid.*, p. 14; 7th Inf Div FLINTLOCK Rpt, Vol. IX, RCT 32 Rpt of Opn PORCELAIN (Kwajalein) Island, and Jnl, 31 Jan–6 Feb 44 (hereafter cited as RCT 32 Rpt and RCT 32 Jnl), p. 30.

[59] Marshall, Kwajalein Notes, Vol. I, p. 7; RCT 32 Rpt, p. 30.

[60] RCT 184 Jnl, 1 Feb 44.

[61] Marshall, Kwajalein Notes, Vol. I, p. 14.

got hung up on high stumps. Most of the tractors, after landing their troops, found lateral movement along the beaches so impeded by the litter left by the first wave of infantrymen and engineers that, instead of adhering to the original plan of moving to the flanks before returning seaward, they turned around on the beach or backed into the water. This caused considerable congestion and slowed the fourth wave's approach to the shore. Troops in this wave either waded in or waited for the beach to be cleared.[62] In spite of these difficulties, the first four waves of both battalion landing teams were ashore within fifteen minutes after the designated H Hour.[63]

Build-up of the Assault

While some elements of the first four waves pressed forward in the wake of the artillery barrage and others organized the beaches, additional infantry and units of supporting arms and services continued to come ashore throughout the day.

The 32d Regiment's forward command party landed at 0950 and set up a command post a few yards inland in the center of Red Beach 2.[64] The 184th's advance command post was established on Red Beach 1 at 1235.[65]

The light tanks, carried in LCM's, approached the beach in the fifth wave. Stopped on the reef at 0947, the tank lighters discharged their tanks, which then tried to make shore under their own power. Three light tanks were stranded on the reef. All six of the medium tanks of the sixth wave assigned to Red Beach 2 got ashore, but two destined for Red Beach 1 were held up by the reef and an underwater shell hole. After drying out motors and radios, those tanks that had landed struggled inland across the crowded, shell-torn beach and over the sea wall. Most of

the tanks succeeded in pushing on, but the marshy land behind Red Beach 2 held four up.[66]

At 1205 the 2d and 3d Platoons, Company A, 767th Tank Battalion, were ordered into shore and, with one casualty on the reef, proceeded inland via Blue Beach 1, which was located on the southwest corner of the island to the right of Red Beach 2. The 2d Platoon was sent forward and the 3d Platoon remained on the beach in reserve. The 2d Platoon of Company B reached Red Beach 1 at 1400. It landed without mishap, being guided ashore by four stranded medium tank crewmen of the 1st Platoon who stood on the reef in water up to their armpits and directed the tanks around the underwater hazards. The tanks went forward to support the infantry without delay, using a new route from the beach that had been cleared by bulldozers.[67] The 1st Platoon, Company B, and the 2d Platoon, Company C, brought their twelve mediums in at 1600 while the 1st Battalion, 184th, was still being landed. One medium tank was disabled on the reef; the others went into bivouac. When the 1st and 3d Platoons, Company C, were sent to Red Beach 2 by error between 1630 and 1700, they were kept ashore overnight and re-embarked late the next day to participate with the 17th Infantry Regiment in the forthcoming operations on Burton Island.[68]

[62] RCT 32 Jnl, 1 Feb 44, Msg 18.

[63] 7th Inf Div G-3 Jnl, 1 Feb 44, Msg 45; 767th Tk Bn Jnl, 1 Feb 44, p. 4; Marshall, Kwajalein Notes, Vol. I, p. 3.

[64] RCT 32 Jnl, 1 Feb 44, Msg 18a.

[65] RCT 184 Jnl, 1 Feb 44.

[66] Marshall, Kwajalein Notes, Vol. I, pp. 9, 15, 94.

[67] RCT 32 Jnl, 1 Feb 44, Msg 50; Marshall, Kwajalein Notes, Vol. I, p. 9; 767th Tk Bn Jnl, 1 Feb 44, p. 4.

[68] 767th Tk Bn Jnl, 1 Feb 44, p. 6; Leach, Tanks on Kwajalein Atoll.

BULLDOZER CLEARS ROUTE *from beach (above) to facilitate the movement of M4 medium tanks supporting the infantry (below).*

Combat engineers found their problems fewer than had been anticipated. Without much difficulty they cleared the beach of enemy explosives, set up demolition dumps, and replenished forward ammunition supplies. They later joined the shore party engineers in smoothing out the rough passage from the beach to the western section of the island highway (Wallace Road) with bulldozers and in repairing that section of the highway. The first of the supply DUKW's came ashore just before noon. Seven were sent forward over the new route with grenades, 75-mm. shells, and other ammunition.[69] The matériel dropped from the LVT's was gathered by engineers and put in a dump about fifty yards inland. Regimental supply personnel arrived at Red Beach 2 about 1115. They later established a supply point well inland in the wake of the assault forces.[70]

One platoon of the 184th Regiment's 81-mm. mortars erroneously landed at 1025 on Red Beach 2, but was quickly moved to Red Beach 1 to support the regiment's attack.[71] Late in the afternoon the 1st Platoon of the 91st Chemical Company, which was attached to the 32d Regiment, was emplaced near the southern limit of Red Beach 2, having been landed during the morning and early afternoon. Extra ammunition with which to fire night missions, however, was unavailable until early the next morning. The 2d Platoon, 91st Chemical Company, landed at 1630 on Red Beach 1 in support of the 184th. After having been afloat in landing craft for seven hours, it came ashore in four crowded amphtracks with its mortars unassembled. The weapons were assembled near the lagoon shore about 150 yards from Red Beach 1, and a fire direction center was established near the mortars.[72]

The Cannon Companies of the two regimental combat teams landed one platoon at a time with each battalion. Some of the 75-mm. howitzers were packed ashore, while others were waterproofed and towed over the reef from landing craft. The howitzers of the 32d Regiment were emplaced by 1700 in the southwest corner of a natural clearing just beyond the beachhead line, which lay about 250 yards inland.[73] As early as 1330 one section of the 184th's Cannon Company was firing from a position on the lagoon shore line; about three hours later three more pieces were in battery formation with it. The remaining platoon landed about 1900 and went into bivouac.[74]

Each of the nine battalion landing teams at southern Kwajalein was assigned a collecting platoon of the 7th Medical Battalion. The first to land was the 1st Platoon, Company B, which came in at Red Beach 2 with the 1st Battalion, 32d Regiment, at 1130. An hour later the 3d Platoon, Company C, landed on Red Beach 1 with the 3d Battalion, 184th. Each platoon set up a collecting station on the beach and evacuated casualties by LVT's to the transport. When the shore party medical sections were ready on the beaches, evacuation of casualties was turned over to them, and the collecting platoons, each now reinforced by a second, moved inland from the beaches to set up two collecting stations. Before night, all collecting platoons and headquarters of each medical company

[69] RCT 32 Jnl, 1 Feb 44, Msg 54.
[70] Marshall, Kwajalein Notes, Vol. I, p. 95; RCT 32 Rpt, p. 34.
[71] 7th Inf Div FLINTLOCK Rpt, Vol. XI, RCT 184 Rpt of Opns, BLT 184–1 Rpt of Opns, Jnl, 1 Feb 44, p. 87.
[72] 91st Chemical Co Rpt of Participation in Kwajalein Opns, 18 Feb 44, pp. 131–41.
[73] RCT 32 Rpt, p. 22.
[74] RCT 184 Rpt, p. 43.

75-MM. HOWITZER IN ACTION *against enemy positions across the lagoon.*

were ashore.[75] Evacuation of the injured along the highway to the beaches was swift. Because of the small number of casualties, only one platoon was needed to operate a collecting station in each regimental zone. Men of the other two platoons were sent forward to act as litter bearers, thus accelerating the medical service. About 1530 the 7th Infantry Division Medical Battalion headquarters and headquarters detachment established the battalion command post about 200 yards inland, midway between the two beaches. The 1st Platoon, Company D, 7th Infantry Division Medical Battalion, landed some three hours later and was held in reserve near the command post pending the establishment of a clearing station, which was not put into operation until the morning of 4 February.[76]

On Red Beach 1 a switchboard set up by the 75th JASCO and wire laid by 7th Infantry Division Signal Company elements connected the two regimental command posts with each other and with that of the 7th Division on Carlson Island, and also linked the six battalions with the division artillery batteries. Amphibian tractors laid 4,500 yards of submarine cable along the atoll reef between the two islands. Later, the ebb and flow of the sea dragged the cable over the sharp coral and broke it from time to time, but cable laying details continually repaired the damage.[77]

The 2d Battalion, 32d Regiment, was available for support from the moment the

---

[75] 7th Inf Div Med Bn Rpt of Activities During FLINTLOCK Opn, 22 Jan–8 Feb 44, pp. 13, 14.
[76] *Ibid.,* pp. 14, 15.
[77] RCT 184 Rpt, p. 37.

landings began; its four assault waves had embarked in amphibian tractors and its four supporting waves in landing craft shortly after sunrise. They were ordered ashore at 1035. After the first waves had landed, the LVT's returned to pick up the troops of the four supporting waves at the edge of the reef. Early in the afternoon they reorganized near the beach and started eastward in column of companies. The 3d Battalion, 32d, spent most of the day at sea, coming ashore in the afternoon. This battalion, the regimental reserve, was not committed until the next day.[78]

The 2d Battalion, 184th Regiment, the support battalion, landed on Red Beach 1 between 1330 and 1630, formed a column of companies to mop up the area behind the 3d Battalion, and later established a defensive perimeter for the night. The 1st Battalion, in reserve, landed between 1800 and 1930 and crowded into the limited bivouac area near the lagoon.[79]

Throughout 1 February the Southern Landing Force thus built up its assault and support elements on the western end of Kwajalein Island as rapidly as reef and beaches could be crossed. Their task was relatively easy because of the light opposition encountered on the beaches. The confusion that had marked the landing of assault and support units at Tarawa was nowhere apparent at Kwajalein. Naval, artillery, and aerial bombardment had done their work well. The troops had been carried ashore on schedule and in sufficient number to sustain the assault. The ship-to-shore movement was an eminent success.

---

[78] RCT 32 Jnl, 1 Feb 44, Msgs 29a, 35, 101.
[79] RCT 184 Rpt.

CHAPTER XV

Reduction of the Main Defenses of Kwajalein Island

The Push Inland: First Day

There was one main highway on Kwajalein Island, which completely circled it, paralleling the shore line for most of its length and inland from the beach about a hundred yards. (*See Map V.*) The northern (lagoon) section of the highway was known as Will Road; the southern (ocean) section, as Wallace Road. At the western end of the island, the loop ran somewhat farther inland, but there, and at various points along the ocean shore, secondary roads branched from the highway to installations nearer the water. Approximately twenty cross-island roads short-circuited the main loop. In the narrow, northeastern end of the island among the various buildings, these cross-island roads were near enough together to seem like streets of a village. Air photographs showed that the small airfield near the center of the island was still under construction just before the landings. It consisted of a single runway paralleled on the north by a narrower strip used for dispersal. Between the dispersal strip and the runway, wooded areas had been separated by two transverse clearings and further divided by straight narrow roads that ran almost all the way across the island from ocean to lagoon. Less than one eighth of the runway had been paved in concrete.[1]

Construction materials for the Japanese installations on Kwajalein were delivered to the lagoon at wooden docks directly north of the center of the airfield and at a long coral-filled pier nearer the northeastern end of the island. The docks, referred to in the operation maps as Center Pier, were shaped like a wide capital H, and were accessible to boats of shallow draft only. The long pier, designated Nob Pier, almost a mile farther northeast along the lagoon shore, projected westward across the reef for some five hundred yards to reach deep water. It was shaped much like a hocky stick with a wide blade projecting at an angle from its long slender causeway.

Just west of the airfield and lying within the western loop of the island highway was a depressed area of land, largely cleared except for some brush, designated Wart Area on operation maps. It stretched from Will Road on the north to a fringe of trees near Wallace Road on the south, a distance of 450 yards; the distance from the highway loop on the west to a semicircle of trees ringing the eastern edge of this clearing was about 500 yards. In this area the

---

[1] 7th Inf Div FLINTLOCK Rpt, Vol. II, FO 1, Opns Map; JICPOA Bull 48-44, Jul 44, p. 1.

Japanese had set up a radio direction finder with auxiliary radio installations in four buildings. About 1,500 yards farther east, at the eastern end of the runway, another clearing, approximately 300 yards by 600 yards, extended along the ocean shore. It was crossed by Wallace Road, by two cross-island roads (Cox and Carl Roads), and by an antitank ditch.

Commencing near the base of Center Pier and extending along the lagoon side of the island to the northeastern tip, the Japanese had constructed most of their buildings. North of the base of Nob Pier these structures filled most of the area within the loop of the highway.

The Advance From the Beaches

The beachhead line lay about 250 yards inland, along the western loop of the main island highway, which there ran north and south roughly parallel to the two Red Beaches. The shore rose just behind the beaches to an island rim a few yards wide and about ten feet above sea level. East of this higher ground as far as the beachhead line were marshy dips covered with thick underbrush. Vegetation was thickest behind Red Beach 2, in the line of the 32d Regiment advance. The northern zone, which was drier, having been shaded only by tall coconut palms more widely spaced, contained several buildings strung along an additional loop of secondary road that linked the northwest point and the highway. From the shell-pocked reef and torn-up terrain along the beach itself, the advance had to be made through debris and soft ground, both of which presented great difficulty to tanks and other vehicles.

The northern boundary of the 32d Regiment's zone ran a little north of the middle of the island, from Red Beach 2 to a road junction at the western edge of Wart Area. The ocean shore on the regiment's right curved southeast, widening the area from about 275 yards at the beach to about 400 yards at the beachhead line. Within the 32d's zone the enemy defenses, referred to as Wet Strong Point, were expected to consist of pillboxes and antiaircraft gun positions, directly back of Red Beach 2, and a closely associated network of installations along the ocean shore.

As the 1st Battalion, 32d Infantry, advanced after landing on Red Beach 2, it discovered the enemy defenses surprisingly weak. Although several log shelters not indicated on the operations map were met, the group of prepared firing positions at Wet Strong Point was found to be nonexistent. Moreover, very few dead Japanese were counted by the 1st Battalion as it moved toward the beachhead line with Company A on the right, Company B in the inner zone at the left, and part of Company C following in reserve. The battalion reported only light, scattered enemy resistance to its advance.[2] *(See Map VI.)* No large pillboxes remained to be demolished. Only a few of the enemy were discovered in small underground shelters. Japanese riflemen usually preferred to let the line pass, withholding fire until more profitable targets appeared. The advance platoons were at the north-south portion of Wallace Road within an hour after the landing. The rest came up more slowly, but at 1130 the battalion was at the western edge of the Wart Area clearing.

In the northern zone, the 3d Battalion, 184th Infantry, experienced more resistance during this phase of the battle than was met in the southern zone. Except for twenty-two men from Company K who

[2] RCT 32 Jnl, 1 Feb 44, Msgs 23a, 26, 28, 33a, 36, 54a, 68; Marshall, Kwajalein Notes, Vol. I, p. 14.

had been carried by a disabled LVT to Red Beach 2, and twenty-one men transferred from another damaged tractor to one in the fourth wave, the first two waves of the 3d Battalion on Red Beach 1 contained all the troops of Companies K, I, and L, plus the 3d Platoon, Company C, 13th Engineer Battalion.[3]

Ahead of them lay a network of several pillboxes, which still contained live Japanese in spite of the heavy preliminary bombardment. These were silenced in short order in a series of almost simultaneous actions in which many varieties of weapons were used. Typical of the action at this juncture was the experience of two infantrymen of Company K, Pvt. Parvee Rasberry and Pfc. Paul Roper. The two men had landed near the left of Red Beach 1 and had run about twenty-five yards inland when they came under fire from one of the pillboxes in the area. Quickly taking shelter in a shell hole, they started lobbing grenades at the enemy position about fifteen yards ahead. The Japanese merely threw the grenades back and the volley kept up until a flame thrower was brought forward. That, too, proved ineffective; the flames only hit the box and bounced back. Finally, Private Rasberry got out of his foxhole, crawled to within about five yards of the pillbox and threw in a white phosphorus smoke grenade. This flushed several Japanese from their cover into open positions where they could be taken under rifle fire. Those who weren't hit ran back to the pillbox. Rasberry threw white phosphorous grenades until he had none left, by which time about eight of the enemy had been killed. At this juncture, T. Sgt. Graydon Kickul of Company L was able to crawl up to the pillbox and on top of it. He emptied his M1 rifle into it, killing the remainder of the Japanese inside.

To make doubly certain that the job was done, an amphibian tank was then brought forward to fire both its flame thrower and its 37-mm. gun into the aperture.

In much the same manner, all of the pillboxes were taken out or sufficiently neutralized to permit bypassing. When the work was completed, the assault Companies L and I passed through the first landing wave and continued on up the island. Company K now went into battalion reserve and, to the rear of the assault wave, continued to mop up positions that were bypassed as the attack progressed.[4] Company I on the right and Company L on the left moved rapidly forward under protection of artillery from Carlson Island. The 184th Infantry was receiving direct support from the 57th Field Artillery, which at 0947 had already established communications with its forward observers in the 3d Battalion's front lines.[5]

Meanwhile, the 49th Field Artillery was furnishing direct support to the 32d Infantry and at 0949 had its forward observers for Battery A reporting at a point 150 yards inland from Red Beach 2.[6] The remaining three battalions of divisional artillery continued general support by dropping barrages successively farther inland. During the initial phase neither battalion had effective support from tanks, and the LVT(A)'s were left behind near the beaches. In the southern sector the swampy terrain held up the tanks until the infantrymen and engineers were well beyond the beachhead line. In the northern sector the two medium tanks that had not foundered on the reef or at the approach

---

[3] Marshall, Kwajalein Notes, Vol. I, pp. 10–11.

[4] *Ibid.*, Vol. I, pp. 10–13.

[5] 7th Inf Div FLINTLOCK Rpt, Vol. XII, 7th Inf Div Arty Rpt, Jnl, 1 Feb 44, Msg 23.

[6] *Ibid.*, Msg 24.

to the beach joined the 3d Battalion, 184th Infantry, just before it reached the beach-head line.[7]

Enemy dead, estimated at 250, lay scattered among the desolate ruins and tangled wreckage of the coconut grove or in the rubble and debris of shattered buildings behind Red Beach 1. Although for over half an hour hidden Japanese stragglers fired on the beach and harassed the advancing troops, both advance companies of the 184th reported insignificant opposition. By 1135 they had come up to the north-south sector of Wallace Road and had reorganized for the next stage of the advance.[8]

The Second Phase

The next objective of the two assault battalions was the line of Wilma Road, a north-south road that ran east of Wart Area and west of the landing strips, connecting Will Road on the north with the ocean-shore stretch of Wallace Road.

The zone ahead of the 32d Infantry included the southern part of Wart Area at the left and at the right some 550 yards of the shore stretch of Wallace Road, together with a band of wooded ground between that road and the ocean. The shore defenses in this section were grouped in two organized systems, designated Whistler Strong Point and Wheeler Strong Point. Each was thought to consist of machine gun and antiaircraft gun positions fronting the ocean, and a line of rifle pits and connecting trench just inland.[9]

After halting at the beachhead line, Company B furnished covering fire over Wart Area while Company A continued to advance, with Company C behind it, along the wooded ground that stretched from the clearing to the ocean shore.[10] The forward

company was out of communication with the battalion for over half an hour. At 1220 it was reported to be progressing against rifle and machine gun fire only, and to have pushed to a point 250 yards west of Wilma Road.[11] Whistler Strong Point had proved to be unoccupied.

Moving on toward Wheeler Strong Point, Company A encountered its first organized resistance of the day from pillboxes along the ocean shore and suffered ten or eleven casualties. At 1330 steps were taken to shift the burden of the assault from the 32d Regiment's 1st Battalion to its 2d, commanded by Lt. Col. Glen A. Nelson. Company C, which had been following behind Company A, was sent northeastward to clean up the dispersal area east of Wilma Road. Companies A and B were to be relieved by the 2d Battalion. As the latter came abreast of Wheeler Strong Point, it was fired upon from three pillboxes that Company A had failed to mop up completely. These were attacked and wiped out by infantrymen with the assistance of a platoon of medium tanks that had moved ahead to support the 2d Battalion.[12]

Meanwhile, to the north, the 3d Battalion, 184th, was finding the resistance somewhat tougher, as it had earlier in the morning. Before jumping off for the second

[7] 7th Inf Div FLINTLOCK Rpt, Vol. XI, RCT 184 Rpt of Opns, BLT 184-3, Chronological Rpt of Opns (hereafter cited as BLT 184-3 Rpt), p. 1.
[8] RCT 184 Jnl, 011135 Feb 44, 011240 Feb 44. (All messages of the 184th Infantry's Journal are time-dated in this manner and not numbered. The first two digits represent the day of the month, the last four the time of day.) Marshall, Kwajalein Notes, Vol. I, pp. 94–95.
[9] 7th Inf Div FLINTLOCK Rpt, Vol. II, FO 2, 6 Jan 44, Opns Map, Phase II.
[10] Marshall, Kwajalein Notes, Vol. I, p. 14.
[11] RCT 32 Jnl, 1 Feb 44, Msg 57a.
[12] *Ibid.*, Msgs 75, 75a, 92; Marshall, Kwajalein Notes, Vol. I, pp. 15–16.

FLAME THROWER *in use against a Japanese blockhouse.*

phase of the attack, the battalion reorgan- ized. Company K took up the right half of the battalion line along the north-south segment of Wallace Road to furnish cover- ing fire over Wart Area, and Company I shifted to the rear of Company L, support- ing its advance at a distance of about two hundred yards.[13] Jumping off at noon, Company L fought for twenty minutes to reduce a bunker of reinforced concrete that had an extension constructed of logs and sand. Halfway between Will Road and the lagoon shore, it had been spotted as a pillbox but proved instead to be a very large shelter. Flame throwers proved in- effective, and the occupants emerged one at a time only after high-explosive and white phosphorus charges were used.[14]

Rifle fire and thick underbrush along Will Road north of the direction finder site, as well as machine gun and small arms fire, slowed Company L's progress. By 1310, nevertheless, it had come to the po- sitions defending Wilma Road, and at 1450 reported that the road in its zone was secured.[15] Company I pushed southeast- ward through the wreckage of a group of buildings to establish contact along Wilma Road with the left-hand elements of the 32d Regiment. Some difficulty in achiev- ing contact arose from the fact that Com- pany C of the 32d had continued beyond Wilma Road into the dispersal area of the airfield, which was actually within the 184th Regiment zone of action.[16]

---

[13] BLT 184-3 Rpt, p. 2.
[14] RCT 184 Jnl, 011205 Feb 44, 011240 Feb 44.
[15] *Ibid.*, 011450 Feb 44.
[16] Marshall, Kwajalein Notes, Vol. I, pp. 16, 17.

Seizure of the Airfield Begins

The area east of Wilma Road contained the airfield. Two bands of wooded ground, studded with fortified positions and laced with trenches, lay along and back of the lagoon and ocean beaches on either side of the airfield. In the center of the field, between the airstrips, stretched a third wooded area about a hundred yards wide. The rest of the sector had been cleared of trees by the Japanese. Immediately east of Wilma Road was a major dispersal area, shaped much like a fishhook, curving away from the line of advance at the right to a barbed point on the regimental boundary, and broadening at the left into the western terminus of the airstrips. This terminus was a single clearing, 300 yards from north to south and 75 yards from west to east. The two airstrips—one a runway strip and the other a dispersal strip—extended eastward about 1,200 yards to another unbroken cleared area. The northern (dispersal) strip was about 50, and the southern over 100 yards wide. The boundary between the zones of the 184th and 32d Regiments had been set along the southern (runway) strip, about one fourth of the distance from its northern edge. Bombardment had shattered most of the trees not previously cleared by the Japanese from the wide area extending from Will Road on the north to Wallace Road on the south. Except for a jumble of trunks, branches, and fronds in the area between the airstrips and between the southern strip and Wallace Road, the island seemed to have become one broad clearing between coastal fringes of vegetation.

Some of the enemy held out at the western end of the field as the advance battalions continued the attack and the 2d Battalion, 32d Infantry, moved forward to pass through the 1st Battalion.[17] No firm defensive position commanding the entire width of the island had been established, however. The bulk of the defenders had simply retired eastward.

Three coastal defense positions were anticipated on the ocean side along the shore. They were labeled on the operations map Worden, Canary, and Cat Strong Points.[18] Worden Strong Point was believed to contain a covered artillery position for a field piece, a heavy antiaircraft gun, four machine gun emplacements, a network of rifle trenches, and some unidentified buildings. Canary Strong Point was thought to include two groups of positions, each similar to Worden and separated by over a hundred yards of brush-covered ground, in which the presence of pillboxes and connecting trenches was suspected but not definitely established. Worden was 200 yards beyond the Wilma Road line, and Canary about 800 yards farther. Four hundred and fifty yards beyond Canary was Cat Strong Point, extending along some three hundred yards of ocean shore south of the airfield's eastern end. The troops of the 32d Infantry would not reach it until the next day.

The attack eastward began to move into the airfield area as early as 1440.[19] An air attack on the defenses at Canary Strong Point, south of the middle of the airfield, was not thought safe because of the presence of American troops within 500 yards of the target. Artillery fire, however, was heavy; 300 rounds of 105-mm. and 155-mm. artillery fire from Carlson Island was delivered between 1405 and 1425. Company A, 32d Infantry, remained tempo-

---

[17] RCT 32 Jnl, 1 Feb 44, Msg 104.
[18] 7th Inf Div FO 2, Opns Map, Phase II.
[19] RCT 32 Jnl, 1 Feb 44, Msg 92; RCT 184 Jnl, 011442 Feb 44, 011550 Feb 44; 7th Inf Div Arty Rpt, Jnl, 1 Feb 44, Msg 99.

rarily near the south end of Wilma Road, mopping up enemy positions, while Company B pushed forward about 100 yards beyond the road. Company C, after passing through the western dispersal area, continued eastward into the wooded area between the airstrips, well into the zone of the 184th Regiment.[20]

The progress of the 1st Battalion, 32d, from Wilma Road along the ocean side of the island continued to be somewhat more rapid than that of the 3d Battalion, 184th, in its zone. Company B, 32d Infantry, met only scattered resistance during its first two hundred yards of advance, while Companies L and I, 184th, ran at once upon large underground shelters and defenses as well as rifle fire. Moreover, a fuel dump that had been ignited by artillery fire from Carlson Island exploded and temporarily barred the 184th's advance.[21]

Any attempt of the enemy to reinforce his troops already in the wooded strip between the lagoon and Will Road was prevented by a creeping barrage along Will Road and by a concentration from 155-mm. howitzers upon an assembly of Japanese troops observed near the northeastern end of the island.[22] Organized enemy resistance to the 3d Battalion, 184th, was also forestalled by sixty rounds from the 57th Field Artillery Battalion, dropped on a nearer concentration of the enemy forces between the airfield and the lagoon.[23]

At 1525, Company L, 184th Infantry, was reported to be two hundred yards east of Wilma Road, while Company I of the same regiment was at the northwestern corner of the airfield.[24] On the right, Company C, 32d Infantry, had moved into the wooded panel between the airstrips, pursuing a few of the withdrawing enemy. Company B, 32d Infantry, pushed through the ruined concrete-mixing plant and the

other debris at Worden Strong Point, leaving the mopping up of all bunkers to Company A. Company B then moved forward against Canary Strong Point, preceded by an artillery preparation that commenced at 1515. By 1540 friendly troops were so close to the target that artillery fire had to be discontinued.

At 1525 Company B, 32d Infantry, was ordered to hold while Company E of the 2d Battalion passed through and commenced reducing the defensive positions in the western section of Canary Strong Point. Some of these positions, which extended along each side of Wallace Road, were defended by Japanese who ducked and crawled through rubble heaps and bunkers in such a way that Lt. John L. Young, commanding Company E, became convinced that they were using connecting tunnels. For an hour the fighting persisted, but not more than ten enemy dead could be counted above ground.[25]

Company E continued through a litter of small works, moving so slowly that it was necessary to commit Company F, which undertook a flanking movement at the left. The maneuver was intended to cut the strong point off, but the company promptly ran into fire that slowed its advance to about fifty yards in thirty minutes. It then became clear that the whole movement had been stopped. The attack was consequently broken off at 1800 and defensive positions were organized for the night.[26] At 1820 the 32d Regimental Com-

[20] RCT 32 Jnl, Msg 82; Marshall, Kwajalein Notes, Vol. I, p. 16.
[21] 7th Inf Div Arty Rpt, Jnl, 1 Feb 44, Msg 98; Marshall, Kwajalein Notes, Vol. I, p. 95.
[22] 7th Inf Div Arty Rpt, Jnl, 1 Feb 44, Msgs 95, 101.
[23] Ibid., Msg 102.
[24] BLT 184-3 Rpt, p. 2.
[25] Marshall, Kwajalein Notes, Vol. I, pp. 16–17.
[26] Ibid., p. 17.

KOREAN LABORERS, *captured on Kwajalein, point out the location of enemy positions on a map.*

bat Team casualties were reported at seven dead and twenty-three wounded.[27]

In the 184th Regiment's zone, the attack stopped at 1700, when Company L arrived at the western edge of a group of ruined storage buildings that extended as far as the H Docks (Center Pier).[28] Defensive perimeters were prepared. The day's casualties in the 184th's 3d Battalion were reported to be ten killed and thirteen wounded.[29]

The enemy losses on Kwajalein at the close of the day's fighting were estimated at five hundred killed and eleven captured. Approximately 450 of the dead Japanese counted were in the zone of the 184th, and this regiment also was responsible for the capture of ten of the eleven prisoners taken.[30]

Of course, a large share of the enemy casualties must be attributed to the heavy bombardment from ships and aircraft and from artillery based on Carlson. Estimates made by assault troops and by others, including doctors following the assault, indicated that the preparatory bombardment caused from 50 to 75 percent of all Japanese casualties on Kwajalein Island. These estimates probably run high, but there can be no doubt that the preliminary fire, especially from ships' guns and shore-based artillery, was exceptionally effective.[31]

[27] RCT 32 Jnl, 1 Feb 44, Msg 134.
[28] BLT 184-3 Rpt, p. 2; Marshall, Kwajalein Notes, Vol. I, p. 96.
[29] RCT 184 Jnl, 011745 Feb 44.
[30] RCT 32 Jnl, 1 Feb 44, Msgs 134, 142a, 147b.
[31] Col Claudius H. M. Roberts *et al.*, Report on

The first day's field artillery operations, however, were not without cost to the American units involved. When Battery C, 145th Field Artillery, fired its first round, one gun had a premature burst of a fuzed projectile, causing two casualties. A few minutes later, a muzzle burst in Battery A occurred, seriously wounding five men. Not long afterward, just after 1000, the principal air observer, Capt. George W. Tysen, USN, and his pilot, Ensign William J. Sayers, USNR, in a spotting plane from *Minneapolis* flew below the safety level into a curtain of artillery shells from Carlson Island. The plane was struck and destroyed in mid-air.[32]

The two forward battalions established defensive perimeters that crossed the terrain on each side of the airfield but then looped westward along its edges and joined in the dispersal area near Wilma Road. In the northern zone Companies L and I, 184th Infantry, shared the most advanced position, with Company L on the left. Company K, except for one platoon sent to support Company L, extended along Will Road and linked the two forward companies with those of the 2d Battalion, 184th, east of Wilma Road.[33] In the southern zone, Company F, 32d Infantry, alone held the forward line from the ocean beach to the southern edge of the landing strip. The remainder of 2d Battalion, 32d, took up positions west and northwest of Company F. Three antitank guns were set up at equal intervals, interspersed with machine guns, in Company F's easterly line. The men were well dug in, two or three men to a foxhole.[34]

Between the southernmost position of Company I, 184th Infantry, and the northernmost position of Company F, 32d Infantry, the width of the landing strip intervened; moreover, Company F's line lay about 250 yards farther east than that of Company I. The wide gap was devoid of cover for either defending or attacking troops, but to guard against the possibility of infiltration, Company C was again sent forward early in the morning of 2 February to guard the area.[35]

The First Night on Kwajalein Island

When darkness fell on Kwajalein Island after the first day of battle, the front lines crossed the island at points more than one fourth of the distance from the landing beaches to the northeastern tip. Six infantry battalions were ashore, supported by four tank companies (forty-four medium and eighteen light tanks were operative), five self-propelled 75-mm. guns, and two platoons of 4.2-inch chemical mortars. The two Red Beaches had been fully organized, cleared of enemy explosives, graded by bulldozers, and linked with the island's road system. Shell holes in the highways had been filled, debris removed, and supply points established. Command posts were established in each battalion area, and regimental command posts were set up about fifty yards inland, near the northern limits of each of the two beaches. The 13th Engineer Battalion had its command post near that of the 184th Infantry, while the 767th Tank Battalion's was a hundred yards east of Red Beach 2.[36]

Kwajalein and Eniwetok Operations, 14 Mar 44 (hereafter cited as Roberts Report), pp. 34ff. The Roberts Mission was sent to the Marshalls to evaluate the effect of both U.S. and enemy weapons and report its findings to General Richardson.

[32] 7th Inf Div Arty Rpt, Jnl, 1 Feb 44, Msgs 21, 31, 32; TF 51 Marshalls Rpt, Incl A, p. 6.
[33] BLT 184-3 Rpt, 1 Feb 44, p. 1.
[34] Marshall, Kwajalein Notes, Vol. I, pp. 17–18.
[35] *Ibid.*, p. 18.
[36] 7th Inf Div FLINTLOCK Rpt, Vol. VII, G-4 Rpt, Annex B, p. 3; 767th Tk Bn Jnl, 1 Feb 44, pp. 4–5.

105-MM. HOWITZER CREW IN ACTION *on Carlson Island.*

In the lagoon, the destroyer *Sigsbee* was stationed to furnish searchlight illumination of a zone crossing the island at the eastern end of the airfield. It was scheduled to light the area during the first half of each hour.[37] Provision was made for harassing fire to be delivered into the areas east and north of the illuminated zone from the divisional artillery on Carlson Island, the regimental Cannon Companies, and the twelve mortars of the 91st Chemical Company.[38]

While the men were being soaked by a chill rain in the perimeter foxholes and in bivouac areas nearer the landing beaches, plans for the next day's operations were reviewed at the regimental command post. Intelligence from prisoners and from enemy documents indicated that about 1,500 Japanese remained alive on Kwajalein Island. Contrary to an earlier estimate that only small arms and light machine guns remained, the enemy was known to be able still to use some artillery, although his heavier 5-inch guns had been destroyed.[39]

Despite a hard day, the divisional artillery batteries on Carlson prepared for the night's action. During the day they had fired 20,949 rounds of 105-mm. and 759 rounds of 155-mm. shells, most of them during the artillery preparation from 0800 to 1200.[40] A strong wind had swept the smoke and dust away from the guns and

[37] TF 51 Marshalls Rpt, Incl A, p. 6.
[38] RCT 184 Rpt, p. 2.
[39] RCT 184 Jnl, 012400 Feb 44.
[40] These figures are calculated from the 7th Inf Div Arty Jnl, 1 Feb 44, Msg 134, which lists rounds expended between shorter intervals than those of the Southern Artillery Report. For 1 February 1944, the latter gives the figures for 155-mm. as 873 and for 105-mm. as 28,120 rounds between 0600 on 1 February and 0600 on 2 February 1944.

cooled the crews as they maintained a rate of fire of from three to four rounds per minute. Cooks, clerks, and drivers participated as ammunition handlers, while the guns were manned by teams of eight, permitting rest periods for three or four men at a time. The crews broke open pallets and passed tons of ammunition. "The men can stand more than the guns," said Lt. Col. George D. Preston, commanding the 145th Field Artillery.[41]

The 49th and 57th Field Artillery Battalions prepared to deliver night barrages east of the battalions that they were supporting. The 2d Battalion, 32d Infantry, had reached an area dangerously near that on which the guns of the 57th Field Artillery had registered in front of the 184th less than an hour earlier, and that artillery battalion had to swing its fire closer to the lagoon and farther from the 184th's night perimeter. The 32d's late advance also delayed, until twilight, the registration of the 49th. The first shells from the 49th Field Artillery's preparatory fire fell among troops of the 32d Infantry. After the 49th's range had been corrected, however, later barrages were repeatedly requested during the night. A total of 4,556 rounds was expended by the unit between 1800 and 0600.[42]

Naval gunfire on 1 February totaled 6,574 rounds of which 1,342 were 14-inch shells from four battleships, 397 rounds were 8-inch projectiles from three cruisers, and 4,835 rounds were 5-inch shells fired from battleships, cruisers, and five destroyers. In addition to the fire preparatory to landing, naval guns were repeatedly employed in close support of the infantry advance as it moved up Kwajalein Island.[43]

As the day's advance had entered the last stage, General Corlett and the rear echelon of his staff moved ashore to the command post on Carlson Island previously held by the advance party under General Ready.[44] General Holland Smith, commanding the V Amphibious Corps, remained aboard the flagship *Rocky Mount* with Admiral Turner.

During the day's operations the enemy had fought primarily from underground shelters and pillboxes. A few large bunkers and interconnected positions had delayed the advance until details "peeled off" to dispose of them while the remainder of the American line continued forward. Certain positions thought to have been wiped out by grenades, flame throwers, and high-explosive charges or projectiles remained quiet for hours, only to have surviving occupants recover and resume the battle by any means remaining to them. Those Japanese who fired rifles from trees or underbrush were relatively few and scattered. The organized resistance that occasionally developed in the open had provided a series of skirmishes for small details working with the tanks but had resulted in no large-scale encounters.

After dark, however, a large number of the enemy emerged from bunkers and air raid shelters and tried to disrupt the invading force by a series of counterattacks upon the forward perimeters. Individual enemy riflemen and machine gun squads sought to infiltrate along the flanks of the American line or between the two regiments. To the men in the foxholes it was a long night full of action and confusion.[45]

At the northern tip of the island, three enemy dual-purpose guns continued in action, dropping shells at various points

[41] Marshall, Kwajalein Notes, Vol. III, p. 26.

[42] 7th Inf Div Arty Rpt, Jnl, 1 Feb 44, Msgs 137, 138, and 2 Feb 44, Msg 43; 49th FA Bn AAR, p. 3.

[43] TF 51 Marshalls Rpt, Incl E, App 1, p. 3.

[44] 7th Inf Div FLINTLOCK Rpt, Vol. III, 7th Inf Div G-1 Rpt, Annex VIII, p. 2; *Ibid.*, Vol. VI, 7th Inf Div G-3 Jnl, 1 Feb 44, Msg 111.

[45] Marshall, Kwajalein Notes, Vol. I, p. 97.

near the Red Beaches. Japanese mortars, which had registered along the northern end of Will Road late in the afternoon, struck repeatedly during the night.[46] The enemy directed an antiaircraft gun, mounted on Nob Pier, against the destroyer *Sigsbee* to suppress the searchlight illumination it was furnishing. When the destroyer succeeded in silencing the gun, another was brought to bear from the same position, and when that was knocked out, enemy artillery on Burton Island tried unsuccessfully to hit *Sigsbee*. Though it seemed to annoy the Japanese, illumination by searchlight did not serve the needs of the infantry as well as did flares and star shells closer to their front lines.[47]

Naval gunfire from the lagoon, and the division and regimental artillery deprived the Japanese of any opportunity to deliver blows with great force. Nevertheless, they were able to mount a series of counterattacks covered in part by their own sporadic artillery and mortar fire. A number of these were broken up by American artillery while still in the preparatory stages, but several had to be repulsed by the infantry in close-range fighting.[48]

In addition to concerted attacks, the Japanese tried persistently to infiltrate in small groups. In the 32d Regiment's zone, flares over the ground in front of Company F revealed the enemy to the Americans, but enough got through to justify a warning order to the 1st Battalion, 32d, to be ready to come to the support of the 2d Battalion. From the panel between the airstrips, intermittent enemy machine gun fire from the flank passed over the forward troops, most of it too high to do any damage.[49] Similar tactics in the 184th's zone brought Japanese riflemen deep within the American lines. One Japanese was killed by a sentry as far west as the message center on Wolf Point, near the northern end of Red Beach 1.[50]

One attack almost attained the proportions of a successful break-through in the American defenses but was not exploited by the enemy, either because of ignorance of his opportunity or because of insufficient strength. This attack was launched against the 3d Battalion, 184th Infantry, and started at about 0130.[51] During a heavy rain squall in the last hour before midnight, the Japanese had moved back into positions that they had vacated in the afternoon. They had located Company L's machine guns in the course of an earlier assault, and proceeded to lay down a dense concentration of light mortar fire on the portion of Company L's line nearest to the lagoon. Three mortar shells fell directly on the heavy machine gun position, wounding several men and killing one. A light machine gun went out of operation nearby, and the remainder of the 1st Platoon, Company L, was forced into a temporary, hasty withdrawal. While some of the enemy infiltrated through this gap and struck the left of the 2d Platoon, the heavy machine gun in the center of that part of Company L's line was swung to the left and fired over the previous location of the 1st Platoon. By this fire on the Japanese flank, a machine gun was silenced and Will Road was closed to the enemy.

While the 1st Platoon withdrew, a call for reinforcements and a resupply of am-

---

[46] RCT 184 Jnl, 011800 Feb 44; Marshall, Kwajalein Notes, Vol. I, p. 18.

[47] TF 51 Marshalls Rpt, Incl E, App 2, p. 8.

[48] BLT 184-3 Rpt, p. 3; 7th Inf Div FLINTLOCK Rpt, Vol. IX, RCT 32 Rpt of Opns, BLT 32-2 Jnl, 012355, 020320 Feb 44.

[49] RCT 32 Jnl, 1 Feb 44, Msg 149c, and 2 Feb 44, Msgs 1, 2.

[50] RCT 184 Rpt, S-1 Rpt, 9 Feb 44, p. 1.

[51] RCT 184 Jnl, 020137 Feb 44; Marshall, Kwajalein Notes, Vol. I, pp. 97–98.

munition had been sent to the regimental command post. Company C, 184th Infantry, was sent forward but the thin lines were restored even before the reinforcements had arrived. The two machine gun sections of Company C were placed at the extremities of the 1st Platoon line with the rifle platoons in supporting positions. From division artillery heavy fire was sent into the area directly in front of Company L, starting at 0158, and the immediate threat of a break-through in this area was forestalled.[52]

During the early hours of morning, enemy offensive action dwindled to occasional harassing fire. Just before dawn, mortar fire hit one of the machine gun crews that had come forward as reinforcement to Company L, 184th Infantry, causing six casualties.[53] About 0600 steps were being taken for the day's attack by the 2d Battalion, 32d Infantry, when another shell fell squarely beneath one of the antitank guns in Company F's line killing two, wounding one, and disabling the gun.[54]

The 3d Battalion, 184th, was to be relieved at the end of this first dismal night on Kwajalein. It had sustained casualties of 14 killed and 54 wounded for the entire period of its fighting on the island.[55] The 2d Battalion of the same regiment was ordered to move through the 3d's forward positions and take up the attack. In the 32d regimental zone, the 2d Battalion was to continue in the line. Fresh troops would relieve that unit later in the morning.

Second Day's Action

The second day's action on Kwajalein Island required more co-operation between the two regimental combat teams than had been necessary on the previous day. General Corlett had ordered the two

assault regiments to launch a co-ordinated attack at 0715. The 32d Regiment on the right, with Company A, 767th Tank Battalion, attached, was to drive rapidly to the northern tip of the island. The 184th Regiment, with Company B, 767th Tank Battalion, attached, was to push hard on the left, breach fortified positions, assist the advance of the 32d Infantry across the tank trap and push rapidly to the end of the island. Division artillery was ordered to support the attack by a fifteen-minute preparation commencing at 0700 and thereafter by successive concentrations. Artillery was to cease fire during a scheduled twenty-minute air strike by naval planes to commence at 0800.[56]

Following the preparatory fire, in which the battleship *Idaho,* the cruiser *Minneapolis,* four destroyers, and five field artillery battalions on Carlson participated, the attack opened. The 2d Battalion, 184th Infantry, passed through the 3d Battalion of the same regiment during the hour after 0715, Company E on the left and Company F on the right. Company G followed about 150 yards behind as a mopping-up force, while the 1st Battalion came on in close support. Each company of the leading battalion was strengthened by one section of heavy machine guns, one 37-mm. antitank gun, five medium tanks, and two light tanks.[57]

On the other side of the island, as the 2d Battalion, 32d Infantry, began to advance,

[52] 7th Inf Div Arty Rpt, Jnl, 2 Feb 44, Msg 6; BLT 184-1 Rpt, p. 4.
[53] BLT 184-1 Rpt, p. 5.
[54] Marshall, Kwajalein Notes, Vol. I, p. 18.
[55] *Ibid.,* Vol. I, p. 98.
[56] 7th Inf Div FLINTLOCK Rpt, Vol. II, FO 3, 1 Feb 44.
[57] 7th Inf Div FLINTLOCK Rpt, Vol. XI, RCT 184 Rpt of Opns, BLT 184-2 Rpt of Opns (hereafter cited as BLT 184-2 Rpt), pp. 3-4; TF 51 Marshalls Rpt, Incl E, App 2, pp. 8-9; Marshall, Kwajalein Notes, Vol. I, pp. 98-99.

37-MM. ANTITANK GUN FIRING *on an enemy strongpoint.*

enemy dual-purpose gun and mortar fire struck the leading elements, killing two men and wounding one. At 0800 fifteen dive bombers commenced their scheduled strike against the area in which the dual-purpose guns had been observed from the air, and the battalion pushed forward with its tanks according to plan. Company G was in front, with Company E in close support and Company F in reserve.[58]

Occupation of the Airfield Is Completed

The first stage of the second day's action would bring the leading battalions to the eastern end of the airfield.[59] Carl Road crossed the island there, approximately 800 yards east of the 32d Regiment's starting line and 1,000 yards east of the 184th's. The zone to be covered by the 2d Battal-

ion, 32d, contained the westerly portion of Canary Strong Point, just short of which the battalion had spent the night, and all of Cat Strong Point, some 500 yards farther along the ocean shore. The dense vegetation between the shore and Wallace Road and the taller coconut palms between the road and the southern edge of the airfield had been badly blasted and burned by the bombardment, but they were less thoroughly flattened than those at the western end of the island. The tank trap given such prominence in the division's field orders cut left diagonally across Carl Road in front of the 32d Infantry, but

---

[58] Marshall, Kwajalein Notes, Vol. I, p. 18.

[59] Terrain description is based on operations map and aerial photographs now in files of OCMH. The description of the defenses is also based on the map and photographs as corrected by JICPOA Bull 48-44.

most of its length was in the area beyond the road.

Because of the northward curve of the island, the area between the airfield and the ocean narrowed quite sharply at the end of the airfield nearest Carl Road, and the regimental boundary down the middle of the island cut diagonally across the airfield's eastern end. Near Carl Road the wider portion of the 32d's zone was thus open ground, consisting of the end of the landing strip and part of the dispersal space just north of it. The 184th Infantry's zone of advance for several hundred yards ranged from the northern edge of the landing strip to the lagoon. The central, wooded panel between airstrips was at the right; next was the dispersal strip, which curved southward at the far end; to its north was the wooded area between the airfield and Will Road; and between the road and the lagoon beach was a curving belt about seventy-five to a hundred yards wide in which, commencing in the area of Center Pier, there was a continuous series of buildings. Although bombardment and air strikes had wrecked the docks and destroyed most of the buildings and a direct hit during the naval bombardment of 30 January had sent an ammunition dump skyward with devastating results in a wide area near the base of the docks, a number of active gun positions had been spotted along the lagoon. Also, in the area near Carl Road, where the thickly wooded strip between the dispersal strip and Will Road greatly widened, some enemy resistance might be expected.

It was thought, as the battalions jumped off toward Carl Road for the first phase of the second day's attack, that the 184th could expect more difficulty than the 32d, unless Cat Strong Point proved to be formidable. Enemy riflemen who had taken positions behind the advanced perimeters of the 3d Battalion, 184th, fired on the 2d Battalion as it passed through the 3d. Return fire carried past them and some of it fell among the 3d Battalion, causing four casualties.[60] By 0816 the entire 2d Battalion had passed the 3d's advanced positions.[61]

At first the advance of the 2d Battalion was cautious as the men felt their way forward, but after they began to familiarize themselves with the terrain ahead they pushed forward rapidly. Scattered enemy points of resistance were encountered, mostly small pillboxes, sometimes with interconnecting trenches but with no shelters. The positions on the lagoon shore had been mostly knocked out by the artillery. The assault waves advanced about two hundred yards before they came into a perimeter of heavy sniper fire from an area that was still studded with trees and underbrush in spite of the preparatory bombardment. Snipers worked from behind rubble heaps and from the ruins of old buildings, but the effect was more harassing than deadly.[62]

By 0900 the advance of the leading companies had passed the H Docks and was continuing. The 1st Battalion was closely following the assault, mopping up rear areas and eliminating snipers. In the assault waves the medium tanks and infantry advanced abreast. Tanks sprayed the treetops with their .30-caliber machine gun fire, coming to a stop when it was necessary to turn their 75-mm. guns against pillboxes. The standard procedure when one of these positions was encountered was for the tank to advance up to the

---

[60] BLT 184-2 Rpt, p. 61; RCT 184 Jnl, 020732 Feb 44.
[61] RCT 184 Jnl, 020816 Feb 44.
[62] Marshall, Kwajalein Notes, Vol. I, p. 99.

pillbox with two or three infantrymen covering it and one tankman on the ground guiding his vehicle. The tank ordinarily then took its position so that its machine gun could cover the entrance to the pillbox while the 75-mm. gun fired at the wall. Frequently while this action was taking place the infantry wave bypassed the structure and continued beating the ground ahead. By 1040 these maneuvers had succeeded so well that Companies E and F were across Carl Road. As of 1030 the advance had cost twenty-five casualties.[63]

On the opposite shore of the island, the 2d Battalion, 32d Infantry, met greater difficulties, although it did reach Carl Road at the same time as the 184th. Shortly after the strafing attack carried out by naval planes from 0800 to 0820, Company G came across an unexpected tank ditch running from the landing strip to Wallace Road. To avoid this obstruction, the accompanying tanks swung wide left to go along the airstrip, thus exposing the infantrymen to fire from a pillbox on the left. Two of the tanks attempted to silence this position, but failed to do so and moved on toward the airstrip. Three more tanks came along and joined the fusilade, which continued for fifteen minutes. Finally, Capt. Albert W. Pence of Company G succeeded in establishing contact with his supporting tanks and in a few minutes the infantrymen had the position under control.[64]

That part of Company G that was moving along the ocean shore had relatively little trouble, but the platoon on the left ran into considerable organized resistance in the form of riflemen working from trees and shallow fire trenches and of automatic fire from strongly revetted pillboxes. The positions backed up those along the ocean front, and while the latter were the more

conspicuous, the former were the more deadly. It took two hours of fighting for Company G to advance two hundred yards through this belt of works with the aid of tanks and engineer demolition crews. By 0926 they had reached the end of Canary Strong Point.

The 2d Battalion then moved on rapidly until it reached the perimeter of fire from Cat Strong Point where its earlier experience was repeated. Once more it became evident that the beach positions were the outer crust and not the core of resistance. They yielded readily and the right platoon advanced well ahead of the left. But inland from the road were well-concealed tiers of defensive works which, in spite of the artillery fire, were still capable of action. Not until 1020 was Cat Strong Point finally cleared on the right, and not until 1040 did the left platoon finally reach Carl Road abreast of the 184th Infantry.[65]

The Area of the Main Tank Trap

Upon crossing Carl Road, the two regiments began the second stage of their attack of 2 February. A section between Carl Road and Nora Road, some three hundred yards farther along the island, was to be traversed. Will Road continued to parallel the lagoon beach. Wallace Road, at a point a hundred yards beyond Carl Road, swung left away from the ocean for a hundred yards to join Nora Road, thus narrowing the distance between Will and Wallace Roads.

A deep tank trap lay immediately before the 32d Infantry. The longer section of this trap ran for two hundred yards straight

[63] BLT 184-2 Rpt, p. 4.
[64] Marshall, Kwajalein Notes, Vol. I, p. 19.
[65] RCT 32 Jnl, 2 Feb 44, Msgs 30, 31, 32, 33; Marshall, Kwajalein Notes, Vol. I, p. 19.

east from Carl Road to the bend in Wallace Road; and, from the other side of the highway at that point, a shorter section extended for ninety yards south to the ocean beach. Just beyond the angle of the trap, between the long bend in Wallace Road and the ocean shore and short of the Nora Road line, lay one of the most extensive and elaborately organized sets of defensive positions on the island. Designated as Corn Strong Point, it extended inland to a depth of about a hundred yards and was believed to contain three pillboxes and an open artillery position, both near the beach, and up to seven machine gun emplacements inland. These positions were interspersed with storage pits and antitank trenches.

North of the main tank trap a long rifle trench ran in an irregular line across the island diagonally from Corn Strong Point to a point near the junction of Carl Road with Will Road. The 184th Infantry had come upon its northern extremity just before reaching the Carl Road line. The trench, with a connected loop in the middle of the island, extended through most of the ground to be covered by the 184th's right elements. It was clear that the long rifle trench, the tank trap, and the associated gun emplacements of Corn Strong Point were intended to be the main defense system obstructing movement from the western part of Kwajalein Island, containing the airfield, into the northeastern portion, containing most of the installations. Along this line the Japanese were expected to make their most determined stand.

For the initial assault on the tank trap and Corn Strong Point, the 32d Infantry's 3d Battalion was ordered to pass through its 2d Battalion at Carl Road and to lead the attack. These fresh troops were to be supported by the tanks of Companies A

and D, 767th Tank Battalion and, from the left flank, by the tanks of Company B, which would be temporarily detached from the 184th.[66] Preparatory and supporting fire from the artillery on Carlson Island and from the 32d's Cannon Company in Wart Area was to be co-ordinated with the tank and infantry movements. While the new assault units were moving up, the enemy in Corn Strong Point was kept under heavy artillery bombardment and was isolated from possible reinforcement by naval gunfire.[67] Enemy guns that were still active in the northeastern end of the island were struck by dive bombers. The jump-off was ordered for 1245.

A series of delays deferred this crucial attack over an hour. To assemble the staff and co-ordinate the plans for employing tanks, artillery, and infantry while the 3d Battalion made its approach march, proved difficult to arrange. The time for the assault had passed before the planning difficulties were resolved. Then came notice of an air strike to be made at 1315— later postponed, on Admiral Turner's order, to 1330—thus necessitating the suspension of all artillery fire.[68] Since the attack on Corn Strong Point was to be immediately preceded by a heavy artillery barrage, the whole operation was postponed to 1400.

The tanks of Company A, 767th Tank Battalion, lined up along Carl Road to fire against the strong point, while those from Company B took positions almost at right angles to that road and prepared to strike the enemy from the left flank during the first stage of the attack. One of the batteries on Carlson continued to fire during

---

[66] RCT 32 Jnl, 2 Feb 44, Msg 34a; 7th Inf Div FO 2, Opns Map, Phase II.
[67] RCT 32 Jnl, p. 121.
[68] *Ibid.*, Msgs 37, 43.

the air strike, and the Cannon Company's howitzers also laid a preparation on the target area before the advance commenced at 1400.[69] Then, while the artillery lifted fire to ground northeast of the target, the tanks and infantry approached the tank trap in a 225-yard advance across open ground. The tanks poured machine gun fire into the area. Thirty yards behind them the troops came forward to the shelter of the tank ditch without receiving an enemy shot. The Japanese were pinned down.[70]

While the left wing of infantry troops started to push across the wide tank barrier, the tanks on their left momentarily broke off fire from the flank. A few tanks from Company A, 767th Tank Battalion, moved toward the ocean to bypass the deep ditch, and the others after a brief hesitation laid a base of fire to cover the infantry's advance. The tanks hesitated to poke out along the flimsy wooden bridge by which Wallace Road cut through the angle of the tank trap.

At this stage, a concentration of white phosphorus shells commenced to fall into the area in which Company I, 32d Infantry, was moving, and some two score of the men were burned. After hesitating briefly the infantry moved steadily to the tank ditch.

There the troops remained for some time because the medium tanks pulled back claiming they could not get over the ditch. This impasse was finally broken when two light and two medium tanks made their way along the ocean beach around the right end of the ditch and took the pillboxes in Corn Strong Point under fire. The infantry wave then pushed forward and with the aid of engineers proceeded to destroy that strong point in detail. There were no American casualties. An estimated hundred Japanese were killed in the area, the majority by demolition charges carried forward by engineer details while rifle and BAR men covered them. Little or no defense was put up against these tactics. The Japanese remained huddled in their shelters in spite of efforts made to coax them out to surrender. Only one prisoner was taken in the whole area. Grenades were thrown into the shelters, and those who survived were then destroyed by demolition charges. Altogether, it took about thirty-five minutes to reduce Corn Strong Point once the American infantry got beyond the tank trap.[71]

Contact between the forward battalion of the 32d Infantry and that of the 184th was temporarily lost during this fray, and Company K, 32d Infantry, moved through the left platoon of Company I to establish the contact firmly as soon as Corn Strong Point was taken. Advance to the Nora Road line seemed practicable within the time remaining before taking defensive positions for the night. To escape spending the night in an area too heavily wooded for security, the 3d Battalion, 32d Infantry, planned to advance northeast of the junction of Nora Road and Wallace Road, even though that would place its perimeter slightly forward of the 184th's front-line elements, which were resting just short of Nora Road itself.[72]

Meanwhile, the 2d Battalion, 184th, had crossed Carl Road before 1040 but was held up until 1245 in order to advance

---

[69] 7th Inf Div Arty Rpt, Jnl, 2 Feb 44, Msgs 91, 99, 100, 101, 104, 108. According to this journal, all battalions ceased fire between 1327 and 1407; however, at 1350 the 32d Infantry's journal records that the 49th Field Artillery Battalion had continued to fire during the air strike. See also Marshall, Kwajalein Notes, Vol. I, p. 20.
[70] Marshall, Kwajalein Notes, Vol. I, p. 20.
[71] RCT 32 Jnl, 2 Feb 44, p. 128; Marshall, Kwajalein Notes, Vol. I, p. 21.
[72] Marshall, Kwajalein Notes, Vol. I, p. 21.

evenly with the 32d. At that time it moved out with Company F on the right and Company E on the left along the lagoon. For the first forty-five minutes no serious resistance was met. There was no tank obstacle in the area and the enemy's positions along the lagoon shore were less formidable than had been expected. At 1330, however, the 184th had to lend its medium tanks to the 32d Infantry as the latter moved against Corn Strong Point. This left the infantry unprotected at a time when they began to meet their first serious resistance. The tanks returned about an hour later but were so low on ammunition and fuel that they had to be sent back to Wolf Strong Point for resupply. Without this tank support the infantry advance was stalled. Altogether, the 184th suffered over sixty casualties by the end of the day, including the loss of Company F's commanding officer. At 1630 Company G was sent forward to relieve Company F.[73]

When the time arrived to organize night defenses, the forward perimeter of the 184th, instead of being located on Nora Road as planned, was withdrawn to a line only seventy-five to a hundred yards northeast of Carl Road.[74] This necessitated an even greater withdrawal on the part of the 32d Regiment. From a line well beyond Nora Road the 3d Battalion, 32d, fell back to another somewhat short of the road and took positions in the abandoned trenches and shell craters of Corn Strong Point. The line bent westerly from Wallace Road to reach the regimental boundary at a point about a hundred yards beyond the main portion held by the 2d Battalion, 184th Infantry.[75]

Situation at the End of the Second Day

As night closed in the naval planes retired to their carriers, having made seventy sorties over Kwajalein Island dropping 40 tons of bombs and expending 20,800 rounds of .50-caliber ammunition in special missions and general ground support. The close support carriers and battleships, with their screens, cruised a few miles south of Kwajalein Island. No enemy aircraft had been discovered operating in the entire Marshall Islands area.[76]

During 2 February the transports had continued unloading the supply and ammunition for dumps on Carlson, Carlos, and Kwajalein Islands. A forward ammunition dump and maintenance point was set up between Wilma Road and the airfield and maintained by DUKW's until their withdrawal during the late afternoon for service in the next day's assault on Burton Island. By the end of 2 February the unloading of matériel for Carlos and Carlson had reached a point where it could be estimated that it would be completed by noon of the 3d. The shore parties on Kwajalein Island were reinforced during the day by elements of the defense force. Green Beach 4, facing the lagoon at the western corner of the island, was put into use during the afternoon.[77]

American casualties recorded on 2 February included 11 killed in action and 241 wounded, of whom 34 were returned to duty.[78] Evacuation of the wounded on 2 February had been rapid, especially after the arrival of the ambulances during the afternoon. Litter squads took the wounded to the battalion aid stations for treatment, after which they were brought along the

[73] RCT 184 Jnl, 021330 Feb 44, 021831 Feb 44; 767th Tk Bn Jnl, p. 6; Marshall, Kwajalein Notes, Vol. I, p. 100.
[74] BLT 184-2 Rpt, p. 4.
[75] Ibid., p. 4; Marshall, Kwajalein Notes, Vol. I, p. 22.
[76] TF 51 Marshalls Rpt, Incl F, p. 4.
[77] Ibid., p. 109, and Incl A, p. 7.
[78] 7th Inf Div FLINTLOCK Rpt, Vol. VII, G-4 Rpt, Annex C, Medical Rpt, p. 127.

BATTALION AID STATION *near the beach and corpsmen administering blood plasma to a casualty.*

main highways in ambulances to the two collecting stations. At the beach, the shore party medical section evacuated them to the transports in LVT's. Late in the afternoon, the collecting station of Company B, 7th Medical Battalion, which served the 32d Regimental Combat Team, moved along Wallace Road to a position some seven hundred yards east of Red Beach 2. No clearing station had yet been established.[79]

The enemy was believed to be near the end of his strength. His casualties were thought to be from 1,000 to 1,200 dead. One of the few captured prisoners declared the remaining defenses in ruins, communications broken, and only 200 to 300 of the remaining soldiers able to resist.[80] In such circumstances, the stage was set for the characteristic "banzai" attack. General Corlett's headquarters warned, "Be alert for counterattack at anytime day or night, it's bound to come. The Jap makes his suicide counterattack at dawn on the day after his cause becomes hopeless. Watch out tomorrow morning."[81]

The night's operations nevertheless proved to be relatively quiet. Enemy artillery fired some white phosphorus in front of both regiments, dropped a mortar shell near the tanks bivouacked at the western end of the airfield, and after midnight sent over a substantial volume of grenades and small arms, automatic, and mortar fire,

[79] 7th Inf Div Med Bn Rpt of Activity During FLINTLOCK Opn, 2 Feb 44, pp. 10, 11.
[80] 7th Inf Div FLINTLOCK Rpt, Vol. III, G-1 Rpt, Jnl, 2 Feb 44, p. 9; RCT 32 Jnl, 022030 Feb 44.
[81] RCT 32 Jnl, 2 Feb 44, Msgs 71, 72.

such as might be preliminary to a counter-attack. Yelling and the throwing of grenades continued in front of Company G, 184th Infantry, but no major counter-attack developed, and after 0320 the front line quieted down.[82] From the 32d Infantry's side of the island, firing and star shells on the lagoon side could be observed, but no corresponding action, not even active evening patrols, disturbed the waiting men in their own zone.[83]

The night did not pass without some casualties, however. At approximately 2300 an enemy shell burst above the position of the 2d Platoon, 91st Chemical Company, causing a conflagration that wounded seven men.[84] Soon thereafter one of the 155-mm. howitzers in Battery B, 145th Field Artillery Battalion, suffered a premature burst that split the tube, sent one large piece four hundred yards through the air, and set the nearest powder cases ablaze. One man was killed at once, three

later died of wounds, and thirteen others were wounded, of whom five had to be immediately evacuated. Live ammunition was hastily removed to safety, the fire gotten under control, and the position saved.[85]

The situation at the end of the second day's fighting on Kwajalein Island encouraged expectations of a speedy victory on the following day. For the next day's operations, General Corlett ordered the two assault regiments: "Organize vigorous attack 0715 tomorrow. . . . Finish the job not later than 1500 3 February. The Northern Force [at Roi-Namur] has finished the job. . . ."[86]

---

[82] *Ibid.*, pp. 136–39; Marshall, Kwajalein Notes, Vol. I, p. 101.

[83] RCT 32 Jnl, 3 Feb 44, p. 139.

[84] 91st Chemical Co Rpt of Participation in Kwajalein Opns, 18 Feb 44, p. 137.

[85] 145th FA Bn Jnl, 3 Feb 44, pp. 187–88; Marshall, Kwajalein Notes, Vol. III, pp. 27–29.

[86] RCT 32 Jnl, 2 Feb 44, Msg 71.

CHAPTER XVI

Kwajalein Island: The Third Day

From the line of departure of 3 February to the northeastern extremity, Kwajalein Island curved and narrowed for about 2,000 yards.[1] Halfway along the lagoon shore was Nob Pier, while on the ocean side the distance around the outside of the curve from Corn Strong Point to Nathan Road, which extends across the island from Nob Pier, was approximately 1,500 yards. The island was over 600 yards wide where the day's advance was to start but narrowed to almost 300 yards at Nathan Road. *(Map 11)*

Nathan Road was the day's first objective. At the left, between the lagoon and Will Road, the band of buildings that had begun near Center Pier continued unbroken. Another concentration of buildings lay in the middle of the island some 250 yards north of Nora Road, in a diamond-shaped area of approximately 250 by 350 yards. Here, according to a captured enemy map, were the headquarters, communications center, shops, and other installations of the Admiralty section, as distinguished from those related to the airfield. Except along its southeastern side, the area of these buildings had been cleared, and a loop of secondary road connected it with Will Road. The third aggregation of enemy buildings to be encountered in the area before Nathan Road was

the southern section of the heavily built-up area that stretched to the end of the island. Buildings extended, within a grid of cross-island and north-south streets, from a wooded area some 500 yards south of Nathan Road to the northern highway loop. Halfway between Nora and Nathan Roads, among the southernmost buildings of this northern aggregation, was Noel Road, which also linked the two main island highways.

Photographic reconnaissance of the part of Kwajalein Island yet to be captured on 3 February had been limited by the heavy woods. Coastal installations stood out most clearly, and these appeared to be considerably stronger on the ocean side. South of Nathan Road two concentrations had been detected along the ocean shore. The first, organized around 300 yards of trench, lay parallel to the shore, 600 to 900 yards beyond Corn Strong Point, from which the right elements of the 32d Infantry were to start. In the narrow area between the trench and the ocean, two covered artillery positions and five pillboxes were anticipated. Immediately beyond the trench the second concentration, designated as Nap Strong Point, consisted of nearly 400 yards of organized positions in which three heavy

---

[1] Description based upon 7th Inf Div Opns Map, JICPOA Bull 48-44.

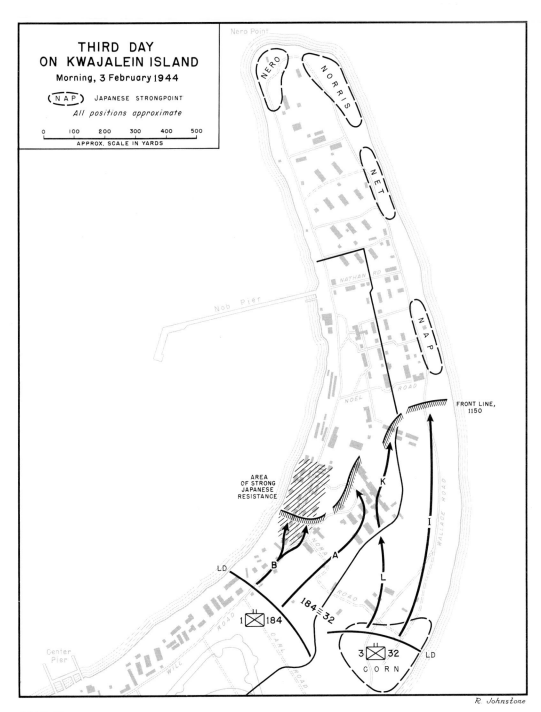

THIRD DAY
ON KWAJALEIN ISLAND
Morning, 3 February 1944

(NAP) JAPANESE STRONGPOINT

All positions approximate

APPROX. SCALE IN YARDS
0   100   200   300   400   500

Nero Point

NERO

NORRIS

NET

NAP

NATHAN RD

Nob Pier

NAP

FRONT LINE,
1150

NOEL   ROAD

AREA
OF STRONG
JAPANESE
RESISTANCE

K

I

WALLACE ROAD

A

NORA   ROAD

B

L

LD

ROAD

1 ☒ 184

184 ≡ 32

3 ☒ 32

CORN

LD

Center
Pier

WILL   ROAD   CARL   ROAD

R. Johnstone

MAP 11

and five light machine gun emplacements had been observed and at least one pillbox was expected.

The Plan for 3 February

The two regiments faced, on what was expected to be the last day of attack, the island's area of densest construction. Estimates of remaining Japanese fortified positions other than those along the shores had been made from information supplied by Japanese prisoners and the captured Marshalls natives but, although the latter had warned of reinforced concrete shelters among the other structures in the northern portion of the island, their actual number and strength was not anticipated.[2]

Progress on Kwajalein Island on 3 February required co-ordinated movement through strong defenses and heavy concentrations of enemy troops. The axis of advance would turn gradually from northeast to north, as the troops advanced along the narrowing curve of the island. Except for a brief loop to the east to bring all of the Admiralty area into the 184th Infantry's zone, the regimental boundary continued along the middle of the island. To make the swing along the island's curve while maintaining alignments of the two regimental fronts demanded greater rapidity of advance in the 32d Infantry zone.

General Corlett's plan for 3 February anticipated rapid occupation of the rest of the island. It called for a "vigorous attack," beginning at 0715.[3] At 0700 a ten-minute artillery preparation would begin in which the eighteen heavy regimental mortars would supplement the division artillery in hitting Kwajalein Island, while the naval gunfire was being directed on Burton Island.[4] During this preparatory fire, the 1st Battalion, 184th Infantry, was to pass through the 2d Battalion and jump off from the line of departure at 0715, Company A on the right, Company B on the left, and Company C in reserve. Each company was to have a detachment of the 13th Engineers, a platoon of heavy machine guns, and one 37-mm. antitank gun. The engineers were to prepare the charges to blow up enemy shelters. Each of the leading companies would be supported by four medium tanks, and in addition two light tanks would operate with Company A on the right.[5]

The 32d Infantry's attack was to be carried by the 3d Battalion, Company I on the right along the ocean shore, Company K on the left between Wallace Road and the regimental boundary, and Company L mopping up behind Company K. One platoon of medium tanks and two light tanks were to support the assault, with a second platoon of mediums in reserve. A destroyer would furnish naval gunfire on call, and air support would continue as on the previous days. The 1st Battalion was to pass through the 2d Battalion and follow in close support, covering any gaps in depth that might develop.[6]

The Attack of the 32d Infantry

The execution of the plan began at 0705, with the ten-minute preparatory fire. The troops jumped off on schedule while the artillery continued to fire ahead of the troops in a creeping barrage. When the 1st Battalion, 184th Infantry, had come abreast of the 32d Infantry, the latter moved forward across a hundred yards of

---

[2] Marshall, Kwajalein Notes, Vol. I, pp. 68, 101.
[3] RCT 32 Jnl, 2 Feb 44, Msg 71.
[4] RCT 184 Jnl, 021830 Feb 44.
[5] RCT 184 Rpt, pp. 53–54.
[6] RCT 32 Rpt, p. 5.

brush to a woods that had been under bombardment. No fire was received until the troops had pressed though the woods for another two hundred yards. Only ruins of a few structures were found there, but about 150 yards to the northwest was the corner of the Admiralty area, where a large concrete pillbox partly commanded the 32d Infantry's route of advance. Protected by the trees, most of Companies K and I passed beyond this installation, while Company K's support platoon and two of the medium tanks turned left to attack it. Driven into the open by demolition charges and 75-mm. shells, the enemy occupants ran out one by one to seek shelter among nearby buildings. Lt. Col. John M. Finn, executive officer of the 32d Infantry, and Capt. Sanford I. Wolff, observer from the 33d Infantry Division, shot them as they ran. The Japanese buildings on the left flank could not be cleared unless Company K moved into the field of fire of Company A, 184th Infantry, which was just beginning to push along the southwestern edge of the Admiralty area. A local arrangement was therefore made by Colonel Finn and 1st Lt. Norvin E. Smith, commanding Company A. Company L, 32d Infantry, with the support platoon of Company A, 184th Infantry, would mop up the building area by house-to-house action; the remainder of Company A would continue north, and in so doing protect Company K's left flank. Company L would also maintain connection between the two battalions. The arrangement in effect modified the regimental boundary.[7]

Enemy positions in the 32d Infantry's zone were not only scattered but also such as to enable rapid movement without detailed search of all cover. The more thorough mopping up could be done by support elements. General Corlett ordered the 32d

Infantry to "keep smashing ahead."[8] The growing gap between the leading elements of the two regiments was, however, a cause of increasing concern to Colonel Finn. By shortly before noon the right wing had pushed through the first aggregation of defenses along the ocean shore and had reached Noel Road. The 32d Infantry's line bent southwest from that point to a point about two hundred yards north of the Admiralty area. The 184th Infantry's lines extended from the southwestern edge of the Admiralty area southwest to the lagoon shore about a hundred yards from Nora Road.[9] Between the two regiments there was a vertical gap including most of the Admiralty area. To care for this and any other strain on the lengthening gap between the two regiments, the 1st Battalion, 32d Infantry, had been sent forward at 0900. Early in the afternoon Company B relieved Company L, which had been mopping up in the Admiralty area; Company L then moved north to fill in the vertical gap; Company C filled in south of Company L along the gap; and Company A, in reserve, stood ready to shift to the south of Company C should the gap become longer.[10]

Had the enemy defense been co-ordinated, the long spearhead on the eastern side of the island might have been struck effectively from the west, but actually the danger most apparent to the 32d Infantry's command was that of fire from the zone of the 184th. In fact, small arms fire from the 184th's zone did fall from time to time east of the Admiralty area.[11] As the 184th Infantry swung north, the line of fire could increase this risk.

[7] Marshall, Kwajalein Notes, Vol. I, p. 80.
[8] RCT 32 Jnl, 3 Feb 44, Msg 17.
[9] Ibid., 3 Feb 44, pp. 155–56.
[10] Ibid., 3 Feb 44, pp. 144, 157.
[11] Ibid., 3 Feb 44, p. 160.

The Morning Action in the 184th Infantry's Zone

The division plan for 3 February had envisioned heavy opposition in front of the 32d Infantry and very little of consequence facing the 184th. Within thirty minutes of the move northeastward, however, the 1st Battalion, 184th Infantry, had run into the first of the many surprises it was to encounter during the day.

The Early Phase of the Attack

After passing through the 2d Battalion, 184th Infantry, and continuing into the area temporarily penetrated on the previous afternoon, the 1st Battalion had reached the line of departure at 0715 in accordance with orders.[12] The advance was started without supporting tanks, which had failed to arrive because of a misunderstanding about their rendezvous with infantry guides.[13] In the first 150 yards Company B, along the lagoon, and Company A, at the right, advanced through rubble and broken trees west of Nora Road without more than scattered rifle fire from Japanese riflemen and occasional light machine gun fire from pillboxes. Their momentum carried them on for another seventy-five yards with such rapidity that the prospects for swift advance seemed excellent. Company B cleaned out an air raid shelter with grenades and shot down fleeing Japanese wearing arm bands like those of the American troops. Both companies were advancing over ground that had been under American mortar fire just before the jump-off. At 0806 enemy opposition was reported to be weak.[14]

Then Company B looked ahead at a sight for which no warnings had prepared them. As far as could be seen along either

side of Will Road—along the lagoon and in the Admiralty area—amid dust and smoke, lay the dense ruins of frame structures, the shattered walls of concrete buildings, some of them very large, and a confused tangle of trees and rubble. Interspersed among the wrecked buildings were several underground shelters with great earthen mounds above them, and concrete blockhouses, intact and active. At the nearer edge of this formidable barrier was a great, round blockhouse of reinforced concrete; fifty yards beyond the blockhouse, among the buildings, two huge shelters could be seen side by side. Thick, reinforced concrete, steel plates, logs, and a blanket of sand several feet thick had enabled them to withstand artillery fire without significant damage. Smaller bunkers at their right were part of the system of organized defensive positions that the men of Company B had to reduce. As the line approached the blockhouse, enemy fire strengthened.

The Split in Company B

Capt. Charles A. White, the Company B commander, had placed two rifle platoons in line at the start of the morning's attack. The blockhouse was almost entirely in the zone of the 1st Platoon, on the right. Just to the east of the built-up position lay a long, open corridor where a building had once stood. All that remained was the concrete floor.[15]

The company had come up to the block-

[12] RCT 184 Jnl, 030745 Feb 44; RCT 184 Rpt, BLT 184-1 Rpt, p. 7.
[13] BLT 184-1 Rpt, p. 7.
[14] RCT 184 Jnl, 030806 Feb 44; Marshall, Kwajalein Notes, Vol. I, p. 24.
[15] Marshall, Kwajalein Notes, Vol. I, pp. 24ff. Unless otherwise noted, the following account of the action of Company B is taken from this source.

house with no supporting weapons. Before any attack was made, it was decided to wait until the heavier pieces could be brought to bear. 1st Lt. Harold D. Klatt, commander of the 1st Platoon, upon receiving a 37-mm. antitank gun, the first heavy weapon to be brought up, moved it to the entrance of the blockhouse, and the crew fired several rounds into it. Nothing seemed to happen as a result of these shells, so the gun was withdrawn. While the 1st Platoon had been working on the position from the right, the 2d Platoon, under 2d Lt. Frank D. Kaplan, had meanwhile swung more to the left toward the lagoon, partly to pass the blockhouse and partly to follow the curve of the lagoon shore.

After his 1st Platoon had withdrawn its antitank gun, Lieutenant Klatt decided to bypass the position to the right and leave it for the tanks and reserve company to finish when they came up from the rear. To keep from being too badly mauled by the enemy still in the blockhouse, however, the platoon had to take maximum advantage of cover. Lieutenant Klatt ordered his men to move by bounds, swinging just to the right of the open corridor provided by the demolished building's floor. Several things happened now almost simultaneously: In the course of moving forward the 1st Platoon broke up into small groups and thus became a whole series of more or less independent bodies, each engaged in some small mission; the Japanese in the blockhouse, seeing that they were about to be bypassed, evidently decided to make some attempt to get out and back to other positions in the rear; and Lieutenant Klatt discovered that he was actually lost—in the piles of rubble and debris that littered the whole area. Although the men of Lieutenant Kaplan's 2d Platoon were not more than twenty yards away on a straight line, they could not be seen; nor could Lieutenant Klatt's operator reach them on his radio.

The men of the 1st Platoon gave their full attention to their own situation. Their most immediate problem seemed to be the elimination of the Japanese who were trying to escape from the blockhouse. Wherever they could, the men took up firing positions and cut down the enemy, one by one, as they appeared at the entrances. Elsewhere, Japanese in trees, in numerous supporting pillboxes and shelters, and even under and behind the rubble piles, began a counterfire on the little groups. Some of the platoon broke off fire at the blockhouse and began to search through the debris for the sources of the harassment. Others crouched in shell holes or behind the piles of rubble trying to find the enemy from the relatively protected vantage points. Meanwhile, medium tanks had at last moved up the road from the rear and approached the blockhouse. There they stopped and sat idly since neither Lieutenant Klatt nor any of his men could get to them to tell the crews what had to be done.

The truth is that it would probably have made little difference at this point whether the infantrymen could have reached the tanks. The improvised telephone sets that had been installed on the rear of the tanks for the Kwajalein operation were usually shorted out because their boxes were inadequately waterproofed. The only sure way for Klatt to have contacted a tank would have been to rap on its outside with a rifle butt. This would have entailed stopping the tank and opening its hatch while the infantry and tank commanders conferred. In a close-fire fight such as this, the danger to all parties concerned would have been too great to warrant the risk.[16]

---

[16] USAFICPA Participation Rpt Kwajalein and Eniwetok, pp. 176–78; 767th Tk Bn FLINTLOCK Rpt, 28 Feb 44, p. 66.

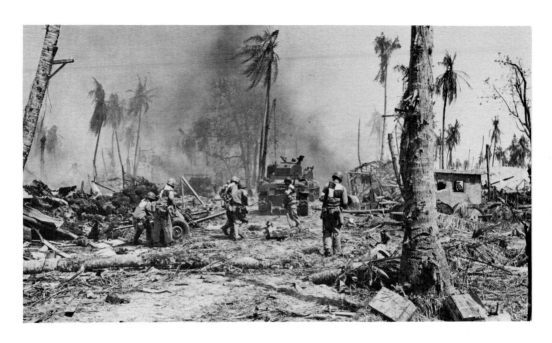

TANK-INFANTRY ATTACK *amid the rubble of the fortifications on Kwajalein. A 37-mm. antitank gun being brought into position (above); infantrymen, supported by M4 tanks, prepare to attack (below).*

While the 1st Platoon had been working around the right of the big blockhouse, the 2d Platoon had moved to the left and then halted to reorganize and wait for the 1st Platoon to re-establish contact. Ahead of his men, Lieutenant Kaplan could see nothing but debris. From the littered ground and from a small wharf that jutted out into the lagoon, rifle fire was being received in fairly heavy volume. To eliminate this, the platoon commander decided to call in artillery fire, but he asked the artillery forward observer to confine it, if possible, to the area between the lagoon and the road. He did not know exactly where the 1st Platoon was, but suspected it might be ahead of him. When the fire was finally brought in, some of it spilled across the road and began bursting within 20 to 25 yards of Lieutenant Klatt's men. Klatt sensed that the bursts were from American artillery, and, as they appeared to be getting closer, he yelled for his men to pull back behind the blockhouse. In one case four men had just left a crater when the exact spot on which they had been lying was hit by a shell. The 1st Platoon reorganized and took up a position approximately on a line with the blockhouse.

The Second Attack

More than an hour had elapsed since the company first entered the area, and battalion headquarters was beginning to notice that there had been no advance in the Company B area. Headquarters called Captain White so frequently for information that the company commander finally left his command post to join Lieutenant Klatt in the debris ahead. Before he left for the front line he committed part of his 3d Platoon along the lagoon shore where, according to an air observer, some Japanese were gathering for a counterattack.

Upon his arrival at the front lines, Captain White reorganized his whole line, bringing up machine guns to cover the gap between his two assault platoons and lining up the tanks for a co-ordinated drive against the numerous shelters that lay ahead. Because of the failure of previous tactics against these positions, the tanks were now to precede the infantry, moving slowly and firing all their weapons at targets of opportunity. The infantry, under cover of this fire, would move directly up to the shelters and throw in satchel charges.

Company B's second attack began at approximately 0945. Two hours and a half had elapsed since the initial effort had begun, and no appreciable gains had been registered since the company had first reached the fortified area.

The new tactics proved unsatisfactory from the first. The fire from the tanks was directed at random and proved to be more dangerous to the infantry than the action of the enemy. When Captain White sought to co-ordinate the work of tanks and infantry, the problem of communications again became a major one. The phones on the rear of the vehicles would not work, and the company commander had to scramble up on the top of the turret and beat a tattoo with the butt of his weapon to get the attention of the men in the lead tank. By the time he had told the commander what he wanted, the whole platoon of tanks had become separated from the infantry, and each tank was proceeding on an independent mission. For the time being, the value of the tanks was lost to the infantry. Moreover, the two assault platoons, pushing through the rubble, had themselves once more become separated and all co-ordination between them was lost.

On the left, between the highway and

the lagoon, all of the 2d Platoon and part of the 3d were driving forward steadily. Each pile of debris was investigated, blown up with satchel charges, and then set afire. Working in small groups, the men on the left moved forward one hundred yards in an hour. Conditions were such that two details working less than ten yards apart did not know of each other's presence. The high piles of splintered wood and smashed concrete, together with the dense smoke that now covered the area, isolated and split up the various actions. Japanese who fired from under the debris, sometimes at almost point-blank range, had to be routed out.

On the right, Lieutenant Klatt's platoon had also separated into small groups to carry the fight to the shelters and piles of debris in its area. Captain White, after his episode with the tanks, tried to re-establish a solid company front and sent his runner to Lieutenant Klatt with orders to close the gap between himself and Lieutenant Kaplan. Klatt replied that this was impossible until the big blockhouse, now to his left rear, had been cleaned out. White, upon receiving this message, ordered his runner to take a detail from company headquarters and see if he could knock out the blockhouse. The runner, together with the company bugler and the mail orderly, moved up with two satchel charges and threw them inside. There was a terrific explosion, but there seemed to have been little damage done to the position. The company's executive officer reported that there were many signs of Japanese still inside, and a platoon of Company C was brought forward to work on the position and keep it under surveillance. Enemy soldiers were still being killed there late in the evening as they tried to wriggle out and escape.

Captain White had followed the action at the blockhouse by again trying to get the two assault platoons of his company in direct contact. He moved up the road and found Lieutenant Kaplan. After failing once more to get satisfactory co-ordination in tank-infantry efforts, the company commander began the task of extending the 2d Platoon's right flank to meet Lieutenant Klatt's left. Between Will Road and the point at which he judged the 1st Platoon's right elements to be, there were three large shelter-type buildings, one close to the road and the other two well back from it. The latter were definitely concrete reinforced shelters, but the former could not be identified.

There appeared to be no enemy in any of these shelters, but to make sure a 37-mm. antitank gun was brought forward and placed on the road to bear on the nearest building. It fired several rounds of high explosive and canister, which completely wrecked the structure and set fire to it. Much to the chagrin of the whole company, the building was later found to contain virtually all the sake, beer, and candy that the Japanese had on the island. Only a few bottles of beer were saved.

Meanwhile, without the company commander's knowledge, a small patrol of the 1st Platoon had reached the farthest inland of the two remaining shelters. Two of the men, Sgt. Melvin L. Higgins and Pvt. Arthur T. Contreras, after taking cover in a shell hole and surveying the two buildings, decided to throw satchel charges in the main entrance and see what would happen. By this time the company had used so many of the charges that it had exhausted the supply in the regimental dump. The company executive officer, however, had brought up several blocks of Composition C, a high explosive, and members of the company were improvising satchel charges by tying the blocks together and putting them into gas mask carriers. Two of these improvised charges were now made up, and each of the two men ran twenty-five yards over to the entrance, threw one in, and ducked back to the cover of the shell hole. The explosion shook the building but caused no appreciable damage. Another charge was placed with the same apparent lack of effect. As he ran back for cover, however, Higgins noticed two Japanese machine guns between the left-hand building and the road. There seemed to be no enemy around these weapons, but almost directly behind them was a little trench, which made Higgins suspicious. Instead of running over to the guns, he went over to one of two medium tanks nearby, talked the crews into opening their hatches, and pointed out the machine guns. The tank lumbered toward the position. As it did so, a white flag began waving a short distance behind the guns. Nevertheless, the tank opened fire and a few moments later Sergeant Higgins crawled forward and found twelve dead enemy soldiers directly behind the guns in a camouflaged ditch, from which they could have fired at anyone curious enough to approach.

The action of the tank had, it appeared, opened the way for a resumption of contact between the two platoons. Without either knowing of the other's actions, Kaplan and Klatt each sent patrols to find the other. The group from the 1st Platoon consisted of only two men, S. Sgt. Roland H. Hartl and Pfc. Solteros E. Valenzuela. That from the 2d Platoon was composed of ten men under the command of Sgt. Warren Kannely. Both groups were concerned with the shelter into which Higgins and Contreras had just thrown charges.

Neither group knew of the other's presence.

Sergeant Hartl's group reached the building first. Hartl came up to the front entrance from the southeast side. The building was, therefore, interposed between himself and Kannely. Hartl and Valenzuela crept up to the entrance, looked in, and saw nothing. Hartl got to his feet, nonchalantly pulled the pin on an offensive grenade, and tossed it in the door. Then the two men sprinted out of sight from everyone around a big pile of rubbish, and Hartl stopped and took a long drink of water from his canteen.

At the moment Sergeant Hartl's grenade exploded, Pfc. Harold S. Pratt was creeping up on the entrance from the opposite direction with another improvised satchel charge. He had not seen Hartl, nor had Hartl seen him. Only a moment after the grenade exploded, Pratt heaved his charge in the entrance, yelled "Fire in the hole" at the top of his voice, and ducked back toward the point where Sergeant Kannely and his patrol were hiding in shell holes, twenty yards away. At that moment several things happened quickly. The charge exploded. Japanese came streaming out of the shelter at two entrances, shooting rifles, brandishing bayonets, and throwing grenades as they rushed pell-mell toward Sergeant Kannely and his men. Sergeant Hartl dropped his canteen, and he and Valenzuela dove for the shell craters in which the 2d Platoon's patrol was hiding. Sergeant Higgins and his group on the opposite side took up fire on the screaming Japanese. For ten minutes the whole area was a melee of struggling men. Grenades were exploding and rifle bullets flying in all directions. One Japanese machine gun opened fire from beyond the shelters and enemy soldiers began taking up the fire from under heaps

A .30-CALIBER MACHINE GUN *emplacement on Kwajalein.*

of wreckage and from trees nearby. The combined action of Kannely's and Higgins' groups soon killed all the Japanese who had come from the shelter, but in the process Kannely and two others of his group had been killed and several seriously wounded, including Valenzuela. The remainder were now under heavy fire from enemy machine guns and riflemen. Pratt crawled back to the road and asked Captain White, who was still standing near the wrecked and burning storage house, to send tanks, machine guns, and litter bearers into the area. He explained what had happened. The company commander immediately sent two tanks off the road toward the shelters. The tanks soon drove the Japanese out of their hiding places and silenced the machine guns, but in the process also fired on Sergeant Higgins'

group, which was still hiding on the opposite side of the shelters. Neither Higgins nor any of his men could see the tanks or the machine guns, but they could hear them; and the volume of fire meant only one thing to them, a Japanese counterattack. T. Sgt. Ernest Tognietti, the platoon sergeant, who had now come forward to join Higgins, ordered a withdrawal to a line of machine guns that Lieutenant Klatt had set up forty yards to the south of the shelters. Behind this defensive position, the platoon leader reorganized his platoon and ordered the men to hold.

In the 2d Platoon area, meanwhile, Lieutenant Kaplan had still been trying to push his men forward on the lagoon side of the road beyond the sake storage house. Because of the debris he had not seen the action involving Sergeant Kannely's patrol and was unaware of the casualties incurred there. When the opposition of the Japanese became stronger along his immediate front, shortly after this incident, the platoon leader came back along the road to see Captain White and find out whether he could have more tank support. The company commander informed him of Kannely's death and of the fact that only two of the ten men sent to the right of the road were left. He advised Kaplan to hold up his attack until the whole company front could be reorganized. It was now 1230. Before Company B could launch a third attack through the area, the whole attack plan for the 184th Infantry was changed.

Action of Company A

At Nora Road, Company A, 184th Infantry, had also found a totally unexpected group of buildings, pillboxes, and shelters through which it moved during sharp fighting.[17] Enemy riflemen behind fallen trees and piles of debris kept up a heavy fire as six or more defended points were brought under control. When two medium tanks and one light tank, with one self-propelled 75-mm. howitzer, reported at 0830, they joined in the attack. The company's progress was more rapid than that of Company B, past whose right wing it continued as far as the Admiralty area. The eight large structures and twelve or more smaller buildings of this area had been thoroughly bombed and shelled, but active blockhouses and shelters were scattered among them. To comb the enemy from the wreckage and clear out the shelters was certain to take a long time and perhaps more than one company's strength. Company A suffered several casualties as it began the task, although

resistance was less determined than that encountered by Company B.[18] Company A pushed about a hundred yards beyond the Admiralty area before it was ordered to advance slowly rather than move too far beyond Company B. At its right, Company K, 32d Infantry, continued to advance and took over a wider front. Company A's right platoon was pulled back behind the left and Company K moved forward somewhat to the west of the established regimental boundary.[19]

The Revised Plan of Attack

Company B, 184th Infantry, was faced with a situation that it could not handle alone. It could not move ahead, leaving mopping up to supporting units. The enemy was too numerous and too firmly established and the terrain continued to be so badly disrupted that co-ordinated action could not be maintained. Shortly before noon, the regiment produced a revised plan of attack. The 2d Battalion, 184th Infantry, was to move through the right wing of the 1st Battalion and then swing left, taking over the entire regimental zone from a line a hundred yards southwest of Noel Road. The 1st Battalion was itself to swing left and shift the direction of its attack to a broad front parallel to the lagoon.[20] This order was modified by a division order at 1225.[21] The 2d Battalion, 184th Infantry, was limited to a northern boundary that curved from Noel Road to the juncture of the lagoon and Nathan Road. The 32d Infantry was to take over all the island north of that point, pinching

[17] BLT 184-1 Rpt, p. 7.

[18] Marshall, Kwajalein Notes, Vol. I, p. 60.

[19] BLT 184-1 Rpt, p. 7.

[20] RCT 184 Jnl, 031150 Feb 44.

[21] 7th Inf Div FLINTLOCK Rpt, Vol. VI, 7th Inf Div G-3 Jnl, 3 Feb 44, Msg 72.

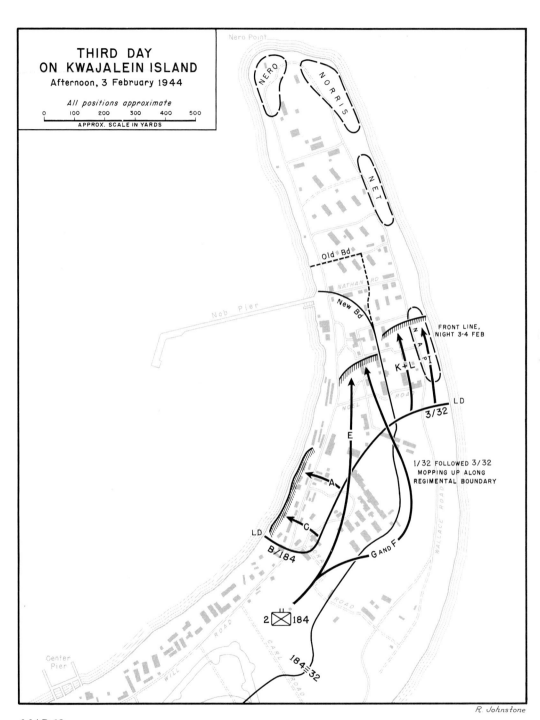

THIRD DAY
ON KWAJALEIN ISLAND
Afternoon, 3 February 1944

All positions approximate

0   100   200   300   400   500
APPROX. SCALE IN YARDS

Nero Point

NERO

NORRIS

NET

Old Bd

NATHAN RD

Nob Pier

New Bd

FRONT LINE,
NIGHT 3-4 FEB

K + L

NOEL

LD
3/32

E

1/32 FOLLOWED 3/32
MOPPING UP ALONG
REGIMENTAL BOUNDARY

A

C

LD

B/184

G AND F

WALLACE ROAD

2 ⊠ 184

184 ═ 32

WILL   ROAD

CARL   ROAD

ROAD

Center
Pier

R. Johnstone

MAP 12

off the 184th's zone there. The 1st Battalion, 184th Infantry, was to attack toward the lagoon but over a less extended front. By 1330, maneuvers to carry out the new plan of attack were in progress. *(Map 12)*

Execution of Attack in the 184th's Zone

At the time when the revised plan of operations was adopted, the enemy was being engaged along an irregular front that extended from the Noel Road line on the ocean side to the northwestern edge of the Admiralty area, and thence westward to the lagoon at a point about a hundred yards north of Nora Road. The 32d Infantry was three hundred yards nearer Nathan Road than the 184th, the right wing of which was in turn well ahead of its left and able to advance more freely. The 2d Battalion, 184th Infantry, which had been mopping up in the rear, moved forward at once, only six hours after being relieved, with Company G at the right, Company F behind G, and Company E at the left.[22] The battalion was to march along the eastern edge of the regimental zone to the area in which Company A was operating, to pass through or around Company A, and to swing northwest toward Nob Pier and the lagoon. It expected to reach the northern edge of Company A's area at approximately 1430. Shortly after the 2d Battalion moved off in the attack, Companies A and C were to turn west and approach the lagoon with the former on the right. Company B was to serve as the hinge, furnishing fire in front of Company C from the south until Company C itself masked B. Then Company B was to swing around to the lagoon beach.[23]

As the 2d Battalion approached the Admiralty area about 1400, a conflagration among its ruined structures made move-

ment through it impossible.[24] Company E kept to the left of it; Company G, followed by Company F, went to the right, losing contact. Company E had expected to reach a line at least partly held by Company A. A guide was killed on the way forward, and the company moved uncertainly through the welter to what was thought to be its line of departure. Company A was not there; it had already been pulled back in order to reorganize for its new attack toward the lagoon. A gap between Company A and Company E thus developed directly northwest of the burning Admiralty area. Company G and Company F passed by Company A over ground well east of the regimental boundary, then turned northwest toward their line of departure. When Company G renewed contact with Company E, after at least half an hour, G had lost touch with the left-hand elements of the 32d Infantry.[25]

Lt. Col. Carl H. Aulich and the forward echelon of the 2d Battalion, 184th Infantry, command post came up to a tentative location northeast of the Admiralty area amid heavy rifle fire, smoke, and confusion. Attempts to co-ordinate the movements of the 2d Battalion with those of Company A, with which it was to maintain contact on its left, proved inordinately difficult.[26]

About 1545 Company A was joined by two medium tanks and Company C by two mediums and two M10 tank destroyers. The attack was mounted by 1605 on the western edge of the built-up Admiralty area along a three-hundred-yard front,

[22] BLT 184-2 Rpt, p. 6.
[23] BLT 184-1 Rpt, p. 8.
[24] Marshall, Kwajalein Notes, Vol. I, p. 60.
[25] *Ibid.*, pp. 62–64.
[26] *Ibid.*, pp. 73–74.

with Company A's right wing somewhat south of Noel Road. Ten minutes later the advance toward the lagoon began. From the line of departure to Will Road, a distance of about seventy-five yards, movement was steady and opposition quickly overcome. Will Road was crossed shortly after 1630. The enemy was much more firmly established between the highway and the beach, in pillboxes, blockhouses, and strong shelters. Mortar fire on this area kept the enemy down until the tanks and infantry approached. The co-ordinated work of tanks, infantry, and demolition teams ran smoothly. At 1800 they were at the lagoon.[27]

Company C began to mask Company B's fire about 1630, releasing the latter to re-form on Company C's left wing, in the vicinity of Will and Nora Roads. Company A received a counterattack from about twenty of the enemy on its right flank, just as its advance was ending, but destroyed the attacking force. There was still no contact with Company E.[28]

Company E had started its attack before those of either Company G or the 1st Battalion. At 1440 it began moving northwest.[29] Somewhat more than half an hour later Company E was reported to have crossed Noel Road, with Company G on its right. Two medium and two light tanks, taken over from the 1st Battalion, moved forward with each of the companies, and each had one squad of engineer troops with demolitions. Enemy rifle fire was heavy. The men broke up into small groups, proceeding unevenly in the general direction of Nob Pier. Between 1830 and 1900, Capt. Peter Blaettler, Company E's commander, was seriously wounded.[30] Control from the battalion command post had been lost—that element was hugging the ground to avoid sharp fire from enemy

riflemen. Colonel Aulich had become separated from the main part of his battalion and was to remain so until the next morning. To all intents and purposes he had lost command of his unit.[31]

The 2d Battalion's attack was pushed along the eastern side of Will Road toward Nathan Road, but as sunset approached it became evident not only that Company E would not reach Nob Pier but also that across Will Road on the left flank there was an area with many strong enemy defense positions too powerful to be occupied in the forty-five minutes before dark.[32]

Action of the 32d Infantry After Change of Plans

The 3d Battalion, 32d Infantry, with the support of Company C of the same regiment, pushed rapidly toward Nathan Road to execute its mission under the revised plan of attack, which became effective at 1330. On the extreme right wing, Company I achieved excellent co-ordination of infantry-engineer teams with medium tanks, and rapidly reduced Nap Strong Point, which proved to be only weakly defended. The company was reported at 1355 to have reached Nathan Road.[33] Company K, in the inner zone, had much more difficulty. Its route lay through a maze of ruined buildings, debris, connecting trenches, and still active pillboxes, as well as shelters crowded with hiding enemy. The terrain and poor communications prevented tank-infantry co-operation, and while the tanks were reduc-

[27] BLT 184-1 Rpt, p. 9.
[28] Marshall, Kwajalein Notes, Vol. I, p. 72.
[29] BLT 184-2 Rpt, p. 7.
[30] *Ibid.*, p. 8.
[31] Marshall, Kwajalein Notes, Vol. I, p. 73.
[32] *Ibid.*, p. 74.
[33] RCT 32 Jnl, 3 Feb 44, p. 163.

ing enemy positions the infantry had to work near rather than with them.[34] Company K was about two hundred yards to the left rear when Company I reportedly reached the road. Company L, in fulfillment of an understanding reached during the morning by the two leading battalions, was withdrawn from the Admiralty area to cover the gap on the left of the 3d Battalion's front when it was found that Company A, 184th Infantry, had pulled back for its new mission under the revised plan.[35] Behind L, Company C, in support, received heavy rifle fire from the left, by which Capt. Charles W. Murphy, Jr., the company commander, was wounded.[36] Company B and then Company A, 32d Infantry, were both committed to mopping up the Admiralty area, from which they moved north toward Noel Road.[37]

As the reports sent back to regimental headquarters were persistently conflicting and confused, it proved impossible to co-ordinate company movements. Perhaps even more important was the battered and shattered condition of the terrain. The terrible pounding to which Kwajalein had been submitted by artillery and naval shells was not an unmixed blessing to the infantry. The difficulty of getting around the rubble and other physical impedimenta tended to diffuse units and keep their flanks dangling. In the middle of the island near Noel Road the conditions of battle and terrain made co-ordination almost out of question since enemy fire was being delivered against the advancing battalions from positions between them and even to their rear.[38]

Company I, 32d Infantry, remained near Nathan Road, unable to advance until the line at the left came up. General Corlett came ashore and at 1640 held a telephone conference with his assistant division commander, General Ready, Colonel O'Sullivan of the 184th Infantry, and Colonel Logie of the 32d Infantry. He was reassured concerning the progress of the attack.[39] Thinking ahead to the remaining enemy blockhouses and other concrete positions that might still be in the northern portion beyond Nathan Road, General Corlett arranged for naval gunfire to be spotted. This fire, from a heavy cruiser, was to be controlled through the naval liaison officer with the 32d Regiment, and it was to be delivered wherever the regiments desired. The regimental commanders later decided, however, that they were not yet in position to use this support. The main effort, they felt, had first to be the straightening of the line across the island.[40]

Between 1630 and 1730 Company K was moved up beside Company I by a maneuver that enabled Company I to furnish protection for its rear while it moved. Company L then advanced along the same route. As it moved, fire hit it from its left flank, possibly originating among friendly troops. The company did not complete its mission. It stopped for the night in the middle of the island between Noel and Nathan roads and its exact position was not accurately reported until next morning.[41]

Situation on the Night of 3 February

All planes had returned to their carriers by 1857. The 3d of February had been a

[34] Marshall, Kwajalein Notes, Vol. I, pp. 82–83.
[35] RCT 32 Jnl, 3 Feb 44, p. 165.
[36] *Ibid.*, p. 164.
[37] *Ibid.*, p. 171.
[38] Marshall, Kwajalein Notes, Vol. I, p. 83.
[39] RCT 32 Jnl, 3 Feb 43, p. 171.
[40] *Ibid.*, p. 174.
[41] Marshall, Kwajalein Notes, Vol. I, pp. 43–44.

quiet day for the planes over Kwajalein Island, where patrol and observation duty rather than air strikes had occupied them.[42] Admiral Reeves' carrier group, part of Task Force 58, departed during the evening for Majuro to refuel. One group of small escort carriers remained to furnish protection for the remainder of the battle for Kwajalein. The lagoon anchorages had filled steadily during the day. Transports carrying the reserve force, which it was clear would not be committed in this action, came into the lagoon from their previous station east of the atoll. All the transports of the attacking force were also at anchor. One group was so nearly unloaded that it could plan to depart for Funafuti early in the morning.[43]

The eight LST's and three LCT's of the Kwajalein Island Defense Group, which arrived about noon on 2 February, had unloaded enough men and material to undertake the general defense of the western end of the island as far as Wilma Road. The group had brought ashore and emplaced its 40-mm. antiaircraft batteries on the western beaches.[44]

During the day, Green Beach 4, the westernmost portion of the lagoon shore, became the principal scene of shore party operations. Pontoon strips brought by LST's were lashed together to form the first of two causeway piers there, and progress was well advanced toward the completion of a good road connection from the beach to the island's highway system. All beach and shore parties were consolidated. One of the transport groups shifted its unloading operations from Carlos Island to Kwajalein Island. The hospital ship *Relief* anchored in the lagoon at noon and began to take aboard the casualties already in the sick bays of the transports and to receive others directly from the beaches.

Those on Kwajalein Island were carried directly from beach to ship in landing craft, thus avoiding the previous days' delays caused by transferring the wounded from LVT's to boats at the edge of the reef. Heavy engineer equipment began to come ashore, although the main stream of such traffic was not to be released until the beachhead was better prepared.[45]

The advance along the axis of Kwajalein Island on 3 February had progressed about 1,000 yards. The hard fighting had been more costly than on either of the preceding days. Fifty-four were reported killed in action, and 255 wounded of which 60 were returned to duty.[46] The enemy, however, had paid heavily in lives as well as in lost ground. The 32d Infantry estimated that 300 had been killed on its side of the island, and the 184th estimated at least 800 and perhaps 1,000 in its zone. In the one huge blockhouse alone, 200 dead had been found, many of them evidently suicides.[47]

Neither of the regiments had reached Nathan Road in spite of optimistic reports to regimental headquarters. The 32d Infantry was on one of the smaller streets among the cantonments, a road that paralleled Nathan Road about 150 yards south. At the extreme right of the eastern zone was Company I and at the left of the zone, Company L. Holding a line that folded back from Company L's left flank as far as Carl Road were Companies B and A. Companies K and M were bent

[42] TF 51 Marshalls Rpt, Incl F, p. 5.
[43] *Ibid.*, Incl A, p. 8.
[44] 7th Inf Div G-3 Periodic Rpt 4, 031700 Feb 44.
[45] 7th Inf Div FLINTLOCK Rpt, Vol. VII, 7th Inf Div G-4 Jnl, 3 Feb 44, Incl 3, p. 4.
[46] *Ibid.*, Annex 3, Incl 1, p. 127.
[47] RCT 184 Jnl, 031930 Feb 44; 7th Inf Div FLINTLOCK Rpt, Vol. III, G-1 Jnl, 3 Feb 44, p. 14, and G-1 Rpt, p. 2; RCT 32 Jnl, 3 Feb 44, p. 181.

PONTON PIERS AT GREEN BEACH 4

back along the ocean shore. Company C, which had been supporting the 3d Battalion during the afternoon, was to be placed across the zone behind the two forward companies despite some remaining uncertainty about its release for that mission by the 1st Battalion, which was expected to lead the assault next day, and even though no one knew exactly where Company L was located. In the last minutes of daylight, largely on the initiative of 1st Lt. Ramon Nelson, a platoon leader temporarily in command of Company C, that company started marching to its widely dispersed position while its other officers were still in conference with battalion and regimental commanders over the orders to move. Its elements were separated during the movement and its exact situation was not well understood at regimental headquarters until next morning.[48] From Carl Road back to Wilma Road, the 2d Battalion, 32d Infantry, covered the regimental zone; and from Wilma Road to the end of the island, on order of General Ready, the division's shore party provided defense of supply installations.

The 184th Infantry was about seventy yards farther south than the 32d Infantry. The two leading companies, E and G, had pushed into an area between Will Road and buildings on the left of Company L, 32d Infantry. West of the highway, as well as in front of the two companies at the north and in the uncleared buildings on the east, the enemy had control. A gap actually existed in the rear of Company E in a portion of the island over which no

[48] RCT 32 Jnl, 3 Feb 44, pp. 183–88; Marshall, Kwajalein Notes, Vol. I, p. 85.

contact with Company A had been established. Thus, the energetic push toward Nathan Road and Nob Pier had moved these companies into a salient. Heavy and light machine guns were set up to cover the areas at the left and front, but from the ruined structures on the right, rifle fire on Company G was heavy and incessant during the night, its accuracy improving with approaching daylight. The 3d Battalion, 184th Infantry, held the sector from Nora Road to the western edge of Center Pier. Defense of the supply installations in the remaining portion of the island as far west as Red Beach 1 was the mission of the shore party and, in part, of the 184th Infantry's Cannon Company.[49]

Eagerness to reach the Nob Pier line on 3 February had induced the leading elements of both regiments to advance with all possible speed, without paying full attention to local security. Night found them in positions in which they were intermingled with the enemy, sometimes at such close range that fighting was restrained for fear of damage to friendly troops. At many points along the front, and at several spots in the rear, flickering fires lighted up adjacent areas and silhouetted moving men.

Typical of the experiences all along the line on this evening were those that befell Company C, 32d Infantry.[50] This unit had begun moving into position across the rear of the 3d Battalion, 32d Infantry, at approximately 1930. It was then nearly dark. There had been little time to investigate the ground the company covered, but in the gathering dusk, three large Japanese shelters and one pyramidal tent were found in the defensive area. The men of Company C felt that Japanese were still hiding under the canvas and were reasonably certain that the shelters contained several enemy soldiers. The men were torn

between two courses of action: clean out the enemy, or simply let them remain where they were until morning. Because the company radio was not working and no information could be passed on to neighboring units that Company C was actually moving in across the rear of the front line, the latter course was chosen. There was some fear that firing in the rear might be misinterpreted by the forward companies. Any pitched battle in the area would be almost certain to draw heavy American fire from the front and flanks.

Company C "bedded down" in the midst of the enemy. The darkness and uncertainty of its position prevented its digging in. Behind the men of Company C were 150 yards of ground filled with debris that had not been investigated or cleaned out. On the right, 150 yards away, Company K had placed its flank on the ocean shore and extended forward and inland in a great arc. On the left, its exact whereabouts unknown to Company C, was the 184th. To the rear, two great fires burned brightly, casting a red light over the whole area. At five-minute intervals flares and star shells from the mortar sections and ships drifted over the front, and sometimes directly over troops in the eastern zone. From 2000 to almost 0300 moonlight also faintly illuminated the area.

Whenever the illumination became unusually bright, enemy machine guns swept Company C's area, and from time to time mortar shells and grenades landed among the men. American BAR's, directed against scattered Japanese, threw bursts of

---

[49] RCT 184 Rpt, p. 96 (see map); *Ibid.*, BLT 184-3 Jnl, 3 Feb 44, p. 3. This journal mistakenly substitutes Carl Road for Nora Road.

[50] Marshall, Kwajalein Notes, Vol. I pp. 85ff. Unless otherwise noted, the account of Company C's action on the night of 3–4 February is drawn from this account.

fire from the company's rear. When fire became too heavy in certain parts of their area, elements of Company C tried to move to more favorable positions. Somewhere during these movements six men of the mortar section of the weapons platoon were killed, although their presence was not missed until next morning.

Japanese were in the areas south of the front line in greater numbers than on either of the preceding nights of the Kwajalein Island operation. They prowled in the forward area all night. Some incidents occurred as far to the rear as Corn Strong Point, more than a thousand yards from the 32d Infantry's advanced position.[51] Japanese came out of shelters, screaming and yelling, throwing grenades, and charging at the men in foxholes. They fired rifles and threw grenades from buildings that offered places of advantage. In a pocket northeast of the Admiralty area, they greatly harassed the companies near them.

Attacks from the north and from the lagoon shore were also attempted by enemy troops at various times during the night. Just after sunset, a bugle could be heard sounding among the enemy shelters near the base of Nob Pier, and shortly afterward a headlong counterattack by screaming Japanese was made toward Company E and Company G, 184th Infantry. As the Japanese tried to cross Will Road, they were cut down to the last man.[52] Five prospective attacks were broken up before they were actually in progress by barrages along the entire front from mortars and from the supporting batteries of artillery on Carlson Island.[53]

Just before 0400, nevertheless, heavy enemy mortar and dual-purpose gunfire, which struck Companies I and L, 32d Infantry, was closely followed by a surprise

attack by an unknown number of enemy. This effort was beaten off and no other was tried for an hour. Then a second organized attack came and was also repulsed by Companies I and L.[54] Sometime after midnight, an effort by a group of the enemy to come ashore from the lagoon reef at a point opposite Company A, 184th Infantry, was foiled by automatic fire. Infiltration by individual Japanese was repeatedly stopped in the Company A area. In the morning twenty-seven enemy dead were found there.[55] About 0530 an attack by from thirty to forty Japanese upon the front line of Company E, 184th Infantry, wilted under the bursts from the machine guns set up there.[56] This attempt was the last of the night's futile sorties by enemy groups. From various positions beyond Nathan Road, enemy machine gun, mortar, and artillery fire was directed into the forward area at irregular intervals during the night, sometimes coinciding so closely with the fire from Carlson Island that Japanese monitoring of the artillery radio was suspected.[57]

The 49th Field Artillery Battalion fired 1,492 rounds of ammunition on Kwajalein Island between 1800 and 0600, and the 47th Field Artillery Battalion fired 716.[58] In position near Carl and Will Roads, the six 81-mm. mortars of the 3d Battalion, 32d Infantry, sent approximately 1,500 rounds into the enemy area after dark, and the 60-mm. mortars with the companies

[51] RCT 32 Jnl, 3 Feb 44, p. 186; Marshall, Kwajalein Notes, Vol. I, p. 115.
[52] RCT 184 Jnl, 032000 Feb 44; Marshall, Kwajalein Notes, Vol. I, pp. 44–45.
[53] 57th FA Bn AAR, p. 137.
[54] RCT 32 Jnl, 4 Feb 44, p. 189.
[55] Marshall, Kwajalein Notes, Vol. I, p. 75.
[56] Ibid., p. 44.
[57] Ibid., pp. 115–16; 7th Inf Div FLINTLOCK Rpt, Vol. XII, 7th Inf Div Arty Rpt, Jnl, 4 Feb 44, Msg 3.
[58] 7th Inf Div Arty Rpt, Jnl, 4 Feb 44, p. 29.

were also active.[59] Harassing fire ceased at 0600 as the artillery was made ready for the morning's preparatory fire at 0700. The 49th Field Artillery Battalion, however, shelled the northern end of the island during that period in the last of several attempts to silence enemy guns.[60]

Thus as dawn broke on the morning of 4 February the men of the 32d and 184th Regiments prepared to make their final drive to the northern tip of Kwajalein Island. The complete capture of the island was taking longer than had been expected. In spite of the excellence of both naval gunfire and land-based artillery, this northern sector of Kwajalein had proved still to contain a sizable number of Japanese well concealed among the damaged buildings and in underground shelters and pillboxes. Infantrymen, engineers, and tanks, working separately and in co-ordination, still had to feel their way cautiously among the remnants of the enemy's defenses. Another hard day's fighting remained ahead.

[59] Marshall, Kwajalein Notes, Vol. I, p. 75.
[60] 7th Inf Div Arty Rpt, Jnl, 4 Feb 44, Msg 21.

CHAPTER XVII

End of the Battle for Southern Kwajalein

Kwajalein Island Secured

Plans for the Attack of 4 February

Occupation of Kwajalein Island had reached an advanced stage by the morning of 4 February. The end of enemy resistance during the day could definitely be anticipated. The advance from the western beach had covered more than three fourths of the island's length and considerably more than three fourths of its area. The stretch that remained was less than 1,000 yards long and 400 yards wide, a section containing the ruins of about thirty buildings amid the scorched and battered remnants of many trees.[1] The ground north of Nathan Road was divided into segments by four east-west roads at intervals of approximately 100 yards and, some 300 yards farther north, by the loop of the island highway. The ocean shore was studded with pillboxes, gun positions, machine gun emplacements, antitank sea wall barricades, and shelters. Most of these works were oriented toward attack from the water rather than along the island from the south, and all had been heavily pounded by naval gunfire, artillery fire, and air bombing. The interior could be presumed to hold concrete shelters and earth-and-log bunkers resembling those that had proved to be such substantial obstacles to the advance of the previous day. *(Map 13)*

Plans for the attack on 4 February had been made during the night of the 3d in partial misconception of the actual location of the front-line troops. At division and regimental headquarters it was supposed that the Nob Pier–Nathan Road line had been reached. The 2d Battalion, 184th Infantry, was understood to have reached the base of the pier, and the 3d Battalion, 32d Infantry, was believed to be on the Nathan Road line, from which the 32d Infantry was to take over the entire assault to the end of the island. These estimates were based on the overoptimistic reports of the front-line units, issued the evening before, and had not been contradicted during the night. Nor was there full recognition of the condition of the areas directly behind the reported front lines. As indicated, the late afternoon drive on 3 February had been pushed forward with little attention to the task of mopping up the enemy troops hiding under rubble piles, in shelters, and in the few buildings still left standing. Reserve units had not been able to complete the task. Until the remnants of the enemy force thus bypassed could be destroyed, confusion would exist,

---

[1] Terrain description drawn from 7th Inf Div Opns Map, JICPOA Bull 48-44.

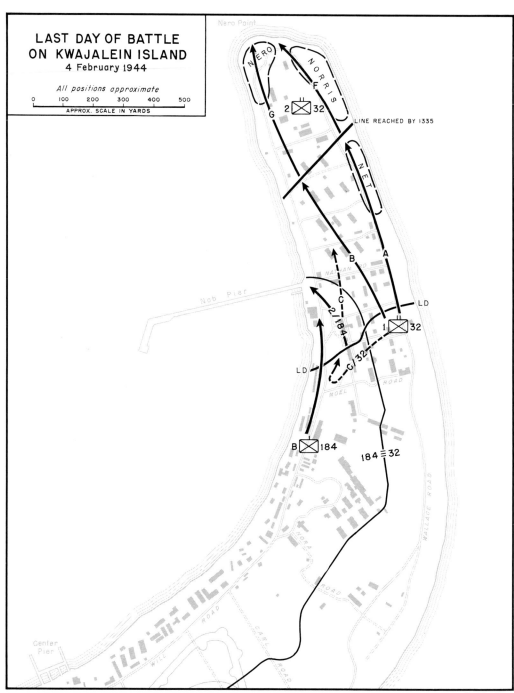

LAST DAY OF BATTLE
ON KWAJALEIN ISLAND
4 February 1944

All positions approximate

0   100   200   300   400   500
APPROX. SCALE IN YARDS

Nero Point

NERO

NORRIS

F

2 ⊠ 32

G

LINE REACHED BY 1335

NET

B

A

Nob Pier

C

LD

2/184

1 ⊠ 32

LD

C/32

NOEL   ROAD

B ⊠ 184

184 ≡ 32

WALLACE ROAD

ROAD

Center
Pier

WILL   ROAD

CARL
ROAD

R. Johnstone

MAP 13

communications would be disrupted, and the attack delayed.

An exact knowledge of the location of various units still could not be had as morning approached. Company and battalion commanders did not know where many of the components of their units were, and radio contact with the rear continued to be poor. In the 184th Infantry zone of action, moreover, one entire section of enemy-held territory—that south of Nob Pier between Will Road and the lagoon—had not even been entered, although regimental and division headquarters assumed that it had been seized. The 2d Battalion, 184th Infantry, which had been charged with the capture of this ground, had failed to enter it by dark on 3 February and planned to complete its mission early the next morning.

Regimental orders for the 32d Infantry attack of 4 February called for the 1st Battalion to attack through the front lines held by the 3d Battalion, 32d Infantry, and by the 2d Battalion, 184th Infantry. It was to jump off at 0715, following fifteen minutes of preparatory fire by artillery and naval guns.[2] In order to execute this attack, however, it was thought necessary to get all companies of the 1st Battalion into position before dawn. Company A was to form the right of the battalion line, Company B the center, and Company C the left. At the moment this plan was decided upon, Companies A and B were in reserve some distance to the left rear of the 3d Battalion line, and Company C was stretched out across the rear of the front in a badly disorganized state. The weapons platoon of the latter company was "missing" after becoming involved in the previous night's counterattack, having actually pulled back to the ocean shore.

To launch the attack as early as possible,

Colonel Logie about midnight ordered 1st Lt. Robert J. Kretzer, the Company C commander, to move his men to the lagoon side of the island before dawn. Company A would relieve Company C in its earlier position at approximately 0230. Lieutenant Kretzer, realizing that such a movement would be extremely dangerous under the conditions then existing behind the front lines, made a personal reconnaissance of the route his company would follow and visited the command posts of the 184th's advance companies, notifying them that Company C would be moving through the area later in the night.

Company A arrived in the area behind the front lines at 0230, as ordered, but because of the confusion the relief was not completed until 0400. By that time the moon had gone down, but fires and flares still cast enough light over the area to silhouette moving men. Lieutenant Kretzer executed his move to the lagoon shore in the simplest manner possible. After organizing his company, he simply faced them to the left and marched them westward in a long column. At one time two of the platoons became separated in the debris, but they found each other again quite accidentally. At another time the column passed close to a Japanese shelter. The men could hear the enemy soldiers talking inside. As the rear marched along the side of the dugout, four enemy soldiers came charging out of it straight for the last few men. A Japanese officer, swinging a saber and yelling, threw a grenade from about thirty feet away. The Americans, who could see the trail of sparks as it sailed toward them, scattered in all directions. Two men were wounded in the explosion, but the four Japanese were all killed in ex-

---

[2] RCT 32 Jnl, 3 Feb 44, pp. 182–83.

change. During the rest of the march two other Company C men were hit in the legs by rifle fire. By 0530 the company was in position somewhere in the rear of the 184th Infantry line.[3]

Morning Attack of 4 February

Sunrise on 4 February came at a few minutes after 0700. It found the forward elements of the attacking force intermingled with the defending enemy in a wide zone between Noel and Nathan Roads. The attack began in considerable confusion. Companies A and B, 32d Infantry, moved forward on the right according to plan. Supporting tanks were with them from the start. Ten medium tanks preceded the main body of the infantry by about fifty yards, and four light tanks moved along the ocean beach. Before either company reached the front-line positions of the 3d Battalion, however, they had become involved in a full-scale battle with the Japanese who had been bypassed the day before and who now poured heavy fire on the companies as they advanced toward the line of departure. By 0730 the 32d Infantry attack had almost stalled as groups of infantrymen turned aside to clean out the positions that poured fire into their ranks. It was not until 1000 that the two 1st Battalion companies reached the lines held by the 3d Battalion. Company L, 32d Infantry, was finally pinched out by Company B at 1030.[4]

Until after 1000 the whereabouts of Company C on the lagoon side of the island was unknown at the 32d Infantry command post because of failure of the company's radio communications.[5] During this period Lieutenant Kretzer found himself confronted by a peculiar situation. The 2d Battalion, 184th Infantry, was still fol-

lowing the orders issued to it the day before and, despite the presence of Company C in its rear, it proceeded to complete mopping up the last 300 yards between it and Nathan Road as well as the area between Will Road and the lagoon. Without further orders from his own battalion, Lieutenant Kretzer could do nothing but wait until the units to the front moved out of his way.[6]

As many Japanese had been bypassed in the 184th's zone as had been overlooked on the ocean side of the island. Company G, 184th Infantry, had serious difficulty even in organizing the attack upon which Lieutenant Kretzer's unit was waiting. Besides withstanding counterattacks, Company G had been under fire in its perimeter throughout the night from enemy riflemen firing from every direction but west. When daylight came, riflemen—especially in buildings along the eastern edge of the perimeter—pinned the unit down and prevented it from forming for an attack at 0715. Low in ammunition, hampered by unevacuated wounded, and facing an extensive air raid shelter in the center of the perimeter in which a large contingent of the enemy was believed to have taken refuge, the company decided to await the arrival of tanks. When the tanks arrived, fire was directed into the shelter, and the first large-scale surrender on Kwajalein took place. Thirty-one Koreans and one Japanese scurried out of the structure with their hands up and much of their clothing removed. One of the tanks herded them to the rear.[7]

Company C, 32d Infantry, began the

---

[3] Marshall, Kwajalein Notes, Vol. I, p. 90.
[4] RCT 32 Jnl, 4 Feb 44, pp. 197–99.
[5] *Ibid.*, p. 197.
[6] Marshall, Kwajalein Notes, Vol. I, p. 91.
[7] *Ibid.*, pp. 76–77; BLT 184-2 Rpt, p. 9.

day by capturing many prisoners while waiting for the battalion ahead of it to move. Aided by tanks of Company B, 767th Tank Battalion, the platoon on the left brought five Koreans up from an underground shelter. Then, covering the Koreans with BAR's, the unit moved from shelter to shelter while the prisoners persuaded others to surrender. In less than an hour thirty-three of the enemy were taken in this fashion.[8]

In the area between the Admiralty ruins and Noel Road the 1st Battalion, 184th Infantry, began mopping up at daybreak. When at 0830 an order was received from the regimental commander to send one company to participate in the assault, Company B was attached to the 2d Battalion, which ordered it to attack along the lagoon shore from the northern limit of the 1st Battalion's night perimeter.[9] The company moved along Will Road in columns of platoons, crossed its line of departure at approximately 0900, and worked through the area in the rear of Companies E and G, at the same time swinging toward the lagoon.[10]

The action of Company B, as had been hoped by Colonel O'Sullivan, commander of the 184th Infantry, cleared out many of the Japanese who had been harassing the 2d Battalion and gave Company C, 32d Infantry, a chance to move through the front lines and proceed with its attack to the north. At approximately 1100 Lieutenant Kretzer pushed his company beyond Nathan Road for the first time, and shortly before 1200 the unit came abreast 1st Battalion, 32d Infantry, the right flank of which had reached Nate Road, two hundred yards north of Nathan, in a badly disorganized condition a short time before.[11] Some of the tanks were approximately three hundred yards ahead, ap-

proaching the northern highway loop, but orders had been issued for the 1st Battalion to halt its advance pending relief by the 2d Battalion, 32d Infantry. The latter unit was to carry the battle for Kwajalein Island through to the end.

Completion of the Mission of the 184th Infantry

At daylight on 4 February the actual disposition of the forward troops became known to 184th Infantry headquarters, and the plan of attack in that regiment's zone was modified. The movement of Company B, 184th Infantry, and the use of Japanese-speaking teams to induce surrender were the earliest of several steps taken to restore motion to the northward attack and to control the enemy within the area south of Nathan Road. To drive to Nob Pier and secure that structure, "the remnants of all three companies" of the 2d Battalion were placed under the command of Capt. Rene E. Maysonave of Company G, with orders to bypass Company B whenever B should be held up.[12] Shortly after 1300 Captain Maysonave's consolidated unit swept by Company B's right wing and took up the attack on the base of Nob Pier. The 2d Battalion cut off any enemy withdrawal across Nathan Road and sent patrols, by tank, on foot, and in a small boat, out to the pier's end. No enemy was found on the pier.[13] By 1435 all resistance had ceased along the lagoon side of the island from Nob Pier back to Green Beach 4.

The surrender of a considerable number

---

[8] Marshall, Kwajalein Notes, Vol. I, p. 91.
[9] BLT 184-1 Opns Rpt, p. 10.
[10] BLT 184-2 Rpt, p. 9.
[11] RCT 32 Jnl, 4 Feb 44, p. 203.
[12] BLT 184-2 Rpt, p. 9.
[13] RCT 184 Jnl, 041350 Feb 44

of Japanese and Koreans continued to be a notable feature of the action of 4 February. Only a remnant of the original garrison was still capable of fighting. Fragments of the enemy force, after several days in isolation and without water, abandoned their shelters. From the first hour of the renewed attack until darkness, the compounds filled with a stream of prisoners.

Maj. Jackson C. Gillis, intelligence officer of the 184th Infantry, accompanied Company B with a loudspeaker and a nisei interpreter. After heavy tank fire on shelters, the loudspeaker went into action. The enemy was promised food and water and immunity from further harm if he came out and surrendered. When the loudspeaker broke down, prisoners were recruited to talk directly to the men in the shelters, in some cases even going down among them. Though two Koreans were tortured by the Japanese in one shelter that they entered on such a mission, before the end of the morning over ninety prisoners were taken by the 184th. The 32d Infantry used the same method beyond Nathan Road.[14]

The Afternoon Attack of the 2d Battalion, 32d Infantry

The 2d Battalion, 32d Infantry, passed through the 1st Battalion at 1345 to complete the assault along Kwajalein Island.[15] All forward movement of the 1st Battalion had stopped, its line consisting of a series of small, exhausted groups in a dense confusion of debris. The ground was interlaced with innumerable trenches and foul with bodies of the enemy, many of them long dead. Some of the corpses had been mangled by maneuvering tanks, adding greatly to the nauseating stench that blighted the area.[16]

Company F, on the right, held its position until Company G brought the left wing in line; then both advanced. After going for seventy-five yards, Company F and its seven supporting tanks came to a large blockhouse into which the tanks directed their fire. While Company F was thus engaged, Company G moved ahead for about a hundred yards, occasionally coming under fire from Company F. Both companies eventually resumed their progress with the left still far advanced; they cleared the surface and underground shelters of living enemy all the way to Nero Point at the end of the island. Camouflaged dugouts and ruined concrete blockhouses and shelters contained Japanese against whom it was necessary to employ scores of satchel charges, hundreds of grenades, and, ultimately, flame throwers.

The 1st Platoon, Company G, on the extreme left, reached Nero Point at 1515 and reported its arrival to the regimental command post. The men then sat around on the beach and discussed the battle, oblivious of further combat behind them.

The 3d Platoon, Company F, nearer the island's center, in the meantime came upon three long concrete shelters, side by side. The first was sixty feet long and about six feet above ground. Its left end had been blown off and a hole had been broken in the top near the right end, but the remainder held some of the enemy. Under command of S. Sgt. Raymond Borucki, the platoon started to pass the structure after hurling two satchel charges in an entrance.

---

[14] RCT 32 Jnl, 4 Feb 44, p. 204; RCT 184 Jnl, 041349 Feb 44.

[15] RCT 32 Jnl, 4 Feb 44, p. 207.

[16] Marshall, Kwajalein Notes, Vol. I, pp. 102ff. Unless otherwise noted, the action of the 32d Infantry on the afternoon of 4 February is drawn from this account.

Finding that living enemy were still inside, they then threw in more heavy demolition charges and many grenades. Pvt. Elmer Collins and Pfc. Franklin S. Farr volunteered to investigate. They crawled to a door, walked in, and found themselves facing several of the enemy. Firing as fast as they could, they hurriedly backed out, dropped to the ground, and threw in grenades while their comrades fired into the doorway. Another squad covered a second entrance most effectively. When Collins and Farr re-entered, the only man they saw alive was the leader of the other squad, S. Sgt. Eugene M. Rider; he had just come in through the other entrance on the same mission. All the enemy were dead. After this operation, which required nearly half an hour, the 3d Platoon, Company F, took the two remaining shelters in a similar manner.

Machine gun bullets began to whine over the heads of the 1st Platoon, Company G, on the beach. The men investigated. Soon they were back in action, mopping up circular 5-inch twin-mount gun positions and other places concealing small numbers of the enemy, and helping to establish a cordon within which to confine the remnants of the enemy at the island's tip.

Company F's methodical movement among the enemy positions in its path subjected it to well-aimed rifle fire, which inflicted numerous casualties and delayed the last stages of the battle. Obstinate Japanese resistance continued as evening approached. About 1900, Captain Pence, commanding Company G, walked over to Company F's area to confer with Capt. Mark E. Barber, and was shot by an observant enemy rifleman before he could heed the warning shouts of men in Company F's forward line. Even with the

battle's end so near, the troops became increasingly cautious.

At dusk tanks were brought up to reduce the last 150 yards of the island. The tanks remained for only a few minutes, but they either drove to cover or killed the enemy riflemen who had been pinning down Company F. The attack again got underway and continued until 1920, when the entire northern end of the island was secured.

Even before that time, General Corlett had announced the island of Kwajalein secured. At 1610 he radioed to Admiral Turner: "All organized resistance . . . has ceased. The troops have been organized for mopping up operations." [17]

The cost of the fourth day's fighting had been somewhat higher than that of the preceding day. The number killed in action on Kwajalein Island and adjacent Burton Island came to 65; 252 men were wounded.[18]

The operation had been a model one in almost every respect. The attacking force had achieved strategic surprise. The Japanese were not expecting a landing in the central Marshalls and were generally unprepared to meet one when it came. To a degree, even tactical surprise was won since it was obvious that the enemy was better prepared to meet an invasion either from the lagoon shore or from the ocean side than from the end of the island where it came. Except for the occasional failure of tank-infantry co-ordination, no important deficiency had been revealed in the execution of the plan. Artillery preparation, naval gunfire, and aerial bombardment had softened up the target in a fashion unexcelled at any other time in the

[17] RCT 32 Jnl, 4 Feb 44, p. 212.
[18] 7th Inf Div FLINTLOCK Rpt, Vol. VII, G-4 Rpt, p. 127, Annex C, Incl 3.

Pacific war. The ship-to-shore movement had been conducted expeditiously and without serious hitch. Supplies flowed ashore and to the front lines smoothly and without interruption. The infantry-engineer teams assisted by tanks moved steadily, if somewhat more slowly than had been anticipated, up the axis of the island clearing the enemy from shelters and pillboxes. American casualties were light. All together, the battle for Kwajalein Island represented the ideal for all military operations—a good plan, ably executed.

Completing the Conquest of Southern Kwajalein

The Southern Attack Force, which had captured Kwajalein Island after establishing supporting units on Carlson, Carlos, and the channel islands, was also charged with the seizure of the many other islets and coral outcroppings of southern Kwajalein Atoll north as far as Bennett Island (Bigej) on the eastern leg of the atoll and Cohen Island (Ennugenliggelap) on the southwestern leg. *(See Map 9.)* Running north from Kwajalein Island on the eastern leg, these included in order, Byron, Buster, Burton (Ebeye), Burnet, Blakenship (Loi), Beverly (South Gugegwe), Berlin (North Gugegwe), Benson, and Bennett.[19] Running north from Chauncey (Gehh) lay Chester, Clarence (Torrulj), Clement (Mann), Clifford (Legan), Clifton (Eller), and Cohen. No specific times for the capture of these outlying islands had been set, since the situation on Kwajalein Island was to be the determining factor in governing the timing of the landings on each.

Chauncey Island

During 1 February the troops that had landed by mistake on Chauncey Island

that morning were removed without completing the occupation. The infantry went to Cecil Island, and the reconnaissance troops were brought back aboard their high-speed transport, *Overton*. Only a small force of eleven sailors was left to guard the barges on the nearby reef, but when the enemy opened fire on these men it was decided to send reinforcements ashore from *Overton* and complete the occupation of the island without further delay.[20]

Between 0800 and 0900 on 2 February elements of the 7th Reconnaissance Troop landed from *Overton* on the northwestern end of Chauncey. Four 60-mm. mortars were set up at once and began a searching fire over the island. For twenty minutes the APD also shelled the ocean side.[21] Three platoons formed abreast and moved along the island through the thick woods, with the headquarters platoon in the center rear. None of the enemy was discovered until the left wing of the line had reached that part of the island opposite the beached tugboat. Then the silence was broken by heavy machine gun and rifle fire, falling mostly on the left center of the American force.[22]

A long mound of earth, about five feet high and sloping at both ends, was discovered to be undefended. Investigation of the end of the mound brought rifle fire from nearby trees, and it soon became apparent that the Japanese were concentrated about twenty yards beyond the mound in a shallow trench behind a rock parapet. Over their heads was a tent, camouflaged with

---

[19] Byron, Buster, Burnet, and Benson had no known native names. See JICPOA Bull 53-43, 1 Dec 43, map facing p. 2; 7th Inf Div FLINTLOCK Rpt, Vol. II, FO 1, 19 Feb 44, map.

[20] 7th Cav Rcn Tr Rpt, p. 6.

[21] *Ibid.*, p. 7.

[22] Marshall, Kwajalein Notes, Vol. II, pp. 22–27. Unless otherwise noted, the account of the capture of Chauncey Island is drawn from this source.

palm fronds and masked by the deep shade of tropical vegetation.

To overcome this position the 1st and 3d Platoons, on the flanks, moved forward far enough to assault the position obliquely, while the 2d Platoon crawled near enough to direct machine gun fire at the parapet and to throw grenades into the position beyond it. For about forty-five minutes a fire fight ensued, and only after a bazooka rocket exploded inside the tent in which the Japanese were concealed were they finally subdued.

A count of the enemy dead revealed that sixty-five had fallen in the action. Out on the tugboat, to which troopers of the 2d Platoon rowed in rubber boats, twelve others were found dead, possibly from shelling by *Overton*. In a small landing barge were thirteen others, and along the beach were thirty-five more probably killed by air attacks earlier in the day. While the American flag was being raised on the beached Japanese tugboat, charts and other documents were found containing intelligence material that was to prove of considerable assistance in completing the capture of Kwajalein. The rest of Chauncey was soon secured without further trouble. The total American loss on the island that day was fourteen wounded.[23]

Burton Island

Among the islands in southern Kwajalein known to have Japanese garrisons, Burton was believed to be second to Kwajalein Island in importance. A plan for its capture was prepared before and during the approach from the Hawaiian Islands, and perfected after arrival at the atoll. The assault forces were to be drawn from the 17th Infantry.[24]

This regiment had completed its mission of taking Carlos and Carlson Islands on 31 January and had been assembled on Carlos to reorganize and re-equip while holding itself in readiness on 1 February to support the attack on Kwajalein Island, if necessary. When such employment was deemed to be unlikely, it was decided to make the landing on Burton Island at 0930 on 3 February.[25]

Terrain and Enemy Defenses

The southern extremity of Burton Island is less than three miles north of Kwajalein Island, and there are two minute outcroppings of the atoll reef between them. Along a straight axis, Burton extends almost directly north for 1,800 yards, its width being an unvarying 250 yards. The southern end curves to the southwest and is shaped somewhat like the bow of a freighter; the northern shore line runs squarely east and west.[26] *(Map 14)*

Before being heavily bombarded, it had had more than 120 machine shops, warehouses, and other buildings. Coconut palms dotted most of the island, but along the ocean shore the major vegetation was sand brush and small mangrove trees. The most conspicuous clearing was a concrete apron for seaplanes, extending 100 yards in width for about 300 yards along the lagoon shore in the northern quarter of the island. Jutting a hundred yards into the lagoon from the apron were two concrete seaplane ramps, and nearby were large hangars and repair shops. From the southern edge of the hangar area to the southwestern point of the island, a narrow, surfaced road paralleled the lagoon beach

---

[23] 7th Cav Rcn Tr Rpt, p. 8.
[24] RCT 17 Rpt, p. 5.
[25] *Ibid.*, S-3 Rpt, p. 3.
[26] 7th Inf Div FLINTLOCK Rpt, Vol. II, 7th Inf Div FO 4, 1 Feb 44, Opns Map.

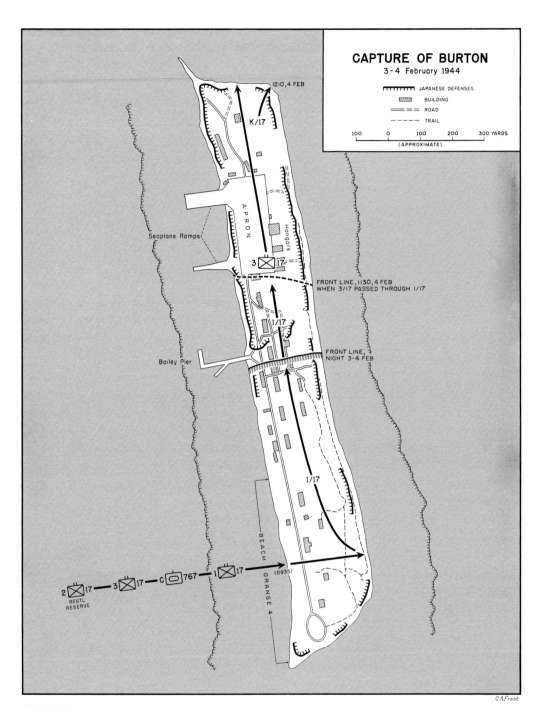

CAPTURE OF BURTON
3-4 February 1944

▭▭▭▭	JAPANESE DEFENSES
▨▨	BUILDING
═══	ROAD
— — —	TRAIL

100   0   100   200   300 YARDS
(APPROXIMATE)

1210, 4 FEB

K/17

APRON

Seaplane Ramps

Hangars

3 ⊠ 17

FRONT LINE, 1130, 4 FEB
WHEN 3/17 PASSED THROUGH 1/17

1/17

Bailey Pier

FRONT LINE,
NIGHT 3-4 FEB

1/17

2 ⊠ 17   3 ⊠ 17   C ▭ 767   1 ⊠ 17
REGTL
RESERVE

BEACH ORANGE 4

(0935)

C.A.Frost

MAP 14

BURTON (EBEYE) ISLAND *from the air. The tip of Kwajalein is visible in upper right.*

for 1,200 yards. From the northern side of the seaplane area, a curving road with several spurs ran to the northwestern point. Trails extended along the ocean shore.

In addition to the seaplane area and the roads, one of the most noticeable of the enemy's improvements at Burton Island was a concrete pier 160 yards long extending into the lagoon from a point almost midway along the coast. Known to the attacking force as Bailey Pier, it was shaped like an L, with the arm jutting north at right angles to the main stem, but with a spur extending obliquely southwest halfway out from shore. At the pier's base were several buildings and two high radio masts.

Preliminary air reconnaissance indicated that Burton was defended by pillboxes and machine gun emplacements near the beaches and surrounding the seaplane area. The enemy had evidently originally expected an attack to come from the ocean side, where the shore could be more closely approached by ships of deep draught. Prepared positions had been organized to meet such an assault. Much attention had recently been given, however, to defense of the lagoon side. On the lagoon beach and near the hangars a number of pillboxes and machine gun emplacements had been spotted. One heavy and eight medium antiaircraft guns had also been observed near the apron.[27]

[27] JICPOA Bull 48-44, pp. 21ff. Also see above, Ch. XIII, p. 23.

JAPANESE ENTRENCHMENTS ON BURTON

The lagoon beach had been designated by the invading force as Orange and marked off into four sections, of which that farthest south was known as Orange 4. On Orange 4, a stretch about five hundred yards in length, the defenses seemed lightest, and here the landing was to be made. After getting ashore and making a left turn, the attacking force would move northward along the axis of the island.[28]

On 2 February, Maj. Maynard E. Weaver, executive officer of the 1st Battalion, 17th Infantry, with engineer officers and representatives of other elements of the regiment, made an offshore reconnaissance of Burton Island from the destroyer *Franks,* which was supplemented by a two-hour seaplane flight by Major Weaver. These investigations confirmed the earlier choice of Orange 4 and revealed defenses that had been concealed by vegetation before the bombardment.[29]

The Landings and First Day's Action

The 17th Infantry was to hit Orange Beach at 0930, 3 February. The last details of the assault plan, including naval participation, were co-ordinated during the night of 2–3 February.[30] The first four waves of the 1st Battalion had already embarked from Carlos Island in two LST's, and the first waves of the 3d Battalion were in two other LST's. The 2d Battalion, in reserve, was in a transport equipped with LCVP's.

---

[28] 7th Inf Div FO 4, 1 Feb 44, Opns Map and p. 1.
[29] RCT 17 Rpt, p. 5.
[30] *Ibid.,* S-3 Rpt, p. 3.

To support the landing, not only the platoon of light tanks from Company D, 767th Tank Battalion, but also the seventeen mediums of Company C that had been landed by error on Kwajalein Island, were assigned to the force. The amphibian tanks of Company A, 708th Amphibian Tank Battalion, were also ready. During the night the regimental field order for the attack was distributed. Harassing artillery fire was thrown at Burton from the 155-mm. howitzers emplaced on Carlson, supplementing the pounding that had been given the island by the guns of *Minneapolis* and *San Francisco* during the afternoon.[31]

The landings on Orange Beach 4 followed the standard pattern. At 0730 the 5-inch and 8-inch guns began firing.[32] Half an hour later the artillery on Carlson Island again opened fire. The 145th Field Artillery Battalion sent 981 rounds of 155-mm., while the 31st and 48th Battalions fired so intense a barrage of 105-mm. that the enemy were driven to cover and the ground over which the attack was to move was devastated.[33] The bombardment was suspended for air strike from 0845 to 0906 in which carrier planes dropped thirty-three tons of general purpose bombs and fired 88,000 rounds of .50-caliber ammunition. Artillery fire was lifted inland at 0933 and farther inland at 0951. The bombardment had been so effective that at the beach itself and for the first two hundred yards no live enemy was encountered.[34]

The 1st Battalion, 17th Infantry, commanded by Colonel Hartl, landed in LVT's with two companies abreast. Despite the mechanical failure of one tractor and a collision between two others, the first three waves made the shore without casualty.[35] An LCI gunboat moved shoreward on each flank of the first wave, blasting the area near the beach with rockets and machine gun fire. The amphibian tanks and tractors directed their machine guns into the few palm trees that still retained enough foliage to conceal snipers. At various points about 150 yards offshore the reef was hit, and then the tractors ground their way through the foamy water to make the beach at 0935.[36] Far off at the left, a machine gun on the end of the pier fired among the boats of the fourth wave and caused the first casualties of the landing. Four men were wounded. An LVT containing artillery observers drew machine gun fire from Buster Island but this was quickly silenced by counterfire from the 31st Field Artillery Battalion.[37] While the men still afloat were meeting the fire, those on shore reorganized and formed a line of attack.

Company A, under Capt. Richard H. Natzke, was on the right and Company C, commanded by 1st Lt. George E. Linebaugh, was on the left, each reinforced by a platoon of heavy machine guns from Company D. Company B, the remainder of Company D, and one platoon from the 50th Engineer Battalion were in reserve. After traversing the southern end of the island, the line started toward the northern end. The amphibian tanks moved at its left flank, pouring fire ahead of the troops. The ground was thoroughly torn up and strewn with debris, but few enemy

---

[31] 145th FA Bn AAR, p. 172; TF 51 Marshalls Rpt, Incl E, p. 4.

[32] TF 51 Marshalls Rpt, Incl E, App 2, p. 10.

[33] 7th Inf Div FLINTLOCK Rpt, Vol. XII, 7th Inf Div Arty Rpt, Jnl, 3 Feb 44, Msgs 13, 87; 31st FA Bn AAR, Jnl, p. 90; 145th FA Bn AAR, p. 173.

[34] 7th Inf Div Arty Rpt, Jnl, 3 Feb 44, Msgs 23, 26; RCT 17 Jnl, 3 Feb 44, Msg 17; TF 51 Marshalls Rpt, Incl F, p. 5.

[35] Marshall, Kwajalein Notes, Vol. II, pp. 31, 42.

[36] RCT 17 Jnl, 3 Feb 44, Msg 14.

[37] 31st FA Bn AAR, p. 68.

JAPANESE BOMBPROOF SHELTER *of reinforced concrete and steel. Note steel door visible in the lower part of the entrance.*

dead were seen. Almost an hour passed after the first wave hit the beach before the first general contact with the enemy was made. When the battalion was stretched across the island on a line even with the northern limit of Orange Beach 4, it received small arms fire at all points. The enemy had come up from shelters after the artillery barrage moved northward and was taking full advantage of the plentiful cover. Bursts of Japanese machine gun fire swept diagonally across the front from positions near the beaches.[38]

Supporting tanks began to cross the landing beaches at 1016.[39] They assembled at the southwestern point of the island and then struggled through the rubble north toward the line of attack. A tank trap across the island was easily passed,

but the island was too narrow to make use of more than four tanks on the line at a time, and co-ordination with the infantry was unsatisfactory.[40]

The attacking force met its strongest opposition on the extreme left, along the lagoon shore, where Company C bore the brunt. At the right, movement was deliberately retarded to keep the line even; Company A could have gone forward much more rapidly than it did. Enemy resistance consisted of individual and small-group activity, without apparent general plan or direction. Japanese troops

[38] Marshall, Kwajalein Notes, Vol. II, pp. 32–33, 43.
[39] 7th Inf Div FLINTLOCK Rpt, Vol. VI, 7th Inf Div G–3 Jnl, 3 Feb 44, Msg 39.
[40] Marshall, Kwajalein Notes, Vol. II, pp. 34–35.

were armed with .25-caliber rifles, 7.7-mm. and 13-mm. machine guns, and one 77-mm. dual-purpose antiaircraft gun that was still in operation after the bombardment. Some of the Japanese, and even the Korean laborers among them, had taken up crudely improvised dynamite throwers and spears made of bayonets attached to poles.[41]

Most machine gun positions were eliminated by directed artillery or mortar fire. Some were destroyed by tanks. In the forward line demolition charges were used by the infantrymen, while combat engineers worked among the supporting elements. The enemy, following a pattern of behavior now familiar to the American troops, remained in shelters until they were blasted out by explosive charges, flame throwers, and sometimes bazookas. Holes were made by repeated point-blank fire from the 75-mm. guns of the tanks and by the self-propelled M8's, of which four came ashore in the afternoon. More often, hand-placed charges were used to create working space for flame throwers. Although this type of work on the larger shelters was frequently left for the engineers by the advancing front-line infantry, the work of the 1st Battalion in eliminating riflemen lurking in rubble heaps and among the trees was very thorough and the advance, while persistent, was slow. The rear was well secured.[42]

Progress on the extreme left wing was slowed not only by the many active pillboxes but also by the large number of individual rifle pits in which the enemy lay concealed under palm fronds, waiting as usual for opportunities to fire or to throw grenades upon our troops from behind. First the 2d Platoon, Company C, and then the 3d carried the advance in this zone. The 3d thoroughly cleared one hole

after another and in one place eliminated a group of the enemy firing from a large excavated pigpen.[43]

Although one tank had made an advanced reconnaissance as far as the base of Bailey Pier, the line was about a hundred yards south of the pier when, shortly before 1700, Company B passed through Company C to take over the front at the left. About 1900 consolidation for the night began. The forward elements of the 1st Battalion were strung across the island on a line just south of Bailey Pier, and the area inland from the landing beaches and to the rear of the 1st Battalion was covered by the 3d Battalion.[44]

Evacuated from Burton Island during 3 February were twenty litter cases and twenty-three ambulatory wounded. The 1st and 3d Platoons, Company A, 7th Medical Battalion, had landed within the first ten minutes, set up a collecting station near the beach, and operated together under company control. They had used five ¼-ton trucks converted to ambulances and had also served as the shore party medical section in evacuating wounded by LVT's to ships.[45]

On Burton during the night of 3–4 February constant illumination and artillery, mortar, machine gun, and naval fire helped to to forestall any counterattack that might have been organized. An enemy 77-mm. dual-purpose gun was silenced by the intermittent counterbattery fire of 81-mm. mortars, which was later

---

[41] Ibid., pp. 36–38; RCT 17 Rpt, p. 7.

[42] Marshall, Kwajalein Notes, Vol. II, pp. 35–36; RCT 17 Rpt, Engineers Rpt, p. 3.

[43] Marshall, Kwajalein Notes, Vol. II, pp. 48–51.

[44] RCT 17 Jnl, 3 Feb 44, Msg 102; 7th Inf Div FLINTLOCK Rpt, Vol. VIII, S-3 Periodic Rpt No. 2, 3 Feb 44.

[45] RCT 17 Rpt, Medical Rpt, FLINTLOCK, p. 52; 7th Inf Div Med Bn AAR, p. 14.

found to have killed several Japanese relief crews. In the half light of dawn the enemy attempted several counterattacks, none of which materialized into any serious threats. The last was broken up at about 0700 with the aid of called artillery concentrations.[46]

Completion of the Conquest of Burton

When on the second morning the attack was resumed at 0730, the main enemy resistance had shifted to the eastern side of the island. The Japanese had reoccupied four pillboxes close to the American front line on the ocean side, and were able to hold up Company A until, with the aid of self-propelled mounts, the company took the positions.[47] During the morning, a flight of five Navy bombers made two runs over targets that had been spotted with the aid of information from a prisoner. The planes dropped a total of two and three-quarters tons on an ammunition dump, a shelter, and a heavy machine gun that had an excellent field of fire across the hangar apron. Direct hits on these targets apparently disheartened the enemy. Not a single shot was fired by them at any later time during the operation.[48] They remained buried in their dugouts until forced out or until they killed themselves.

By 1130, when the 3d Battalion passed through and took up the assault, Company B had moved about 350 yards to the southern edge of the concrete apron, and on the right Company A was fifty to seventy-five yards farther back. On the left Company L advanced behind the tanks across the open area, while on the right Company K pushed swiftly through the heavily bombarded section of hangars, repair shops, small buildings, trenches, and shelters, arriving at the northeastern cor-

ner of the island at 1210. After this the last of the enemy were readily mopped up. By 1337 the island was fully secured.[49]

The official estimate of the enemy dead totaled almost 450. Seven Japanese were captured. The 17th Infantry lost seven killed in action. Eighty-two were wounded.[50]

Final Mop-up

During the two days in which Burton Island was being captured (3 and 4 February), two pairs of smaller islands south and north of it were also brought under American control. Detachments of amphibian tanks were dispatched on 3 February to Buster and Byron, two tiny outcroppings above the main reef between Kwajalein and Burton. The amphibian tanks met no opposition. Troops of the 2d Battalion, 17th Infantry, landed the following day on Burnet and Blakenship north of Burton. On the former, about forty natives cheerfully submitted to capture. On the latter, somewhat more than a score of marooned Japanese sailors and Korean laborers had to be clubbed or bayonetted into submission before the island could be declared secure at 1212.[51]

For the continuation of the mop-up on 5 February, the 2d Battalion, 17th Infantry, less a beach combat team and the

---

[46] RCT 17 Rpt, p. 6, and Jnl, 4 Feb 44, Msg 9; Marshall, Kwajalein Notes, Vol. II, p. 38; 31st FA Bn Jnl, 4 Feb 44.
[47] RCT 17 Rpt, p. 7; Marshall, Kwajalein Notes, Vol. II, pp. 39–40.
[48] TF 51 Marshalls Rpt, Annex F, p. 5; Marshall, Kwajalein Notes, Vol. II, pp. 39–40.
[49] RCT 17 Rpt, p. 7 and Jnl, 4 Feb 44, Msgs 55, 60; 7th Inf Div G-3 Jnl, 4 Feb 44, Msg 57.
[50] RCT 17 Rpt, pp. 7, 20; 7th Med Bn AAR, pp. 14–15.
[51] RCT 17 Rpt, pp. 6, 7, and Jnl, 3 Feb 44, Msg 76, 4 Feb 44, Msgs 14, 39; 708th Amph Tk Bn, Sp Action Rpt, 12 Mar 44, p. 3.

BUILDINGS AND SHELTERS *after heavy air and artillery bombardment.*

Blakenship security detail, was organized into an Eastern Force and a Western Force, each consisting of a reinforced rifle company. The Eastern Force went first to the northern end of the southeastern leg of Kwajalein Atoll and worked south toward Bennett Island. In succession it visited Ashberry, August, Barney, Augustine, and Bascome Islands, meeting no resistance, but finding seven natives on Augustine Island.[52] *(See Map 9.)*

The Western Force moved northward from Carlos Island. Clement, Clarence, and Clifford Islands were quickly secured and without opposition.[53] On Clifton a small Japanese force had to be subdued before the island could be declared secured. Troops of Company E met some desultory machine gun fire as they moved up the island from the landing beach on the southern tip. From a wounded prisoner it was learned that over a hundred sailors had come ashore from ships that had been bombed in the lagoon and had brought with them antiaircraft machine guns and other weapons. This little force could offer no serious resistance to the attackers, although one American soldier was killed and four others were wounded. By nightfall the island was declared secure. The enemy had lost 101 killed, many of them suicides. The next day neighboring Cohen Island was occupied without opposition.[54]

Meanwhile, the remaining islands on the southeastern leg of the atoll were being seized by other units of the 17th Infantry,

[52] RCT 17 Rpt, pp. 9–10.
[53] *Ibid.*; Marshall, Kwajalein Notes, Vol. II, pp. 55–56.
[54] Marshall, Kwajalein Notes, Vol. II, pp. 56–64.

the 7th Cavalry Reconnaissance Troop, and a detachment from the 184th Infantry. At 0930, 5 February, the 3d Battalion, 17th Infantry, made an unopposed landing on the northern end of Beverly Island and completed its occupation in less than an hour, having discovered only three Japanese on the island. Simultaneously, the 1st Battalion, 17th Infantry, landed on Berlin. After moving slowly through the underbrush some distance up the island from the southern end, the attackers encountered some small arms fire from dugouts, costing them altogether three men killed and four wounded. These dugouts were quickly demolished and by 1514 Berlin was secured. One hundred and ninety-eight enemy were killed and one captured. Immediately thereafter, Company C, preceded by a platoon of medium tanks, crossed the reef to Benson Island. The crossing was unopposed and the advance up the island was rapid. One Japanese was killed and two natives taken prisoner at the cost of one American killed and one wounded.[55]

The task of capturing Bennett Island was assigned to the 7th Reconnaissance Troop, which was to repeat the procedure it had followed in capturing Carter and Cecil Islands on D Day. The troops were taken from Carlos through the lagoon to a point near Bennett in the high-speed transports *Manley* and *Overton* and disembarked before dawn. In rubber boats they moved ashore, landing at the northern point of the island at 0600. Hastily, before daybreak, a defensive position was established there. At dawn the force moved out, with the 3d Platoon in front, the 1st Platoon on the left flank, the headquarters platoon supporting the center rear, and the 2d Platoon acting as rear guard.[56]

About a hundred yards from the line of departure, the advance platoon came across a well-protected bunker containing an unknown number of Japanese. Neither grenades, bazookas, nor clusters of grenades were powerful enough to destroy the position, so Captain Gritta, commanding officer, ordered it bypassed. The 1st and 3d Platoons then moved forward to meet an attack of Japanese infantry approaching from the south. After a brief exchange of machine gun and small arms fire, fifteen of the enemy were killed and one machine gun was captured, another knocked out. As the front line continued toward the center of the island, it came across another bunker, which appeared to be much stronger than the first.

Meanwhile, Captain Gritta had called for reinforcements. The 3d Battalion, 184th Infantry, had been standing by in floating reserve to assist in the capture of Berlin or Beverly, if necessary. The battalion was ordered instead to Bennett, where the resistance appeared to be heavier. Accompanied by two medium tanks and under command of Lt. Col. William B. Moore, executive officer of the 17th Infantry, this reserve force began to come ashore on Bennett about 1100. The unit moved up at once, getting into the front lines shortly before noon. Meanwhile, the destroyer *Noel* had moved to a station west of Bennett in order to furnish fire on call.[57]

In the absence of other orders, Colonel Moore and his infantrymen took over the ocean side of the island while Captain Gritta's troop covered that nearest the lagoon. By this time the occupants of the first dugout had committed suicide, and after the tanks subdued the second dugout the

---

[55] RCT 17 Rpt, pp. 7–8.
[56] 7th Cav Rcn Tr AAR, pp. 9–10.
[57] *Ibid.*; 7th Inf Div G-3 Jnl, 5 Feb 44, Msgs 5, 7; TF 51 Marshalls Rpt, Incl E, App 2.

advance southward along the island began. After hardly more than twenty-five yards' progress, machine gun fire from a pier on the right stopped the advance for a few minutes while mortar and tank fire knocked out the machine guns.[58]

The attack was almost halfway to the southern tip before division orders authorized Colonel Moore to take command of the operation. The 7th Cavalry Reconnaissance Troop withdrew to the beach, and the infantry, supported by two light and two medium tanks, completed the attack. Early in the afternoon the troop overcame another set of pillboxes near the center of the island. Through the dense underbrush the process of mopping up was continued until 1642, when the island was reported fully secured. At the cost of one killed and two wounded in the 7th Cavalry Reconnaissance Troop and no casual-

ties among other components, Bennett Island had been captured and some ninety-four Japanese had been killed or had died by their own hands.[59]

The Southern Landing Force thus completed its mission, with losses for the entire operation in southern Kwajalein reported as 142 killed, 845 wounded, and two missing in action. The best estimate of enemy losses was 4,938 dead and 206 prisoners, 79 of whom were Japanese and 127 Korean.[60] Meanwhile, some forty-five miles to the north, operations of the Northern Landing Force against the sixty-two islands of the upper half of Kwajalein Atoll were also nearing completion.

[58] RCT 17 Rpt, p. 9; 7th Inf Div G-3 Jnl, 5 Feb 44, pp. 68, 88.

[59] RCT 17 Rpt, p. 9; 7th Inf Div G-3 Jnl, 5 Feb 44, pp. 149–51.

[60] 7th Inf Div FLINTLOCK Rpt, Vol. III, G-1 Rpt, pp. 18, 19, 70.

CHAPTER XVIII

The Capture of Majuro
and Roi-Namur

Majuro

On the same day that the first landings were being made on Kwajalein Atoll, American forces with far less difficulty were occupying Majuro Atoll about 265 nautical miles to the southeast. Majuro was correctly believed to be only lightly defended, if at all, and the configuration of the atoll plus its location on the eastern rim of the Marshalls made it an ideal location for an advance naval base. Hence the decision to include its capture as a secondary phase of the FLINTLOCK operation.

The atoll contains a large lagoon, about twenty-six miles long and six miles wide, surrounded by a narrow ribbon of islets covered with low-lying vegetation and connected by submarine reefs. *(Map 15)* Some portions of this rim are distinguishable as separate islands. The largest of these, Majuro Island, extends from the southwestern corner of the atoll about fifteen miles east. Between Majuro Island and Dalap Island, twelve miles to the east, there is a string of small islets. On the eastern leg of the atoll north of Dalap lie Uliga and Darrit Islands. The northern side of the atoll is irregular and broken. Along it, and elsewhere around the lagoon are many tiny islets too small to be of any consequence. Near the middle of the

northern leg are the two best entrance channels, separated by Eroj Island. Calalin Pass, to which the attacking force was directed, was that at the east, lying between Eroj and Calalin Islands.[1]

The Majuro Attack Group (Task Group 51.2), commanded by Admiral Hill, left Pearl Harbor on 23 January in company with the Reserve Force destined for Kwajalein. The ground forces committed to Majuro consisted of the 2d Battalion, 106th Infantry, reinforced, of the 27th Infantry Division, under command of Colonel Sheldon, and of the V Amphibious Corps Reconnaissance Company, commanded by Capt. James L. Jones, USMC. These troops, totaling over 1,500 officers and men, were carried aboard the transport *Cambria*, which also served as Admiral Hill's flagship, and the high-speed transport *Kane*.

Protection was initially provided by the cruiser *Portland*, escort carriers *Nassau* and *Natoma Bay*, and later by Destroyer Division 96, consisting of *Bullard*, *Black*, *Kidd*, and *Chauncey*, which rendezvoused with the attack group at sea after a voyage from Funafuti. Three mine sweepers, *Chandler*, *Sage*, and *Oracle* and the LST *482*, carrying

---

[1] Office of Naval Intelligence (ONI), The Assault on Kwajalein and Majuro, Washington, 1944, 2 vols., Vol. I, p. 7 (map).

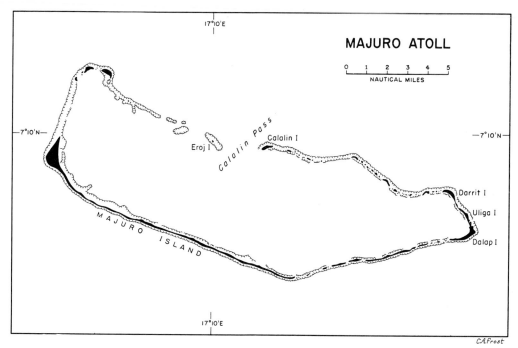

MAP 15

the amphibious vehicles for the landing, completed the group.[2]

At 0300 on 30 January, the Majuro group broke off from the remainder of the convoy bound for Kwajalein and headed directly for its target.[3] About two hours later *Kane* sped forward alone and reached Calalin Pass about 2130 that evening. Under cover of darkness she launched her rubber boats that were to carry ashore the first American troops to land on a possession held by the Japanese before the outbreak of the war. Led by 1st Lt. Harvey C. Weeks, USMC, elements of the V Amphibious Corps Reconnaissance Company landed on Calalin Island close to the entrance to the pass. They found one native and at 2345 reported by radio that he had told them that about 300 to 400 enemy were on Darrit Island, but that none were elsewhere on the atoll.[4]

Meanwhile, *Kane* had continued around the eastern end of the atoll and at 0200 on 31 January commenced to land the remainder of the reconnaissance company, under Captain Jones, on Dalap Island. Proceeding north along the island, they found a native from whom they learned, in direct contradiction of the earlier report, that all but four of the enemy had left Majuro more than a year earlier and that those four Japanese were at the other end of the atoll on Majuro Island. Confirmation of this second account was next obtained from an English-speaking half-caste, Michael Madison, who was discovered on Uliga Island. By this time Ad-

[2] TG 51.2 Action Rpt, Majuro Atoll, Marshall Islands, 15 Feb 44, Incl A, pp. 2, 8.

[3] *Ibid.*, p. 11.

[4] V Phib Corps FLINTLOCK Rpt, Incl J, V Phib Corps Amph Rcn Co, War Diary, Sundance Atoll, 20 Jan 44, Annex H, p. 2.

miral Hill's ships had commenced their scheduled naval gunfire on Darrit Island at 0600, and Captain Jones had some difficulty in getting in touch with the flagship by radio to call off the fire, which was not needed since no known enemy was on the island. Finally, after about fifteen minutes, radio contact was established and the naval bombardment of the eastern section of the atoll ceased.

A detail from the reconnaissance company then walked across the reef from Uliga to Darrit and verified the report that had prompted suspension of the bombardment. They found the village on Darrit deserted and installations only partly damaged by the naval gunfire. Incomplete buildings and useful construction material were also discovered.[5]

That afternoon the marines of the reconnaissance company boarded *Kane* to be taken to Majuro Island itself, where it was hoped they would find the remnant of Japanese reported to be still in the atoll. At 2145 that evening a detail of forty-two men landed from rubber boats and commenced patrolling the island. Only one Japanese was discovered, a Warrant Officer Nagata of the Imperial Japanese Navy, who had been left as overseer of Japanese property in Majuro. Several machine guns and a small store of dynamite and hand grenades were taken, and with that the "capture" of Majuro Atoll was completed.[6]

D Day: Northern Kwajalein

The 4th Marine Division's plan for the capture of the northern half of Kwajalein Atoll was in most respects a duplicate of that of the 7th Infantry Division's for the southern half. The principal target was Roi-Namur, twin islands on the northern tip of the atoll, connected only by a strip of

sandy beach and an artificial causeway. The day before the main landing was undertaken, adjacent islands were to be captured in order to make safe the passage of naval vessels into the lagoon and provide location for artillery to support the assault on Roi-Namur. This preliminary task was assigned to a special landing group (designated Ivan Landing Group) commanded by General Underhill. It consisted of the 25th Marines (reinforced), the 14th Marines (Artillery), Company D (Scout) of the 4th Tank Battalion, and other attached units.

Ivan and Jacob

At 0900 on 31 January the 1st Battalion, 25th Marines, plus the Scout Company, was to make simultaneous landings from the ocean side on Ivan (Mellu) and Jacob (Ennuebing) Islands, which guarded the deep water pass into the lagoon. *(See Map 10.)* After the lagoon had been swept for mines, the 2d and 3d Battalions of the same regiment were to move in and land on Albert (Ennumennet) and Allen (Ennubir) Islands, which lay southeast of Namur. If time permitted, the 3d Battalion was then to capture Abraham (Ennugarret) Island thus completing the chain surrounding Roi-Namur. The four battalions of the artillery regiment (14th Marines) were to be emplaced respectively on Ivan, Jacob, Albert, and Allen, from which positions they could support the next day's landings on Roi and Namur.[7] Only enough amphibian tractors (from the 10th Amphibian Tractor Battalion) were available to carry two landing teams at a time,

---

[5] *Ibid.*, Annex E, pp. 2–3.
[6] *Ibid.*, Annex H, pp. 4–6.
[7] 4th Marine Div Opn Plan 3-43 (Revised), 30 Dec 43; 4th Marine Div Final Rpt FLINTLOCK, 17 Mar 44, Incl C, Rpt of Gen Underhill, CG Ivan Landing Group, p. 1.

the 1st and 2d Battalions. The plan called for the 1st Battalion to release its tractors to the 3d upon completion of the capture of Ivan and Jacob.[8] This shortage of amphibian tractors, the inevitable complications involved in making five separate landings in one day, and other factors yet to be mentioned led to such confusion and delay that all of the plans for D Day quickly went awry.

At 0535 on 31 January Admiral Conolly's flagship, *Appalachian,* in convoy with the transports and fire support ships of the Northern Attack Force took station southwest of Ivan and Jacob Islands and commenced preparing for the initial attack on northern Kwajalein. The sky was overcast; a 19-knot wind blew from the northeast, which meant that the amphibian craft bound for Ivan and Jacob would have to buck both wind and sea.[9]

Shortly before sunrise Conolly's fire support ships took station, and at 0651 *Biloxi* and *Maryland* commenced shelling. In addition to these two vessels, the landings were to be supported by the old battleships *Tennessee* and *Colorado,* the heavy cruisers *Louisville, Mobile,* and *Indianapolis,* the light cruiser *Santa Fe,* escort carriers *Sangamon, Suwanee,* and *Chenango,* seventeen destroyers, one destroyer escort, and three mine sweepers. At 0715 naval gunfire was checked to permit a scheduled air strike by planes from the escort carriers. This was completed within eight minutes, and the naval guns again took up the blasting of Roi and Namur.

Meanwhile, the troops that were to land on Ivan and Jacob were facing unexpected difficulties getting debarked from their transports into landing craft and transferred into the amphibian tractors, which had been carried aboard LST's. Before the operation, landing team commanders had estimated that their debarkation interval would be about sixty minutes. This proved to be grossly optimistic. Once the troops were loaded in their assigned landing craft they had to make their way through choppy seas to the LST area for transfer to amphibian tractors. At this juncture all semblance of control broke down.

Landing craft were about two hours late in reaching the LST area. Choppy seas and a head wind were partly responsible for the delays. Boat control officers left the tractors in frantic search for the landing craft and failed to return in time to lead the LVT's to the line of departure. Tractors were damaged or swamped while milling around their mother LST's waiting for the troops to show up. Radios in LVT's were drowned out. One LST weighed anchor and shifted position before completing the disembarkation of all its tractors. The elevator on another broke down so that those LVT's loaded on the topside deck could not be disembarked on time. In short, almost every conceivable mishap occurred to delay and foul up what, under even the best of circumstances, was a complicated maneuver.[10]

---

[8] 4th Marine Div Final Rpt FLINTLOCK, 17 Mar 44, Incl C, p. 1.

[9] 4th Marine Div Jnl, 31 Jan–2 Feb 44, Roi-Namur, Operational Narrative, 31 Jan 44, p. 2. The following narrative of the landings on Ivan and Jacob is derived from this source and from the following: TF 53 Rpt Roi-Namur, 23 Feb 44, Incl A, pp. 10–14; 4th Marine Div Final Rpt FLINTLOCK, 17 Mar 44; *Ibid.,* Incl C, Rpt of CG Ivan Landing Group; *Ibid.,* Incl F, Rpt of RCT 25; 1st Bn 25th Marines Rpt of Activities, 16 Feb 44; 10th Amph Trac Bn Rpt of Opns During the FLINTLOCK Opn, 17 Mar 44; 14th Marines Opns Rpt. Also, the authors are indebted to the U.S. Marine Corps Historical Division for permission to read the first three chapters of a draft study of Marine Corps operations in the Marshalls prepared by Lt. Col. Robert D. Heinl, USMC.

[10] See reports of platoon leaders of the 10th Amphibian Tractor Battalion in 10th Amph Trac Bn Rpt FLINTLOCK.

At 0825 another air strike was launched against Roi and Namur and ten minutes later the naval ships again resumed fire. By this time it had become apparent to the control officer who was stationed aboard the destroyer *Phelps* on the line of departure that the scheduled H Hour could not be met and he so advised Admiral Conolly. The admiral postponed the time of landing by thirty minutes and advised the planes that were to deliver a last-minute bombing and strafing on the beaches to coordinate their actions with the progress of the landing waves, holding their strike until the tractors were twenty minutes off the beach.

Not until 0917 were enough tractors present on the line of departure to warrant starting the final movement forward. As the first wave moved toward the beaches of Ivan, Col. Samuel C. Cumming, commanding officer of the 25th Marines, radioed, "Good luck to first Marine to land on Japanese soil."[11] Ahead of the troops bound for Jacob moved a wave of armored amphibians and ahead of them a wave of LCI gunboats. Eleven hundred yards off the shore these ugly little vessels released their barrage of rockets and immediately thereafter the final air strike against the beaches of Ivan and Jacob was delivered. As the LCI's lay to in the water, the wave of amphibian tanks passed through to pound the beaches with 37-mm. shells. These then deployed to port and starboard and the troop-laden amphibian tractors moved to the shore. The first tractor touched the coral beaches of Jacob at 0952, almost a full hour behind the original schedule.

The landing on Ivan, carried out in the same manner, was even further delayed. Unable to negotiate the reefs on the seaward side the Scout Company, contrary to orders, moved into the lagoon and landed on the southeast beach about 0955. There they quickly built up a firing line across the southern end of the island from east to west. When the remainder of the Ivan Landing Group (C Company) landed on the southwest (seaward) side of the island at 1015, they quickly established liaison with the Scout Company and together the two units moved up the island.[12]

There was only token resistance on Ivan and Jacob. By 1015 Jacob was reported secured with thirteen Japanese killed and three taken prisoner. An hour and a half later Ivan was completely overrun with seventeen enemy killed and two taken prisoner. By early afternoon the 3d Battalion, 14th Marines (75-mm. pack howitzers), had been carried ashore to Jacob Island in LVT's, and the 4th Battalion (105-mm. howitzers) was landed on Ivan from LCM's.[13] With this accomplished, the regiment's attention could now be turned to the capture of Albert, Allen, and Abraham Islands on the other (eastern) flank of Roi-Namur.

Albert and Allen

The plan for the next stage of D-Day operations called for the 2d Battalion, 25th Marines, commanded by Lt. Col. Lewis C. Hudson, to capture Allen Island, and for the 3d Battalion, 25th Marines, under command of Lt. Col. Justice M. Chambers, to take Albert and, if possible, Abraham. A Hour for landing on Albert and Allen was 1430; B Hour for landing on Abraham

---

[11] 4th Marine Div Jnl, 31 Jan 44, p. 6. Colonel Cumming was in error. Marines of the V Amphibious Corps Reconnaissance Company had landed the night before at Majuro.

[12] 1st Bn 25th Marines Rpt, p. 1.

[13] 14th Marines Rpt FLINTLOCK, p. 1.

was 1600. The 2d Battalion had already been boated in LVT's (except for one wave, which was in LCVP's) and was standing by as the reserve force for the Ivan-Jacob landings. There had not been enough LVT's, however, to carry the 3d Battalion, which had to wait until early afternoon in LCVP's until the 1st Battalion had released sufficient tractors to carry the 3d to its destination.[14]

The first step was to clear the passes and the lagoon off the southern shore of Roi-Namur of any possible mines. By 1116 the mine sweepers had moved under cover of smoke through Jacob Pass and within 1,500 yards of Albert Island. As the sweepers retired southward into the lagoon, Albert and Allen were bombed and strafed by carrier aircraft, and LCI's moved close in to add to their 20-mm. and 40-mm. fire to the din. Then, about noon, as both mine sweepers and LCI's moved out of Jacob Pass back into the ocean, six torpedo planes and seven bombers delivered an attack on Albert and four bombers hit Allen. As soon as this was completed naval fire from two destroyers, *Porterfield* and *Haraden,* was resumed. Meanwhile the larger vessels were pouring shells into Namur. At 1210 Admiral Conolly sent the order, "Desire MARYLAND move in really close this afternoon for counter battery and counter blockhouse fire, using pointer fire for both main and secondary batteries."[15] Thus was born the affectionate title "Close-in Conolly," which was endowed upon the admiral for the rest of the war and never failed to endear him to soldiers and marines who liked the comfortable feeling of battleships and cruisers close behind their own unarmored backs.

Meanwhile, another mix-up in the landing plan had occurred. As naval gunfire and mine-sweeping operations were pro-

ceeding inside the lagoon, the landing craft and vehicles to carry the 2d and 3d Battalions, 25th Marines, to Allen and Albert were supposed to be forming in transfer areas about 3,000 yards southeast of the Ivan-Jacob line of departure, which was marked by the destroyer *Phelps.* Up to 1130 no boats or LVT's were anywhere near these areas. About this time *Phelps,* which had been acting as central control vessel for all D-Day landings, received orders to leave station as control vessel and proceed into the lagoon to deliver fire support missions. In obedience to these instructions *Phelps* announced over her bull horn to the SC 997, aboard which rode General Underhill, "Am going to support minesweepers. Take over." Whereupon the destroyer steamed through Ivan Pass into the lagoon, leaving the job of boat control to the surprised party aboard the subchaser. Unfortunately the SC 997 had been furnished none of the plans for boat control and furthermore had an insufficient number of radios aboard to carry on proper communications with the milling tractors and landing craft. To compound the confusion, most of the tractors of the 2d Battalion Landing Team took out after *Phelps* and started to follow her through the pass.

General Underhill immediately ordered SC 997 to overtake the retreating troops. Their tractors and landing craft were ordered by megaphone to return to the proper transfer area. En route, the newly appointed control vessel collected a few

[14] This account of the Albert, Allen, and Abraham landings is derived from the following sources: 4th Marine Div Final Rpt FLINTLOCK, Incls C and F; 4th Marine Div Jnl, 31 Jan 44; 2d Bn 25th Marines Rpt, 20 Feb 44; 3d Bn 25th Marines Rpt, 9 Feb 44; 10th Amph Trac Bn Rpt FLINTLOCK; TF 53 Rpt Roi-Namur, Incl A.

[15] 4th Marine Div Jnl, 31 Jan 44, p. 15.

aimlessly wandering tractors as well as most of the boats carrying the 3d Battalion Landing Team. Then Admiral Conolly was informed that the assault troops for Allen and Albert would probably be ready in the transfer areas by 1230. With this information, A Hour was postponed to 1430.[16]

By about 1250 a few more tractors had come into the transfer area, and General Underhill then ordered the SC *997* to lead the two assault battalion landing teams through Jacob Pass to *Phelps,* which was now lying off Albert and Allen waiting to direct the final attack. By this time Colonel Chambers' 3d Battalion had only enough LVT's to make up the first wave and a half. The remainder of these vehicles, which were supposed to have been released by the 1st Battalion, were either sunk or otherwise incapacitated, still drawn up on the beaches of Ivan or Jacob, or simply lost in the melee. General Underhill ordered Chambers to make do with what he had and proceed with the scheduled attack.[17]

At 1342 *Phelps,* which was now stationed on the line of departure, radioed to Admiral Conolly that the first wave of tractors was not going to meet the 1430 A Hour and recommended that it be delayed by half an hour. It was so ordered. At 1420 the scheduled last-minute air attack was ordered to be executed. Six bombers and one torpedo plane bombed Allen and six bombers and five torpedo planes covered Albert for fifteen minutes. Immediately upon suspension of this attack, the LCI(G)'s moved forward from the line of departure followed by a wave of armored amphibian tractors, which were followed in turn by the amphtracks and landing craft carrying the assault troops. The three destroyers that had been shelling the beach up to this time were ordered to cease fire at

1450. As the waves moved closer to the beaches, the LCI(G)'s opened up with their 40-mm. and 20-mm. guns and their 4.5-inch barrage rockets. On Albert a tremendous explosion was observed as a result of the barrage. Meanwhile, nine dive bombers and nine torpedo bombers from the escort carrier *Suwannee* were sent in to bomb and strafe Sally Point, the southeast promontory of Namur. At 1513 the first wave of the 3d Battalion, 25th Marines, touched ground on Albert, and about five minutes later the leading troops of the 2d Battalion hit Allen.[18]

Resistance on both islands was light. Within twenty minutes after the first touchdown, the 3d Battalion had pushed across Albert, and killed the ten Japanese present at the cost of one marine killed and seven wounded. The 2d Battalion had only a little more difficulty. On the northern half of Allen they ran into about a platoon of Japanese, but after sustaining seven casualties the attackers killed the twenty-four enemy and declared the island secure. Then Company G, supported by five armored amphibians, pushed across the reef to Andrew Island, a little sandspit south of Allen, and took it without suffering casualties. Before dark the 75-mm. pack howitzers of the 1st and 2d Battalions, 14th Marines, had been landed respectively on Allen and Albert, thus completing the bracketing of the main targets of Roi and Namur from both sides.[19] All that remained to complete the day's operations was the capture of Abraham Island lying immediately southeast of Namur.

---

[16] This account is derived from General Underhill's report, 29 Feb 44, in 4th Marine Div Final Rpt FLINTLOCK, Annex C.

[17] *Ibid.,* p. 4.

[18] 4th Marine Div Jnl, 31 Jan 44, pp. 19–24.

[19] 14th Marines Rpt FLINTLOCK, pp. 1–2.

Abraham

Plans for the capture of Abraham were greatly complicated by the premature departure from Albert of all but two LVT's. This situation came about as a result of a midstream modification of plans and ignorance on the part of the LVT commanders of the proposed scheme for landing on Abraham. After leaving Hawaii and while still aboard ship, General Underhill received a change of D-Day plans to include the capture of Abraham about 1600. This plan was supposed to have been forwarded to the commander of the 10th Amphibian Tractor Battalion and his subordinate commanders on the morning of D Day. In the confusion that attended the transfer of troops to the LVT's, the change of orders was not received by the tractor units. Hence they were under the impression that once Allen and Albert were secured they were at liberty to return to the LST's to take on much-needed fuel.[20]

Late in the afternoon, Colonel Cumming, commanding officer of the 25th Marines, conferred with Colonel Chambers, the 3d Battalion commander, on the feasibility of an immediate landing on Abraham. It was agreed and subsequently ordered that B Hour for the landing would be 1800. No artillery support would be available because the pack howitzers had not yet had time to get into position and register. It was too late to establish contact with the naval fire support ships to get naval gunfire support, and although a request was made for air support, it was refused. This meant that the only preliminary fire that Chambers could count on would be from his own 60-mm. and 81-mm. mortars plus the half-tracks that had been attached to his battalion for the invasion of Albert.[21]

Before the hour for jumping off arrived, two more LVT's were commandeered, bringing the total number available for the attack to four. The commanding officer of Company A, 4th Tank Battalion, 1st Lt. Robert E. Stevenson, personally reconnoitered the depth of water by wading almost the whole distance to Abraham. A small sandspit lying between Albert and Abraham (called Albert Junior) was occupied without any opposition except for light fire from Abraham. Then, starting at 1750, the half-tracks and mortars delivered a ten-minute preparatory fire against Abraham, and 81-mm. mortars laid smoke on the landing beach. With 120 officers and men of Company L aboard, the four LVT's hit the beach on schedule. After putting up a token resistance the few enemy on the island withdrew. Within thirty minutes two rifle companies (Companies L and K, reinforced) had been shuttled to the island. By 1915 the initial occupation of the island was completed, although

[20] 4th Marine Div Final Rpt FLINTLOCK, Annex C, p. 5; 10th Amph Trac Bn Rpt FLINTLOCK, p. 3; 3d Bn 25th Marine Rpt, p. 1.
Part of the confusion resulted from a conflicting interpretation of orders. The Northern Landing Force Operation Plan 3-43 of 31 December 1943 provided that at the completion of Phase I on D Day, the LVT's should revert to division control. Since the tractors had not been apprised of the decision to take Abraham, their commanders assumed that with the securing of Allen and Albert, Phase I was completed and they were free to return to the LST area (10th Amph Trac Bn Rpt FLINTLOCK, p. 3). On the other hand, General Underhill's Ivan Landing Group order directed the LVT's attached to 3d Battalion, 25th Marines, to return to their LST's only when released by his command. According to this interpretation, ". . . there was no authority for LVT(A)'s to detach themselves from CT-25 or leave ALBERT or ALLEN until ordered by C.G., IVAN Landing Group or by C.O., CT-25 and no release had been given." (4th Marine Div Final Rpt FLINTLOCK, Annex C, p. 5.)
[21] The account of the capture of Abraham is derived from 4th Marine Div Final Rpt FLINTLOCK, Incl F, Rpt of RCT 25, and 3d Bn 25th Marines Rpt.

NAMUR *as it appeared before (above) and during (below) the bombardment.*

mopping-up operations continued for several hours. Six enemy were killed and others appear to have escaped to Namur after darkness set in.

Immediately upon its capture, steps were taken to convert Abraham Island into a base for regimental weapons to support the next day's attack on Namur, which lay only 460 yards away. Ammunition and supplies were brought from Albert throughout the night. Battery B of the 4th Special Weapons Battalion and the 75-mm. platoon of the regimental Weapons Company were landed. Before daylight the entire north coast bristled with flat-trajectory weapons and mortars. The total fire power located on Abraham came to five 75-mm. half-tracks, seventeen 37-mm. guns, four 81-mm. mortars, nine 60-mm. mortars, and sixty-one machine guns. The 24th Marines, which next day would attack Namur, would have reason to be thankful for all this additional support on their right flank.

Thus, by the close of D Day the 25th Marines had captured five islands flanking the main target of Roi-Namur. Four battalions of artillery (three of 75-mm. pack howitzers and one of 105-mm. howitzers) had been emplaced, and all but the one 105-mm. battalion had commenced registration. Mortars, machine guns, and regimental weapons in considerable number had gone into position to support the right flank of the assault on Namur. An estimated 135 Japanese had been killed at the cost of eighteen marines killed, eight missing, and forty wounded in action.[22]

On D Day, Roi and Namur had both been subjected to constant bombardment from air and from sea. The lagoon off the southern landing beaches had been swept and found clear of mines. Under cover of darkness an underwater demolition team had reconnoitered south of Roi and Namur to within fifty yards of the beaches and found no mines or obstructions.

On the night of 31 January–1 February, as the marines and sailors ashore and afloat anxiously awaited the dawn that would initiate the main assault on northern Kwajalein, three destroyers kept up an intermittent fire on those islands to harass the Japanese and prevent them from resting up for the coming attacks. Star shells from the destroyers from time to time pierced the murky darkness. The LST's of the initial group stayed at anchor inside the lagoon, fueling their embarked LVT's and otherwise preparing for the main assault. The flagship *Appalachian* lay to just outside the lagoon, as did the ships of Transport Division 26, which spent the night disembarking ammunition and supplies to Ivan and Jacob. The remainder of the large ships of the Northern Attack Force cruised at sea waiting the signal to return to the attack area at daylight.[23]

Initial Landings on Roi and Namur

The plan for the main assault on Roi-Namur called for simultaneous landings by the 23d Marine Regimental Combat Team on Red Beaches 2 and Red 3 on the lagoon (south) shore of Roi and of the 24th Marine Regimental Combat Team on Green Beaches 1 and Green 2 on the lagoon shore of Namur (*Map VII*). Each regiment would attack with two battalions abreast and one in reserve. The assault waves were to be carried in LVT's, which would be preceded by armored amphibians as far as the shore line. LCI gunboats, as usual,

---

[22] 4th Marine Div Jnl, Operational Narrative, 1 Feb 44, p. 1; 4th Marine Div Final Rpt FLINTLOCK, Incl F, p. 3.

[23] TF 53 Rpt Roi-Namur, p. 6, Incl A, p. 14.

would lead the waves close in to shore, firing their guns and rockets as they went. W Hour for Roi and Namur was to be 0900 on 1 February.[24]

The original plan had called for the transfer of the troops of the 23d and 24th Regimental Combat Teams from their transports to LST's outside the lagoon on the afternoon of D Day while the outlying islands were being captured. Then, in the early morning hours of 1 February, the LST's were to launch their troop-laden amphibian tractors, which would proceed into the lagoon under their own power and take station on the line of departure. Because of the many difficulties that had beset the LVT's on D Day, this plan was changed. After the troop transfer had been completed, the LST's were ordered to move into the lagoon themselves early on the 1st before discharging their amphibian tractors.[25]

While the LST's got under way preparatory to moving into the lagoon and making ready to put their amphibian tractors into the water, naval ships and planes commenced their final softening up of the target. At 0650 the first bombardment began when *Santa Fe, Maryland, Indianapolis, Biloxi, Mustin,* and *Russell* opened fire on Roi, and twenty minutes later *Tennessee, Colorado, Louisville, Mobile, Morris,* and *Anderson* commenced pounding Namur. Artillery fire commenced at 0645 with the 1st and 2d Battalions, 14th Marines, firing on the beaches of Namur and the 3d and 4th Battalions on those of Roi.[26]

Meanwhile, the assault troops were struggling, as often as not unsuccessfully, to get into their LVT's and move toward the line of departure. The 23d Marines were to be carried to their beaches by the tractors of the 4th Amphibian Tractor Battalion, which had rested idle aboard their

LST's outside the lagoon on D Day. To the 24th Marines bound for Namur were assigned the tractors of the 10th Amphibian Tractor Battalion that had participated in the preceding day's actions.

The troubles that had beset the 10th Amphibian Tractor Battalion on D Day were titanic. They had been launched too far from the line of departure in the first place. They had had to buck adverse winds and unexpectedly choppy seas. Radio failures had tremendously complicated the problem of control, causing still further delay and much unnecessary travel through the water. All of this spelled excessive fuel consumption and many of the tractors ran out of gas before the day was over. For an LVT to run out of fuel in a choppy sea was usually disastrous. This model, the LVT(2), shipped water easily and its bilge pumps could not be manually operated. Thus, when the gasoline supply was gone the vehicle could not be pumped out and usually sank. In addition, many of the tractors of the 10th Battalion had not been released from their duties on D Day until after dark, were unable to get back to their mother LST's for refueling, and had spent the night on various outlying islands. Thus, as the hour for descending on Namur approached, the 24th Marines could muster only 62 of the 110 tractors that had been assigned to them.[27] A hurried call was sent out for LCVP's to make up the difference. Since the regimental commander, Col. Franklin A. Hart, USMC, had not yet received the report of the pre-

---

[24] 4th Marine Div Opn Plan 3-43 (Revised).
[25] TF 53 Rpt Roi-Namur, p. 6.
[26] 4th Marine Div Jnl, Operational Narrative, 1 Feb 44, p. 1; 14th Marines Rpt FLINTLOCK, p. 2.
[27] 10th Amph Trac Bn Rpt FLINTLOCK, 1st Ind by CG 4th Marine Div, 27 Mar 44; 4th Marine Div Final Rpt FLINTLOCK, Incl E, Rpt of RCT 24, p. 6.

vious night's beach reconnaissance by the underwater demolition team, he was not sure whether there was enough water off the beach to float LCVP's. Hence he had to make last-minute changes in the scheduled wave formation. In the zone of the 2d Battalion, which was destined for Green Beach 2, the original fourth wave was ordered to go in as the second and third waves on the left of the line. This was because Company E, which had originally been designated as reserve, had all of its twelve amphibian tractors available whereas Company G, designated the left assault company, had only three.[28]

To the left, off the beaches of Roi, the 23d Marines were having their own share of problems. Their LST's were late in arriving on station inside the lagoon and once there they encountered serious difficulties in disembarking their tractors. Elevators jammed when the effort was made to lower the LVT's stowed on the top decks into the tank decks for launching. To add to these mechanical failures, the naval personnel of the LST's were for the most part inexperienced. Some of these ships had been rushed from their Ohio River building yards to San Diego only a few days before final departure for the Marshalls. Their crews had had only the most rudimentary basic training and very little time to work with the troops and the equipment. On one LST, only one man in the entire crew professed to having actually seen an LVT lowered down the elevator from the main deck to the tank deck.[29]

As soon as Admiral Conolly was made fully aware of this series of delays, he realized that the original W Hour of 1000 could not possibly be met. Accordingly, at 0853 the time for the first landing was postponed an hour, and shortly thereafter fire support ships were ordered to adjust their schedules to the new W Hour.[30]

As tractors and landing craft struggled to reach the line of departure and form in some semblance of orderly boat waves, naval ships and planes continued their devastating attack on the landing beaches and inland. At 1026 naval and artillery fire ceased as sixteen torpedo bombers and dive bombers from the light carrier *Cabot* flew in to drop their 2,000-pound bombs on assigned targets. Ten minutes later fifteen dive bombers arrived from *Intrepid* to drop their loads, followed by a dozen fighters from the same ship, who flew in low and strafed the landing beaches. At 1055 Admiral Conolly ordered all planes out of immediate area of the islands and ships and artillery were told to resume fire. Roi and Namur were covered with such towering plumes of smoke that one air observer reported the ceiling to be "absolutely zero."[31]

At the line of departure, marked again by the destroyer *Phelps*, confusion still reigned as W Hour approached and then passed. Off the beaches of Roi, Col. Louis R. Jones, commanding the 23d Marines, was out of radio contact with the commander of the 4th Amphibian Tractor Battalion. Radios had been doused with rain and salt water and, as had been the case the day before, very few were functioning. Lt. Col. Edward J. Dillon, commanding the 2d Battalion, 23d Marines, reported that he was completely out of touch with the regimental commander, and similar

---

[28] 2d.Bn 24th Marines, Narrative of Battle Roi-Namur, p. 1.

[29] 4th Marine Div Final Rpt FLINTLOCK, Incl D, Rpt of RCT 23; Ltr, Adm Richard L. Conolly to Jeter A. Isely, 31 Aug 49, in Princeton University Library.

[30] 4th Marine Div Jnl, Operational Narrative, 1 Feb 44, p. 3.

[31] *Ibid.*, p. 4.

communications difficulties beset other units.[32]

By the time the 1st Battalion, 23d Marines, reached the line of departure it was after 1000, the time originally set for the initial landing. Neither the troops nor their officers had yet received word of the delay in W Hour and therefore "felt that they had failed miserably to perform their mission."[33] In one case, the naval wave commander had lost some of the LVT's en route to the line of departure and the senior Marine officer had to hold up the wave until the missing tractors could be located. In the case of the fourth wave, consisting of LCM's carrying tanks, no wave commander ever appeared to guide the craft into the line of departure. Since no radio contact could be established, dispatch boats had to be sent out to locate the missing tanks and lead them into position. Not until 1045, roughly an hour and a half behind schedule, were all the tractors and boats of this battalion ready on or near the line of departure to make the run for the beach.[34]

At the same time Colonel Dillon of the 2d Battalion, 23d Marines, was having his share of grief. At 1040 he got word from the commanding officer of Company E that the elevator on the company's LST had jammed and that some of his tractors would be delayed reaching the line of departure. Since this company was scheduled for the first two waves, readjustment in the wave formation was required. Dillon simply ordered all tractors afloat to proceed independently to the line of departure and form themselves into a third and a fourth wave in the order of their arrival.[35]

Eleven o'clock came and went and still no order had been given to land the troops. The 23d Regiment had enough of its tractors in the area of the line of departure to

start the assault, but the 24th on its right was still not ready. The run from the line of departure to the beach, it was estimated, would take thirty-three minutes, but by 1027 there were still not enough tractors on the line of departure off of Namur to make an orderly attack. At 1041 Colonel Hart reported that his waves were still not ready for the attack and at about the same time Admiral Conolly advised the fire support ships that W Hour might be delayed another fifteen minutes.[36] Colonel Hart meanwhile was under the impression that W Hour would be delayed indefinitely until his troops could form in sufficient number and in correct enough order to make a sustained attack.

By 1110, however, both Admiral Conolly and General Schmidt decided that there had been enough delay. The stunning blows delivered by aerial bombardment and naval gunfire might soon wear off and the tractors' fuel supply could not last forever.[37] Therefore, *Phelps* was granted permission to send in the first wave, and at 1112 the flag Baker was hauled down from her yardarm giving the signal to start for shore. Off the beaches of Roi this was welcome news to the anxious troops of the 23d Marines, who had for some time been drawn up in fairly good formation on the line of departure. Colonel Jones some minutes before had been impatiently demanding of the control craft in his area why the first wave had not been sent in. But to

[32] 4th Marine Div Final Rpt FLINTLOCK, Incl D; 2d Bn 23d Marines Rpt of Landing Opns Roi-Namur, 14 Feb 44, p. 3.
[33] Rpt of BLT 1, RCT 23, 4th Marine Div, FLINTLOCK, 10 Feb 44, p. 3.
[34] *Ibid.*, pp. 3–4.
[35] 2d Bn 23d Marines Rpt of Landing Opns Roi-Namur, p. 3.
[36] 4th Marine Div Jnl, 1 Feb 44, p. 12.
[37] Ltr, Adm R. L. Conolly to Jeter A. Isely, 31 Aug 49.

LANDING CRAFT HEAD FOR BEACH AT NAMUR

Colonel Hart lying off Namur the order was an unwelcome surprise. Indeed, the first indication he received that the order to land had been executed came only when he spotted the tractors of his 3d Battalion Landing Team start off for the beach. Thinking they had jumped the gun, he immediately dispatched a control vessel to intercept them, but then observed that the tractors carrying the 23d Regimental Combat Team had also started for the line of departure. In view of this, there was nothing to do but send in those of his straggling waves that were on or near the line and trust to fortune that the landing would not be too chaotic.[38]

Ahead went the LCI gunboats, behind them the armored amphibians, and behind them the infantry in tractors, followed by tanks in LCM's. On Roi the 1st Battalion, 23d Marines, landed on the left on Red Beach 2, and the 2d Battalion on the right on Red Beach 3. Armored amphibians of the 1st Battalion touched down at 1133 and moved inland to the antitank trench to take up firing positions. There they continued firing their 37-mm. guns and .30-caliber machine guns across the entire landing team zone of action. One of the armored amphibians was hit by .50-caliber fire from the rear, killing one marine. Shortly thereafter a platoon of the LVT(A)'s moved around the left flank through the water and over Wendy Point to open fire on Norbert Circle at the west end of the northern runway. By 1158 the first two waves of infantry had landed, somewhat west of the assigned zone, but

---

[38] 4th Marine Div Final Rpt FLINTLOCK, Annex D, p. 3, Annex E, p. 7.

not sufficiently so to prevent their taking up assigned positions. Resistance up to this point was characterized as very light. On the right the assault wave of the 2d Battalion, 23d Marines, reached shore at 1150, passing through the armored amphibians. The heavy pall of smoke that covered the island obscured the vision of the first troops to get ashore, and for that reason four tractors of the right assault company (Company F) landed on the right of the regimental boundary line between Red Beach 3 and Green Beach 1. There they silenced a few Japanese positions still operating before moving northwest into their proper zone of action.[39]

On Namur, the first troops hit the shore about 1145. On the left was the 3d Battalion, 24th Marines, and on the right the 2d Battalion. On the left the first wave of the 3d Battalion did not land on Green Beach 1 until 1200. Its substitute reserve company, Company B, got ashore about forty-five minutes later. The 2d Battalion Combat Team, at Green Beach 2, was somewhat prompter. Its first troops got ashore at about 1145, although by the time they landed the first and second waves had become scrambled. Company G, in reserve, landed at only about 50 percent strength somewhat later than scheduled and was followed piecemeal by the balance of the reserves as they were able to secure LCVP's. Very little fire was encountered except friendly fire from the rear. The armored amphibians that had led the tractors into the beach had been ordered to land and precede the assault troops up to a hundred yards inland. Instead, they halted offshore and let the tractors pass through them. This created an unexpected traffic congestion in a movement that was already far from orderly. Worse still, the amphibians kept up their fire at the beach through the troops as the latter worked inland, causing some casualties and more indignation among the infantry.[40]

The Capture of Roi

The main effort in the attack on Roi was on the right in the zone assigned to Colonel Dillon's 2d Battalion, 23d Marines. The battalion had been ordered to land on Red Beach 3 and move up the east coast of the island where, according to photographic intelligence, most of the enemy's hangars, buildings, and other aviation base facilities were. To this landing team had been assigned a full company of armored amphibians plus most of the division's medium tank company (Company C, 4th Tank Battalion, less one platoon) and an additional platoon of light tanks from Company A. The tanks were to land from LCM's in two waves immediately following the first two waves of infantry.[41]

The first two waves of infantry landed easily. Colonel Dillon, on receiving word that there were no obstacles present either under water or on the beaches themselves, ordered his two waves of tanks to come in.[42] The LCM's carrying the tanks were supposed to proceed through a channel immediately west of Tokyo Pier, but since the pier had been demolished some of the coxswains failed to find the channel and the first platoon of medium tanks grounded on the coral shelf about two hundred

---

[39] 1st Bn 23d Marines Rpt FLINTLOCK, p. 5; 2d Bn 23d Marines Rpt of Landing Opns Roi-Namur, p. 4.

[40] 4th Marines Div Final Rpt FLINTLOCK, Annex E, p. 8; 2d Bn 24th Marines Narrative of Battle Roi-Namur, p. 2.

[41] 2d Bn 23d Marines Opn Order 2-44, 19 Jan 44.

[42] This account of action in the zone of the 2d Battalion, 23d Marines, is derived, unless otherwise noted, from 2d Bn 23d Mar Rpt of Landing Opns Roi-Namur, pp. 4-5.

MEDIUM TANKS *move across the airfield on Roi Island.*

yards offshore. About half of the vehicles had to drive through water up to five and a half feet deep before touching ground, but each LCM carried aboard an extra tank man who waded through water ahead of the tank and guided it around potholes, so all reached shore safely. Once ashore, the tanks were temporarily held up by an antitank ditch directly behind the beach. Proceeding eastward in column they quickly found a place where the ditch had been filled in by preliminary bombardment and made their way across. Once over the ditch, the tanks assumed a line formation and moved directly across the airfield toward the first objective line.[43]

Behind them came the first waves of infantry. Resistance was light and scattered. "The air and naval gunfire bombard-ment," reported the battalion commander, "had reduced the entire zone of action to a shambles."[44] One pillbox located in the middle of the sand strip connecting Roi and Namur was still intact and functioning, and some fire was still coming from positions among the debris of the beach defenses, along the eastern edge of the island, and in the southeast corner of the airfield. Otherwise, the enemy was silent.

In spite of the weakness of the opposition, the troops moved forward cautiously. It was their first experience under fire and

[43] 4th Tk Bn Rpt FLINTLOCK, 31 Mar 44, Incl C, Rpt of Co C, p. 1.
[44] 2d Bn 23d Mar Rpt of Landing Opns Roi-Namur, p. 5.

they had expected to meet much heavier resistance than they actually did. Also, they thought it necessary to investigate almost every square foot of ground on the not unlikely chance that Japanese would be hiding under the debris of demolished fortifications.

Tanks and troops moved forward together and in about half an hour reached the first objective line (0-1 line) located about 200 to 350 yards inland from the shore line. Once there, the medium tank company commander radioed his liaison officer on the beach, requesting permission to cross the 0-1 line. Unfortunately, the frequencies assigned to the tanks and to supporting aircraft were so close together that they caused mutual interference, and the message could not be gotten through. What bothered the tank commander was that the enemy antitank guns, located in the blockhouses on the northern edge of the airfield, might still be operating and he was afraid to leave his vehicles immobilized on the open runway. Failing to establish radio contact, the tanks proceeded across the line without permission. Shortly thereafter, front-line elements of the infantry followed the tanks, also without orders to do so.[45]

On the left of the 2d Battalion, the 1st Battalion, 23d Marines, commanded by Lt. Col. Hewin O. Hammond, had landed on Red Beach 2. They, too, found the resistance unexpectedly light. A group of pillboxes thought to be located on Wendy Point, the southwest promontory of the island, proved to have been wiped out by preliminary bombardment. As in the case of the 2d Battalion, the infantrymen pushed on ahead of the 0-1 line without orders, following the medium tanks ahead of them. There were a number of reasons for this: the runway that marked the line

was so covered by debris as to be unrecognizable; radio communications between the landing team commander and his assault company commanders failed; and platoon leaders found it hard to maintain control because, in the words of one sergeant, "the men wanted to kill a Jap so they went out on their own."[46]

By 1311 Colonel Jones, the 23d's commander, was ashore and radioed back to General Schmidt, "This is a pip. No opposition near the beach. Located scattered machine gun fire vicinity of split between . . . [Roi] and . . . [Namur]. Landing teams moving in to 0-1 line. Little or no opposition." Fifteen minutes later he followed this announcement with the message, "Give us the word and we will take the rest of the island."[47]

In spite of this optimism, division headquarters was disturbed that front-line elements had crossed the 0-1 line without orders and that the tanks were operating independently to the north of the line. Any attempt at a co-ordinated push to the northern shore of the island was out of the question until some order had been brought out of the confusion that existed on the front. Furthermore, neither close air support nor naval call fire could be utilized until the front line had been stabilized. At 1325 General Schmidt notified Colonel Jones to await orders for further attack and urged him to get his tanks under control and bring them back to the 0-1 line.[48]

Finally, the order came to push off in a co-ordinated attack from the 0-1 line at

---

[45] 4th Tk Bn Rpt FLINTLOCK, Incl C, p. 2; 2d Bn 23d Mar Rpt of Landing Opns Roi-Namur, p. 5.

[46] Rpt of BLT 1, RCT 23, 4th Marine Div, FLINTLOCK, 10 Feb 44, p. 3; *Ibid.*, Incl, Rpt of Co A, p. 5.

[47] 4th Marine Div Jnl, 1 Feb 44, pp. 21–22.

[48] *Ibid.*

1530.[49] About the same time the 2d Battalion, 23d Marines, assigned to the eastern (right) zone of Roi, moved out closely behind its supporting medium tanks. From left to right (west to east) were Companies E, G, and F.[50] In reserve was the 3d Battalion Landing Team of the 23d Regiment, which had come ashore at about 1450. Its duty was to defend the right flank of Roi to the 0-1 line. Troops of the reserve landing team not thus occupied were to support the advance of the 2d Battalion to the north shore of Roi.[51]

On the left, Company E met practically no opposition and reached its objective by 1600. On the right and in the center the going was somewhat rougher, although at no time did the enemy offer any really serious obstruction to the progress of Companies G and F. The first obstacle to be encountered was a concrete administration building with steel doors, which by some freak of chance had not been touched by naval gunfire, planes, or artillery. Troops of Company F advanced toward it cautiously but received no fire. One man was sent forward toward the door under cover of fire. He kicked it open and tossed in a grenade. Only one Japanese was found inside and the grenade disposed of him.

A few minutes later the company commander called for a dive bombing attack on a blockhouse located about 500 yards north of the 0-1 line. This installation was constructed of reinforced concrete approximately three feet thick and had three gun ports, one each facing north, east, and west, another indication of the enemy's mistaken assumption that the Americans would attack from the sea rather than the lagoon shore. Two heavy hits had been made on the blockhouse, one apparently by 14-inch or 16-inch shells and the other by an aerial bomb. Nevertheless, the position had not been demolished and Colonel Dillon asked for a dive bombing attack against it. The air support commander refused the request because the front-line troops were less than three hundred yards away from the target, too close for safety.

Dillon then ordered Company G to take the blockhouse. The company commander first sent forward a 75-mm. half-track, which fired five rounds against the steel door. At this point, a demolition squad came up and its commander volunteered to knock out the position with explosives. While the half-track continued to fire, infantry platoons moved up on each flank of the installation. The demolition squad placed charges at the ports and pushed Bangalore torpedoes through a shell hole in the roof. "Cease fire" was then ordered and, after hand grenades were thrown inside the door, half a squad of infantry went in to investigate. Unfortunately, the engineers of the demolition squad had not got the word to cease fire and had placed a shaped charge at one of the ports while the infantry was still inside. Luckily, no one was hurt, but as the company commander reported, "a very undignified and hurried exit was made by all concerned."[52] Inside were found three heavy machine guns, a quantity of ammunition, and the bodies of three Japanese.

---

[49] The time of attack of 1530 had been sent by radio; subsequently a verbal order from the commanding officer of the 23d Marines set this back to 1515. This caused some confusion in the minds of battalion commanders, but did not seriously interfere with the attack. (2d Bn 23d Mar Rpt of Landing Opns Roi-Namur, p. 5.)

[50] This account of the movement of 2d Battalion, 23d Marines, from 0-1 line is derived from 2d Bn 23d Mar Rpt of Landing Opns Roi-Namur, pp. 5-6, and inclosed reports of Companies E, F, and G.

[51] 3d Bn 23d Marines Record of Events, 31 Jan-5 Feb 44, 12 Feb 44, p. 2.

[52] 2d Bn 23d Mar Rpt of Landing Opns Roi-Namur, Incl L, Rpt of Co G, p. 4.

NEUTRALIZING A CONCRETE BLOCKHOUSE

Extending east from the blockhouse, overlooking the beach, was a system of trenches and machine gun positions, some connected by tunnels. Here the few remaining Japanese put up a feeble resistance. Most of those who had stayed in the trenches were already dead. The pillboxes were still firing but these were taken out by the demolition squad of Company F aided by the 37-mm. guns from the division special weapons battalion. Companies F and G then moved on to Nat Circle in the northeast corner of Roi and wiped out what few enemy remained in that area by 1700. The 2d Battalion then secured for the day and set up night defensive positions.[53]

Meanwhile, in the left (west) half of Roi, the 1st Battalion, 23d Marines, was having an even easier time in accomplishing its objectives. Company A had landed on the left, Company B on the right, with Company C coming in somewhat later as reserve. By 1215 the battalion commander learned that his Company A had passed beyond the 0-1 line and immediately ordered its withdrawal. This took some time to accomplish, as the company commander could establish no radio contact with his platoon leaders and had to rely on runners to get the order through. Gradually, the forward platoon was drawn back and preparations made to start a co-ordinated attack to the north.[54]

At 1530 the battalion commander called a conference of all company commanders

---

[53] *Ibid.*, Incl L, p. 5; *Ibid.*, Incl K, Rpt of Co F, p. 2.
[54] Rpt of BLT 1, RCT 23, 4th Mar Div, FLINTLOCK, p. 5; *Ibid.*, Incl, Rpt of Co A, p. 2.

and ordered the reserve Company C to pass through Company A and press the attack up the west coast of Roi. It was to be supported by one platoon of the weapons company, a platoon of medium tanks, and three half-tracks. Company B on the right was to hold its position on the 0-1 line.[55]

Company C jumped off at 1600 hugging the west coast of the island. Infantry and demolitions engineers moved forward slowly behind the tanks, meeting only light rifle and machine gun fire. A few scattered enemy riflemen continued to fire as the troops approached the north shore. These were quickly disposed of by the tanks firing 75-mm. and machine guns. The preliminary bombardment had virtually annihilated the enemy in this part of Roi. In one trench on the north coast were discovered forty to fifty recently killed Japanese—the only enemy, dead or alive, encountered. By 1800 Company C reached the northwest corner of the island at Norbert Circle and was ready to secure for the night. Casualties during the day for the entire battalion had come to only three killed and eleven wounded.[56]

Thus, by early evening, marines of the 23d Regimental Combat Team had, with comparative ease, established a firm beachhead on the lagoon shore of Roi and had captured most of the land lying along the east and west coasts. All that remained was for the small pocket in the center of the airfield to be mopped up.[57]

The only feature to mar the complete success of the day's ground fighting was a rash of indiscriminate firing that broke out all over Roi, starting about 1800 and lasting for more than half an hour. The sources were not clearly established, but on later investigation it was obvious that trigger-happy, green marines both on Roi and on Namur were responsible. Following this episode, Lt. Col. John J. Cosgrove, Jr., commanding officer of the 3d Battalion, 23d Marines, concluded "that fire discipline was poor, . . . that 95% of those firing had no definite idea as to why they were firing . . . [and] . . . that a large portion of those firing were doing so because they wanted to be able to say they had fired at a Jap."[58]

As night settled down, fire discipline was once again restored, and the marines on Roi rested in their shelters and foxholes uninterrupted by enemy counterattack. For all practical purposes the island was secured. All that remained next day was to mop up the few remaining Japanese, and this was accomplished without much difficulty.

Credit for the ease with which Roi was taken goes largely to the preliminary bombardment by naval guns and aircraft and Marine artillery. Colonel Dillon, commanding the 2d Battalion, 23d Marines, estimated that of the 400 Japanese dead in the eastern half of the island, 250 were killed by action prior to W Hour.[59] Since most of the resistance encountered on Roi was in the zone of this battalion, it is reasonable to believe that a similar ratio obtained on the rest of the island.

But to the eastward, affairs were not proceeding so smoothly for the 24th Regi-

---

[55] *Ibid.*, Incl, Rpt of Co B, p. 2, and Incl, Rpt of Co C, p. 2.

[56] *Ibid.*, Incl, Rpt of Co C, p. 3, and Incl, Rpt of Bn Executive Officer, p. 4.

[57] During the afternoon's fighting on Roi, Pfc. Richard B. Anderson won (posthumously) the Medal of Honor by covering an armed grenade with his body, thereby saving the other men sharing his foxhole from injury. (Citation quoted in Carl W. Proehl, *The Fourth Marine Division in World War II* (Washington, 1946), p. 12.)

[58] 3d Bn 23d Marines Record of Events, 31 Jan–5 Feb 44, Incl D, p. 4.

[59] 2d Bn 23d Marines Rpt of Landing Opns Roi-Namur, p. 6.

mental Combat Team. Namur was proving a much harder nut to crack.

The Capture of Namur

An air observer flying over the beaches of Namur about twenty minutes after the initial landing reported, "There is no enemy resistance. . . . Don't think a bird could be alive." [60] This was somewhat of an exaggeration. The troops of the 24th Marines were to encounter considerably more resistance on Namur than was being met on Roi. Roi was almost all airfield, open and uncluttered by many buildings or much vegetation. Namur, on the other hand, contained the bulk of the shelters and buildings housing the aviation and other personnel located in northern Kwajalein. Furthermore, it was thickly covered with underbrush that even the heavy preliminary bombardment had not succeeded in burning off. [61] Here was congregated the majority of enemy troops assigned to the twin islands. They were concealed among the numerous buildings scattered through the area and were afforded ample protection by the thick vegetation that remained standing.

The four assault companies of the 3d and 2d Battalion Landing Teams had landed on Green Beaches 1 and 2 respectively between 1145 and 1200. From left to right they were Companies I, K, E, and F. Because of the shortage of amphibian tractors, the original reserve companies of each of these battalion landing teams could not be boated soon enough to perform the missions assigned to them, so the reserve landing team, the 1st Battalion, 24th Marines, which was already boated in LCVP's behind the line of departure, was ordered to send one assault company to the 2d Battalion and another to the 3d Battalion to substitute for the reserve companies. Thus, Company B landed about 1245 as reserve for the 3d Battalion on Green Beach 1 and Company A got ashore shortly after 1300 to act as reserve for the 2d Battalion on the right half of the island. The plans called for the assault companies to proceed inland a hundred yards before pausing, in order to place the assault troops inside the perimeter defense of the island. All four companies were then to move as rapidly as possible on to the initial objective (O-1) line, which was marked by Sycamore Boulevard, a road running athwart the island about 400 to 500 yards inland of the beach. [62]

Of the two battalion landing teams allocated to Namur, that on the left had the easier going at first. About 1200 Company I landed on the extreme left and most of Company K came in on its immediate right. One platoon of Company K was sent to Pauline Point, the name given to the tiny spit of land that lay between Roi and Namur. This was the only unit that landed exactly on the proper beach as directed by the landing diagram. [63] Enemy resistance to the initial landing was light

[60] 4th Marine Div Jnl, 1 Feb 44, p. 18.

[61] The napalm bomb, which was later demonstrated to be so effective in burning off vegetation, had not yet made its appearance in the Pacific. It was first employed at Tinian in July 1944.

[62] 4th Marine Div Final Rpt FLINTLOCK, Incl E, Rpt of RCT 24, pp. 2, 8.

[63] The account of the activities of the 3d Battalion Landing Team, 24th Marines Regimental Combat Team, is derived from 4th Marine Div Final Rpt FLINTLOCK, Incl E, Rpt of RCT 24, and Lt Col A. R. Brunelli, USMC, The Capture of Namur Island, Kwajalein Atoll, Marshall Islands, 1–2 February 1944, MS, U.S. Marine Corps Schools, Record Section. Colonel Brunelli was battalion commander and prepared this monograph as a historical tactical study for the Amphibious Warfare School, Marine Corps Schools, Quantico, Senior Course, 1946–47. In the absence of any known official battalion action report, this monograph has been used.

NAMUR ISLAND BEACHHEAD. *Men and equipment crowd the narrow beach before advancing inland.*

and unorganized. What fire there was from pillboxes, shell holes, and debris was neither mutually supporting nor co-ordinated. Nevertheless, the enemy had not been entirely silenced by the heavy preparatory fire and from the remains of the blockhouses and concrete air raid shelters he was able to pour out enough fire to slow down the progress of the attack.

In spite of this, Companies I and K moved ahead in skirmish line, leaving some positions to be mopped up by the reserves. Company B, the reserve company, landed about 1245 and commenced mopping up. Fifteen minutes later, three light tanks of the 3d Platoon, Company B, 4th Tank Battalion, got ashore but were almost immediately bogged down. The beach was congested with men and sup-plies and in trying to get around the congestion, two tanks were bellied up in the soft sand that had been churned up by the preliminary bombardment. The one remaining tank got inland about thirty yards, where it slipped into a shell hole and threw a track, thus immobilizing itself for the time being.[64]

By 1400, about two hours after their touchdown on the beach, both of the assault companies of the 3d Battalion had reached the 0-1 line on Sycamore Boulevard. There they were ordered to stand by and prepare for a co-ordinated attack northward with the 2d Battalion Landing Team on their right. The jump-off was to be 1630.

---

[64] 4th Tk Bn Rpt FLINTLOCK, Incl B, Rpt of Co B, p. 2.

During the two hours and a half of delay before pushing forward the assault, other elements of the battalion landed and various shifts were made along the forward line. The plan called for the left flank of the attack north of 0-1 line to be supported by machine guns and other weapons based on Pauline Point. Between 1430 and 1533 Company M, the weapons company, emplaced its 81-mm. mortars and some of its heavy machine guns on Pauline Point. Company L, which had initially been scheduled to act as battalion reserve, was finally boated, got ashore at 1531, and was ordered to release one assault team to Company I and to relieve Company B in reserve. Company B then relieved Company K on the 0-1 line, while the latter was shifted to Pauline Point. Thus, as the hour for the jump-off approached, Companies I and B rested on the 0-1 line from left to right; Company L was in reserve to their rear; and Company K occupied Pauline Point along with elements of the regimental weapons company.

On Green Beach 2, Companies E and F, from left to right, came ashore within five minutes of each other around noon. Within ten minutes the landing team reserve, Company G, started to land to the right of Yokohama Pier, which was on the boundary between Green Beaches 1 and 2. At 1215 landing team headquarters came ashore, followed approximately five minutes later by the weapons company (Company H) less its detached machine gun platoons. By early afternoon ten light tanks of the 1st and 2d Platoons, Company B, 4th Tank Battalion, were safely ashore and in a tank assembly area about sixty yards inland.[65]

As on the rest of the island, initial resistance in this zone of action was light. It had been anticipated that Sally Point, the southeast promontory of Namur, would be alive with Japanese weapons. Since the landing beaches extending to the west of Sally Point were concave in shape, this would have been an ideal position for enfilade fire against the shore line and the approaches thereto. That such was not the case can be attributed to the effectiveness of the preliminary air, naval, and artillery bombardment as well as to the supporting fires from the 3d Battalion Landing Team of the 25th Marines, which had emplaced so many weapons on Abraham Island the night before.

Only desultory fire greeted the assault troops as they pushed inland toward the 0-1 line. At first they were temporarily delayed by an unexpected antitank ditch that extended laterally behind part of Green Beach 2. Most of the amphibian tractors found it impossible to get across this obstacle and had to discharge their troops at the edge of the shore instead of proceeding a hundred yards inland as originally planned.

As the infantrymen moved forward, naval gunfire began to fall too close for comfort, and on the request of the battalion commander all naval ships were ordered to cease fire at 1250. By that time the artillery regiment would have completed its schedule of fire. One final dive-bombing attack was delivered against

[65] This account of action of the 2d Battalion Landing Team, 24th Regimental Combat Team, is derived from 4th Marine Div Final Rpt FLINTLOCK, Incl E, 24th Marines Rpt; 2d Bn 24th Marines Narrative of Battle of Roi-Namur; Lt Col Richard C. Rothwell, USMC, A Study of an Amphibious Operation, The Battle of Namur, 31 Jan 44-2 Feb 44, Kwajalein Operation, Second Battalion, Twenty-Fourth Marines, 4th Marine Division, MS, Marine Corps Schools, Record Section. Colonel Rothwell served as battalion executive officer on Namur and prepared this monograph for Amphibious Warfare School, Marine Corps Schools, Senior Course, 1946-47.

Natalie Point on the northeastern tip of the island. Thereafter, the fighting was too close and the advance of front-line elements too uneven to justify the use of further support fires. The infantry would have to rely on its own weapons.

By 1300 elements of both assault companies of the 2d Battalion, 24th Marines, were on or close to the 0-1 line. On the right, Company F had overrun Sally Point and cleared out two machine guns that had fired a few rounds at the advancing marines. On the left, one boat team of Company E had quickly occupied Yokohama Pier without opposition while the rest of the company moved slowly through the underbrush and debris toward the 0-1 line. In the absence of any well-distinguished landmarks, Company E veered somewhat to the right of its zone of action and later became intermingled on the 0-1 line with elements of Company F.[66] The reserve company, G, had been landed in its entirety on the left half of Green Beach 2. It moved straight ahead in the expectation of coming up on the rear of Company E. But since that company had moved to the right, Company G found itself unexpectedly in the position of being in the assault on the battalion left. There, it met with sporadic machine gun and rifle fire and by 1300 was able to move only about 175 yards from the beach.

Up to this point progress in the zone of the 24th Marines had been fairly steady in spite of the confusion incident to dispatching of boat waves from the line of departure, the failure of the armored amphibians to precede the troops inland, and the somewhat piecemeal landing. Resistance was light and scattered, and the main impediment to the advancing troops was the thickness of the underbrush and the presence of a multitude of only half-destroyed

buildings and installations, which had to be thoroughly investigated before the advance could proceed.

Then, shortly after 1300, an incident occurred that brought the advance to an abrupt halt and temporarily threw out of gear all plans for an orderly movement across the island to the north shore. With a tremendous roar a revetted building exploded in the zone of Company F.[67] Immediately a thick cloud of pungent black smoke billowed upward a thousand feet and covered the entire island. The odor was so acrid that many thought a gas storehouse had been blown up. At the 2d Battalion command post there was a frenzied search for gas masks that had been discarded as unnecessary impedimenta. Down came a rain of large concrete fragments, twisted pieces of steel, shrapnel, and torpedo heads. Casualties to American troops in the immediate area ran from fifty to a hundred, of whom about twenty were killed, either by concussion or by the falling debris. In a few minutes two other less violent explosions occurred somewhat forward of Company F's front lines. Altogether these three explosions accounted

---

[66] The "boat team" or "assault and demolitions team" represented an innovation in Marine Corps assault tactics. Each team in the assault companies consisted of a light machine gun group of four men, a demolitions group of five men, a bazooka group of three men, a support group consisting of two BAR teams, and an officer in charge. The reserve companies were organized into similar boat teams minus the machine gun elements. Each type of team was capable of embarking in entirety in an LVT(2). (4th Marine Div Final Rpt FLINTLOCK, Incl E, Rpt of RCT 24, p. 4.)

[67] The exact time of this incident is not clearly established. The regimental action report sets it at 1245 (4th Marine Div Final Rpt FLINTLOCK, Incl E, Rpt of RCT 24, p. 9). Colonel Rothwell's monograph puts it at 1305 (Rothwell, Battle of Namur, p. 22). 1305 seems to be the more accurate since the first report made by an aerial observer of the explosion was at 1308 (4th Marine Div Jnl, 1 Feb 44, p. 21).

A JAPANESE TORPEDO WARHEAD MAGAZINE *explodes on Namur. Note splashes in the water caused by falling debris.*

for more than 50 percent of all the casualties suffered on Namur by the 2d Battalion Landing Team of the 24th Marines.[68]

The cause of this disaster was not clearly understood at the time, but subsequent investigation makes it reasonably certain that at least the first explosion was set off by a Marine demolitions group. These men had moved forward under cover of rifle fire and placed a shaped charge to penetrate the wall of the building near the ground. Once this was done, a sixteen-pound satchel charge was tossed into the building and immediately thereafter it blew up. What had been thought to be a possible gun position turned out to be a torpedo warhead magazine.[69]

The immediate results of the explosions were to stop any further co-ordinated forward movement in the zone of the 2d Battalion and to delay the organization of units already near the 0-1 line. All radio communication between battalion and the assault companies was knocked out and the battalion commander, Lt. Col. Francis

[68] 4th Marine Div Final Rpt FLINTLOCK, Incl E, Rpt of RCT 24, p. 9.

[69] These conclusions are based on a monograph entitled The Battle of Roi-Namur, Marshall Islands, prepared by Joseph E. Lo Prete for Marine Corps Schools, Amphibious Warfare School, Junior Course, 8th Class, MS, pp. 8–9. Major Lo Prete was one of the few surviving eyewitnesses to the incident and reiterated his conclusion as to the cause of the explosion in an interview with P. A. Crowl, at Quantico, 16 November 1951. The regimental commander of the 24th RCT, Franklin A. Hart, confirms this explanation of the event. (Interv, P. A. Crowl with Lt Gen Franklin A. Hart, 16 Nov 51.)

H. Brink, had to rely exclusively on runners. Individual boat teams on the front line had already become intermingled and after the explosion the company commanders found it virtually impossible to reorganize their units into any semblance of order or integrity. Moreover, the enemy was becoming more active. Japanese machine gun and rifle fire now enfiladed the entire right half of the 0-1 line.

Nevertheless, Company G on the left succeeded in pushing forward to the 0-1 line by about 1330. Meanwhile, Company A had landed shortly after the first explosion and had moved immediately to Sally Point behind Company F. About 1430 it was attached to the 2d Battalion Landing Team and ordered to pass through Company F and continue the attack on order. By 1545 Company A was in position on the 0-1 line along Sycamore Boulevard from the sea to a point about two hundred yards northwest. There, it came under fire from either flank of its line. Two light tanks were ordered forward to take out the installation close to the sea on the right. At the same time fifteen LVT(A)'s were ordered to proceed through the water along the east coast of Namur and take the same blockhouse under fire. Meanwhile, on the left of the battalion's zone, Company C had landed and was ordered to relieve Company E, the latter to go into battalion reserve.[70]

1630 was the jump-off hour prescribed by the regimental commander, Colonel Hart, for a two-battalion push from the 0-1 line to the north shore. On the regimental left the 3d Battalion Landing Team had been in position for almost two and a half hours and launched its attack as scheduled. Unfortunately during the long delay on 0-1, the Japanese had been able to recover from the shock of the initial heavy

shelling and put up much stiffer resistance than they had yet been able to make. The fighting was too close and the front lines too hard to identify to justify the use of artillery, naval call fire, or close aerial support.[71]

In the right zone, the 2d Battalion Landing Team was experiencing greater difficulty in getting organized for the attack to the north coast. Not until about 1700 did Company C get into position to relieve Company E on the battalion left. Also, the light tanks were late in arriving and the attack did not get under way until 1730. Many of the small units of Companies E, F, and G had not received the word that they were to retire into the reserve area, so when the attack jumped off there were elements of five companies intermingled in the assault. As the troops advanced behind the tanks, they came under steady fire from the large blockhouse on the right and from small arms all along the line. Progress on the battalion left was fairly steady, but on the right the line remained pinned down by fire from the blockhouse.[72]

Communication between tanks and infantry was faulty and co-ordination between the two generally poor. Tanks frequently moved out of sight or fire range of the troops that were supposed to be supporting them and engaged in independent fire fights. Infantrymen in their turn often

---

[70] Rothwell, Battle of Namur, pp. 25–26.

[71] Brunelli, The Capture of Namur Island, p. 15.

It was in this phase of the action that 1st Lt. John V. Power met his death and won the Medal of Honor. While setting a demolition charge on a Japanese pillbox, he was wounded in the stomach. Refusing to withdraw from the fight he pressed forward against another pillbox, stopping the flow of blood with his left hand and firing with his right. After emptying his carbine into this second pillbox he stopped to reload and was shot again in the stomach and head and killed. (Citation quoted in Proehl, *The Fourth Marine Division in World War II*, p. 11.)

[72] R. C. Rothwell, Battle of Namur, p. 27.

MARINES TAKE COVER *from Japanese small arms fire. Note the split-toed footgear on the dead Japanese soldier in the foreground (below).*

failed to keep pace with the tanks, even when it was possible, or to provide them with the support that was their due. It was during this phase that Capt. James L. Denig, who commanded Company B of the 4th Tank Battalion, got separated from his own tanks as well as his supporting infantry unit. As he stopped to get his bearings, six Japanese leaped out of the underbrush and swarmed over his tank. One of them dropped a grenade down the visual signal port, which had been left open to allow the foul air to escape from the turret. The explosion that followed mortally wounded Denig and killed his driver, and only by the timely intervention of some infantrymen who happened on the scene was the remainder of the crew rescued.[73]

As nightfall approached some tanks pushed forward as far as the north shore, but had to pull back for want of fuel or infantry support. A few of the troops also got as far as Narcissus Street, which ran parallel to the north coast less than a hundred yards from the shore line. This was the ultimate extent of Marine progress on 1 February. About 1820 the regimental commander ordered the rest of the island to be taken but it soon became apparent that this would be impossible before nightfall, and at 1930 the order came down to dig in on a perimeter defense, hold the ground gained, and prepare to continue the attack the following morning. By that time the 3d Battalion Landing Team had two companies abreast on a line about 175 yards north of the 0-1 line, or halfway between Sycamore Boulevard and the north shore. The 2d Battalion Landing Team's line was tied in with the 3d's and then bent back to the east to the point where the 0-1 line met the eastern shore.[74]

The night was far from restful. Japanese who had been bypassed during the day came to life to harass the Americans from the rear. Others infiltrated from the front. To compound the confusion, trigger-happy marines in the rear areas kept up a running fire that seriously endangered troops at the front. The only organized Japanese counterattack occurred just at daybreak. Company I had lost contact with Company B on its right, thus facilitating enemy infiltration of the line. About a hundred Japanese, organized into groups of ten to twenty, fell upon the two companies in a desperate charge that took thirty-five minutes of intense hand-to-hand fighting to repulse.[75] Meanwhile, Company L was ordered into the front line, and Company K was moved from Pauline Point to Namur as landing team reserve.[76]

For the final push to the northern shore, the 24th Regimental Combat Team was to have for the first time the additional fire power of the division's medium tanks. These had been detached from the 23d Marines the previous evening and had already made one sortie up the west coast of Namur as far as Natalie Point and helped to break up the dawn counterattack.[77]

At 0900 the 3d Battalion Landing Team, supported by the mediums, resumed the attack up the left half of Namur. Company

[73] 4th Tk Bn Rpt FLINTLOCK, Incl B, Co B Rpt, pp. 4–5.

[74] 4th Marine Div Final Rpt FLINTLOCK, Incl E, Rpt of RCT 24, p. 11.

[75] During this counterattack, Pvt. Richard K. Sorenson saved the lives of five of his companions by hurling his own body on a Japanese hand grenade. For this action, which he survived, he was awarded the Medal of Honor. (Citation quoted in Proehl, *The Fourth Marine Division in World War II*, p. 12.)

[76] 4th Marine Div Final Rpt FLINTLOCK, Incl E, Rpt of RCT 24, pp. 11–12; Brunelli, The Capture of Namur, p. 17.

[77] 4th Tk Bn Rpt FLINTLOCK, Incl C, Co C Rpt, pp. 2–3.

MARINES ATTACK BLOCKHOUSE. *Note the Japanese crawling out from under the shelter in right center (below).*

K was on the left, Company I in the middle, and Company L on the right. Company B went into battalion reserve. In the right sector of the island the attack was delayed until about 1000 because of the late arrival of the light tanks that were to support it. Meanwhile, command had been transferred from the 2d to the 1st Battalion Landing Team, the latter under Lt. Col. Aquilla J. Dyess. Dyess had a conglomerate command. In addition to Companies A, C, and E, which held positions on the front line from right to left, elements of Companies F and G still remained on the front line in spite of the fact that their parent units had been withdrawn into the rear area.

Both battalion landing teams pushed steadily forward along the west and east coasts. By 1100 the 3d Battalion had reached Nora Point, the northwestern tip of the island. By that time, the two battalions were within visual contact of each other. The supporting tanks were then sent to the rear and the infantry, aided by half-tracks, continued the fight. By 1215 the 1st Battalion and Company L had secured Natalie Point and, except for mopping up, the battle was ended. During this final assault, Colonel Dyess personally led his battalion against the final pocket of Japanese resistance. While standing in the parapet of an antitank trench directing a group of infantry in a flanking attack against the last enemy position, he was killed by enemy machine gun fire.[78]

At 1418 on 2 February General Schmidt, commanding the 4th Marine Division, officially announced the end of organized resistance on Namur.[79] All that remained was to mop up the few live Japanese still concealed in the underbrush and debris of Namur and to secure the rest of the islets of the northern half of Kwajalein Atoll.

This latter task was assigned to the 25th Regimental Combat Team, which had made the initial D-Day assault on the islands immediately adjoining Roi-Namur and which had since been in division reserve. Between 2 February and 7 February this regiment occupied some fifty-five islands in the northern part of the atoll. Since it was at first believed that there might be enemy garrisons on these islands, artillery concentrations were fired from Allen and Albert, but this was unnecessary and was discontinued. No opposition was encountered and the natives proved friendly and anxious to be taken into American custody.

Thus, with the capture of Roi-Namur and surrounding islands, U.S. forces completed the occupation of the northern half of Kwajalein Atoll. In approximately two and a half days of fighting, the 4th Marine Division had suffered only 737 casualties, of which 190 were killed or died of wounds.[80] Enemy losses totaled 3,563 including 3,472 enemy dead, 51 Japanese prisoners of war, and 40 Korean laborers captured.[81]

In comparison to Tarawa, the operation was both easy and cheap in terms of lives expended. The reasons for this are not hard to discover. The enemy garrison in northern Kwajalein was fewer in number than that on Tarawa by about a thousand. The Japanese had not been expecting such a deep penetration into the Central Pacific and were generally caught off balance.

---

[78] For his aggressive leadership he was posthumously awarded the Medal of Honor. (Citation quoted in Proehl, *The Fourth Marine Division in World War II*, p. 11.)

[79] 4th Marine Div Final Rpt FLINTLOCK, Incl A, p. 32.

[80] 4th Marine Div Final Rpt FLINTLOCK, Incl I, Med Rpt, p. 4.

[81] V Phib Corps FLINTLOCK Rpt, Incl D, G-2 Rpt, p. 12.

Their fortifications were not particularly strong nor were they well enough emplaced to resist an invasion from the lagoon shore. Hydrographic conditions were favorable for an amphibious landing, and the Marines of the 4th Marine Division were much better supplied with the necessary amphibious equipment to effect such a landing than had been the 2d Marine Division at Betio. Finally, and most significant, was the tremendous quantity of shells and bombs thrown into and dropped on the target before the main landings took place. Admiral Conolly's Northern Attack Force conclusively demonstrated that in small-island amphibious operations a prolonged preliminary bombardment could preclude a high casualty list.

CHAPTER XIX

The Seizure of Eniwetok Atoll

Plans and Preparations

The easy capture of Kwajalein Atoll provided the Central Pacific forces with an unexpected opportunity to advance their schedule of operations. Since the original directive of 20 July 1943, plans had been formulated by Admiral Nimitz, with the concurrence of the Joint Chiefs of Staff, for an expansion of the American offensive in the Central Pacific. These plans had contemplated the capture of Eniwetok Atoll, on or about 1 May 1944, in preparation for a possible seizure of Truk or other islands in the Carolines. A strike by the main elements of the Pacific Fleet against Truk had been tentatively scheduled for 24 March 1944, prior to the landings on Eniwetok and Truk.[1] The 27th Infantry Division had been alerted on 13 January 1944 to prepare for the seizure of Eniwetok.[2] Preparations for this new move were already in their preliminary stage when the landings in the Marshalls took place.

The possibility that the operations against Kwajalein might be concluded early enough to step up the advance against Eniwetok had been considered by Admiral Nimitz and other naval planners even before the Marshalls operation was launched. Admiral Spruance later recalled that before sailing for Kwajalein from Pearl Harbor he had received the first aerial photographs of Eniwetok indicating that the atoll was only lightly defended,

but other indications were that the garrison was being reinforced by several thousand troops. He reported these findings to Nimitz and expressed the hope that immediately upon the conclusion of the Kwajalein-Majuro operation he might proceed to the capture of Eniwetok rather than send his fleet to the South Pacific for the attack against Kavieng, which the Joint Chiefs of Staff had scheduled for 1 April 1944.[3]

By 2 February it had become apparent that Kwajalein could be completely secured without the commitment of the reserve troops—the 22d Marines and the 106th Infantry (less 2d Battalion). Admiral Nimitz radioed Spruance asking his recommendation on proceeding immediately to the capture of Eniwetok, covering it with a carrier strike against Truk. After consulting with Admiral Turner and General Holland Smith at Kwajalein, Admiral Spruance recommended approval, and the decision to strike at Eniwetok was confirmed.[4]

On 3 February, Admiral Hill, who had commanded the brief assault on Majuro,

---

[1] Memo, CINCPOA for JCS, 13 Jan 44, CINCPOA Serial 004, Campaign Plan GRANITE.
[2] Rad, COMGENCENPAC to CG 27th Inf Div, 13 Jan 44, in 27th Inf Div G-3 Jnl, 13 Jan 44.
[3] Ltr, Vice Adm Raymond A. Spruance to Jeter A. Isely, 14 Jan 49, filed in Princeton University Library; Morison, Aleutians, Gilberts and Marshalls, p. 285.
[4] Ltr, Vice Adm Raymond A. Spruance to Maj Gen Harry J. Malony, 6 Jan 49, filed in OCMH; Ltr, Spruance to Isely, 14 Jan 49.

was flown by seaplane to Kwajalein. He proceeded at once to a series of conferences with Admirals Spruance and Turner, and from these conferences the basic plans for the invasion of Eniwetok were formulated.[5]

No operation that preceded or followed it in the Central Pacific had the same impromptu character that marked the seizure of Eniwetok. Formal planning may be said to have begun no earlier than 3 February and lasted until 15 February, the day on which the expedition sailed for Kwajalein lagoon. The invasion force was assembled in a seven-day period, beginning with the conclusion of the Kwajalein campaign and ending the moment the ships sailed into the open sea. While the expedition against Eniwetok was not exactly makeshift, it was, by previous standards, thrown together hurriedly without the meticulous preparation that characterized most large-scale amphibious operations.

The plan for the seizure of Eniwetok included the ambitious project of a full-scale carrier strike against Truk, which lay about 670 nautical miles southwest of Eniwetok Atoll. Truk had long been known to Americans as the "Gibraltar of the Pacific" and the "Japanese Pearl Harbor." It possessed the best fleet anchorage in all the Japanese Mandated Islands and since July 1942 had been the base for the *Combined Fleet,* now under command of Admiral Koga. Also, Truk served as headquarters for the *6th Fleet* (submarines) and was an important air base and staging point between Japan and the South Pacific.[6]

Admiral Mitscher's fast carrier force (Task Force 58) was assigned the job of conducting a full-scale strike against Truk on 16 February, partly to cover the Eniwetok landing but, more important, to hit the *Combined Fleet,* which was thought to be still based there, as well as to damage the

airfields and destroy any planes that might be found there. After completion of the move against the eastern Carolines, Mitscher's task force was to proceed on northwest and strike at the Marianas, if feasible.[7]

Eniwetok Atoll, the target assigned to Admiral Hill's task group, lies 330 nautical miles northwest of Kwajalein.[8] It is a typical Central Pacific coral atoll with a circular reef surrounding a lagoon, which at its widest point is seventeen miles from east to west and twenty-one miles from north to south. Some thirty small islands rise from the reef, most of them along the eastern half. The main islands, three in number, were Engebi in the north, Parry in the southeast, and Eniwetok in the south. There were, at the time of the invasion, only two deep-water passages into the lagoon. One, called Wide Passage, was located at the extreme southern end of the lagoon to the west of Eniwetok Island. The other was Deep Passage, lying between Parry and Japtan Islands. *(Map 16)*

When planning for the operation began, intelligence of the atoll was vague. One reconnaissance mission, flown from the Gilberts on 28 December, had managed to reach the atoll and take air photographs from an altitude of 20,000 feet. Other aerial photos, taken during the neutralization strikes that accompanied the Kwajalein landings, became available during the planning period, and additional photographs were dropped from planes onto the

---

[5] Commander Eniwetok Expeditionary Group (TG 51.11) (Adm H. W. Hill) Report of Eniwetok Operations, 7 Mar 44 (hereafter cited as TG 51.11 Eniwetok Rpt), p. 1.

[6] Morison, *Aleutians, Gilberts and Marshalls,* pp. 315–17.

[7] CINCPAC-CINCPOA Opns in POA, Feb 44, Annex B.

[8] JICPOA Bull 3-44, 20 Jan 44, pp. 1–5.

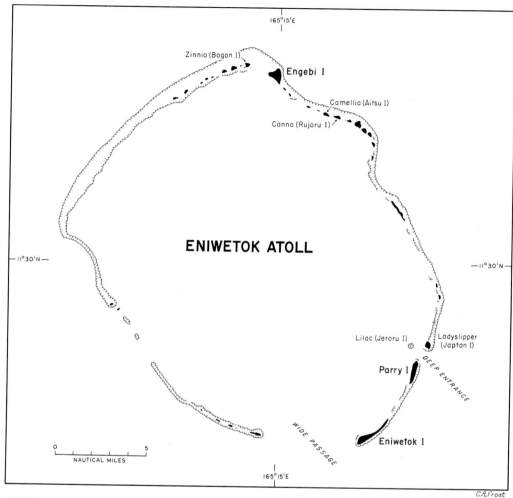

165°15'E

Zinnia (Bogon I)

Engebi I

Camellia (Aitsu I)

Canna (Rujoru I)

ENIWETOK ATOLL

—11°30'N—   —11°30'N—

Lilac (Jeroru I)   Ladyslipper
                         (Japtan I)

Parry I

DEEP ENTRANCE

0   5
NAUTICAL MILES

WIDE PASSAGE

Eniwetok I

165°15'E

C.R.Frost

MAP 16

ships of the invasion convoy while the vessels were en route to the target.[9]

Until early January, the best American intelligence sources indicated that there were only about 700 Japanese in the atoll, mostly concentrated on Engebi Island, which contained the only airstrip in the area. Late in January, however, it became apparent that the atoll might have been recently reinforced. From documents captured at Kwajalein, the presence of the Japanese *1st Amphibious Brigade* in the Marshalls became known. American intelligence staffs at that time knew it as the *1st Mobile Shipborne Brigade* and surmised from its designation that it might be stationed aboard ships so as to be transferred readily from one atoll to another. The brigade had been traced to Truk, thence eastward, but had been lost by American submarines be-

[9] COMINCH P-002, p. IV-7.

fore its arrival at its ultimate destination. The ships had not been located during the invasion strikes. Captured documents from Kwajalein and a prisoner of war who had formerly been a member of the Kwajalein detachment of the brigade confirmed the planners' fears that the main strength of the unit was at Eniwetok. This information, received during the first week of planning, caused the estimate of the Eniwetok Atoll garrison to be revised upward to 2,900–4,000 troops. Air photographs taken during the assault on Kwajalein indicated that most of the above-ground installations on Engebi showed a considerable increase in the foxhole and trench systems, but failed to disclose any indication of troops on Parry beyond the location of a few new foxholes. On Eniwetok Island, approximately fifty new foxholes were discovered as well as indications of small enemy forces near the southwest end of the island. On the basis of interpretations made from these later photographs, it was assumed that the main body of the Japanese garrison, whatever its strength, would be found on Engebi, and that Parry and Eniwetok Islands would be only lightly defended.[10]

Composition of the Force

The Eniwetok expedition was to be much smaller than the one that had just captured Kwajalein. In organizing it, Admiral Hill modeled his force after the Majuro Landing Force rather than adopt the more elaborate task force organization for Kwajalein. The force was known as the Eniwetok Expeditionary Group. Admiral Hill's flagship was the attack transport *Cambria,* which had been converted to an amphibious headquarters ship by the addition of much additional radio equipment and other communications facilities. The troops with their supplies and equipment were to be lifted aboard five attack transports, one transport, two attack cargo ships, one cargo ship, one dock landing ship, two high-speed (destroyer) transports, and nine LST's. This transport group, which also included six LCI's, was to be screened en route by ten destroyers. The naval fire support group, commanded by Rear Adm. Jesse B. Oldendorf, USN, contained three battleships, three heavy cruisers, and seven destroyers. Air support would be provided by an escort carrier group containing three escort carriers and three destroyers, and a fast carrier group (Task Group 58.4, detached from Admiral Mitscher's carrier task force) containing one heavy carrier (CV), two light carriers (CVL), two heavy cruisers, one light antiaircraft cruiser (CL(AA)), and eight destroyers. Finally, a group of three mine sweepers was attached.[11]

The assault troops assigned to the expedition consisted mainly of the 106th Infantry Regiment, reinforced (less the 2d Battalion), commanded by Col. Russell A. Ayers, USA, and the 22d Marine Regimental Combat Team commanded by Col. John T. Walker, USMC. Both were joined under a temporary command echelon entitled Tactical Group One, V Amphibious Corps, commanded by Brig. Gen. Thomas E. Watson, USMC. This command also included several other units that had been detached from the Kwajalein attack forces after completing their duties there. These included the V Amphibious Corps Reconnaissance Company, the Scout Company (Company D) of the 4th Marine Tank Division, Company A of the 708th Amphibian Tank Battalion (17 amphibian

---

[10] RCT 106 Unit Opns Rpt DOWNSIDE, 25 May 44, p. 10; TG 51.11 Eniwetok Rpt, pp. 1–2.
[11] TG 51.11 Eniwetok Rpt, Incl A, pp. 1–4.

CHART 3—TASK ORGANIZATION OF MAJOR COMMANDS FOR THE ATTACK ON ENIWETOK
ATOLL

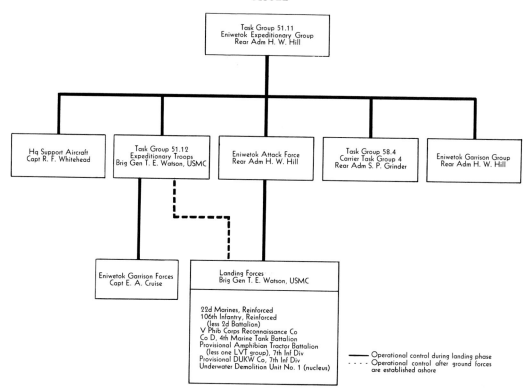

tanks), the 708th Amphibian Tractor Battalion (less one LVT group) totaling 102 LVT's, a provisional DUKW company of the 7th Infantry Division (30 DUKW's and 4 LVT's), and part of Demolition Team 1. The total landing force came to 7,997 men.[12]

Except for those units that had participated in the landings at Kwajalein, the assault troops assigned to Eniwetok lacked the intense training that usually preceded amphibious invasions in the Pacific. The 106th Regiment had received some amphibious training in the Hawaiian area in the early autumn of 1943 when it had been thought that the entire 27th Division would invade Nauru, but subsequent specialized

training had been only sketchy because of the last-minute assignment of the unit to the reserve force for the Kwajalein operation.[13] The 22d Marines, stationed on Samoa since mid-1942, had only moved to the Hawaiian area in November of 1943, and its eleventh-hour training too was sketchy.[14] Both units suffered from want of realistic amphibious rehearsals. About all they had been able to accomplish before sailing for Kwajalein were simple practices

[12] RCT 106 FO 2, Annex B, 12 Feb 44, p. 1; CINCPAC-CINCPOA Opns in POA, Feb 44, Annex B, p. 7.
[13] USAFICPA Participation Rpt Kwajalein and Eniwetok Opns, p. 199.
[14] Bevan G. Cass, ed., *History of the Sixth Marine Division* (Washington, 1948), p. 8.

in ship-to-shore movements. Not enough amphtracks were available and there were no DUKW's. During the operation itself most of the troops were landed in amphtracks for their first time. The Marine artillery battalion landed for its first time in DUKW's. The rehearsal held on the island of Maui had not permitted any appreciable advance inland, no combat firing, no infantry-tank team movement. In short, the troops destined for Eniwetok were greener than most going into actual amphibious combat for the first time.[15]

Tactical Plans

Initially, the target date recommended was 12 February, but was later changed to 15 February, and finally established for the 17th of that month.[16] The assault was originally divided into four phases. Phase I was to take place on D Day, 17 February. Following the usual preliminary gunfire, aerial bombardment, and mine sweeping operations, the Reconnaissance Company, V Amphibious Corps, was to land initially on Camellia (Aitsu) and Canna (Rujoru) Islands southeast of Engebi. At the same time the scout company (Company D), 4th Marine Tank Battalion, was to land on Zinnia (Bogon) Island northwest of Engebi to prevent any escape of the enemy from Engebi in that direction. Once Camellia and Canna were secured, the 2d Separate Pack Howitzer Battalion (Marine) with 75-mm. pack howitzers was to land on Camellia, and the 104th Field Artillery Battalion (Army) with 105-mm. howitzers was to land on Canna. The two battalions were then to prepare to support the next day's attack on Engebi. Phase II was to commence on 18 February. The 22d Marine Regiment was to land on the lagoon shore of Engebi with two battalions abreast

and capture that island. One platoon of the 106th Infantry's Cannon Company, consisting of two self-propelled 105-mm. guns, was to support the marines. The 106th Regimental Combat Team was to act as group reserve during this phase. During Phase III of the operation, Eniwetok and Parry Islands in the southern sector of the atoll were to be seized, the date depending upon the progress of the attack on Engebi. The 106th Infantry with the 2d Separate Tank Company (Marine medium tanks) attached, was to land in column of battalions on Eniwetok Island and capture it. One battalion of the 22d Marines was to be prepared to land in support if necessary, while the remaining marines were to occupy the other small islands in the northern sector of the atoll. It was presumed that Eniwetok Island would be only lightly defended, so the 106th was ordered to be prepared to land on Parry Island within two hours after the initial assault on Eniwetok. During Phase IV, the remainder of the islands in the atoll were to be occupied by troops of both the Marine and the Army regiments.[17]

Preliminary Air Operations

As the Eniwetok Expeditionary Group sailed from Kwajalein lagoon on 15 February, Marc Mitscher's mighty flotilla of fast carriers was moving swiftly westward toward that most fearsome of all of Japan's island bases in the Central Pacific—Truk. With three of its fast carrier groups (the fourth was detached to support the Eniwetok landings), Task Force 58 set sail from

---

[15] CG Tactical Group 1, V Amphibious Corps (Gen Watson), Special Report Concerning FLINTLOCK and CATCHPOLE Operations, 1 Mar 44 (hereafter cited as Tac Gp 1 Sp Rpt), p. 7.
[16] TG 51.11 Eniwetok Rpt, p. 2.
[17] Tac Gp 1 Opn Order 2-44, 10 Feb 44.

Majuro on 12 February. Operating under the command of Admiral Spruance, who carried his flag aboard the new battleship *New Jersey,* Task Force 58 consisted of 5 heavy carriers, 4 light carriers, 6 battleships, 10 cruisers of various sizes, and 28 destroyers.[18] After refueling at sea, Mitscher's ships arrived off of Truk in the early morning of 17 February (Tokyo time) and launched their first fighter sweep of seventy planes, which attacked aircraft and airfields at dawn. The strike was eminently successful. A total destruction of 128 enemy planes (72 on the ground and 56 in the air) was credited to the U.S. naval pilots with the loss of only four American planes.[19] Immediately after the fighter strike, eighteen torpedo bombers dropped fragmentary clusters on most of the airfields, rendering them temporarily unserviceable. Next day the main strike against shipping in the harbor was made. Naval planners had hoped to catch a sizable element of the *Combined Fleet* at Truk, where it had been sighted two weeks earlier by Marine reconnaissance planes. Unfortunately, Admiral Koga was alert to the impending danger and had set sail with most of his fleet for Palau before the U.S. carriers arrived. Nevertheless, the Japanese merchant marine suffered a severe blow as a result of the strikes. A total of about 200,000 tons of merchant shipping was destroyed in the harbor. Also, while the carrier planes were working over Truk itself, Admiral Spruance's support ships were able to intercept and sink one light cruiser and one destroyer trying to escape from the area. A third Japanese destroyer got away.

Meanwhile, the fourth fast carrier group (Task Group 58.4), which had been attached to Admiral Hill's command, proceeded directly against Eniwetok on 16 February, the day before the expeditionary force arrived. There, the planes destroyed all buildings of any consequence, rendered the airfield at Engebi temporarily useless, and demolished one of the two coastal defense guns on the northeast corner of that island. The airfield was pitted with bomb craters, and an estimated fourteen enemy aircraft were destroyed on the ground. In addition, last-minute aerial photographs were taken and delivered to Admiral Hill's flagship, *Cambria,* at sea en route to the target.[20]

Japanese Defenses on Eniwetok Atoll

Although before the attack on Pearl Harbor the Japanese Navy had conducted extensive construction projects in the Marshall Islands, Eniwetok had been largely overlooked. Up to that time Japanese plans called for the atoll to be used only as a fuel storage depot, and on 5 September 1941, the *4th Fleet* ordered 1,416,000 yen ($336,583.20) to be set aside for the construction of a fuel tank, feed pipe, and living quarters for the personnel to man the depot.[21]

Evidently, the first Japanese garrison on Eniwetok was a small detachment of six men sent from the *61st Guard Force* at Kwa-

---

[18] This account of the Truk strike is derived from the following sources: CINCPAC-CINCPOA Opns in POA, Feb 44, Incl B, pars. 164–219; Office of the Secretary of Defense, Weapons Systems Evaluation Group, Staff Study 4, Operational Experience of Fast Carrier Task Forces in World War II, 15 August 1951, pp. 163–64; Morison, *Aleutians, Gilberts and Marshalls,* pp. 315–32.

[19] CINCPAC-CINCPOA Opns in POA, Feb 44, par. 177. These claims are probably exaggerated. Morison estimates Japanese losses in the air to be over thirty and on the ground about forty. (Morison, *Aleutians, Gilberts and Marshalls,* p. 320.)

[20] TG 51.11 Eniwetok Rpt, Incl A, p. 38.

[21] Special Forces, Early Series, Vol. 10, NA 12255, WDC 161009.

jalein to man a special lookout station.[22] In November 1942 about three hundred construction workers landed at Engebi. The next month about five hundred workers of the *4th Fleet Construction Department* were sent to Eniwetok to construct an airfield. The field was completed in June or July of 1943, whereupon the majority of the construction personnel were transferred to Kwajalein. Sometime between August and October 1943 a small naval garrison force, never totaling more than sixty-one men, arrived at the atoll to garrison Engebi and its air base. This garrison maintained three lookout stations, a branch naval post office, a battery of two 12-cm. guns, and two twin-mount 13-mm. machine guns. The tiny force was the only ground combat unit on Eniwetok Atoll before the arrival of the *1st Amphibious Brigade* on 4 January 1944.[23]

Thus Eniwetok Atoll was left practically unprotected, with no major system of prepared defenses. The *1st Amphibious Brigade* arrived less than a month and a half before the American landings and barely had time to dig in. The contrast between the Japanese capacities here and at Kwajalein are obvious. In the latter atoll the fortifications had taken years to construct. Some of the units at Kwajalein had been there since before Pearl Harbor and were certainly prepared to defend the base long before U.S. forces attacked it. At Eniwetok, over 2,500 troops were dumped on a lonely atoll almost barren of defenses only six weeks before the American landings.

The *1st Amphibious Brigade,* which totaled 3,940 troops, may have originally been intended to serve as a mobile reserve force for the entire Marshalls area, to be based at Kwajalein and rushed to other threatened atolls. But when the brigade reached Truk on 27 December it was ordered to be parceled out to Wotje, Maloelap, Kwaja-

lein, and Eniwetok to reinforce the garrisons on those atolls. The brigade left Truk on 30 December, reaching Eniwetok on 4 January. There, the Eniwetok detachment consisting of 2,586 troops was detached and the convoy left for Kwajalein and elsewhere.[24]

In addition to the 2,586 troops of the brigade, there were stationed on Eniwetok Atoll at the time of the attack almost a thousand other enemy personnel: civilian employees of the brigade; fifty-nine men of the *61st Guard Force Detachment,* which had been there since October of 1943; air personnel that were in the process of being evacuated; a small survey party of about fifty men; Japanese and Korean construction workers; laborers hired by the Sankyu Transportation Company; and an unknown number of naval stragglers. This brought the total to about 3,500, but of this number only the brigade and the *61st Guard Force Detachment* could be considered effective combat troops.[25] Thus, in terms of numbers alone, Eniwetok housed more combat troops than Kwajalein, but this difference was more than offset by the comparative paucity of fortifications on Eniwetok Atoll.

Contrary to American expectations, the bulk of the enemy personnel at the time of the landings was located on Parry Island rather than on Engebi. Parry was the headquarters of Maj. Gen. Yoshimi Nishida, who commanded the brigade, and on

---

[22] JICPOA Translation 3998, *6th Base Force Secret Directive* 104-43.

[23] JICPOA Bull 89-44, Japanese Defense of Eniwetok Atoll, 12 Jun 44, p. 3.

[24] The 729 men for the Wotje detachment were caught at Kwajalein by the American invasion. (JICPOA Bull 88-44, *1st Amphibious Brigade,* Japanese Army, 13 Jun 44, pp. 6–7.)

[25] JICPOA Bull 89-44, Japanese Defense of Eniwetok Atoll, 12 Jun 44, pp. 4–5.

this island Nishida had stationed the bri- gade reserve and the Parry Island garrison, totaling 1,115 troops, with almost 250 other personnel. The troops had with them a total of thirty-six heavy grenade dis- chargers, thirty-six light machine guns, six heavy machine guns, ten 81-mm. mortars, three 20-mm. automatic guns, two moun- tain guns, one 20-mm. cannon, and three light tanks.

The defense plans for Parry were out- lined in a brigade order dated 5 February 1944. About one half of the troops were disposed at the water's edge, where they were to be grouped into strong points about 140 feet apart. The defense of the beaches was to be supported by mountain guns, 20-mm. automatic guns, and other weap- ons. The mountain guns and 20-mm.'s were to fire first. Light and heavy machine guns were to fire on landing craft before and after they reached the underwater ob- stacles. Next, mortars and grenade throw- ers were to deliver concentrated fire against the enemy at the beaches and were to cover the sectors between fortified areas and strong points. To facilitate the employ- ment of artillery and heavy weapons, the order called for fields of fire to be cleared through coconut groves. The order gave quite explicit instructions for measures against tanks: "Destroy enemy tanks when they are stopped by obstacles by means of hollow charge anti-tank rifle grenades, close-in attack, land mines, water mines, and Molotov cocktails. Especially at night, have a part of the force attack them." [26]

The order made it very clear that the brigade was not expected to survive an American assault once it had established a beachhead. Any troops remaining after the Americans had landed in force were to assemble in a central area. Then, the order continued, ". . . sick and wounded who

cannot endure the battle will commit sui- cide. [Others] . . . will reorganize, return to battle as a unit, and die fighting." [27]

The Japanese were able to construct very few installations and gun positions above ground on Parry in the short time that the brigade was there. With very few exceptions, the defenses consisted of fox- holes and trenches. These fell into two categories, the old and the new. The old foxholes and trenches were located on the ocean side, were well constructed, and often lined with rocks or coconut logs. Relying on their estimate of American am- phibious tactics as demonstrated at Tara- wa, the Japanese more recently had undertaken heavier defenses on the lagoon side. These were freshly and hastily con- structed, and therefore much inferior. All entrenchments were well camouflaged, although the camouflage was superior on the ocean side. A typical strong point con- sisted of a spider-web pattern of entrench- ments. In the center of the web was a large personnel shelter lined and covered with coconut logs. Strips of corrugated iron and a thick layer of sand were placed over the log roof. The center was surrounded by a circle of foxholes ten to fifteen feet apart, mostly roofed over with corrugated iron. These holes were connected with one an- other by narrow trenches or tunnels. The trenches and tunnels on the outer edge of the web were in turn joined by radial trenches and tunnels to the shelter or con- trol foxhole in the center of the position. The entire web was extremely well camou- flaged and very difficult to locate. Parry was honeycombed with positions of this sort. [28]

---

[26] *Ibid.*, pp. 31–32.
[27] *Ibid.*, p. 34.
[28] TG 51.11 Eniwetok Rpt, Incl A, p. 62; Tac Gp 1 Sp Rpt, Incl C, p. 1.

On neighboring Eniwetok Island were stationed 779 Japanese combat troops of the brigade plus 24 civilian employees and 5 naval personnel manning the lookout station. The island was commanded by Lt. Col. Masahiro Hashida, and the garrison originally possessed a total of two flame throwers, thirteen grenade dischargers, twelve light machine guns, two heavy machine guns, one 50-mm. mortar, eleven 81-mm. mortars, one 20-mm. automatic gun, three 20-mm. cannons, and three light tanks.[29] The garrison was divided into five forces, three on the lagoon shore, one placed so as to cut off the narrow eastern neck of the island, and one to be held in reserve. The three lagoon shore forces were to place their weapons so as to obtain interlocking bands of fire over the surface of the lagoon. The force in the east was to protect the rear of the three lagoon shore forces from any American units landing on the northern tip of the island. The reserve force was placed to the rear of the forces on the lagoon shore, near the western tip of the island.[30]

As on Parry, the defenses consisted mostly of foxholes and trenches. Those on Eniwetok Island were better constructed and better camouflaged. After the capture of Kwajalein, the Japanese had begun construction of concrete pillboxes on the southwest tip of the island and had dug additional foxholes. Land mines were also found on Eniwetok.[31]

On Engebi, at the northern tip of the atoll, the garrison consisted of about 692 members of the *1st Amphibious Brigade* plus 54 naval personnel of the *61st Guard Force Detachment* and an additional 500 noncombat personnel. The garrison was commanded by Col. Toshio Yano. Its total weapon strength came to two flame throwers, thirteen grenade dispatchers,

twelve light machine guns, four heavy machine guns, two 37-mm. guns, one 50-mm. mortar, eleven 81-mm. mortars, one 20-mm. automatic gun, two 20-mm. cannons, two mountain guns, three light tanks, and two 12-cm. coast defense guns.[32]

Colonel Yano on 10 February made a very accurate estimate of American intentions:

The enemy will bomb this island either with carrier or land based planes and will bombard us from all sides with battleships and heavy cruisers. Directly following these bombardments, an amphibious force landing will be carried out.

It will be extremely difficult for the enemy to land here from the open sea because of the high waves and rugged reefs.

[Therefore] it is expected that they will . . . enter the atoll and carry out landing operations from the lagoon . . . making assaults on outlying islands, they will approach this island from all directions.[33]

Yano accordingly planned to concentrate his defensive system on the lagoon shore of this triangularly shaped island. The Japanese defenders were ordered to ". . . lure the enemy to the water's edge and then annihilate him with withering fire and continuous attacks." Most of the

[29] JICPOA Bulls 88-44 and 89-44. In addition the island may have contained two 75-mm. mountain guns (JICPOA Bull 89-44), although this was denied in Admiral Hill's report (TG 51.11 Eniwetok Rpt, Incl A, pp. 62-63).
[30] Reproduction of Japanese map in JICPOA Bull 89-44 p. 35.
The compass directions given here are not exact. Eniwetok Island does not lie due east and west, but is shaped like an arc. One end faces west but the rest of the island curves gradually so that the opposite tip faces approximately north-northeast. The bulk of the island, however, runs generally along an east-west axis, so to avoid confusion, locations on the island and direction of movement are stated in terms of cardinal compass points.
[31] TG 51.11 Eniwetok Rpt, Incl A, pp. 62-63.
[32] JICPOA Bulls 88-44 and 89-44.
[33] JICPOA Bull 89-44, p. 24.

prepared defenses and over half of the brigade detachment were concentrated at the center of the lagoon shore. The approach to this strong point was flanked by the fire of two 75-mm. mountain guns on the northwest corner and two 20-mm. machine cannon in the southern part of the concentration itself, as well as two 37-mm. guns emplaced on the southern tip. Frontal fire could be delivered by the 20-mm. automatic guns and the three tanks, each mounting 37-mm. guns.

Besides the main area of defense on the lagoon shore, three other strong points were established, one in each of the three apexes of the island triangle. The south corner contained the *2d Rifle Company* (less one rifle platoon) plus the 37-mm. gun platoon detached from Yano's artillery company. The west corner was composed of the artillery company (less its 37-mm. gun platoon) plus the rifle platoon detached from the *2d Rifle Company.* In the north corner of the island was located the *61st Guard Detachment,* manning the two 12-cm. coast defense guns.

Before the arrival of the *1st Amphibious Brigade,* the defensive system had been predicated on an assault from the ocean, for it was on the ocean sides of the island that the better-prepared and older trenches and dugouts were found. Not until after the arrival of the brigade were hasty efforts made toward fully organizing a defensive system along the lagoon shore. While the lagoon foxholes and trenches were numerous, they were hurriedly and rather poorly constructed. Most of them were located about three hundred yards inland and parallel to the lagoon beach. Dugouts of coconut log and earthwork embankments as well as some concrete pillboxes were on Engebi. The concrete was less than one foot in thickness, not reinforced, and had

a very low resistance to penetration and blast.[34]

The effectiveness of the Japanese defense of Eniwetok Atoll cannot, however, be estimated on the basis of Japanese plans, for by the time the first American troops landed on the atoll the enemy's strength had been greatly reduced. Air strikes were successful in inflicting considerable damage on installations and weapons and in causing a large number of casualties. The raids reduced the ammunition supplies and food stores. The medical situation at Eniwetok was very poor in the first place, and the reduction of food rations lowered the health and energy of the Japanese to such an extent that many were physically incapable of carrying on their assigned duties. Moreover, the frequency of the raids resulted in constant interruption to the work schedule and forced the Japanese to work at odd hours, often at night. These factors, together with the speed of the American advance from Kwajalein to Eniwetok, meant that the Japanese were only partially prepared before the preinvasion bombardment. This bombardment had the further effect of causing more damage and casualties, and partially, though not completely, disrupting organized resistance.[35]

---

[34] TG 51.11 Eniwetok Rpt, Incl A, p. 61; Tac Gp 1 Sp Rpt, p. 4.

[35] For Japanese accounts of the damage done by the preliminary aerial bombardment see: JICPOA Translation 7603, Excerpts Taken from the Diary of a Member of the *1st Amph Brigade;* JICPOA Translation 7811, Complete Translation of the Diary of 2d Lt Kakino; JICPOA Translation 6808, Excerpts from the Diary of Cpl Masamichi Kitama, *1st Bn Arty Co, 1st Amph Brigade;* JICPOA Translation 7005, Diary of WO Shionoya; JICPOA Translation 8200, Extracts from the Diary of NCO Norio Miyada; JICPOA Preliminary Interrogation Rpt 47, Interrogation of Sgt Takumi Furukawa, *Transportation Squad,* Captured 19 Feb 44 on Engebi.

The Seizure of Engebi Island

The two sections of Admiral Hill's Eniwetok Expeditionary Group arrived off the southeast coast of Eniwetok Atoll during the early morning of 17 February. The fire support ships separated for bombardment missions against Engebi, southwestern Eniwetok Island, and the islands flanking Deep Entrance, while the escort carrier group diverged to take station northeast of the atoll.[36] Naval gunfire opened at 0659 without eliciting return fire from the enemy. At 0750 the ships halted their bombardment for air attacks against Engebi and Eniwetok. These were completed at 0825 and 0907, respectively, and the firing ships then resumed their bombardment. Meanwhile, at 0700 mine sweepers commenced sweeping a channel through Wide Passage. LST's, though temporarily held up as the mine sweeper *Sage* swept a moored mine inside the lagoon, followed. Then the fire support ships and the main transport group steamed through Deep Passage, pouring 40-mm. automatic fire on Parry, Lilac (Jeroru), and Japtan Islands without response. Somewhat more than three hours later, the attack force reached its first stations in the northern part of the lagoon and preparations were begun for the initial landings on Canna and Camellia Islands, southeast of Engebi.

H Hour for the first landings was set at 1230, but unexpected delays developed. The subchaser, SC *1066*, which was supposed to act as convoy guide, took station off the wrong island. The high-speed transport *Kane* sent her boats to the wrong LST, and the Marine artillery battery was delayed in getting boated and to the line of departure. As a result, the commanding officer of SC *1066* was relieved as was the commander of the Marine 2d Separate Pack Howitzer Battalion.[37]

In spite of these contretemps, the first amphtracks, carrying troops of the V Amphibious Corps Reconnaissance Company and supported by two destroyers, made unopposed landings on Canna and Camellia Islands at 1318. Shortly before 1400 the landing troops reported that no enemy was present, and the 75-mm. pieces of the 2d Separate Pack Howitzer Battalion and the 105-mm. howitzers of the 104th Field Artillery Battalion were taken ashore in DUKW's manned by the provisional DUKW company of the 7th Infantry Division. As at Kwajalein, some of the DUKW's carrying the 105-mm. pieces were fitted with special A-frames for use in unloading after landing. Guns, five units of fire, and gun crews were landed without difficulty. At 1602 all artillery had reached the beach and within half an hour was in position and prepared to register on Engebi. Registration was carried out without cessation of naval gunfire and was completed by 1902. About forty minutes later night harassing fires were commenced against Engebi. The mean range for the pack howitzer battalion was 6,900 yards and for the field artillery battalion, 8,100 yards. Fires throughout the night were executed at the rate of two rounds per gun per minute for five minutes every half hour.[38]

While the artillery was being emplaced, the naval underwater demolition unit reconnoitered the lagoon beaches off Engebi. As the battleships *Colorado* and *Tennessee*, destroyers *Heermann* and *McCord,* and one LCI(G) fired over their heads, the doughty

---

[36] This account of D-Day activities, unless otherwise indicated, is derived from the following sources: TG 51.11 Eniwetok Rpt, Incl A, pp. 18–20, 64, 85; Tac Gp 1 Jnl, 17 Feb 44.

[37] Morison, *Aleutians, Gilberts and Marshalls*, p. 291; Tac Gp 1 Jnl, 17 Feb 44, Msg 83.

[38] TG 51.11 Eniwetok Rpt, Incl A, p. 85.

swimmers went as close as fifty yards from the shore. In spite of intermittent machine gun fire from the beaches, the team accomplished its mission without casualties. No underwater obstacles were discovered, and boat lanes and shoal spots were buoyed.

After securing Canna and Camellia, the Reconnaissance Company landed, against no opposition, on the three islands northwest of Camellia and on two small unnamed islands west of Canna. These landings were made to offer security to the artillery units against possible Japanese infiltration during the night. In addition, the scout company of the 4th Marine Tank Battalion was ordered to land on Zinnia (Bogon), just west of Engebi, to forestall the possibility of Japanese escaping from Engebi. This latter plan miscarried somewhat when some of the rubber boats carrying the scout company got lost in the dark and had to return to their mother ship, the APD *Schley*. The remainder, however, under the company commander, succeeded in landing at a point two islands below Zinnia and by 0315 worked their way northward to the proper island, which they found unoccupied.

Thus D-Day operations were carried through successfully in spite of some minor delays and errors in landing. No American casualties were sustained. The stage was set for the attack on Engebi.[39]

The plan for the main attack on 18 February called for an assault by the 22d Marines against the lagoon shore of Engebi. W Hour was set at 0845. The two landing beaches extended 750 yards along the lagoon, with a finger pier as a dividing marker. *(Map 17)* The 1st Battalion, 22d Marines, was to land on White Beach 1 on the right, the 2d Battalion on Blue Beach 3 at the left. The two battalions were to be supported by medium tanks of the 2d Separate Tank Company, and a platoon from the Cannon Company, 106th Infantry, with two 105-mm. self-propelled guns. The 3d Marine Battalion was in regimental reserve while the 1st and 3d Battalions, 106th Infantry, waited aboard ship, prepared to support the attack if necessary.

At 0655 *Colorado* and *Louisville* began shelling the northern and eastern part of the island. *Tennessee* and *Pennsylvania* moved at dawn to deliver close-range destructive fire against beach defenses from flanking positions on each side of the boat lanes. At 0720 two destroyers, *Phelps* and *Hall,* moved into position as direct support ships, but because of the smoke and dust rising from the island, *Hall* was unable to fire. Just before 0800 the naval guns ceased fire to allow a half-hour air strike to take place. This was completed ahead of schedule and naval fire was resumed at 0811 and increased steadily in intensity until just before the first troops landed. Shortly after the air strike was lifted, artillery on Canna and Camellia joined the naval guns and began to fire on the beaches at maximum rate until just after the first wave landed at 0844, whereupon the artillery barrage was lifted inland to the center of the island for another five minutes. Thereafter, because of the smallness of the island, very few call missions were fired.

As usual, LCI gunboats preceded the first wave firing rockets and 40-mm. guns. On each flank of the first wave were five

---

[39] The following account of the action on Engebi on 18 February is, unless otherwise indicated, derived from: TG 51.11 Eniwetok Rpt, Incl A, pp. 2, 6, 21–24, 67; Tac Gp 1 Jnl, 18 Feb 44; 22d Marines Reinforced, Rpt on CATCHPOLE Opn, 9 Mar 44, pp. 6ff; Lt Col Arthur H. Weinberger, USMC, A Study of Amphibious Tactics—The Capture of Engebi Island, a monograph prepared for the 10th Section, Marine Corps School, Amphibious Warfare School, Senior Class.

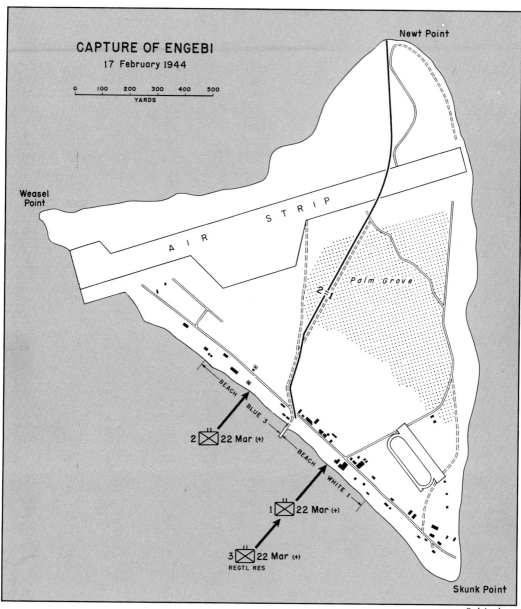

CAPTURE OF ENGEBI

17 February 1944

0   100   200   300   400   500

YARDS

Newt Point

Weasel Point

A I R   S T R I P

Palm Grove

BEACH BLUE 3

2 ⊠ 22 Mar (+)

BEACH WHITE I

1 ⊠ 22 Mar (+)

3 ⊠ 22 Mar (+)
REGTL RES

Skunk Point

R. Johnstone

MAP 17

armored amphibians; seven others were in
V formation in the center. As the leading
waves moved slowly from the line of departure, smoke and dust from the heavy
bombardment swept out over the water
obscuring the beaches from the crews and
disguising the gradual divergence of the
two assault battalions. The first waves of

ATTACK ON ENGEBI.

amphibian tractors tended to guide on LCI's operating to their flanks, and when the LCI's swung out from their direct approach to the beach and moved parallel to it, the leading LVT's tended to follow suit. Thus there was a gap between the two assault battalions by the time they reached the beach.

The armored amphibians moved quickly inland about a hundred yards, firing their 37-mm. guns at likely targets. Behind the first three waves of troops came the medium tank company, boated in LCM's. These landed on schedule with one unfortunate exception. One of the LCM's commenced to ship water because of a premature partial lowering of the bow ramp. In the tank this craft was carrying the crew was "buttoned up" and remained oblivious to frantic warnings as the craft filled up

and sank in forty feet of water, five hundred yards from the shore. Only one man escaped as the tank sank to the bottom of the lagoon.[40]

Enemy opposition on the beach was at first light. Almost the only noteworthy resistance came from a few automatic guns on Skunk Point, the southeastern tip of the island. Company A on the right of the 1st Battalion found its right flank exposed and had to delay the attack until the aid of a tank platoon was obtained. On the left, the 2d Battalion pushed forward rapidly, bypassing isolated points of resistance. These consisted chiefly of "spider-web" covered foxholes, similar to those that were to be encountered in greater number on Parry and Eniwetok Islands.

[40] USS *Ashland* Action Rpt Eniwetok Atoll, 3 May 44, p. 1.

The 2d Battalion overran the airfield quickly and within less than an hour tanks had pushed forward as far as the northern part of the island. By 0925 the troops were so far inland that the scheduled naval gunfire had to be called off. At 0955 the 3d Battalion in reserve was landed and started the tedious job of ferreting the Japanese out of various tunnels and covered foxholes that had been bypassed by the assault battalions.

The only organized resistance occurred in the zone of the 1st Battalion in the area of Skunk Point. There, a large number of Japanese put up a stiff fight, but were slowly forced northward along the island's eastern shore and eventually isolated and cut down. This took time, not only because of the stubborness of the Japanese but also because of the heavy underbrush through which the marines had to move.

At 1450, about six hours after the initial landing, the island was declared secured. Mopping up continued, however, until the following afternoon. Meanwhile, before dark on 18 February the 3d Battalion and the 2d Separate Tank Company re-embarked for operations against Parry and Eniwetok. Total Marine casualties came to 85 killed and missing, and 521 wounded in action. In exchange, 1,276 of the enemy were killed and 16 prisoners of war taken.[41]

On the 18th and 19th of February the Scout and Reconnaissance Companies completed the search of all the smaller islands between Engebi and the major targets in southern Eniwetok Atoll.[42]

The Capture of Eniwetok Island

Before the arrival of the task force at Eniwetok, Phase III of the operation had been planned to include the capture of both Eniwetok and Parry Islands the day after Engebi was secured. Little was known about the defenses or garrisons of those two islands when this plan was drawn. It was hoped that information gathered at the targets would be sufficient to elaborate upon the original scheme of maneuver or to change it.

During the capture of Camellia and Canna Islands on 17 February, the V Amphibious Corps Reconnaissance Company had captured several natives who said that a thousand Japanese soldiers were stationed on Parry and Eniwetok. Attempts to verify this information proved futile, and its reliability was doubted because the prisoners questioned seemed to have no very clear idea as to what the numbers given really meant. On 18 February Japanese documents and prisoners taken on Engebi indicated that Eniwetok Island was defended by 556 soldiers, and that Parry's garrison came to 326, including General Nishida's brigade headquarters.[43]

In view of this increase in the estimated strength of the enemy garrison on Eniwetok Island, Admiral Hill modified his orders. The original plan called for sending the 106th Infantry into Eniwetok in column of battalions, then two hours later withdrawing one battalion to support the 22d Marines' attack on Parry. The new order called for the two battalions of the 106th to land abreast on Yellow Beaches 1 and 2 on the lagoon shore of Eniwetok. (Map 18) Attached was the 2d Separate Tank Battalion (Marine) and the 3d Battalion, 22d Marines, in reserve.[44] Immediately upon receipt of this change of orders,

[41] JICPOA Item 89-44, CINCPAC Analysis, Feb 44.
[42] TG 51.11 Eniwetok Rpt, Incl A, p. 23.
[43] RCT 106 FO 4, 181500 Feb 44; RCT 106 Rpt of Opns at Eniwetok, Incl 4, p. 1; TG 51.11 Eniwetok Rpt, Incl A, p. 58.
[44] RCT 106 Rpt on Amph Opns, 13 Mar 44, p. 18.

Colonel Ayers, commanding the 106th Regimental Combat Team, called a meeting of the members of his staff and other interested officers aboard the transport *Custer*. There, he set forth in detail his new plan of operation. The 1st Battalion was ordered to land on the right on Yellow Beach 2 and was charged with making the main effort to the west to clear the lower end of the island. The 3d Battalion was to land on Yellow Beach 1 and form a covering line just east of a road that bisected the island from the lagoon to the ocean shore. Only one company was to be employed for this maneuver, the purpose of which was to seal off the eastern end of the island against possible Japanese infiltration while the 1st Battalion was capturing the western end where most of the enemy defenses were presumed to be. The remainder of the 3d Battalion was to stand in regimental reserve in readiness to assist the 1st Battalion if necessary. After the west end of the island was cleared, the 1st Battalion was then to pass through the 3d Battalion and clean out the rest of the island.

The 3d Battalion, whose primary job was merely to conduct a holding action, was instructed to take only the combat equipment necessary for temporary action on the island. Its orders were: "If rifle fire is drawn, dont't sit and take it if [you] . . . can clean it out. But don't try to take the rest of the island—limited movement only."[45] Two platoons of medium tanks were assigned the 1st Battalion, the third platoon to be in reserve. Light tanks were ordered to remain aboard ship.

The Assault

The scheduled time for the landing on Eniwetok was 0900, 18 February. At 0710 two cruisers and two destroyers took position on the flanks of the boat lanes and commenced to deliver fire on the landing beaches at close range. Half an hour later a third destroyer commenced delivering interdiction fire east of the landing beaches and in another thirty minutes a fourth destroyer took position off the ocean side of the island and commenced bombardment from there. The amount of naval fire placed on Eniwetok was considerably less than that for either of the other two main targets. Whereas a total of 1,179.7 tons of naval shells had been fired on Engebi and 944.4 tons were to be used on Parry, Eniwetok Island received only 204.6 tons altogether.[46] Also, the attackers of Eniwetok were at a disadvantage since they did not have any preliminary artillery bombardment to support their landing.

Here as elsewhere in Eniwetok Atoll, the problem of delivering effective fire from naval ships differed from that in other parts of the Pacific. In former atoll operations, the main job for naval gunfire was to destroy heavy defenses, mostly above ground, such as pillboxes, blockhouses, and bomb shelters, all visible from the ships at close range. With a few exceptions on Engebi, this type of target was not in evidence at Eniwetok, the main defenses being covered foxholes and trench systems. Close-in direct fire could not be effectively delivered against these, because they were invisible from the ships and because at close range naval shells with their flat trajectory fire simply overshot the targets. A higher angle of fire was necessary, so Admiral Hill ordered his ships to increase their range once they had completed the destruction of all visible targets.[47]

45 *Ibid.*, p. 19.
46 Tac Gp 1, V Phib Corps, Rpt on Naval Gunfire Support During CATCHPOLE Opn, 19 Mar 44, p. 2; TG 51.11 Eniwetok Rpt, Incl A, p. 69.
47 TG 51.11 Eniwetok Rpt, Incl A, p. 77.

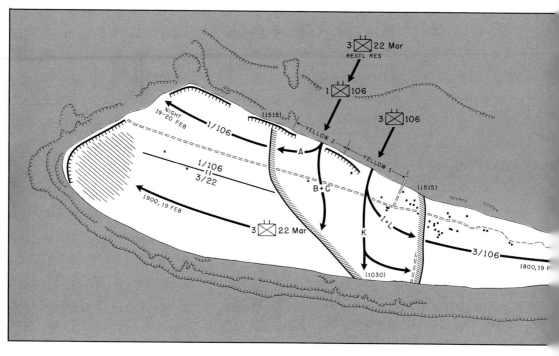

MAP 18

At 0810 naval gunfire was checked for fifteen minutes to allow carrier planes to bomb and strafe the beaches. LCI gunboats followed with a last-minute rocket saturation of the landing area and then turned right to deliver a special rocket bombardment against the western end of the island. Meanwhile, six LST's, each with seventeen LVT's aboard, had disembarked their contingents of assault troops at approximately 0730. There the amphtracks circled, waiting the arrival of the medium tanks of the 2d Separate Tank Company, which had been boated aboard LCM's the night before in the northern part of the atoll and were moving slowly through twenty-five miles of choppy water toward the line of departure off of Eniwetok Island. Fearful of a delay in the arrival of the tanks, Admiral Hill postponed

H Hour fifteen minutes. It shortly became apparent that the LCM's would arrive on schedule, so at 0909 the first wave drew up on the line of departure.

On the left in the zone of the 3d Battalion, Lt. Col. Harold I. Mizony, battalion commander, had Company L at the left and Company K on the right, with Company I following as reserve. Company L was to pivot on the pier on the left of Yellow Beach 1, turn left, and extend its line toward the ocean beaches. Company K was to open a corridor across the island behind it and then mop up in the rear of Company L's right flank near the ocean shore. In the right zone, Lt. Col. Winslow Cornett had planned a somewhat similar deployment for his 1st Battalion landing on Yellow Beach 2. Company B was to push straight inland along the battalion

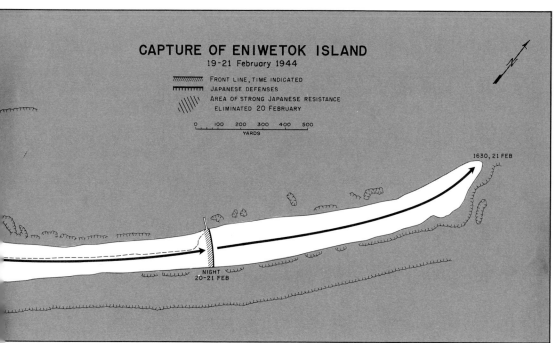

CAPTURE OF ENIWETOK ISLAND
19-21 February 1944

```
//////////   FRONT LINE, TIME INDICATED
mmmmm   JAPANESE DEFENSES
\\\\\\   AREA OF STRONG JAPANESE RESISTANCE
         ELIMINATED 20 FEBRUARY
```

```
0    100   200   300   400   500
            YARDS
```

1630, 21 FEB

NIGHT
20-21 FEB

H. Damon

boundary until it had crossed the east-west trail about a third of the way across the island. Then it was to swing to the right until its left wing reached out to the ocean. Company A was to land on the right half of Yellow Beach 2, pivot to the right, tie in with Company B, and together the two would move west to the end of the island. Company C, in reserve, was to advance to just south of the trail and secure a perimeter there, establishing a point for the battalion command post.

At 0917, just two minutes after the scheduled H Hour, the first wave hit the beach.[48] The landing plans went somewhat awry at the very outset. The island rose abruptly from the shore where a steep bluff eight or more feet high denied further progress to the LVT's. While some struggled to climb it, others remained on the beach or backed off, cluttering the landing area and tending to force later waves to come ashore beyond the assigned beach limits. Men dropped from LVT's onto the sand and obtained shelter behind the vehicles or the defilade next to the bluff, but enemy automatic and mortar fire caught some units and contributed to their disorganization. The enemy's plan of defense required sturdy opposition to the landings themselves. Preparatory fire had left the Japanese still

_____
[48] Unless otherwise indicated the following account of the morning's action on Eniwetok Island is derived from: RCT 106 Rpt on Amph Opns, 13 Mar 44; RCT 106 Jnl, 18 Feb 44; Tac Gp 1 Jnl, 18 Feb 44; War Department Special Staff Historical Division, Operations on Eniwetok Atoll, MS in OCMH. (This monograph was prepared by Edmund G. Love, historian attached to the 106th Regimental Combat Team during the Eniwetok operation. It is cited hereafter as Love, Opns on Eniwetok.)

INVASION OF ENIWETOK. *Landing craft pass support warships as they fire on the beach defenses of the island.*

able to resist from prepared positions directly inland from the beach and, in particular, from well-concealed positions that enfiladed parts of Yellow Beach 2.

Company B, on the left (east) of Yellow Beach 2, met difficulties at once. Its left and right flanks landed at the proper points, but the rest of the company was set ashore to the right and left of the designated positions. In front of the 3d Platoon at the left was an enemy strong point that had not been neutralized by preparatory fire. It consisted of a spider-web network of firing pits and radiating trenches, artfully concealed by vegetation, from which automatic and rifle fire and grenades struck the troops on the shore. As the men pushed inland through the position, the Japanese struck them from the flank or rear and then shifted by underground passages to other hidden vantage points. The enemy had to be rooted out by tactics improvised on the spot.

2d Lt. Ralph W. Hills and Pfc. William Hollowiak, caught within the strong point, at first merely lay on the ground shooting the enemy as they rose in their pits to fire toward the beach. Hollowiak found this method too slow. He got Hills to cover him while he crawled forward and fired into a hole, after which he would lift the covering frond and throw in a grenade. Then he in turn covered Hills while the 1st Platoon leader repeated the process. Hollowiak picked up a Japanese rifle and took ammunition from every dead Japanese and obtained grenades from all the wounded or dead Americans in his path. Scrambling forward in this fashion, the two men alone killed perhaps twenty of the enemy and knocked out seven or eight of the positions in fairly rapid sequence, thus neutralizing enough of the east side of the strong point so that Company K's right

wing could also press on toward the ocean.

1st Lt. Arthur Klein and one section of Company B's weapons platoon were set ashore on the westernmost portion of the beach. They made their way with some difficulty along the shore through Company A before striking inland from that part of Yellow Beach 2 originally assigned to Company B. The section reached the road by crossing the right side of the enemy strong point from which, however, the Japanese were no longer resisting; they then waited for Company A to arrive. Klein moved eastward alone along the road until he came upon Lieutenant Hills and Private Hollowiak, leaving the rest of his group to await Company A. He joined the Company B main body, which cleared the last of the enemy positions in the defense system there with the aid of an amphibian tank and its 37-mm. gun. In the absence of the company commander, Klein took command and reorganized the elements of Company B along the road, with the exception of the group he had led ashore, starting them on the second phase of their mission. By 1145 the left flank, under Lieutenant Hills, had pushed across the island jointly with elements of Company K, had subdued another enemy defense position, and had captured five native prisoners. Contact between Lieutenant Hills' detail and the remainder of Company B had been lost, however, during this advance. The right wing of Company B, about thirty men with rifles and carbines, was itself quickly divided into many small groups, separated by dense underbrush, and gaps also developed on both of its flanks.

Company A landed on the right (west) part of Yellow Beach 2 and struggled through a thick tangle of underbrush to the crest of the knoll on which it was to pivot to the west. Its right flank was cov-

MACHINE GUN SQUAD FIRING *its .30-caliber water-cooled weapon on an enemy position.*

ered by a patrol of four men under S. Sgt. Joseph A. Jasinski. Although the main body of the company made no contact with the enemy until it turned, the patrol encountered the first of a series of dugout and trench defenses almost immediately. The company's right flank also ran upon the eastern limits of these works shortly after it started inland but it was able to proceed well ahead of the hard-pressed patrol. Reinforcements, including two amphibian tanks with 37-mm. guns and some light tanks, were sent back, and the destruction of the enemy in these positions went forward rapidly. About 1330 the line from the lagoon inland was straightened.

Company C was expected to land behind Company B and to advance southward in the rear of Company B's turning movement to the west, beyond the trail. 1st Lt. Robert T. Bates, company commander, brought part of his unit ashore in one long line on Yellow Beach 2 in the fifth and sixth waves. The beach was already badly congested. Four boatloads of Company C were accidently brought in west of Yellow Beach 2, beyond the point at which Lieutenant Klein's section of Company B had landed. Three of the boats, a little apart from the others, were under heavy small arms fire for the last 150 yards; when the men in them started to rush across the beach, they were cut down by heavy fire from enemy machine guns. The machine guns were mounted on jutting points that permitted enfilade. Mortar fire also fell upon the attacking elements as some of the Americans sheltered behind their boats threw grenades into the area beyond the sea wall. Out of fifty-three men in the three boats, twenty were killed, fifteen were wounded, and only eighteen escaped unhurt in a fight that lasted over four hours. They were saved from complete annihilation by the westward advance of Company A along the lagoon shore.

The 1st Platoon of Company C had proceeded from the left side of Yellow Beach 2 without mishap and took up a front-line position in one of the gaps in the Company B line. They were under the mistaken impression that Company B was actually ahead of them. Shortly before noon, the platoon engaged in a stiff fire fight with a number of Japanese entrenched in a position beyond the trail. It was joined on the right by the 2d Platoon, Company B.

At noon, therefore, the front line of the 1st Battalion, 106th Infantry, was in the shape of an S, extending from the lagoon to the ocean. On the lagoon side, near the southwestern edge of Yellow Beach 2, the flank patrol of Company A was trying to work its way through an uninterrupted series of spider-web defenses. On the ocean side, a small detachment of Company B was digging in among the pits and trenches of an enemy position that they, with elements of Company K, had just captured. Between these two extremities, Company A extended from the lagoon to the trail, while Company C and Company B, intermingled, held a line running southerly through brush and palm grove, from trail to ocean. In the curving corridor crossing the island between the two battalions, Company K was then swinging to the eastward from the ocean side, having detached two squads to support Company B. A platoon of the 106th's Cannon Company, with two 75-mm. guns, was also in Company B's rear. Such was the situation

when the Japanese launched a counterattack.

The Japanese Counterattack

The American plan of attack, to establish a line holding the enemy at the east while the western end of the island was swept clear for field artillery emplacements, inadvertently brought the assaulting forces inland through outposts of the main enemy defensive system. In the western end of the island, the Japanese construction that had been noted in reconnaissance photographs was in fact part of an elaborate system. Underground and surface positions, including concrete pillboxes, immobilized tanks, and wire barricades, had been prepared to resist landings on that corner of Eniwetok Island. To meet the American attack after it penetrated the island farther east, the enemy abandoned all but the most important of the positions and sent between 300 and 400 men to deliver a counterattack. Well out of sight, they moved east in the brush on the southern side of the road and when they came to the American line shortly after noon, struck it on both sides of the trail.

Detachments of the enemy hit in quick succession and with severe effect parts of the American line extending southward as far as the ocean shore from a point just north of the trail. At some points, the Japanese actually broke through before they were cut down. In the center, their assault was prefaced by a concentrated mortar barrage and pressed home with extremely heavy small arms fire. Company B's line was temporarily broken but was re-formed under the determined leadership of Lieutenant Klein. The machine gunners of Companies B and D stood firm and finally stopped the enemy's advance. From positions about thirty yards west of their farthest progress, the Japanese then sent heavy automatic fire over the ground they had so recently assailed. The remnants of Company B, supported by elements of Company K and by machine guns, eventually wore the enemy down. At the extreme left of the American line, next to the ocean, a bitter five-minute hand-to-hand fight with knives and grenades checked one Japanese assault. A second charge was stopped by a supporting squad from Company K, aided by Sgt. William Toppin, a BAR man with Company I. By 1245 the counterattack had spent its force. The American line had been thinned but not broken.

Capture of Southwestern portion of the Island

The American attack to the west was now resumed. Company A on the right wing made slow progress through the enemy positions near the lagoon, but the mingled elements of Companies C and B, even after being reorganized and supported by three Cannon Company guns, could not push through the line taken up by the enemy at the end of his counterattack. Although it steadily reduced the Japanese positions, the attacking force was unable to move forward.

At 1245 Colonel Ayers ordered the 3d Battalion, 22d Marines, the reserve battalion, to land as soon as possible after 1330 to relieve the left half of the 1st Battalion line.[49] It had become apparent that one battalion was not sufficient to clear the western portion of the island. The 3d Battalion, 106th Infantry, had already been ordered at 1205 to attack to the eastern end of the island,[50] so the only alternative was to send in the Marines. The 3d Battalion, 22d Marines, commanded by Maj.

Clair W. Shisler, USMC, was ashore by 1425, passed through the 1st Battalion about an hour later and by 1605 had established contact with Company A. The boundary line between the Marine and Army battalions was to run down the middle of the island.[51] As the Marine battalion moved through the area south of the Japanese defensive positions that Lieutenant Klein's small force had engaged for the preceding three hours, it quickly straightened the line. Movement accelerated after 1645.[52]

Following the relief of the 1st Battalion on the left side of the line, Company C took over part of Company A's line on the right. Company B, after completing the reduction of a stubbornly defended pillbox near Yellow Beach 2, rested, reorganized, and eventually moved up to support the other two companies. About 1830 the swift movement of the marines on the left of the line had reached the last Japanese defensive position in the southwest corner of the island. As darkness approached, a gap existed between the Marine and 1st Battalion positions.

To deny to the enemy an opportunity for his customary aggressive night tactics, Colonel Ayers at 1850 ordered that the attack be pressed during the night.[53] Colonel Cornett then ordered Company B to relieve Company A. During these last minutes of daylight, Company A decided to continue its advance, which brought it abruptly to the seashore before Company B had arrived. In the darkness, units of the three companies joined in an irregular perimeter near the beach on the western

[49] RCT 106 Rpt of Opns at Eniwetok, Incl 5.
[50] RCT 106 Jnl, 19 Feb 44, Msg 43.
[51] Love, Opns on Eniwetok, pp. 56–57.
[52] RCT 106 Jnl, 19 Feb 44, Msg 72.
[53] *Ibid.*, Msgs 78, 82.

MARINES PREPARE TO ATTACK *a Japanese defensive position. Note flame thrower, which was frequently used to rout the defenders from their dug-in positions.*

corner of the lagoon shore. The Marines' right flank rested on the battalion boundary more than a hundred yards from the 1st Battalion's position. A gap existed through which the enemy could readily infiltrate. At 0910 a counterattack all along the Marines' front was repulsed, but from a deep shelter that had been missed, or through the gap between battalions, one group of about thirty Japanese succeeded in striking the Marine battalion command post.[54]

On the morning of 20 February the action on the western end of the island was concluded with some heavy fighting. The 3d Battalion, 22d Marines, found one of the main enemy defenses, manned by a strong and determined force, at the southwestern corner of the island in its zone. A combined force of light and medium tanks, five guns from the Cannon Company, 106th Infantry, and a supporting rifle company from the 1st Battalion, 106th Infantry, joined the Marines in destroying the enemy during the day.[55] The back of enemy resistance had been broken before the second night, and, except for small parties trying to infiltrate, no attacks upon the southern force were made during the night on Eniwetok Island. Early on the third morning the Marines and the tanks re-embarked in preparation for one more assault landing, that on Parry Island.

---

[54] Tac Gp 1 Unit Rpt 4, 20 Feb 44, p. 1.

[55] RCT 106 Jnl, 20 Feb 44, Msgs 101, 116, 120, 124, 135; RCT 106 Rpt of Opns at Eniwetok; Love, Opns on Eniwetok, p. 70.

The 1st Battalion, 106th Infantry, besides sending Company A to support the Marine unit on 20 February, mopped up its zone. Next day, after the withdrawal of the Marines, the battalion ran a line across the island from the pier and mopped up to the western end. Company A, at the right, finished first and returned to the battalion area near the landing beach. Company B, in the center, reached the end of the island a little later and then went for a swim. Company C, on the ocean side, found twenty-two of the enemy in hiding and destroyed them in a fire fight that sent some bullets over the heads of Company B's swimmers. Company B came out of the water, dressed, and rejoined the fight. The western end of Eniwetok Island was finally clear of Japanese. When the 3d Battalion left on 22 February on the LSD *Ashland* to be in floating reserve for the Parry Island action, the 1st Battalion assumed responsibility for the eastern part of Eniwetok Island as well. One more mopping up of the whole island took place on the 22d.[56]

Action of the 3d Battalion

The 3d Battalion, under Colonel Mizony, landed on Yellow Beach 1 simultaneously with the 1st Battalion at 0917 on 19 February. Company L was on the left, Company K on the right, Company I following in support. Beach conditions were quite similar to those on Yellow Beach 2. Enemy installations in the sandbank itself had been wrecked by the preparatory fire, but the damage to other covered defenses along the shore failed to neutralize them. When the assault squads of the first wave found themselves in the same sort of strong point as that holding up Company B on their right, they too had to investigate all

holes. Supporting troops working over the same ground later found some of the enemy still there.

Company L, at the extreme left, readily made its way beyond the trail, but there its right wing was engaged by two pillboxes. One platoon then went on ahead to the ocean beach, arriving there at 1010. It swung left to take up the eastward-facing line, found a hole covered by a palm frond, and a grenade was dropped. Following the explosion, the sounds of a familiar Christian hymn came from within the hole. Further investigation revealed an old man, the natives' chief, with six companions, and in another shelter nearby were twenty-six others. None had been hurt by the American fire. A sociable exchange of souvenirs and cigarettes ensued, after which the prisoners progressed to the beach.[57] Company L's line was established at the western edge of the area designated on the maps as a village. All the structures had been flattened except some concrete revetments. The enemy moved into position behind these barriers while the American line held a stationary position for over an hour, under a Japanese mortar barrage.

Company K's progress to the ocean side was impeded first by the eastern edge of the enemy strong point on which Lieutenant Hills and Private Hollowiak were working, next by a thick tangle of underbrush beyond the trail, and finally by an especially difficult area along the ocean shore. A belt of bushes rising six to twelve feet high, growing densely in a fringe of from ten to thirty-five yards in width, paralleled that shore for most of its length. In it, the enemy had concealed firing positions from which they inflicted so much damage that the entire area had to be

[56] Love, Opns on Eniwetok, p. 73.
[57] *Ibid.*, p. 77.

combed painstakingly during the movement along the island. As Company K began to swing east, it started to work through this barrier. At the same time, some of its units were engaged in repelling the major counterattack from the west.

The attack to the east, which was begun at 1515, was undertaken by Company L on the left and by Company I on the right. The latter company passed through Company L's right flank to take over that half of the line. Company K followed the advance as battalion reserve. After a fifteen-minute air strike the attack began.[58] Company L was able to sweep forward more rapidly than Company I because of the latter's difficulties with the belt of brush along the ocean. Contact was maintained during the remainder of the day, and as night fell, Colonel Mizony pulled back Company L sufficiently to straighten the line. For the remainder of the drive along the island, the company on the right was designated as the base unit. Thus, the entire line was paced by the slow advance on the extreme right wing. Barrages from artillery and naval guns failed to solve the problem. Light tanks were brought forward to run up and down through the brush; the bushes bent over as they passed and rose back in place behind them. Sgt. William A. Forsyth of the 2d Platoon, Company I, was sent to investigate after the tanks had run over one hidden Japanese position several times. He found what appeared to be a frond-covered hole, lifted the cover, and found two of the enemy grinning up at him. When all fire from this particular area had ceased, the whole platoon waded in and found the bodies of twenty-one Japanese.

One of the light tanks engaged in the task of reducing the enemy positions in the heavy foliage struck a land mine late in the afternoon while it was at the upper end of its run, some two hundred yards ahead of the infantry. Unable to move because of a lost track, the vehicle's occupants remained unresponsive to every effort to communicate with them. A small patrol managed to reach the tank and banged on its side, but the occupants, sure that the noise came from Japanese, refused to unbutton. The patrol retired. Just before sunset the vehicle's commander cautiously opened the turret, looked around and then crawled out to inspect the damage, leaving the turret open. As he reached the ground he was subjected to a fusillade of fire from several Japanese nearby and was forced to crawl, wounded, under the tank for protection. The enemy then came out of hiding and dropped a series of grenades and fired rifles into the open turret. Only two of the crew survived this attack, one of them the man lying underneath the vehicle. The 3d Battalion had continued to advance after dark, following the orders issued by Colonel Ayers. The night was dark, but frequent illumination was furnished by mortar flares. Its progress was slow and brought it to the tank at 0200. The Japanese, using the vehicle as a fortress, put up a stubborn fight at that point. When they were finally driven off, they left over forty bodies behind them.

The line moved forward twenty-five yards farther, again ran into heavy enemy fire and, at 0430, dug in for the remainder of the night. Naval guns continued, at intervals, to illuminate the enemy area with star shells. When daylight came at 0700, both Company L and Company I renewed the attack. At 1030, after two hard fire fights with the enemy in the brush belt, Company I was relieved by Company K.

---

[58] COMINCH P-002, p. II-19.

The line had reached the island's slender waist. No strong organized resistance was met thereafter but the brush was beaten continuously and slowly. Artillery and naval gunfire furnished support and drove the enemy from a machine gun nest observed near the center of the island. At a tank ditch that crossed the island from shore to shore, the enemy left rather clearly marked channels through a field of improvised land mines, and the attack was not seriously delayed by the obstacle. Gunfire destroyed other mines ahead of the advance.[59] Movement continued through thick smoke from brush fires in the center of the island, fires that detonated duds from the naval bombardment at considerable danger to American troops. During the second night, white phosphorus naval shells kept the eastern end of the island ablaze. Several casualties resulted from indiscriminate shooting and grenading in one of the company perimeters. Preceded by time fire to explode mines and harass the foe, the troops reached the tip of the island at 1630, 21 February.

Thus, in two and a half days Eniwetok Island was secured with a loss of 37 Americans killed and 94 wounded in action. Except for 23 prisoners taken, the total Japanese garrison of about 800 men was killed.[60] The capture of the island had been much slower than planners had anticipated. This was in part due to the relatively small amount of preparatory bombardment (as compared with that placed on other islands in the atoll), in part to the heavy underbrush that covered most of the eastern end of the island, and in part to the cleverness with which the enemy had constructed and concealed his underground entrenchments. However, some of the responsibility for the delay must be laid to the extreme caution that the troops of the 3d Battalion,

106th Infantry, displayed in their movement eastward.

Parry Island

The unexpected delay in the seizure of Eniwetok Island and the commitment of the 1st and 3d Battalions of the 106th Infantry in its reduction had caused a major change in plans for the seizure of Parry Island. Instead of a landing being made there on the same day as at Eniwetok Island, the initial invasion was postponed until the latter was secured.

Plans and Preparations

The delay in attacking Parry Island permitted better preparation than had been possible for the assault on Eniwetok Island. The most striking contrast was in the volume of preliminary fire, for which ample incentive was found in the report of prisoners that the Japanese force there was larger than on the other islands, and in the evidence supplied by a captured map of the enemy's prepared defenses.[61] For three days bombs and naval and artillery shells pounded the target. Naval shells dropped on the target totaled 944.4 tons, considerably more than the weight delivered on Eniwetok Island; the weight of artillery shells came to 245 tons, and bombs added 99 tons more.[62] The 104th Field Artillery Battalion had begun landing on Eniwetok Island late in the afternoon of 19 February and had completed its registration on Parry by noon the next day.[63] The 2d Sep-

---

[59] Love, Opns on Eniwetok, pp. 73–95.
[60] Morison, *Aleutians, Gilberts and Marshalls*, p. 304.
[61] TG 51.11 Eniwetok Rpt, Incl A, p. 60. A copy of the captured map is attached to this report.
[62] CINCPAC-CINCPOA Opns in POA, Feb 44, Annex B, p. 21.
[63] RCT 106 Jnl, 19 Feb 44, Msg 49.

PARRY ISLAND UNDER PRELIMINARY BOMBARDMENT

arate Pack Howitzer Battalion had landed on Japtan Island before noon on 20 February and joined in the preparation.[64]

The extra time was also used to give the landing forces of the first few waves some rest on LST's. The 3d Battalion, 22d Marines, was withdrawn accordingly from Eniwetok Island. Since the defense battalion had arrived at Engebi, the 1st and 2d Battalion Landing Teams of the 22d Marines were brought from there to southern Eniwetok in transports. To the main body of the landing troops, the two reconnaissance units that had completed the investigation of all the small islands were attached. The task group reserve was to consist of the 3d Battalion, 106th Infantry, kept in readiness afloat, and a battalion consisting of five improvised rifle companies, each of a hundred men, drawn

from the 10th Marine Defense Battalion shortly after its arrival on 21 February.[65]

The expedition was running low on ammunition and weapons. Naval and artillery shells were carefully apportioned. From all the ships, available grenades and demolition charges were gathered. To supplement them, 775 grenades and 1,500 percussion caps were flown in from Kwajalein while the attack was in progress. Other units surrendered BAR's and rifles to equip the 22d Marines.[66]

The regiment's plan of attack was completed and approved during the afternoon of 21 February in time to be fully understood by the participants. At 0900 the following morning, the touchdown was to be

[64] Tac Gp 1 Sp Rpt, p. 9.
[65] *Ibid.*
[66] *Ibid.*, p. 10.

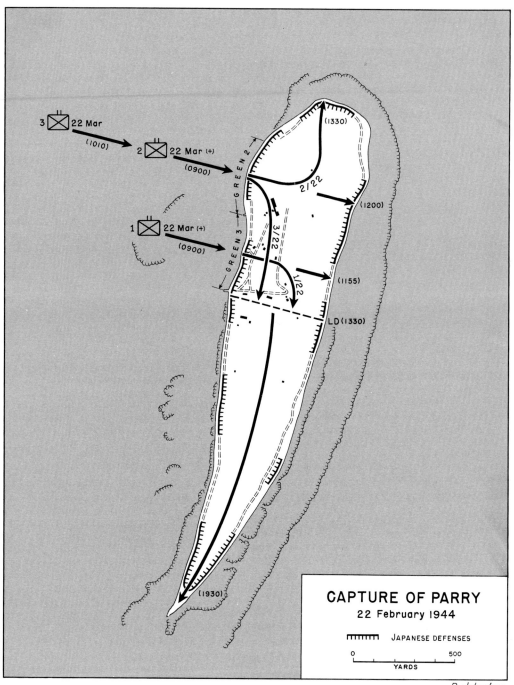

3 ⊠ 22 Mar
(1010)

2 ⊠ 22 Mar (+)
(0900)

1 ⊠ 22 Mar (+)
(0900)

GREEN 2

GREEN 3

(1330)

2/22

(1200)

3/22

1/22

(1155)

LD (1330)

(1930)

CAPTURE OF PARRY
22 February 1944

⟱⟱⟱ JAPANESE DEFENSES

0   500
YARDS

R. Johnstone

MAP 19

made on about six hundred yards of sandy beach just north of the pier on the lagoon side. *(Map 19)* From right to left, the 1st and 2d Battalions, 22d Marines, would go in abreast in the hard-worked LVT's and landing craft, and land between two areas developed as strong points by the defenders. The 3d Battalion would be in regimental reserve. The amphibian tanks of the 708th Amphibian Tractor Battalion would, for the third time at Eniwetok Atoll, slightly precede the waves of assault troops on the flanks and in the center, to deliver cross fires against enemy resistance at the beach. Medium tanks were to land in the third wave in LCM's. After seizing the beachhead, tanks and infantry were to press forward to the ocean side of the island, which at this point was about five hundred yards eastward from the landing beaches. An artillery barrage across the island south of the pier would block reinforcement from the southern part of the island, while the two portions of the attacking force prepared for the next phase of the operation.[67] The 2d Battalion, 22d Marines, at the left, was to clear the Japanese from the northern lobe of the island while the 1st Battalion would attack to the right and capture the southern portion.

The Seizure of Parry

The preliminary naval and air bombardment of Parry Island opened at dawn on 22 February. The battleships *Tennessee* and *Pennsylvania* took positions only 1,500 yards north of the landing area and not only mauled it with their big guns but also covered it with their 40-mm. automatic weapons batteries. From the other side of the boat lanes, the heavy cruisers *Indianapolis* and *Louisville* and the destroyer *Hailey* also fired. Smoke and dust blew out over

the lagoon without masking the target for the battleships but with serious consequences for the other three warships and for the landing craft that started ashore at 0845. Three of the LCI(G)'s that approached through the haze with the first wave to fire rockets were hit by 5-inch shells from *Hailey,* killing thirteen and wounding forty-seven.[68] Some LVT's landed outside the designated beaches, thus widening the front and making necessary the suspension of artillery fire in their vicinity. Other tractors crisscrossed or fell behind, so that the landing teams had difficulty in reorganizing on the beaches.

While the tractors made their fifteen-minute run from the line of departure, two formations of planes bombed Parry in the last of 219 sorties made during the six days of action at Eniwetok Atoll. This time they only bombed the island, omitting strafing runs because of the type of defense trench systems on Parry Island.[69]

The first troops struck Green Beaches 2 and 3 at 0900, with a wave of tractors and one of LCM's carrying medium tanks directly behind them. Heavy machine gun and mortar fire greeted the marines at the water's edge. As they tried to form an assault line, enfilading machine gun fire also struck them from a concealed position on the pier at the right. The machine guns were silenced by grenades and by shells from the amphibian tanks. Then the assault passed inland. Some of the enemy in trenches and foxholes in the dune line on the beach, men who had survived the bombardment, were overcome in hand-to-hand fighting. Most of the Japanese had either taken refuge in covered defense sys-

[67] TG 51.11 Eniwetok Rpt, Incl A, pp. 9, 10.
[68] *Ibid.,* pp. 10, 72, 92.
[69] *Ibid.,* p. 10; CINCPAC-CINCPOA Opns in POA, Feb 44, Annex B, p. 20.

tems farther inland or had been beyond the range of the main preparatory fire in positions along the ocean shore.[70]

Prepared defenses on Parry were much like those on Eniwetok Island.[71] Foxholes, covered shelters, and gun emplacements, sometimes open but often covered, were organized into strong points fronting and flanking the most favorable landing beaches. They extended in depth as much as the size of the island would permit. Spider-web systems provided much the same difficulty as on Eniwetok Island. A large shelter would be excavated, then lined and roofed with heavy coconut logs. Corrugated iron sheets, sand, and palm fronds covered it. In a circle around this shelter, covered foxholes of varying depth were placed from ten to fifteen feet apart. Radial trenches and tunnels connected each of these holes with the central position, while peripheral tunnels connected them with each other. Often oil drums with the two ends removed, when placed end to end and covered with earth, served as tunnel passages. Foxholes were also dug at the bases of coconut palms, hidden by the roots. In addition to these covered positions, on Parry Island many open trenches had been prepared along the shore.

Marines found the best method of securing areas containing such defense systems to consist of three phases. Infantry-tank teams first pushed rapidly ahead to assigned objectives. Demolitions and flame thrower parties followed and cleared out each hole, trench, and shelter. Small teams of three or four men worked together in covering such operations, then mopped up the remaining Japanese in the position. Among the demolitions teams, the favorite weapon was a hand grenade taped to a block of explosive.

About 1000, shells from Japanese 77-mm. field pieces began to strike from the right flank among the leading units of the 1st Battalion, 22d Marines. Neither an air strike nor naval gunfire could be directed on the source without danger to friendly troops and tanks, but the urgency of the request for such support finally prevailed. Five salvos from 5-inch naval guns, although damaging to our troops and tanks, did smash the enemy's guns and break his resistance to the advance. Before 1010 the front line had pushed forward about three hundred yards inland from the beach. Additional forces were being committed or made ready. The 3d Battalion, 22d Marines, started ashore at 1001 to take position on the right half of what was to be the southward-moving line of attack. From Eniwetok Island, the 3d Battalion, 106th Infantry, was preparing to move to Parry as reserve. The two reconnaissance companies joined the attack early in the afternoon, but the 106th Battalion was to remain afloat.[72]

At 1330 the 2d Battalion, 22d Marines, had reached the northern end of Parry and was mopping up while the other two battalions were in line abreast due east of the pier and about to begin their main attack to the south. A fifteen-minute barrage by field artillery from the adjacent islands and by naval guns on the enemy's flanks had just been concluded. The southern force extended across the island, with the medium tanks about a hundred yards in front of them.[73] Ahead of the tanks, the destroyer *Hailey* fired on call until it was hitting only the most southern target areas. As the attack jumped off, the troops pressed through thick underbrush and

[70] Tac Gp 1 Sp Rpt, p. 11.
[71] TG 51.11 Eniwetok Rpt, Incl A, p. 62.
[72] Tac Gp 1 Sp Rpt, p. 11.
[73] *Ibid.*, pp. 11, 12.

continued over an area in which land mines had been strewn promiscuously. Overrunning a series of trench and foxhole defenses, they gathered speed until, at 1930, resistance ceased and the end of the island was in sight. At that time the island was reported secured. The two battalions dug in for the night, prepared to mop up in the morning.

To forestall enemy infiltration or counterattacks, both ends of the island were illuminated by star shell and searchlight from a cruiser and three destroyers. Enemy movement was quickly detected and suppressed. In a long series of fruitless attempts to strike back, small groups of Japanese invited destruction.

Tanks and infantry scoured Parry Island on 23 February. The 3d Battalion, 106th Infantry, landed that morning to assume its duties as a garrison force. With all possible speed, other Army and Marine units withdrew from the island and prepared to depart from the atoll.[74]

Total American casualties on Eniwetok came to 1,096, with 262 killed, 757 wounded, and 77 missing in action. Sixty-six Japanese and Korean prisoners of war were taken; the rest of the enemy garrison was destroyed.[75] Eniwetok Atoll was completely under American control.

---

[74] TG 51.11 Eniwetok Rpt, Incl A, pp. 72, 73.

[75] *Ibid.*, Incl F.

CHAPTER XX

Consolidating the Victory

With the fighting on Eniwetok Atoll ended, U.S. forces in the Central Pacific were now free to consolidate the gains achieved by the capture of the three key positions in the Marshalls group. Three tasks remained before them. First, a host of undefended and lightly defended atolls and islands in the area had to be occupied. Secondly, air and naval bases had to be constructed to support the continued drive across the Central Pacific. Finally, the by-passed strongholds of Wotje, Mille, Jaluit, Maloelap, and Truk had to be kept under constant aerial bombardment to assure their neutralization.

Mop-up in the Marshalls

The job of occupying the various atolls and islands that the Japanese had chosen not to fortify fell largely to the 22d Marine Regimental Combat Team, with a slight assist from the 111th Infantry Regiment.[1] First to be occupied were the atolls of Wotho, Ujae, and Lae, lying immediately to the westward of Kwajalein. A detachment of about 350 marines from the 1st Battalion, 22d Marines, accompanied by eight amphibian tractors, all loaded aboard an LST, landed unopposed on Wotho Atoll on 8 March and subsequently encountered twelve Japanese, the crew of a plane that had recently crash-landed on the reef. All twelve committed suicide. Two days later the same force

landed without opposition on Ujae, where it discovered six enemy operators of a weather station that had previously been bombed out by American planes. Five of the Japanese committed suicide; the sixth was taken prisoner. On 13 March a landing was made on Lae Atoll. No Japanese were on the island and the natives reported that none had ever been there. The same proved to be true of Lib Island southwest of Lae.

Next to fall under American control were a number of atolls lying southeast of Kwajalein. The job of occupying these was assigned to two groups of about 325 troops each from the 3d Battalion, 22d Marines, to which were attached seven amphibian tractors, all loaded on an LST. Both groups of this force proceeded in company to Ailinglapalap Atoll for the first phase of their operation. Before any landing in force was attempted, a native was picked up who revealed that the crews of two Japanese picket boats, numbering about forty men and equipped with four machine guns and numerous rifles, were on the main island of the atoll. On the night of 20 March and the following morning, the

---

[1] This account of the occupation of the minor atolls and islands in the Marshalls is derived from: 22d Marines Reinforced, Rpt of Operations into the Lesser Marshalls, 6 Apr 44; TU 57.10.9 Rpt, Reconnaissance of Ailinglapalap, Kili, Ebon, and Namorik Atolls, 30 Mar 44; Co I, 111th Inf Regt, Rpt on Opns, Occupation of Ujelang, 27 Apr 44, in 111th Inf Regt Unit History, 1 Jan–31 Dec 44.

entire force of marines, numbering about 650, was landed without opposition. The Japanese were discovered drawn up in a prepared position, which was successfully assaulted. Thirty-seven of the enemy were killed, two taken prisoners and two or three escaped. The marines suffered three wounded. The escaped enemy were pursued around the island for a while, but the hunt was finally abandoned as futile and the marines returned to their LST to proceed to the next objective. One group went on to Namu Atoll, where it landed without opposition on 24 March. There, were found seven Japanese including one woman and four children, all of whom voluntarily surrendered. The second group proceeded to Namorik Atoll and landed on 26 March. Natives reported one unarmed Japanese on the atoll but after extensive patrolling failed to locate him, the search was finally abandoned as a waste of time.

To a detachment from the 2d Battalion, 22d Marines, fell the task of securing the group of atolls and islands lying northeast of Kwajalein. Aerial reconnaissance and the interrogation of natives indicated that Ailinginae and Rongerik Atolls were uninhabited, so the marines were ordered not to investigate them unless it should be subsequently discovered that Japanese had fled to these places after other atolls in the northern group had been captured. The first of these to be visited was Bikini, later to become famed as the site of postwar U.S. experiments with the atomic bomb. It was invaded on 28 March, and the five Japanese located on the atoll committed suicide. Three days later unopposed landings were made on Rongelap Atoll, where eleven Japanese were reported but none discovered. The same day a detachment from the 3d Battalion, 22d Marines, landed on Ailuk Atoll and discovered no enemy

there. Within a few days the same force had invested the Mejit Islands and Likiep and Utirik Atolls, netting a small bag of enemy stragglers. Finally, late in April, Company I of the 111th Infantry Regiment completed the occupation of the lesser Marshalls by capturing Ujelang Atoll, which lies about 140 nautical miles southwest of Eniwetok. The landing was made without opposition on 22 April and eighteen Japanese were flushed out and killed. Thus ended the American occupation of the Marshall Islands with the exception of Wotje, Mille, Jaluit, and Maloelap, which were left to "wither on the vine" subject to constant harassment by American planes and ships.

Building the Marshalls Bases

Immediately after Majuro Atoll was occupied, naval Seabees went ashore on Dalap Island to commence construction of an airstrip.[2] When this was completed in March, it measured 4,800 by 445 feet and was thereafter constantly in use for raids against Mille, Wotje, Maloelap, and Jaluit. A naval base was established on the atoll to support two Marine dive bomber squadrons, half of a Marine patrol squadron, and temporary staging for one Army fighter group flying out of Makin against the bypassed Marshalls. In addition, Majuro provided a fleet anchorage (without shore-based facilities), medical facilities for

[2] This account is derived from: Building the Navy's Bases in World War II, History of the Bureau of Yards and Docks and the Civil Engineer Corps, 1940–1946, Vol. II, prepared under the general supervision of the Director of Naval History, Washington, 1947, filed in Naval Records and History Division; U.S. Naval Administration in World War II, CINCPAC, Marshalls-Gilberts Area, Part IV, first draft prepared under general supervision of Director of Naval History, filed in Naval Records and History Division.

the fleet, and a loran transmitting station. Repair ships and submarine and destroyer tenders, together with tankers and supply ships, rode at anchor in the lagoon to supply the needs of whatever elements of the fleet passed through. Majuro, along with Eniwetok and Kwajalein, was to serve as a primary staging base for the American forces when they attacked the Marianas from June through August of 1944.

On Roi-Namur the 121st Naval Construction Battalion went ashore on 5 February, only three days after the island was declared secured. A day later it was joined by the 109th Naval Construction Battalion, and Seabees set to work immediately repairing and enlarging the Japanese airstrip on Roi. Progress was temporarily interrupted on 13 February when a flight of enemy bombers launched a heavy attack against Roi, setting fire to a bomb dump. Altogether the Seabees suffered 157 personnel casualties, and the 109th Battalion lost 75 percent of its material and 35 percent of its equipment. Nevertheless work continued, and on 15 May the field on Roi was commissioned, with a hundred planes based there. Long before the final commissioning of the field, it was in daily use as a base for strikes against Wotje, Jaluit, and Kusaie, and subsequently it became one of the primary bases for raids against Truk.

In March the 74th and 107th Naval Construction Battalions went ashore on Kwajalein Island, where they rebuilt the Japanese runway into a 6,300-foot coral-surfaced strip with two 80-foot taxiways and 102 hard stands for heavy bombers. In addition, water-front facilities were developed to provide for minor fleet repairs, the Japanese pier reaching into the lagoon was restored, a 250-ton pontoon drydock was assembled, and a 2,000-ton floating dock was provided. On nearby Ebeye other Seabees developed a seaplane base, which was completed by April. Kwajalein Island was to become the primary base for Army bombers flying against Truk. On Eniwetok Atoll Seabees began repairs and construction work late in February. By 5 March the airstrip on Engebi was able to accommodate three Army medium bombers (B-25's), which went into action against enemy shipping at Kusaie five days later. By 20 March a 6,000-foot airstrip had been completed on Eniwetok Island as well. Parry Island was used as a small-boat repair base and a seaplane base, the ramp and facilities for servicing seaplanes being ready for use early in May.

Eniwetok Atoll thereafter served as an advanced fleet anchorage without shore-based facilities, as well as an air base capable of handling two heavy seaplane patrol squadrons, two fighter squadrons, one half of a night fighter squadron, one scout bomber squadron, two heavy bomber squadrons, and one photographic squadron. From May through October 1944, Army squadrons staging through Eniwetok and Navy and Marine squadrons based there flew continuous sorties against Truk and Ponape. In addition, Navy bombers staging through Eniwetok delivered low-level bombing and strafing attacks against Wake, and daily reconnaissance of Wake was conducted by seaplanes based on Parry.

Neutralizing the Bypassed Atolls

From February 1944 until the close of the war, that area of the middle Pacific containing the Gilberts, Marshalls, and eastern Carolines became virtually an American lake through which ships and troops passed freely with little danger of enemy interception. The reason, of course, was that the capture of key bases in the Marshalls and the establishment of airfields thereon made it possible for the superior American air arm to keep the atolls still remaining in Japanese hands under constant surveillance and bombardment.

By the time of the capture of Kwajalein, Japanese aircraft in the eastern Marshalls (Mille, Wotje, Jaluit, and Maloelap) had been either completely destroyed by Army and Navy aircraft or evacuated.[3]

Thereafter, the main effort of American aircraft was to prevent these bases from being reinforced and rehabilitated and to bomb out and starve out the enemy abandoned there. After mid-March, when the base at Majuro was completed, Army medium bombers flew regular flights out of Tarawa and Makin, bombed two of the bypassed islands, landed at Majuro for rearming and refueling, and then bombed the other two targets on the way home. At the same time ten fighter squadrons and two bomber squadrons of the 4th Marine Air Base Defense Wing at Kwajalein flew a steady series of sorties against the same islands. After June 1944, Marine flyers assumed sole responsibility for these targets.[4]

In March two heavy bomber groups of the Seventh Army Air Force moved onto Kwajalein for the primary purpose of conducting bombing raids against Truk.[5] In conjunction with planes of the Thirteenth Army Air Force based in the South Pacific, bombers of the Seventh, flying out of Kwajalein and staging through Eniwetok, kept Truk effectively neutralized from April 1944 until the end of the war.[6]

[3] USSBS, *The American Campaign Against Wotje, Maloelap, Mille and Jaluit*, p. 35.

[4] Robert Sherrod, *History of Marine Corps Aviation in World War II* (Washington: Combat Forces Press, 1952), Ch. VII. Mr. Sherrod has kindly allowed the authors to read this book in galley proof.

[5] Craven and Cate, *AAF IV*, p. 672.

[6] *Ibid.*, pp. 683–86; USSBS, *The Reduction of Truk*.

CHAPTER XXI

Tactical and Strategic Consequences of the Marshalls Operation

Writing soon after the capture of the Marshalls, General Holland Smith reported, "Recommendations made and acted upon . . . as a result of the Gilberts offensive proved sound. In the attack of coral atolls, very few recommendations can be made to improve upon the basic techniques previously recommended and utilized in the Marshalls . . ." [1] As a matter of fact, after the capture of Eniwetok it was found unnecessary to seize any more well-defended atolls in the Pacific. Thereafter, all major landing operations were conducted against larger island masses ranging in size from such small volcanic islands as Iwo Jima and Ie Shima to such comparatively large land masses as Luzon and New Guinea.

In the latter phases of the Pacific war, then, many new problems presented themselves on which the experience in either the Gilberts or the Marshalls had no particular bearing. Large bodies of troops of corps and army size had to be maneuvered over relatively vast areas of land. Campaigns were to be measured in months, not days. The burden of supply, transportation, and medical care and evacuation were correspondingly increased. Tactical aviation assumed a new role. On Luzon and again at Okinawa, fighter and bomber planes were to be used extensively in close support of ground troops that had penetrated far inland from their original beachheads. Fleet tactics, too, underwent considerable revision. Continuous attrition of Japanese naval and air strength plus the mighty build-up of American naval power freed the U.S. Fleet from the cautious hit-and-run tactics it had been compelled to resort to as late as February 1944. For the most part thereafter, the fleets that struck succeeding objectives in conjunction with landing forces came prepared to stay at least until all serious ground resistance had been eliminated. In the Marianas, the Palaus, the Philippines, Iwo Jima, and, finally, Okinawa, the U.S. Fleet stayed close offshore of the land targets for prolonged periods of time, ready to render constant support to ground troops as they pressed forward toward their objectives. And this in spite of the growing menace of the Japanese *Kamikaze* (suicide) *Corps,* which mounted steadily from October 1944 to May 1945.

Yet notwithstanding these changes the

[1] V Phib Corps FLINTLOCK Rpt.

progress of the war in the Pacific was to bring about, one aspect of most of the subsequent campaigns remained basically unchanged—the technique of the amphibious landing. Insofar as this phase of Pacific warfare was concerned, Holland Smith's generalization that "very few recommendations can be made to improve upon the basic techniques previously recommended and utilized in the Marshalls" proved quite valid. The techniques that had been perfected in the capture of tiny atolls in the Central Pacific proved applicable, and were in fact applied, with only minor variations in most of the subsequent island landings as U.S. and Allied forces worked their way closer and closer to the heart of the Japanese Empire.

In the Marshalls operations some important innovations were made in the techniques and equipment of American amphibious assault procedure. The amphibious headquarters ship, which had already seen action in the Mediterranean theater, was first introduced into the Pacific at Kwajalein, where it conclusively demonstrated its value. For the first time there also, infantry landing craft were equipped with both 40-mm. guns and rockets and were effectively employed to lay down a last-minute barrage just before the troops landed. Underwater demolition teams demonstrated their ability to swim close to shore into the very teeth of the enemy under the protective cover of naval fire. The DUKW saw its first action on any large scale at Kwajalein and proved its immense value as a cargo and artillery carrier. At Eniwetok naval star shells were for the first time extensively employed to illuminate areas behind friendly lines and thereby impose a serious check on the standard Japanese tactic of night infiltration.

With the conclusion of the Marshalls operation, the standard pattern of American amphibious landings was set and was thereafter followed with a high degree of consistency by U.S. forces whenever they attacked an enemy beachhead in the Pacific. A few new items of equipment and a few new techniques were to be evolved that would improve still further on this pattern, but they introduced no major changes. After February 1944, standard procedure called for as heavy and as prolonged preliminary naval and aerial bombardment of the beachhead as conditions permitted. Where feasible, this was supplemented by the emplacement of land-based field artillery on islands near the main landing beaches before the principal landings were made. Underwater demolition teams searched the shore line and the shallow water offshore for obstacles and mines and detonated them where necessary. Just before the landings, a last-minute preparatory fire was delivered by shallow-draft vessels of various types firing a variety of missiles from 20-mm. shells up through 4.5-inch rockets. The assault troops, boated insofar as possible in amphibian tractors, landed in waves and pressed the attack forward, followed by waves of tanks, artillery, and supplies and equipment, which were carried in amphibian tractors, amphibian trucks, and landing craft and ships of all sorts and sizes. Naval and land-based aircraft kept the enemy under continuous pressure and naval ships, where possible, supplied close and deep support to the troops as they advanced forward.

Some of these elements of force were omitted in subsequent island landings in the Pacific, especially in the various amphibious operations on the New Guinea coast, where enemy opposition was relatively light and such a preponderant display of power was unnecessary. But most of the techniques were employed in the major landings and all of them were used with brilliant success at Tinian and Okinawa. By the close of the Marshalls campaign, the basic pattern for the Pacific style of amphibious assault was set and any subsequent deviations therefrom were minor.[2]

Strategically speaking, the easy capture of main bases in the Marshalls, coupled with the successful raid on Truk, was of utmost significance in its influence on the course of the future conduct of the war in the Pacific. First, the combined operations against the Marshalls and Truk served to confirm and reinforce the opinions already held by the Joint Chiefs of Staff and other strategic planners that the Central Pacific drive offered the most profitable route by which Allied forces could deliver a death blow against the Japanese Empire. Second, the strike against Truk revealed that base to be far weaker than had originally been supposed by most American planners and led to the final decision to bypass it altogether. Finally, the economy of force with which the Marshalls had been taken and the removal of Truk from the list of prospective targets made available to Admiral Nimitz a large body of trained troops that could now be employed to accelerate the Central Pacific drive to a far greater degree than had originally been planned.

In the spring of 1943, the Joint Chiefs of Staff had decided that the main effort in the war against Japan should be made along the Central Pacific axis, with a simultaneous but subsidiary effort to be launched through the South and Southwest Pacific. This decision had been reached in spite of the strong recommendations by General MacArthur that his own theater be given paramount consideration in Pacific plan-

ning.[3] The quick victories in the Marshalls confirmed the original judgment of the Joint Chiefs and strengthened their resolution to continue the main pressure along the Central Pacific axis. Two questions, however, called for immediate solution. The first was whether to launch the next attack in Admiral Nimitz's theater against the Marianas. The second was whether or not to bypass Truk, keeping it neutralized from the newly acquired bases in the Marshalls and letting it "wither on the vine."

The feasibility of an attack against the Marianas had long been discussed and debated among members of the Joint Chiefs of Staff, their subordinate committees, and theater staffs in the Southwest and Central Pacific. Admiral King had firmly declared that the capture of the Marianas was the "key to success" in the Pacific war,[4] and he was supported in that opinion by the Army Air Forces representative on the Joint Chiefs of Staff, General Henry H. Arnold, who wanted the Marianas as bases for B-29 raids against the Japanese homeland.[5]

In the meetings of the Combined Chiefs

[2] For more details on Pacific amphibious operations after February 1944 see: Isely and Crowl, *The U.S. Marines and Amphibious War;* Appleman *et al., Okinawa;* M. Hamlin Cannon, *Leyte: Return to the Philippines,* UNITED STATES ARMY IN WORLD WAR II (Washington, 1954); and the following forthcoming volumes in the Pacific series of UNITED STATES ARMY IN WORLD WAR II, to be published by the Office of the Chief of Military History, Department of the Army: Robert Ross Smith, *The Approach to the Philippines;* John Miller, jr., CARTWHEEL, The Reduction of Rabaul; Philip A. Crowl, Campaign in the Marianas; Robert Ross Smith and M. Hamlin Cannon, Triumph in the Philippines.
[3] See above, Ch. I.
[4] Min, 92d mtg CCS, 21 May 43, TRIDENT Conference, pp. 429–37. For a more detailed discussion of the planning for the Marianas see Philip A. Crowl, Campaign in the Marianas.
[5] Min, 109th mtg JPS, 27 Oct 43; Min, 123d and 124th mtgs JCS, 15 and 17 Nov 43; Henry H. Arnold, *Global Mission* (New York: Harper & Brothers, 1949), pp. 476–80.

of Staff held in Cairo in November and December 1943, the King-Arnold argument was accepted by the Allied strategic planners. The advance westward through the Central Pacific, through the mandated islands to the Palaus, and north to the Marianas was approved. Again, it was stated that Central Pacific operations were to have priority over those of the Southwest Pacific.[6]

On the basis of the Combined Chiefs' decision, Admiral Nimitz had issued a tentative plan of operations on 13 January 1944, designated GRANITE. Initial landings in the Marshalls were to be undertaken on 31 January. Late in March a carrier strike against Truk was to be executed, and in May amphibious landings were to be made in the western Marshalls. Landings on Truk and Mortlock in the Carolines would be initiated on 1 August. If Truk were bypassed, the Palaus would be invaded instead on approximately the same date. Amphibious operations against the Marianas were to begin about 1 November.[7]

The early successes in the Marshalls operation and the successful carrier raid against Truk of 17–18 February enabled Admiral Nimitz to step up this program considerably. He became more convinced than ever of the feasibility of bypassing Truk and so recommended to the Joint Chiefs of Staff. He advocated instead an invasion of the Marianas on 15 June, to be followed by the seizure of Ulithi Atoll, about 360 miles southwest of Guam; the capture of Yap Island, a Japanese air base 100 miles southwest of Ulithi; and the capture or neutralization of the Palaus, about 300 miles still farther to the southwest. Woleai, in the Carolines, 360 miles due south of Guam, should also be captured, he recommended, to assure the neutralization of Truk and to protect the lines

of communication from the Marianas to Yap and Ulithi.[8]

With these and other recommendations in hand, the Joint Chiefs of Staff issued on 12 March a new operational directive for action in the Pacific during 1944. General MacArthur was ordered to cancel the proposed Kavieng operation and complete the neutralization of Rabaul with the minimum of forces. Following the development of Manus Island in the Admiralties as an air and fleet base, he was to occupy Hollandia on or about 15 April and conduct operations along the New Guinea coast preparatory to an invasion of the Palaus and Mindanao, southernmost of the Philippines. Admiral Nimitz was ordered to cancel his plans for seizing Truk and expedite the neutralization of Truk and other islands in that immediate area. Nimitz was also to conduct carrier strikes against the Marianas, the Palaus, the Carolines, and other profitable targets. The Marianas were to be invaded on 15 June 1944, after which Central Pacific forces were to move to the Palaus.[9]

Thus, with the successful conclusion of the campaign in the Marshalls, it became possible to launch the drive against the Marianas at a far earlier date than had originally been anticipated. Truk was to

[6] CCS 417, 2 Dec 43, title: Overall Plan for the Defeat of Japan; CCS 397 (Revised), 3 Dec 43, title: Specific Operations for the Defeat of Japan, 1944; CCS 426/1, 6 Dec 43, title: Rpt to the President and Prime Minister. All foregoing documents located in bound volume of SEXTANT papers, copy in G-3 files.
[7] CINCPAC-CINCPOA, Campaign Plan GRANITE, 13 Jan 44, Naval History Div.
[8] JCS Memo for Information 200, 7 Mar 44, sub: Sequence and Timing of Operations, Central Pacific Campaign, a Rpt by CINCPOA, ABC 384 Pacific (1–17–43) Sec. 3a; Supplementary Min, 140th mtg JCS, 7 Mar 44.
[9] JCS 713/4, 12 Mar 44, title: Future Operations in the Pacific.

be bypassed and kept neutralized by aircraft operating chiefly out of the newly seized Marshalls bases. These bases were also to be put to good use in staging fleet elements that would later be used not only against the Marianas but also against the Palaus and the Philippines themselves. Most important, the early and quick capture of the Marshalls released a volume of manpower for early employment against the Marianas. Originally, Admiral Nimitz had allocated the task of seizing Eniwetok to the 2d Marine Division and two regimental combat teams of the 27th Infantry Division. When it was found possible to employ the reserve force initially assigned to Kwajalein for this task, the 2d Marine Division and the two regimental combat teams of the 27th Division were immediately set upon the task of training for the forthcoming Marianas campaign. The decision to bypass Truk freed still more ground forces for future operations. In January 1944, Nimitz had earmarked three Marine divisions, two Army divisions, and an independent Marine regiment for the capture of Truk and adjacent atolls.[10] Three of these divisions (the 2d and 4th Marine Division and the 27th Infantry Division) were now free to be trained for employment in the invasion of Saipan. Two others, the 3d Marine Division and the 77th Infantry Division, as well as the 22d Marine Regiment, were to be used against Guam.

With the quick termination of the capture of the main Japanese bases in the Marshall Islands, the drive of U.S. forces through the Central Pacific against Japan was greatly speeded up. Any previous doubt as to where would lie the "main effort" against the enemy was permanently dispelled.

"Thus," to quote Admiral Nimitz again, "we get on with the war."[11]

---

[10] CINCPAC-CINCPOA, Outline Plan for Operations in Pacific Ocean Areas, 13 Jan 44.
[11] *Ibid.*

Concordance of Code and Native Names for Islands in Kwajalein Atoll

Code	Native
Abraham	Ennugarret
Albert	Ennumennet
Allen	Ennubirr
Arlington	Gagan
August	Omelek
Bascome	Meck
Bennett	Bigej
Berlin	North Gugegwe
Beverly	South Gugegwe
Blakenship	Loi
Burlesque	Roi
Burton	Ebeye
Camouflage	Namur
Carlos	Ennylabegan
Carlson	Enubuj
Carter	Gea
Cecil	Ninni
Chauncey	Gehh
Clement	Mann
Clifford	Legan
Clifton	Eller
Cohen	Ennugenliggelap
Homer	Boggerik
Ivan	Mellu
Jacob	Ennuebing
Porcelain	Kwajalein

Bibliographical Note

This volume is based primarily on the official records of the U.S. armed services and of the planners of strategy, both American and Allied. Supplementing these are the interviews conducted by official Army historians in the field while the fighting was going on and postwar interviews and correspondence of the authors with the chief participants. Special preliminary studies, officially sponsored by the various armed services or by their respective service schools, have been consulted and full use has been made of the pertinent published works. Finally, the authors of this volume have been especially fortunate in having access to the wealth of Japanese records available in this country both in their original form and in translation.

Official Records

Strategic Planning

Materials concerning strategic planning on the highest Allied and U.S. levels are to be found in the records of the Combined Chiefs of Staff (Allied) and the U.S. Joint Chiefs of Staff and its subordinate committees. Copies of these records were kept for the Army by the Strategy Policy Group of the Operations Division and are identified by the initials ABC. They may be obtained through the G-3 Division of the General Staff. Other papers concerning the planning for the Gilberts and Marshalls operations are to be found in the OPD central files currently located in the Departmental Records Branch, Adjutant General's Office (DRB AGO), in Alexandria, Virginia.

U.S. Army

The official U.S. Army records constitute the backbone of the study. They fall into three general categories—operation plans (or field orders), after action reports, and unit journals. The after action reports used include those of the highest theater command, Headquarters, U.S. Army Forces in the Central Pacific Area (USAFICPA), divisions, regiments, battalions, and attached units. The journals consulted were those on the level of division, regiment, and battalion. Generally speaking, the daily journal has been found to be the most reliable and most complete of all official records. The after action reports are usually little more than a recapitulation of the main events of the day as recorded in the journals, but they do furnish convenient guides to an understanding of the course of the battle. Usually, but not always, the lower the echelon, the more reliable and more detailed is the after action report. Most of these records are in the custody of DRB AGO, although many administration files and some unit journals are in the Kansas City Records Center, AGO.

U.S. Navy

For the Navy, the same types of records have been used except that it has not been felt necessary to consult ships' logs, which are the naval equivalent of the unit journal. The naval action reports [1] covered include those of the Commander in Chief U.S. Fleet and Chief of Naval Operations (Ernest J. King, *Official Report, Covering Combat Operations Up to March 1, 1944,* Washington, 1944); Commander in Chief U.S. Pacific Fleet and U.S. Pacific Ocean Areas (CINCPAC-CINCPOA, Operations in the Pacific Ocean Areas [monthly from September 1943 through February 1944]); various subordinate Pacific Fleet task forces, and individual ships. All World War II U.S. Navy records are located in the Classified Operational Records Branch, Naval History Division, and copies of most of those used in this volume can be found in DRB AGO or in the Records and Research Section, Historical Branch, G-3, Headquarters, U.S. Marine Corps.

U.S. Marine Corps

The action reports and daily journals of the Marine Corps units have been covered in the same manner as those of the Army. The issuing authorities range from V Amphibious Corps to battalion. These records are also located in the Records and Research Section, Historical Branch, G-3, Headquarters, U.S. Marine Corps.

Interviews, Field Histories, and Letters

Each of the Army operations described here was covered by a field historian and a team of specialists sent by Headquarters, U.S. Army Forces in the Central Pacific Area, to accompany the troops during the actual fighting. For Makin and southern Kwajalein the historian was Lt. Col. S. L. A. Marshall; for Eniwetok it was Capt. Edmund G. Love, coauthor of this volume.

The original notes of their interviews and firsthand observations are filed in the Office of the Chief of Military History, Department of the Army (OCMH). It was at Makin and Kwajalein that Colonel Marshall first developed the techniques of combat interviewing for which he became famous during and after World War II, and which, with variations, have been adopted by the U.S. Army and U.S. Marine Corps.

Since the beginning of the preparation of this volume the authors have consulted, either by personal interview or through correspondence, more than a score of officers who participated in the operations. Their names are listed here: [2]

Maj. Gen. Archibald V. Arnold, USA, Col. Russell G. Ayers, USA, Lt. Gen. Stephen J. Chamberlin, USA, Admiral Richard L. Conolly, USN, Maj. Gen. Charles H. Corlett, USA (Ret.), Col. Winslow Cornett, USA (Ret.), Lt. Col. Victor Croizat, USMC, Col. William A. Eareckson, USAF, Col. Charles B. Ferris, USA, Col. Wallace M. Greene, Jr., USMC, Lt. Gen. Franklin A. Hart, USMC, Vice Adm. Harry W. Hill, USN, Col. Gerard W. Kelley, USA, Col. S. L. A. Marshall, USAR, Fleet Admiral Chester W. Nimitz, USN, Lt. Gen. Robert C. Richardson, Jr., USA (Ret.), General Harry Schmidt, USMC (Ret.), Lt. Gen. Julian C. Smith, USMC (Ret.), Maj. Gen. Ralph C. Smith, USA (Ret.), Admiral Raymond A. Spruance, USN (Ret.), Admiral Richmond

---

[1] Army and Navy nomenclature differs here. The same report is called "after action report" by the Army and "action report" by the Navy. The U.S. Marine Corps for the most part uses the Navy term. Other variations that occasionally appear are "special action report," "operations report," and "participation report."

[2] Ranks are those held as of date of letter or interview.

Kelley Turner, USN (Ret.), Lt. Gen. Thomas E. Watson, USMC (Ret.).

The letters and reports of interviews of the above are filed in OCMH. Another important collection of letters from leading figures in the Pacific campaigns of World War II is located in the Princeton University Library with the manuscript copies of *The U.S. Marines and Amphibious War* by Jeter A. Isely and Philip A. Crowl (Princeton: Princeton University Press, 1951).

Special Studies

Among other sources used were several special studies prepared after the operations, either under the official auspices of particular commands or by individuals attending service schools or attached to the historical sections of the various services. In the former category are: History of United States Army Forces Middle Pacific and Predecessor Commands During World War II, 7 December 1941–2 September 1942, 60 vols., MS in OCMH; Office of Naval Intelligence (ONI), The Assault on Kwajalein and Majuro, 2 vols. (Washington, 1945); Commander in Chief U.S. Fleet (COMINCH), Publication P-002, Amphibious Operations in the Marshall Islands, January–February, 1944, 20 May 1944; Office of the Secretary of Defense, Weapons Evaluation Group, Staff Study No. 4, Operational Experience of Fast Carrier Task Forces in World War II, 15 August 1951, MS in OCMH; Operational History of the Seventh Air Force, 7 December 1941–6 November 1943, and Operational History of the Seventh Air Force, 6 November 1943–31 July 1944, MSS in Air University Historical Liaison Office.

Individual special studies consulted are: Sgt. Frederick A. Baxter, Armored Force Action on Makin, MS in OCMH; Lt. Col. A. R. Brunelli, USMC, The Capture of Namur Island, Kwajalein Atoll, Marshall Islands, 1–2 February 1944, MS in Record Section, Marine Corps Schools (RSMCS); Lt. Col. Robert D. Heinl, USMC, Marine Corps Operations in the Marshalls, MS (unfinished) in Records and Research Section, Historical Branch, G-3, Headquarters, U.S. Marine Corps; 1st Lt. Paul R. Leach, Jr., Tanks on Kwajalein Atoll, MS in OCMH; Capt. Joseph E. Lo Prete, USMC, The Battle of Roi-Namur, Marshall Islands, MS in RSMCS; Cpl. Millard Rogers, The Artillery Action of the Battle of Kwajalein Atoll, MS in OCMH; Lt. Col. Richard Rothwell, USMC, A Study of an Amphibious Operation, The Battle of Namur, 31 January 1944–2 February 1944, Kwajalein Operation, Second Battalion, Twenty Fourth Marines, 4th Marine Division, MS in RSMCS; Lt. Col. Arthur H. Weinberger, USMC, A Study of Amphibious Tactics—The Capture of Engebi Island, MS in RSMCS.

Japanese Records

The National Archives houses a tremendous number of original Japanese records of World War II in the collection called World War II Seized Enemy Records. After the war the G-2 Section of General Headquarters, Far East Command (GHQ FEC), directed a group of Japanese officers to prepare a series of special studies of Japanese operations, based on their personal recollections and on the official Japanese records in Tokyo. These were translated and incorporated into a series entitled Japanese Studies in World War II, manuscript copies of which are filed in OCMH. Those studies used in the preparation of this volume are numbered 50,

55, and 72. The largest collection of translated captured enemy records is contained in the bulletins and translations prepared during the war by Headquarters, Commander in Chief Pacific Fleet and Pacific Ocean Areas and by the Joint Intelligence Center, Pacific Ocean Areas (JICPOA). Complete collections are deposited in the Classified Operational Records Branch, World War II, Office of Naval History, and in the Records and Research Section, Historical Branch, G-3, Headquarters, U.S. Marine Corps.

Published Works

Arnold, Henry H., *Global Mission* (New York: Harper & Brothers, 1949). Personal memoirs of the Commanding General, U.S. Air Force.

Cass, Bevan G., ed., *History of the Sixth Marine Division* (Washington, 1948).

Craven, Wesley Frank, and James Lea Cate, eds., THE ARMY AIR FORCES IN WORLD WAR II, Vol. IV, *The Pacific: Guadalcanal to Saipan, August 1942 to July 1944* (Chicago: University of Chicago Press, 1950). A volume in the U.S. Army Air Forces official history of Army air operations.

Historical Division, War Department, *The Capture of Makin, 20 November–24 November 1943,* AMERICAN FORCES IN ACTION SERIES (Washington, 1946). One of a series of detailed but undocumented combat studies prepared during the war mostly for the benefit of hospitalized veterans. A documented manuscript version of this monograph is in the custody of OCMH.

Heinl, Lt. Col. Robert D., Jr., USMC, and Lt. Col. John A. Crown, USMC, *The Marshalls: Increasing the Tempo,* Historical Branch, G-3 Division, Headquarters, U.S. Marine Corps (Washington, 1954). The final official Marine Corps history of operations in the Marshalls. This monograph was not published until after the present volume was completed.

Isely, Jeter A., and Philip A. Crowl, *The U.S. Marines and Amphibious War* (Princeton: Princeton University Press, 1951). A survey of prewar developments in amphibious warfare and of the amphibious phase of the Pacific campaigns in which Marines participated.

Johnston, Richard W., *Follow Me, The Story of the Second Marine Division in World War II* (New York: Random House, 1948).

King, Ernest J., *Fleet Admiral King, A Naval Record* (New York: W. W. Norton & Company, Inc., 1952). Personal memoirs of the Commander in Chief U.S. Fleet and Chief of Naval Operations.

Love, Edmund G., *The 27th Infantry Division in World War II* (Washington: Infantry Journal Press, 1949).

Love, Edmund G., *The Hourglass: A History of the 7th Infantry Division in World War II* (Washington: Infantry Journal Press, 1950).

Marshall, Lt. Col. S. L. A., *Island Victory* (Washington: Infantry Journal Press, 1944). An intimate contemporary history of infantry action on Kwajalein by the official Army historian who accompanied the troops there.

Miller, John, jr., *Guadalcanal: The First Offensive,* UNITED STATES ARMY IN WORLD WAR II (Washington, 1949). As in the case of the other volumes in this series, cited below, this is the final official Army history of the operation.

Morison, Samuel E., HISTORY OF UNITED STATES NAVAL OPERATIONS IN WORLD WAR II, Vol. IV, *Coral Sea, Midway and Submarine Actions,*

May 1942–August 1942 (Boston: Little, Brown and Company, 1949); Vol. VI, *Breaking the Bismarcks Barrier, 22 July 1942– 1 May 1944* (Boston: Little, Brown and Company, 1950); Vol. VII, *Aleutians, Gilberts and Marshalls* (Boston: Little, Brown and Company, 1951). Semiofficial.

Morton, Louis, *The Fall of the Philippines,* UNITED STATES ARMY IN WORLD WAR II (Washington, 1953).

Myers, Denys P., *Handbook of the League of Nations* (Boston: World Peace Foundation, 1935).

Proehl, Carl W., ed., *The Fourth Marine Division in World War II* (Washington, 1946).

Robson, R. W., *The Pacific Islands Year Book* (Sydney, Australia: Pacific Publications, Ltd., 1943). A descriptive survey of the islands of the Pacific, their history, geography, culture, etc.

Smith, Holland M., *Coral and Brass* (New York: Charles Scribner's Sons, 1949). Personal memoirs of the Commanding General, V Amphibious Corps.

Smith, Robert Ross, *The Approach to the Philippines,* UNITED STATES ARMY IN WORLD WAR II (Washington, 1953).

Stockman, Capt. James R., USMC, *The Battle for Tarawa,* Historical Section, Division of Public Information, Headquarters, U.S. Marine Corps (Washington, 1947). The final official Marine Corps history of the operation.

United States Strategic Bombing Survey (Pacific), Naval Analysis Division, *The Campaigns of the Pacific War* (Washington, 1946); *Interrogations of Japanese Officials,* 2 vols. (Washington, 1946); *The American Campaign Against Wotje, Maloelap, Mille and Jaluit* (Washington, 1947); *The Reduction of Truk* (Washington, 1947).

List of Abbreviations

AA	Antiaircraft	CM-IN	Classified message, incoming
AAF	Army Air Forces		
AAR	After action report	CM-OUT	Classified message, outgoing
AGC	General communications vessel		
		CNO	Chief of Naval Operations
AK	Cargo ship		
AKA	Cargo ship, attack	Co	Company
ALP	Air liaison party	CO	Commanding officer
AM	Mine sweeper	CofS	Chief of Staff
Amph	Amphibious	COMCENPAC	Commander, Central Pacific Area
AP	Transport		
APA	Transport, attack	COMCENPACFOR	Commander, Central Pacific Forces
APD	Transport (high-speed)		
		COMGENCENPAC	Commanding General, Central Pacific Area
App	Appendix		
Arty	Artillery		
		COMINCH	Commander in Chief, U.S. Fleet
BAR	Browning automatic rifle	CTF	Commander Task Force
BLT	Battalion landing team	CV	Aircraft carrier
		CVE	Aircraft carrier, escort
Bn	Battalion		
Bull	Bulletin	CVL	Aircraft carrier, small
Cav	Cavalry		
CCS	Combined Chiefs of Staff	D-3	Operations officer or section (Marines)
CENPAC	Central Pacific Area	Div	Division
CENPACFOR	Central Pacific Forces	DMS	Mine sweeper (converted destroyer)
CG	Commanding general	DRB AGO	Departmental Records Branch, Adjutant General's Office, Alexandria, Virginia
CINCPAC	Commander in Chief, U.S. Pacific Fleet		
CINCPOA	Commander in Chief, Pacific Ocean Areas	DUKW	Amphibian truck, 2½ tons
CL(AA)	Light cruiser, antiaircraft	FA	Field Artillery
		FO	Field Order

G-1	Personnel section of a general staff	LCM	Landing craft, mechanized
G-2	Intelligence section of a general staff	LCS	Landing craft, support
G-3	Operations section of a general staff	LCVP	Landing craft, vehicle and personnel
G-4	Supply section of a general staff	LSD	Landing ship, dock
		LST	Landing ship, tank
Gp	Group	LT	Landing Team
		Ltr	Letter
HD SSUSA	Historical Division, SSUSA	LVT	Landing vehicle, tracked
		LVT(1)	Landing vehicle, tracked, unarmored (Mark I) ("Alligator")
ICPOA	Intelligence Center, Pacific Ocean Areas		
IJN	Imperial Japanese Navy	LVT(2)	Landing vehicle, tracked, unarmored (Mark II) ("Water Buffalo")
IMTFE	International Military Tribunal for the Far East		
		LVT(A)	Landing vehicle, tracked, armored
Incl	Inclosure		
Inf	Infantry	Med	Medical
Interv	Interview	Memo	Memorandum
IPS	International Prosecution Section, IMTFE	Min	Minutes
		MS	Manuscript
		Msg	Message
		Mtg	Meeting
JASCO	Joint Assault Signal Company		
		NA	National Archives
JCS	Joint Chiefs of Staff		
JICPOA	Joint Intelligence Center, Pacific Ocean Areas	OCMH	Office of the Chief of Military History
		OPD	Operations Division, War Department General Staff
Jnl	Journal		
JPS	Joint Staff Planners		
JSSC	Joint Strategic Survey Committee	Opn	Operation
		Ord	Ordnance
JWPC	Joint War Plans Committee		
		PACMIRS	Pacific Military Intelligence Research Section
KCRC	Kansas City Records Center, AGO		
		Phib	Amphibious
		POA	Pacific Ocean Areas
LCI	Landing craft, infantry		
		Rad	Radiogram
LCI(G)	Landing craft, infantry, gunboat	R.A.N.	Royal Australian Navy

Rcn	Reconnaissance	Tac	Tactical
RCT	Regimental Combat Team	TF	Task Force
		TG	Task Group
Regt	Regiment	Tk	Tank
R.N.	Royal Navy	Trac	Tractor
Rpt	Report	TU	Task Unit
S-1	Personnel section of a regiment or smaller unit	USA	U.S. Army
		USAFICPA	U.S. Army Forces in the Central Pacific Area
S-4	Supply section of a regiment or smaller unit		
		USAFMIDPAC	U.S. Army Forces, Middle Pacific
SAR	Special Action Report	USMC	U.S. Marine Corps
SC	Subchaser	USMCR	U.S. Marine Corps Reserve
Sec	Section		
SNLF	Special Naval Landing Force	USN	U.S. Navy
		USNR	U.S. Naval Reserve
Sp	Special	USSBS	U.S. Strategic Bombing Survey
SSUSA	Special Staff, U.S. Army		
Sub	Subject		
SWPA	Southwest Pacific Area	WDC	Washington Document Center

Glossary of Code Names

CARTWHEEL   MacArthur's drive against Rabaul
ELKTON   MacArthur's plan for recapture of Rabaul
FLINTLOCK   The Marshall Islands operation
GALVANIC   The Gilberts-Nauru operation
GRANITE   Nimitz' plan for operations in 1944
ORANGE   Prewar plan of operations in event of war with Japan
RAINBOW   Various plans prepared between 1939 and 1941 to meet Axis aggression involving more than one enemy
RENO   MacArthur's plan for advancing along north coast of New Guinea and thence to Mindanao
SEXTANT   International conference at Cairo, 22–26 November and 3–7 December 1943
TRIDENT   International conference at Washington, 12–25 May 1943

Basic Military Map Symbols*

Symbols within a rectangle indicate a military unit, within a triangle an observation post, and within a circle a supply point.

Military Units—Identification

Antiaircraft Artillery . . . .

Armored Command . . . .

Army Air Forces . . . .

Artillery, except Antiaircraft and Coast Artillery . . . .

Cavalry, Horse . . . .

Cavalry, Mechanized . . . .

Chemical Warfare Service . . . .

Coast Artillery . . . .

Engineers . . . .

Infantry . . . .

Medical Corps . . . .

Ordnance Department . . . .

Quartermaster Corps . . . .

Signal Corps . . . .

Tank Destroyer . . . .

Transportation Corps . . . .

Veterinary Corps . . . .

Airborne units are designated by combining a gull wing symbol with the arm or service symbol:

Airborne Artillery . . . .

Airborne Infantry . . . .

*For complete listing of symbols see FM 21–30, from which these are taken.

Size Symbols

The following symbols placed either in boundary lines or above the rectangle, triangle, or circle inclosing the identifying arm or service symbol indicate the size of military organization:

Squad	●
Section	● ●
Platoon	● ● ●
Company, troop, battery, Air Force flight	I
Battalion, cavalry squadron, or Air Force squadron	I I
Regiment or group; combat team (with abbreviation CT following identifying numeral)	I I I
Brigade, Combat Command of Armored Division, or Air Force Wing	X
Division or Command of an Air Force	XX
Corps or Air Force	XXX
Army	XXXX
Group of Armies	XXXXX

EXAMPLES

The letter or number to the left of the symbol indicates the unit designation; that to the right, the designation of the parent unit to which it belongs. Letters or numbers above or below boundary lines designate the units separated by the lines:

Company A, 137th Infantry	A ⊠ 137
8th Field Artillery Battalion	⊡ 8
Combat Command A, 1st Armored Division	A ⊡ I
Observation Post, 23d Infantry	△ 23
Command Post, 5th Infantry Division	⊠ 5
Boundary between 137th and 138th Infantry	—137 III— 138

Weapons

Machine gun	●→
Gun	●
Gun battery	⊔⊔⊔
Howitzer or Mortar	◆
Tank	◇
Self-propelled gun	⬡

UNITED STATES ARMY IN WORLD WAR II

The following volumes have been published:

The War Department
Chief of Staff: Prewar Plans and Preparations
Washington Command Post: The Operations Division
Strategic Planning for Coalition Warfare: 1941–1942
Strategic Planning for Coalition Warfare: 1943–1944
Global Logistics and Strategy: 1940–1943
Global Logistics and Strategy: 1943–1945
The Army and Economic Mobilization
The Army and Industrial Manpower

The Army Ground Forces
The Organization of Ground Combat Troops
The Procurement and Training of Ground Combat Troops

The Army Service Forces
The Organization and Role of the Army Service Forces

The Western Hemisphere
The Framework of Hemisphere Defense
Guarding the United States and Its Outposts

The War in the Pacific
The Fall of the Philippines
Guadalcanal: The First Offensive
Victory in Papua
CARTWHEEL: The Reduction of Rabaul
Seizure of the Gilberts and Marshalls
Campaign in the Marianas
The Approach to the Philippines
Leyte: The Return to the Philippines
Triumph in the Philippines
Okinawa: The Last Battle
Strategy and Command: The First Two Years

The Mediterranean Theater of Operations
Northwest Africa: Seizing the Initiative in the West
Sicily and the Surrender of Italy
Salerno to Cassino
Cassino to the Alps

The European Theater of Operations
Cross-Channel Attack
Breakout and Pursuit
The Lorraine Campaign
The Siegfried Line Campaign
The Ardennes: Battle of the Bulge
The Last Offensive
Riviera to the Rhine
The Supreme Command
Logistical Support of the Armies, Volume I
Logistical Support of the Armies, Volume II

Index

PIN : 038769-006